social problems

Holt, Rinehart and Winston, Inc.

New York • Chicago • San Francisco • Atlanta
Dallas • Montreal • Toronto • London • Sydney

social problems

Frank R. Scarpitti
University of Delaware

SOCIAL PROBLEMS by Frank R. Scarpitti
Copyright © 1974 by Holt, Rinehart and Winston, Inc.

Holt, Rinehart and Winston Inc.
383 Madison Avenue
New York, N. Y. 10017

Library of Congress Catalog Card Number 73-20207
ISBN 0-03-011471-3

Printed in the United States of America
456789 032 98765432

A Leogryph Book

Project director: **George R. Allen**
Design: **Ladislav Svatos**
Line art: **Vantage Art**
Production: **Cobb-Dunlop, Inc.**

"The Demolition Worker" by Herb Goro from *The Block* by Herb
Goro © 1970 by Herb Goro.

"An Urban Bill of Rights" from "Wither Urban Society?" by
Philip M. Hauser. Reprinted with permission from the National
League of Cities © 1970.

"Postcivilization" from "The Death of the City: A Frightened
Look at Post-Civilization" by Kenneth E. Boulding. Reprinted
from *The Historian and the City* edited by John Burchard and
Oscar Handlin © 1963 by the Massachusetts Institute of
Technology and the President and Fellows of Harvard College

"Goodbye to All That" from "Does the Family Have a Future?"
by Suzanne Keller © 1971 by The Journal of Comparative Family
Studies.

"Redefining Fatherhood: Notes after Six Months" by David
Steinberg in *The Future of the Family* edited by Louise K.
Howe © 1972 by David Steinberg. Reprinted by permission of the
author.

"Black Immigrant," excerpted from "Time and Tide," by John A.
Williams. This selection is from *The Immigrant Experience,*
edited and with an introduction by Thomas C. Wheeler.
Copyright © 1971 by The Dial Press. Reprinted with permission of
the publisher.

contents

preface

purpose

This text for the Social Problems course provides a comprehensive sociological analysis of the major problems confronting American society, based on the best of recent research as well as on classic sociological studies. The book is suitable for use either in a course sequence including the introductory course in sociology, or in a separate course, since all sociological concepts it utilizes are clearly explained to the student before they are used in exposition. The complexity of the problems considered has drawn sociologists of many differing perspectives to the task of analysis and explanation. This text draws freely on the insights of all schools.

organization

The book is divided into three sections. In the first, Social Disorganization, problems of traditional social institutions and conditions that threaten social cohesion are considered. Chapters are devoted to the family and to prejudice and discrimination, among others. The second section, Deviant Behavior, is given over to problems that are primarily the result of deviation from social norms, such as mental disorder, crime and the use of drugs. The chapters of the third section, Technology and Social Change, are concerned with problems related to the institutions of society's macro-structure, such as the communications media, government and business.

The instructor may, if he wishes, resequence chapters to fit his own course organization. Chapter One, Urbanization, provides a background for understanding many of the problems later discussed; all other chapters may be utilized in any order, depending on the instructor's desire for emphasis, and some may be omitted entirely. The book has been designed for maximum flexibility in course use.

Each chapter begins with a discussion of the problematic nature of present conditions, and an account of the development of social consciousness concerning them. This provides an introduction to the detailed discussion of the scope of the problem that follows. Each chapter ends with an account of responses made to the problem, whether governmental or private, and an assessment of the possibilities for solution of the problem. A summary follows each chapter.

The text features an introduction designed to orient the student to the sociological consideration of social problems. An epilogue at the end of the book discusses the variety of proposals, from revolution to social engineering, that have been put forward as a way to end social problems. The book also includes, as an appendix, a discussion of the methodology sociologists use to gather and interpret data.

readability

Throughout the text, an effort has been made to present the subject matter in clear and readable form. Each chapter is broken down into several topics, permitting the student to move one step at a time in studying otherwise difficult matters. The language used in discussing sociological concepts is familiar. Even complicated concepts are presented using a minimum of professional terminology; when such terms are used, however, they are immediately defined. Though published studies provide a basis for much of the discussion, illustrations and examples are frequently drawn from the students' own environment, the behavior of family, friends and community.

readings

In addition to the text, the book contains thirty-three readings, ranging in length from 1000 to 3500 words. Their inclusion permits the book to fulfill the function of a reader as well as a text. The selections are from sociology and allied disciplines, as well as from journalistic and literary sources. Many provide the student with examples of sociological work, both investigative and theoretical; others, more personal than scientific, are statements by or about those whom social problems touch most closely. The readings are placed within the text, to relate them directly to the material being presented.

additional features

Included in the book as a kind of running commentary are quotations from literary, sociological and political sources. Some are aphoristic, some discursive. They provide commentary on the difficulties through which institutions, individuals and groups within our society are passing.

Sequences of photographs placed at the beginning of each chapter provide visual representations of aspects of the problem. Each chapter includes line art, which presents statistics in graphic and chart form. Five phototopics, or picture sequences with a brief text, deal with American women, the elderly, youth, and the critical problems of land use and strip-mining.

acknowledgements

Many people have been of great help to me in the preparation of this book. I would like to thank my colleagues at the University of Delaware, Dennis Wenger, Howard Harlan, and Shigeo Nohara, for the benefit of their advice, and the staff of Latham Publishing Enterprises for their editorial help. Mr. Richard Owen of Holt, Rinehart and Winston contributed valuable criticism and editorial advice, as did two anonymous academic readers. I dedicate the book, with thanks for their help and support, to my wife Ellen, and my children Susan and Jeffrey.

introduction

Anyone who reads a newspaper knows that America is a society full of problems: a child dies of lead poisoning in a city hospital; racial tensions rise as black students are bused from the inner city to suburban schools; robbery and murder occur with frightening frequency; a middle-class youth dies of a drug overdose; a large corporation plans resort development and inspires opposition from groups organized to save the wilderness. The toll of individual misery and misfortune and the din of group conflict sometimes seem endless.

In the following chapters, a number of these conflicts and conditions will be examined carefully from a particular perspective: that of sociology. Not all the problems that exist in a society are the concern of the sociologist, however. Like a careful investigator in any field, he must discriminate between those conditions he can usefully examine from those that lie beyond his competence. Which problems are truly *social* problems?

In *The Sociological Imagination,* C. Wright Mills notes the clear distinction that exists between private troubles on the one hand and public issues on the other.

> Troubles occur within the character of the individual and within the range of his immediate relations with others; they have to do with his self and with those limited areas of social life of which he is directly and personally aware. . . . A trouble is a private matter.[1]

A public issue, however, is a problem which disrupts society as a whole, often involving "a crisis in institutional arrangements."[2] When one man is unemployed, we may examine his character and skills in order to alleviate his personal trouble. When a quarter of the population is unemployed, a public issue exists, demanding reevaluation of the society's economic, political and social institutions. It is public issues with which sociologists are primarily concerned.

In order for a public issue to be termed a social problem, however, it must fulfill two fundamental criteria. First, a large segment of the population must believe that a social problem exists. A widespread condition which most people perceive as an unavoidable fact of life— such as poverty in earlier centuries—is not a social problem. Second, a large segment of the population—or a number of its significant members—must believe that the problem is one which can be resolved through social action. A society which recognizes that it can organize to train doctors, build hospitals and treat patients is one in which poor health or a high rate of infant mortality can be considered a social problem. In a society that finds such conditions lamentable, but can perceive no solution except increased watchfulness over the ill at home and a higher birth rate, no social problem exists.

Thus, social problems consist of objective situations or conditions and subjective interpretations of them. Is the situation problematic and can something be done about it? The answers to these questions are based upon the values of society's members and often create severe value conflict.[3] Rarely is there universal consensus about the undesirability of any social condition. What one person defines as a harmful situation may be defined by another as completely acceptable. The current use of marijuana by large numbers of youths may be seen as immoral and illegal or as an acceptable attempt to relieve boredom and secure temporary euphoria no worse than other socially approved substances designed to do the same thing. One's values dictate the perspective taken.

It is obvious, though, that everyone's values are not given equal weight in defining a social problem. Those persons who are in positions of power have a unique advantage. The people in power are the decision makers, and in America, the individuals who exercise the greatest power are those who control the legal, economic and political institutions. They tend typically to be white, male, middle-aged and upper middle class. They are capable of influencing public opinion and structuring institutions so that what is defined or not defined as a social problem largely reflects their particular value orientation.

Whereas these individuals exert profound influence over both the government and the communications media, they are often, because of their position, unaware of the problems confronting the majority of the American people. It is frequently necessary for groups of people actively to publicize their problems in order to bring them to the attention of the decision makers. The incidence of lung disease among mine workers, for example, was long regarded as a fact of life by mine owners—and even by many workers—until intensive union action influenced the decision makers to enact legislation to provide safeguards against hazardous working conditions and compensation for those affected. Similarly, racial and sexual discrimination were of little concern to the majority of the white male power structure until the black movement and the women's movement made it impossible for the decision makers to avoid confronting the issues. Mass action is often a prerequisite for social change.

Because recognition of a social problem may result in a drastic change in the social and economic *status quo,* those members of society who are in a decision-making capacity tend to be slow-moving and conservative in their attitudes. Slum landlords are no more enthusiastic about providing adequate housing for poor blacks than weapons manufacturers are about cutting the national defense budget. Even social workers must recognize that their jobs depend on the existence of personal and social problems. Any change in social policy is likely to have adverse effects on some people.

Generally, men in power are reluctant to enact changes in social policy unless they believe their own social status to be in jeopardy. During the Depression, for example, the threat of a socialist revolution which would change the class structure and redistribute property was a very disturbing notion to those in positions of wealth and power. By recognizing poverty as a social problem and adopting social policies that alleviated it, the decision makers effectively stabilized their own positions in the social structure.

Ultimately, it is the cost of social problems that lead to reform. Drug rehabilitation programs, community public health centers and job training centers have been provided only when maintenance of the *status quo* became too costly, not just in economic terms, but in terms of crime, social unrest and a disabled population. Changes have been slow to come, but progress has been made over the years. Increasingly, the old explanations of social phenomena are giving way to more scientifically valid ones. Social policy no longer attributes the high nonwhite crime rate to racial inferiority, or poverty to personal laziness. More and more, the decision makers are being forced to recognize that social problems are the product of flaws in the social structure itself. Maintenance of the *status quo* will not solve the problems confronting modern American society.

Sociology and the study of social problems

In any society social problems may be approached from many perspectives and in many different ways. Religion provides a system of values and standards of conduct to which both individual and social action can be compared. The law, embodying traditional concepts of appropriate social behavior and elaborate regulation of its conduct, also provides mechanisms by which some social conditions may be altered.

With the growth of communications media, journalists and other investigators have often exposed to the public view conditions which otherwise would have remained hidden and unattended. Anthropologists, delineating the patterns of action within a culture, and across cultures, have thrown light on the structures by which men interact.

The sociologist, too, has his own perspective on social problems, one which permits an understanding somewhat different from those described above. Who is the sociologist? And how does he approach the study of social problems?

The sociologist is a social scientist, whose work is to study the pattern of interpersonal relationships within society. In his investigations of social problems, the sociologist collects and analyzes data within the context of the society he is studying, using methods common to all science—natural and social—as well as techniques that render more rational the sometimes immense amount of data available on the problems with which he is concerned. Some of the methods he uses are outlined in the Appendix, beginning on Page 633.

Many factors complicate the efforts of the sociologist to understand social problems. Objectivity is the goal of every scientist, but in a society as complex as our own, every social problem tends to be multifaceted and so interwoven with other aspects of society as to render valid many mutually contradictory interpretations of a single set of data.

In evaluating his findings, even in framing his hypotheses, the social researcher is usually under a number of pressures. The beliefs and preferences of those individuals who have authorized his study may have to be accommodated. Even when he works entirely independent of any special interest group, the sociologist remains an individual with his own personal beliefs and biases; he cannot ignore his own preconceptions in evaluating that data. The great German sociologist Max Weber once suggested that the biases of the social scientist should be made public together with his recommendations, in order to create a relevant framework in which to evaluate his theories and interpretations.[4]

The study of social problems is further complicated by the rapidly changing nature of social phenomena. Conclusions which are valid today may be invalid under altered conditions tomorrow. The mere presence of the social researcher may contribute significantly to the creation of new variables in social relationships. Furthermore, the social scientist cannot control his experiments in a manner comparable to that in which the natural scientist may control his. In a society geared to technological precision, these limitations sometimes cast a shadow of doubt over the efficacy of social research. It is too often felt that the findings of a sociologist's analysis, if enacted into law or implemented by public policy, will result in amelioration of the conditions examined. Such a view neglects something the sociologist himself views as given: the fluctuating nature of social phenomena.

Introduction

No single comprehensive theory of the sociology of social problems exists today, but the prevalent approach among American sociologists views the social system as a hierarchical structure in which individual roles and statuses are interrelated so that the collective purposes of the society and the individual objectives of its members may be realized.[5] In an ideal social system, the needs and goals of each member would be smoothly integrated with those of every other member, but real societies all too often seem to serve as breeding grounds for conflict. The sociologist recognizes that the roots of discontent often lie in the social structure itself.

The inability of dominant social values and the behavior which they generate to provide adequately for all members of the society may result from several sources.

One is the process of *social change.* A wide range of phenomena—urbanization, the population explosion, modern war—may be said to have been produced by the technological changes introduced by the industrial revolution; but sociologists see them as the product, to a great extent, of the changes in *social* relationships that the technological changes induced—the changes in patterns of settlement and the nature of work—and which may themselves induce further technological changes. During periods of rapid social change people are more likely to act contrary to the values of their culture than in times of social stability. Sociologist Arnold Rose has posited three reasons for this occurrence:

> (1) sometimes values are no longer helpful in guiding people to adjust to the changed situations they must face; (2) individuals internalize one set of meanings and values in their childhood and then are expected to conform to another; and (3) in times of change people are likely to get out of communication with each other—communication that would allow them to modify their meanings and values to meet the changed situation.[6]

Sociologists often notice a time lag between the occurrence of a phenomenon and the social change in relationships or ideas required to accommodate it; this is called *culture lag.*[7] Advances in medical technology, for example, now make it possible to transplant the heart of a deceased patient into an otherwise normal patient with a diseased heart; however, we have yet to answer fully the question of what exactly constitutes death. Until the philosophical, religious and scientific authorities can agree upon an unequivocal definition, the advance of technology may be perceived as being out of step with the values and beliefs of society.

The slight qualms caused by an uncertain cultural definition of death, however, are usually less important in society than true *value conflicts.* Whether everyone agrees on what death is seems less important than that everyone values life. In a society troubled by social problems, however, the conflicting values held by disparate groups—urban versus rural, young versus old, one religious or ethnic group versus another—are important obstacles to be overcome in the solution of any social problem. Racial integration of the school system, for example, is viewed by some as desirable, since they view equal educational opportunity for blacks and whites as valuable. At the same time, many Americans seek to block integration achieved by busing disadvantaged children from slum neighborhoods into middle-class schools because they value education for their own children, which they feel busing will undermine.

A person growing up in a society of conflicting values may find it difficult to develop his own value code, unless he is firmly socialized into a value system cut off from the larger society, such as the Amish. Modern American society, so various in its ethnic, religious and social makeup, contains few universal value standards against which conflicting values of a less important sort may be set and resolved.

When value commitments are weak and generally ineffective, social roles and patterns of interaction become confused and lack necessary coordination. Such confusion tends to disorganize society to some degree. *Social disorganization* more precisely, occurs when a specific aspect of the social system fails to fulfill adequately the social objectives of all groups and their individual members, relative to standards that groups and individuals share for that system. Social problems obviously are generated by this condition. As Robert K. Merton has indicated, however, "the type of social problem involved in disorganization arises not from people failing to live up to the requirements of their social statuses . . . but from the faulty organization of these statuses into a reasonably coherent social system."[8] Here, ironically enough, conformity to established social roles leads to problem situations.

A *social dysfunction,* on the other hand, occurs when a specific aspect of the social system fails with respect to a specified purpose.[9] Widespread discontent with family life in a society might be considered a condition showing social disorganization. The failure of a school system to provide adequate education for a small minority of students would, on the other hand, be seen as a dysfunction occurring within an institution otherwise operating normally.

Often, an individual whose behavior varies significantly from the social norms established for persons occupying his particular position in the social structure is described as *deviant.*[10] Deviant behavior can be classified as either nonconformity or aberrant, however. The nonconformist publicly challenges existing norms, while the aberrant hides his deviant behavior to escape the penalties for violating norms he does not seek to change. Social opinion is generally more favorable to the nonconformist than to the aberrant. Nonconformity is measured against cultural norms which are relative and changeable, and conformity to one set of norms may involve nonconformity to another.

Some social problems are widely recognized as such—including public health, poverty and crime. These may be referred to as *manifest* social problems; that is, they are problems which have already been acknowledged by the decision makers, and which society has taken measures to solve, or somehow ameliorate.[11] Many social conditions exist, however, which, although they adversely affect a large segment of society, have yet to be recognized as social problems. These are the *latent* social problems—harmful social conditions which have yet to be generally acknowledged.[12]

Social problems sometimes have the habit of being manifest during one period in history and latent during another. Drinking, for instance, was once considered a social problem important enough to inspire a constitutional amendment. At present, the related problem of alcoholism threatens, in the light of other serious problems facing society, to become a latent social problem, its social costs underestimated or misunderstood by society.

As we shall soon see, there is a great deal of uncertainty about how society should respond to social problems. Potential ameliorative efforts are often limited by the values of those in a position to affect change. Some years ago sociologists Richard Fuller and Richard Myers indicated that values "obstruct solutions to conditions defined as social problems because people are unwilling to endorse programs of amelioration which prejudice or require abandonment of their cherished beliefs and institutions."[13] Hence, proposed solutions tend to fall within a narrow range of acceptability and seldom call for anything but minor alterations in existing social arrangements.

Notes

[1] C. Wright Mills, *The Sociological Imagination* (New York: Oxford University Press, 1959) p. 8.

[2] *Ibid,* p. 9.

[3] For a discussion of the role of values in the definition of social problems, see John F. Cuber, William F. Kenkel and Robert A. Harper, *Problems of American Society: Values in Conflict* (New York: Holt, Rinehart and Winston, Inc., 1964), pp. 35–39.

[4] Julien Freund, *The Sociology of Max Weber* (New York: Pantheon Books, 1968) pp. 48–59.

[5] For an authoritative treatment of social systems analysis, see Robert K. Merton, *Social Theory and Social Structure,* enlarged edition (New York: Free Press, 1968).

[6] Arnold M. Rose, *Sociology: The Study of Human Relations* (New York: Alfred A. Knopf, 1965) p. 580.

[7] William F. Ogburn, *Social Change* (New York: Huebsch, 1923) pp. 200–237.

[8] Robert K. Merton and Robert Nisbet, *Contemporary Social Problems* (New York: Harcourt Brace Jovanovich, Inc., 1971) p. 823.

[9] *Ibid.,* p. 839.

[10] *Ibid.,* p. 824.

[11] *Ibid.,* pp. 806–810.

[12] *Ibid.*

[13] Richard C. Fuller and Richard R. Myers, "The Natural History of a Social Problem," *American Sociological Review* 6, June 1941, p. 320.

part

1

social
disorganization

chapter

urbanization

Cities have a long history in organized society. They begin with the first settlements of 3500 B.C. in the Fertile Crescent of Mesopotamia—Ur and Lagash, Jericho and Babylon. Urban problems—the problems of sizeable numbers of people, gathered together to live, to govern, to produce and exchange goods—are as old as the cities themselves. When these problems were made manageable, civilizations flourished. Then, for reasons so diverse scholars continue to argue over them, many of these same civilizations—and cities—declined. Writes the sociologist, Gideon Sjoberg:

> There is a significant relation between the rise and fall of empires and the rise and fall of cities; in a real sense, history is the study of urban graveyards.[1]

The historical fact today sounds something like a threat. In modern America, with its technologically sophisticated communications media, every newspaper reader and television viewer is made instantly aware of the problems American cities are encountering. This was particularly true in the 1960s, with their massive organized demonstrations and ghetto riots. By 1968, not only journalists but politicians and community leaders were examining "the urban crisis" and proposing solutions. President Johnson's message to Congress on urban subjects that year was entitled, "The Crisis of the Cities." The president of the University of California issued a statement called, "What We Must Do: The University and the Urban Crisis." The bishops of the United States Catholic Conference presented a program, "The Church's Response to the Urban Crisis."

In 1973, President Nixon, listing recent developments in urban affairs, asserted in a radio address that "the hour of crisis has passed" in American community life. In support of his statement, he mentioned a number of problems that seem of paramount importance in American cities. The rate of crime, he said, was dropping "in more than half of our major cities." Civil disorders had declined; the air was getting cleaner; the number of people living in substandard housing had been cut more than 50 percent since 1960, and "once again the business world is investing in our downtown areas."[2]

President Nixon's confidence was not shared by many spokesmen for the cities. Making due allowance for partisan sentiment on both sides, it seems fair to say that only the most noticeable expressions of urban unrest have subsided. The problems themselves remain, brought about not by demonstrators or criminals but by the urban condition itself, a problematic situation that has developed out of the rapid urbanization of American society in the past century.

Urbanization is a worldwide phenomenon. Though cities themselves have existed for 5500 years, the urban era is of much more recent date. Sociologists such as Sjoberg make a distinction between preindustrial cities and those which have taken on their characteristic form and complexity since the advent of the Industrial Revolution. In preindustrial times, the vast majority of the population lived in farms and small villages. Modern cities first developed between 1750 and 1850. They were capable of supporting a greater proportion of the population, because civilization had learned to utilize new sources of energy, such as coal and oil, in addition to the older sources, such as horses, oxen and wood. Industrialization and the higher standard of living it brought to cities permitted and encouraged the development of many more specialized occupations, most notably scientists. Scientific contributions, in turn, speeded further technological advance.[3]

In the twentieth century, with the advent of the automobile and increasingly efficient systems of industrial production, a majority of the population has come to live in urban surroundings, both in the United States and in other industrially developed countries. This shift has caused disruptions on a global scale. Because the United States has been in the forefront of technological advance, the effects have been particularly significant here.

City officials and national planners have made some attempt to anticipate and prepare for increased urban congestion; the city of Stockholm has perhaps been most foresighted in its undertakings.[4] But many of our American institutions, designed for an earlier era, have not proved adequate to deal with an increasingly urban society.

Today, three out of four Americans live in an urban setting. That does not necessarily mean they live in a big city. Some 93 million citizens, or 42 percent of the population, live in suburbs or smaller cities. Nevertheless, they are urban in outlook, employment and to a degree in social relations as well. Their problems are the urban problems that will be the scope of this book: health, education, employment, income, discrimination, crime, alcoholism and drug abuse.

The concern of this chapter will be to show how the conditions of American society have been altered to accommodate the rapid urban growth and change of the past century. We will also outline proposals which have been made to alleviate the difficulties and eliminate the disruption that have resulted from urbanization. Reorganization—of financial, social and governmental institutions—is needed, and has in some instances been undertaken. It remains to be seen whether technological change can be matched by social change and social improvement.

The American city

American political thinkers and intellectuals have been suspicious of the impact of cities since the days of the founding fathers, when most Americans still lived on the land. Thomas Jefferson was among the most famous of those to express this concern. In 1787, for example, in a letter to James Madison, he wrote:

> Our governments will remain virtuous for centuries as long as they are chiefly agricultural . . . . When they get piled upon one another in large cities, as they are in Europe, they will become corrupt as in Europe.[5]

In their study of American intellectual attitudes, philosophers Morton and Lucia White quoted the criticism of urban society voiced not only by Jefferson, but also by Emerson, Thoreau, Melville, Poe, Henry Adams, Henry James, Louis Sullivan, Frank Lloyd Wright and John Dewey.[6] Noting that their survey included the names of America's greatest political thinker, greatest essayist, greatest philosopher, greatest educational theorist, greatest novelist, greatest autobiographer and greatest architect, the Whites suggested that "the city planner would make a grave mistake if he were to dismiss that tradition."[7]

Some intellectuals cited by the Whites feared that the city would fail to educate its citizens sufficiently to enable them to participate in a working democracy. Others believed the city pressured individuals toward conformity and discouraged free communication. Sociologists who have sought to analyze urban attitudes do not necessarily find data supporting these contentions. Yet the policy of elected leaders, like that of the intellectuals, has been to praise "grass-roots" democracy and decry the evils of urban politics. The Jeffersonian position is traditional, found in the rhetoric of Jacksonian Democrats, theoreticians for the Southern Confederacy, populists like William Jennings Bryan and prohibitionists.[8]

Despite the concern expressed about them, American cities grew and flourished in the nineteenth century. Both the great seaports of the East Coast—New York, Boston and Philadelphia—and the newer inland cities of Pittsburgh, Chicago and St. Louis prospered as the rich resources of the Midwest and West were opened up. Spreading from Europe to America, the Industrial Revolution developed light and heavy industry, mass-producing industrial and consumer goods; it spurred railroad construction, money markets, and the expansion of governmental and corporate bureaucracies. Even before this era was fully begun, however, the French traveler to America, Alexis de Tocqueville, noted a characteristic of urban populations that he feared would imperil democracy. Visiting America in the 1820s, he observed that "the rabble" of New York and Philadelphia (he was referring to freed blacks and poor artisans) had already been responsible for riots. He wrote:

> I venture to predict that American republics will perish from this circumstance, unless the government succeeds in creating an armed force which, while it remains under the control of the majority, will be independent of the town population and able to repress its excesses.[9]

The cities' population

In 1860, only one out of every six Americans lived in towns or cities larger than 8000. By 1900, nearly one in three did and by 1920, more than half the population was urban. Some of the new city dwellers flocked from the country, allowing the farms they abandoned to return to wilderness.

Another factor that helped increase the population of the cities was the increasing flow of immigrants, who tended most often to settle in cities. In the eighteenth century, the immigrants had been principally English, Scots-Irish and Germans who sought farmland. The nineteenth century brought an influx of Irish, starting with the potato famine of 1848, and a second wave of Germans, following the unsuccessful revolutions of 1848. Both groups became predominantly urban dwellers. The Irish were often contracted for by American employers to do coalmining, railroad construction or other heavy labor. They settled in New York, Boston, Chicago, western Pennsylvania and other industrial centers. The Germans settled in New York, Cincinnati, St. Louis, Baltimore and Milwaukee. By 1855, the Irish-born made up 25 percent of New York's population, the German-born 16 percent.[10]

After the Civil War, the urban population was further augmented by waves of immigrants from south and central Europe. Czech, Hungarian, Polish, Russian and Ukranian peasants were also recruited as contract labor, employed in factories in northern New Jersey, Pittsburgh, Chicago and Detroit. In the 1880s, Jews from the Austro-Hungarian Empire, Poland and Russia, together with sizeable numbers of Italians, began to arrive. The Jews assembled principally in New York; the Italians congregated in New York, Boston, Chicago.

In the cities, members of each national group gathered together in local neighborhoods. There they could patronize restaurants and grocery stores selling their national foods, maintain family and village ties from the homeland, speak their own language and attend churches of their native religion. They established mutual aid societies and a foreign-language press. For the most part, first-generation immigrants were confined to unskilled or semiskilled occupations. Poorly educated, and unfamiliar with the English language, they adapted only gradually to American society. Their voting potential was organized and exploited by the political machines which began to flourish in the latter half of the nineteenth century.

Disruption of family and cultural patterns was often impossible to avoid. In the process of assimilation to American life, the old patterns often lost their hold. The result was family breakup, alcoholism and delinquency, occurring in the context of turbulent city growth.[11]

Twentieth century cities

In the twentieth century, changes in technology made possible a vast increase in the size of cities. Previously, industry and commerce had located along water and rail routes; city-dwellers relied on horse cars, suburban trains or foot to get to work. The development of the automobile freed both employer and employee. Factories could be established away from rail lines, utilizing truck transport; workers could drive to their jobs. The automobile's mode of production, the horizontal assembly line, became standard throughout industry. The new system required much larger amounts of space for its operation than did earlier means of production, so manufacturers gravitated to the suburbs, where land was cheaper. The development of heavy duty transmission lines for electricity enabled the building of factories hundreds of miles away from power sources.

The invention of mechanical refrigeration, together with a vast increase in the types of inexpensive canned foods available, gave less well-to-do people much more mobility and freedom than they previously had.[12] They could now move away from central markets, spend more money on better living accommodations, and migrate from the central cities to low-income suburbs.

Los Angeles as prototype

As early as 1930, the model of the new American megalopolis was beginning to be in evidence: an increasingly decentralized unit, with teeming business districts and slums located at its center and residential and industrial suburbs expanding in ever-widening circles over the surrounding countryside. Los Angeles was the prototype, a city which grew slowly in the era of the horse car, but by leaps and bounds after the popularization of the automobile. Sociologist Robert M. Fogelson, in his study of that "fragmented metropolis,"[13] documents the role of the automobile in the decentralization of both industry and retail trade in Los Angeles. By 1930, prominent department stores were opening branches or relocating outside the downtown area, on Wilshire and Hollywood Boulevards. Steelmakers erected furnaces in Torrance. Oil producers built refineries at El Segundo. Aviation companies constructed hangars in Santa Monica, while motion picture producers located studios in the San Fernando Valley. One outcome of this decentralization was that the commuter railways, plagued by competition from passenger cars, were forced to curtail services and raise fares, therefore depriving themselves of still more customers and eventually being driven out of business. Lack of public transportation caused even further decentralization.

At the core of the new situation is the interaction of increasing numbers of people, all using or seeking to make use of more energy and more materials, all tending to draw together in closer proximity in urban regions, all concentrating to a wholly new degree the by-products of their activities—their demands and consumption, their movements and noise, their wastes and effluents.

Barbara Ward and Rene Dubos

The shifts in population tell the story of change in Los Angeles. Between 1923 and 1931, when the population within ten miles of the central business district expanded 50 percent, the number of people entering downtown Los Angeles increased only 15 percent. And what was true of Los Angeles in the 1920s and 1930s has, to an increasing degree, become the pattern with other metropolitan centers across the United States. Though metropolitan areas have continued to expand, the inward drift of new arrivals to the cities

has been counterbalanced by an outward drain to suburbia of residents, factories and, in the 1960s, by an exodus of white-collar employers as well.

City and suburb

In the period between 1950 and 1970, the population of America's central cities increased by more than a third, from 48 to 64 million, but in the same period the population of the suburban fringe more than doubled, from less than 25 million to 55 million. The shift in population was accompanied by the relocation of jobs and political power. The Bureau of Labor Statistics reported that by 1971, total employment amounted to 26 million in the country's twenty largest standard metropolitan statistical areas. (The Standard Metropolitan Statistical Area is defined by the United States Office of Management and Budget as "a county or group of contiguous counties which contains at least one central city of 50,000 inhabitants or more or 'twin cities' with a combined population of at least 50,000.") Of these employees, 11 million had jobs in central cities and 15 million in the suburban rings.[14] Suburban employees, of course, do not necessarily commute from the central city. More likely, they live in suburban areas, and their ranks are augmented by residents of rural areas outside the suburban ones.

In 1972, the effects of reapportionment, based on the 1970 census, were beginning to be felt. It was estimated that some 290 members of the United States House of Representatives would come from metropolitan areas, and 145 from rural ones. Of the metropolitan total, only 100 would represent districts dominated by central cities. Some 130 Congressmen would come from predominantly suburban areas, while the remaining 60 would represent mixed districts.[15]

phototopic: LAND USE

Housing development and industrial expansion in the United States since World War II have taken place for the most part outside the older central cities. Farmlands have been turned into suburbs and industrial parks, and the interstate highway has replaced the railroad as the important connecting link between cities, changing the look and function of the land. The mobile home park has become a feature of communities large and small. Despite the encroachment of development on areas ever more distant from metropolitan centers, the existing housing units of the inner city continue to decay.

Redevelopment of inner city areas has been sponsored by local, state and federal governments, but in many cases the environment of the inner city remains one of dehumanization, in which social conflict readily develops. Land use practices in all types of communities have recently come under criticism for their devastating effect on America's physical and social environment.

Urban population trends

Since the 1920s, when the United States government enacted legislation limiting foreign immigration, the cities' growth in population has come primarily from internal migration. The greatest number of new arrivals has been blacks from the rural South, moving to both southern cities and northern ones. The New York-New Jersey area has also received substantial numbers of Puerto Ricans; Chicago, Detroit and other north central cities have attracted whites from Appalachia; in the West, Mexican-Americans long settled in the area now seek urban employment.

The black migration to eastern and northern cities began during World War I, when high-paying defense industry jobs attracted many rural blacks. However, blacks in urban centers, mostly working in unskilled or semiskilled jobs, were the first to be laid off and the last to be rehired in the depression of the 1930s. Despite this, black migration northward mounted anew during World War II and after. With defense industry scattered across the country, blacks also began moving westward.

The 1970 census showed that 74 percent of America's black population of 23 million live in metropolitan areas.[16] In the decade since 1960, New York's black population rose from 14 percent to 21 percent of the total; that of Chicago, from 23 to 33 percent; that of Los Angeles, from 14 to 18 percent. Southern cities attracted even greater proportions of blacks. Atlanta had a 51 percent black population; Washington, D.C., 71 percent.[17]

Like earlier immigrant groups, blacks settled in segregated neighborhoods. However, where segregation had been at least in part a matter of choice with foreign-born immigrants, blacks were forced into highly congested ghettos because of racial discrimination. One by-product of racial discrimination was that even middle-class blacks, who could afford better neighborhoods, were forced to reside in ghettos that were predominantly slums.

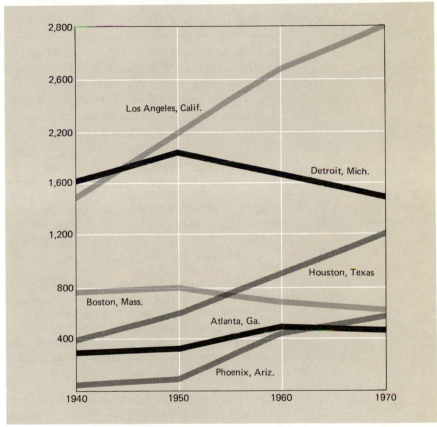

Figure 1-1   Recent growth of selected major urban areas

While blacks and others were moving into the central cities, other groups had begun to move out. Among the immigrants of an earlier era who had achieved assimilation into American society, some members of each group had become more prosperous in their old age than they had been as new arrivals. Their children were better educated and moved into more highly paid skilled and professional occupations. Seeking better housing, and now able to afford it, these groups moved to the better residential areas of the city and to the suburbs. The process has been documented statistically by the sociologist Stanley Lieberson. In a study of census data from 1910 to 1950, for ten ethnic groups in ten cities, Lieberson found that:

> . . . in 1930, the second generation tended to be less centralized in residence than the first generation. In addition, the foreign-born in 1950 were less centralized than the foreign-born in 1930 . . . . Further, the old-new differences held for the most part; new groups were more centralized than old groups in each city. Finally, in eight of the ten cities there was some association between length of residence and degree of centralization; that is, groups with more years of residence in the United States tended to be more decentralized than the relatively recent immigrants.[18]

The nature of the city

Seeking to interrelate technological and economic developments with other factors influencing the city's growth and distinctive character, sociologists since the early years of the century have worked to analyze urban culture in detail. As a starting point, it was necessary to isolate and define the nature of an urban settlement, as opposed to a market town or fortified citadel.

Weber and Simmel

One of the earliest students of urban culture was the German sociologist Max Weber. In 1905, he summed up the attributes of an "ideal-typical" city, basing his initial definition on a comparison of the activities and institutions of cities in preindustrial Europe, the Middle East and Far East. He arrived at this conclusion:

> To constitute a full urban community, a settlement must display a relative predominance of trade-commercial relations with the settlement as a whole displaying the following features: (1) a fortification; (2) a market; (3) a court of its own and at least a partially autonomous law; (4) a related form of association; and (5) at least partial autonomy and autocephaly, thus also an administration by authorities in the election of whom the burghers participated.[19]

His younger friend and colleague, Georg Simmel, also dealt with an "ideal-typical" form of city. But where Weber approached his subject from a socioeconomic point of view, Simmel's concern was the psychological outlook developed by the typical city dweller. Simmel maintained that:

> The psychological basis of the metropolitan type of individuality consists in the intensification of nervous stimulation which results from the swift and uninterrupted changes of outer and inner stimuli . . . . With each crossing of the street, with the tempo and multiplicity of economic, occupational and social life, the city sets up a deep contrast with small town and rural life with reference to the sensory foundation of psychic life.[20]

To protect himself against this more complex environment, the metropolitan type, Simmel believed, became more intellectual, more rational. The fact that the city was also the center of the money economy tended to make the city dweller more matter-of-fact in dealing with men and things, coupling formal justice with inconsiderate hardness. Because he was intellectual and commercially oriented, the metropolitan type became blasé and reserved in his relations with other people. At the same time, the impersonality of the great metropolis granted the individual a unique kind and amount of personal freedom.

The extraordinarily high value which people set upon the vacation periods gives the measure of their discontent with their daily lives. But surely it is a crying absurdity that the emphasis should be on that small fraction of the year. It is to the workaday world itself that pleasantness must be imparted, failing which, the palliative of escape will in time make the resorts as unpleasant as the residences.

Bertrand de Jouvenal

Though frequently leaving the city dweller feeling lonely and isolated, this freedom also created a cosmopolitan atmosphere, in which city dwellers sought increasingly to assert their independence and individuality. The extreme economic division of labor in a metropolis promoted and encouraged such differentiation. So did the fact that social relations were apt to consist of relatively brief contacts with other individuals in specialized spheres—on the job, in the home or through membership in organizations.

Park, Wirth and the Chicago School

During and after World War I, a group of University of Chicago sociologists undertook to adapt and apply these theoretical formulations to the facts of the American city. The leaders of the "Chicago school"—Robert Park, Ernest Burgess and Louis Wirth—wished to particularize the study of urban culture. The first fruit of this endeavor was Park's landmark essay, published in 1916: "The City: Some Suggestions for the Study of Human Behavior in the Urban Environment."[21] Park outlined possible avenues for exploration, based on the assumption that the city could be understood both as a geographical entity and a "moral order." Borrowing a term from the natural sciences, he maintained that cities have an "ecology," or self-contained natural life, which tended to bring about an orderly and typical grouping of their populations and institutions. This ecology, he argued, might be examined in many ways: from the standpoint of population composition, neighborhood development, industrial and vocational specialization, social mobility, collective behavior or urban crowds, the changing influence of church, school and family, or the effectiveness of courts, custom, party politics and the press.

Park's suggestions were extensively taken up and pursued by the "ecological" school of sociologists. Using the empirical method to postulate and substantiate hypothesis, they systematically chronicled and documented many aspects of American urban life. In 1938, Louis Wirth surveyed some of their findings in his essay, "Urbanism as a Way of Life."[22] To Wirth, the distinctive characteristics of urban settlements are large size, population density, social and occupational heterogeneity. He found that these characteristics, partly because of the structures of social organization required for their management, promote "segmental" and "secondary" contacts between individuals, as opposed to the "primary" contacts of folk and rural society. The urbanite described by Wirth is much like Simmel's metropolitan type.

Cities are full of people with whom a certain degree of contact is useful and enjoyable, but you do not want them in your hair. And they do not want you in theirs either.

Jane Jacobs

While Wirth recognized the freedom and individuality which the city permits, he stressed the deleterious effect of urbanism on community life. In modern cities, where mass production techniques and the ideologies of mass communication are prevalent, he saw a leveling influence at work, destroying the social bond by catering to the statistical average rather than to the needs of unique individuals. Wirth's emotional preference was for a community where "primary" contacts remain important.

The study of community

Among sociologists who have studied community since Wirth, some have questioned the extent to which a large urban settlement can be defined as a single community. Sociologist Herbert J. Gans, for example, found the population of central cities to consist not of one urban type but rather of five: (1) the cosmopolites; (2) the unmarried or childless; (3) the "ethnic villagers"; (4) the deprived; (5) the trapped and downward-mobile.[23] Of these five, Gans concluded that only the last two suffered from the problems Wirth described. The cosmopolites had succeeded in creating a distinctive life-style which made conventional neighborhood life unnecessary. The ethnic villagers had managed to establish their own communities through personal and social ties. For many, the city was only a temporary home; once resources for the change were available, they would move to the low-density, "quasi-primary" life of the suburbs. Gans found Wirth's diagnosis of urban life not so much wrong, as too narrow, and out of date.

Sociologist James S. Coleman has noted that there are ways of creating community other than by similarity of experience shared over a long time. Previously unassociated neighborhoods may be drawn together to form a sort of community when confronted with specific events.[24] A crime wave within a few blocks may cause neighbors to form local protective associations or vigilante groups.

After a group of individuals has organized to confront a problem, a residuum of community organization remains and may be directed to other purposes. Interrelated but dissimilar activities—extremely important in cities, where the division of labor and the network of interdependence are highly developed—can also generate interests in common. In a city threatened by an exodus of industry, workers and employers may agree upon the need for tax incentives to encourage new industry. On the other hand, the same groups may disagree on the level of wages to be paid.

There is little doubt, however, that communities in urban America are vastly different now than they were at the time Wirth wrote. Local geographic communities are now highly specialized. Residential suburbs daily export workers. Industrial suburbs and central cities import them. Housing projects in large cities function purely as residential centers; local churches have little influence and political bosses cannot sustain networks of supporters as they used to. College towns and resort communities attract a large proportion of part-time residents, whose attitude towards community problems may be very different from that of the natives. Communities such as retirement settlements attract a very high proportion of individuals of one age group.

Such fragmentation is even more disruptive of community than the city Wirth described, yet, ironically, much of it can be seen as an attempt to regain the primary contacts of the village or the small town, to flee the confusion of modern city life for a simpler and more ordered existence. Sociologist Richard Sennett criticizes this search for what he calls a "purified community."[25] He agrees that conflict in cities is inevitable, but he sees it as an opportunity for personal and social growth impossible to find in the new suburbs. The purified community of the suburbs, supported by affluence, fostered by a consumer society with an elaborate system of mass communication and persuasion, is to Sennett a myth bound to fail because it blinks at the inherent difficulties of social life.

Urban problems

There is some evidence that, as the suburbs grow, they become increasingly like the cities in terms of the problems they encounter—rising costs, rising crime rates, family and social disorder. For the moment, however, these problems are concentrated in the cities, whose institutions of government are being tested by difficult economic and social conditions.

City governments

In America, as elsewhere, the urban settlement developed its distinctive forms of governmental and allied institutions. The most notable was the big-city political machine. Its methods and structure have been outlined by political scientists Edward C. Banfield and James Q. Wilson. The existence of the machine, Banfield and Wilson observe, depends on its ability to control votes. The voters are organized and kept track of through the activities of the ward leader; he, in turn, operates through a network of precinct captains. Votes become available only when the voters place less value on their ballots than on the favors the machine can do for them. The voter who is indifferent to issues, candidates or principles furnishes the best material for the machine. Banfield and Wilson write:

> Workingclass people, especially immigrants unfamiliar with American ways and institutions, have always been the mainstay of the machine. To use the terminology of the politician, the "delivery" wards are also the "river" wards, and they are a long way in both political and geographic distance from the "newspaper" wards. A delivery ward, of course, is one whose votes can be "delivered" by the machine, and a newspaper ward is one in which voters take the newspapers' recommendations seriously. The delivery wards are the river wards because the oldest, hence poorest and most rundown parts of the city are those that lie near the warehouses and the railroad yards. Almost without exception, the lower the average income and the fewer the years of schooling in a ward, the more dependable the ward's allegiance to the machine."[26]

As one moves from the lower middle-class districts to those of the middle class and out to the suburbs of the upper middle class, ties to the machine become weaker and fewer until they cease to exist. As voters become more educated and more assimilated, they espouse the political values of "the Anglo-Saxon Protestant elite,"

> . . . the central idea of which is that politics should be based on public rather than private motives and accordingly should stress the virtues of honesty, impartiality and efficiency.
>
> Whenever the middle class is dominant, this ethos prevails and fixes the character of the political system. If, as seems likely, the middle class will in the long run assimilate the lower class entirely, the final extinction of the machine is probably guaranteed.[27]

At present, although machine politics has lost its dominance in many areas, there remain lower-class enclaves in some central cities and suburbs where the system flourishes.

It would be a mistake to assume, however, that because the machine elects officials to office, it necessarily controls the destiny of that community. Indeed, since the 1920s substantial research has been done by sociologists who maintain that control of most urban communities in fact resides with a "power elite." This elite is defined as a class of citizens who control a disproportionate share of the community's wealth. Through their investment in the community and their attitudes toward it, they exercise a disproportionate influence upon its elected officials.

The first study of the power structure of an urban community to receive widespread recognition was Robert S. and Helen M. Lynd's *Middletown*, published in 1929. In their analysis of Muncie, Ind., the

Lynds found that "Family X" controlled the city in all important respects. More recently, the most influential study to arrive at elitist conclusions has been Floyd Hunter's *Community Power Structure,* a 1953 analysis of decision-makers in Atlanta.

In recent years, the elitist model of community studies has been under attack by sociologists who argue that urban power has in fact become "pluralist" in character—not controlled by any one group, but by a variety of interests. In his 1961 study of New Haven, political scientist Robert Dahl documented that community's evolution from oligarchy to pluralism between 1784 and 1960.[28] The office of mayor, he found, had from 1784 to 1842 been held almost exclusively by men from patrician backgrounds. Between 1842 and 1900, the new self-made men of industry, the entrepreneurs, took over. Since then, "ex-plebes" rising out of working class and lower middle-class families of non-Anglo-Saxon origin have predominated in the office. Under modern conditions, this development has meant more sharing of actual political power than was possible in the past.

Individual communities vary widely, of course. One recent study has attempted to reconcile the claims of elitists with pluralists by correlating specific variables such as population composition, size, age and industrial makeup. Sociologist Michael Aiken, who tabulated findings on community power structures in 57 cities, found that larger cities have more diffused power structures than smaller ones; that older cities have more diffused power structures than younger ones; finally, that growing cities are more likely to have concentrated power configurations, while stagnant and declining cities are more likely to have diffused power structures.[29]

Reform government

Both the influence of the big-city political machine and the control exercised by the power elite have been substantially lessened by the campaigns for reform of city government inaugurated in the last half of the nineteenth century. The exact extent of improvement wrought by reformers has been subject to debate. However, there is no doubt that the introduction of merit examinations for civil servants' jobs deprived ward bosses of a major means to reward the faithful; no longer could politicians dispense low-level jobs as patronage plums. Similarly, the development of the welfare system has enabled the poor to become more economically independent, and less impressed by the traditional precinct captain's means of rewarding allegiance, such as the Thanksgiving turkey or the extra hod of coal at Christmas.

The new style of politics, with its emphasis on honesty, impartiality and efficiency, favors a number of tendencies. As outlined by Banfield and Wilson, they include:

—A limiting of opportunities for members of new minority groups to rise to positions of eminence through the machine.

—A growing demand for "fresh faces," meaning candidates who at least seem free from the taint of professionalism and who also have the technical qualifications and disinterestedness the new politics calls for.

—An increase in professional administrators, on all levels of city government.

—An increasing identification of local, urban issues with national, ideological ones.

—A hastening in the process of centralization of authority, with greater emphasis on disinterested urban planning.[30]

The cost of running a city

Although city governments are faced with ever greater demands for services and higher standards in administration, they possess only limited means for providing them; financial problems impose real limitations on the cities. As wealthier citizens emigrated to the suburbs, their houses were taken over by larger numbers of less affluent residents, causing neighborhoods to deteriorate. However, part of this deterioration can be ascribed to the fact that old buildings in many cities are more lightly taxed than new ones. Landlords thus have felt no incentive to improve their real estate to keep wealthier tenants in occupancy and within city limits.[31] Their profit comes rather from high rents and minimal investment. The eventual effect of a situation such as this is to permit the tax base of the entire community to decline. At the same time, inflation, rising wages and the continued flow of inward migration have increased the amounts of money needed to pay for such civic services as transportation, public welfare, police services, education, sanitation and garbage disposal.

Costs of goods and services provided by state and local governments have escalated in the postwar era. State and local expenditures on social welfare services, for example, increased from $13 billion in 1950 to $68 billion in 1970; on education from $6.5 billion in 1950 to $44 billion in 1970. Police expenditures by state and local governments amounted to $5 billion in 1970. While these statistics include suburban and rural expenditures as well as urban ones, the burden borne by the central cities is proportionately higher than that borne by the suburbs, and the resources available for raising taxes less. Cities must, after all, provide such facilities as public transport and police protection for suburban commuters as well as residents. If the cities raise taxes, they risk accelerating the flight of industry and residents to the suburbs, where such taxes are lower.

High taxes have already caused many businesses to leave the central cities. Low-income job seekers, centered in metropolitan areas, are thus faced with a declining number of jobs. Political scientists Alan Campbell and Donna Shahala write:

The result is higher and higher rates of unemployment and underemployment in these areas . . . . This pattern, of job location, added to education, housing and discrimination has produced an income and poverty distribution which accentuates the disparities between city and suburb. In general, the gap between median family income in the suburb and city is increasing. Average median family income in the central cities in 1960 was $5,940 compared to $6,707 in the suburbs . . . . Estimates for 1967 are $7,813 for the central city family while for the suburban family it has increased to $9,370. Thus, the gap has increased since 1960 from a suburban advantage of $767 to a 1967 advantage of $1,446—a doubling.[32]

Despite the lower median income for the city, the true extent of poverty that exists in the cities remains hidden. Many of America's most wealthy citizens live in the cities, making the median income unrealistically high. Welfare cases are concentrated in central cities in nearly every state. For example, 44.2 percent of New York State's population lives in New York City, while 70.2 percent of the state's welfare load is located there. In Philadelphia, the proportions are 17.8 and 29.6; Boston, 13.6 and 32.0; and in St. Louis 15.5 and 25.5.[33]

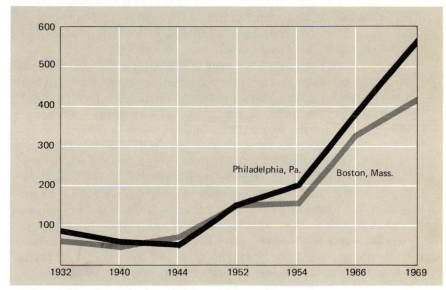

Figure 1–2   Total cost of city services in millions of dollars, selected years 1932–1969, Philadelphia and Boston

In almost every area where services must be provided, the cities are forced to do more with less resources than the suburbs have to do. With crime rates higher in the central cities, the cities must also pay a higher price for police protection. In central cities, a greater share of the population is dependent upon public transportation, so subways, busses and commuter trains must be maintained. Yet city streets are inundated with the cars of commuters from the suburbs. Finally, city schools are called upon to provide the same quality of education that suburban schools provide. But with a smaller percentage of the tax dollar available for their upkeep, classrooms are overcrowded and facilities frequently out-of-date.

Herb Goro
THE DEMOLITION WORKER

It takes about one week to tear down a building. Just about a week, it all depends on how many men you get on it. I'd say about 25 percent of the buildings we tear down are in Harlem and stuff like that—all through 120th, 117th, right up all the way up in Harlem. Then we got some on the other side of Manhattan there—154th Street; then through the Bronx, here. I would say they are about equally shared, fifty-fifty. It's a risky business, demolition is a risky business. The pay is very good. As far as the pay, we get about $5.40 an hour, but it's a dangerous job, very dangerous.

If you looked down there in the records and stuff like that at the union hall, many a wrecker has been killed or hurt, I mean maimed; this is a very tricky business. In fact, it got so it's hard to get a good wrecker nowadays. There is an awful lot of work going on in demolition.

A four-, five-story building, we could take it down in less than a week, that's salvage and all. About 40 or 50 percent of the stuff or more is salvageable. I mean that's all there is to the wrecking business. You have a building, take it down and that's it. Save whatever you can; what you can't save, you destroy.

You know, you can't blame the landlords, I mean about 80 percent of these buildings you'd be surprised when you get into the buildings there, boy, I'm telling you they're polluted, they stink, I'm telling you. You can't blame the landlord, you cannot, that's impossible, you can't. It's like everything else, if you maintain something, I mean, you will always preserve it for the rest of your life. Regardless, I mean, these buildings are up—God Almighty—forty, fifty years and if they took care of these buildings like they should, they'd last another forty, fifty years. It's negligence, it's the people themselves, that's all it is. I'm telling you. It wouldn't be on the landlord, it would be on the people. You got to be a lazy person. As for myself, I moved out from this city. I moved to Long Island. I have a family, I have kids, I have eleven kids. Well, I figured I could raise them out there better than I can in the city. Really, I think it's the people themselves. I realize my job is risky, but the pay is good. It's better than going to a factory—with eleven kids, I could hardly make it. Unless, if you're the type, well, you don't want to work for eleven kids, I could go to welfare and that I've never been on. My wife doesn't work, she does a good day's work with eleven kids.

I happen to be the burner on the job, so just the other day I was burning fire escapes—I burn all the steel and stuff—and I could see some of the people throwing water and garbage out of the window. They have about two years of garbage back there. I asked a woman how the garbage got back there and she said, "I don't know but there is two years of garbage back there." I think the people are too lazy to take it down so they throw it out the window. She claims she wasn't doing it, but it was the other people who were doing it. She was looking out the window and she shouted to me, where could she find a nice place to move to. She was asking me where she could find five rooms, so I told her I didn't know because she had a big family, and she said she wanted to get out of this place. When you see the garbage back there, I don't see how a person would want to live around this place. Maybe these people can't afford to move out, but like myself I was living in Harlem and eventually I was making some money, and I had a family coming, the little ones coming. You figure you got to do better, so we decided to take a chance and buy a home, that's just what I did. We bought a home in **38** Wyandach, Long Island. It's a nice area but it's a long way out.

The conditions, from what I've seen I can't say it's the landlord. I would say it's the people's fault as well as the landlord. Well, you have some landlords who don't like to fix up, so really that makes it difficult for the people. But then not all landlords are alike. Then you have the landlords that do fix up, but the people tear it up, so I don't know why the landlord would want to invest money any further to fix up. Many landlords are afraid to take a chance because if they invest money in the building they may lose it if the city takes it over. It's a fifty-fifty chance.

There is too much garbage in the street. It's the people themselves, not the landlord. I see it, I know it. They're lazy people. That's a lazy person that doesn't want to have anything. There are some people that I know who are very poor and keep a very clean home and there are some women that I know who have children with no father in the home who go out and work. It all depends on the person themselves. The conditions cannot be blamed all on the landlord. The people know better, but I don't think they care. Between 171st and 174th streets on the right-hand side, them houses, I'd say about fifteen years back, 80 percent of them were Jewish people that lived in them houses and they were immaculate. I mean immaculate. Now, within the last ten years, you go there and see them houses now. They're deteriorating. The windows are all broken, they don't have any curtains, they have rags sticking up in the windows and stuff like that. I never seen nothing like it. I'm not Jewish and I'm not prejudiced either. I'm not. Maybe these people are a different breed of people. So help me. My opinion, I think it's the people themselves. I actually believe it's the people themselves, I really do. You look between these two buildings out here, the lot. Look at the garbage you find here. I blame it on the lack of education of these people, the proper education. They just don't care, they don't give a darn. What they need here is better laws or something. The parents are falling down on their responsibility in helping to keep this community clean and not training their children right. That's what I say. The parents themselves have not been brought up right.

The landlord gets so disgusted, you know what I mean, investing money, money, money. One can't blame them, they'll go broke. So what happens, they can't even pay their taxes. And what happens, the city steps in, they take the property over and they condemn the building. Now if the city felt that way about it, what they should do is sponsor the program. Go ahead, do what's right. But they don't want to; all they're doing is grabbing real estate. That's all they want. You watch, in ten years from now they'll probably sell it to a private syndicate so they'll make a co-op or stuff like that, and charge these poor fools thirty dollars a room. It's all a gimmick. It's only common sense. Building projects is all they ever do. They force these poor landlords out, because of the heavy taxes. So what the hell, why don't they lend them the money to pay their taxes.

You know something, you can't blame the people. You can't. You can't blame the people. What can you expect of them? They have a dozen kids and they can't afford to take care of them. I think everything is referred back to the city. It's a complicated affair. Actually, when I talk about these problems, we have to consider every little thing. Every little thing. Like the conditions of living. The conditions of wages. What they earn. What they don't earn. How much they spend for different booze, or whatever you want to call it, liquor. The jobs, education and all that stuff. In plain words, I say that the people are ignorant of the fact. I've been around this racket now for the last twenty some odd years and I've seen what goes on. There are some of these people you have to pity, they don't know any better. That's why I think these people need an education. That's the gospel truth. They should get together, I mean the people that are well-educated, and try to teach these people, you know, that don't have too much happiness and tell them what to do and how to do it. What's right and what's wrong. That's what I say. Because, some of these people, actually, innocently do things that's going to hurt everybody else.

You want to know something? Between you and me, sometimes I'm glad the people don't take care of the place—that's why we have plenty of work.

From
The Block by Herb Goro
(New York: Random House, 1970) pp.35–38.

Conflict in urban centers

The existence of large, heterogeneous populations in urban centers has frequently led to conflict between different special-interest groups. Essentially, such conflicts reflect social, economic, racial and religious cleavages within society as a whole, but they become most intense when acted out in a confined urban setting. Bus drivers and garbage collectors tie up entire urban areas in massive strikes against city authorities. Catholics and non-Catholics debate the legality of providing birth-control information, equipment or abortions in city hospitals. Adolescent Puerto Rican gangs engage in street fights with black or white gangs.

Ethnic minorities traditionally resolved their demands for representation in urban government through the brokerage mechanisms of the big-city political machines. Italian, Jewish and Irish candidates were all given places on party tickets that reflected the strength of the various communities. The system was one which defused many potentially explosive conflict situations. In the postwar years, however, the newest minorities—blacks, Mexicans and Puerto Ricans—have encountered greater difficulty in finding a voice. Although a few politicians have succeeded in building local black or Puerto Rican machines, by and large the established central organizations have failed to respond to these communities' needs and grievances.

The ghetto problem

With the outbreak of widespread rioting in the urban ghettos between 1963 and 1967, increasing study was directed toward conditions within the ghettos. The pattern of racial residential segregation has been statistically documented by sociologist Karl E. Taeuber.[34] Residential segregation has added significance because it leads to segregation in schools, libraries, parks, stores, hospitals and a variety of other local facilities. Taeuber developed an objective index to measure residential segregation, and determine the extent to which it is caused by choice, poverty or discrimination. On his scale, an index of 80 indicated that 80 percent of a given city's blacks would have to be relocated in white neighborhoods if the city were to achieve an integrated pattern of residence. Using census data for 207 cities,

Taeuber found that his index varied from 60.4 in San Jose, Cal., to 98.1 in Fort Lauderdale, Fla. Half the cities had segregation indexes of 87.8 or more, half less. Moreover, by correlating income statistics, Taeuber found that discrimination, rather than poverty or choice, was the prevailing cause.

Seeking to assess the causes and responses to the riots of 1963-67, the National Advisory Commission on Civil Disorders surveyed not only population trends, but also employment, family structure and "social disorganization" in Negro neighborhoods. It found that:

—Negro incomes remained far below those of whites. Negro median family income was only 58 percent of the white median in 1966.
—Unemployment rates for Negroes were still double those for whites in every category.
—Negro workers were concentrated in the lowest-skilled and lowest-paid occupations. These jobs often involved substandard wages, low status in the eyes of both employer and employee, little or no chance for meaningful advancement, and unpleasant or exhausting duties.
—The abandonment by many Negro males of their families affected children growing up in the racial ghetto. In 1966, 8.9 percent of all white households had a female head, but 23.7 percent of all Negro households had a female head.
—The relatively high incidence of prostitution, dope addiction, casual sex affairs and crime in racial ghettoes created "an environmental jungle" characterized by personal insecurity and tension.[35]

Anthropologist Oscar Lewis sought to explain the social characteristics of urban residents confined to racial ghettos by means of the concept of "lower-class" culture, or the "culture of poverty." Anthropologist Charles Valentine points rather to structural conditions of the larger society as the cause of behavior such as the Commission describes.[36] Yet many authorities believe that "lower-class individuals" represent only a fraction of the residential population of racial ghettos. Working-class and even some middle-class residents make up the balance. The problem of the ghettos appears to be that, as more blacks graduate from lower class to working class and subsequently to middle class, there is no space available for them to establish exclusively working- and middle-class enclaves. Because the ghettos are so restricted in area, the demand for living space is too great, and when a neighborhood "goes black," lower-class blacks move in right along with more prosperous ones. As a result, streets become littered with garbage; vandalism and the crime rate rise.

The expansion of racial and cultural minorities outside the ghettos is therefore likely to bring on community conflicts. White civic associations and protective leagues protest the erection of public housing that will house blacks, or withdraw their children from public schools to which blacks are admitted. Alternatively, white middle-class and even working-class urban residents move to the suburbs. The incentive to move is increased by the fact that, with less expensive police, transport and welfare budgets, suburban sales and property taxes are relatively low. More money can be allotted to better equipped schools, hospitals and recreational facilities.

Society and power in suburbia

Suburban residential communities develop a distinctive form of social organization and political power structure. In the suburban community, Herbert J. Gans found that people purchase homes "with only a sidelong glance" at the people who will be their neighbors to make sure that they appear to be compatible.[37] Ethnic neighborhoods do not transplant themselves; ethnic minorities become integrated with native whites and with one another.

Once people have moved in, they establish relationships on the basis of propinquity. Women become involved with neighbors on the block or street front. Homeowners, concerned with maintaining the value and status image of their houses, must make sure that neighbors share their concern, and thus every block develops a social system devoted to exerting the control needed to see that houses and lawns are kept up. Finally, people join clubs, churches and civic organizations for the purpose of finding friends. Most people do not remain active in the organizations to which they have flocked, but the organizations persist and are an important part of life in the suburbs, at least for an active minority.

Concerning political structure, political scientist Murray Stedman observes that politics in the suburbs are dominated by the nonpartisan approach, in contrast to state, national and big-city politics. He writes:

> Much of suburban politics is concerned with family-related issues. In particular, questions concerning the schools and housing attract continuing interest and attention. Occasionally in the limelight are such additional subjects as the police, recreational facilities and "corruption." In short, the politics of small communities tends to be focussed on local issues. Local government in the suburbs usually pays very careful attention to the interests of its constituents.[38]

This pattern continues, despite the fact that today a large proportion of the economic activity of metropolitan areas is being concentrated in suburbs. In this situation, more thoughtful decisions relating to zoning and land use are needed. By their nature, such matters often need county-wide or even region-wide consideration, but there is as yet no political organization on which the suburban constituency can focus for decisions of this kind. The result may be that, while local taxes are hotly and heavily debated, decisions about the placement of highways and the development of land will be handled at the state and federal level, without proper attention being given to the effects of such development on the locality involved. Some suburbs, such as Greenwich, Conn., have been able to set standards for new development. But less wealthy and less well-organized communities—the majority—are often the victims of decisions that take from them the very qualities their residents moved from the city to find. They find that the city has followed them, and that their suburban governments are no more powerful to resist an unwanted change than are the ossified structures for decision making which the city governments embody.

Intervention by the Federal Government

Since the 1930s, the Federal Government has undertaken a variety of programs that affect urban residents to a great degree. Funds spent on public welfare programs, education, health, transportation and housing supplement budgets already appropriated by state and municipal agencies. Federal spending has had diverse effects, but not always the ones anticipated.

Housing

One field in which the Federal Government has been especially active is home building. The Federal Home Loan Bank system in 1932, the Home Owner's Loan Corporation and Federal Farm Mortgage Corporation of 1933, and the National Housing Act of 1934, setting up the Federal Housing Administration, were all steps to the creation of a Federal policy that facilitated home ownership. The Federal Housing Administration and, to a lesser extent, the Veterans' Administration functioned as an incentive to single-family house construction. By insuring mortgages, they established minimum standards for facilities to be included and land use to be offered by developers. In this case, the effect of Federal intervention was an increase in the trend toward decentralization.

By contrast, Federal and state programs to encourage the construction of low cost public housing in urban centers, and urban renewal programs are much more recent and quite modest in scope. Congress inaugurated Federal public housing support with the Housing Act of 1937, but large scale urban renewal did not get underway until the Housing Act of 1949.

Sociologist Nathan Glazer has compared the relative success of Federal housing programs. He writes:

> Urban renewal, which began in 1949, even with the large areas which have been cleared in some American cities, is small potatoes compared to the central policy of encouraging single-family home building and ownership. In contrast to some 600,000 units of public housing that have been built during the history of the public housing program and 80,000 that have been built under urban renewal, over 5,000,000 units have been built under FHA home mortgage programs.[39]

A major part of the problem in urban renewal has been that Federal funds were used to buy up tracts of inner-city land which was then sold to private developers who could use the land for nonhousing purposes or for luxury housing. Not surprisingly, they chose the most profitable forms of construction, which was almost never low-income housing. Surveying the results of urban renewal, planner Morton Schussheim found that through June, 1965, the reconstruction of urban renewal land was mainly for institutional and public uses (37 percent), and for commercial and industrial use (27 percent).[40] Only 36 percent was for housing. Prior to 1963, most of the new housing was designed for upper middle-income occupancy, reflecting the desire of city officials to attract or hold such people as residents while building up the real estate tax base. Under new policy directives from Housing Administrator Robert C. Weaver, the localities began to turn increasingly to moderate- and low-income housing reuses; even so, by 1965, only about one-third of the new housing was for such families.

Everyone values everything differently today. The basic question is how to plan for a pluralistic democracy where no one agrees on anything.

Richard Weinstein

Black leaders have complained that "urban renewal" was nothing more than "Negro removal." In fact, Schussheim reported that 60 percent of the families displaced were black, though they numbered less than a third of the populations in the cities involved.[41] Students of architecture and city planning argue that urban renewal and public housing projects too often have been characterized by shortsighted planning and shoddy construction. In 1961, the architectural critic, Jane Jacobs, wrote:

> Look at what we have built with the first several billions: low-income projects that have become worse centers of delinquency, vandalism and general social hopelessness than the slums they were supposed to replace. Middle-income housing projects which are truly models of dullness and regimentation. . . . luxury housing projects that mitigate their inanity, or try to, with a vapid vulgarity. Cultural centers that are unable to support a good bookstore. Civic centers that are avoided by everyone but bums . . . . Promenades that go from noplace to nowhere and have no promenaders. Expressways that eviscerate great cities. This is not the rebuilding of cities. This is the sacking of cities.[42]

Sociologists have also concluded that in some instances urban renewal disrupted established neighborhoods without providing adequate means for their residents to regroup. Herbert J. Gans, in his study of the West End in Boston, found that 60 percent of the tenants of that neighborhood had been expected to move into public housing when their area was cleared; only 10 percent actually did.[43]

Model cities

By the 1960s, the focus of Federal aid to the urban underprivileged had shifted from providing better housing to more comprehensive programs. The omnibus housing bill of 1966 established a "Model

Cities" program. Under Title II, cities were entitled to seek Federal grants for a comprehensive attack on urban blight. These funds could be used for programs in education, antipoverty and social welfare programs, as well as more traditional construction programs aimed at stopping physical decay. Model Cities grants went to pay for emergency street repairs, bookmobiles, ambulance services, methadone maintenance clinics for narcotics addicts, sanitation services and day-care centers for working mothers.

The breadth of the problems to be attacked is indicated by the variety of uses to which Federal funds have been put. But to a certain extent cities are handicapped by the very breadth of these problems. In a free society, there is no way in which governmental agencies can prohibit the inward migration of poor citizens to the cities. In the same way, cities can only indirectly influence the decisions of established citizens and corporations to leave or stay in the city. They can do this by offering tax incentives and other inducements to stay.

Cities are themselves municipal corporations chartered by the states. Their powers to expand their boundaries, levy taxes and otherwise govern are limited by state laws. For grants in urban renewal and other improvement projects, they must apply to Federal and state agencies. Thus, to a very real degree, cities are incapable of directing their own destinies. The decisions affecting them are too often made in corporation boardrooms, in state capitals—where legislators are subject to the demands of rural constituents also—and in Washington.

reading:

Philip M. Hauser
AN URBAN BILL OF RIGHTS

The urban crisis will worsen during the 1970s and, short of major reordering of national priorities and great increases in urban expenditures, will probably grow increasingly severe until the end of the century. This is likely to be true in respect of virtually all urban problems—physical, personal, social, economic, and governmental. There is as yet no indication that this nation will do very much to bring under control during the seventies the acute and chronic problems which plague our cities and which threaten the viability of American society.

It may be anticipated, therefore, that during the seventies air and water pollution will continue to threaten health and life; housing supply and quality will remain inadequate; slums will continue to be centers of physical rot and social pathology; air and surface traffic will continue to congest urban areas and the commuters' crisis will not abate; urban design will continue to fall far short of meeting requirements; crime and delinquency will continue at high levels; organized crime will continue to thrive with virtually the same immunity it has enjoyed for half a century; drug addiction and alcoholism will continue to serve as avenues for escape for increasing numbers of people unable to cope; the revolt of youth will not only continue but, in all likelihood, will escalate at both extremes—the hippies who seek escape and the activists who seek confrontation; the revolt of the blacks will also escalate as the gap between what they desire and what they have continues to grow; the public schools will transform the United States into a caste society stratified by race and economic status as they continue to fail to provide the poor and minority groups with adequate education; poverty will continue to remind this most affluent of all nations that it has grave systemic disorders; tax reform is likely to continue to be a promise rather than a reality; welfare provisions will continue to be inadequate and constitute a continuous source of irritation both to welfare recipients and to taxpayers; payments will still be made to massive agricultural enterprises for not growing crops; consumer protection will remain inadequate as "caveat emptor" lingers as a relic of the past; the House of Representatives and the state legislatures will remain malapportioned through continued use of the gerrymander despite the "one-man-one-vote" rule; the dead hand of the South will continue its reactionary grip on the federal legislative process by reason of the combination of the one-party system and seniority rules; the "New Federalism" will demonstrate the continued disinterest of state governments in urban problems and demonstrate again that state governments are more inept, more calloused, more subject to special interest pressures and more corrupt than the federal government; military expenditures will remain at astronomical levels . . . .

The urban crisis which afflicts this nation is the product of the gap that exists between the 20th century technological and demographic world we have created and the 19th and prior century ideologies, values and institutions which we have inherited. The United States is the world's most dramatic example of our developments which have transformed this nation from an agrarian society to an urban and metropolitan order—from the "little community" to the "mass society."

These developments are the population explosion, the population implosion, the population displosion and the accelerating tempo of technological change. The population explosion refers to the remarkable acceleration in the rate of population growth. The population implosion refers to the increasing concentration of people on relatively small portions of the earth's surface—better known as urbanization. The population displosion refers to the increasing diversity of peoples who share not only the same geographic area but, also, the same life space—social, economic, and political activities. The acceleration of technological change requires no elaboration in this age in which men have now twice walked on the moon . . . .

. . . Insight into this situation is afforded by a concept a former professor of mine at the University of Chicago, William F. Ogburn, a gentleman from Georgia, introduced into the literature—namely the concept of "cultural lag." Professor Ogburn perceived that the different elements in our society and culture change at different rates so that some things "lag" behind others . . . .

. . . As recently as 1960, there were 39 states in this Union in which the urban population constituted a majority of the people. But there was not a single state in the Union in which the urban population controlled the state legislature. In my judgment, there was never an example of civil disobedience as injurious to the American people as the civil disobedience of the state legislatures which deliberately defied federal and state constitutional mandates on reapportionment. This rural minority so callously ignored urban problems that they forced the urban population to turn to the federal government for resolution of their problems.

It is rather naive to say that the federal government usurped states' rights. What has happened is that the state legislatures have committed suicide by not joining the 20th century . . . .

46   There is major need for an Urban Bill of Rights to supplement the present Bill of Rights drawn in an agrarian setting. The founding fathers did not, nor could they have been expected to, anticipate the population explosion, implosion and displosion and the great technical changes which the United States has experienced since its founding.

What is presented below is a proposed Urban Bill of Rights to be added to the Constitution to pave the way for the closing of the gap between our technological and social worlds

Every person in the United States is to have the right to:

1. Opportunity, freedom and security to enable him to achieve optimal development.
2. A physical, social and political setting for effective socialization, including formal education, to enable him to acquire the basic skills, the saleable skills and the civic skills to assume the obligations and responsibilities as well as the rights of citizenship.
3. Opportunity for maximum length of life in good health.
4. An environment controlled in the interest of society, physical and social, free from pollution and adverse population densities and including adequate housing.
5. Opportunity for employment commensurate with his education and skill, assuring him an adequate and uninterrupted income flow, preferably for services performed.
6. Knowledge and means of limiting family size in a context consistent with family, community, national and world welfare.
7. Equality and impartiality in the administration of justice in a manner to protect the interests of society, even while safeguarding the interests of the person.
8. A system of governance, federal, state and local, consistent with the realities of the metropolitan order and based on democratic principles, including representative government and majority rule.
9. Full access to the fruits of economic growth and the benefits of science, technology and the arts.
10. Opportunity to live in a peaceful world in which all conflicts of interest are resolved by adjudicative means, not physical force, including conflicts on the international as well as the domestic front. This means among other things the renouncement of war as an instrument of national policy—even at the expense of subordinating national sovereignty to international organizations and forms of government . . . .

. . . it is to be noted that the proposed rights include such fundamental things, necessary in the urban interdependent and highly vulnerable society, as opportunity and security, including assured employment and assured income flow . . . . Especially significant is the provision to make the interests of society paramount over those of the individual—a provision that would in effect modify present provisions in the Constitution which place the rights of the person above those of society. The present Constitutional provisions, as interpreted by the U.S. Supreme Court, actually prevent urban areas in the nation from dealing effectively with organized crime with which cities have been afflicted for over half a century. Finally, and perhaps most important, the new bill of rights includes the right to be free from the use of physical force in the resolution of conflicts of interest—on the domestic as well as the international front. This on the domestic front would, among other things, outlaw the use of force in the settlement of labor-management strife—would outlaw both the strike and the lockout and require adjudicative means of settlement. The use of brute force to settle labor-management conflict is another survival from the past which is generally injurious to the entire nation.

Also worthy of special attention is the provision for government based on representative government and majority rule, neither of which the American people have yet achieved. Suppression of the right to vote, gerrymandering and malapportionment have characterized the Congress and the state legislature . . . .

Finally, to deal with contemporary problems, both the conservative and liberal approaches must be abandoned in favor of a social engineering approach. The conservative turns to the past for an answer to 20th century problems. The liberal too often manifests emotion, zeal and determination to deal with the 20th century problems. Both approaches are hopelessly outmoded. What is needed is the social engineering approach—the application of knowledge based on research to the resolution of problems. Social engineering is needed to deal with social problems in the same sense that physical engineering is utilized to solve physical problems and biomedical engineering (medicine and surgery) to meet biomedical problems. Our society has come to recognize the role of the physical and biomedical engineer but has yet to recognize and accept the social engineer . . . .

. . . It may take the century from 1950 to 2050 for the social sciences to gain comparable respectability and acceptance so that the social engineer is permitted to apply knowledge to the solution of social problems.

But it is a moot question as to whether we shall remain a viable society to 2050. It may well be that the chaos with which we are beset will engulf us and drag us down into the drain of history as a nation which achieved the miraculous in technology but could not adapt itself to the new world man created rapidly enough to survive . . . .

From
"Whither Urban Society?" by Philip M. Hauser
in *Cities in the 70's*
(Washington, D.C.: National League of Cities, 1970) pp. 15-21.

Proposals for change

The most recent proposals for improving conditions in cities have called for a dual approach. On the one hand, the Federal government, under President Nixon, has inaugurated a policy of revenue sharing. On the other hand, political scientists such as Campbell and Shahala argue that state governments must assume a more constructive role.[44]

In January, 1970, President Nixon proposed his revenue sharing plan, under which taxes collected by the Federal government would be funneled back to state, city and other local governments. In the fall of 1972, Congress enacted a bill authorizing $30 billion worth of expenditures for this purpose, to be spread over five years. The bill will give to state governments a rising amount, from $1.95 billion in 1972 to $2.85 billion by 1976; it allots another $3.5 billion annually to local governments for "high-priority expenditures," specifically public safety, environmental protecton and transportation.

When originally proposed, revenue sharing was greeted with enthusiasm by mayors and governors. By 1973, when the program went into effect, it began meeting with objections. Federal administrators apparently believed that revenue sharing was meant to replace, rather than supplement, existing urban renewal and civic improvement programs. Funds for low-income housing projects and Model Cities undertakings ceased to become available, or were doled out for temporary purposes. Local officials protested that they needed revenue sharing and the other expenditures as well.

At this point, it is too early to tell how successfully revenue sharing

48

will operate. However, as Campbell and Shahala observe, the states themselves possess capacities for urban improvement. To some extent, they have already taken steps. Campbell and Shahala write:

> Governor Rockefeller did force the New York State legislature to establish an Urban Development Corporation. Governor Hughes of New Jersey did present to his legislature the only full-fledged state urban program ever proposed, but other governors and legislators have simply found excuses ranging from the constitutional to the political for inaction.[45]

New city forms

Seeking to expand their tax base, and develop a coordinated attack on such problems as transportation and air pollution, cities have tried to extend their boundaries. Such extensions are regulated by state law—and state laws tend to impede the process by requiring referendums or enabling legislation. Annexation has traditionally been the most commonly proposed remedy. It has been used in recent years by Houston, Dallas, Fort Worth, San Antonio and Oklahoma City. However, writes the urbanologist Daniel Grant:

> Opposition to annexation is almost always strong in the suburbs, with any one of several arguments being sufficient to secure a negative referendum vote: higher taxes, a corrupt or incompetent central city government, false promises in the delivery of services, and annexation as a devious tax-grabbing scheme. . . . In short, annexation is virtually dead in the older and larger metropolitan areas, particularly in the North and East, as a device for permitting a city to keep up with its growth.[46]

A second means for restructuring local government is the extension of a city's boundaries to include the entire county and the consolidation of city and county governments into one. Baton Rouge, Jacksonville, Indianapolis and Nashville have all used this method since World War II.

Still another device, commonly proposed but almost never adopted, is the metropolitan federation, with city governments operating with partial independence, and limited powers delegated to the federation. Although state governments have been willing to pass enabling legislation for cities wishing to consolidate with counties, they have done very little to encourage or permit the establishment of metropolitan federations in the United States. The best-known examples of metropolitan federation are the governments of Greater London and Metropolitan Toronto. In each case, the structure was established by an Act of Parliament without the requirement of a popular referendum. The closest thing to a metropolitan federation in the United States is the metro government of Dade County and Miami. Voters there narrowly adopted a two-tier form of government in 1957. Grant writes:

> In practice, Dade County's metro is more nearly a "municipalized county" than it is a federation of municipalities, since the cities as such are not

represented on the board of commissioners. But even with its lawsuits, recurring referendum fights, and financial limitations, this new approach to governing a metropolitan area has offered new hope and has stimulated the imagination of many other cities.[47]

The most common reorganizational device is the special district, a semiautonomous authority set up to handle transport, housing, schools or some other single function of government. While special districts have proved popular with administrators, they are subject to a wide range of criticisms. For example, they separate the program under consideration from the mainstream of city affairs but make it vulnerable to the pressures of a specialized clientele; they atomize local government and make comprehensive planning of local programs a virtual impossibility.

Another approach to solving the problems of the urban center is the creation of satellite cities, or "new towns." As originally envisioned by the English social planner, Ebenezer Howard, the "new town" was to be a completely self-contained community in the country, near the metropolis. It would contain not only residential but also cultural facilities, offices and an industrial park to provide employment. In the United States, perhaps 20 communities have been built that are true "new towns," all since World War II. They include Reston, Va.; the Irvine Ranch, in Orange County, Cal.; and Columbia, Md., the most successfully integrated project to date. By the time of its completion in 1980, Columbia is expected to have cost $2 billion and to house a population of 110,000 in seven villages.[48]

Neighborhood control

Within the central cities, recent years have seen several attempts to return neighborhoods to local control. One theory of local organization is that advocated by the late activist Saul Alinsky, and employed in a number of cities through his Industrial Areas Federation—such as The Woodlawn Organization (TWO) in Chicago, FIGHT in Rochester and BUILD in Buffalo. Alinsky's groups seek to bring pressure to bear on civic authorities by mobilizing public opinion in low-income neighborhoods. The Students for a Democratic Society also began a number of projects for local community action in Chicago, Cleveland, Newark and Oakland. The SDS groups were primarily ideological, however, and much of their activity are of an evangelical sort.

A more practical approach, argues legal expert Milton Kotler, is seeking the transfer of public authority to the neighborhood through the legal establishment of a neighborhood corporation.[49] The first example of this type of organization is the East Central Citizens Organization of Columbus, Ohio. Set up in 1965, it has been followed by the formation of some seventy similar neighborhood corporations in different parts of the country. ECCO is located in a poor neighborhood of Columbus one mile square, with 6500 residents. With a 1969 budget of $202,947, consisting mainly of a grant from the United

States Office of Economic Opportunity, it oversaw a variety of programs. Its youth center offered educational facilities, nurseries for retarded children and adult education; other activities sponsored by ECCO included the rehabilitation of homes in cooperation with the city government, local operation of the state employment office, health programs and a credit union.[50]

ECCO must compete for power with other antipoverty programs sponsored by the Federal government, including the Columbus Community Action Agency and the Model Cities Agency. This type of bureaucratic rivalry hinders effective planning in other cities as well. Some authorities believe that the best solution to the cities' problems lies not in specific programs geared toward improvement of housing, transportation or education, but in programs intended to raise living standards across the board. Various ways to do this have been suggested, including family assistance payments, a guaranteed annual wage, and a negative income tax that will enable every family's income to rise above the poverty level. However, none of these proposals has yet been enacted into law.

The political and social change required to implement many of the neighborhood control programs proposed for urban areas would be time-consuming and painstaking to bring about. Knowing this, planner John Friedmann still believes they constitute the only sensible way to proceed, and approvingly cites Thomas Jefferson, the foe of cities, on the matter:

> For Jefferson, the elementary unit of "good and safe" government is the "republic of the ward," a subunit of the county. The criterion of how much effective power is to be internalized at each level of government is *competence*.[51]

Many planners see the matter differently, however, and some economists and technologists assert that the present problems of the city are problems of transition. They see changes in social and physical structure for the city brought about through centralized authority rather than by local control, largely because of the technological realities of the present and future.

---

reading: **Kenneth E. Boulding**
POSTCIVILIZATION

We are now passing through a period of transition in the state of man quite as large and as far reaching as the transition from precivilized to civilized society. I call this the transition from civilization to postcivilization. This idea is shocking to many people who still think that what is going on in the world today is a simple extention of the movement from precivilized to civilized society. In fact, however, I think we have to recognize that we are moving towards a state of man which is as different from civilization as civilization itself was from the precivilized societies which preceded it. This is what we mean by the innocent term "economic development." There is something ironic in the reflection that just at the moment when civilization has, in effect, extended itself over the whole world and when precivilized societies exist only in rapidly declining pockets, postcivilization is stalking on the heels of civilization itself and is creating the same kind of disruption and disturbance in civilized societies that civilization produces on precivilized societies.

Just as civilization is a product of the food surplus which proceeds from agriculture, which represents a higher level of organization of food production than primitive hunting and food gathering, so postcivilization is a product of science, that is, of a higher level of organization of human knowledge and the organization of this knowledge into know-how. The result of this is an increase in the productivity of human labor, especially in the production of commodities, which is quantitatively so large as to create a qualitatively different kind of society. The food surplus upon which classical civilization rested was extremely meager. In the Roman Empire at its height, for instance, it is doubtful whether more than twenty or twenty-five per cent of the total population were in nonfood-producing occupations. That is, it took about seventy-five per cent of the total population to feed the hundred per cent, and only twenty to twenty-five per cent could be spared to fight wars, to establish states, and to build the great monuments of civilization, both of architecture and of literature.

In the United States at the moment, which is the part of the world furthest advanced toward postcivilization, we can now produce all our food requirements with about ten per cent of the population and still have an embarrassing agricultural surplus. This is a change in an order of magnitude. We can now devote ninety per cent of the population to nonagricultural pursuits. In the production of many other commodities, the increase in the productivity of labor is even more spectacular, and with the coming of automation, we may find even another order of magnitude change in this quantity . . . . The prices of those commodities in the production of which technical improvement has occurred have fallen drastically relative to those commodities and services the production of which has been technologically stagnant. Furthermore, no end is at present in sight for this process. It is doubtful whether we have even reached the mid-point of this enormous process of change. We devote increasing resources to technological improvements and to the advance of knowledge and up to now there seems to be little in the way of diminishing returns to this activity. . . . It is by no means impossible to suppose a world at the end of this process in which we can produce our whole food supply with one per cent of the population, in which we can produce all basic commodities such as clothing, housing, and so on with perhaps another two or three per cent or perhaps at most ten per cent, and in which, therefore, economic life revolves very largely around the organization of personal services. We have not yet begun to think out the details of such an economy. It is clear that many of its institutions and forms of organization will be very different from what is now familiar to us . . . .

Just as civilization almost always produces a disastrous impact upon the precivilized societies with which it comes into contact—witness for instance the sad history of the American Indians—it also seems all too probable that the impact of postcivilized on civilized societies will be equally disastrous. There are three major aspects of this breakdown of the institutions of civilization. The first is the breakdown of the system of national defense . . . . The breakdown is the result partly of a diminution in the cost of transport of violence which, coupled with the increase in the range of the deadly missile, has shattered what might be called the classical system of unconditional national security. These two phenomena have destroyed what I call "unconditional viability" even for the largest nations, and in particular have rendered the cities of the world pitilessly vulnerable.

The second symptom of the disintegration of civilization is the population explosion in the civilized countries, and even in the incipient postcivilized countries. Classical civilization maintained whatever equilibrium it had because its high birth rates were offset by high death rates. In the ideal type of civilized society, we might suppose a birth and death rate of about forty with an expectation of life at birth of twenty-five. In postcivilized society, the expectation of life at birth rises to seventy. An equilibrium of population under these circumstances requires birth and death rates of about fourteen per thousand. The first impact of postcivilized techniques, however, on civilized society is frequently a dramatic reduction in the death rate. In many tropical countries, for instance, in the last twenty years, death rates have been reduced from twenty-five or thirty per thousand to about ten per thousand simply as a result of the introduction of DDT and relatively primitive measures of public health. The birth rate, however, stays up at forty with the result that these societies are now suffering a three per cent per annum population increase. This puts a burden on them in the current investment in human resources which may be more than they can bear, and it may therefore prevent them from making the transition into postcivilization. Postcivilized society requires as one of its conditions a large investment in human resources, that is, education. A poor, civilized society may prove to be incapable of devoting enough resources to education in the face of the three per cent per annum increase and in the face of its enormous numbers of children. Under these circumstances, it can easily regress towards even lower levels of civilization until the death rate rises once again or until some methods of population control are adopted. There are many parts of the world today in which we may be repeating the history of Ireland from 1700 to 1846—a gloomy prospect indeed.

It is the third aspect of the disintegration of civilization with which we are mainly concerned here, however. This is the disintegration of what might be called the classical city. The classical city is a well-integrated social organization. It has clearly defined boundaries and limits and it earns its living by a judicious combination of politics (that is, exploitation), production, and trade. It is unsanitary, so that its death rate is high; it almost certainly does not reproduce itself, and it continually renews itself by drawing on the excess population as well as on the excess food supply of the country. There is a sharp differentiation between the culture of the city and of the country. The city is also a focus of loyalty and even the national state is frequently only an extension—or a colony—of the capital city.

In postcivilization all the conditions which gave rise to the classical city have gone. The parameters of the great equations of society have changed to the point where the classical city is no longer included as one of the solutions. The things which give rise to the need for concentrations all disappear. The city is now, for instance, utterly defenseless; it is a sitting duck for the H-bomb, and so called civil defense in the cities becomes little more than an obscene attempt to persuade the civilian population that they are thoroughly expendable in a modern war. The diminution in the cost of transport both of commodities and of communications has greatly diminished the value of concentrations of population for the purposes of trade and human intercourse. The classical city is based fundamentally on the necessity for face-to-face communication. For many purposes even today this necessity remains. The telephone, for instance, is not an adequate substitute for a personal conversation simply because it uses so restricted a channel that much of the nuances of communication which are transmitted, for instance, through gesture are lost. The possibility of communication by means of modulated light beams, however, has opened up an enormous number of long-distance channels, and it may well be that in the not-too-distant future we shall each sit in our own studies and conduct long-distance televised conferences with people all over the world. We are very far from having exhausted the implications, both political and economic, of the communications revolution in which we are living. Stock markets and legislative assemblies, for instance, in a physical sense are civilized rather than postcivilized institutions, and one doubts whether they will survive another fifty or one hundred years with the present type of development.

The impact of the automobile on the city is one stage in its disintegration, and this has been well-documented. We are all familiar, I am sure, with the notion of Los Angeles as the first postcivilized urban agglomeration—an agglomeration created by and poisoned by the automobile. Under no circumstances could Los Angeles be called a city in the classical sense of the word. We must now recognize, indeed, I think, that California has become the first example of what I would call the "state city," that is, an urban agglomeration state-wide in its extent. Even the Shasta Dam has become a weekend playground for people from Los Angeles, and of course, the tentacles of the Los Angeles water system tend to engulf the whole West!. . . The notion of the United States as consisting essentially of three or four loose, sprawling megalopolises separated by stretches of empty countryside is by no means remote.

We can almost say that the city is destroyed by its own success. The paradox here is that by the time ninety per cent of the population are urban, the city has really ceased to have any meaning in itself. The converse of this phenomenon is the disappearance of rural life as a distinctive and peculiar subculture within the society. Over large parts of the United States this has already happened. The Iowa farmer has an occupational subculture but he does not have a rural subculture. He is merely an ex-urbanite who happens to be living on a farm, and he earns his living by thoroughly urban methods. He is, furthermore, a professional, usually with a college degree, and he is far more remote, say, from the European peasant than he is from the American factory engineer.

We may very well ask ourselves, therefore, whether we visualize a period in the not very distant future when in postcivilized societies, the city will really have disappeared altogether as an entity. We can even visualize a society in which the population is spread very evenly over the world in almost self-sufficient households, each circulating and processing everlastingly its own water supply through its own algae, each deriving all the power it needs from its own solar batteries, each in communication with anybody it wants to communicate with through its personalized television, each with immediate access to all the cultural resources of the world through channels of communications to libraries and other cultural repositories, each basking in the security of an invisible and cybernetic world state in which each man shall live under his vine and his own fig tree and none shall make him afraid. There may be a few radioactive holes to mark the sites of the older cities and a few interesting ruins that have escaped destruction. This vision is, of course, pure science fiction, but in these days one must not despise science fiction as a way of keeping up with the news.

Some modifications of this rather idyllic picture have to be made even in postcivilization, I suspect. A high level postcivilized stable technology would almost have to be based on the oceans for sources for its basic raw materials, as the mines and the fossil fuels will very soon be gone. There will, therefore, be some manufacturing concentrations around the shores of the world. We may even see a revival of the form of the classical city for pure pleasure where people can enjoy the luxury of walking and of face-to-face communication. Inequality of income in such a society is likely to be reflected in the fact that the poor will drive vehicles and the rich will walk. We are already, I think, beginning to see this movement in the movement of the rich into the city centers and the development of the mall. These cities, however, will be stage sets—they will arise out of the very freedom and luxury of the society **54** rather than out of its necessities.

Just as we are deeply ambivalent toward the classical city and towards civilizations, so we are likely to be equally ambivalent towards postcivilization and we are likely to find a deep nostalgia for the city. Even in the new Jerusalem (the mile-cube city, we may observe perhaps only just around the corner as being the only practical way of having twenty million people living together) there will be nostalgia for the old Jerusalem and for Athens. We may well find a new race of prophets extolling the virtues of civilization—its purity, honesty, and simplicity, its closeness to nature, and its closeness to God by contrast with the even deadlier vices of postcivilized society . . . .

From
"The Death of the City: A Frightened Look at Postcivilization,"
in *The Historian and the City,* edited by Oscar Handlin and John Burchard
(Cambridge, Mass.: MIT Press and Harvard University Press, 1963) pp. 133–145.

Notes

[1] Gideon Sjoberg, "The Origin and Evolution of Cities," in *Cities: Their Origin, Growth and Human Impact* (San Francisco: W.H. Freeman and Company, 1973) p. 24.

[2] *The New York Times,* March 5, 1973, p. 1.

[3] Sjoberg, *op. cit.,* p. 26.

[4] For an account of Stockholm's limited success, see Göran Sidenbladh, "Stockholm: A Planned City," in *Cities: Their Origin, Growth and Human Impact, op. cit.,* pp. 187-194.

[5] Thomas Jefferson, quoted by Murray S. Stedman, Jr., in *Urban Politics* (Cambridge, Massachusetts: Winthrop Publishers, 1972) p. 21.

[6] Morton and Lucia White, "The American Intellectual versus the American City," *Daedalus,* Winter, 1961, pp. 166-178.

[7] *Ibid,* p. 177.

[8] Francis E. Rourke, "Urbanism and American Democracy," *Ethics,* July, 1964, pp. 255-268.

[9] Alexis de Tocqueville, *Democracy in America,* trans. by Henry Reeve (New York: Knopf, 1945) Vol. 1, p. 290.

[10] Nathan Glazer and Daniel P. Moynihan, *Beyond the Melting Pot* (Cambridge, Massachusetts: M.I.T. Press, 1963) p. 9.

[11] W. I. Thomas and Florian Znaniecki, *The Polish Peasant in Europe and America* (New York: Dover, reissued 1958).

[12] Edward C. Banfield, *The Unheavenly City* (Boston: Little, Brown and Company, 1970) p. 25.

[13] Robert M. Fogelson, "The Fragmented Metropolis: Los Angeles, 1850-1930," in *The City in American Life,* Paul Kramer and Frederick L. Holborn, eds. (New York: G. P. Putnam's Sons, 1970) pp. 236, 328.

[14] United States Bureau of the Census, *Statistical Abstract of the United States,* 93rd edition (Washington, D.C., 1972) p. 223.

[15] Stedman, *op. cit.,* p. 160.

[16] *Statistical Abstract,* op. cit., p. 16.

[17] *Ibid.,* p. 23.

[18] Stanley Lieberson, *Ethnic Patterns in American Cities* (New York: The Free Press, 1963) p. 109.

[19] Max Weber, "The Nature of the City," in Richard Sennett, ed., *Classic Essays in the Culture of Cities* (New York: Appleton-Century-Crofts, 1969) p. 38.

[20] Georg Simmel, "The Metropolis and Mental Life," in Sennett, ed., *op. cit.,* p. 48.

[21] Robert Park, "The City: Suggestions for the Investigation of Human Behavior in the Urban Environment," in Sennett (ed.), *op. cit.*

[22] Louis Wirth, "Urbanism as a Way of Life," in Sennett (ed.), *op. cit.*

[23] Herbert Gans, *People and Plans* (New York: Basic Books, 1968), pp. 35-49.

[24] James S. Coleman, "Community Disorganization and Conflict," in Robert K. Merton and Robert Nisbet, eds., *Contemporary Social Problems* (New York: Harcourt Brace, Jovanovich, 1971), pp. 658-674.

[25] Richard Sennett, *The Uses of Disorder* (New York: Knopf, 1970), passim.

[26] Edward C. Banfield and James Q. Wilson, *City Politics* (Cambridge, Massachusetts: Harvard University Press, 1963), p. 118.

[27] *Ibid.*, p. 123.

[28] Robert A. Dahl, *Who Governs? Democracy and Power in an American City* (New Haven: Yale University Press, 1961).

[29] Michael Aiken, "The Distribution of Community Power: Structural Bases and Social Consequences," in Michael Aiken and Paul E. Mott, eds., *The Structure of Community Power* (New York: Random House, 1970), pp. 494-495.

[30] Banfield and Wilson, *op. cit.*, pp. 331-335.

[31] "The Great Urban Tax Tangle," *Fortune*, March 1965, pp. 106 ff.

[32] Alan K. Campbell and Donna E. Shahala, "Problems Unsolved Solutions Untried: The Urban Crisis," in Alan K. Campbell, ed., *The States and the Urban Crisis* (Englewood Cliffs, N.J., Prentice-Hall, 1970) p. 18.

[33] *Ibid.*, p. 18.

[34] Karl E. Taeuber, "Residential Segregation," in *Cities: Their Origin, Growth and Human Impact, op. cit.*, p. 274.

[35] *Report of the National Advisory Commission on Civil Disorders* (New York: Bantam Books, 1968) pp. 251-262.

[36] Charles A. Valentine, *Culture and Poverty* (Chicago: The University of Chicago Press, 1968), p. 129 and passim.

[37] Gans, *op. cit.*, pp. 134-135.

[38] Stedman, *op. cit.*, p. 163.

[39] Nathan Glazer, "Housing Problems and Housing Policies," *The Public Interest*, Spring, 1970, p. 30.

[40] Morton J. Schussheim, "Housing in Perspective," *The Public Interest*, Spring, 1970, pp. 27-43.

[41] *Ibid.*

[42] Jane Jacobs, *The Death and Life of Great American Cities* (New York: Random House, 1961) p. 4.

[43] Herbert J. Gans, *The Urban Villagers* (New York: The Free Press, 1962) p. 321.

[44] Campbell and Shahala, *op. cit.*, p. 25.

[45] *Ibid.*, p. 32.

[46] Daniel Grant, "Urban Needs and State Response: Local Government Reorganization," in Campbell (ed.), *op. cit.*, p. 67.

[47] *Ibid.*, p. 72.

[48] Gurney Breckenfeld, *Columbia and the New Cities* (New York: Ives Washburn, 1971) pp. 301-303.

[49] Milton Kotler, *Neighborhood Government* (Indianapolis: Bobbs-Merrill Company, 1969) pp. 44-48.

[50] *Ibid.*, p. 72.

[51] John Friedmann, *Transactive Planning* (New York: Doubleday Anchor, 1973) p. 219.

Summary

Urban problems—those of large numbers of people settled together—are as old as cities themselves, and cities have existed since 3500 B.C. The urban crisis in the United States today is a modern version of these problems, but the solution to them is complicated by the large scope and interconnected nature of modern urbanization. The phenomenal growth of the American city has been made possible by technological advances—modern methods of production and communication; the train and then the automobile as a means of transport—and by economic growth. American society has attempted to accommodate this rapid urban development, but solutions to the cities' difficulties are complicated by social and political patterns which adjust more slowly than necessary to changed conditions.

Despite the suspicions of political thinkers such as Jefferson, American cities have flourished since colonial times. Fed by immigrants from rural areas and countries abroad, city populations expanded enormously during the nineteenth century. As each new wave of immigrants arrived, they gathered together in ethnic neighborhoods, often retaining the traditional social customs of the "old country."

Disruption of these traditional ethnic patterns was inevitable, however, as technological changes and economic prosperity made possible a vast increase in the size of urban areas. The personal automobile freed both employer and employee from the concentrated city center. As industries and businesses moved out to lower-taxed land in the urban fringe, they were soon followed by city dwellers who sought the less congested living of residential suburbs. The city of the computer age is an increasingly decentralized unit, with teeming business and slum districts at its center, surrounded by ever-widening circles of industrial and residential suburbs.

The flight to the suburbs has been counterbalanced by a continued inward drift of new city dwellers. Recently, the largest immigrant group has been rural, southern blacks. Like earlier ethnic groups, they have settled in segregated communities. Because of systematic exclusion from other city areas and economic distress, these black areas soon became congested ghettos marked by poverty and social discontent.

Sociologists have interpreted urban settlements by such concepts as the "cosmopolitan personality" of the urban dweller, and they continue to investigate the nature of "community" within urban areas, attempting to understand factors which affect the processes of urban life.

The American city gave rise to a distinctive form of political structure, the Political Machine, which for decades ruled the major cities through systems of patronage and ethnic loyalty. At the same time, much of the political power in cities over the years has resided in wealthy elites of businessmen and established families, most characteristic of cities where official governmental bodies have failed to respond to pressing social ills.

As wealthy homeowners and large industries relocate outside the city's boundaries, the city's tax base has declined drastically, making it difficult to raise sufficient revenue to maintain city services. These financial problems have come in a time of rising costs for all manner of services—transportation, sanitation, police, education, and welfare aid for an increasingly large population unable to find employment. Unable to raise funds to meet these problems, the cities have turned for aid to state governments and to the federal government.

Since the 1930s, the federal government has financially assisted the cities in providing services and programs dealing with welfare, education, health, transportation, and housing. The Model Cities program, begun in the 1960s, has emphasized a comprehensive approach to a range of neighborhood problems, while recent revenue sharing efforts have attempted to give more tax funds back to the states and localities from which they were collected.

Alternatives to present modes of city organization have recently been devised in response to the cities' problems. Annexation of suburbs and consolidation of city-county governments are two methods intended to provide better services to city residents. Self-contained satellite cities are being built outside major urban areas. Yet another attempted solution proposes to transfer public authority to neighborhood governmental units.

The technological changes that made rapid urbanization possible have since been succeeded by others. It remains to be seen whether successful solutions to the urban problems of the present day can be found before the new technologies impose still more difficulties on an almost completely urbanized nation.

chapter

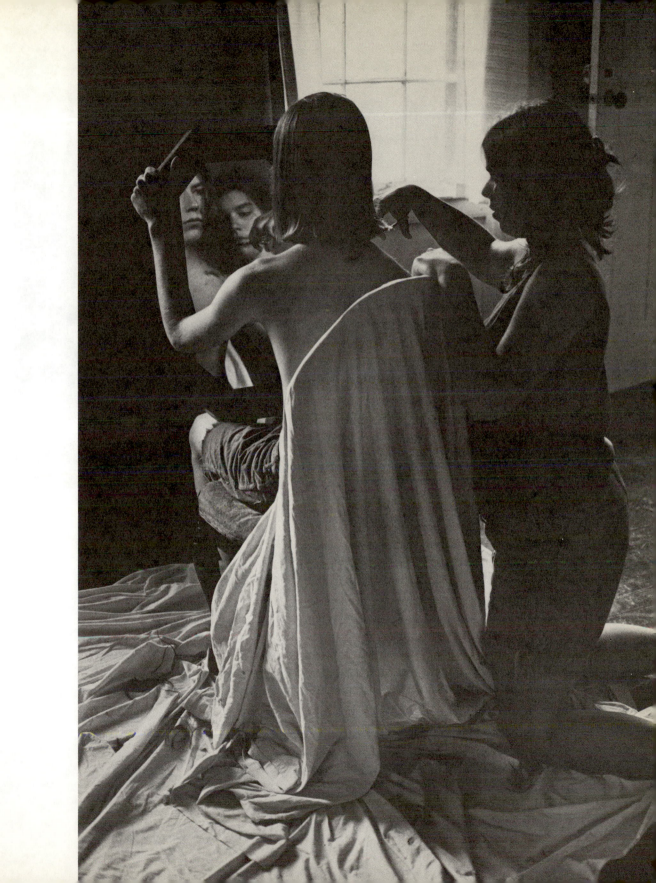

family

To the producers of American television commercials, it is obvious what the family's function in America is: to consume. With few exceptions, commercials depict a mother and father and two children, one boy, one girl, enjoying either their home or their car. They are companionable, mobile and happy. The commercials are true, to a certain extent; the "average" American family these days does have two children, they are mobile and they do consume products and services at a very high rate.

Yet there is mounting evidence that as a unit of social organization, the American family is unstable. Out of every 100 American marriages, 37 end in divorce. The past decade has witnessed the growth of a "generation gap" between parents and their children in which parental precepts are openly disregarded by children almost as soon as the children learn to talk back. Changes in sexual mores have made drastic inroads on the fidelity presumed to be the standard in conjugal relationships. Roles within the family structure are subject to strain. More married women are working than ever before, yet husbands who have traditionally been regarded as family providers in many cases are working harder than ever themselves, to the exclusion of their role as parent.

Observers of the family today, from sociologists to filmmakers, are the latest in a long line of experts who have, throughout our history, been preoccupied with the family's worth. Continued concern would seem to be justified, since the family has functioned as an institution basic to almost all societies. Society entrusts it with the regulation of sexual activity and procreation, the socialization of children, the physical care of its members, and makes it the focus of psychological support and emotional security for the individual. Almost always, of course, the family has shared these functions with other social institutions such as the church, school or work place. And the family has adapted itself to the needs of society to some extent in all of these areas. Yet so high a rate of family dissolution, and such drastic conflict within the family units which stay together, seem to indicate either that society is pushing the family to do too much, or that it has itself taken over so many of the functions that, as an institution, the family no longer has a function to serve, unless it be that of consumption. The possibility exists that the American family is not a vital social unit but a hollow shell.

Because the lives of so many Americans revolve around the families within which they live, some perspective on changes in the institution and its functions is particularly important. Alternatives to present-day family life and solutions to its problems have in the past decade been forthcoming from a great variety of groups within our society. It seems useful to examine both the family's problems and some proposed solutions here, as well as to give some account of how the family has functioned—or failed to function—as an institution in the past.

Trends in American family life

The family has been an important unit of social organization in this country since its earliest days. Whereas in Latin America the first European presence was primarily a rapacious one—the invaders intended to take what wealth they could and return to Europe—in North America the early Europeans came with the hope of colonizing and settling the land. Settlement was accomplished, for the most part, by small groups of families. The relative stability of American society, up to the present, can be partially ascribed to the establishment and reinforcement of these early family patterns.

Colonial families

Much of early American family life took place within communal or utopian societies, such as that of the Puritans of New England. In Puritan families, the father was vested with total authority. His wife and children were to respect and obey him in all worldly matters. But the family itself was subject to the strict religious, social and moral norms of the community. Social control was generally effective; what deviations did occur were harshly sanctioned. As the colony prospered, stresses in the communal arrangements grew greater. Deviant or dissatisfied members departed, often at the express bidding of the community. Those banished from one community founded another.

But social stresses could not be altogether avoided. Lawsuits involving property rights, farming and grazing rights increased markedly, both in the new communities and the old. The communal system could not respond adequately to these problems, especially when subjected to outside pressures. With the influx of new cultural groups, family life in New England and other areas took on the character of European family life of the time.

The colonial period was one in which the institutions of property and family were virtually inseparable. That a family's landholdings would be wholly retained by its heirs was guaranteed by the British legalisms of Primogeniture and Entail, by which the first-born son or a network of family relations inherited property. Under this system the "leading families" of the colonial period evolved into units of social power more important than legislatures, whose powers were severely limited. Within such families, the husband and father still enjoyed complete authority, though the wife might be entrusted with the actual management of the household.

With the revolution, Primogeniture and Entail were abolished. Most of the landed estates were broken up as a result, a move which gave impetus not only to national expansion, but to much greater freedom within the social structure. Both of these conditions had an effect on the family patterns which were to emerge in the nineteenth century.

Nineteenth century families

Ideas of communal living reappeared in the nineteenth century and many experiments were tried. The Oneida Community in New York State practiced an idealistic form of free love and held property in common; Socialist experiments, such as that at New Harmony, Ind., lasted for years in the 1840s. The Mormons, organizing themselves in response to a religious vision, practiced polygamy in all their settlements, a custom so opposed to prevailing norms they were forced to move further westward. In Utah, their settlement flourished with its polygynous family structure intact; acceptance of monogamy was a condition of Utah's acceptance into the Union in 1896. From this fact alone, it is clear that the major expansion of the country and the consolidation of its enterprises was in the hands of families of a different character.

The family unit which faced the challenges of settlement on the American frontier was usually of the extended type, in which three generations lived together as a single large household. In such families the authority of the husband and father was virtually that of an Old Testament patriarch. The wife and mother was responsible for the ordering of the household, and for the domestic training of female children. Grandmothers and aunts, if present, shared in these responsibilities. The children helped work the land, and because there was much to be done, large families were preferred. Typically the extended family included married children as well as their spouses.

On the frontier, the extended family was often the sole unit of social organization, sustained by strong religious beliefs, a rigid moral code and hard cooperative work. Significantly, the family patterns of many of the European immigrants who came to America after 1840 were well suited to the frontier situation. The communities established by Germans, Scandinavians, Poles and others resembled, in their social structure, the towns and villages the immigrants had left in Europe, as well as those they encountered in the new world.

Although the family patterns of the frontier were very similar to patterns developed earlier in Europe, those which accompanied the rise of American cities and towns were historically unique. New family structures developed in response to the Industrial Revolution and the growth of cities.

In preindustrial society, the family had produced most of the major needs of a society—food, clothing, even shelter. The coming of factory production relieved the family of most of these functions. Improved systems of transportation, most notably the railroad and the steamboat, made possible a wider and faster distribution of goods as well, eliminating family-based distribution systems which were local in nature.

*Of all the relations that ever I see
My old fleshly kindred are furthest from me
So bad and so ugly, so hateful they feel
To see them and hate them increases my zeal*

   *O how ugly they look!
   How ugly they look!
   How nasty they feel!*

From a Shaker hymn

As industrialism began to usurp the production and distribution functions of the family, however, it created a growing need for labor. Prospective workers were drawn off the land and into the growing towns and cities. Farm girls were employed in early textile mills, largely because the making of cloth had been part of their domestic function at home. Mechanics and engineers were drawn to the workshops that produced the machines of the new age. Increasing numbers of men, women and children were required to run the machines and factories of the industrial age.

By mid-century, several new trends in family life were evident. Women, no longer bound to the home, were freed from parental authority—though "on their honor" to respect their upbringing. The strains of this situation may account for the trend to earlier marriages that emerged at this time. It was in this period too that the pressure of business began to fall on the husband and father, reducing his time for participating in family life. In the growing middle classes, the responsibility for home life fell increasingly to the wife. Moreover, there were indications of growing permissiveness in child-rearing. These trends became even more pronounced after the Civil War.

The war itself freed from slavery a vast number of blacks whose family life had been overwhelmingly affected by the circumstances of the institution. As their masters' property, slaves were economic assets, to be bought, sold and even bred at will. In such conditions, any family attachments that developed were at best inconvenient. Formalized marriage was generally denied to slaves, though intercourse was encouraged, since the children of such unions constituted additional economic assets. Fathers were not allowed to assume any familial responsibility, however, and the slave child was normally born into a family where a mother was the only parent.[1] Even among freed blacks this pattern persisted for some time. In a society of rapid industrial expansion and continuing immigration, few fathers could support a family: There was no place for uneducated, unskilled black labor. The available work was mostly in the agricultural south and paid poorly. Consequently, the black mother, normally working as a domestic or a nursemaid, was the family provider by default.

Into the expanding industrial economy which characterized the United States after the Civil War, and into the cities which were its locus, came millions of immigrants. The families which immigrated after about 1865 came increasingly from Southern and Central Europe. In family customs these immigrants, Italians and Jews and Slavic peoples, varied widely, but most groups were characterized by some sort of extended family arrangement, common in the rural villages and towns of the countries from which they had come.

Although it was primarily the men who worked in the industries of the new country, many immigrant women and children were employed there, too, since they could be hired for wages less than those paid to men. When the immigrant husband was sole provider, the wife was forced into the home, much as the middle-class wife had been earlier, but without the community connections that had characterized her life in Europe. Child-raising became primarily her responsibility, though the husband often retained the authority characteristic of the extended family arrangement. Combating whatever ethnic standards the immigrant mother might inculcate, however, were the schools of the period, whose policy was to "Americanize" the immigrant child. Under these conditions, ethnic family patterns were slowly broken down by an increasingly urbanized, industrialized environment. The national mood, if not the national policy, was "assimilation." Intermarriage—between ethnic groups and across religious lines—became common. Substituted for the distinctive customs and life of the ethnic community—more slowly and at a later date than the American middle class, but just as surely—was the nuclear family of the twentieth century.

Twentieth century families

Although the American family has shown itself capable of incredible strength and energy, it has also revealed unsuspected submissiveness to any "legitimate" authority that challenges it. During frontier days it amply demonstrated its ability to monitor itself and insure its survival; but when government and business appeared and took over, it readily submitted to outside direction. There are many examples of this submission, from the effect of public education in freeing the children from family influence, to the destruction of entire communities by large business enterprises.

Such destruction began in small ways and proceeded by almost imperceptible degrees. Its effect on family cohesiveness was the more detrimental because many of its manifestations were entrenched and solidified before they were even noted.

The advent of large business enterprises decimated small independent stores and, with them, the neighborhoods to which they catered. The ripple effect spread to the destruction of local institutions, such as parish churches, which had focused on service to the family as a unit. The organizations that took their place—such as labor unions—tended to engage the loyalties of specific individuals rather than of whole families, and over the years did much to loosen family ties.

The destruction of neighborhoods also brought in its wake a growing concentration of more and more people in smaller and smaller areas. Urbanization acquired a momentum of its own and eventually resulted in the conditions graphically described by an early writer on urban conditions:

> The city home has been so stripped and depleted and backed to the wall that in sections like Manhattan it bids fair to lose out entirely. Family life, too, seems to be going by the board. Soaring of land values and pyramiding of rents pinch the city dweller into ever narrowing quarters where for the advantage of location he sacrifices one after another of the comforts of home. The press for space takes away the front yard and then the back yard. It takes away pets and plants and penalizes him for having children, so he gives up the nursery. The parlor and sitting room are narrowed and combined. He is forced to exchange the four poster for an in-a-door bed, the kitchen becomes a kitchenette and the dining room a dinette, while the pantry has all but vanished. The home declines as a family headquarters, a place for eating, sleeping, and passing leisure. It becomes a mere address, a place where members of the family leave things they do not care to carry around with them. Unless he submits to the clipping process he must submit to what is more uncompromising, the increasing cost of retaining these ancient comforts.[2]

Thus, in the aggregate, the consequences of industrialization finally altered the very fabric of family life and changed the traditional roles of its members.

Sociological perspectives

The viewpoint we bring to bear on the problems of the family must inevitably influence the conclusions we reach. In current sociology, two broad perspectives on family problems may be distinguished: the evolutionary and the revisionist approach.

The evolutionary approach

Most sociologists maintain that the American family, though beset by formidable problems, has maintained a modicum of stability by evolving together with other institutions, and accommodating itself to the changes taking place in the larger society. It continues to serve the vital functions of producing children, assuming responsibility for their early socialization and forming the framework within which sexual activity can legitimately take place.

The modern industrial state is, of course, the major external reality to which the family has had to adjust. By demanding greater geographical mobility, industrialization rendered the extended family of earlier eras obsolete, and substituted a smaller, less cumbersome unit better suited to traveling from job to job. This modern "nuclear" family, according to sociologists Talcott Parsons and Robert F. Bales, is a more specialized unit than its predecessor, and for that very reason even more important.[3]

These adjustments have had both positive and negative effects. The father's increased absence from the home, for instance, was at first seen as potentially disruptive but actually resulted in a democratization of family relationships. Some researchers see a change from an authoritarian to a corporatelike family structure.[4]

Such adjustments imply an essentially passive and malleable family structure. But one observer, sociologist William J. Goode, has modified this view somewhat by suggesting a reciprocal relationship between family and society: he believes that the family may, in fact, have been a source of independent change, and that change within it facilitated the more comprehensive changes of industrialization.[5]

. The social changes of the twentieth century have further accentuated this interdependence. In a society increasingly dedicated to success and upward mobility, more and more mothers as well as fathers have been required to turn their lives outward. More married women now work than ever before in our history, sharing their husbands' preoccupation with the acquisition of greater wealth and position. The larger and more varied family units of earlier days probably also served to cushion the shocks of generational conflicts. In our urban and industrial society, children as well as parents have become subject to influences and interests outside the home. Parental authority is no longer an unquestioned fact, and open disagreement with one's elders no longer unthinkable. In recent years this has led to what is now called the "generation gap," although, in fact, such a gap may always have existed in America.

The revisionist approach

The revisionist, unlike the evolutionist, maintains that there is a *qualitative* difference in today's problems as compared to those of the past, reflecting a qualitative difference in the structure and functions of the contemporary family. He believes, moreover, that these problems are potentially so disruptive as to threaten the family's very survival as an institution. In the climate of contemporary life, old problems such as the generation gap, the role of women and alienation in the family have acquired new and ominous meanings.

W. F. Ogburn, one of the first to study these problems from this viewpoint, concluded that the family is in deep trouble.[6] The importance of its traditional functions—providing its members with food, clothing, protection and support against hardships and threats from the environment—could hardly be overstated. But in contemporary America, he feels, it has lost these functions and failed to assume any significant new ones. In effect, like many a good executive with a gift for organization, it has worked itself out of a job.

Whether the family has evolved, or whether it has been changed beyond recognition can perhaps best be determined by examining the specific components of family structure and the stresses to which modern life subjects them.

---

reading: **Suzanne Keller**
GOODBY TO ALL THAT

All in all, it would appear that the social importance of the family relative to other significant social arenas will . . . decline. Even today when the family still exerts a strong emotional and sentimental hold its social weight is not what it once was. All of us ideally are still born in intact families but not all of us need to establish families to survive. Marriage and children continue to be extolled as supreme social and personal goals but they are no longer—especially for men—indispensable for a meaningful existence. As individual self-sufficiency, fed by economic affluence or economic self-restraint, increases, so does one's exemption from unwanted economic as well as kinship responsibilities. Today the important frontiers seem to lie elsewhere, in science, politics, and outer space. This must affect the attractions of family life for both men and women. For men, because they will see less and less reason to assume full economic and social responsibilities for four to five human beings in addition to themselves as it becomes more difficult and less necessary to do so. This, together with the continued decline of patriarchal authority and male dominance—even in the illusory forms in which they have managed to hang on—will remove some of the psychic rewards which prompted many men to marry, while the disappearance of lineage as mainstays of the social and class order will deprive paternity of its social justification. For women, the household may soon prove too small for the scope of their ambitions and power drives. Until recently these were directed first of all to their children, secondarily to their mates. But with the decline of parental control over children a major erstwhile source of challenge and creativity is removed from the family sphere. This must weaken the mother-wife complex, historically sustained by the necessity and exaltation of motherhood and the taboo on illegitimacy.

Above all, the move towards worldwide population and birth control must affect the salience of parenthood for men and women, as a shift of cultural emphasis and individual priorities deflates maternity as woman's chief social purpose and paternity as the prod to male exertions in the world of work. Very soon, I suspect, the cultural presses of the world will slant their messages against the bearing and rearing of children. Maternity, far from being a duty, not even a right, will then become a rare privilege to be granted to a select and qualified few. Perhaps the day is not far off when reproduction will be confined to a fraction of the population, and what was once inescapable necessity may become voluntary, planned, choice. Just as agricultural societies in which everyone had to produce food were once superseded by industrial societies in which a scant six per cent now produce food for all, so one day the few may produce children for the many.

This along with changing attitudes towards sex, abortion, adoption, illegitimacy, the spread of the pill, better knowledge of human behavior, and a growing scepticism that the family is the only proper crucible for child-rearing, creates a powerful recipe for change. World-wide demands for greater and better opportunities for self-development and a growing awareness that these opportunities are inextricably enhanced or curtailed by the family as a prime determinant of life-chances, will play a major role in this change. Equal opportunity, it is now clear, cannot stop at the crib but must start there. "It is idle" commented Dr. Robert S. Morrison, a Cornell biologist, "to talk of a society of equal opportunity as long as that society abandons its newcomers solely to their families for their most impressionable years." (New York Times, October 30, 1966). One of the great, still largely unchallenged, injustices may well be that one cannot choose one's parents.

From
"Does the Family Have a Future?", by Suzanne Keller
Journal of Comparative Family Studies, Spring 1971.

Marriage

The single most important factor determining the quality of family life is the quality of the marriage that supports it. In preindustrial days, a number of basic social and economic functions served, in effect, to solder the union between husband and wife. Enlightened self-interest, if nothing else, dictated the expedience of staying together under almost any circumstances.

As these functions changed, the "ties that bind" married couples changed with them. Sheer survival was no longer a paramount preoccupation, and emotional needs assumed greater importance. Marriage was now expected to supply not only security from physical want, but also emotional and sexual fulfillment, an antidote against the abrasiveness of contemporary life, a haven from the loneliness and isolation of city existence. It was a tall order; increasingly, marriages have warped or broken apart under the new burdens placed on them.

Paradoxically, the changed function of marriage contained the *potential* for a more personally satisfying relationship between husband and wife; the trouble was that it also removed certain buffers to marital conflict which the earlier extended family had provided. Modern nuclear family structure often results in excessive mutual dependence of husband and wife, especially after the children are grown and gone. In such an atmosphere the importance of even minor discord can become greatly magnified. However, according to at least one sociologist, Jetse Sprey, it is not conflict per se but *unresolved* conflict that takes its greatest toll on marriage.[7] Too often neither partner knows how to compromise; for lack of such constructive flexibility marital disputes reach a deadlock, and generally the no-man's land of discord may begin to loom larger than the areas of agreement between husband and wife. Today's divorce trends, Sprey maintains, indicate one of the ways in which such deadlocks are resolved.

> *It is no longer respectable, as it once was, to marry for anything but love. Love has changed from a peripheral concern of the family into its primary justification. Indeed, the pursuit of love through family life has become, for many, the very purpose of life itself.*
>
> Alvin Toffler

Sociologist John Scanzoni, too, found considerable conflict within modern marriage, and even his finding that conflict was still more prevalent among divorced persons than among those who remained married provides indirect validation of Sprey's point; his study of dissolved marriages indicates a pattern of refusal to compromise among the men.[8] Their frequency of compromise was only one-third that of husbands from ongoing marriages; the frequency among wives from both groups was approximately equal.

Divorce rates

In America today, 37 out of every 100 marriages end in divorce. Add to those the cases of desertion and separation—on which figures are harder to come by—and one might gain a view of family change and breakup that the most gloomy prophet would find corroboration for his stand. But to look at these figures in isolation may be misleading, since a majority of those involved in one divorce marry again. And since single-parent families are becoming more and more common among the middle class, such figures tend to say more about marriage than about family—two concepts no longer as inextricably linked as they were in the past. Nonetheless, consideration of the interlocking divorce and remarriage rates is essential for an overview of modern American society.

After varying periods of unhappiness and readjustment, most divorced persons eventually remarry; and the likelihood of these second marriages proving successful is almost as great as that for first marriages. Thus, the high divorce rate does not indicate disenchantment with the institution of marriage. Quite the contrary: most people have such high hopes for it that they are willing to risk a second try.

In the past, the trend in the rate of divorce has been an overall generational rise every thirty years or so, to a new rate which remains in effect for another generation. Thus, in the 1920s, the rate was approximately 1.5 per 1000 population, which was much higher than the nineteenth century figure. In the mid-1940s it jumped to about 2.5 per 1000 population, and stayed at that figure until 1964. By 1971 it had risen to 3.7 per 1000 population.[9]

Divorce rates reflect regional, residential, racial, religious, national, class and age influences. Indeed, almost any factor that increases tension and difficulties tends to increase the divorce rate in the affected segment of the population.

Of the geographical regions in the United States, the Pacific area—including Washington, Oregon, California, Alaska and Hawaii—has the highest divorce rates (4.3 per 1000 population in 1969). In all regions, the urban figure is higher than the rural one: in 1971, the number of divorced persons in farm communities was 1.8 per 1000 population; in nonfarm areas, 5.3 per 1000 population. The racial factor clearly has a strong effect on the number of divorces: the 1971 figure for divorced persons among the white population was 4.8 per 1000; among Negro and other racial groups, 8.8 per 1000 population.

Religion is another important variable, although one must be cautious in assuming a direct cause-and-effect relationship. The divorce rate is higher among Protestants, apparently reflecting the Catholic Church's adamant stand against the dissolution of marriage. On the other hand the difference between the two groups is not significant, and is at least partly neutralized by a higher separation figure among Catholics. Apparently religion is a significant factor influencing divorce in religiously "mixed" marriages; but the highest rate of all is found among couples with no religious affiliation at all.

Satisfaction with the level of income and achievement—in short, "status"—seems to play a role as well. John Scanzoni has studied the role in marital dissolution of the relation between a husband's income and his wife's satisfaction with the husband's achievement.[10] It is interesting to note that wives of manual workers who considered their husbands' incomes inadequate had a higher incidence of divorce than those who were satisfied with their husband's income level. Strangely enough, however, the study showed that the income of the dissolved-marriage group was in fact higher than that of manual workers in the still-married group. In other words, the crucial factor leading to divorce seems to have been the wife's dissatisfaction with the husband's achievement—and possibly her sense of being in a lower social stratum—rather than the actual lack of money.

The early years of marriage produce the greatest strain and hence the highest divorce rate. In the 1920s, the third and fourth years of marriage carried the greatest divorce risk; today, most divorces occur within the first two years.[11]

Very often, any similarity between the actual cause of divorce and the legal grounds upon which it is claimed is purely coincidental. Approximately 52 percent of all divorce cases are based on a claim of "cruelty"; the true reason may be drunkenness (only 1.8 percent claimed this as the cause), nonsupport (1.5 percent), adultery (1.3 percent) or even just plain incompatibility. Perhaps cruelty is a less embarrassing claim than some of the true reasons; it also tends to be more readily provable in court. In any event, studies attest to the fact that cruelty is not always the real motive. For example, in a study of the marital separations granted by one Catholic Chancery—where people are more likely to express the real causes of their dissatisfaction than in civil court—the following reasons were listed in order of their importance: drink, adultery, irresponsibility, temperament, in-laws, sex, mental factors, religion and money.

Attitudinal changes

The trends of the future are difficult to predict with any accuracy; but some factors seem to point strongly toward an incipient rise in divorce rates.

Most important among them is probably the new attitude toward divorce which is developing in the country—an attitude reflected in the following statement by Morton Hunt:

> We have not yet opened our minds to the possibilities that divorce may be a creative rather than a destructive act, that it may be a better choice for all concerned (including the children) than trying to repair a defunct marriage, and that divorcing people should be aided rather than impeded in their efforts to make the break and to live successfully in the post-marital world.[12]

If the viewpoint Hunt advocates becomes widespread, it is likely to result in a liberalization of divorce laws, and new trends in marriage and divorce rates.

More and more people are already perceiving divorce as a potentially constructive and healthy way of dealing with an otherwise intractable situation. Rather than considering it "the end of the world," they see it as the gateway to a better marriage in the future, or, in many cases, to more congenial alternative life-styles.

Further, the attitude that a married couple should stay together "for the sake of the children" is gradually giving way to the belief (borne out by research) that an unhappy marriage may be more detrimental to their emotional stability than divorce and single-parent families.[13] Since much of the damage is done by parents' attitudes during the predivorce period, the emotional strain on children is significantly reduced if the parents remain calm and amicable, and include the children in discussions of the pending divorce.

Another factor which may portend increasing divorce rates is the changing attitude of women toward themselves and their relationship to the social and economic structure. Since it is becoming increasingly easier for women to support themselves, and to establish reasonably fulfilling lives outside the institution of marriage, they are presumably less afraid of striking out on their own. It bears remembering, however, that even now, 2 million of the 5.6 percent of United States families headed by women (46 percent of whom are divorced or separated) live below the poverty level.[14] The fact is that the average working woman is still earning considerably less than her male counterpart. Furthermore, according to the Citizens Advisory Council on the Status of Women, "Where the divorce results in economic hardship, greater hardship is visited on the wife and children than on the husband." In only a small percentage of cases, the Council declared, did the courts grant alimony; in general, fathers contributed less than half the costs of child support after divorce; and court orders for alimony and child support were difficult to enforce.

Separation

The largest group of people involved in the dissolution of marriages is composed not of the divorced, but of the separated, about whom there is relatively little information. According to the United States census, the separation category includes those who are legally separated, those who are waiting for a divorce, and cases of desertion—numerically the largest group. The 1960 census lists 60 separated women and 43 divorced women per 1000 married women aged 14 years and over.[15]

Desertion has been called "the poor man's divorce," and the reason is, indeed, very often purely economic rather than vindictive; but this does not greatly ameliorate its harmful impact. Desertion is likely to result in many other disruptive family situations than are precipitated by divorce: since the marital conflict is *unofficially* resolved, it remains only *half* resolved; no legally binding provisions exist for alimony, child support or visitation rights.

The desertion rate is particularly high among the black population—probably for the above-cited financial reasons. Further evidence for this is provided by the observation that, as the income level among black people rises, their divorce and desertion patterns become similar to those among whites.

Since black men have often been victims of discriminatory employment policies, the wife in the lower-class black household has traditionally provided the economic support for the family. Often, she has carried the entire burden of maintaining the family's emotional and psychological stability. With the growing strength of a black consciousness, and somewhat improved opportunities, the black male has begun to claim a more active role in his own family as well as in society at large. This will undoubtedly affect future trends in desertion, divorce and illegitimacy.

Illegitimacy

Marriage legalizes mating and defines the status of children. In some cultures, biological fatherhood is secondary to legal fatherhood. It is the inheritance of name and status that counts, and marriage facilitates the transfer of these "essentials."

In our American culture, illegitimacy has been for the most part socially stigmatized, but it usually has not in itself impeded social mobility. In a comparatively open society the illegitimate child is *theoretically* as free to make his fortune as the child with legal status. The thread of family inheritance can be broken without denying the child the benefits of the larger social and economic structure. Today more people than ever before are realizing the inherent cruelty of stigmatizing illegitimate children; but this liberalization of attitude has not yet produced much *concrete* effort to improve their lot.

The crux of the problem is that the illegitimate child often lacks even a semblance of family life, and thus is denied the benefits of early socialization in the home. This can adversely affect not only the individual children involved but also the families they themselves will found as adults. Without the support of parents and at least some general preparation for his role as an adult, the child is likely to be severely handicapped in his own ability to function as a parent or a marriage partner.

Seen from this vantage point, illegitimacy remains qualitatively the same problem it has been in the past. And in view of the fact that it is currently on the rise, especially among the poor, the problems connected with it cry out for solution more urgently than ever.

Role change in the family

As the family has accommodated—or been forced to accommodate— itself to changes in the larger society, the roles of family members have been subject to change. Several of these changes have already been noted earlier in this chapter. Here we will discuss recent role changes in more detail.

Much of the dissatisfaction with marriage in our time would seem to involve uncertainty concerning these changes; change almost always produces strain.

Wife and mother

At the present time the wife is probably the most controversial member of the family. Her function is being reevaluated in terms of the new "Women's Lib" consciousness, which emerged in the sixties and has already effected major changes in many spheres.

Not all women were or are dissatisfied with their role of mother and housekeeper; but a sizeable number—especially among the educated—felt sufficiently stifled to become the vanguard of activism for social, economic and political change. The consequences for the family are gradually becoming dramatically visible.

Once before, a generation ago, world conditions had given women the chance for emancipation, but the challenge was not taken up. World War II had brought large numbers out of their homes for jobs and careers. But when their men returned they retreated.

If this retreat caused frustration, it remained for the most part unvoiced. Although less confined by custom than her mother and grandmother had been, a married woman was still expected to find fulfillment in the role of wife and mother. Holding a routine outside job reflected adversely on her husband's abilities as a provider; having a "career"—a word always used in quotes—carried social stigma; and dissatisfaction with traditional roles implied personal deviance rather than a flaw in the social structure.

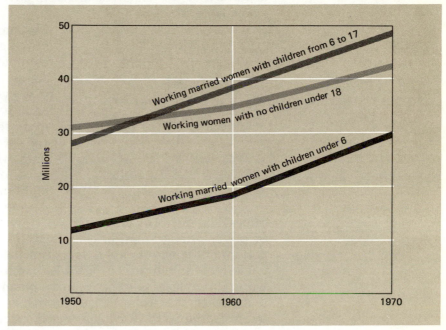

Figure 2–1   Working married women in the United States according to existence and age of children.

The problem worsened with the years. The woman of earlier eras had been too burdened with the work of running a large and complicated household to have much time for self-analysis; and her formal education was too limited to create much of a disparity between her potential and the actual chores that filled her days. The nuclear family structure (and the socioeconomic conditions that fostered it) changed this situation in many ways, and the changes were more intensely experienced by the wife and mother than by other family members.

As the size of the family contracted she became aware of a new quality in her life: isolation. Her husband worked outside the home and her children spent much time at school and with friends. The task of raising and disciplining them was, in any case, a self-limiting one. If she had made it her sole aim in life (as her upbringing encouraged her to do), the day when the youngest child left home was a tragic one. The mother-housekeeper now became predominantly a housekeeper—an occupation which carried negligible status in the "outside" world. Indeed, it was accorded only token acknowledgment even within the family, despite the fact that in an age of specialization she remained one of the few members of society prepared to exercise multiple functions: housekeeper, cook, laundress, governess, practical nurse, social secretary, confidante, seamstress, teacher and chauffeur—in addition to whatever professional skills she may have developed in her youth. She was not only overqualified, but, with the departure of her children, underemployed to the point of feeling expendable.

The family inspires a curious dualism of thought. We tend to regard it uneasily as a final manifestation of tribal society, somehow inappropriate to a democratic, industrial age, but, at the same time, we have become ever more aware of its possibilities as an instrument of social reconstruction.

Robert Nisbet

When the Women's Liberation movement appeared, at first only a few housewives gave it open allegiance, nor did a majority approve of it even silently. Undoubtedly, many were restrained by timidity or by fear of the ridicule which some of the early radicals inspired. Many (rightly or wrongly) felt unequal to the competition equality might bring. But with the passage of time, the leaders became less radical and the followers less conservative. Today women in all parts of the country and of all classes seem determined to change the pattern of their lives, and thus that of their families.

The most significant change seems to be their wholesale return to work. Often this single change in a woman's life acts as a catalyst for many others. Far from being disruptive to the family, a wife's outside interests frequently lead to increased understanding of her husband's problems. Children soon adapt to their mother's work schedule, especially when their father participates in the household tasks. Finally, and perhaps most unexpectedly, a woman's status within her family changes for the better.[16] According to C. Arnott:

> Often husbands were more interested in getting their wives involved in careers than were the women themselves . . . Resulting shared interests should help prevent a gap in understanding between husband and wife in the empty nest years. The future seems promising. It is probable that when the wife's work means challenge rather than underemployment it can enrich the marital relationship, and take some of the pressure off the intimate interdependencies of the nuclear family, pressure which led to increased marital and family problems in past years.[17]

Husband and father

The Women's Liberation movement has obviously affected not only the housewife, but the husband and father as well.

Although men have played what seem to be the more dominant and satisfying roles in our society, they too have been restricted to the extent that their traditional functions as masters and protectors have limited the expression of their individual needs.

Alienation from these needs has plagued men as well as women, the married as well as the single. Industrialization and technological advances have provided greater opportunity for personal achievement, but have also worked against harmonious integration of the various areas of our lives. This pressure to compartmentalize his life has been very keenly felt by the head of the nuclear family.

At work he is expected to be—or at least to seem—impervious to the pressures of his job. In a competitive society these pressures can be great, fatiguing in mind and body. Under such circumstances, he needs his home as a refuge, a place for rest, solitude and escape, rather than active involvement and intense relationships with other family members.

When his emotional and psychological investment in his work is excessive, he may expect too much of his family without being able (or willing) to fulfill his own responsibilities toward it. Psychologist Kenneth Keniston notes:

> . . . In a chaotic and increasingly incomprehensible world, the family provides a small, relatively stable universe where "things make sense." Given work which demands emotional restraint and control, the family provides a haven for the "release" of feelings. . . . Given the tenuous relationship to the future engendered by chronic social change, children in the family provide a concrete link to the future. Given the shattering of the community, the family provides a pseudo-community which partly tells a man who he is and where he stands. Given the fragmentations of social roles on the wider scene, the family provides a narrow stage, within which life promises to be of a piece. . . .[18]

Seen from this vantage point, a husband's acceptance of his wife's new life-style, involving as it does a lessening of financial pressures and increased understanding of mutual problems, becomes less surprising.

---

reading: **David Steinberg**
REDEFINING FATHERHOOD: NOTES AFTER SIX MONTHS

Dylan is napping. A chance for me to unwind and settle into writing. Dylan is six months old. I still find it hard to write in tune with his schedule. Like now I've just started and he's woken up crying. I have to stop and take care of him.

When Susan was pregnant, I imagined that writing and taking care of a baby would fit together well. I figured that as long as I was home taking care of him I would do some writing as well. It seems incredible now that I could have so completely misunderstood what it would be like to have a baby.

I have resisted the shift from working on my schedule to working on Dylan's. I've tried to hold onto my old pattern, and built up a lot of resentment in the process. Now as I begin to accept the new pattern and find that I can work with it, I feel better all around.

After six months I'm finally letting go of my old life for the new one that includes Dylan. I see now that my old life is really gone and that the job is to build a new one that I like as well or better. Letting go means that my energy can go into building instead of mourning what has died. One day, I cried at the ocean, saying goodbye to a life that I had loved and had worked hard to create.

Having a baby has brought an astounding amount of day-to-day work. It's not that doing the work has been so hard. It's what gets lost in the shuffle; time to sit and relax, to talk about things that are hard to say, to sort out feelings and become whole again, Sunday-morning pancakes in bed.

Recently, though, I've gotten better at making the time to work out tensions, unraveling all the muck that's built up over these months. I'm fitting into a new rhythm, making use of free space as it becomes available.

The consumerism of the baby industry is overwhelming. So many special fancy things to buy so that you can feel like a good parent and provider. Dylan does fine with his used crib, toys made from little things around the house. There are a dozen ways to use a plastic infant seat, and a hundred things to do with a single piece of cloth.

Once a salesman came to sell us a piece of baby furniture that converted into fourteen different things, all of which, he insisted, we would buy sooner or later. It cost four hundred dollars. When we didn't buy one he accused us of not caring about our baby. He said he made eighteen sales pitches a week, fourteen "successful." I believe him.

We don't have very much money, and don't have any immediate prospects of earning more. I could make more money, but I would have to give up a lot, including my relationship with Dylan. So far it hasn't been worth it.

So far, Dylan hasn't dramatically changed how much money we need. We've moved into a two-bedroom place, so the rent is a little higher. We spend more freely on conveniences to make up for the time Dylan consumes. And I guess we'll need a car now in place of the scooter that's served us so well. Before Dylan we were spending about three hundred a month. Now we spend about four hundred.

Susan and I both agree that neither of us should work full time. We'll both work and share taking care of Dylan. That way we'll both have outside lives in addition to a baby. Susan is driving a school bus and teaching piano. I'm free-lancing and writing a book.

I get an empty feeling when people ask me what I'm doing. Most of my energy in the last six months has focused on Dylan, on taking care of him and getting used to his being here. But I still have enough man-work expectations in me that I feel uncomfortable just saying that.

I'm not willing to be the second, somewhat foreign, parent. I tried that for a couple of days in a pique of frustration with Dylan. I felt distant and alienated from him almost immediately. It was horrible. I decided it was better to share responsibility for him, which we've done ever since.

Right after Dylan was born, we both spent almost all of our time with him. We both cleared out a month when there was nothing else we had to do. As other demands pressed, we began setting aside time to be alone. I took three hours a day for writing and Susan took three hours in return.

Now, with both of us working, it's a bit more complicated. We've drawn up a schedule, evenly dividing housework, cooking, miscellaneous chores, and Dylan. It feels a little formal and cumbersome, but it's helping me get into honest work-sharing habits, and it's relieved

84 a lot of other-person-not-doing-his-share tension. If the schedule becomes too burdensome, we'll do something else instead. I think once sharing work comes naturally the strict sense of schedule will loosen up by itself.

I wish now that I had prepared myself better for having a baby. I let myself get caught by surprise, and then felt resentful, as if I had been cheated out of something I couldn't quite define.

Having Dylan has made me feel confused, overwhelmed, uncertain, then bitter and resentful. The feeling of being up against a situation that I couldn't handle, that was too much for me. So many things needing to be done, so many emotional pieces to be put together, and my energy outside of Dylan very, very low. Everything has seemed very complicated. I have felt the jaws of middle-aged American mediocrity open wide.

Often my anger and frustration come out at Susan. It seems ridiculous to rage at Dylan, and I'm too defensive to blame myself. Whatever goes wrong somehow becomes Susan's fault.

The more I am ready to have things come out badly from time to time, the more I allow myself to be imperfect, the less angry I get at Susan.

I knew nothing about babies when Dylan was born. I'm an only child and never spent any time at all with babies. My confidence in myself as a father was very shaky. I felt deeply afraid of Dylan, always fighting an urge to close my eyes and shove responsibility for him over to Susan. I could hold myself together as long as everything went smoothly, but when something unusual happened I quickly panicked. I got very depressed at my lack of intuitive baby sense.

One evening, feeling very tense, I let all the fears and insecurities come tumbling out in a heap. Seeing it all together, I got even more scared. I cried for a long time. I felt completely weak, that I had failed at something very important.

Once I admitted all that to myself, and to Susan, I stopped putting up such a brave front and allowed myself to have times when I just couldn't handle being with Dylan. Starting from where I was, instead of where I wanted to be, I could face my weaknesses and work against them. I began to see that there were times when I was really good with Dylan, when I really did have good baby sense.

I had wanted to jump right in, confident and competent, and be a father who enjoyed taking care of his baby half the time. I wanted to cut all the American-father bullshit out of me in one slice. I learned again that coming out from under basic cultural habits isn't that easy or dramatic. But after six months' work I can see that it's happening after all. And that makes me feel that it's been worth all the trauma and tension after all.

Writing about all this is making me jumpy. I'd better stop and do something else for a while.

My fear of Dylan comes from feeling so much responsibility for him. When he cries I'm supposed to make something right. If I don't know how to do that, I panic. I do best when I'm ready to make mistakes, even serious ones.

I know that I will make major mistakes with Dylan, and that I'll cause him a good amount of grief. I try to keep that in front of me, to expect it, and to accept it when it happens.

As soon as I get oriented to one of Dylan's patterns, he changes and a whole new pattern begins to evolve. It's like standing up in a roller coaster, a little unnerving. I'm finding that the more I accept this constant change, the more I can enjoy the dynamics of it, the constant growing. Dylan is deepening my sense of change as a way of life.

When I trust my intuitive sense with Dylan, I generally do pretty well. It's when I lose touch with that intuition that things fall apart.

85   Susan wanted to have a baby at least a year before I did. Being a father was a rather

frightening idea to me. I kept waiting to be more together, to have my life be somehow more resolved. Susan said that I could wait forever before things would be exactly right, that the only way to feel good about being a father was to have a baby and work through the hassles. That made sense to me. We decided to have a baby. Susan became pregnant immediately.

Sometimes I've thought that we should have waited a little longer, maybe another year. That then the adjustment wouldn't have been so traumatic. Now I think that adjusting to a baby is a traumatic process by its nature, and that it would have been the same thing a year later.

Deciding to have a baby was a little like when we decided to start our own school. A chance to do it right without artificial external limits. A chance to see what happens when we can't blame anything on what other people made impossible.

While Susan was pregnant, my relationship with her, and my relationship with myself, went through a beautiful time of growing and deepening. It was a very exciting time. I think now that I was getting ready for Dylan, unconsciously preparing for the upheaval that my conscious mind refused to acknowledge.

I feel myself moving out of stereotyped father roles into a relationship with Dylan that comes from me, that expresses who I am and how I feel. It leads me into some pretty strange situations, but as long as I'm clear on what I want I won't become nervous about the strangeness.

I've gone through a similar process in building my relationship with Susan around our particular personalities. The sense of creatively building the relationship that best suits us has been one of the most exciting things I've ever done. There's been lots of doubt and uncertainty, but we've built something that I find very nourishing and beautiful, that gives me strength and energy.

Remembering how uncertain I felt after we got married and seeing how far we've come from there gives me courage to work out all the stuff with Dylan. After all, six months is really a short time. It took about two years of being married for Susan and me to become ourselves instead of playing out traditional young-couple roles.

It really helps me hold on when I keep my eyes on the prize. It's so easy to take values and roles for granted, particularly basic ideas about being a husband or a father. By looking carefully at what's going on I can shape what I really want and throw out the garbage. Then I'm actively deciding who I want to be and what kind of life I'm going to lead.

Another help is being close to other people who are building new life patterns that suit their needs. I learn from what they do, and with their support I don't feel so self-conscious about rejecting TV-America.

It would be easy to fall into sitting around the house all the time. Doing things with Dylan often seems like a lot of trouble. But he's really pretty flexible. The more we've dared try with him, the more seems possible. He goes to sleep in strange places and survives being carried home on a bus. He jounces around the city in his back pack, goes on long car trips peacefully and has been camping in the country, diapers and all, for a week at a time.

Having a baby doesn't need to mean settling into a regular, repetitive life pattern. I can't go on as before, but whether the basic quality of my life changes now is up to me. I like the flexible, spontaneous, growing, changing life I've been living, so I'll work hard to find a way to integrate that with Dylan's demands.

It's always a shock when I remember that Dylan is related to me in a more basic way than that I take care of him, to realize that he is of my body, grown from my seed. My son. Occasionally it hits me from behind. I still don't know what to make of it. I suffer from not

having been pregnant.

Dylan has been sleeping for three hours while I've been writing. Susan has gone to her bus-driving job. When he wakes up he's going to be hungry. I'd better go make a bottle.

Most of our friends don't have babies and don't relate to Dylan very closely. I remember that before we had Dylan I often felt put upon by the noise and demands of friends' babies. I feel that same tension now from the other side of the fence. I can see how couples with babies tend to socialize with each other almost exclusively. Still, I don't want to give up my relationships with friends who don't have babies. We'll have to work something out.

We exchange child care one afternoon a week with another couple. The free time has been important to me as a period of regeneration. A break from Dylan's unending presence, a chance to walk undisturbed along the ocean, to have some daylight time alone with Susan.

I would like to be living in a larger family group. It would help to have other people share responsibility for Dylan and help with the basic work he requires. It would also be good for Dylan to have intimate relationships with other adults than Susan and me. We have pursued various possible living arrangements with friends, but right now none feels good enough to actually do.

Dylan makes it much harder for me to control my environment, to plan ahead, to predict what's going to happen. He makes me realize how important control and planning have been to me. Now I'll have to loosen up, learn to flow more easily with things as they happen. Again I'm thrown into growing.

I can't impose my rules on Dylan. All my persuasive skills, the ones I use to get other people to do things my way, are totally useless with him. It forces me to accept the validity of his rules and then learn to integrate that with my real needs. The trick is to become less of a control freak without sacrificing myself to Dylan entirely.

Being with Dylan gives me a chance to express my intuitive, feminine, yin-self. As a man, it's easy to always be in situations that call for aggressive, rational, manipulative perspectives and skills. With Dylan I move out of that more completely than I ever have before. As a result I feel myself growing in all kinds of new ways. The clear importance of these new skills in caring for Dylan helps me respect and value them as they develop.

All of this would not be possible if I were working nine to five. That I'm not is no accident. Organizing my life to make room for a close relationship with Dylan has been a conscious deliberate process.

There's more about nine-to-five work than the scheduled hours away from home. There's the coming home tired and grouchy and tense, or being deadened by the boredom of tedious work. Whatever the spirit of my work, it carries over into the rest of my life.

I enjoy most of the time I spend with Dylan—taking care of him, playing with him, watching him change and grow. He is one of the most important parts of my life right now. There are other important parts, like my relationship with Susan, my work, being with other people. I don't want to give them up for Dylan, or him for them. There is as much total space as I have energy to clear and care for.

In struggling to define myself as a husband, I've found that I can open myself to real contact with Susan and feel good about that relationship and about myself. Now with Dylan I am in that same process of discovering new strength and energy. The last six months have been difficult for me, but this kind of growing never comes easy.

From
The Future of the Family Edited by Louise K. Howe
(New York: Simon and Schuster, 1972) pp. 368–378.

The child

In the past, the family assumed the major responsibility for developing the child's character and preparing him for adulthood. The preparation was by no means always successful; maladjusted children are not a phenomenon restricted to contemporary society. Not all children accepted their parents' values and goals, and a generation gap of some sort has probably been a characteristic common to all parent-child relationships. But, for better or worse, socialization of children was primarily the function of the family which, in a rural economy, had greater opportunity to fulfill it.

Today, by contrast, other social institutions have acquired a great deal of control over children's upbringing, and the demands of modern society have further modified such socializing power as the family retains. Less and less time is available to develop close ties between parents (especially fathers) and children. According to Urie Bronfenbrenner:

> Urbanization, child labor laws, the abolishment of apprentice systems, commuting, centralized schools, zoning ordinances, the working mother, the experts' advice to be permissive, the seductive power of television for keeping children occupied, the delegation and professionalization of child care—all these manifestations of progress have operated to decrease opportunity for contact between children and parents, or, for that matter, adults in general.[19]

Growing up is therefore more complicated than it used to be. Children's need for direction and values which can serve as a foundation for growth remains as strong as ever, but satisfaction of this need is becoming harder to achieve. There are too many roles and alternative life-styles to make one unequivocal choice, and the child may be attracted to such a variety of models that he finds it impossible to achieve a cohesive self-image.[20]

Particularly since World War II, many changes have occurred in patterns of child rearing in the United States, but their essence may be conveyed in a single sentence: **Children used to be brought up by their parents.**

Urie Bronfenbrenner

Even if the child were willing to base his commitments on the values and behavioral examples of his parents—which would run counter to a natural (and, to some extent, socially reinforced) rebellion against parental norms—he might still find his identity fragmented. Many parents are themselves presently experiencing confusion and doubt concerning their own roles.

In the midst of these uncertainties, the child must bridge the gap between the needs of childhood and the demands of adulthood—an especially wide gap in American culture. Rather than facilitating the transition, our present culture in some ways seems to emphasize discontinuity between childhood and adulthood. Dependence is intensely cultivated—even exploited—during childhood, while independence and a high degree of self-sufficiency are expected of the adult. Yet the early heavy dependence on parents involves emotional dangers, and may deter the child from ultimately assuming responsibility for his own life.

Of course the problem cannot be placed solely on the doorstep of the American family. The family structure itself has been forced to accommodate the other social and economic institutions of a changing society; it is only fair to expect these institutions to assume their proper share in the socialization of children. Schools, for example, could address themselves more realistically to the transitional problems faced by children, and could supplement parental efforts to insure their maturing into independence.

One result of efforts being made in this direction is "children's lib"—a somewhat facetious term for attempts on the part of youth to gain more control over their own education, which may lead to a modernization of outdated socialization practices in the schools and within the family.

Older family members

Among the most disadvantaged victims of our technological society are older family members, parents and grandparents whose role in the family structure has been virtually eliminated. In the extended family of rural America, older relatives were respected for their experience. Living in the same household, or in close proximity to family members, they were instrumental in the socialization of children and in upholding traditional family practices. Today, at increasingly earlier ages, the older person is often deprived of economic and social status (though still quite capable of working and contributing to the economy), and is expected to provide a meaningful, independent life for himself apart from the activities of the younger generations. In our social structure, says Bronfenbrenner:

> Increasingly often, housing projects, or even entire neighborhoods, cater to families at a particular stage of the life cycle or career line, and social life becomes organized on a similar basis, with the result that, at all levels, contacts become limited to persons of one's own age and station. In short, we are coming to live in a society that is segregated not only by race and class, but also by age.[21]

In such a situation older people have limited options. Many choose to remain in their old, ethnic neighborhoods, even as these fall victim to the bulldozers of urban renewal and the spread of crime and violence, because the familiar surroundings provide their only remaining link with a meaningful past. Those who would like to escape the loneliness and hardship of their urban existence are often trapped by their economic situation; inflation rapidly consumes social security benefits, pension and savings.

Some older people, endowed with greater economic or spiritual resources, manage to adjust to their difficult situation. They may, for example, return to the labor market on a part-time basis, serving as consultants or volunteers. The instinct for survival in an industrialized society often prompts this return to the job market in order to hold on to a symbol of American "worth" and status.

Others turn to retirement villages. These communities provide an opportunity to develop new social relationships in a slow-paced, congenial atmosphere; but at the same time they reinforce the tendency to isolate the aged from the mainstream of our society. Also, those among the elderly who have led active and purposeful lives tend to feel "lost" away from their jobs and old neighborhoods, and find that the slow pace of living leads to atrophy of mental and physical powers. For them, the companionship of peers cannot replace the satisfaction of being a needed member of a heterogeneous community.

Another alternative for the aged person is, of course, to move in with one of the children. In our society this solution is not a popular one, although it seems to be somewhat less traumatic for all concerned than it was in the past.

Finally, it is significant to note that many of the elderly are rejecting the passive, ineffectual role assigned them, and are becoming activists on their own behalf. In several urban senior citizen housing projects, for example, members have banded together to provide mutual protection against crime. Many lobby on their own or in organized groups to promote legislation beneficial to the aged. And a growing number of older men and women are flouting convention, both to ease loneliness and to maintain their economic independence: couples set up house together without benefit of a marriage license, so that the woman can still receive full social security benefits. Through these and other active efforts, today's senior citizens are creating new and important roles for themselves which demand the recognition of younger members of our society.

Responses to family problems

The contemporary situation of the family is a difficult one. Will the family of the future still have a meaningful role to perform? Will it, in fact, survive at all?

Many sociologists are addressing themselves to this question. Barrington Moore, Jr. suggests that the family is obsolete, and that those who assemble data on the number of marriages taking place today to prove it is still alive are prisoners of the status quo.[22] Most of his colleagues do not go this far. Sociologist B. Farber maintains that marriage has lost its permanence since people no longer value it for its own sake, but believes that it retains a pragmatic value if it meets the needs of the individuals involved.[23] Goode regards the family as a buffer between the individual and society.[24]

Leaving theory to the theorists, ordinary Americans are making specific efforts to deal with their individual marital and family dysfunctions. In previous sections we have touched upon some of these responses. Here we will cover these and others in greater depth, since they suggest important possibilities and trends for marriage and family organization in the future.

Legal changes

Legislation tends to be a fairly accurate gauge of the strength of changing attitudes. The fact that controversy continues on issues such as abortion repeal, divorce and antidiscrimination laws creates uncertainty about future trends in these areas and even suggests the possibility of backlash. But for the present the courts appear to be working toward redress of legislative imbalances which have limited women's economic freedom and social mobility.

In January, 1973, the Supreme Court declared that a state could not prevent a woman from having an abortion at any time during the first three months of pregnancy, a ruling which invalidated the abortion laws of Texas and Georgia and implied the illegality of such laws in forty-four other states. Although women were not granted absolute right to abortion on demand, the ruling represents a significant challenge to the legal authority of the State and the moral authority of the Church (primarily the Roman Catholic Church, but also the Mormon Church) to control and define the role of women. Presumably abortion on demand will result in a lower illegitimacy rate, although one criticism of the imposed time limit is that the young and poor (who most often need an abortion after the twelfth week) will be faced with the alternatives of illegal abortion or giving birth to an illegitimate (or unwanted) child. There should also be fewer "forced" marriages—those dictated by pregnancy rather than inclination. Also, the ruling contributes at least in theory to greater social freedom for women, since pregnancy will no longer be as powerful a deterrent to premarital sex as it once was.[25]

There has also been considerable activism to alleviate discriminatory employment and education practices. The government has issued guidelines which prohibit newspapers from classifying jobs according to sex, and in 1967 announced that contractors and subcontractors whose employment practices discriminate against women would risk a loss of federal subsidies. Although intended to curb abuses in private industry, this injunction has thus far been most effectively used by women's groups against educational institutions which receive federal aid.

A more recent Supreme Court decision will affect hundreds of state and federal laws that currently discriminate against women. The Court ruled that the armed forces could not legally require female members to prove that they supplied over half their husband's support in order to claim dependents' benefits, so long as such benefits were automatically granted to male servicemen. That judg-

ment carried the implication that all laws containing gender classifications would henceforth be regarded as "inherently suspect"—a
corollary which women's groups intend to utilize in pending cases
involving discriminatory federal and state laws, Social Security biases
and unequal employment opportunities.[26]

Concerning divorce laws and benefits, no changes have yet been
made which significantly alter the status of divorced men and
women. But the National Organization for Women (NOW) is engaged
in major efforts to change present divorce laws to provide divorced
women with the requisite job training to offset the employment
disadvantages resulting from years spent at housework. Changing
attitudes towards divorce are likely to bring about legislative rectifi-
cation of this problem. One alternative, proposed by NOW, is a
federalized welfare system which would exempt any guardian or
single parent of a young child from the work requirement. Another
option which may become increasingly available (and indispensable)
to working mothers, whether married or divorced, is the use of
federally subsidized developmental child-care facilities.

Day care: child-raising by the state

One of the most significant responses to the problems of women who
desire or need to work is the creation of day-care centers. Some
observers contend that such facilities "will beneficiently reorder the
existing relationships between sexes, generations and social classes";
that they will, in fact, have many significant results beyond enabling
women to enter the job market. Sheila Rothman notes:

> They will once and for all resolve the conflict between the child's welfare
> and the mother's welfare—for the centers will offer advantages that
> neither the nuclear middle-class family nor the economically deprived
> lower-class family can match . . . the day care centers will free the
> suburban child from the intense and overbearing pressures of the nuclear
> family, and therefore fit him better for an adult life in the outside society.
> For the lower-class child, the centers will offer exemplary medical and
> dental care, the chance to use the latest educational play equipment, and
> the skilled guidance of experts who will help the youngster to cope with
> the deficiencies of his own family life.[27]

Historically, day-care projects have not always fulfilled the expectations of those who promote them nor satisfied the needs of those
who use them. Public facilities in one program, for example, were
subsidized for the poor (those earning under $4,320 per year); but a
family with four children and an income of $8,500 was required to pay
the full fee—$2700 per year for each child. The effect of such
inequities is to turn day-care centers into segregated communities of
poor children. To make matters worse, such facilities are often
inadequately regulated by municipal and state governments. Staff
members are not always properly trained for the responsibilities
entrusted to them, nor are they, in general, employed fulltime.

Perhaps the most serious criticism leveled at the day-care concept is that mothers—especially among the poor—may be coerced into the labor force and into using day-care facilities whether they wish to or not:

> Today . . . we are entering a new stage, wherein the government, under the threat of withholding relief, can compel the poor to put their children in the centers.[28]

One alternative (similar to that proposed by NOW) would provide federal fund appropriations for a general family-assistance program. Despite the potential abuses inherent in such a concept, some believe it to be more practicable as well as constitutionally sounder than coercive day-care proposals. Mothers would have the option of working while entrusting supervision of preschoolers to others, or staying at home and caring for the children themselves until they reached school age.

Single-parent families

The expansion of day-care facilities will also be of enormous importance for the single-parent family. This small but growing category has lately been the recipient of increasing attention and recognition.

Both those directly involved and observers are beginning to consider the single-parent family unit a semipermanent or even permanent state, rather than a transitory one born of adverse circumstances. There are people who are by nature and temperament unsuited for marriage, but not at all unsuited to parenthood. It is clearly better for a child to be raised in a happy single-parent home than in an unhappy conjugal one.

If this viewpoint gains wider acceptance—and indications are that it will—it may eventually be possible for single people to adopt children, thereby fulfilling their own lives and helping to relieve the pressure on adoption institutions, whose services cannot, in any case, compare with the tender, loving care of a devoted single parent.

Communal families

An alternative to the nuclear family—one which radically alters the traditional roles and division of labor among partners—is the cooperative or communal household.

In general, communes provide for a sharing of household expenses and duties. All members participate in the task of keeping the household economically viable, either by working at an outside job as in urban cooperatives, or by farming the land, as in some rural communes.

The idea of communes is not new in America—cooperative living was tried in certain nineteenth-century rural communities—nor is it typefied by any single structure or pattern of living. Some communes, for example, discourage conventional marital relationships to the point of actually requiring a group sexual arrangement, while others are composed of strictly monogamous couples. Cooperative lifestyles also differ according to the environment—whether urban or rural—and according to the skills and backgrounds of the participants.

Child-rearing practices are equally varied. For example, in some urban groups composed of couples who primarily wish to create a supportive environment for each other and to divide household expenses, child care may simply entail babysitting duties, since the children are sent outside the household for schooling, and are allowed to socialize with children from outside the group.

Living Groups—		

1. Single Individuals
    a. 1 male adult
    b. 1 female adult
    c. 1 non–adult
        (child)
	2. Single adult with children
	    a. 1 male or female with 1
	        child
	    b. 1 male or female with 2
	        or more children
		3. 1 Pair of adults +
		    a. 1 male—1 female—0 children
		    b. 1 male—1 female with one
		        child
		    c. 1 male—1 female with 2 or
		        more children

4. Commune of Pairs
    a. 2 or more males,
        2 or more fe-
        males
    b. 2 or more males,
        2 or more fe-
        males with chil-
        dren of pair
    c. 2 or more males,
        2 or more fe-
        males, children
        shared
	5. Communes—not paired
	    a. 2 or more males—2 or
	        more females
	    b. (a)—all children within
	        group
	    c. (a)—children reared out-
	        side group
	        (kibbutz–type
	        arrangement)
		6. Communes—Mixed Group-
		    ings
		    a. Some pairs, some singles,
		        children shared
		    b. children with biological
		        parents
		    c. children outside group

7. Sex Groupings
    a. males in one
        group, females
        in one group
    b. males + children
    c. females + children
    d. (a) with children
        in separate sex
        group
	8. Traditional
	    a. one male, one female
	    b. one male, one female,
	        one child
	    c. one male, one female,
	        2 or more children
		9. Community or Neighborhood
		    Groupings
		    a. All family structures living
		        in certain area, grouped in
		        mutual helping roles
		    b. (a) grouped according to
		        interests, age etc.

Figure 2–2   Some alternative family structures

In several rural communes child care, especially care of infants, is primarily the responsibility of the mothers, though some functions may be performed collectively.

As the children mature, they are assured of love and emotional support not only by their biological parents but by their communal "mothers" and "fathers" as well, though "coddling" is notably absent. Indeed, in the communes observed in one study the children were encouraged and expected to behave autonomously at an early age; neither parents nor other commune members were prepared to devote much time to them.

A strikingly different attitude toward child-rearing obtains among the Hutterites, one of the largest communal groups in the United States. Like the Amish and Mennonites, they are Anabaptists who practice their religious beliefs (including pacifism) in daily life. This is undoubtedly a factor in the lack of crime and violence (or any observable hostility, for that matter), and the rarity of family conflict. Their methods of satisfying family functions and socializing children further strengthen the spirit of harmony among them.

The Hutterites live in groups of about a dozen families on communally owned farms. Almost all goods and services are provided and shared by the group, which employs scientific farming methods and modern technology in the manufacture of many of its own tools and machinery. (Despite their technical orientation, they strongly discourage exposure to mass media.)

After their children have been weaned, they are placed in central day nurseries, where formal education begins at age two-and-a-half. After-school care is the responsibility of older brothers and sisters. Between the ages of five and six, the children are taken out of nursery school, given a few simple chores, and allowed to play for much of the day. Religious education (in German) and secular education (in English) begins at the age of six, at a schoolhouse owned by the commune. Supervision and discipline after school hours are in the hands of a religious teacher. All children of the commune between the ages of 5 to 15 eat their meals in their own dining room, apart from the adults. At 15 they are baptized to signify entrance into adulthood, and from then on are expected to assume adult roles.

It should be emphasized that this community grew out of a unique situation. Like members of the Israeli kibbutzes, the Hutterites share a common religious heritage, and, again like kibbutz members, are united by common goals such as mutual economic aid and joint socialization of children. Whether similar living patterns can be established by other segments of American society is difficult to determine; the question is whether sufficient collective motivation can surmount differences in background, class, and goals.

Open marriage

In theory, if not always in practice, the cooperative household provides a framework within which husband and wife can share roles. Both participate in the raising of their children; both can contribute to the economic support of the household; and additional help is always available when needed, in the form of reciprocal aid among the participants in the communal structure.

Cooperative living, then, suggests a pattern in which the family can fulfill its traditional function through new modes without excessively burdening any one member. But this is merely a structural outline. It does not necessarily eliminate marital conflict, nor does it deal with a possible resistance to role sharing. These are essentially problems of attitude, and of one partner's inability or unwillingness to understand and accommodate the other's emotional and psychological growth. Traditional marriage has been a victim of such problems; open marriage is one of the most recent responses.

George and Nena O'Neill, who first suggested and systematically explored the concept, describe it as an attempt to incorporate into marriage the twin needs of relatedness and freedom, regardless of the outward form of the arrangement (group marriage, communal living, etc.).[29] In part, it is a state of mind that not only entails but also fosters patterns of behavior resulting in a new mental outlook.

The goal is "to strip marriage of its antiquated ideals and romantic tinsel," thus enabling the one-to-one relationship to fulfill the needs for "intimacy, trust, affection, affiliation and the validation of experience."[30]

Marriage does require commitment, but, according to the O'Neills, the traditional marriage contract demands unrealistic and unreasonable commitments.

To some degree, every "closed" marriage is a trap which blocks separate experiences and strives for an impossible closeness—a merging of husband and wife into a single entity. Open marriage, on the other hand, provides the opportunity for mental and emotional freedom within the context of a mutually supportive relationship of trust and liking, untainted by possessiveness.

Open marriage seeks to preserve the advantage of an in-depth relationship—which became more and more necessary with manifold changes in society—while removing the restrictions which work to destroy the relationship.

Though one of the most important facets of open marriage is the creation of its personal meaning by the couple involved without regard to tradition and rules, the O'Neills suggest certain juxtapositions that can serve as guidelines in "rewriting" the marriage contract:

The Old Contract Demands	The Open Contract Offers
Ownership of the mate	Undependent living
Denial of the self	Personal growth
Playing the couples game	Individual freedom
Rigid role behavior	Flexible roles
Absolute fidelity	Mutual trust
Total exclusivity	Expansion through openness[31]

In summary, open marriage is based on living in the present, in terms of realistic expectations. It postulates privacy; open and honest communication; role flexibility; open companionship; equality; separate identities; and a trust which implies an ability to forgive, and to treat the separate needs and relationships of the mate without fear, suspicion, or resentment.

The most significant aspect of the open marriage concept is its emphasis on changes which are compatible with the realities of contemporary society. It offers a way to make a viable commitment in the present, without restrictive tentacles to shackle the future.

Notes

[1] F. Ivan Nye and Felix M. Berardo, *The Family: Its Structure and Interaction* (New York: The Macmillan Company, 1973) p. 92.

[2] Quoted in Floyd M. Martinson, *Family in Society* (New York: Dodd, Mead & Co., 1970) p. 82.

[3] Talcott Parsons and Robert F. Bales, *Family, Socialization and Interaction Process* (Glencoe, Ill.: The Free Press, 1955), pp. 3-34.

[4] Robert O. Blood and Donald M. Wolfe, *Husbands and Wives* (New York: The Free Press, 1960).

[5] William O. Goode "Changes in Family Patterns" in *The Family and Change*, John Edwards, ed. (New York: Knopf, 1969).

[6] William F. Ogburn and Clark Tibbitts, "The Family and its Functions" in *Recent Social Trends in the United States*, Report of the President's Research Committee on Social Trends, (New York: McGraw-Hill Book Co., 1933).

[7] Jetse Sprey, "The Family as a System in Conflict," *Journal of Marriage and the Family*, Vol. 31, No. 4, Nov. 1969, p. 699.

[8] John Scanzoni, "A Social System Analysis of Dissolved and Existing Marriages," *Journal of Marriage and the Family*, Vol. 30, August 1968, p. 454.

[9] U.S. Bureau of the Census, *Statistical Abstract of the United States: 1972* (93rd edition) Washington, D.C. 1972, p. 63.

[10] Scanzoni, *op. cit.*, p. 454.

[11] *Statistical Abstract* 1972, *op. cit.*, p. 62.

[12] Morton Hunt "Help Wanted, Divorce Counselor," in *Contemporary American Family*, W. Goode, ed., (New York: N.Y. Times Book Ser., 1971) p. 226.

[13] Judson T. Landis, "A Comparison of Children from Divorced and Nondivorced Unhappy Marriages," *Family Life Coordinator*, Vol. 11, July 1962, pp. 61-65.

[14] *Statistical Abstract* 1972, *op. cit.*, p. 329.

[15] Goode, in Edwards, ed., *op. cit.*, p. 56.

[16] S. Orden and N. Bradburn "Working Wives and Marital Happiness," *American Journal of Sociology* 74, Jan. 1969, p.407.

[17] C. Arnott, "Husbands' Attitude and Wives' Commitment to Employment," *Journal of Marriage and the Family,* Vol. 34, No. 4, Nov. 1972, p. 683.

[18] Kenneth Keniston, *The Uncommitted,* (New York: Harcourt, Brace Jovanovich, 1965) pp. 258-259.

[19] Urie Bronfenbrenner, *Two Worlds of Childhood: U. S. and U. S. S. R.* (New York: Russell Sage Foundation, 1970) p. 103.

[20] Keniston, *op. cit.*, p. 204.

[21] Bronfenbrenner, *op. cit.*, p. 104.

[22] Barrington Moore, Jr. "Thoughts on the Future of the Family," in *Personality and Social Life* (New York: Random House, 1967) pp. 72-81.

[23] Bernard Farber, *Family Organization: An Introduction* (San Francisco: Chandler Publishing Company, 1964) p. 60.

[24] William O. Goode, *World Revolution and Family Patterns* (Glencoe, Ill.: The Free Press, 1963).

[25] *Facts on File,* January 1973.

[26] *The New York Times,* Sunday, May 20, 1973.

[27] Sheila M. Rothman, "Other People's Children, the Day Care Experience in America" *The Public Interest,* No. 30, Winter 1973, p. 21.

[28] *Ibid.,* p. 22.

[29] Nena O'Neill and George O'Neill, *Open Marriage* (New York: M. Evans and Company, Inc., 1972) p. 53.

[30] O'Neill and O'Neill, *op. cit.,* p. 71.

[31] *Ibid.,* pp. 72-73.

Summary

Although it has always been a basic unit of social organization in American society, the family has recently shown distinct signs of strain. Increased rates of divorce and confusion of roles within the family seem to indicate the family is both unstable and weak as an institution in a society which has assumed many of the family's former functions.

In early American families the husband was, as in Europe, dominant over his wife and children, though all were subject to strict community standards, imposed by religion in the case of the Puritans; in colonial America, family and property were virtually inseparable, and the leading families were often more important social forces than legislatures. As the country expanded in the nineteenth century, new varieties of family structure became prominent. Communal experiments were attempted but they had little lasting influence. On the frontier, extended, three-generation families were the basis of social organization, self-sufficient agents of production and socialization. In the cities, as industrialization took hold, families no longer were the primary agents of production and distribution. Men, women and children worked in factories and were less tied to family groupings than previously. As immigrants flowed to the United States, their extended family patterns too were broken down by "Americanization" and industrialization. Slave families were denied any legal basis until after the Civil War, and black family life was required to establish itself after the Civil War with very little support from the larger society.

Urbanization, industrialization and the growth of institutions like government and business all influenced family structure, so that by 1900 the nuclear family of the present day had begun to emerge.

Most sociologists view American family development as adjustment to change, but some, pointing to the record of family difficulties and to the assumption by schools, businesses and government of many of the functions the family once served, see it as leading to obsolescence.

The condition of marriage, within which the family operates for the most part, is an important factor in determining the quality of family life. Earlier in our history, marriage was most often a permanent tie. Husbands and wives fulfilled social and economic needs for one another. Today, a fast-paced complex society fulfills those needs, but creates emotional needs for fulfillment within marriage. Some marriages break under the strain. Divorce, separation and desertion are increasingly common in America, but the fact that a majority of divorced persons remarry indicates many people still rely on marriage to fulfill emotional needs.

Roles within the family are presently changing. Increased exposure to the career world during World War II, increased education, and dwindling family size all have contributed to American women's reevaluation of their family role. The Women's Liberation movement has demanded independence and respect for all women. In recognizing women's independence, men too have begun to question their own role within the family, where for so long they were expected to be sole breadwinner and authority figure. Children, because of schools and their increased association with their own age group, and because of the growth and influence of communications media are less dependent upon their families for value guidance than they used to be. Older family members have become increasingly detached from the family unit and are forced to make lives for themselves within their own age group.

Recent Supreme Court decisions supporting abortion and a working woman's right to claim dependents facilitate an expansion of woman's role in society. Day care centers enable women to work as often and as long as men, and enable a single parent to raise a family. Together with a more positive attitude to divorce, these responses to family problems are changing society and the family. Communal living, which has a long tradition in American family life, has also been revived, together with sometimes rigorous but less parent-centered child-rearing. And within traditional marriage, new flexibility is being developed.

chapter

prejudice
and
discrimination

Prejudice and discrimination damage the cooperation between different groups that is essential in a well-functioning society. As Emile Durkheim observed, society is "before all else an active cooperation."[1] The collective conscience, made up of common sentiments and beliefs, requires joint action. Prejudice and discrimination erode this community of belief and action.

In American society, prejudice and discrimination have often led to actions that go against the society's collective ideals. In the past the result has often been the virtual colonization of minorities: the Indians were reduced to a reservation population, the blacks were enslaved, and Spanish-speaking peoples lost their lands in American territorial expansion.

Although America's period of expansion is over, social problems resulting from prejudice and discrimination continue to affect daily life for millions of people in our society. Among America's minorities, education, housing, health, job opportunities, mental and physical security are undermined by prejudice and discrimination. These deprivations in turn threaten the stability of the whole society.

Prejudice and discrimination dehumanize their victims by treating them little better than animals, as Frantz Fanon has pointed out.[2] The decision to reject the dehumanization is a turning point for the colonized person. In America, Indians resisted the process of dehumanization during colonial times. Similar struggles continued in the slave revolts of the nineteenth century. Resistance has recently culminated in the civil rights confrontations and legislative actions of the 1950s and 1960s, and the movements for political power and self-determination in the 1970s.

As America's minorities move toward self-determination, how much progress is being made against the divisiveness of prejudice and discrimination? Is American society capable of the pluralism that can accommodate such groups? Have older methods of incorporation into American life, such as assimilation, become obsolete? Is separatism a realistic possibility? Can prejudice and discrimination, and their attendant social problems, be eliminated without violence?

Whatever answers evolve in the future, there is increasing evidence that the inner conflicts that have separated America's ideals from its practices create social disorder that could rip apart an already strained collective unity. Because of this fact, a close look at prejudice and discrimination in America has a special urgency.

Understanding prejudice

The study of prejudice has increased since World War II, provoked by the death of six million Jewish people in Europe, the violence accompanying efforts to regain human dignity in America and in colonial nations, the growing numbers of oppressed minorities making their resentments known to the rest of society.

To prejudge other men's notions before we have looked into them is not to show their darkness but to put out our own eyes.

Locke

What is prejudice? The word goes back to one in Latin, meaning prejudgment. The Romans used it to refer to preliminary legal decisions. Today it normally implies a preconceived opinion, often an unfavorable one. Although some prejudgment is necessary to meet the demands of fast paced contemporary complex societies, some flexibility of mind is necessary to allow for new information, or a change in circumstances. Gordon W. Allport points out that a prejudgment becomes a prejudice only if it cannot be reversed by new knowledge. In *The Nature Of Prejudice,* he defines prejudice as "an avertive or hostile attitude toward a person who belongs to a group, simply because he belongs to that group, and is therefore presumed to have the objectionable qualities ascribed to that group."[3] Such a preconceived and hostile attitude can be applied to people because of their race, religion, ethnic background or other kind of group membership.

While prejudice is an *attitude* held by an individual or group, discrimination is an *act* that does not necessarily imply prejudice but may stem from it. Prejudice reflects sentiments that may be held only by an individual, but discrimination relates to the general practices within the social structure of a culture. A person may feel a prejudice and never translate it into a discriminatory action. Prejudice and discrimination can exist independent of each other.

The term "discrimination" also has a Latin origin, going back to the word for divide or separate. Even in its ancient sense, the word provides an elementry understanding of the harm that can be done to a society through discrimination. In its modern usage, to discriminate also means to make a distinction, which may be either in favor of or opposed to a person or thing, on the basis of membership in a group rather than on the basis of individual attributes. Discrimination ignores individual merit or behavior and makes its distinctions on the basis of categories.

Allport outlines the different levels of actions that flow from prejudice, from the mild form of an ethnic slur to the most violent form, extermination. The first level is a verbal expression of prejudice, such as: "I don't like colored people." At the next level, the prejudiced person avoids the members of the group he dislikes. This does no direct harm to the disliked group; rather, the burden of avoidance is maintained by the prejudiced person. The comment, "When I see colored people in a neighborhood, I get away," illustrates this kind of avoidance.

The third level of action resulting from prejudice is discrimination. This stage moves the burden to the victim: members of the disliked group are excluded from certain types of jobs, housing and education. *Segregation* enforces discrimination by law or custom, resulting in an institutionalization of prejudiced behavior, separate toilet facilities for white and black people for example.

The next level brings physical abuse: members of a disliked group are attacked, as when Mexican-Americans were beaten in the streets of Los Angeles during World War II. Fifth, and most violent, is extermination: victims of prejudice are eliminated, as in pogroms and genocide. The massacres of Indians in America and the lynching of blacks after the Civil War were prejudiced behavior in its most violent form.

The danger of open expression of hostility in even a mild form is that it can lead to more intense levels of prejudicial action. For example, because of Hitler's racial slurs against the Jews, the Germans proceeded to avoid the Jews, even in cases where they had previously been friendly. This avoidance facilitated the Nuremberg laws, which compelled segregation. Then, in a climate of repression, burning a synagogue or attacking a Jew on the street seemed natural. Allport writes, "The final step in the macabre progression was the ovens at Auschwitz."[4]

Psychological aspects of prejudice

What leads people to such brutal expressions of hostility against others simply because they belong to one group or another? In personalities exhibiting deep character-conditioned prejudice, Allport found a core of insecurity—this kind of person is afraid of himself and his consciousness. He fears change as well as his social environment. Unable to live with himself or others, he organizes his attitudes to match his condition. "It is not his specific social attitudes that are malformed to start with; it is rather his own ego that is crippled."[5]

A society, as well as an individual, may also exhibit psychological disorders that can lead to prejudice and the use of scapegoats to solve its problems. Hitler used the Jews as scapegoats for Germany's misfortunes. T. W. Adorno and his associates reviewed this scapegoat mechanism at length in their study of anti-Semitism, *The Authoritarian Personality*.[6] Impersonal social processes, which seem beyond the control of individuals, alienate the person from his society. The alienated person then experiences the fear and uncertainty of disorientation, which he attempts to displace onto the prejudiced group. The victims of prejudice are blamed for the disorder that has been created by society's dysfunction.

Some prejudiced people look upon their victims in a seemingly more detached way, however. Adorno found that in interviews with prejudiced people the notion that Jews or blacks were a "problem" came up regularly. Using the word "problem" gives the impression of scientific detachment, of mature and objective thinking. Although there may be problems in relations between Jews and others, speaking of the "Jewish problem" (or the "black problem") changes the focus. The victims of prejudice become objects, rather than subjects, as if they were a part of an equation in mathematics. The prejudiced person sees himself as a wise judge who will manipulate the objects through some action which will solve the problem.

Socio-economic factors

When psychological factors are accompanied by economic factors—as when a group that suffers from cultural discrimination also posesses wealth desired by others—the setting for violent abuse is established. For example, the American settlers' interest in the mineral wealth of lands belonging to the Indians added a particular hostility to an already existing cultural discrimination. The fight for gold in California also led to increasingly violent prejudice and discrimination against the Mexican Americans. The clash of economic interests seems to blur awareness of individual differences. In the gold excitement in California, any one of the 8000 Mexicans, 5000 Chileans and Peruvians and other Spanish-speaking foreigners in California simply became a "greaser." In *The Chicanos,* Feliciano Rivera and Matt S. Meir note the connections between economics, prejudice and violence in the California experience. The "pattern" of Anglo exclusion, based on economic, nationalistic and racist attitudes, quickly moved from suspicion to threats, violence, restrictive legislation, litigation and back to violence.[7]

At times, a society's changing economic needs play a greater role than physical attack in the expression of prejudice and discrimination. The institution of slavery began to wane in the South when lowered profits in the tobacco market caused a switch away from that crop and made field hands unnecessary; the number of slaves increased again when cheap labor was required for the profitable development of the cotton industry. Today, cultural discrimination against the Puerto Ricans facilitates their exploitation as cheap labor.

Psychological and economic factors merge with sociological elements in many instances of prejudiced action. Among the social factors Adorno found enhanced the growth of prejudice in individuals are: "upward social mobility, identification of the higher class to whom they wish to belong themselves, recognition of universal competition as a measuring rod for what a person is worth, and the wish to keep down the potential threat of disinherited masses."[8]

Such social factors can be noticed in manifestations of prejudice in America. Lower middle class workers from various ethnic backgrounds see blacks or other discriminated groups as a potential threat, and stress competition as the ultimate proof of personal merit. Both groups are excluded from higher positions by the prejudices of people with more power.

During the nineteenth century period of immigration from Europe, each ethnic group saw the others as a threat, even though all suffered from discrimination by the dominant social groups. Irish and Italian workers, for example, battled each other for jobs in the coal mines; German Jews who were gaining acceptance in America resented the more impoverished Eastern European Jews who immigrated later in the century.

In a time of social and personal disorientation, scapegoats provide an easy answer to social problems. Luciano J. Iorizzo and Salvatore Mondello ascribe the birth of the stereotype of the "lawless" Italian to the violence of the 1870s: "the stereotype of Italians as lawless was formed during that decade and subsequently transferred to the later arriving South Italians."[9]

reading: **John A. Williams**
BLACK IMMIGRANT

Like most American blacks, with the coming of what has been called the "black revolution" I thought more and more about where my family came from. Other immigrants had roots in Europe or Asia; they could return to those homes and feel a sense of continuity. Not so with the Negro immigrant.

My father's family was a mess. There was an Uncle Bernie in the family, as white as this page, with blue eyes. A couple of cousins have freckles, and in the correct sunlight, red hair. Still, my father's name was John Henry and some part of the pure black South must have touched his ancestors at one time.

Ola, my mother's name, always struck me as odd, and Mississippi was a great state in numbers of slaves. It happened then that I went to Africa twice and in Nigeria found my mother's name. It has two meanings: in the eastern region, the land of the Ibo who make up the dominant tribe, it means "courageous one" and "keeper of the beautiful house." In the western region where the Yoruba live, it means "he who wants to be chief." All three fit very well.

I told this to my mother and showed her slides of buses with her name on them, but she remained unimpressed. She has always been concerned with the here and now; the problem of finding roots was an intellectual one for which she had little time in her life. She only knew that her parents had given her the name; she did not recall any grandparents or great aunts having it, and yet through the curious routes of the mind she was given it, an African name.

Because Negroes were excluded from American society, many of us turned with a vengeance to Africa and African "culture" with the coming of the revolution in the late fifties and early sixties.

We didn't seem to feel or notice that the independence sweeping Africa was at best tenuous, filled with economic considerations that were still very much tied to Europe; nor did we pay attention to the sudden rising of the "black elite" on that continent who were just as officious and just as cruel and greedy as the Europeans had been. We were so eager for a small sign of black self-assertion in this great white-dominated world that we accepted African independence without reservation.

I had met a number of African students and they always seemed to me somewhat distant; and I had worked for a time with an organization concerned with the politics of the African countries. Like many organizations with like interests in this country, we were always backing the wrong man to become premier. So it happened that I became one of the few, very few American Negroes, compared to the black population in the United States, to visit Africa, and I went twice, in 1964 and in 1965.

I met American blacks who had fled the United States and its segregated social systems who were anxious to return to New York, Chicago, Detroit—wherever they came from, for they had discovered that Africa, after all, was not a place of refuge for them. Many African communities in the western part of the continent set aside a small portion of their villages for people who did not have family or tribal ties; in Nigeria this part of the village is called the Sabongari, and a man may live in it all his life and not ever really belong to the community. The American blacks did not live in these areas, but they were just as effectively cut off. As a result, American blacks and whites in Africa tended to be closer there than at home. Single Negro women from the States tended to fare better; these usually were with the foreign service or the Peace Corps.

One of the saddest cases involved a young Negro man who had worked at the U.S. satellite tracking center in Kano, Nigeria. He resigned from what obviously was a challenging and lucrative position as an engineer to help the Nigerians; he planned to teach electrical engineering. The Nigerians did not accept his offer and he had to move into the Sobongari, where he did odd jobs in order to survive.

I traveled through ten countries trying to see reflections of my family, but what was most obvious was that the white man had done as effective a job on the Africans in their own land as he had done with blacks in America, for everywhere those Africans who could appeared to be living by or trying to live by the standards of the European. In the Congo and in Nigeria many of the young women wore wigs; I even saw a couple of young men with the processed hair one used to see ocasionally on young "hip" Negroes here. . . .

I see this as a most dangerous time for the black immigrant. After eight generations his patience has run out. What nonsense is it that he cannot have as much as those who have been here but one generation and contributed far, far less? It is dangerous because the black man can no longer be turned away with faulty education, the dregs of a technological system already outmoded, and the clichés of the past. But the system is not now geared to even care more than adequately for the white population, which in any case regards what it has as being too much for the Negro. The clash appears to be inevitable, which is fitting because the system was established on nearly free black labor in the first place.

Negroes held in slavery, in fact, could be said, as Ralph Ellison has said, to have subsidized immigration. They were the backbone of an agricultural society, providing the wealth therefrom to kick off the industrial revolutions, which in turn required more labor, cheap, of course, from Europe.

The most unlikely white coalitions have been formed; white immigrant neighborhoods have spawned the likes of Daley of Chicago and Louise Day Hicks of Boston and Spiro Agnew of Maryland.

Disaster can only be deflected by the back-to-the-ghetto movements by educated blacks who are taking the time to help train Negroes who haven't had their opportunities. And what we say at the conclusion of meetings or seminars with the man in the street is that when we do come out, we're coming out bad. That means with all the skills, education, and tools this society demands—plus whatever else is necessary to secure a place and function in it as a black human being.

In America the black immigrant looks around the world and sees that it is the nonwhites who have the poorest educations, and he asks, "Is that an accident?" He sees that it is the nonwhites who are always starving, and he asks, "Is that an accident?" He sees that it is the nonwhites who have the highest death rates, and he asks, "Is that an accident?" More and more by circumstances, by awareness, he is being drawn outside his nation to other nonwhites because he is weary of the global "accidents." He is coming to know that his salvation lies with these liaisons because white America has demonstrated time and again that it doesn't mean what it says.

From
"Time and Tide: Roots of Black Awareness"
by John A. Williams,
in *The Immigrant Experience,* edited by Thomas C. Wheeler
(Baltimore: Penguin Books, Inc., 1971) pp. 133-134; 145-149.

The roots of prejudice in America

The origins of prejudice in the United States go back to European attitudes at the time when America was discovered and settled. The Europeans' inability to understand peoples with dissimilar cultures, languages, religions and racial and ethnic backgrounds contributed to discrimination so severe that it led to the destruction of the native American population and slavery for the Africans. European religious animosities also crossed the Atlantic to America, where the victims of prejudice were considered savage heathens or enemies of the majority's religion. At the time of colonial independence, although the Constitution proclaimed individual liberty, local restrictive laws and customs rooted in old world attitudes still applied to various minority groups, including blacks, Indians, Catholics and Jews.[10]

Destruction of indian cultures

The exact size of the indigenous population in North America at the time of the Europeans' arrival is unknown; scholars have estimated it as at least one million. These native Americans represented diverse languages and cultures; within this diversity, however, certain similarities have been observed. John Collier has noted that most tribes functioned democratically; they had a "worldview cooperative, not exploitive, toward nature, and actively tolerant toward the multiplicities of difference."[11]

The westward expansion of European settlers and their descendents destroyed most of the original American population's way of life. By 1800 the number of Indians had been reduced to 600,000, and 50 years later it was less than half that number. The Indians were killed defending their lands, or died when they were forced to leave—4000 Cherokees died in 1834 on a forced march from their homeland in Georgia to reservations in Arkansas and Oklahoma.[12] Thousands died from starvation and disease; in 1837, smallpox reduced the Mandan population from 1600 to 31.

The story of the Sioux illustrates the process by which prejudice and economic factors led to violent forms of discrimination against the native population. The Sioux, once a proud people who hunted and led a nomadic life, were forced off their lands by the discovery of gold and a new push of European immigrants. When their reservation was established in 1889, the Sioux became government wards, subject to changing and contradictory policies.[13] The following year, the U. S. Army, mistakenly thinking the Sioux "Ghost Dances" were a preparation for warfare, massacred 200 Indian women and children and 98 disarmed warriors at Wounded Knee.[14]

The dispossession of the Mexicans

The dispossession of the Mexican-Americans paralleled that of the Indians: prejudice against the Mexicans arising from cultural differences and conflicting economic interests, led to violent discrimination.[15]

Anglo-American attitudes toward the frontier stressed the individual and the personal benefit he could gain from the land. The Spanish-Mexican view emphasized the community rather than the individual. Land ownership among the Mexicans involved length of occupancy and use, with less importance attached to boundaries, surveys, and grant registration—proofs of ownership required by Anglo-Americans.

After defeat in the Mexican war, the Mexican-American lost any grounds for argument. Stan Steiner, in his book, *La Raza* comments: "In the valley of the Rio Grande the murder of the Mexicans at least equaled, if not surpassed the lynching of Negroes in the South during the late nineteenth and early twentieth centuries."[16] Like the Indians, the Mexican-Americans often became impoverished outcasts in what had once been their community home.

Slavery and after

The first black slaves brought to this country in 1619 were treated like white indentured servants, able to earn their freedom after working for a time or being converted to Christianity.[17] Economic life soon required different arrangements, however, and Virginia enacted the first laws recognizing slavery in 1661: gradually, other colonies passed restrictive laws. Since American law was based on English law, which had no precedent for slavery, so the laws that came to govern slaves in this country evolved from English property laws. Because slaves were considered property, not people, they had no civil rights. Slaves were forbidden to enter contracts; their marriages were not considered legally binding, families could be separated by the slaveholder, slaves could be sold, given as free gifts and used in prizes and raffles. Children inherited their perpetual status as slaves from their mothers. As Alphonso Pinkney has described American slavery: "The attitudes which ultimately developed toward the slaves and the behavioral component of these attitudes, led to a system of human bondage without parallel in human history."[18]

Thus it is in the United States that the prejudice which repels the Negroes seems to increase in proportion as they are emancipated, and inequality is sanctioned by the manners while it is effaced from the laws of the country.

Alexis de Toqueville

Like the Indians, the black slaves often rebelled at the conditions forced upon them. A total of 250 slave revolts occurred before slavery ended. In a forty year period ending in 1850, 100,000 blacks escaped from slavery. The number of "free blacks" grew from 59,557 in 1790 to 448,070 in the last census before the Civil War.

After the Emancipation Proclamation and the end of the Civil War, black people experienced a brief period in which they held full civil rights. Thousands registered to vote, some blacks were elected to Congress or held high state offices in the South. It seemed that the ideals of democracy might finally become reality. However, as Frederick Douglass said of Reconstruction's failure, "there was more care for the sublime superstructure of the republic than for the solid foundations upon which it could alone be upheld."[19] Prejudices and economic forces once again impeded the trends to equality: the hard-won achievements of Radical Reconstruction were destroyed.

Discrimination was soon enforced by law, supported by custom, and propped up with pseudo-scientific theories. Historian C. Vann Woodward delineated the re-emergence of racial prejudice at the end of the nineteenth century: "At the very time that imperialism was sweeping the country, the doctrine of racism reached a crest of acceptability and popularity among respectable scholarly and intellectual circles."[20] Books, magazines, and other forms of communication spread the prejudices to the American people. Institutionalized racism became part of the American way of life.

By the turn of the century, the basis for our present problems of prejudice and discrimination had emerged. The Indians and Mexican-Americans, deprived of their lands, were struggling against destitution. On the reservations, the Indians suffered from indignities that affected their daily living conditions as well as their sense of cultural identity. In California, the Mexicans had been reduced to 10 percent of the total population; those in the Los Angeles area lived in a segregated area of the city, worked at low-paying jobs and were allowed little chance to improve their position.

At the turn of the century, American conquest also created another large immigrant group that was also to face the problems of prejudice and discrimination. When Puerto Rico passed from Spanish domination to American domination in 1898, its residents became American citizens. They began moving to the mainland, especially New York. When the Puerto Ricans came to the continent, they found themselves in the same slums once occupied by European ethnic groups, victims of similar stereotyping, and faced with the additional discriminations inflicted on those who are black or brown in America.

The black population, beginning its modern exodus from the rural South to the northern cities, also inherited the deprivations of previous immigrant groups. Poor housing, inadequate schools, economic exploitation—the same discriminatory conditions that had afflicted the immigrants from Europe—awaited the black immigrants from the South. But the black people searching for greater opportunity in the cities encountered the additional obstacle of racism.

At the beginning of this century, W.E.B. Du Bois accurately predicted that "the problem of the Twentieth century is the problem of the color-line."[21] The unfolding century has revealed the difficulties of bridging it.

Prejudice and discrimination today

Is our society moving toward community and away from the divisive effects of prejudice and discrimination? Or is it sinking more deeply into institutional racism and divisiveness?

Current social conditions indicate the scope of the problems resulting from prejudice and discrimination. The minority groups experiencing the worst discrimination—the black population, the American Indians, Mexican-Americans, Puerto Ricans and other immigrants—usually are forced to live in isolation from the rest of society. This colonial-type segregation has been most apparent among the American Indians, cut off from the rest of American society on reservations for more than a century, and the Mexican-Americans, scattered in remote rural poverty throughout the Southwest. Recently Mexican Americans and Indians have been moving to the cities, where they join other minority immigrants in urban segregation.

Although one out of every ten people in the United States is black, and in many cities blacks form a third or more of the population, the environments of the black and white population are so separate that the two races seem to live in two different countries, unable to cross borders, known to each other mainly through stereotypes created by the communications media. Because of the divisive effects of discrimination, 23 million people are unable to share fully in the life of the total society; and the society becomes more divided as the rest of the people try to maintain barriers. Kenneth B. Clark has described the resulting situation: "The dark ghettos are social, political, educational and—above all—economic colonies. Their inhabitants are subject peoples, victims of the greed, cruelty, insensitivity, guilt, and fear of their masters."[22]

Violence

The most basic right in a society is the right to life. The violent manifestation of prejudice destroys this right. Physical attack and elimination of populations, the two most extreme levels of prejudiced action, have taken many lives in the United States, and left a heritage of violence in majority-minority relationships. The number of Indians massacred during colonization may never by known; in this century, over 1000 black people were lynched by the time of World War I. A crowd of 3000 people in Tennessee once came to watch a black person being burned alive.[23] So much violence against minorities has encouraged violence in return; in 1967 alone racial disorders involving blacks and police occurred in 56 cities and resulted in 84 deaths, over 9000 arrests, and millions of dollars in property damage.[24]

The violence created by discrimination has afflicted many minority groups in America. An anti-Catholic mob burned a convent in Massachusetts in 1831; anti-Greek riots took place from Boise, Idaho to Roanoke, Virginia (in one anti-Greek riot in 1909, a mob caused $250,000 in damages and drove 1000 people out of town).[25] A Jewish man was lynched in Georgia in 1915 and picture postcards of his hanging sold in Georgia drugstores.[26] In Wyoming, a mob of whites invaded a Chinese community in 1885, killed 16 people and burned their homes to the ground.[27]

Violence against minority groups continues today in seemingly more isolated instances but with the same effects. In South Dakota, in 1973, Raymond Yellow Thunder, an Indian, was beaten by a white gang and thrown into an American Legion dance hall half-naked, then found dead the next day.[28] His death preceded Indian demonstrations at Wounded Knee.

The violence against minority groups is often an institutional violence. Such problems as police brutality and unjust enforcement of the law particularly strike minority groups. Steiner records the deaths of five Mexican-Americans killed by the police in one urban district within one year, including one 15-year-old boy killed on the street during a summer day by a policeman who said his gun accidently fired.

The Kerner Report analyzing civil disorders documented minority resentments against the police: in the area of a riot in Denver, 82 percent of the people believed that there was police brutality; in the Watts area of Los Angeles, 74 percent of the black men believed the police lacked respect for them or used insulting language to blacks.[29] Policemen are not seen as people from the community who help maintain order within the community, but rather as outsiders who do not live in the communities where they work and who help enforce a white man's domination in the lives of the people.

In response to these problems, some members of minority groups have formed their own self-defense units, or engaged in guerilla warfare attacks on policemen. Attacks on policemen (or on white people in general) seem to follow the same prejudicial pattern as attacks on minority people: usually a policeman is not known as an individual, but attacked because of his membership in a group—the police. As in any violent expression of prejudice, such attacks offer no hope of alleviating the problems that give rise to them.

Besides institutional violence, there is another kind of violence caused by severe discrimination: violence to the quality of life. The black legislator Julian Bond once described this kind of violence:

> Four out of every five Americans are more affluent than any other people in history. They have reached that affluence by degrading the fifth person, the poor Black and Brown Americans and others who have neither the power nor the resources to significantly improve their lot . . . we need to discover who is and who isn't violent in America. Violence is black children going to school for twelve years and receiving five years of education. Violence is 30 million hungry stomachs in the most affluent nation on earth. Violence is having Black people represent a disproportionate share of inductees and casualties in Vietnam. Violence is an economy that believes in socialism for the rich and capitalism for the poor. Violence is spending $900 per second to stifle the Vietnamese, but only $77 a year to feed a hungry person at home. Violence is J. Edgar Hoover listening to your telephone conversation. Violence is an assistant attorney general proposing concentration camps for white and black militants.[30]

Crime

Prejudice and discrimination that force minorities into urban ghettos create a climate of violence that leads to crime among members of minority groups. As long ago as 1870, gangs of young people prowled the urban poor neighborhoods. Police were unable to maintain order as thousands of poor European immigrants were entering the slums. Today crime in America has reached such proportions that there is one murder every half-hour in the United States, and one violent crime, such as rape, robbery and murder every 54 seconds.[31] This increase in crime particularly affects minority groups who live in conditions that make crime more likely. The chances of a black person's being robbed, raped, or violently assaulted are more than two and one-half times a white person's risks.[32] Unjust administration of the law makes the minority person more likely to be arrested and convicted, and sentenced to a longer term in prison.

Political scientists Louis L. Knowles and Kenneth Prewitt summarize the inequities involving discriminated groups in the United States:

> At every stage in the law enforcement process, from arrest to parole or execution, a greater proportion of the defendants or prisoners is black than at the previous stage. Such a situation is an inevitable consequence of a system designed to enforce laws made by whites and operating through a structure created and staffed by whites. The cultural myopia of a white society permeates our judicial system, making it inherently incapable of delivering justice to people of color.[33]

The sense that the society is unjust and that the representatives of the law are oppressors contributes to disrespect for society's laws. Knowles and Prewitt explain that for blacks, Mexican-Americans and Indians, the law means white oppression. "The unequal dispensation of justice is a result both of the origin of legal institutions and their present operation by white citizens who do not recognize the worth of non-white cultures."[34]

Inequality of opportunity

Any group that suffers from discrimination in America can illustrate the inequities of opportunity in the society. The problems of Spanish-speaking people in the United States are indicative. Of more than nine million people of Spanish background in the United States today, over four and one-half million are Mexican-American, the second largest minority group; only blacks outnumber them. However, among all minority groups the Mexican-Americans have the second smallest median income; only the Indians earn less. In every occupational category, the Mexican-Americans earn 20 to 40 percent less than Anglo-Americans.[35]

The more than one-and-a-half million Puerto Ricans in this country also suffer from inequities of opportunity. Puerto Ricans form the major part of the Spanish-speaking population in New York City, and the educational failure confronting these students is so critical that Senator Jacob Javits charged the city has violated the 1964 Civil Rights Act in its denial of equal educational opportunity. In one Board of Education report, 86 percent of the city's Spanish-speaking students were below normal reading levels; an estimated 100,000 Spanish-speaking children in the city's schools speak almost no English. Over 57 percent of the Spanish-speaking students in the city's schools drop out before completing high school, compared with 46 percent for black students and 29 percent for white students. Because of cultural and linguistic prejudice, the failures of the educational system to serve the needs of its students are seen predominantly among the Spanish-speaking.

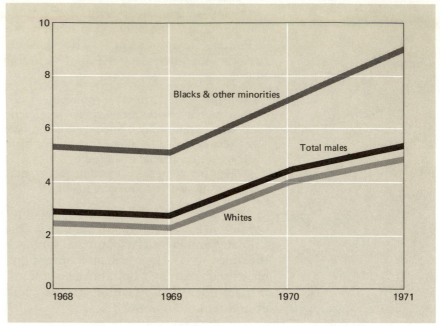

Figure 3–1   Percentages of unemployment, males, age 16 and over

Despair

The despair caused by such difficulties in American society is illustrated by statistics on drug addiction, mental illness, and suicide. In New York City, where about half of all the addicts in the country live, 46 percent of the people reported to the narcotics register in 1968 were black, and 23 percent were Puerto Rican. The rate of drug addiction in central Harlem was reported to be seven times higher than in the rest of the city.[36]

A high rate of mental illness also exists among the black and Puerto Rican population. The living conditions in the ghettos, the lack of adequate psychiatric help available to the poor, along with the frustrations and fears of a difficult existence, may contribute to this. Manuel Maldonado-Denis, a Puerto-Rican sociologist, says the problems of alienation and identity in Puerto Rico's colonial situation lead to an ambiguity, an uncertainty about who and what they are. Second-generation Puerto Ricans on the mainland are rejected by the American society and, when they return to Puerto Rico, are rejected there as well. He thinks that the "abnormally high rate of mental illness among Puerto Ricans living on the mainland is directly or indirectly related to this problem of identity and alienation."[37]

The frustrations of discrimination are also visible among American Indians. At the Pine Ridge Reservation in South Dakota, John Kifner recently reported a high rate of suicide attempts, alcoholism, broken

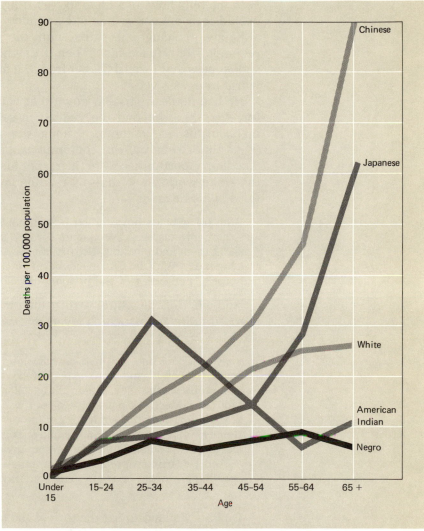

Figure 3–2   Deaths from suicide, United States 1959–1961

family structures, feelings of futility and inferiority. The school dropout rate is 81 percent by twelfth grade. Over half the families receive welfare; unemployment reaches 70 percent in the winter. The annual income per capita on the reservation is $846. The reservation presented a "bleak picture of some of the worst poverty in America," Kifner wrote. "Abandoned, rusted cars cluster around tumble-down shacks and litter the prairie hills, the best acres of which are grazed by white man's cattle."[38]

Resistance to prejudice and discrimination

The movements against prejudice and discrimination grew out of the experiences of idealists like W.E.B. DuBois. In *The Souls of Black Folk,* he tells how as a child in New England the first realization of prejudice swept across him like a shadow when he went to school. In a happy exchange of cards with the other children, one child peremptorily refused his. "Then it dawned upon me with a certain suddenness that I was different from the others . . . shut out from their world by a vast veil.[39]

He had no desire to tear down that veil; instead, he felt contempt for everything beyond the veil. Such self-protective psychological mechanisms are common among the victims of discrimination.

As time went by, the contempt began to fade, for he saw the dazzling opportunities were theirs, not his. He decided to get some of the white world's awards—by reading law, or healing, or telling the tales in his head.

> With other black boys the strife was not so fiercely sunny; their youth shrunk into tasteless sycophancy, or into silent hatred of the pale world about them and mocking distrust of everything white; or wasted itself in a bitter cry, Why did God make me an outcast and a stranger in mine own house? The shades of the prisonhouse closed round about us all . . .[40]

And what of the white world which tried to be gracious when he reached more sophisticated levels as a writer and intellectual of his day?

> They approach me in a half-hesitant sort of way, eye me curiously or compassionately, and then, instead of saying directly, How does it feel to be a problem? they say, I know an excellent colored man in my town; or, I fought at Mechanicsville, or; Do not these Southern outrages make your blood boil? At these I smile, or am interested, or reduce the boiling to a simmer as the occassion may require. To the real question, How does it feel to be a problem? I answer seldom a word.
>
> And yet, being a problem is a strange experience,—peculiar even for one who has never been anything else, save perhaps in babyhood and in Europe.[41]

Du Bois was writing at the turn of the century, but his experiences have been repeated countless times since then. For many, the effects of prejudice led to a bitter rage. For some like Du Bois, the sense of injustice also led to the movements for human dignity. He and other young blacks demanded aggressive action for human brotherhood in the Niagara Movement of 1906; by 1910 the young radicals had joined with educators and social workers in forming the NAACP. As John Hope Franklin wrote, "The presence of Dr. Du Bois on the staff branded the organization as radical from the beginning."[42] At this stage, however, the radicalism was more rhetorical than real.

While the NAACP worked to end segregation and gain the right to vote for all black people, another group, the Urban League, was formed in 1911 to help blacks who were moving into urban centers and to gain new opportunities for blacks in industry. The gains made by these groups formed a necessary prelude to the long marches for civil rights in the 1950s.

The civil rights movement

In 1954 the Supreme Court held that segregation in the public schools was unconstitutional and must be ended. The separation of races in the schools had become fully effective in the South in the 1890s; its overthrow by the Court was a major inroad on the systems of institutional racism. Inroads on other institutionalized discriminatory practices were soon forced.

. . . leadership within the respective groups is taking the reverse side of the coin of discrimination and emphasizing the positive side of discriminatory concepts. But far too few leaders are willing to realize the philosophical implications of the reversal. . . . they are using derogatory terms tagged on their group years ago by an uneducated white majority as proofs of racism inherent in the white man, rather than using the stone rejected by the builders to form a new edifice.

Vine Deloria, Jr.

The Montgomery Bus Boycott, led by Dr. Martin Luther King Jr., began after a black woman was arrested in December, 1955, for refusing to give up her seat to a white man in the "colored" section of a bus. It ended when the Supreme Court ruled against segregation on Montgomery buses. Dr. King's philosophy of nonviolent resistance involved several basic ideas: the perception of discrimination as evil; an active resistance to it; an attempt to use understanding to persuade those opposed; resolution to work against the forces of discrimination rather than against people; acceptance of suffering without striking back; and belief in the triumph of justice.

As the movement grew, white resistance increased. Attempts to desegregate schools—from the 1956 effort at the University of Alabama to those at elementary and secondary schools in many cities—occasioned mob violence against blacks and the use of National Guard troops. When, in 1957, whites resisted nine black students trying to enter Central High School in Little Rock, Arkansas, President Eisenhower ordered troops to the city, the first use of federal troops in defense of black peoples' rights in the South since Reconstruction.

A new generation

The "sit-in" movement began in 1960, when black college students at a segregated lunch counter in North Carolina were refused service and stayed in their places. Soon, black and white people were joining together in sit-in protests around the country. Some 70,000 people took part in the sit-in movement through a period of a year and a half;

over 3000 were arrested. Black college students then began the Student Nonviolent Coordinating Committee (SNCC), and nonviolent demonstrations spread to segregated beaches and churches. Over 1000 people joined in "freedom rides," to protest segregated buses. Their efforts led to an order by the Interstate Commerce Commission against segregation on buses and in terminals. Another important step in the civil rights struggle was the voter registration drive.

In the summer of 1963, efforts to end discrimination on the one hand and resistance to these efforts on the other brought demonstrations, bombings, the arrest of thousands of people. Some 250,000 people joined the March on Washington that August, the largest gathering in history to demonstrate for civil rights.

The next year, Congress passed the Civil Rights Act of 1964, which had many provisions against segregation, such as those outlawing segregation in public places and in programs receiving federal help. The Act established a sixth-grade education as sufficient proof of literacy for voting and gave the Attorney General authority to act in school and equal protection cases.

Attempts to register black voters sometimes resulted in white retaliation. Three volunteers were murdered in the 1964 Mississippi Summer Project of voter registration and "freedom schools"; 1000 people were arrested. Three people also died as a result of the march from Selma to Montgomery in the campaign for the right to vote. The march—which contributed to passage of the Voting Rights Act of 1965, greatly facilitating the registration and vote for southern blacks— also proved to be the final large demonstration in the civil rights movement, in which black and white people had worked together to end legal discrimination in many areas of American life.

Black power

By 1965, the fight against prejudice and discrimination had moved to the northern cities, where many rural blacks had migrated. Many were unable to find jobs or join unions and lacked the training to deal with modern technology. Families were crowded into slums and displaced in impersonal housing projects; and children failed to learn in schools not geared to deal with their education problems. As Martin Luther King had personified the southern blacks' resentments, Malcolm X personified the urban blacks' frustrations. Turning away from the goal of integration, Malcolm X sought group solidarity, joining with the black people of Africa in a struggle for basic rights in political, social, and economic spheres. He urged positive identification—pride in being black.

Black power first emerged as a concept in a speech to a crowd of poor people in Mississippi by Stokely Carmichael, Chairman of SNCC. Later he and Charles Hamilton explained the concept in their book *Black Power*. Black power is "a call for black people in this country to unite, to recognize their heritage, to build a sense of community," they wrote. "It is a call for black people to begin to define their own goals, to lead their own organizations and to support those organizations."[43] It also rejects the dominant society's values and institutions.

You watch. I will be labeled as, at best, an "irresponsible" black man. I have always felt about this accusation that the black "leader" whom white men consider to be "responsible" is invariably the black "leader" who never gets any results. . . . Yes, I have cherished my "demagogue" role. I know that societies often have killed the people who have helped to change those societies.

Malcolm X

Pointing out that ethnic groups traditionally have found social and political strength by setting up their own institutions to represent their needs within the society, Carmichael and Hamilton set the theme for ethnic self-determination and a rejection of old ideas of assimilation. Their fundamental premise is: *Before a group can enter the open society, it must first close ranks.*

In the racial violence of the 1960s, Martin Luther King, Malcolm X, and many others were killed; groups like the Black Panthers developed a more militant position; and the white society became more fearful. Despite its tendencies to violent action, black power appeared as a promising indication of the vitality of the black community. The drive for economic, political and social power gained momentum; pride in blackness led to new confidence; and black solidarity began to have effects in the larger society.

Self-determination among other groups

Other minorities seeking establishment of their rights have since followed the black example. Political, social and economic development among Mexican-Americans took place in the 1960s, through the efforts of the Chicano movement.[44] Beginning with the Delano grape strike of 1965, Cesar Chavez emerged as an advocate of nonviolent reform among Chicano agricultural workers. The efforts resulted in a contract signed with growers of about 50 percent of the table grapes from California in 1970. On another front, Fries López Tijerina tried to reclaim the New Mexico lands once owned by the Hispanic-Mexican peoples, now owned by Anglo-American ranchers and the American government. In Denver, Colorado, "Corky" Gonzales led another Mexican-American group toward such goals as better housing and education in a new Chicano society. José Angel Gutiérrez, working in Crystal City, Texas, started La Raza Unida to gain political, economic and social control of areas of south Texas.

Puerto Rican groups have also translated cultural pride and self-determination into a positive force. Striving for improved educational opportunities for young Puerto Ricans, Puerto Rican educators began bilingual programs from grade school through college. Mobile street theaters and dance groups worked to build cultural identity. The Young Lords Party, which later became the Puerto Rican Revolutionary Worker's Organization, sought radical social reform. On American college campuses, Puerto Rican and Afro-American groups sometimes joined their efforts in third world coalitions.

The Indians also began to organize. The Indian population more than doubled between 1950 and 1970—from 343,410 to 792,730 in 1970—and new leaders worked for greater self-determination. The contemporary American Indian Movement, which began in 1968 in Minneapolis, Minnesota, has led demonstrations in various places. The prolonged Indian take-over of Wounded Knee dramatized Indian grievances. Other Indian groups are attempting to regain tribal lands, or to receive adequate compensation for property taken from them through the years. They are also seeking community control over their schools and other facilities.

Movements which began as a reaction to prejudice and discrimination have evolved into a new social and political force. People from various ethnic groups have begun to emphasize their cultural heritage and question previous ideas of assimilation. However, it is yet to be seen whether the new vitality of the minority groups will lead to more divisiveness or to improved relations among all the members of the society.

Beyond prejudice and discrimination

While some violent manifestations of prejudice still occur, the period of racial hostility in which thousands of lynchings could take place without arousing disgust and anger has ended. Legalized discrimination has been greatly reduced by the civil rights movement. But the less intense levels of prejudiced behavior continue—discrimination by custom, as in housing; by institutions, as in education and in communications. These discriminatory practices still result in unequal opportunities for members of minority groups, and in the continuation of prejudiced stereotypes which slow further progress.

Progress in education

Education particularly illustrates the complexity of the problem of prejudice and discrimination. Despite the twenty years of political and social change that followed from the Supreme Court's 1954 decision, much *de facto* segregation remains. In recent years, resistance to desegregation has been demonstrated in New York, Michigan, and other northern states; the resistance in the South is of long standing. Furthermore, segregated education increases in cities across the country, as more white people move to the suburbs.

No satisfactory answers have yet been found to remedy the situation, although it seems clear that no one simple solution will work. For a time, decentralization was urged, to restore educational power to local communities and to begin to correct inequities. But decentralization easily leads to power battles between hostile racial groups, as the essential goal, improved education for the child, is lost in the antagonisms. Bussing was considered an answer by some; again, hostile reactions diverted attention from the goal of improved education. The merging of suburban and city school systems also has an uncertain future in the face of legal and parental opposition. Educational developments relating to integration and educational quality are discussed in more detail in Chapter Six.

Yet some promising developments are taking place. One is the growth of private and public schools that stress quality education and cultural pride for minority children. Schools like Harlem Prep, the Rough Rock Demonstration School (on a Navajo reservation in Arizona), and bilingual schools for Puerto Rican and Mexican-American children build learning achievement through pride in one's own culture. Respect for the child and his culture includes confidence in the child's ability to learn, rather than the condescension often found in educational attitudes toward minority children. Other hopeful trends are the growth of open admissions plans, which broaden opportunities for minority students to enter college, and the development of community colleges in urban neighborhoods. These colleges address themselves to the needs of people of many ages within minority communities, and often are staffed by educators from minority backgrounds. Within a ghetto neighborhood, such colleges can be centers for cultural and community development.

The development of schools encouraging pride in cultural identity while equipping students with the skills to facilitate achievement in the larger society is reflected by the increasing level of education in the black community. Researchers Ben J. Wattenberg and Richard Scammon have analyzed the new trends.[45] They found that from 1960 to 1970, the percentage of black males finishing high school jumped from 36 to 54 percent; among black women, the figure went from 41 to 61 percent. Along with this, the educational gap between young blacks and whites has been almost eliminated. At the college level, the gap between the number of blacks and whites enrolled has been closing rapidly—from 16 percent in 1965 to nine percent in 1971. In the same short period, the number of black people in college almost doubled, while the white enrollment went up only slightly. Such statistics do not take into account the differences in the quality of education provided for black and white students; nonetheless, they do indicate significant changes.

Economic progress

The economic gaps between minority populations and the majority remain large. Yet there is some ground for optimism about change. Wattenberg and Scammon note that slightly more than half the black families now are in the middle-class range and that young blacks have made striking gains. They find that in the North and West, black husband-wife families whose head of household is under 35 went from 78 percent of white income in 1959 to 96 percent in 1970. However, nationally, black men between 25 and 34 earn 80 percent of white income levels. Significantly, where husband and wife both work, the black family now earns more than the white.

Although black unemployment rates have been higher than those of the white population, the unemployment rate for married black adult men over the past dozen years has been cut in half. Most black family men are now working.

The study also indicates that blacks are now able to get better jobs. Between 1960 and 1970, blacks working at jobs as craftsmen, operatives, and white-collar workers jumped by 76 percent. By 1970, 64 percent of blacks working had middle-class jobs. Great gains were made in the number of nonwhites who were able to find employment as teachers and social workers. Blacks also made breakthroughs in the skilled trades, enrolling in apprentice jobs and joining unions such as those in construction.

At the same time, Wattenberg and Scammon cite less promising figures. Although the percentage of blacks in poverty was cut almost in half, those receiving welfare tripled from 1.3 million in 1960 to over 4.8 million in 1971. It is still true that less than half of those receiving welfare in this country are black, but the number of black people on the welfare rolls is four times higher than their percentage in the total population. Six out of ten black families in poverty were headed by women.

Political progress

In 1973, Thomas Bradley, a black, was elected mayor of Los Angeles by 56 percent of the vote in a city where blacks make up less than a fifth of the total population. A black mayor of the third largest city in the country, personifies black political gains in the early 1970s.

A less optimistic trend for future black political power also can be observed, however: the political consolidation of city and suburban areas, which reduces the percentage of black people within the new political unit. In Jacksonville, Florida, as the whites moved to suburban areas and the blacks approached 50 percent of the city population, a "Metrogovernment" consolidation of Jacksonville and the suburban area was proposed for better city management. In analyzing the Jacksonville consolidation, Lee Sloan and Robert M. French conclude that what happened there is an old story—when blacks seemed to be moving toward their share of political power, "the rules of the game were changed."[46] Such consolidation can have important practical advantages; it provides more income and a more rational basis for city services. But it strips power from the urban black majority, and again creates a climate of neglect of black needs.

When blacks do gain political power, commensurate economic gains are not necessarily achieved. Robert Curvin, who organized the black and Puerto Rican coalition at the convention which nominated Kenneth Gibson for major of Newark, New Jersey, discussed results after Gibson's first year in office and found that, "Black power in city hall will not necessarily deliver the solutions to the problems faced by black people in urban areas."[47] Not only are there two racial Newarks, there are also two economic Newarks: one is mostly black and without economic power; the other is the thriving white business community.

The role of communications

A study by sociologists Paula B. Johnson, David O. Sears and John B. McConahay[48] indicates a growing awareness of the role of communications in minority problems. In an analysis of Los Angeles newspapers from 1892 to 1968, they found that the press had given little attention to blacks through the twentieth century; that the coverage of blacks had diminished from 1892 until just before the Watts riot in Los Angeles, went up during the riot, then returned to pre-riot level afterward. Over the years the content of press coverage changed from reinforcing stereotypes of black life to stressing conflict. The study showed that blacks received about 20 percent of the space which they should have received according to their percentage of the local population, and that coverage of everyday life declined from nine percent in the period 1892-1919 to three percent in the 1965-1966 years. The study also notes that the question of press coverage may involve class bias as well, since powerless people are not considered to be worth much news coverage.

Most white Americans are physically isolated from blacks. The white person's few physical contacts are so structured that blacks are psychologically invisible to him as well. The mass media could potentially fill an important gap, communicating to whites the attitudes, feelings and life styles of black people. But the media reflect and are controlled by the white world. The Kerner Report revealed that less than five percent of the people holding editorial jobs in the news business were black, and that less than one percent of supervisors and editors were black—and most of these worked for organizations owned by blacks.[49] Even newspapers and radio stations serving the black community have often been owned by white people.

Because of these factors, the question of communications is an important issue among minority groups. In several communities, blacks are beginning to buy out the white owners of newspapers and radio stations. Others see public-access television as a way to provide better media coverage of the needs of minority people. Without a more adequate understanding of these needs, progress will be slowed; discrimination in communications facilitates the prejudgments that contribute to discrimination in housing, education and jobs.

Assimilation, pluralism, or separatism?

In the past, immigrants were expected to shed their previous cultures and fit into American life and culture as quickly and as completely as possible. According to the melting-pot theory, the pasts of many people merged into a newer, better product—the American way of life. A "contributions" theory pervaded: these diverse cultures each contributed to American life. Still, it was expected that, after having contributed Irish songs or Italian foods, the immigrant would move out of an ethnic neighborhood, speak English and adopt American cultural values by the third generation.

Many people have begun to reevaluate this process of assimilation. Some sociologists question whether the ethnic background of immigrants has truly been erased. In *Beyond the Melting Pot*, Nathan Glazer and Daniel P. Moynihan suggest that ethnic background is a continuing basis for identity and for social conflict in America.

Assimilation had been thought of as the process by which a new homogeneous entity was created from different cultures, comparable to a biological process by which the body takes in different types of matter and converts it into cells adapted to the whole body. But in recent years, rather than stressing homogeneity, more emphasis has been placed on the need to preserve the distinct cultures, and understand how they function for the individual and in society.

Older views picture America as a land of opportunity, where by competitive struggle each person can gain access to individual opportunities through individual merit. Sociologist Glen H. Elder Jr. has contrasted this individual achievement approach with the revolutionary-collectivist approach, which advocates the subordination of self to a collective cause and authority.[50] The achievements of individual blacks do not necessarily lead to change, but the power of collective action and black solidarity may. (The same contrasting approaches might be observed among other groups discriminated against. Formerly, an individual woman's achievements would be thought to lead to a breakdown of discrimination; recently, collective action by women has been emphasized.) Studying the attitudes of black youths, Elder concluded that both approaches were gaining with the young black population. This point of view expresses an ideal: a pluralistic community in which blacks can affirm their racial identity, contribute to the social, economic, and cultural life of their people, and freely participate in relationships with whites that are characterized by friendship and interdependence.

Whitney M. Young, Jr. stated the ideal another way: "In the context of positive pluralism, black people would enter the dominant white society with a sense of roots," he wrote. "By now, we ought to see the fatal flaws of the old melting-pot theory, which sought to strip people of culture and traditions in order to transform everyone into middle-class, white Anglo-Saxons."[51]

Sociologist Andrew Greeley also rejected the notion that groups must be assimilated into American culture. Instead, he argued for an American culture which understands its diversity. Citing the conclusion of French anthropologist Claude Lévi-Strauss that diversity is necessary for human society, Greeley finds that though differences between peoples are the focus of social conflict, the differences are not likely to be eliminated. "The critical question is how to use these tensions and diversities to create a richer, fuller human society instead of a narrow, frightened and suspicious society."[52]

Some would maintain that the differences are so sharp that the only resolution is separation. This has been the practical outcome of the white retreat into the suburbs. As Americans have fled farther from the minority communities, however, the social fabric has become more strained. Separatism has also been proposed by blacks such as the late Marcus Garvey, whose back-to-Africa movement once involved thousands of people. Separatism always will have some appeal; yet it can never lead to the conditions necessary for a harmonious society because it avoids the issues causing divisions.

Prejudice and discrimination feed upon an insecurity which fears diversity. Psychological, economic and social disorder combine in hostility against discriminated groups. Yet the categories that make people objects of prejudice are not immutable: they change, and the violence directed against one group hardly seems comprehensible some years later.

---

reading: **Paul Jacobs and Saul Landau with Eve Pell AMERICA INSCRUTABLE**

In mythical America, the first stop of the white immigrants who came to the country during the period of unlimited immigration was the cities along the Eastern Seaboard. There, in the legendary America, they lived together in slum areas, maintaining their Old World cultures, eating their own kinds of foods, practicing their own religions, and still speaking the language of their homelands.

Then, goes the myth, the children and grandchildren of the immigrants become assimilated into the American mainstream. The acculturation process is accompanied by the development of tension between the first generation of immigrants and the second, which is not familiar with old ways, cannot speak the language of their parents, and rejects the old customs. The second generation is in turn succeeded by another, for whom the past is not so disturbing; they have become so sure of their American identity that they are able to find a source of pride in their foreign heritage. In the meantime, the original ghetto changes, as the descendants of the original immigrants move out. It becomes a harbor for a new wave of immigrants who prepare, in their turn, to be melted down into homogeneous Americans.

This social process has a mythical economic parallel in which the immigrant groups begin at the bottom of the work ladder, performing the most difficult, least desirable and lowest-paid jobs. In the acculturation process, they move up the economic scale, and the newer immigrant groups take their place on the lower rungs.

Like all myths, the one about America as the melting pot of the world does have some basis in fact. It is true that a great many white immigrants and descendants of white immigrants have achieved political power, financial success, and considerable social status. The walls that once separated these groups from the white Americans who preceded them have been broken down. But a great many Americans still live in enclaves, separated from each other and from the mainstream by their colors, countries of origin, ethnic backgrounds, and religions.

In Milwaukee, Wisconsin, Gary, Indiana, and other cities, the sense of Slavic identity is still so strong that the cry of "Black Power" was met with the cry of "Polish Power." Whole wards of Slavs voted against black candidates and fiercely resisted attempts to break segregated housing patterns.

On Long Island, in New York, the "Golden Ghettos" are towns where virtually no one but middle-class Jews live, isolated in their social and cultural life from the gentiles who surround them. In Los Angeles, crowds of Jews, young ones as well as those from older generations, throng Fairfax Avenue, which has become a Jewish street with Jewish restaurants, kosher meat markets, fish stores, and bookstores featuring Hebrew books and Hebrew records.

In every American city, the ghettos are almost totally black. In the barrios, from metropolitan New York to rural California, Spanish is the spoken language, even in the third and fourth generations. In fact, one of the demands being made by the younger Spanish-speaking groups is that the schools of the South and Far West use Spanish along with English as a teaching language.

New Little Tokyos are growing up in the cities where most of the Japanese-Americans live, while in San Francisco those Chinese-Americans who cannot afford the fantastically high rents of Chinatown move out to the edges of the city, where they clump together in what will soon be Little Chinatowns. On weekends, though, they return to the older and larger Chinatown, anxious to visit with their families, eat in familiar restaurants, do their shopping, and see their friends. Here, too, in the streets of Chinatown, the young have taken a new interest in things Chinese; they identify themselves, openly and proudly, as Asians.

What America is witnessing is a new kind of clustering together of ethnic groups. They are perhaps afraid of being isolated from the familiar and reassuring. In a country that seems to be spinning apart in a centrifugal storm of politics and social upheaval, one's own special identity becomes increasingly essential for survival.

While more than twenty million blacks continue to live in ghettos; while Orientals, Mexicans, Filipinos, and other colored people remain in their racial enclaves; while millions of white Europeans cling to their neighborhoods and their old languages—other white Americans cling tenaciously to the idea that America is truly a great melting pot. They are not aware of the fact that in 1960 at least nineteen million Americans still had a mother tongue, a primary language other than English, and that approximately half of these people were born in America, and that 15 percent of them are third generation.

Society was willing to absorb only those white immigrants who assimilated most easily, accepted racism most readily. Poles in Milwaukee, Italians in New York, Jews in Los Angeles, to mention just a few examples, practice open racism toward one or more minority groups; to do otherwise would be un-American, they think, and might reveal their uneasy feelings about their true status in the United States.

The assimilated immigrant is the one who has blended into the kind of America seen in TV commercials which glorify the middle-class way of life, so attractive to the truck driver who

hates niggers and curses them in Polish or Italian. To be truly assimilated is to have only memories of the Old World culture, romanticized myths about the "good old days." By the third and fourth generation there is a truly assimilated progeny whose grandfathers are as foreign a cultural type to them as a Georgia slave is to a black auto worker in Detroit. To be sure, a cultural heritage remains—food, religion, certain family behavior patterns.

But if the third-generation European immigrant tries to merge successfully into the middle class, he must join the American of the TV screen. And if he remains in the working class and continues to live in an Old World enclave, he will affirm his Americanism through racist attitudes toward blacks and newly arrived immigrants. In both cases, a blending of cultures does occur. In one, a bland, homogenized representative of suburban America emerges; his origins are distinguished only by a "sky" or "itz" at the end of his name. In the other, a bitter acceptance of the worst of of both cultures occurs; primitive and reactionary Old World attitudes are combined with notions of white supremacy and worship of gaudy consumer goods.

Immigrants from Europe encountered white America's racism, and a new outlet was provided for the ancient hostilities which had permeated their lives in the old countries. There, Norwegians and Danes hated Swedes, northern Italians despised Sicilians, Poles persecuted Jews, Serbs killed Croatians, the Irish fought the English, the Germans made war on the French, and the French felt nothing but disdain for the Spanish.

But now, in the New World, the old hatreds and feuds were put aside as the Europeans tried to become Americans. And to become an American meant accepting the white stereotype of the black, brown, red, and yellow-skinned peoples. Religious, national, and regional prejudices of Europe were converted to the color prejudices of America. The American culture was so thoroughly suffused with racism that the immigrants found it comparatively easy to adjust to the new society. That aspect of America was familiar to them; only the objects of the hatred were different. So the newcomers quickly and passionately adopted precisely that part of the American heritage which was destined to keep democracy from ever functioning properly. Descendants of the first Virginia slaveholders have little in common with the sons and grandsons of midwestern Polish steelworkers. Virginians have accepted very few Polish Old World patterns, but second- and third-generation Poles have assimilated the racist heritage of the first Americans. Ironically, the melting pot did work—but only in one direction.

D. H. Lawrence once expressed his judgment of this country. It was harsh, but fitting.

The American landscape has never been at one with the white man. Never. And white men have probably never felt so bitter anywhere, as here in America, where the very landscape in its very beauty seems a bit devilish and grinning, opposed to us.

The desire to extirpate the Indian. And the contradictory desire to glorify him. Both are rampant still, today. . . .

But you have there the myth of the essential white America. All the other stuff, the love, the democracy . . . is a sort of by-play. The essential American soul is hard, isolated, stoic, and a killer. It has never yet melted.

From
"America the Myth,"
in *To Serve the Devil*
by Paul Jacobs and Saul Landau with Eve Pell
(New York: Vintage Books, 1971) Vol. I, pp. XXX-XXXV.

Notes

[1] Emile Durkheim, *The Elementary Forms of Religious Life,* trans. Joseph Ward Swain (London: Allen & Unwin; New York: The Macmillan Co., 1915), pp. 465-466.

[2] Frantz Fanon, *The Wretched of the Earth,* Preface by Jean-Paul Sartre, trans. by Constance Farrington (New York: Grove Press, Inc., 1968) pp. 42-43.

[3] Gordon W. Allport, *The Nature of Prejudice* (Cambridge, Mass.: Addison-Wesley Publishing Co., 1954) p. 7.

[4] *Ibid.,* p. 15.

[5] *Ibid.,* p. 396.

[6] T. W. Adorno, Else Frenkel-Brunswik, Daniel J. Levinson, R. Nevitt Sanford, *The Authoritarian Personality* (New York: Harper & Brothers, 1950) p. 618.

[7] Matt S. Meier and Feliciano Rivera, *The Chicanos* (New York: Hill and Wang, 1972) p. 76.

[8] Adorno, *op. cit.,* p. 700.

[9] Luciano J. Iorizzo and Salvatore Mondello, *The Italian-Americans* (New York: Twayne Publishers, Inc., 1971) p. 35.

[10] See John Higham, *Strangers in the Land: Patterns of American Nativism 1860-1925* (New Brunswick, N.J.: Rutgers University Press, 1955), and Gustavus Myers, *History of Bigotry in the United States* (New York: Random House, 1943).

[11] John Collier, "The United States Indian," in *Understanding Minority Groups,* Joseph B. Gittler, ed., (New York: John Wiley & Sons., Inc., 1956) p. 34.

[12] Information on the Indians is based on: Murray L. Wax, *Indian Americans: Unity and Diversity* (Englewood Cliffs, N.J.: Prentice-Hall, Inc., 1971).

[13] Thomas F. Gossett, *Race: The History of an Idea in America* (New York: Schocken Books, 1965) pp. 232-233.

[14] John Kifner, "At Wounded Knee, Two Worlds Collide," *New York Times,* 24 March 1973, p. 14.

[15] Information on Mexican Americans based on: Matt S. Meier and Feliciano Rivera, *op. cit.*

[16] Stan Steiner, *La Raza: The Mexican Americans* (New York: Harper, 1970) p. 24.

[17] Information based on Alphonso Pinkney, *Black Americans* (Englewood Cliff, N.J.: Prentice-Hall, Inc., 1969).

[18] *Ibid.,* p. 8.

[19] Frederick Douglass, *Life and Times of Frederick Douglass* (New York: Collier Books, 1962) p. 502.

[20] C. Vann Woodward, *The Strange Career of Jim Crow* (New York: Oxford University Press, 1966) p. 74.

[21] William E. B. Du Bois, *The Souls of Black Folk* (Chicago: A. C. McClurg & Co., 1903) introduction.

[22] Kenneth B. Clark, *Dark Ghetto* (New York: Harper & Row, Publishers, 1965) p. 11.

[23] John Hope Franklin, *From Slavery to Freedom: A History of Negro Americans*, Third Edition (New York, Alfred A. Knopf, 1947, 1956, 1967) p. 439.

[24] Pinkney, *op. cit.*, pp. 205-206.

[25] Oscar Handlin, *A Pictorial History of Immigration* (New York: Crown Publishers, 1972) p. 250.

[26] Lenora E. Berson, *The Negroes and the Jews* (New York: Random House, 1971) p. 30.

[27] Alphonso Pinkney, *The American Way of Violence* (New York: Random House Vintage Books, 1972) p. 73.

[28] Kifner, *op. cit.*, p. 14.

[29] *Report of the National Advisory Commission on Civil Disorders* (New York: Bantam Books, 1968) p. 302.

[30] Julian Bond in *Black Business Enterprise: Historical and Contemporary Perspectives*, Ronald W. Bailey, ed., (New York: Basic Books, Inc., 1971) pp. viii, ix.

[31] Pinkney, *The American Way of Violence, op. cit.*, p. 6.

[32] Ben J. Wattenberg and Richard M. Scammon, "Black Progress and Liberal Rhetoric," *Commentary*, Vol. 55, No. 4, April 1973, p. 40.

[33] Louis L. Knowles and Kenneth Prewitt, eds., *Institutional Racism in America*, (Englewood Cliffs, N.J.: Prentice-Hall, Inc., 1969) pp. 58-59.

[34] *Ibid.*, pp. 76-77.

[35] Meier and Rivera, *op. cit.*, p. 280.

[36] Statistics from Pinkney, *Black Americans, op. cit.*, p. 134; Joseph P. Fitzpatrick, *Puerto Rican Americans: The Meaning of Migration to the Mainland* (Englewood Cliffs, N.J.: Prentice-Hall, Inc., 1971), p. 172; Kenneth Clark, *Youth in the Ghetto* (New York: Harlem Youth Opportunities Unlimited, 1964) pp. 144-145.

[37] Manuel Maldonado-Denis, *Puerto Rico: A Socio-Historic Interpretation*, trans. by Elena Vialo (New York: Random House, 1972) pp. 320-321.

[38] Kifner, *op. cit.*, p. 14.

[39] Du Bois, *op. cit.*, p. 1.

[40] *Ibid.*, p. 2.

[41] *Ibid.*, p. 3.

[42] Franklin, *op. cit.*, p. 447.

[43] Stokely Carmichael and Charles V. Hamilton, *Black Power: The Politics of Liberation in America* (New York: Random House, 1967) pp. 37, 44.

[44] This account of the Chicano movement is based on that of Meier and Rivera, *op. cit.*, pp. 250-276.

[45] Wattenberg and Scammon, *op. cit.*, pp. 35-44.

[46] Lee Sloan and Robert M. French, "Black Rule in the Urban South?" *Transaction*, Vol. 9, Nos. 1/2, Nov./Dec. 1971, pp. 29-34.

[47] Robert Curvin, "Black Power in City Hall," *Society*, Vol. 9, No. 10, Sept./Oct. 1972, pp. 55-58.

[48] Paula B. Johnson, David O. Sears, John B. McConahay, "Black Invisibility, the Press, and the Los Angeles Riot," *American Journal of Sociology*, Vol. 76, No. 4, Jan. 1971, pp. 698-721.

[49] *Report of the National Advisory Commission on Civil Disorders.* p. 384.

[50] Glen H. Elder Jr., "Intergroup Attitudes and Social Ascent among Negro Boys," *American Journal of Sociology*, Vol. 76, No. 4, Jan. 1971, pp. 673-697.

[51] Whitney M. Young, Jr., *Beyond Racism: Building an Open Society* (New York: McGraw-Hill Book Co., 1969) p. 152.

[52] Andrew M. Greeley, *Why Can't They Be Like Us?* (New York, Dutton, 1971) pp. 15-16.

1 *part*

**Social
disorganization**

Summary

Prejudice and discrimination endanger American society by
damaging the community of belief and action which enables that
society to function.

Prejudice can be defined as a preconceived, hostile attitude
toward a person based on his membership in a group.
Discrimination is the favorable or unfavorable distinction of one
person on the basis of his membership in a group, rather than on
the basis of his qualities as an individual. The most prevalent kind
of discrimination practiced in America is the denial of certain
kinds of jobs, housing, education, and other benefits of society to
members of specific racial and ethnic minorities.

Psychological factors, such as fear of change, socio-economic
factors, such as competition for job opportunities, and sociological
factors, such as the desire for social prestige and power, combine
to perpetuate prejudice in American society.

The Europeans who colonized America brought prejudice with
them. Unable to appreciate the different cultures they found, and
bearing particular animosity for people of "pagan" religion, they
took little care to respect America's native inhabitants, who
remained outside the community of belief. As American society
developed, the prejudice which permitted such actions persisted.
Black slaves were considered property, rather than human beings.
Indians and Mexican-Americans were conquered, then exploited,
but never recognized as having a claim to treatment on the same
level as the dominant European groups.

Though slavery was abolished, blacks continued to be
discriminated against by social custom and by law. These
sanctions were accompanied by an ideology stressing white
superiority, fully developed by the turn of the twentieth century,
which we have come to recognize as racism.

Discrimination against other groups—Puerto Ricans, Mexican-
Americans, Orientals, American Indians—has also been practiced
by the larger society. Procedures for dealing with these groups
parallel those used in keeping blacks from full participation in
American life.

Prejudice and discrimination are responsible for the segregation
of minority groups in urban ghettos or on Federal reservations. The
effect of such segregation is often to increase the difficulties of
living for the minority involved. Crime, disease, disorder in
minority life are in large part ascribable to segregation.
Discrimination in hiring limits job opportunities for minorities.
Poor education limits opportunities still further.

Discrimination is so deeply rooted in American society that to
reverse it to any degree has required radical action. Black attempts
to combat it began early in this century and culminated in the Civil

Rights Movement of the 1950s and 1960s. The 1954 Supreme Court decision against segregation in the public schools gave the movement impetus. A later development of the movement was the drive for Black Power, both political and economic, and a search for African cultural roots. Other minorities subject to discrimination have in general followed the non-violent confrontation methods advocated by Martin Luther King, Jr. Groups such as the Black Panthers have advocated violent resistance to the oppression of prejudice and discrimination. Sometimes these methods have been advocated by other minorities as well.

Minorities have made some progress against discrimination in educational, economic and political fields. In education and in employment, the federal government has been an active agent in changing discriminatory practice. In politics, an increasing number of minority candidates are winning elections not only in minority areas, but city-wide in such places as Los Angeles, which is predominantly white. Progress has also been made in communications, where minorities have insisted on more objective treatment.

Minority resistance to prejudice and discrimination has revived the ethnic identity of national groups once thought to have been "assimilated" into American society. While such a revival has often served to counter black and other minority demands, it has stimulated discussion of pluralism, rather than assimilation, as a goal for American society. Conflicts between groups have in some instances become sharper than they were before, but American society may be moving toward a recognition of diversity in individual and group relations.

chapter

poverty

Many Americans have a tendency to view poverty as the young regard old age—something that happens only to "others," whether individuals or nations—yet poverty is very much a part of the American scene, a fact hard to believe about the world's wealthiest nation. Poverty is a relative rather than an absolute state: America's poor may not be the emaciated skeletons that arouse horrified pity in newspaper photos of underdeveloped countries, but their plight is often quite as acute, even if less dramatically obvious. The very fact of our national wealth magnifies their condition by comparison. In most other countries, even moderate wealth is reserved for relatively few; in the United States, it constitutes the accepted middle-class standard, which the poor see portrayed as the norm on TV and in the other mass media. Their exclusion from this norm has, as sociologists S. M. Miller and Pamela Roby point out, "surreptitiously ushered in the issue of inequality in the affluent society."[1]

Such inequality extends far beyond mere inability to afford the luxuries of life. It generates a vicious cycle in which poor education leads to restricted job opportunity, thus to a reinforcement of low income and resultant lack of the "upward mobility" that is one of the prized traditions of the American way of life. Low income also means poor housing—in areas of high crime and inadequate police protection—and comparatively poor health, with limited access to proper medical care.

The poor in this country are a minority, but an appreciable one: in

1970, 25.5 million Americans fell into the government-defined poverty category,[2] and $14 billion would have been needed to raise their incomes above the poverty level.[3]

These underprivileged millions represent a problem of mounting urgency for the entire nation. Poverty spawns crime—especially in urban areas, where the discrepancy between living standards is more obvious and causes more bitterness and despair. But neither blight nor economic stagnation is confined to the cities. Appalachia has become a synonym for catastrophic and widespread hopelessness; and many similar areas, less well publicized, exist throughout the country.

During the 1960s, as the nation grew increasingly aware of existing inequities and their potential for political and social disruption, poverty became a high priority issue. "Equal opportunity" had become little more than a slogan, and traditional remedies had failed to improve its efficacy.

It is an odd fact that such money as the poor have frequently buys less for them than it does for the wealthy. The poor cannot economize by buying in large quantities; they cannot take advantage of seasonal sales; they have difficulty in obtaining credit, and when they do, they must pay higher interest rates because they constitute poor risks and take longer to repay loans. Finally, the tax structure, which affords the rich loopholes such as oil depletion allowances, depreciation on property and equipment, expense accounts, and numerous legally deductible expenses, mitigates against those in the lowest income brackets.

All these factors, combined with many less tangible ones (such as their lack of the status which money bestows), have long conspired to keep the poor poor, and their numbers growing at a rapid rate despite recent government activity.

America's attitudes to the poor

Several observers have pointed out a curious American ambivalence toward the poor. Sociologist Paul Jacobs notes: "On the one hand, we believe achievement is related primarily to self reliance and self help: on the other we have been forced to concede that failure cannot always be laid at the door of the individual."[4]

This ambivalence has historical roots. Eighteenth-century Americans did not consider poverty a social problem. In their view society was hierarchical, consisting of a gradation of permanently established classes. The upper classes, composed of the rich, powerful, and educated, required deference from the indigent and ignorant lower classes, but in return gave them help in time of need, often on a person-to-person basis. Relief was a local matter, and charity a neighborly duty. Little stigma was attached to poverty, which rich and poor alike considered part of the immutable natural law.

The winds of change originated in England, where the industrial revolution was beginning to produce a free labor market as well as unexpected social disorganization. The 1795 Speenhamland Law, designed to establish a protected labor market, introduced the concept of the "right to live", providing wage subsidies based on a scale calibrated with the price of bread and thus assuring the worker of a minimum income regardless of his earnings. The result was a reinforcement of the old paternalistic system. The worker had little reason to work, or to maintain quality standards. He produced barely enough to earn his minimum, and received as a supplement aid from the community.

The Poor Law Reform of 1834 abolished the "right to live" and the practice of community relief, substituting the principle of relief from a publicly maintained live-in institution, from which the poor were required to labor. Both the principle and abuses of this workhouse system spread to Jacksonian America, where the surge of people into the vast western expanses had broken the colonial pattern of communities. The poor were no longer neighbors one had known for years, but a group of strangers, whose situation seemed incomprehensible in view of the New World's unlimited opportunities. It was easy to conclude that their failure was due to some personal flaw—that they were poor as a result of vice or depravity.

The more charitable insisted that these poor people were not depraved by nature, but had merely succumbed to too many temptations. Hence, it was necessary to protect them from the weakness of their natures. The solution here, as in England, was to concentrate the poor within workhouses or almshouses where, "for their own good," they would be subjected to rigorous remedial discipline in the form of long hours of hard work.

The gap between theory and practice soon became evident. Since most of those assigned to almshouses were not poor due to vice but to ill health, the work regime could not be enforced; the almshouses soon degenerated into degrading human warehouses, largely populated by the remnants of successive immigration waves. Thus, by the middle of the nineteenth century, the almshouse inmate was doubly a stranger to the well-to-do American, who could identify neither with his poverty nor his alien nationality. Prosperous and preferring to ignore the inconvenient, he returned to the more genteel practice of private charity.

By the turn of the century, the average citizen's attitude was no longer as simplistic as that of his counterpart a century earlier: greater understanding of the complexities of poverty generated new alternatives to institutionalization. Community social workers were active in settlement houses. Sociologists embarked on studies of the causes of poverty. Journalists popularized their findings, alerting their readers to the effects of urbanization and immigration, the economic fluctuations that caused periodic unemployment, and the resulting hardships, such as disease or early death of the breadwinner.

As the country became more urbanized and industrialized, the number of jobs available to the untrained poor declined, and the ensuing labor surplus increased with each wave of immigration. In consequence, immigrants became a special concern of socially conscious Americans, such as Jacob Riis and Samuel Gompers. But much remained undone during the subsequent decades; and suddenly, in 1929, the stock market crash and the Great Depression made the poverty problem nationwide.

During the 1930s, Roosevelt's New Deal program gradually reversed the economic catastrophe which had overtaken the country, initiating national government participation in aid to the poor, and also changing the nature of public aid: a distinction was made between the unemployable, who received direct relief, and the able-bodied poor, who were put to work on federal projects. Jobs and relief funds were also made available to the states through the Social Security Act and the establishment of the Works Progress Administration. In the private sector, employer and employee assumed responsibility for the prevention of hardship: a tax on employers provided for unemployment compensation, and a tax on employees established retirement pensions.

With the advent of World War II, the country entered upon a productive period in which poverty all but disappeared from public view. The postwar boom continued into the 1950s, when alternating (and sometimes overlapping) periods of inflation and depression weakened the economy. By the 1960s, poverty once more confronted the nation as a visible major issue.

In some ways our current thinking about the poor has become sophisticated, although in other ways the old ambivalence persists. Public programs to aid the disadvantaged have expanded, presumably with voter consent; but simultaneously, hostility toward the poor appears to grow as well. A 1964 poll revealed that only 20 percent of respondents advocated a decrease in governmental relief expenditures, yet close to 70 percent maintained that many of those on the relief roles did not belong there and had obtained aid under false pretenses. A large majority continued to believe that poverty is not the result of unalterable circumstances, and that being on relief, if not always due to laziness, at least encourages laziness.

For many Americans, the major intimation of this fact that poverty had not yet been eradicated was the publication of Michael Harrington's *The Other America*,[5] which did much to explode the comfortable myth of egalitarian society. Other observers added new dimensions to the discussion of the situation, by delineating a "culture of poverty,"[6] and pointing to contributing factors such as racial discrimination, and widespread alienation from middle-class values.

During his brief term in office, President John F. Kennedy initiated several programs to deal with the needs of the underprivileged, both at home and abroad; but it was President Lyndon B. Johnson whose legislative program focused on a national "War on Poverty," and who related the poverty issue to the civil rights movement. His plans were hampered by the rising costs of an escalating war in Southeast Asia, and only a few of his aims were to come to fruition.

Definitions of poverty

Poverty, which may at first glance seem a simple and concrete term, is surprisingly hard to define. Many definitions highlight one or the other of its many dimensions; the outstanding common denominator is the implication of "not enough."

But, depending on the viewpoint, "not enough" may involve a deficit of essentials, or of amenities possessed by the majority, or of luxuries enjoyed by the few; poverty may mean having no food, no TV set, or no yacht.

The critera are impossibly hard to define. Theorists often make subtle distinctions that combine economics with more abstract components, by taking into account the emotional impact that accompanies these deficits. Economist J. K. Galbraith, for example, is most impressed with the sense of degradation from which the poor suffer; he feels that "people are poverty-stricken when their income, even if adequate for survival, falls markedly behind that of the community."[7]

Economic definitions

The government adopted some time ago the criterion of monetary income as one of its principal yardsticks of poverty, and within this category distinguished between the fixed income line and the relative income line.

Figure 4–1   Income Levels

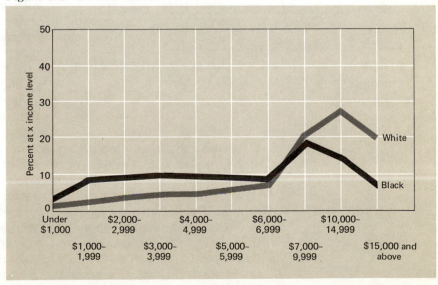

The fixed approach defines poverty in terms of specific cash income. This is often unsatisfactory, because such a standard necessitates constant revision in accordance with rising inflation and other economic factors. In the 1950s, for example, Galbraith suggested a poverty line at $1000 cash income per family.[8] This soon became obsolete, and in 1962 Leon Keyserling suggested a poverty level of $4000 for a family of four, with an additional classification for "deprived" families, those with a cash income between $4000 and $9000.[9] This placed 46 percent of the entire population in the poor and deprived group. Other scholars offered alternative guidelines; in 1966, Oscar Ornati subdivided poverty into three levels of minimum subsistence, minimum adequacy, and minimum comfort,[10] while Herman Miller advocated the use of local welfare standards.[11]

None of these proposals was sufficiently objective to provide reliable figures. To remedy this, Mollie Orshansky, a social insurance research analyst with the Social Security Administration, suggested food as the principal criterion for a basic standard of living.[12] Following some senators' visit to rural Mississippi, a Citizens' Board of Inquiry into hunger and malnutrition had unearthed some unexpected evidence: contrary to common belief, hunger and malnutrition were widespread not only in southern states like Mississippi, but were to be found in all parts of the country, including cities such as New York, Boston, Cleveland and Baltimore.[13] The use of this yardstick was further facilitated by the fact that standards for acceptable nutrition had already been established by the National Research Council, and that cost estimates for this nutritional minimum were regularly published by the Department of Agriculture.

It may seem obvious that the first need of the poor is money, but the obvious is worth stating here because it is too often forgotten in the discussion of comprehensive antipoverty programs . . . Most of the poor cannot alter their status. To them, incentives are meaningless.

Bruno Stein

On an average, a third of the family income is spent on food, and Orshansky established the poverty line at the amount spent for food multiplied by three. By this standard, approximately 34 million Americans (15-20 percent of the total population) were poor. In 1963 the Council of Economic Advisers defined as poor any family of two or more with an annual income below $3000, and any single person living alone with an annual income below $1500. This standard placed 33.4 million persons in the poverty category.

The relative income approach considers the concept of relative poverty ignored by the fixed approach. To this end, Victor Fuchs proposed a statistical measure—the median family income: those families should be defined as poor whose income amounted to less than half of the nation's median family income. This definition also had several drawbacks—notably its arbitrariness—but its advantage lay in its ability to accommodate changing economic conditions.[14]

In 1964 the Social Security Administration made a study to ascertain the characteristics of the poor in relation to the total population; among the poor, the percentage of childless families was found to be higher than in the general population, whereas the percentage of poor families with four or more children was less than that of the general population. In consequence of these and related findings the Social Security Administration developed "poverty thresholds" defining categories of "poor" and "near poor." These thresholds were computed for 124 different kinds of families, reflecting differences such as sex of the breadwinner, number of dependent children and type of residence. They were based on food consumption surveys conducted by the Agriculture Department, and the aim was to determine sufficient food needed for minimum adequate nutrition. A "low cost plan" was applied to the near-poor, and an "economy food plan" to the poor, postulating daily costs of 70 cents per person.

This concept, which came to be known as the Social Security Administration's poverty index, was criticized for taking into account only actual current income, and for its exclusive reference to food, despite the well known fact that for many of the poor, particularly blacks and large families, housing represented another critical factor.

The problem of deciding who the poor actually are is further complicated by the growing list of goods and services once considered luxuries that eventually turn into necessities. At one time an attempt was made to use the criterion of income balancing expenditure, but this too proved unsatisfactory: with the increasing national habit of installment buying, income deficits began to show up in high-income families, who could not be considered for relief.

Nor is unemployment a reliable index. Bureau of Labor Statistics data indicate that the median 1966 income of the families of workers unemployed in March 1967 was $6,530—an amount nearly double that of a nonfarm family of four designated as poor. A further complication that must be briefly noted is the concept of "relativity"; as long as there is a range of incomes in the country, the people at the bottom of the range will be poor relative to those at the top.

Despite its shortcomings, the Social Security Administration's index of "poor" and "near-poor" continues to be used by the Office of Economic Opportunity as a basis for guidelines for those programs where one criterion of eligibility is income. These guidelines, periodically revised to reflect increases in consumer prices, are also used for other purposes, such as determination of eligibility for allowances and reimbursements, data collection and various statistical purposes.

Sociocultural definitions

Defining poverty necessarily involves the labeling of certain individuals and groups as "poor"; and its impact on those so labeled is readily comparable to that on other groups, such as the mentally disturbed.

The writings of authorities in both fields illustrate this dramatically. Sociologist Lewis Coser maintains that "the very granting of relief, the very assignment of the person to the category of the poor, is forthcoming only at the price of a degradation of the person so assigned."[15] Georg Simmel declared that "it is not personal destiny or personal conditions which determine the position [of poverty] but rather the fact that others—individuals, associations, or social totalities—attempt to correct this state of affairs. . . . The sociological category of poverty emerges only when those who suffer from want are receiving assistance."[16]

On a psychological level, the poor must often contend not only with the misguided condescension of benefactors, but also with those whose affluence barely exceeds their own. Members of the lower middle class, who live in close proximity to the poor and work at jobs to which the poor aspire, often feel that the poor cause their neighborhoods to deteriorate into slums, and their children's schools to breed criminals. The blue-collar and white-collar workers who make up this group have incomes frequently too low for a decent standard of living, but too high to qualify for welfare assistance. Stuggling to make ends meet, they oppose any action designed to aid people only a little worse off than they are, while raising their own tax burden.

Two further psychosociological distinctions deserve mention. Coser addresses himself to the effects of personal (or private) as against impersonal (or professional) interaction between donor and recipient. He tends to favor the impersonality which normally characterizes the relationship between professional welfare worker and client, because it may spare the latter at least some of the humiliations to which the private charity recipient is subjected.

The bureaucratic structure itself distinguishes sharply between the unemployed welfare recipient and the recipient of unemployment compensation, who is almost totally exempt from the stigma of poverty. Receipt of unemployment compensation is an earned right, comparable to any other insurance payment. The agency official exerts a minimum of authority over the client, who has no need to pretend to indigence or to camouflage any other financial benefits he may be obtaining. Compensation recipients have been known to arrive for their weekly appointments in cabs, or to have checks forwarded to Europe, where they have gone by habit. The agency official may ask for periodic reports concerning the recipient's job-searching activities, but may not pressure the client into accepting a job at terms different from the preceding one.

Who are the poor?

The poor are not only hard to define, they are difficult to pinpoint as a group. As already indicated, poverty in the United States is not confined to any particular region, though it is most acute in the South, where nearly half the population qualifies as poor or near-poor. But in 1962, even in the North Central region approximately three out of ten families were classified as poor, as against one-fifth of all families in the West and North East.[17]

Among those between 16 and 64, the largest single group are mothers of small children living without husbands, while children under 16 and senior citizens over 64 together constitute 57 percent of the poor in the entire country. Persistent myths notwithstanding, government data indicate that only 12 percent of the indigent are physically capable of working but do not hold down jobs. Of these, 1.5 percent are ablebodied men, while the rest are mostly women with household and child-rearing responsibilities too extensive to permit the holding of outside jobs. About 25 percent of the indigent work, but do not earn enough to raise themselves and their families above the poverty line. One explanation lies in the fact that in 1971, although over half the breadwinners of poor families were employed, only a fifth of them worked full-time during the entire year. Further, only two out of ten of the working poor held jobs requiring high skill and commanding relatively high wages.

Although one in five persons (39.9 million) was poor in the early 1960s, and only one in eight (25.5 million) is considered poor today, these statistics do not present a rosy situation, since most of the improvement occurred in the first half of the decade. Thereafter conditions remained stationary for a few years, and in 1970, for the first time since 1959, poverty increased significantly by 1.2 million over the 1969 level of 24.3 million. The cause of this is not exactly known, but economists tend to lay the blame on two key factors: the business slump of 1970, which reduced the number of employed as well as total working hours; and the simultaneous 6 percent rise in the cost of living.

The urban poor were the hardest hit. A report by the Department of Labor's Bureau of Labor Statistics for 1970,[18] analyzing the country's one hundred largest metropolitan areas, indicated that the overall unemployment rate in poor urban neighborhoods had risen from 5.5 percent in 1969 to 7.6 percent in 1970. Among teenagers in underprivileged neighborhoods, total unemployment rose from 19.9 percent to 24 percent. This rate reflects an increase from 27.9 percent to 35.8 percent for black teenagers, and a jump from 13.8 percent to 16.3 percent among whites.

Despite these figures, the Bureau found that white workers as a group were disproportionately affected by unemployment in poverty neighborhoods, given their greater numbers, and as a result the ratio of black-to-white unemployment rates went down. The total rate of white unemployment rose from 3.1 percent in 1969 to 5.7 percent in 1970, while black unemployment rose from 4.3 percent to 7.1 percent.

In 1970, the Census Bureau poverty level category spanned an income range from $2000 for a single male of nonfarm domicile to $4000 for a family of seven. This means that 25.5 million citizens of the world's wealthiest country were now within the poverty category. In 1971 and 1972, the nationwide unemployment rate continued to fluctuate between 5 and 6 percent. As of April, 1973, 4.2 million people were out of work, and the same groups continued to be over-represented among the jobless.

It is interesting to note that, despite upward and downward fluctuations of the poverty line during the past two decades, the relative distribution of wealth has remained constant. According to the Bureau of the Census, the gap between rich and poor remained unchanged between 1947 and 1970: the wealthiest fifth of the population received 42 percent of the national income, while the poorest fifth received 5.5 percent.

Where do the poor live?

The geographical distribution of poverty is still in a state of flux, as it has been for much of the second half of the twentieth century. The basic direction of the underprivileged seeking a better life continues to be a movement from south to north, from rural environment to urban environment, from agriculture to industry.

Since the breakdown of the South's agricultural system in the nineteenth century, laborers engaged in agricultural work dropped from 53 percent of the population in 1870 to 27 percent in 1920, and in 1967 to 5 percent. Although the migrant poor are predominantly black, the group also includes many whites—especially farmers drawn to the cities by relatively high wages. The total number of farm emigrants has dwindled during the last decade, but still amounts to about a million people a year. Between 1959 and 1966, the number of poor farm households declined by two-thirds, with a concomitant reduction in demand for hired hands.[19] Another sizeable group consists of tenant farmers and sharecroppers forced to leave the land they worked because it was diverted to more profitable uses. Not all those displaced sought their fortune in the big cities; many settled near their former homes, thus extending rural poverty to the surrounding villages and small towns. Today, only 25 percent of the rural poor still live on farms.[20]

There is yet another type of migrant, perhaps more disadvantaged than all others: the migrant agricultural worker. His plight is exemplified by an account published in *The New York Times* of March 17, 1973.[21] The article details the treatment of migrant black field crews, hired to pick the crops on the large tomato plantations of Southern Florida. The workers on one plantation not far from Miami were promised the standard field hand wages of 25¢ per 25-pound "lug" of tomatoes picked, payable on a weekly basis, except for $2 given out daily for food. Although they worked ten and a half hours a day, they never received any wages, on the grounds that these were "owed" to the crew boss for room, board, transportation, and other expenses. Such procedures are by no means rare in Florida and other states employing migrant labor. Agencies such as the federally funded Rural Legal Services have tried repeatedly to seek legal redress, but these so far have met with scant success.

Poverty and the social structure

A process of social reorganization often accompanies the geographical relocation of the poor. In the cities, racial and ethnic minorities usually live in relatively small, encapsulated neighborhoods. The concentration of large numbers of people in run-down neighborhoods breeds a special kind of big-city poverty with distinct characteristics. Crime, drug addiction, poor mental and physical health are only a few of its components. In the United States, this is especially true of blacks, who bear the country's greatest burden of deprivation and discrimination.

Two other socially distinct groups of disenfranchised poor are the aged and women. For both of these groups, the outlook is perhaps a shade better than it was a few years ago: though woman's fight for equality did not originate among the poor, some of its tangible and intangible results are now beginning to filter down. A case in point is the current emphasis on bettering the working conditions of domestics through the organization of unions and the enforcement of the minimum wage laws.

In 1972 the 4.7 million elderly poor received a 20 percent increase in Social Security payments; only a few of the retired people in this group were thereby raised above the Government's poverty line. To the majority the increase makes little difference; their greatest problem, financially as well as psychologically, is lack of employment and the absence of any hope of ever again obtaining work. Beset by ill health and discrimination against older workers on the one hand, rising costs of living and insufficient retirement benefits on the other, they find themselves in a hopeless dilemma. Moreover, many of these people, comfortably off during their working lives, must now adjust to a reduced standard of living just when adjustment to new circumstances is most difficult.

A distinct correlation exists between poverty levels and extent of education. Approximately half the heads of low-income families have completed less than one year of high school, and 73 percent never finished high school. But despite this, and despite the fact that lack of education is both a cause and an effect of poverty, almost all occupations are represented among the poor. The proportion is lowest in the professions (10 to 20 percent) and in public administration (8.2 percent), and highest in agriculture, forestry and fishing (67 percent). In the personal-service job category, the poverty rate runs over 50 percent, and in fields such as entertainment, recreational services, retail trade and construction work it amounts to 20 to 30 percent.[22]

In 1970, 37 percent of all indigent families were headed by women breadwinners, and the number is growing steadily.[23] This family structure is doubly critical, because it means more children are growing up under circumstances considered socially undesirable. Female-headed households provide the homes of 44 percent of all poor children.[24] To make matters worse, poverty in this group is especially hard to eradicate: even during the employment boom between 1947 and 1960, when the median family income of male-headed households rose by 43 percent, the median income of female-headed households increased by only 3 percent. This was due not only to the lower pay commanded by women, but also to their limited availability for employment.

Social characteristics

The poor are discriminated against not only in housing and employment, but also because of their lack of other basic necessities. Wherever they are, they get the worst education, the worst food, the worst health care.

Schools in poor neighborhoods are almost universally over-crowded and understaffed. The teachers are overworked and their pupils largely undermotivated—often for physical reasons directly attributable to undernourishment. During the depression, Chicago schoolteachers were instructed always to ask a child what he had had to eat that day before punishing him for misbehaving.[25] This ruling grew out of the discovery that many of the children were obliged to subsist on little but potatoes and an occasional candy bar, a diet that tends to forestall weight loss but is totally inadequate from a nutritional and health viewpoint.

Conditions for many children have not yet changed appreciably, as Dr. Harold Wise, an internist affiliated with New York City's Monte-fiore Hospital and a Bronx neighborhood health center points out:

> We see hunger over a weekend, the period immediately before the next welfare check is due, and a lot of malnutrition mostly manifested in iron deficiency anemia, and susceptibility to infection. Doctors and nurses . . . - sometimes shell out of their own pockets to tide a family over a weekend. Malnutrition is more prevalent in the children, but it is seen also in the adults.[26]

Few gulfs are as wide as that separating theory from practice in the case of health care for the poor. In theory, the picture could hardly be improved upon: when the indigent become sick, at any hour of the day or night, they are admitted free of charge to well run and usually university-affiliated teaching hospitals; they are cared for by top medical specialists, who donate services for which the wealthy pay enormous fees.

In practice, a statement by Mrs. Janice Bradshaw of Pueblo, Colorado, quoted by Sargent Shriver, makes clear the disparity between theory and practice:

Poverty is taking your children to the hospital and spending the whole day waiting with no one even taking your name, and then coming back the next, and the next, until they finally get around to you. . . . Poverty is having a child with glaucoma and watching that eye condition grow worse every day, while the welfare officials send you to the private agencies and the private agencies send you back to the welfare, and when you ask the welfare officials to refer you to this special hospital they say they can't— and then when you say it is prejudice because you are a Negro, they deny it flatly and they shout at you: "Name one white child we have referred there." When you name twenty-five, they sit down, and they shut up, and they finally refer you, but it is too late.[27]

The poor in the United States are to be found everywhere, and because of their situation do not or cannot reverse the tide of deprivation and discrimination. For the 25.5 million people affected— and that number is rising—it remains difficult to single out one overriding cause, but for the individuals themselves, as Mrs. Bradshaw declared, poverty remains "a personal thing."

reading: **David Caplovitz**
THE LOW-INCOME MARKETING SYSTEM

The problems of low-income consumers stem from the same set of forces that have created that special system of sales-and-credit—the quasi-traditional economy—catering to their wants. Any program of action must therefore take into account the conditions that have brought this system into being.

. . . this marketing system is in many respects a deviant one, in which unethical and illegal practices abound. Nevertheless, it can persist because it fulfills social functions that are presently not fulfilled by more legitimate institutions. The system's paramount function is to allow those who fail to meet the requirements of the impersonal, bureaucratic economy to become consumers of products costing substantial sums. Families with almost no claim to credit—the welfare family, for example—are nevertheless able to buy major durables in this market. Through the various mechanisms we have examined, the poorest risks are shunted to a special class of merchants who are ready to accept great risk. A close association probably exists between the amount of risk that merchants in this system are willing to accept and their readiness to employ unethical and illegal tactics. It may even be that under the present marketing arrangements in our society, unethical practices are an inevitable consequence of serving the wants of the poorest risks. Society now virtually presents the very poor risks with twin options: of foregoing major purchases or of being exploited.

Of course, the poor risks are always free to do without the goods that are available to them only in this special system of marketing. But—and this is as much a part of the misfortune of the low-income consumer as the exploitative merchant—consumption in our society, as in many others, is more than a matter of getting and having material conveniences. Equally important, Americans in all walks of life are trained to consume *in order to win the respect of others and to maintain their self-respect.* These social pressures to consume are perhaps inevitable in a society characterized by a rising standard of living. As was observed by the French economist, Emile Levasseur, more than half a century ago:

In fact the [American] laborer does spend more than the laborer in France. But it is because he desires to, and because he must adjust his life to a higher standard of living *in order not to be looked down upon by his fellows.*

Compounding the force of a rising standard of living is the fact that most low-income families (many of which belong to minority racial and ethnic groups) have little opportunity to base their self-respect and the respect granted them by others on occupational, educational, or other accomplishments. And this poverty of opportunity may only reinforce the significance of consumption in that pattern which we have called "compensatory consumption."

The power of this special marketing system rests on more than its readiness to give credit to poor risks. The local merchants and peddlers—unhampered by bureaucratic procedure—are able to personalize their services. This has particular importance for those low-income families who come from more traditionalistic cultures and are consequently intimidated by that impersonality that pervades the major downtown stores. When they do venture into the more bureaucratic marketplace, some of these consumers, because of their manners, dress, and language problems, find themselves greeted with suspicion rather than with carefully contrived courtesy. By catering to the traditionalism of their customers, the local merchants and peddlers undoubtedly attract many who meet the formal credit requirements of the more legitimate economy but who find its social atmosphere cold, remote, and repelling. Their attention to social relations, as well as accepting great risk, help the neighborhood merchants to develop their "captive markets."

The consumer's traditionalism also makes for the *dys*functions of the system. The local merchants not only cater to traditional values, they exploit them for their own ends by imposing upon their naive customers terms of exchange that are far worse than those they could obtain if they knew where and how to shop.

Courses of action directed at the dysfunctions of the low-income marketing system will be effective only if they take account of the functions of that system. Two correlative kinds of action must be considered: changing the consumer through education and changing the marketing system through legislation.

From
David Caplovitz, *The Poor Pay More*
(New York: Free Press, 1967) pp. 179-182.

Concepts of poverty

Of all the definitions of poverty, those that consider it purely in economic terms have been found most inadequate. The income-deficit explanation does not, for example, do justice to relative poverty. Its deficiencies become more glaring the wider the framework in which we apply it. Lack of money may be an adequate explanation for the poverty of a welfare recipient who cannot stretch the monthly check to cover rent and food; but is it equally adequate in explaining the position of the wealthy professional man whose temporarily overextended resources delay payment of the $2500 rent on his triplex penthouse?

The poverty of a black mother unable to feed her children is not the same as that of a member of the upper middle class in even catastrophic financial straits, though both suffer from an absence of ready cash. The Negro mother is destitute; the professional man is bankrupt. Destitution is a stepping-stone to nothing but further destitution; bankruptcy has often proved a stepping-stone to even greater fortune, as several nineteenth century industrialists discovered.[28]

The enormous difference between these two hypothetical individuals brings us to a concept which has occupied many sophisticated thinkers: inequality. Some of the specific forms and effects of inequality, which lend it such sociological importance, deserve more detailed examination.

The culture of poverty

The phrase "the culture of poverty", was coined by an anthropologist, Oscar Lewis, who studied the structure underlying the state of poverty both chronologically and geographically—as a set of attitudes and responses passed down from generation to generation among the poor of the United States and, in remarkably similar form, among the disadvantaged of many other countries.[29]

Poverty is a great enemy to human happiness; it certainly destroys liberty, and it makes some virtues impracticable and others extremely difficult.

Samuel Johnson

The reason for the emergence and perpetuation of a culture of poverty is that it provides rewards which enable the poor to adjust to their chronic deprivation and the resultant despair. It flourishes predominantly in societies where there is a cash economy, wage labor, and production for profit; a persistently high rate of unemployment or underemployment for unskilled labor; low wages; and a lack of social, political or economic organization provided to serve the low-income population. Also, the dominant class in such societies normally stresses values such as the accumulation of wealth and property, upward mobility, and thrift, and explains low economic status as the result of personal inadequacy or inferiority.[30]

In response to these conditions, the poor adopt a way of life that is typified in the urban and rural slums. It consists of a multitude of interwoven social, economic and psychological factors. Its perpetuation is natural too, since children exposed to it from birth learn how to adapt to it very early in order to survive.

The culture of poverty is both a symptom and a result of the fact that the underprivileged are denied participation in many institutions of the larger society, and that those with which they are in contact often offer punitive rather than supportive experiences. Examples are the public relief system, which provides minimum subsistence at the price of dignity, pride and privacy; or the police, who are regarded as an authority to run from in fear rather than one to turn to for help.

The values of the dominant society are largely irrelevant to the lives of the poor. They may, for example, pay lip service to the sanctity of legal marriage. But common-law unions are better suited to jobless men and to women who fear being tied to unreliable providers. Poor mothers are less concerned with their children's legal status than are women of the middle and upper classes; legitimacy is not as important as having exclusive rights to their children if they leave the men who fathered them. Nor is the prestige of marriage as important as having exclusive rights to whatever property may have accumulated.

Absence of financial resources prevents the disadvantaged from participating in many of society's institutions, and for these their own culture has provided substitutes. The poor, for instance, cannot usually obtain loans from banks; as a result informal credit sources are organized within their own immediate neighborhoods, often on a temporary basis. Indeed, lack of continuity and organization are key features of the culture of poverty, which even extends to the makeup of the family. Discontinuity is visible in the children's brief childhood, in the frequent abandoning of wives and children, in a strong present-time orientation and in lack of impulse control. The thinking of the poor is not characterized by planning for the future. They know that the future will be exactly like the present; and the fact of having some kind of indigenous culture—the culture of poverty—binds them together as a social group to make that knowledge bearable.

The socialist view

Traditional theories of poverty tend to attribute it to a flaw in the individual; most recent theories attribute it to flaws in the social system. For socialist Michael Harrington, whose book *The Other America* (1962) alerted Americans to stark want in their midst, poverty is the result of our capitalist society's commitment to the wrong priorities. Capitalism, he maintains, may have made us the richest country in the world, but it has led to an "affluence . . . so misshapen that it does not even meet the needs of the majority of the people."[31] The poor have been ruthlessly sacrificed to the technological progress the system has generated, and as technology advances, its victims among the poor continue to increase. He acknowledges that a few reforms have alleviated some of the worst evils; but they are stop-gap measures that are overwhelmed in a welter of raw problems.

In Harrington's view, the capitalistic system itself is the cause of mass poverty, and its continuance is incompatible with the solution of our national problems; relief can come only when capitalism is replaced by socialism. He cites three reasons for his views: the class structure, private, corporate power, and the self-destructive tendency of affluence.

The inequalities of capitalist class divisions, built into the very system, are demonstrable in many areas. Harrington cites housing as one dramatic example; he points to the fact that housing shortages for the wealthy are not only improved more rapidly than those of the poor, but also at the expense of housing for the poor. The same process is observable in public transportation, education and the development of affluent suburbs at the expense of the inner cities. Poverty, in short, is practically synonymous with the inequality upon which capitalism is built.

The uses of poverty

Theories have also been advanced that analyze the uses of inequality and, by extension, the reasons for its perpetuation. Sociologist Herbert Gans has applied the technique of functional analysis, which Robert Merton[32] had used some 20 years before to explain the perpetuation of the political machine system, to explain the continuance of poverty and inequality. Gans has isolated numerous economic, social and political functions served by the existence of poverty, and thus succeeds in making his point.[33]

First on his list of positive functions is the fact that the existence of the poor insures a labor pool to do jobs that are repulsive, dangerous, underpaid, undignified or menial. But the poor do much more than that: they insure the perpetuation of higher-level occupations that either minister to the poor or protect the nonpoor against them; they use up goods that would otherwise go to waste (second-hand clothes and furniture, stale bread). Because they are powerless, they absorb the brunt of the discomfort attendant upon society's growth; land required for renewal projects, expressways, and cultural and educational facilities, is usually acquired at the expense of the poor, who have no means to resist displacement. Lastly, they even help to solidify the present political process, by providing the Democratic party with an almost guaranteed constituency.

Gans does not portray an appealing condition; but fortunately he has also suggested some solutions for it, to be discussed, together with governmental and other responses, in the rest of this chapter.

Responses to poverty

Though the Kennedy administration had already instituted a number of poverty relief measures, it was President Johnson who in 1964 declared "unconditional war on poverty in the United States" as part of his plans for the "Great Society".

The "war on poverty"

Governmental aid programs undertaken by the Johnson administration can be divided into four general categories: human resource development, social insurance, cash-income support, and income-in-kind. President Johnson's orientation favored the first kind, giving the poor the opportunity to help themselves rather than keeping them in perpetual bondage through "hand-outs." The preamble to the Economic Opportunity Act, passed in August 1964, explicitly stressed "the opportunity for education and training" and the "opportunity to work," which was to be made available through the Office of Economic Opportunity (OEO).

The OEO began with an allocation of $784 million; by 1968 its budget had risen to $1.9 billion, a sum that financed a great variety of programs. The Job Corps for men and women between 16 and 21, the Neighborhood Youth Corps for teenagers, the Work Experience Program for the unemployed and the Adult Basic Education Program, all provided vocational training or part-time employment. The Rural Loans and Small Business Loans Programs provided loans to farm families and to small businesses, many owned by members of minority groups. The Community Action Program, the most extensive and most controversial of the OEO programs, gave financial support to local authorities for projects such as day care, remedial education, consumer education, legal aid, birth control programs, aid to the aged. Migrant Programs guaranteed to migrant workers the basic necessities, such as housing and child-care facilities. The Volunteers in Service to America, better known as VISTA, was a kind of domestic Peace Corps, in which volunteers ranging in age from 18 to 80 worked on Indian reservations, in hospitals and institutions for the mentally ill, in schools, urban and rural slum areas, and migrant labor camps. Head Start is the widely known program that prepared disadvantaged preschoolers for regular school attendance through preparatory education, medical care and nutritional aid.

It is to be expected that enterprises as numerous and far-reaching as those of OEO would include failure as well as successes. Nor are its accomplishments easy to assess, in view of the political controversy that has surrounded the Office. Initiated by a Democratic administration, it was widely rejected by Republicans and also aroused opposition among some Southern Democrats, who feared that the programs might accelerate racial integration.

In addition to its major activities, OEO also ran a number of more modestly funded "special emphasis programs." The impact of OEO's Legal Services has been considerable. For the poor, as former Supreme Court Justice Abe Fortas said, "the law has always been the hostile policeman on the beat, the landlord who has come to serve an eviction notice, the installment seller who has come to repossess."[34] At the same time, generations of discrimination have taught the disadvantaged to distrust the lawyers of the larger society from which their low status excludes them.

The Legal Services program was specifically designed to give the poor access to reliable legal help. By 1968 it was operating 850 law offices in low-income neighborhoods all over the country, and its 1800 qualified lawyers were giving assistance to 475,000 indigent clients. Their caseloads ranged from the settlement of domestic difficulties to the successful challenge of an eviction regulation. In fact, the lawyers of the Legal Services program actively looked for precedent-setting cases which might help to eradicate some of the inequities to which the poor have been subject. They brought suits against cities, public officials and even OEO itself.

The program's educational activities gave the poor a working knowledge of the legal structure and acquainted them with their rights as citizens. Through cooperation of Legal Services lawyers and local civic groups, by the end of fiscal 1967 nearly two million people had received basic legal education.

The OEO Family Planning program (the subject of some controversy in its early years) was added to the group of special emphasis programs in 1969. In addition to its educational functions, it provides birth control devices. These were formerly supplied only to married women living with their husbands, but are now available to all women.

The Office of Economic Opportunity and its local community action agencies (CAAs) constituted the first network of public agencies exclusively devoted to the underprivileged making a concerted attack on the whole range of their problems. Its system of coordination, involving federal, state, local, public and private agencies, was designed to end fragmentation and to insure the availability of help to all who needed it. To cite one example: its program of coordinating manpower services involved state employment services, who sent counselors to neighborhood centers to provide information on job finding. In addition, the Labor Department placed its own "coordinators" in the major cities to urge the state employment services to develop outreach programs of their own and to give special help to the hard-core unemployed. Out of these joint efforts developed the Concentrated Employment Program (CEP), whose purpose was to bring all manpower services under a single administration. In 1966 the same concept was used for the model cities program.

Social insurance programs

Income maintenance and public assistance programs had already been established during earlier administrations—notably by Franklin Roosevelt's New Deal—but were expanded during the war on poverty. By 1967, governmental cash transfers to the indigent totaled $48.6 billion, which represented 8 percent of total personal income. Indirect expenditures for goods and services included $8 billion for health and hospitals and $3 billion for public housing and additional welfare services.[35] The major social insurance and public assistance programs are Social Security or, officially, Old Age, Survivors, Disability, and Health Insurance (OASDHI), which is exclusively federal; state governments also participate.

The principal difference between these programs and the assistance programs administered by OEO lies in their orientation: the former were designed in aid of "insecurity" rather than in aid of poverty, and tend to benefit people with sudden economic reverses rather than the chronically poor. In the words of economist James Tobin, "There is no unemployment compensation for the man who has never had a job, no OASDHI payment for the man with an insufficient history of covered employment."[36]

Social Security is both the largest and by all accounts the most successful of the income maintenance programs, since it serves two functions. Although designed as an income maintenance system, it actually provides more cash assistance to the needy than does public assistance: 35 percent of social security benefits go to poor households.[37]

The group most difficult to reach and most difficult to assist once reached is the "hard-core unemployed." Private-enterprise personnel departments exist for the very purpose of screening out members of this group, which includes "undesirables" who lack education and experience, are high insurance risks, or have police records.

In 1968 President Johnson appealed to the business community to liberalize its hiring policies, and a number of business leaders responded. Henry Ford II organized the National Alliance of Businessmen which, in turn, organized the Jobs in Business Sector program known as JOBS. Major employers in fifty large cities reacted to the program more favorably than was expected. Within six months, 165,000 new permanent jobs had been set up and approximately 40,000 filled, not including the 100,000 teenagers for whom summer jobs were found.[38]

*Figure 4–2   Breakdown of those receiving Aid to Families
with Dependent Children as of 1969, according to year in
which they began receiving aid.*

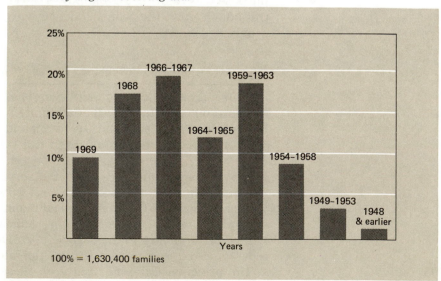

Economic researcher James Sundquist suggests that the motives animating the business leaders were not exclusively altruistic. The spread of rioting may have played a part in jogging their consciences:

> Business leaders began saying to one another that they had a collective responsibility to help solve the problem of ghetto unemployment—if they didn't, who would? Only the government, obviously, through taxes levied on them. So they were receptive when the government proposed to cooperate by paying the extra costs that training and employing the disadvantaged would impose . . .[39]

Two other types of programs are intended for people not covered by other forms of assistance. Cash Income Support programs include "welfare," aid to the aged and disabled, old age assistance, veterans' pensions, and aid to families with dependent children (AFDC). AFDC is by far the most frequently criticized category of public welfare, since it allows no payment to families where a man is present. The result in many cases has been involuntary desertion by husbands unable to work for as much money as welfare payments given the wife he deserts. Income-in-kind programs, which provide assistance in obtaining essentials such as food, housing and health care, include the food stamp program, the commodity distribution program, and Medicaid, which provides medical care for welfare recipients.

The organized poor

In order to be effective, aid programs must also motivate the poor to help themselves. Attempts to organize the poor for action on their own behalf have been problematical, probably due to the twin handicaps of lack of education and poor health. Nonetheless, some private groups, usually headed by members of the particular disadvantaged segment which they serve, have made progress.

One of the most active is the National Welfare Rights Organization (NWRO), which concerns itself with the improvement of the public relief system. Its primary objectives are the elimination of restrictive eligibility requirements and education of the people to safeguard their rights. In 1968, for instance, it organized a successful campaign in New York City to insure that welfare clients received special grants to which they were entitled but usually had not received. Another group, the Poor People's Campaign, which grew out of Martin Luther King's Southern Christian Leadership Conference, has been less successful, probably because its concerns have ranged so widely, from hunger in Mississippi to protecting Indian hunting and fishing rights in Oregon.[40]

The black woman, simultaneously disadvantaged because of racial and sex discrimination, has developed her own organizations to fight for higher wages and job security. The Professional Household Workers Association, formed in 1969, serves domestic workers, while black women formed their own caucus within the Manhattan Women's Political Caucus, organized in 1971.

The long overdue organization of farm labor was realized when the United Farm Workers Organizing Committee signed contracts with most of California's table grape growers. Since then, the lot of farm workers has improved in California, but has not yet spread to other areas. In many parts of the country agriculture still uses child labor; it has the third-highest rate of work-connected deaths; and the migrant farm worker's average life expectancy is 49 years.

The curse of poverty has no justification in our age. It is socially as cruel and blind as the practice of cannibalism at the dawn of civilization, when men ate each other because they had not yet learned to take food from the soil or to consume the abundant animal life around them. The time has come for us to civilize ourselves by the total, direct and immediate abolition of poverty.

Martin Luther King, Jr.

The man largely responsible for the unionization of the California grape pickers was Cesar Chavez, a Mexican-American who gained national prominence in 1965. An admirer of Gandhi, Chavez is dedicated to nonviolent struggle; he obtained union recognition for the California grape pickers by means of fasts, strikes and the propagation of a national grape boycott. His organization of the grape pickers is likely to affect other segments of the agricultural labor force.

In the long run, the actions of the organized poor will immediately affect the government's responses to continued poverty. In the next pages we will evaluate the progress of programs to date and take a look at what remains to be done.

reading: **Robert Messer
STATEMENT OF PROTEST**

I think it's come a time when the poor people's got to wake up. They've got to go a'doin' somethin' about this, place o' lettin' people run everythin' over them. I've seen people run over poor people all my life, an' I'm gettin' tired of it fer my part.

You take in this county right here; they're good people long as you go down an' vote fer 'em. Then they'll come back in the next four years an' pat you on the back an' say, "We're gonna give you jobs." You never see 'em no more—till the next four years. Then you'll see 'em come up. "Well, it's the election. You gonna vote fer old man Charlie this time?" Well, a lot of them will go down there, an' they'll ease around, an' they'll do this, an' they'll say they're Christians. Then they'll reach around there, an' they'll give 'em two dollars, an' people'll stick it in their pockets. An' they'll vote four years against their own interests fer two an' a half or two dollars. That's right. They ought not to do that. They ought to be votin' fer a man who'll do somethin' fer them. If you can find him. If you got a man in four years doesn't do nothin' fer you, put him out, an' put in a man that will do it. Jest keep on till you try to find that kind o' man. That's the way I see the poor people's gonna have to do. If they don't, they're gonna be trod right down on their feet, an' these big politicians'll jest be cheatin' them alive to get 'em to vote fer 'em every four years. . . .

An' we got the poorest folk there ever was. An' they'll come around an' say, "Let's have a community meetin'." I've been goin' to community meetin's fer the last four years, an' we got plenty people goin' out to meetin's. I ain't got anythin' to offer 'em myself. I'm gonna be honest about that. I ain't got nothin'. But we got people who got money, the OEO. They'll say, "We'll do somethin' about it. You set up a meetin' an' we'll do somethin'." An' when you set that meetin' up, you'll never see 'em about it, an' they'll never do nothin' about it. We talked about buyin' a well rig. People's drinkin' out o' the creek in Clay County, out o' the branches, an' they got Self-Help money to buy a well rig, an' I don't know what's the reason they won't buy it. I believe if I had the money I'd buy it. I wouldn't stop till I found it.

I don't know what to do about it. We oughta jest walk down an' say, "Stop all of it," say, "Boys, this is the time to change over. We come after you." You believe that'd work? I think that's the only way you're gonna solve the problems.

Now I believe in people havin' jobs. An' that's the only way you can solve the problem a lot o' times. But if you go an' give one man $12,000 or $14,000 a year to run the CAP an' the poor people are gettin' nothin', that's not right either. Why don't you pay a man a salary he can live at, an' take some o' that $12,000 you're givin' him an' let that come down to the poor people to give them somethin'. And the poor people are livin' on $1500, some of 'em a thousand. They're scratchin' any way to get by.

And them Mainstream men, they got jobs sweepin' schoolhouses. They need takin' out o' the schoolhouse though. They need takin' out o' this an' get up there an' build roads an' bridges where people won't have to wade the creek to their knees. Our taxpayers pay fer the schools to be cleaned. They're knockin' people out o' jobs.

And what makes me so sick, the school system won't have nothin' to do with the CAP much. If they got a community building, they want people to go down yonder to the schoolhouse fer adult education class. A woman told me yesterday she wouldn't go. Then she told me she'd go to adult education if it weren't up at the schoolhouse. I told her I wasn't gonna go up to the schoolhouse. We're gonna have it in our own buildin'. We've got a buildin' in Goose Creek. We built it. An' that's where we're gonna hold our meetin's at. What's the reason they can't have it in this center? We got lights. We got plenty o' water in here.

Q. How much do they pay the county judge and the school superintendent?

The county judge? I don't know what they pay him. I don't know what they pay the school superintendent. $7,000, $8,000 a year. I understand they're raisin' it, but I guess the judge'll make around $6,000 a year.

Q. How much do they spend on campaigns?

Oh God! About $20,000, $30,000 every four years. He stays there every year, an' it takes him four years to get that money back. If you buy an office here, you see, you've got to stay there four years to get your money back, about it. They don't get it all off o' the county. They get part of it, but they get other things. That's the reason they don't do nothin'; they got to get that money back. An' that's the way the school system is; they buy it. But they don't be out as much on their politics as the county judge would. They got their districts cut up where they can get elected where they pull. But that day's comin' where they won't have that.

See a good man ain't got a chance. A poor man ain't got a chance now. That's the way they run it, an' that's the way they've had it. It wouldn't be worth nothin' to run down here fer an office. Why they'd jest laugh at me. "Why he ain't got no money." And I've knowed a lot of poor men to run, an' they jest laughed, "Oh, that man can't make it." No wonder he couldn't make it. He didn't have the money to back him. I ain't a'figurin' on runnin' fer nothin'. It wouldn't be no use. I ain't got no money. The people's goin' to have to get behind the election office an' say, "Look here, buddy, that's agin the law." We're gonna have to get shet o' these people, though, that's been a'doin' that an' elect new people. An' then we're gonna stop all that.

I'll tell you the reason the people takes the two dollars. You know, two dollars looks pretty big to the poor man when he's got nothin' to live on. You know, they go to the election, they know they're gonna get the two dollars that day. But they don't have no promise fer a job the day atter. An' I think that if everybody was up on the standard of livin', that they would turn that two dollars down.

You take a poor man today that ain't got a sack o' meal in his house or somethin' like that, two dollars looks pretty big to him. But I wouldn't take the two dollars myself. I'd beg the two dollars 'fore I'd sell my vote fer two dollars. I'd say, buddy, I ain't got a bite, but I don't want your two dollars. But you know a lot o' poor people does that, an' that's a bad thing. I'd like to see that broke up. But one thing that'd do it is fer poor people to get on their feet. They wouldn't be beholdin' to people. Then they'd say we don't have to sell out. We got the money. We've got a job. I believe that'd be one of the answers. I see a poor man, he's got a big bunch o' kids, two or three dollars will help him a big lot sometimes. I've seed the time myself if I had three dollars it'd help me a lot. Sure have.

You know buddy, you take a lot o' these rich people, they want to stay in power. I don't think we should have selfishness, selfish people. I think we should have all alike. But we've got some people that's got respect of persons an' that's all right with your relations, but I don't think that you should go down in that county judge's office an' make diff'rences in people, I think that you should treat everybody alike. You should not send a bulldozer down to the lower end of the county and maybe blacktop a road and never send one to the head of Goose Creek in four years. That's not treatin' your tax money right.

These fellers have been in power so long, an' they got a certain bunch o' people. That's the way they get 'em to stick to 'em. They do that much fer so many people. An' the poor people, they don't do nothin' fer the poor people. The only thing they look at is every four years. You're good people fer three or four months; they shake hands with you to beat the world. An' atter the election, they won't shake hands with you till the next four years. I can tell jest as good, if I fergit about an election, when it's comin' up. They go shakin' hands with you, buddy, an' you know somethin' up. They're out to get elected again. An' if the poor people'd stay away from those elections . . . . They oughta wake up their eyes an' say, "Buddy, we're shet of you. We're gonna put a poor man in who'll do somethin' fer us."

But a lot o' things, the OEO money, I'm gettin' sick of it. They say they're gonna help the poor people. Then they get it all made up an' it's too much, we can't do nothin' fer you, you're not in the category. That's what they say. Let's not talk about helpin' people. If we're gonna help 'em, let's do somethin' about it. I've seed so many things that ain't right, I don't know what to do against it.

I think that the strip minin' coal industry has damaged Kentucky worse than anythin' I've ever seed. It's tore the beauty of the mountains up. And the poor man didn't get anythin' out of it. It went out to the big fellers. That's the way I see the strip mines. But coal mines has helped a lot. If it hadn't been fer some o' that in Clay County, the poor people would o' fared bad. They sure would. They had to work at somethin'. If they couldn't get the big price, they had to work at something to feed their families. But they worked many a day that they didn't get what pay they oughta have. They had to work at it. I've had to work at it; I've had to feed my young'uns. It was the only thing I could get to make any money at all. I could work out in the timber woods or somethin' like that, but I could make more money in the coal mines than I could that. But strip minin' has destroyed this country . . .

168 There's gonna have to be somethin' in East Kentucky besides coal mines. There's gonna have to be some jobs come in fer the young people. You take a feller fifteen years old right now. There's not gonna be any coal. There's not much coal here now in Clay County 'cept little bitty stuff . . . .

Young people they don't want to leave the state. They'd rather stay in Clay County or in Kentucky if there's jobs fer them to do. If they could get a job here an' make as much money . . . they'd come back to make a lot less money. But they go to Lexington. They go to Detroit. They go to Ohio. They go to Georgia. They go to Indianapolis, Indiana. Anywhere they can find work. They work at General Motors. They work at Ford's. And they work at regular jobs. A lot of these boys go off an' do construction. They work on the railroads. People out o' Goose Creek works out on the railroads. Anybody who's got a high school education generally gets a job at a factory.

They don't see nothin' here right now. And they're young people. And they don't know what steps to take to get somethin' in here, to get shet o' politics an' get somethin' in here. I've talked to a lot of big people, an' they say, "You ain't got no roads in Clay County." If a business tries to start up here, I've heard said that they've said we don't need no business, but I don't know if that's true. Let me tell you somethin'. The reason they didn't want business here is they had a right smart o' coal work here at one time, an' they wanted these men to work in the coal mines fer them. And they knowed if there come a decent job here, that they're gonna quit an' go to it. An' these young men all stopped workin' in the coal mines an' left here. The coal operators in Clay County didn't want the WPA in here. They didn't want the Happy Pappies in here. They was mad. They say we can't hire a man to work in our coal mines. But they didn't care about the rock dust I was eatin' or the black lung I was gettin'. Let me go to heck; they're gonna hire another man the next day if they can get him. That's how I feel about it. They don't want these gov'ment programs. They don't want these OEO programs.

From
Our Land Too by Tony Dunbar
(New York: Pantheon, 1971) pp. 178–185.

Changes in government programs

Almost anyone concerned with governmental aid programs agrees that they are in need of some revision; but there is great disagreement about the changes to be made.

James Tobin lists seven principal failings of the present public assistance system: inadequate coverage; anti-family incentives; inadequate benefits; incentives for uneconomic migration; disincentives to work and thrift; excessive surveillance; inequities.[41] In his view, some of the defects could be eliminated by imposing nationwide standards of benefits and eligibility on the states; but a more far-reaching and more economical move would be to establish a system totally financed and administered by the federal government.[42]

Even the most successful of the income maintenance programs—Social Security—could still be improved. Henry J. Aaron believes that the system could be altered to make it more efficient as a means of reducing poverty, without lessening its value as the "basic retirement system" of the majority of Americans. He opposes the raising of benefits across the board, and suggests that the poor would be better served by freeing them from payroll taxes, and by having their benefits determined not by the earning history of the worker but by that of the family as a whole.[43]

In 1966 President Johnson's Council of Economic Advisers suggested a negative income tax as a means to reform public welfare. The concept is not new; it was first proposed in 1943 by economist Milton Friedman, who was troubled by the effect of fluctuating earnings on income tax. Because of graduated tax rates, people with inconstant yearly incomes paid more taxes, in the long run, than people whose (equivalent) income was earned in unvarying annual sums. The system is most detrimental to the poor. Friedman's negative income tax would redress the balance by having the worker pay taxes during good-income years, and having the treasury pay taxes to him during bad-income years.

Later Friedman incorporated the idea of permanent treasury payments to persons who never achieved positive income brackets. Negative income tax payments would be reduced if the worker's earnings increased; but—in a manner analogous to the positive income tax—they would never decrease to the point where increased earnings would become financially undesirable.

Among the negative income tax's advantages are its simplicity, and the relative ease with which it could be incorporated into the present tax structure. Its drawbacks include the cost, and the probability that it would have to subsidize some of the nonpoor as well, in order to maintain its advantage of work incentives.[44]

Such a program was eventually proposed, but by the Nixon administration rather than the Johnson administration. In 1969 the Family Assistance Plan (FAP) was presented to the country in a nationwide television address by the President. Daniel P. Moynihan, a political scientist and veteran of the Kennedy and Johnson administrations, has called it "one of the most ambitious pieces of social legislation in American history."[45] As executive secretary of the Urban Affairs Council and as Assistant to President Nixon for Urban Affairs, he had the opportunity to witness FAP's rise, decline, and fall at first hand.

FAP, with its provisions for guaranteeing incomes to about 20 million people, called for income redistribution not only for individuals but also from wealthy to poor regions of the country. Payments were to decrease as personal income rose; and because of the work incentives written into it, the President described it as "workfare," to distinguish it from welfare.

The program sounded, even to experts, more intricate than it really was. Some legislators never quite grasped the idea of a negative income tax. There was confusion and fear regarding FAP's potential cost, and considerable opposition arose from the large group of middle-class poverty workers who saw their livelihood threatened by a large-scale elimination of poverty FAP would attempt.[46]

So after three years of maneuvering and debate, a measure that many impartial observers felt would have been an outstanding piece of social legislation was defeated. Though the House of Representatives passed it twice, the Senate, as Moynihan points out, never even voted on the measure which President Nixon had designated his number one domestic priority.

The outlook for the future

What is the outlook for improvement? Of the many measures under discussion, only a few promise alleviation on a permanent basis. One of these is the concept of revenue sharing, which calls for the sharing of federal revenues by the states and individual cities, and would deal with some of the current inequities overshadowing the poor.

In his State of the Union message of January 22, 1971, President Nixon proposed a $16 billion investment in renewing state and local government. He asked Congress to allocate $5 billion of this sum to unrestricted funds to be used as the states and localities see fit. An additional $10 billion was to be converted from current grant-in-aid programs, to be used by the states and cities at their discretion for urban and rural development, education and job training, transportation and law enforcement.[47]

The rationale for revenue sharing lies not only in the inequality of resources among the three levels of government, but also in their unequal ability to collect taxes. Cities of all sizes obtain about 85 percent of their revenues through property taxes, whereas states depend largely on sales taxes, from which over 60 percent of their revenue is derived. Since poor people must spend a much larger proportion of their income than the wealthy, sales taxes are far more punitive for them than for the rich, and are therefore called regressive taxes. The federal government, on the other hand, obtains two-thirds of its income from the so-called progressive income taxes, those which are graduated in relation to income. The federal income tax structure is in need of revision to eliminate inequities, but it is still fairer to more citizens than are sales and property taxes. In addition, the federal government has a much more effective machinery for collecting revenues than either the states or the cities.

Yet generally speaking, money spent locally by local government seems to affect the individual citizen much more personally than money spent in the same locality by a larger, more distant government. Such, at least, is the theory of revenue sharing.

In addition to easier collection and more relevant use of taxes, advocates of revenue sharing believe that it will both strengthen state and local governments, and ease the plight of major cities like New York, traditionally slighted in the allocation of funds for basic services. Some feel, though, that revenue sharing should go hand in hand with a general revision of overall tax structure.

However, no treatment can be effective unless the nature of the ailment has been correctly identified. A crucial aspect of the persistence of poverty to which until recently little consideration has been given, is the social inequality it demonstrates. In the final analysis, eradication of poverty depends on, and is almost synonymous with, the eradication of inequality. It is high time, as Herbert Gans points out, "to start thinking about a more egalitarian America, and to develop a model of equality that combines the traditional emphasis on the pursuit of liberty with the newly emerging need to reduce inequality."[48]

The evidence suggests that equality of opportunity cannot be a reality until all those who want opportunity are equally able to compete, and are not held back by poverty-induced poor health and lack of access to sufficient education to make them truly competitive. Under our present system, two individuals of different backgrounds but equal competence in shorthand and typing may, indeed, compete for a secretarial position; but preference will almost invariably be given to the well-groomed, well-spoken, well-educated candidate.

Gans points out that methods for achieving equality have usually been collectivist, with public institutions replacing private ones and with a nationalized industry. Because such methods have usually resulted in the unequal favoring and enrichment of officials, and in restrictions on liberty for the ordinary citizen, he suggests that America develop an individualistic model of equality. Such a process would be complicated but feasible. It calls for a governmental bureaucracy more responsive to average citizens than to pressure groups. Some liberty would have to be surrendered in favor of greater equality, and public debate would determine how much liberty should be given up in exchange for which kind of equality (social, economic, racial or sexual).

Gans' concept includes detailed proposals for the implementation of the radical changes he suggests. But the greatest incentive lies in a point he touches upon only tangentially: the possibility that such total restructuring toward equality would benefit the well-to-do as much as the disadvantaged, because in it lies the hope of curing the "current American malaise"—the poverty of spirit with which we have all become afflicted.

Notes

[1] S. M. Miller and Pamela A. Roby, *The Future of Inequality* (New York: Basic Books, 1970) p. 5.

[2] U.S. Bureau of the Census, *Current Population Reports,* #77. (Washington, D.C.: U.S. Government Printing Office, May 7, 1971).

[3] *Ibid.*

[4] Paul Jacobs, "America's Schizophrenic View of the Poor," in David Boroff (ed.), *The State of the Nation* (Englewood Cliffs, N.J.: Prentice Hall, 1965).

[5] Michael Harrington, *The Other America: Poverty in the United States* (New York: MacMillan, 1962).

[6] Oscar Lewis, *Five Families: Mexican Case Studies in the Culture of Poverty* (New York: Basic Books, 1959).

[7] John Kenneth Galbraith, *The Affluent Society* (Boston: Houghton Mifflin, 1958) p. 323.

[8] *Ibid.*

[9] Leon Keyserling *et al., Poverty and Deprivation in the United States.* Conference on Economic Progress (Washington, D.C.: U.S. Government Printing Office, 1962), pp. 19 ff.

[10] Oscar Ornati, *Poverty Amid Affluence* (New York: Twentieth Century Fund, 1966), p. 13.

[11] Herman P. Miller, *Rich Man, Poor Man* (New York: Crowell, 1964), p. 81.

[12] Mollie Orshansky, "Counting the Poor: Another Look at the Poverty Profile," *Social Security Bulletin,* Jan. 1965; and "The Shape of Poverty in 1966," *Social Security Bulletin,* March 1968.

[13] Citizens' Board of Inquiry into Hunger & Malnutrition in the U.S., *Hunger, U.S.A.* (Washington, D.C.: New Community Press, Inc., 1968).

[14] Victor Fuchs, "Toward a Theory of Poverty," in *The Concept of Poverty.* Task Force on Economic Growth and Opportunity (Washington, D.C.: U.S. Chamber of Commerce, 1956) p. 74.

[15] Lewis A. Coser, "The Sociology of Poverty," *Social Problems,* Vol. 13, Fall, 1965, p. 144.

[16] *Ibid.,* p. 142.

[17] *Poverty and Deprivation in the United States: The Plight of Two-Fifths of a Nation* (Washington, D.C., Conference on Economic Progress, 1962), pp. 40-41.

[18] Bureau of Labor Statistics, *Report for 1970* (Washington, D.C.: U.S. Government Printing Office, 1971).

[19] *Economic Report of the President,* January 1968, pp. 132-38.

[20] James Tobin, "Raising the Incomes of the Poor," in *Agenda for the Nation* (Washington, D.C.: The Brookings Institution, 1968), p. 81.

[21] Wayne King, "Florida Peonage Charges Reflect Plight of Migrants," *The New York Times,* March 17, 1973.

[22] *Poverty and Deprivation in the United States, op. cit.,* p. 45.

[23] Office of Economic Opportunity, *The Poor in 1970: A Chartbook* (Washington, D.C.: U.S. Government Printing Office, 1970), pp. 16, 46, 48, 68.

[24] *Ibid.*

[25] Caroline Bird, *The Invisible Scar* (New York: David McKay Co., Inc., 1966) pp. 27-30.

[26] Citizens' Board of Inquiry into Hunger and Malnutrition in the United States, "Hunger, U.S.A." in *Poverty in America* (Washington, D.C.: New Community Press, Inc., 1969).

[27] Sargent Shriver, "Poverty is a Personal Thing." From the opening statement to the Ad Hoc Subcommittee on Poverty of the House Committee on Education and Labor, April 12, 1965.

[28] *Ibid.*

[29] Lewis, *op. cit., passim.*

[30] Oscar Lewis, "The Culture of Poverty," in *The Study of Slum Culture—Backgrounds of La Vida* (New York: Random House, 1968).

[31] Michael Harrington, "Why We Need Socialism in America," *Dissent,* 17:3, May-June 1970, pp. 240-303.

[32] Robert K. Merton, "Manifest and Latent Functions," in *Social Theory and Social Structure* (Glencoe, Ill.: The Free Press, 1949), pp. 73-138.

[33] Herbert J. Gans, "The Uses of Poverty: The Poor Pay All," *Social Policy,* Vol. 2, July/August 1971, pp. 20-24.

[34] Abe Fortas, quoted in Gans, *Ibid.*

[35] Tobin, *op. cit.,* p. 93.

[36] *Ibid.,* p. 94.

[37] Henry J. Aaron, "Income Transfer Programs," *Monthly Labor Review,* February 1969, p. 53.

[38] James L. Sundquist, "Jobs, Training, and Welfare for the Underclass," in *Agenda for the Nation, op. cit.,* p. 56.

[39] *Ibid.*

[40] Gilbert Steiner, *The State of Welfare* (Washington, D.C.: The Brookings Institution, 1971), p. 281.

[41] Tobin, *op. cit.,* pp. 100-101.

[42] *Ibid.,* p. 103.

[43] Aaron, *op. cit.,* pp. 53-54.

[44] Daniel P. Moynihan, *The Politics of a Guaranteed Income: The Nixon Administration and the Family Assistance Plan* (New York: Random House, 1972).

[45] Daniel P. Moynihan, "The Annals of Politics: Income by Right—I, II, III," *The New Yorker,* January 13, 20, 27, 1973.

[46] *Ibid.*

[47] Maxwell S. Stewart, *Money for Our Cities: Is Revenue Sharing the Answer?* (New York: Public Affairs Pamphlets, 1971).

[48] Herbert J. Gans, "The New Egalitarianism," *Saturday Review,* May 6, 1972, pp. 43-46.

Summary

Poverty is a prominent part of the American scene despite America's position as the world's wealthiest nation. The acceptance of moderate wealth as the norm in America magnifies the condition of the poor. The American economic system, which favors the rich, prevents the condition of the poor from significantly improving.

Americans look at the poor in an ambivalent way. On the one hand, they believe achievement is directly related to effort and tend to blame poverty on the poor. On the other hand, they recognize a disparity in opportunity and seek methods to help.

Defining the poor is difficult. Most definitions contain the implication "not enough." The government defines the poor as those with "not enough" monetary income, both on fixed and relative income lines. The fixed approach defines the poor in terms of specific cash income. The relative approach defines the poor as those whose income amounts to less than half the nation's median family income. Defining the poor labels the poor. Such definition can seriously degrade those within its reach and leave them regarding their condition as a stigma.

Pinpointing the poor as a group is also difficult. They are those moving from South to North, from rural environment to urban environment, and from agriculture to industry seeking a better life. They are those living in overcrowded, run-down, crime-infested neighborhoods. They are those receiving the worst education, food, and health care. The poor are found everywhere and because of their situation do not or cannot reverse the tide of deprivation and discrimination.

Poverty cannot be defined in economic terms alone. Anthropologist Oscar Lewis considered specific attitudes and responses an essential part of poverty passed down from generation to generation. Where conservative theorists have attributed poverty to flaws in the individual, radical theorists have attributed it to flaws in the system. Others have attributed poverty to the idea that it has its uses and thus perpetuates itself. For example, the existence of the poor insures a labor pool for undesirable jobs.

Though President Kennedy initiated numerous poverty relief measures, it was President Johnson who declared "unconditional war on poverty." The Johnson administration undertook aid programs in the areas of human resource development, social insurance, cash-income support, and income-in-kind. Income maintenance and public assistance programs, established during Roosevelt's New Deal, were expanded during the war on poverty. To be effective, such aid programs must motivate the poor to help themselves.

Most persons concerned with governmental aid programs agree they need revision, but can't agree on what revisions to make. The public welfare program, in particular, has been subject to suggestions for reform, such as Milton Friedman's negative income tax and President Nixon's Family Assistance Plan.

Few measures under discussion promise permanent alleviation of poverty conditions. Among measures recently instituted, revenue sharing is designed to rectify tax inequities and improve conditions in the nation's cities where the majority of the poor live. Other measures concentrate on insuring equality in competition for job opportunities.

chapter

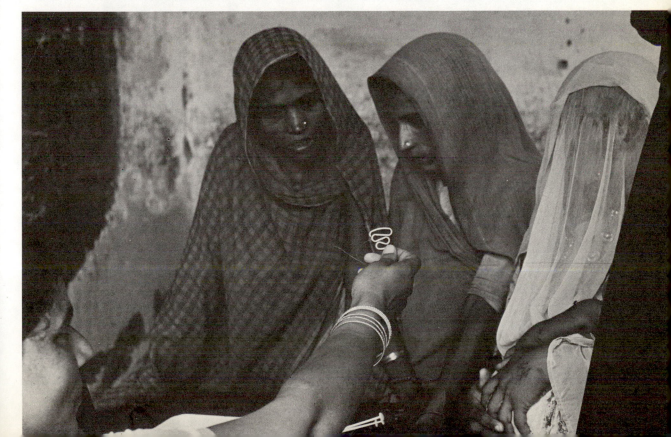

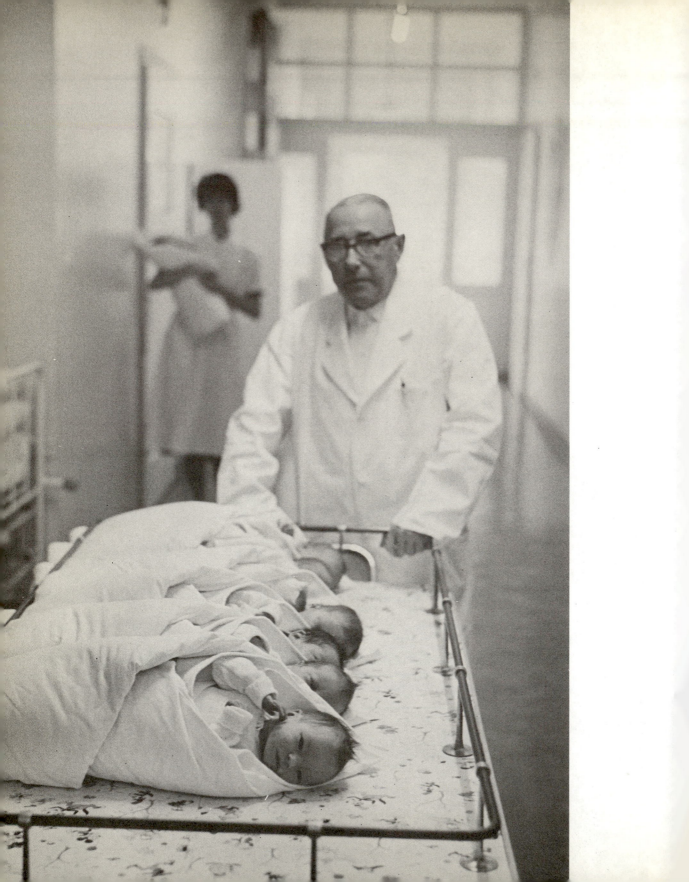

population

Ten thousand years ago, when human beings survived by exploiting the earth's resources through hunting, food-gathering, farming and herding, the entire population of the earth was only about 5.3 million people—less than the number of people who now live in New York City alone. Today the earth's population stands at about 3.8 billion,[1] and it is increasing more rapidly than at any other time in history. This vast population is a comparatively recent phenomenon. As late as 1850, the earth's population was only 1 billion. The fact that so many people now depend on the limited resources of the earth for sustenance is a sobering one, as is the knowledge that, unless some effective means of population control is employed, the earth's present population will double by the year 2007.

Only a third of the world's present population lives in the economically developed countries of North America, Europe, the Soviet Union and Japan, where an advanced technology has permitted a higher standard of living than ever before in the world's history. To maintain this standard, these countries consume a disproportionate amount of the world's limited resources.

Two-thirds of the world's population live in the economically underdeveloped countries of the world—in Africa, Asia and Latin America predominantly. Living standards there have risen, too, as these countries are increasingly penetrated by the technological and social influences of the developed world. But expectations have risen faster than the living standards. In the underdeveloped countries, populations continue to swell out of all proportion to economic advance, and rigid social structures funnel much of the wealth into a few hands. Nor do these countries possess the political power to retain their resources for their own use. Under such circumstances, social disruption is inevitable, as it was in the presently developed countries in the years when technological revolution forced the creation of new patterns of social life.

Surpluses in the developed countries have often been sent to relieve shortages—especially of food—in the underdeveloped countries. Yet such moves would not be necessary if an adequate base for technological advance could be constructed in the underdeveloped world. Besides, they seem to fuel the fires of population growth and make the problem greater. Short of drastic solutions such as war or famine, the means available for controlling the press of population on the world's resources are closely connected with social and attitudinal changes within *all* societies of the world.

Demography, the science of counting people, is concerned not only with the absolute numbers of human beings and with explaining the variations in these numbers, but also with the implications that this vast increase in humanity has on the quality of life, the world's social institutions and the depletion of the world's natural resources.

In order to understand the complexities of the issues of world population growth, it is necessary first to examine the tools of demography and to study the history of population growth and the efforts to control it. Then we will be in a position to consider the consequences of the social pressures created by the recent vast increase in the number of people on the earth. In its implications for America's use of the earth's resources, our relations with the rest of the world's peoples, and our commitment to personal liberty in a world increasingly subject to policy which puts a premium on social control, the population problem compels our attention.

Population processes

Before the sociologist can analyze the clustering of people in cities, study the causes of rapid population growth, or make recommendations for the control of population, he must make accurate measurements of a population and its changes. Changes in the size of a population result from changes in the numbers of births and deaths and the movements of people in or out of an area. These three processes—fertility, mortality and migration—are the components of demography.

Human fertility might seem to be so obvious as not to need explanation, based as it is on the basic biological drives and the necessity to maintain the species. However, each society has different social practices, attitudes and values that influence the number of children a couple may have. A woman is capable of bearing children roughly from age 15 to age 49. Theoretically, a woman can give birth to as many as fifteen or twenty children. The biological capacity for childbearing is called *fecundity,* and social factors produce a large differential between fecundity and fertility—the actual number of births to women in the childbearing age.

The cultural regulation of sexual conduct is universal although sex mores vary widely in detail. Sociologists Kingsley Davis and Judith Blake classify the social variables affecting fertility by the three stages of the reproductive process: exposure to intercourse, exposure to conception and exposure to gestation and birth.[2] The frequency and occasion of a woman's exposure to intercourse reflects the social norms of her group. In India girls are expected to marry in their early teens; in Ireland marriages may be delayed until a woman is in her late twenties. In some societies premarital and extramarital intercourse are proscribed and widows are forbidden to remarry. In such societies, fertility is negatively affected. Certain occupations, particularly those concerned with religion, may require celibacy and enforce it institutionally. Another group of social factors affects the process of conception. In India, failure to conceive a child is considered a grave misfortune; in a modern industrialized society, even voluntary refusal to conceive a child is increasingly accepted behavior. Some societies provide easy access to contraceptives, some do not; the Catholic Church condemns their use altogether. After conception, social norms, often embodied in the law, determine whether the prospective mother has access to, and is willing to undergo, a voluntary abortion.

The incidence of death is, by and large, influenced by economic rather than social factors—good health being a universal social value. Explanations of mortality differentials therefore are concerned with differences in the standard of living. Public health facilities, sanitation conditions, housing, nutritional standards, medical knowledge—factors which affect longevity—are all variables related to the material wealth of a society and how it is distributed.

The infant mortality rate may well be the most sensitive quantitative indicator of social welfare that we possess, since a baby is most vulnerable to adverse living conditions. If fact, there is an almost one-to-one relationship between infant mortality rates and living standards, both between countries and between different groups living within a country.

The movement of people from one geographic area to another is the third factor that affects the size and particularly the age and sex distribution of a population. Movement into an area is called immigration; movement out is called emigration. Typically, those who immigrate are young and, in the early stages of population movement, male. This affects the age and sex distribution of the population left behind, as in the Caribbean in the first half of the twentieth century when there were more women than men. Those who move also tend to be poor and from rural areas. In the cities where they settle, they provide cheap labor.

The nineteenth and first three decades of the twentieth century witnessed the most extensive mass movement in recorded history. Probably a total of 60 million people left Europe in the nineteenth century and perhaps three-fourths of these did not return.[3]

The migration out of Europe during this time is an instance of people freely leaving to enter a new area, but migration between countries is seldom totally free anymore. In 1922, the United States passed the first national quota law which limited both the total number of people admitted and specified the proportion to be admitted from each geographical area, discriminating against all except those from northern and western Europe. Few countries invite immigration today. Canada, Australia and New Zealand do, but are predisposed to welcome those who are young, white and skilled or professionally trained. Emigration is also controlled, as in some Eastern European countries.

Migrations may also be forced, as when Africans were brought to this country as slaves. For both religious and political reasons, India and Pakistan were forced to exchange populations after achieving their independence from Great Britain in 1947. Religious persecution was the major reason for the earliest immigration to the United States and religious and political persecutions were important in forcing many people to migrate from Nazi Germany and areas controlled by Germany during World War II.

The major reason in modern history for people to pull up their stakes and move has been economic—the hope of a better life for themselves and their children. Migration, then, tends to be the demographic process that is most determined by social rather than biological factors and has an effect on size and growth of population that is more complex than may be immediately surmised. The age, class, sex and race of those both entering and leaving a country and moving within a country have a profound impact on both the birth and death rates and the age/sex composition, which together determine the size and rate of growth of a population.

Population measurements

Industrialized countries all collect data on their populations. They keep on-going records of births and deaths and periodically make a total count of their people in the form of a census. The United States Constitution requires a census be taken every ten years to determine the number of representatives from each state to the Congress.

The UN publishes demographic statistics of all the countries of the world. Accurate population statistics are still unavailable in many of the underdeveloped countries, however, because census taking is such an expensive enterprise. Even when a census is taken, people who do not read and write, who are not by culture record keepers, may not remember a baby who was born and died or the exact age of each living child.

In the United States census takers are criticized for not counting some of the population who are hard to find because they do not belong to any particular household, such as young black males in the cities. The Bureau of the Census has in fact admitted an undercount in the 1970 census of perhaps 5 million people. When a reasonably accurate census is taken, however, the information it provides is invaluable in assessing population trends and public needs and planning appropriate policies to meet them.

The most familiar population statistics, crude birth and death rates, are calculated by dividing the number of births and deaths in one year by the population count in the middle of the year. This number is then multiplied by a thousand to show the figure per thousand people.[4] For example, the crude birth rate in India from July, 1971, to July, 1972, was 42 per thousand, the crude death rate, 17 per thousand. The difference between the two, 25 more people a year per thousand, is the crude rate of population change (also expressed as 2.5 percent).[5] Similarly, the difference between immigration and emigration gives the crude rate of net migration. The rates are "crude" because they are gross figures and do not reflect either the sex or age of the population. Sex and age, of course, are factors necessary to determine the fertility rate.

Figure 5-1   Population pyramids, in millions

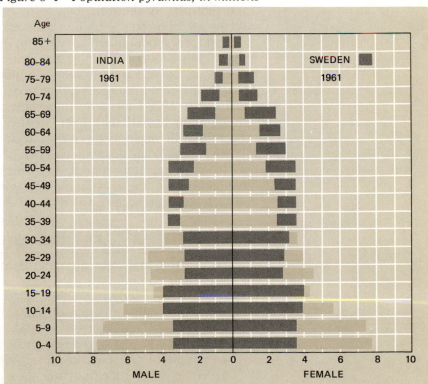

The sex and age distribution within a population gives a clearer picture of population trends and potential growth. It is normally shown by means of "population pyramids,"[6] such as those shown here for India and Sweden. The largest segment of India's population is in the age groups under 15. The number of Indians in these three groups is almost equal to the number in the six groups between 15 and 45, the childbearing ages. After fifteen years, Indians now under 15 will have drastically swollen the number of Indians of childbearing age. Thus even a substantial reduction in the number of births per female won't immediately reduce the population growth rate. Sweden's age structure is a sharp contrast to India's; population is more or less evenly distributed through age groups up to 55. At 55, it tapers off gradually. The number of Swedes in the age groups under 15 is slightly more than half the number between 15 and 45. After fifteen years, the number of Swedes of childbearing age will have increased only minimally. Therefore, any reduction in the birthrate, the number of births per thousand females, would actually reduce the rate of growth of Sweden's population. Distribution of a population in various age groups determines the pattern of the pyramid.

Population growth

Until very recently the world's population has increased almost imperceptibly. By about the beginning of the Christian era, the earth may have supported 250 million people, but another 1650 years were required for the population to reach an estimated half billion. It took only 200 years more to double that figure, however, and only 80 years more to double again and reach 2 billion, the earth's population in 1930. The present total of 3.8 billion, may be doubled in only 35 years, according to 1972 United Nations estimates.

Population growth has been neither a gradual nor an orderly process. An increase in the size and density of the population has followed technological advances as man has achieved greater control over the physical environment. According to V. Gordon Childe, there have been three major technological revolutions in human history and each has been accompanied by a marked increase in population.[7]

Agricultural and urban revolutions

The earliest humans were nomadic hunters and food-gatherers. Of necessity their numbers were very low and scattered. The first great population surge occurred about 8000 B.C. with the agricultural revolution. The domestication of plants and animals and the invention of agricultural tools helped bring about permanent food supplies, a more stable pattern of settlement and a great increase in population.

The building of cities marked another great revolution in humanity's development. With cities came the centralized control of soil and water resources and the organization of great irrigation systems;

cities developed long-distance trade and supported dense populations with specialized work roles and complex social systems.

. . . I want to introduce a new term, which I suggest be used in future discussions of human population and ecology. We should speak of our numbers in "Indian equivalents." An Indian equivalent I define as the average number of Indian citizens required to have the same detrimental effect on land's ability to support human life as would the average American.
. . . let's take an extremely conservative working figure of 25.
Wayne H. Davis

The first great cities arose about 3500 B.C. in Mesopotamia, along the Tigris and Euphrates rivers. Other cities followed in Egypt, Crete, India and later China and parts of Central America. After the Urban Revolution, population rose steadily but very slowly through the growth of the Roman Empire, the European Middle Ages and the Renaissance. Many technological developments during this period encouraged population growth, but mortality rates were high. The lack of medical knowledge left human beings helpless in the face of serious illness or injury. In 1347, bubonic plague, the Black Death, one of the most terrible epidemics in history, erupted in Europe. Conservative estimates indicate that at least one-fourth of Europe's total population died in this epidemic.

Most of the population increase from the mid-seventeenth century on can be traced to the decline in mortality effected by better diets and expanding medical knowledge.

The industrial revolution

The eighteenth and nineteenth centuries witnessed a revolution in technology comparable to the earlier agricultural and urban revolutions. New manufacturing techniques, the fruit of flourishing science and engineering skill, brought about vast increases in the efficient production and distribution of goods in the countries of the West. Medical knowledge increased and new cities were built, incorporating improved sanitation and safe water supplies. The result was a wholesale change in the physical and social world of the European countries and North America, and a pronounced increase of births over deaths.

Economists and philosophers had begun to be concerned, however, about the eventual result of unrestrained population growth. In 1798, Robert Thomas Malthus published his *Population: The First Essay.*[8] Malthus maintained that improvements in technology could not keep up with the rate of population expansion. He forecast hunger, epidemics and war as a result, which would once again reduce the level of population to that of the means of subsistence.

At the turn of the nineteenth century, however, when a reasonable ratio of births to deaths had been achieved within the population of the West, manipulation of fertility and mortality processes came into play. The manipulation was of two types. One, involving the development of birth control methods (discussed on page 203), might be called technological in nature. The other, sociocultural in nature, was related to the social processes operating in industrial society.

By the 1870s, the birth rate in the developing countries began to decline, a trend which continued until the "baby boom" of the 1940s and 1950s. New social conditions had begun to make large families impractical, and people began to realize that their place in the new order of things might relate rather directly to the ways in which they controlled their rate of reproduction. On a farm, large families provided the necessary labor, but in the industrialized city, where housing, food and other basic needs were expensive and education was the key to success, the small family was more practical. The French sociologist, Dumont, termed the phenomenon "social capillarity." Just as a column of water must be thin to rise by capillary action, so must a family be small to rise in the social scale.[9]

In developed countries, despite short-term surges such as the baby boom mentioned above, the birth rate has generally continued to decline. Widespread birth control, lessening religious influences, greater educational and employment opportunities for women and the certainty that most children born will grow to majority have contributed to a lower fertility level in recent years, just as improved diet and medical knowledge contributed to a lower mortality level 200 years earlier.

The underdeveloped nations

Prior to World War II, the nations of Africa, Latin America and Asia (with the exception of Japan) had death rates equivalent to those of Europe during the Middle Ages.[10] After the war, international agencies such as the World Health Organization, Pan American Health Organization, UNICEF and others brought the benefits of twentieth century medicine to underdeveloped nations. Insecticides, antibiotics, preventive public health programs and modern medical techniques were all introduced. The current population explosion in the underdeveloped nations can be attributed to the decline in death rates which resulted.

The reduction of mortality rates was sudden. In Ceylon, for example, the death rate dropped by 43 percent in a single year (1946-1947) as a result of malaria control achieved by spraying fields with DDT.[11] The drop in mortality was imposed from the outside; it was not an organic part of the technological and social development of the Ceylonese. As birth rates outstripped death rates, the underdeveloped nations found themselves with rapidly growing populations that their technological resources could not hope to support and their social system had not evolved to cope with. The values of these countries, which had long been adapted to conditions of subsistence agriculture and high mortality rates, were not easy to change. In India, large families were the norm because only a few of the children born could be expected to survive beyond childhood. The parents depended on the few children who survived to help them provide for the family or village unit and to care for them in their old age. Today, however, all, or most, of the children live. A change of technology is much more rapid than a change in custom. The combination of sharply reduced mortality and continued high fertility has given rise to abnormally young populations. Their reproductive potential poses an unprecedented threat to the economic development of these nations. In the meantime, they must also be fed, cared for and trained to be productive members of society.

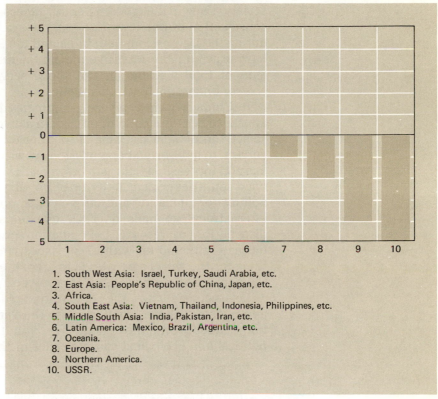

1. South West Asia: Israel, Turkey, Saudi Arabia, etc.
2. East Asia: People's Republic of China, Japan, etc.
3. Africa.
4. South East Asia: Vietnam, Thailand, Indonesia, Philippines, etc.
5. Middle South Asia: India, Pakistan, Iran, etc.
6. Latin America: Mexico, Brazil, Argentina, etc.
7. Oceania.
8. Europe.
9. Northern America.
10. USSR.

Figure 5-2 Increase or decrease of annual rate of population growth between mid-1966 and mid-1972 (percentages)

The scope of the problem

In the advanced or developed countries, where social norms and economic priorities have the potentiality for controlling population growth, the population problem is primarily a problem of the quality of life. Advanced technology helps solve many human problems, but it causes others—congested cities, a depopulated and economically depressed countryside, and pollution of the environment. High-level technologies also consume resources at so fast a rate that industrial nations are beginning to face the problem of scarcity. (In highly developed societies, there is also a gap between population change and social change, for the proportion of the aged within the population has increased, resulting in new strains within the social structure.)

In the underdeveloped countries, however, population growth remains so rapid that the first priority is the development of means by which the survival of these populations may be guaranteed, while at the same time they are struggling toward social progress and technological and industrial advancement. In ancient civilizations, huge resources of manpower were regarded as sources of strength in a society. Even in the modern period, excess labor has been used in the construction of public works—as, for example, in the United States during the Depression. Both India and the People's Republic of China have utilized labor-intensive means for just this purpose. The problems of food distribution and social services, however, if left unsolved, undermine even this tactic.

In China, within a severely regimented social system, problems appear to be closer to solution than in a diverse and loosely organized society like India's. China also appears, if recent estimates are correct, to have brought population growth under control, while India has not. Increasingly, the gap between the developed and underdeveloped countries widens in terms of population growth, industrial and political organization and the power to make its opinions known in international councils on such questions as the proper use and distribution of resources. Population growth and movement are intimately bound up with these issues, and beneficial resolution of them for the world's peoples is to a great extent conditioned by how the population problem itself is resolved.

Let us consider now the comparative growth rates in the developed and underdeveloped countries and the variables that affect population makeup and movement. We will then consider the social, political and ecological consequences of these changes.

reading: Garrett Hardin
THE TRAGEDY OF THE COMMONS

We can make little progress in working toward optimum population size until we explicitly exorcize the spirit of Adam Smith in the field of practical demography. In economic affairs, The Wealth of Nations (1776) popularized the "invisible hand," the idea that an individual who "intends only his own gain," is, as it were, "led by an invisible hand to promote . . . the public interest." Adam Smith did not assert that this was invariably true, and perhaps neither did any of his followers. But he contributed to a dominant tendency of thought that has ever since interfered with positive action based on rational analysis, namely the tendency to assume that decisions reached individually will, in fact, be the best decisions for an entire society. If this assumption is correct it justifies the continuance of our present policy of

192

laissez-faire in reproduction. If it is correct we can assume that men will control their individual fecundity so as to produce the optimal population. If the assumption is not correct, we need to re-examine our individual freedoms to see which ones are defensible.

The rebuttal to the "invisible hand" in population control is to be found in a "scenario" first sketched in a little known pamphlet in 1833 by a mathematical amateur named William Forster Lloyd (1794–1852). We may well call it "The Tragedy of the Commons," using the word "tragedy" as the philosopher Whitehead used it: "The essence of dramatic tragedy is not unhappiness. It resides in the solemnity of the remorseless working of things." He then goes on to say: "This inevitableness of destiny can only be illustrated in terms of human life by incidents which in fact involve unhappiness. For it is only by them that the futility of escape can be made evident in the drama."

The tragedy of the commons develops in this way. Picture a pasture open to all. It is to be expected that each herdsman will try to keep as many cattle as possible on the commons. Such an arrangement may work reasonably satisfactorily for centuries because tribal wars, poaching, and disease keep the numbers of both man and beast well below the "carrying capacity" of the land. Finally, however, comes the day of reckoning, i.e., the day when the long-desired social stability becomes a reality. At this point, the inherent logic of the commons remorselessly generates tragedy.

As a rational being each herdsman seeks to maximize his gain. Explicitly or implicitly, more or less consciously, he asks: "What is the utility to me of adding one more animal to my herd?" This utility has two components:

> 1. A positive component, which is a function of the increment of one animal. Since the herdsman receives all the proceeds from the sale of the additional animal, the positive utility is nearly $+1$.
> 2. A negative component, which is a function of the additional overgrazing created by one more animal. But since the effects of overgrazing are shared by all the herdsmen, the negative utility for any particular decision-making herdsman is only a fraction of -1.

Adding together the component partial utilities, the rational herdsman concludes that the only sensible course for him to pursue is to add another animal to his herd. And another; and another . . . But this is the conclusion reached by each and every rational herdsman sharing a commons. Therein is the tragedy. Each man is locked in to a system that compels him to increase his herd without limit—in a world that is limited. Ruin is the destination toward which all men rush, each pursuing his own best interest in a society that believes in the freedom of the commons. Freedom in a commons brings ruin to all.

Some would say that this is platitudinous, that is, a truth known to all. Would that it were! In a sense it was learned thousands of years ago, but natural selection favors the forces of psychological denial. (The individual benefits as an individual from his ability to deny the truth even though society as a whole, of which he is a part, suffers. Education can counteract the natural tendency to do the wrong thing, but the inexorable succession of generations requires that the basis for this knowledge be constantly refreshed.)

From
"The Tragedy of the Commons" by Garrett Hardin,
in *Science*, Vol. 162, 1968, pp. 244–245.

Growth in the industrialized nations

Low, relatively stable birth and death rates now characterize technologically advanced countries. The United States, with a population of 210.2 million, seems to be headed for "zero population growth" (the situation which results when the increase in population through births and immigration is equal to population loss through deaths and emigration).[12] In the United States, the trend toward smaller families is gaining ground so quickly that an estimated birthrate of 2.1 children per family in September of 1972 was followed in a few months by a revised estimate of 1.8 per family. On the strength of these developing patterns, the U.S. Bureau of the Census projects that there will be 250 to 300 million Americans by the year 2000, 25 to 50 percent more than at present, yet 20 million less than previous forecasts indicated.

Yet it is not at all certain that the United States will reach zero population growth. The rapid growth following World War II has given the American age structure a large number of young adults who, to bring the growth rate to a halt in the near future, would have to limit themselves to one child per couple. Unless they and their children continue a commitment to replacement levels of childbearing, the United States will still be faced with the consequences of a growing population.

Europe's growth rate declined following World War I, with France not even able to replace her population during the Depression; and, although Europe, too, experienced a post-World War II "baby boom," its birth rate soon began a decline which accelerated in the mid-sixties. Growth rates in the highly industrialized western and northern countries of Europe have declined faster than growth rates in southern and eastern countries. The people of West Germany (with a growth rate of 0.2 percent), the United Kingdom (0.5 percent), and Sweden (0.4 percent) have rapidly adopted contraceptive practices. Slightly higher growth rates in Italy (0.7 percent) and Spain (1.0 percent) may be partly due to religious opposition to birth control. In eastern Europe, growth rates are also declining (Poland, 0.9 percent; Czechoslovakia, 0.5 percent; Hungary, 0.3 percent). The use of contraceptives is widespread in eastern European nations, and the practice of abortion is publicly advocated by individual governments.[13]

In the Soviet Union, growth rates have declined almost 50 percent over the last decade. In western areas of the country, birth rates have declined sharply, partly because of a gap in the age structure caused by loss of life in World War II and partly because of Europeanized life-styles. Although birthrates are still high in the Asiatic regions of the Soviet Union, the overall decline in population has caused some official concern, since Soviet plans for agricultural, mineral and industrial developments in the sparsely inhabited lands of the north and east require large labor forces.[14]

Japan's present growth rate is lass than half the Asian average. The most advanced industrial nation in Asia, Japan reacted to a postwar growth spurt with a campaign for control which produced, in Kingsley Davis' words, "the swiftest drop in reproduction that has ever occurred in an entire nation."[15] As a small island nation with a limited supply of arable land and industrial resources, Japan depends largely on imports to maintain its industrial capacity and high standard of living. Without population control, Japan would become unbearably crowded and living standards would decline sharply. Even with control, parts of Japan are very densely populated. A strong tradition of social control has enabled the Japanese to curb population growth and endure very crowded living conditions, but there is still much to be done to further limit growth and control density.

Australia and New Zealand, the only industrialized nations of Oceania, are growing at a slightly greater rate than a decade ago. Along with Canada, these countries still welcome immigrants— particularly skilled workers.[16]

Underdeveloped nations

The highest growth rates are found in the economically underdeveloped nations, which can least afford to support growing populations. Illiteracy, ignorance of contraceptive methods and cultural resistance to smaller families impede efforts to control population. Population growth and economic underdevelopment are closely linked. Much of the wealth and resources of underdeveloped nations, which might be spent on developing new industries and raising living standards, has to be spent on food imports to support the growing population.

Since World War II, the continent of Africa has experienced a progressive decline in mortality; it also displays the world's highest fertility rates. Nations such as Morocco, Nigeria, Ethiopia, Zaire and South Africa show birth rates of almost 50 per 1000, close to three times those of developed nations.[17] Such countries will double in population over the next two decades. Even now population growth is straining the ability of their limited arable lands to produce enough food. A number of African countries have achieved a small industrial base that allows them to engage in some international trade, and thus to acquire food supplies and technical advice for development from outside. Swift population growth takes up any of the slack that develops, however.

Latin America, a close second in the growth race, shows a fertility rate of 38 per 1000, while death rates are now close to those in Europe. Evidence of transition to the patterns prevalent in developed nations can be found in growth rates of countries such as Cuba, Argentina and Uruguay—1.9, 1.5 and 1.2 respectively. Most other Latin American nations have a growth rate of around 3 percent, with a population doubling time of twenty-five years. Mexico, for instance, is expected to double its population in twenty-one years.[18]

Asia is the area of the world in which population growth puts the most desperate burdens on social structure. In most of Asia's countries, from Turkey to Hong Kong, populations will double in thirty years or less. And much of this growth is of the type noted earlier, which places more and more of the population in a younger age category, guaranteeing high growth rates for years to come unless drastic measures are taken.

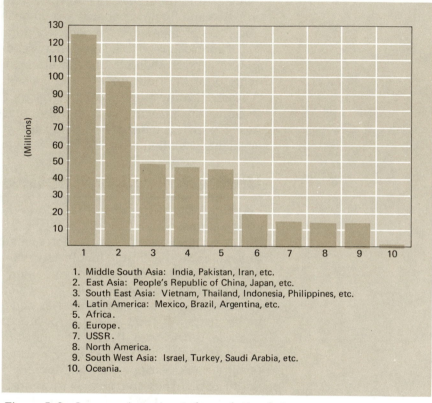

1. Middle South Asia: India, Pakistan, Iran, etc.
2. East Asia: People's Republic of China, Japan, etc.
3. South East Asia: Vietnam, Thailand, Indonesia, Philippines, etc.
4. Latin America: Mexico, Brazil, Argentina, etc.
5. Africa.
6. Europe.
7. USSR.
8. North America.
9. South West Asia: Israel, Turkey, Saudi Arabia, etc.
10. Oceania.

Figure 5–3   Increase in estimated population between mid-1966 and mid-1972

Distribution and density

Although humanity has adjusted to any number of environments, many land areas are simply too hostile to support sizeable populations. Greenland, Antarctica, mountainous areas of Africa and North and South America, and desert regions of North Africa and Asia support only a fraction of the total world population. In fact, world population distribution is so uneven that about half the earth's people are crowded into 5 percent of its land.

Only a few broad generalizations can be made about world distribution patterns: (1) over 90 percent of the world's people live north of the equator; (2) population is concentrated on the rims of the continents, with three-fourths of the world's people living within 600 miles of the sea and two-thirds within 300 miles; (3) population density declines with altitude; 72 percent of the earth's land area is over 656 feet above sea level, but 56 percent of the human race lives below that point.[19]

Aside from these generalizations, there seems to be no neat pattern of world population distribution. Crowded and sparse areas exist in both developed and underdeveloped countries, in the tropics and middle latitudes, in the Old World and the New World. The largest high-density areas, with over 250 people per square mile, are eastern and southern Asia, which are primarily agrarian, and western Europe and the northeastern United States, which are heavily industrialized regions. In some parts of these high-density areas, levels rise to over 1000 people per square mile.[20]

Glenn Trewartha groups the factors affecting distribution into three main classes: (1) physical factors, including climate, terrain, soil, water and space relationships; (2) cultural factors, including social attitudes, stage of economic development and political organization; and (3) demographic factors, including differential birth and death rates and currents of migration.[21] These factors operate in combination; it is almost impossible to separate and assess the effects of a single factor. However, Trewartha postulates that "the role of physical factors in spatial distribution of population declines in direct importance as civilization advances in complexity."[22]

The developed world

The process of urbanization in the United States, as sketched in Chapter One, illustrates some aspects of the process Trewartha postulates, as do the methods and motives through which immigrant populations displaced native American Indian and Spanish cultures, as described in Chapter Three.

At present, with urbanization of the American continent almost complete, population distribution indicates a growing number of depopulated small towns with inadequate facilities for maintaining any but the most skeletal of social organizations, largely composed of the old and poor who are unable to leave. Those towns close to large urban areas are often absorbed and become suburbs, but in the states of the upper Midwest, Iowa and the Dakotas, for example, this is not the case.[23]

Yet those who come to the cities are not always trained or educated for the opportunities that exist there. The high density of central cities, with their slum areas and decaying housing stocks, compared to the relative low-density of the burgeoning suburbs, indicates the economic disparities that influence population distribution.

The vast recent growth of Japan's population has resulted in urbanization unprecedented even in the United States. Over the past 70 years, the Tokyo region has grown in population from about 2.5 million to 37 million, fusing the areas of Kyoto, Osaka, Nagoya, and

Tokyo into a vast megalopolis.[24] An intricate physical and social structure is necessary to focus the activities of such a large population. The Tokaido megalopolis has a more homogeneous population than American cities, and may be less prone to social conflict. Yet such a population is dependent on a high level of economic activity, subject, in Japan's case especially, to international conditions. The failure of conditions conducive to its support would have the most dire social consequences.

Planning has eased some of the problems attendant on urban growth, but besides Japan, it is only in Europe that social policy and population policy have been integrated, especially in the Scandinavian countries. Urbanization for the most part is still an uncontrolled process.

The underdeveloped world

The movement of peoples in the underdeveloped countries parallels that of the industrialized nations. Migration has been from the rural areas to the cities. Urbanization is taking place in' the world's underdeveloped countries at an unprecedented pace. In these countries the population in cities of 100,000 or more grew 67 percent per decade between 1950 and 1970. The overall population of the countries grew 23 percent. At a 67 percent rate of growth, the population of cities of 100,000 or more people will double in thirteen and a half years.[25]

Urban population growth is partly due to a high birth rate and a low death rate in the urban areas themselves. Young people of childbearing age make up a heavy portion of a city's population and account for the high birth rate. Despite numerous deficiencies, health and sanitation in the cities tend to be better than in the country and account for the lower death rates.

However, migration accounts for about half the urban population growth. Whatever economic opportunities an underdeveloped country has for its people are in its cities. People from the countryside move to the cities looking for jobs. Ghettos grow, multiply and spread. The shanty towns of Manila and the squatter settlements outside Lima in Peru are only two examples of such rapid growth. There is no housing available for the newcomers, so they must live as they can—normally in squalor and without proper transportation or other facilities. Although it packs cities with more and more people, migration does not relieve overcrowded rural areas. In most underdeveloped nations an even higher birthrate in these areas keeps the rural population enormous. Despite urban growth in underdeveloped countries, only 15.7 percent of their people lived in cities in 1970.[26] Population density overall in the underdeveloped countries was a staggering 105 persons per square mile, more than twice that of developed countries.

Since the Industrial Revolution, migration has tended to be not only toward the cities but from poorer rural countries to richer industrialized countries. The mass migration to the United States at the turn of the century was of rural people from the poorer, less industrialized areas of Europe to the American cities of the eastern seaboard. This means of opportunity for poor and landless farmers is no longer open to the people of the underdeveloped world. The industrialized nations have closed their doors.

The consequences of growth

Expanding populations increase the demand on food, energy and mineral resources. In recent years, the dramatic ecological consequences of the population explosion—vanishing fisheries, costlier fuels and mineral ores, contaminated air and water— have aroused worldwide concern. The immediate consequences differ from nation to nation, but the long-range consequences concern every human being on earth.

Food

With large areas of arable land and highly efficient agricultural techniques, the United States would not seem to have any urgent concerns about food supplies. There are signs, however, that American agricultural abundance is not inexhaustible. In 1972 the Commission on Population Growth and the American Future reported that faster population growth would soon require the farming of marginal lands, a costly process. The commission members warned that three-child reproduction averages (admittedly higher than present patterns) could lead to 40 to 50 percent increases in farm food prices.[27]

Most advanced industrial nations now either maintain their populations in line with domestic food production or depend on food imports to meet some of their needs. At the present time the United States, Canada, Australia and Argentina are able to produce large quantities of food for export. If, however, population growth creates increased demands for food within those countries, there may be no food left to export.

In the underdeveloped nations, agriculture is typically at the subsistence level, barely keeping pace with population growth at an inadequate level of nutrition. Experts estimate that two-thirds of the 800 million children of Africa, Asia and Latin America now suffer from malnutrition. Natural disasters that affect agriculture can turn subsistence nutritional levels into outright famine. In 1972, crop failures brought on by drought conditions caused severe food shortages in India and Central America and, in Africa, a tragic migration in search of food by millions of nomads across a 2000-mile belt of the south Sahara.[28] The agriculture of underdeveloped nations is clearly inadequate, but not even the most advanced agricultural technology could feed a chronically expanding population. A telling example of the population/food dilemma is that of India. Although India's 1973 grain output is expected to be twice that of 1950, its population is still greater, having grown by two-thirds since then.[29]

Energy and mineral resources

In 1972, the group of experts known as The Club of Rome issued *The Limits of Growth,* a report on the possible effects of depletion of the earth's resources brought about by modern technology. It points out that the United States, with 6 percent of the world's population, consumes 25 percent of the world's nonrenewable natural resources.[30] Worldwide usage rates are increasing faster than population, so that there are more people consuming at the same time that average consumption is rising. Although only the Soviet Union, Japan and West Germany even begin to approach the United States in exploitation of vital raw materials such as chromium, aluminum, copper, petroleum and lead, the most liberal estimate of reserves indicates that continued consumption at this level will lead to severe scarcities and higher costs in the years ahead. To drive home their argument, the experts point to a 500 percent increase in the price of mercury and a 300 percent rise for lead just in the last two or three decades. Within a century, some minerals may be totally exhausted.

The natural inequality of the two powers of population and of production in the earth and that great law of our nature which must constantly keep their effects equal form the great difficulty that to me appears insurmountable in the way to the perfectability of society. All other arguments are of slight and subordinate consideration in comparison of this.

Thomas Robert Malthus 1798

What effect accelerated depletion of these minerals necessary for industry will have on the rising expectations of the underdeveloped nations remains to be seen. *The Limits of Growth* observes that scarcities may bring about political conflicts over the control of resources. In the early 1970s, many experts were predicting that the Arab nations, which control a large portion of the earth's oil resources, would be demanding more and more political and economic concessions from the oil-consuming industrial countries. Regardless of who controls these vital resources, they will continue to be depleted unless present consumption patterns are radically altered, both through population control and changes in economic priorities.

Environmental consequences

Although only industrialized nations are the immediate victims of pollution, contaminants dispersed in the atmosphere and oceans threaten all human beings. Recent scientific research has demonstrated the effects of such pollutants as mercury, industrial and organic wastes and lead. Concentrated DDT and toxic breakdown products have been detected in the body fat of humans from Alaska to New Delhi. Discussing the trade-offs between industrial development and pollution cleanup, the Club of Rome warns us that "the earth is finite. The closer any human activity comes to the limit of the earth's ability to support that activity, the more apparent and unresolvable the trade-offs become."[31] In November, 1972, an agreement to limit the dumping of toxic or noxious substances in the oceans was signed by seventy-nine nations, acknowledging the worldwide implications of pollution.[32]

Although most industrial nations are now earnestly studying ways of preventing environmental damage, underdeveloped countries seem less concerned about the problem. At present they are vitally interested in *building up* new industries, not controlling them. Realizing the difference industrialization can make to the lives of their people, leaders of underdeveloped nations do not want to spend great sums on costly pollution-control research. India's Prime Minister Ghandi put it this way: "How can we speak to those who live in villages and in slums about keeping the oceans, the rivers, and the air clean when their own lives are contaminated at the source."[33]

Social and economic consequences

The smaller a nation's population, the less people to divide its national income. The less people to divide the national income, the greater the amount of money to be spent on food, clothing and shelter for those who do divide it.

Industrially developed nations such as the United States have kept their populations at a reasonably low level, and there is abundant material wealth to be converted to a high standard of living for most of the population. There is enough food to eat, clothing to wear and housing to live in. In the United States, the issue of population growth as viewed by the middle class is normally related to questions about the distribution of our wealth and the social priorities involved in its use. How does overcrowding in cities affect the way people live? How will traffic congestion affect the emotional and mental stability of the city-dweller or bumper-to-bumper commuter? How can enormous wealth, symbolized by concrete and steel skyscrapers, exist minutes away by subway from stultifying ghetto tenements? Most underdeveloped countries are too involved with achieving sustenance levels for their people to consider population growth as anything but an economic problem.

Underdeveloped countries are constantly engaged in trying to raise their people's standard of living. Uncontrolled population growth prevents them from significantly doing so. Most economists believe that to raise the standard of living of its people, a nation with a stable population must invest 3 to 5 percent of its annual income in new income-producing development. Many underdeveloped countries have a population growth rate of 3 percent. For such a country to raise the standard of living of its people requires as high as a 20 percent investment. Poor nations can rarely afford this. They are forced by mushrooming population growth to spend most of their national income on imports of food and other staples. Even when they can afford it, population growth spreads the benefits so thin as to be barely recognizable.

If it were admitted that the creation and care of new human beings is socially motivated, like other forms of behavior, by being a part of the system of rewards and punishments that is built into human relationships, and thus is bound up with the individual's economic and personal interests, it would be apparent that the social structure and economy must be changed before a deliberate reduction in the birth rate can be achieved.

Kingsley Davis

Capital investment is essential to the expansion of an economy. So is a large and skilled labor force. In countries with a huge population growth rate, large numbers of the population are too young to work. Those who must care for these children are likewise economically unproductive. Quality education is scarce in underdeveloped countries, and the incentive to get an education is low because jobs are rarely available even for the educated. The labor force remains proportionately small and unskilled. Reversing this situation calls for large injections of capital investment.

The world's poor are becoming more politically aware, however. They no longer accept poverty as fate or the will of God, and are seeking better economic conditions that they realize are possible. However, increased population growth prevents attainment of better economic conditions, as do the rigid and often exploitive governments and social systems in many of the underdeveloped countries; both block the aspirations of the poor and can only lead to political upheaval in the future. Many sociologists have pointed out that people are satisfied with their lot in life, however hard, so long as it is all they expect; but when expectations change, dissatisfaction grows. We are on the verge of a revolution of rising expectations.

Population planning

In times of drought and famine, the Bushmen of the Kalahari Desert abstain from sexual intercourse. That is the only form of birth control they know, and they do not wish to bring a child into the world at a time when he would not survive and his birth would put a strain on other members of the group. Most of the world's people would rather not adopt the Bushmen method of family planning, but until the twentieth century that was the only absolutely reliable method. Today there are several methods: the problem is to make the knowledge and means of these methods of birth control available on a worldwide scale and to change whatever social attitudes hinder their adoption.

Methods of birth control

In 1822, an Englishman named Francis Place published a treatise on contraception entitled *Illustrations and Proofs of the Principle of Population.* To overcome the strain of postponed marriage, Place advocated early marriage and the use of a contraceptive, namely a sponge. Other nineteenth century advocates of birth control suggested *coitus interruptus* and an astringent douche as effective contraceptives. Whatever the methods advocated, interest in birth control grew during the latter part of the nineteenth century, particularly in western Europe. In 1913, an American, Margaret Sanger, toured western Europe to gather information about contraceptive methods that could be used in the United States. Mrs. Sanger not only initiated the birth control movement in the United States, but also helped start movements in Hawaii, Japan and China.

Some of the more popular birth control methods today include spermicidal agents, the condom, and the diaphragm; none of these methods is completely reliable and the diaphragm must be fitted individually by a doctor. The rhythm method (in which the couple refrains from intercourse during the woman's fertile period) requires careful attention to the calendar and is highly unreliable. The various contraceptive pills require strict adherence to instructions and their effect on women's health is still being debated. The intrauterine device (IUD) requires surgical installation, is not totally reliable and can cause internal bleeding. Surgical sterilization is completely effective, but it is usually irreversible. In some countries abortion is the only means available to avoid unwanted children. In 1937, a French doctor estimated that there were at least 125 illegal abortions for every 100 live births, and in 1961 the estimates ran to a total of 800,000 abortions—equal to the number of live births—occurring in France each year.[34] In Chile, one out of every three pregnancies ends in illegal abortion. In Colombia, the need for medical care after illegal abortion constitutes the second largest cause of hospital admissions.[35]

Family planning

Up to the present, the major effort to control population has been through programs of voluntary family planning. Such programs have been effective for the most part, despite the religious and sometimes the political views of some groups within society.

A family planning program doesn't just help a couple avoid children they don't want; it also helps them have the children they do want. Such a program will normally feature qualified medical personnel to recommend and assist with various contraceptive devices. Advice is given with particular concern for the good of the family: What will be best for the health of both mother and child? How many children can the family support? Will there be enough money to properly educate the children when they're grown? This economically oriented approach has proved successful with American middle-class couples.

The most popular criticism of family planning is that the number of children a couple wants to have is often more than it ought to have. Family planning has also been criticized because not enough people avail themselves of the services, either because they are unaware of the facilities or because family planning takes place in clinics, which tend to frighten people away. Other criticisms include the fact that family planning deals only with married couples, ignoring pregnancies among unmarried women and girls; that in underdeveloped countries medical personnel are often unavailable to implement the program; and that the program's support of the family as a social institution can only encourage increasing birthrates.

The most decisive statement concerning family planning and population growth in the United States is contained in the report of the Commission on Population Growth and the American Future. The result of a two-year study, the report offers sweeping recommendations aimed at improving both the quality and quantity of family planning services currently available in the United States. Among the Commission's recommendations are:

1. The nation should welcome and plan for a stabilized population.
2. States should make contraceptive services and information available to everyone, including minors; responsible sex education courses should be widely available.
3. All restrictions to voluntary sterilization should be eliminated so the decision can be made solely between parent and doctor.
4. States should liberalize abortion laws along the lines of the New York State statute; all levels of government should provide funds for abortion services; abortion should be included in comprehensive health insurance benefits.[36]

While there are still many controversies in the courts concerning the availability of contraceptive devices and conditions under which birth control information can be provided to the public, and while Catholic and other groups have been active in fights to maintain laws against abortion, there seems to have been a general realization in the country at large that provision should be made, by legal change, for many of the Commission's recommendations to be carried out. The Women's Liberation movement has been in the forefront of the fight for more liberalized abortion laws, arguing that a woman should have the right of control over her own body. As noted in Chapter Two, the Supreme Court recently issued a decision that made abortion legal and a matter between the perspective mother and her doctor during the first twelve weeks of pregnancy, and allowed the state to regulate the provision of abortion only during the second twelve weeks.

There are, nevertheless, people who object to the increasingly visible public programs to limit population as a way of improving the quality of life in the United States. Spokesmen for black groups, such as Minister Louis Farakham of the Nation of Islam, have protested that population control is a program to limit the strength and political power of blacks by controlling their numbers. Throughout the world, whether in the advanced or underdeveloped nations, it is the poor who have most of the children. As families ascend the social and economic scale, whether in Japan or Mexico, they tend to have fewer children. The poor in most countries have neither knowledge of birth control methods nor the means for implementing them. Studies have shown that family planning is particularly desired by many lower-class and rural women who have three or four children.[45]

Family planning world-wide

As might be expected, countries such as India actively encourage birth control. Family planning clinics have been established in a large number of Indian urban and rural areas, although they are not always effective because of traditional attitudes favoring large families. In some cases, the government has made payments to men who undergo voluntary sterilization after the birth of their second child. Other Asian nations, such as Pakistan and the Republic of Korea, have programs similar to India's. Japan has had an effective birth control program for years, and China, the world's most populous nation, has made considerable progress in population control.

All the impulses of decent humanity, all the dictates of religion and all the traditions of medicine insist that suffering should be relieved, curable diseases cured, preventable disease prevented. . . . Some might [take] the purely biological view that if men will breed like rabbits they must be allowed to die like rabbits. . . . If ethical principles deny our right to do evil in order that good may come, are we justified in doing good when the foreseeable consequence is evil?   *A. V. Hill*

Countries such as Great Britain, Sweden, Finland and Denmark put great stress on personal welfare and individual choice. Most of these countries grant small family allowances, but contraceptives are readily available, sex education is a regular part of the school curriculum and abortion is essentially legal.

Most international efforts to control population have been carried out through the United Nations. The United Nations established its Population Commission in 1946, but it was not until 1962 that the General Assembly recognized that "economic and social development and population policies are closely interrelated."[37] In 1965, the Economic and Social Control Commission (ECOSOC) requested that advisory and training services for population programs be provided to governments who wanted them.

With the creation of the Population Trust Fund in 1967, all UN agencies with a potential role in the solution of population problems were mobilized: the World Health Organization (WHO) provided family planning services and training; the Children's Fund (UNICEF) assisted with material; the Educational, Scientific, and Cultural Organization (UNESCO) helped with education, mass communications and social services; the Food and Agriculture Organization (FAO) developed programs of Better Family Living through its program of home economics, agricultural extension and community development; the International Labor Organization (ILO) developed information and education for labor and management.

On the regional level, the Economic Commission for Asia and the Far East and the Economic Commission for Africa are beginning to undertake major programs. Regrettably, the Economic Commission for Latin America has not yet exerted any significant influence.

The World Bank has assumed a major role in family planning programs, including loans to Jamaica and Tunisia for construction of family planning facilities in rural areas. A number of private foundations and organizations also perform active or informational functions in the family planning field. Among these are the Ford Foundation, the Population Council, the Population Reference Bureau and the International Planned Parenthood Federation.

Figure 5–4   Appraisal of proposals to limit population growth, by criteria

Proposal	Scientific Readiness	Political Viability	Administrative Feasibility	Economic Capability	Ethical Acceptability	Presumed Effectiveness
A. Extension of voluntary fertility control	High	High on maternal care, moderate to low on abortion	Uncertain in near future	Maternal care too costly for local budget, abortion feasible	High for maternal care, low for abortion	Moderately high
B. Establishment of involuntary fertility control	Low	Low	Low	High	Low	High
C. Intensified educational campaigns	High	Moderate to high	High	Probably high	Generally high	Moderate
D. Incentive programs	High	Moderately low	Low	Low to moderate	Low to moderate	Uncertain
E. Tax and welfare benefits and penalties	High	Moderately low	Low	Low to moderate	Low to moderate	Uncertain
F. Shifts in social and economic institutions	High	Generally high, but low on some specifics	Low	Generally low	Generally high, but uneven	High, over long run
G. Political channels and organizations	High	Low	Low	Moderate	Moderately low	Uncertain
H. Augmented research efforts	Moderate	High	Moderate to high	High	High	Uncertain
Family planning programs	Generally high, but could use improved technology	Moderate to high	Moderate to high	High	Generally high, but uneven, on religious grounds	Moderately high

In 1965, the United States Agency for International Development, which is primarily responsible for foreign aid, announced its intention to provide interested governments with assistance in developing family planning programs. Although only 2 million dollars were earmarked for this program,[38] the policy was a radical departure from the government's earlier position that family planning was not a suitable area for government interference. AID assistance in the field grew rapidly. In 1969-1970, 80 million dollars in aid was channeled through private organizations, UN agencies and direct bilateral aid.[39]

Beyond family planning

In an article with the above title, the population planner Bernard Berelson discusses the nature of proposals which go beyond the family planning concept.[40] Some of them involve measures, such as involuntary fertility control, which would be labelled totalitarian by many in the United States. He rates the proposals by several criteria of acceptability. (See figure 5-4.) Berelson is not alone in thinking that more efforts than family planning will be needed to solve the world's population problem. Kingsley Davis notes that population policy is a dilemma.[41] Politically, it is difficult to advocate anything more than family planning, yet the very acceptability of the family planning concept, with its voluntary decisions about family size, makes it ineffective for population control. He suggests that wide-ranging social and cultural change, involving national population policy rather than national family planning policy, is what is needed. The continued trend to interpret population control as a matter of family planning may indicate that the family is a more durable institution world-wide than it has been presented in our chapter on the family in America. The Report of the Commission on Population Growth and the American Future contains a section whose title must look strangely cold to many: "Women: Alternatives to Childbearing."[42] The Commission lists a variety of these increasingly available to women in America, connected primarily with increased education and employment opportunities. For solution to the problems of population growth worldwide, some such alternative for women throughout the world would seem to be necessary.

The clear-eyed cannot hope for progress in the short run beyond that which family planning efforts may induce. In the race for social development, the desires stimulated in the population of an underdeveloped nation are not those that first lead to so efficient and sensible a movement as limitation of family size. The development of a broader educational program for all classes in these areas must, then, be viewed as a function of population planning, rather than as a separate social endeavor. The population problem is a social problem, but in some countries it is a major political problem as well, though the terms in which it is discussed are often those of class struggle or economic development. In systems where a relatively small middle class or a class of large land-owners controls the political apparatus, there is likely to be little action in population planning or in education unless it is forced through action which does not always stop short of revolution. Countries which have not yet attained a reasonable standard of living for a majority, and are not disposed to do so or are unable, may be those where population planning will be effective only when it is imposed from above, or by revolutionary decree.

Notes

[1] Population Reference Bureau, *1972 World Population Data Sheet* (Washington, 1972).

[2] Kingsley Davis and Judith Blake, "Social Structure and Fertility: An Analytic Framework," *Economic Development and Cultural Change* (Chicago: University of Chicago Press, 1952) Vol. 1, pp. 211-235.

[3] Dennis H. Wrong, *Population and Society,* 3rd ed. (New York: Random House, 1967) p. 73.

[4] Quentin H. Stanford, ed., *The World's Population* (Toronto/New York: Oxford University Press, 1972) pp. 7-8.

[5] Population Reference Bureau, *1972 World Population Data Sheet* (Washington, 1972).

[6] Stanford, *op. cit.,* p. 160.

[7] V. Gordon Childe, cited in Wrong, *op. cit.*

[8] Thomas Robert Malthus, *Population: The First Essay* (Ann Arbor: Ann Arbor Paperbacks, 1959).

[9] United Nations, "Economic and Social Factors Affecting Fertility," in Stanford, *op. cit.,* p. 110.

[10] Philip M. Hauser, ed., *The Population Dilemma,* 2nd ed. (Englewood Cliffs, N.J.: Prentice Hall, 1969) p. 16.

[11] Facts on File 1973, p. 62 A3.

[12] *The New York Times,* Sept. 23, 1972 and Dec. 18, 1972.

[13] Population Reference Bureau, *1972 World Population Data Sheet* (Washington, 1972).

[14] Alfred Sauvy, "Population Problems in Europe and the Soviet Union," in *International Aspects of Overpopulation,* John Barratt and Michael Louw, eds. (London: Macmillan Press, Ltd., 1972) pp. 185-193.

[15] Kingsley Davis, "Fertility and Mortality in the Developed and Underdeveloped Countries," in Stanford, *op. cit.,* p. 58.

[16] C. A. Price, "International Migration," in Barratt and Louw, *op. cit.,* pp. 113-125.

[17] Robert C. Cook, "World Population Projects 1965-2000," in Stanford, *op. cit.,* pp. 24-31.

[18] Population Reference Bureau, *1972 World Population Data Sheet* (Washington, 1972).

[19] David M. Heer, *Society and Population* (Englewood Cliffs, N.J.: Prentice Hall, 1968) p. 23.

[20] Glenn T. Trewartha, *A Geography of Population* (New York: John Wiley and Sons, 1969) pp. 105-108.

[21] *Ibid.,* pp. 74-75.

[22] *Ibid.,* pp. 77-78.

[23] U.S. Commission on Population Growth and the American Future, *Population and the American Future* (New York: New American Library, 1972) p. 130.

[24] C. Nagashema, "Megalopolis in Japan," *Ekistics,* Vol. 140, pp. 6–14.

[25] Kingsley Davis, Introduction to "Burgeoning Cities in Rural Countries," in *Cities: Their Origin, Growth, and Human Impact* (San Francisco: W. H. Freeman and Company, 1973) p. 220.

[26] *Ibid.*

[27] U.S. Commission on Population Growth and the American Future, *op. cit.,* p. 28.

[28] *The New York Times,* June 4, 1973.

[29] Population Reference Bureau, *1972 World Population Data Sheet* (Washington, 1972).

[30] Dennis L. Meadows, *et al., The Limits to Growth, A Report for the Club of Rome's Project on the Predicament of Mankind* (New York: Signet, 1972) pp. 57–75.

[31] *Ibid.,* pp. 78–94.

[32] "World Priorities," *Environment,* Vol. 14, No. 6, July/Aug. 1972, p. 4.

[33] William Petersen, *Population* (New York: Macmillan, 1961) pp. 364–365.

[34] Tadd Fischer, *Our Overcrowded World* (New York: Parent Magazine Press, 1969) p. 72.

[35] *Ibid.,* p. 169.

[36] *Population and the American Future, op. cit.,* pp. 191, 168-170, 171, 177.

[37] Philander P. Claxton, Jr., "The Development of Institutions to Meet the World Population Crisis," U.S. Dept. of State Bulletin, Aug. 16, 1971, p. 169.

[38] Clyde Sanger, "Family Planning in Columbia: A Case Study," in Stanford, *op. cit.,* p. 231.

[39] *Ibid.*

[40] Bernard Berelson, "Beyond Family Planning," *Ekistics,* Vol. 162, pp. 288–291.

[41] Kingsley Davis, "Population Policy—Will Current Programs Succeed," *Science,* Vol. 159, pp. 730–739.

[42] *Population and the American Future, op. cit.* p. 150.

Summary

To comprehend the world-wide problems posed by population growth, it is necessary to study the intimate relationship among sophisticated ways of counting people, cultural and behavioral patterns in the societies of the world, and analyses of the use and limitations of the world's natural resources.

Demography, the science of counting people, involves a study of the processes which cause changes in a given population. These are three: fertility, mortality, and migration. The study of fertility involves social practices, attitudes and values, as well as biological capacities for child-rearing. The study of mortality involves a knowledge of public health facilities, sanitation conditions, housing, nutrition and medical knowledge in a given area. Migration is the study of population movements.

Most countries, when they can afford it, collect data on their populations. This data includes a record of births and deaths, a periodical population count called a census, and crude birth- and death rates.

Knowledge of sex and age distribution within a population can give a fairly clear picture of population trends. Large portions of a population in its youngest age groups indicates a high growth rate.

Technological advances give man greater control over his physical environment. This control permits sharp increases in population size and density. In developed countries, however, advanced birth control methods, and a socially conditioned preference for smaller families have led to declines in population growth rates. In underdeveloped countries, on the other hand, technology has cut mortality rates, but customs and ignorance have kept birth rates high. This combination had led to young populations with high growth rates in countries which can least afford rapid growth.

World population distribution is uneven. Physical, cultural and demographic factors affect distribution. In recent years, the world's population has been increasingly concentrated in cities, in both the developed and underdeveloped countries. Urbanization has diminished rural populations in developed countries. In underdeveloped countries, because of high birth rates, rural areas remain densely populated despite urbanization.

Expanding populations increase demands on food, energy and mineral resources. Some advanced nations maintain their populations in line with domestic food production. Others depend on food imports to meet some of their needs. In underdeveloped countries, however, malnutrition is prevalent; agriculture is typically at the subsistence level, and these nations are too poor to import needed supplies. While population explosion continues in the underdeveloped world, the developed countries demand more and more of the world's resources to keep their own standard of living high.

Developed nations tend to view the population crisis as a problem of the "quality of life." Underdeveloped nations are so involved with feeding, clothing and housing their burgeoning populations, they rarely view it as anything but an economic issue. Underdeveloped nations devote almost all their annual income to maintaining subsistence levels for their people. Little capital is left for the investment necessary to stir economic growth.

A major problem in population control is making the knowledge and means of birth control methods available. Family planning programs sponsored by national governments and by international agencies are operating today around the world. These programs are much more successful in countries where social preference is for small families than in countries where religious and social norms encourage large families.

Most of these programs have been operated on a voluntary basis. Some commentators on the issue, however, view population control as so vital that they have proposed programs which limit births by law, by enforced sterilization, and so forth. At present the social and political implications of these plans have made them unacceptable. Neither control of population growth world-wide nor control of the strain it places on the world's resources has yet been achieved.

chapter

education

Since the time of Socrates, education has been a major issue in every society. Socrates' battle for educational reform in Athens ended abruptly in 399 B.C. when he was sentenced to death for instilling the wrong values in his students. The harshness of the sentence attests to the importance that the ancient Greeks accorded to education; in our own day this issue continues to be equally crucial although the administration of hemlock to controversial educators has gone out of style.

The United States Constitution says nothing about public schools, but the constitutions of all fifty states clearly spell out the community's duty to educate the young. By 1850, nearly all northern states had enacted free education policies, and by 1918 education in every state of the Union was not only free, but compulsory as well.

The broad commitment to public education in the 1800s arose largely out of the growing need for a uniform approach to socialization for the diverse groups entering America. Historian Joel H. Spring writes:

Education during the nineteenth century had been increasingly viewed as an instrument of social control to be used to solve the social problems of crime, poverty, and Americanization of the immigrant. The activities of public school tended to replace the social training of other institutions, such as the family and church. One reason for the extension of school activities was the concern for all education of the great numbers of immigrants arriving from eastern and southern Europe. It was feared that without some form of Americanization immigrants would cause a rapid decay of American institutions.[1]

What was Americanization? Basically it was (and still is) a regimen of values that stressed hard work, fair play, individual initiative, upward social mobility and monetary success. The educational system embodying these tenets was a fairly rigid one; though basic skills were taught, much of the instruction time was given over to value training such as every society has required of its educational institutions, to keep its populace coherent in belief and thought.

There were, of course, a number of children who were left out of the educational process almost entirely. Most blacks, despite the philanthropic efforts that established special institutes following the Civil War, received little training even in basic skills. Child labor in the expanding industries of the nation cut short many a school career. Most women were barred from higher education until the later decades of the nineteenth century, and even then, only the richest or the luckiest could enter the few women's colleges that had been formed.

The Progressive Education Movement, which gathered momentum at the turn of the century, constituted a reaction to the failures of the "imposed" structured schools of the time.[2] It advocated reform in classroom methods and curriculum, hoping to make students more questioning, creative and actively involved in their own education. Philosopher John Dewey, a Progressive, cared less for rigid socialization than for individualism and personal growth. But the Progressive ideas, although generally successful in small private schools, found little acceptance in public education.

As immigration continued to increase, the size and scope of education grew rapidly. Schools had to train students for a new technological world that seemed to grow more complex each year. To accommodate its demands, the education system was forced to expand so quickly that it added to its qualities as an agent of socialization those of the bureaucratic enterprise, in touch with the needs of education. The net result of this rapid growth and change was that the quality of education improved in some respects for most Americans (except blacks); but, at the same time, education became so oriented towards technology and rigid systems of learning that students have grown more and more alienated and dissatisfied with the education provided them. By the 1960s, students and teachers alike claimed that public education had become dehumanizing as well as irrelevant, and demanded fundamental changes in the archaic system.

The goal of quality education for all has always been set before American society as one worth attaining, and steps have been taken over the years to involve all the children of the nation in the educational process. Yet, many voices in America protest that the education currently provided is not equal in quality. Equal access to quality education is the first of today's educational problems this chapter will consider.

In the early years of the country, the financing of a school was one of the first concerns of a new community; a school guaranteed civilization. Such fund-raising was often difficult. Despite the country's wealth, school financing remains a difficult problem today. We will examine a number of factors contributing to it.

The substance of the values and information set forth in America's schools has been forever subject to debate, though certain trends in curriculum and policy are clear. Debates of the 1920s concerned such matters as the teaching of the theory of evolution; today the subjects at issue have changed, and the larger question has been asked: what are schools for? Debate in recent years has grown into social conflict taking place within educational institutions themselves. Curriculum and educational policy is the third problem area with which this chapter is concerned.

Inequality in education

America's commitment to equal education for all its citizens has not changed in theory since the 1850s. But our society has changed greatly; advancing technology and industrialization have given rise to different educational needs, and even the idea of what constitutes education has changed drastically since the beginning of this century.

The most crucial test of this country's broad educational policy came in the 1954 Supreme Court decision that ruled racial segregation in public schools unconstitutional. The Court ordered all public schools desegregated "within a reasonable time limit," thus obliging the federal government to make certain that integration was achieved throughout the country.

The issue of equal access to integrated, quality education became a national one, which continues to be hotly debated today. The busing of children to distant schools—one of the most controversial methods of achieving integration—continues to arouse violent resistance in many quarters, which has slowed the process of integration, especially in the north.

Nonetheless, the 1954 decision has inexorably changed not only American education but society at large as well. The Court decision had been based on conclusive evidence that schooling for blacks was inferior to that for white children, that black schools were financially worse off than white schools, and that the future job opportunities of black and white children were therefore wholly unequal and unfair.

Inequities in other social areas soon became equally apparent to the nation; attention focused especially on inequalities in housing, employment practices, public transportation and public accommodation. Although education had always been regarded as the "great equalizer," black leaders such as Martin Luther King, Jr., doubted that educational equality alone would solve the problems of their people. Even if schools were completely desegregated, this would not, for example, automatically eliminate discriminatory employment practices; and equal schooling would be of little use without equal job opportunity to follow.

Does integration work?

Nearly 20 years after the historic decision, it is painfully evident that desegregation, in spirit and in fact, has so far been a largely unsuccessful process. Even more disturbingly, recent studies by researchers James S. Coleman,[3] Arthur Jensen,[4] Christopher Jencks,[5] and Daniel Moynihan and Frederick Mosteller,[6] all suggest (although the authors differ greatly in many ways) that equal schooling will not in itself insure subsequent equal occupational opportunity and income.

Through the late 1950s and up to 1966, most liberal educators had been convinced that if quality education were offered to everyone in our society, minorities would have equal chances to gain good employment and "a better life." The two basic premises involved in their theory were: (1) educational opportunities must be equal in terms of finances, facilities and faculties; and (2) integration must be sufficiently widespread to give all people access to these educational opportunities.

With these goals in mind, Congress passed the Civil Rights Act of 1964 as the foundation of President Johnson's "Great Society." The Act called for a report, within two years, "concerning the lack of availability of equal educational opportunities for individuals by reason of race, color, religion, or national origins in public educational institutions at all levels in the United States."[7] The resulting study, known now as the "Coleman Report,"[8] came as a shock to many leaders. On one hand, it reported that despite the 12-year-old Court decision, integration continued to be more an ideal than a reality;[9] but on the other, it challenged that ideal by documenting not the difference, but the *lack* of difference between black schools and white schools.

The report concludes that "American public education remains largely unequal in most regions of the country, including all those where Negroes form any significant proportion of the population."[10]

But there were other findings. Segregation was found to be the rule, not the exception.[11] Yet, contrary to popular opinion, the facilities, curricula, and most of the measurable characteristics of teachers in black and white schools were quite similar.[12] The differences in facilities, curricula and teacher quality had little effect on either black or white students' performance on standardized tests,[13] and the single characteristic that showed a consistent relationship to test performance was the one characteristic to which poor black children were denied access: classmates from affluent homes.[14]

In other words, Coleman concluded that schools did little to aid rapid social upward progress; it was family background, not education, which accounted for the huge discrepancy between the achievements of blacks and whites. Many social and educational reformers had been aware of this, but had believed that education would swing the pendulum towards a more equal social situation. The Coleman Report, which highlighted the insignificance of educational differences between blacks and whites, raised many issues and started new controversies. If education does not further social equality, why spend millions on improving the schools? If schools don't make a difference, what will? These questions have been left essentially unanswered, but the debate has increased.

Jencks's book, *Inequality,* which relies on the Coleman data, generally reaches roughly similar conclusions; he finds that schools are *unequal* in wealth and facilities, but neither of these factors matters when it comes to making money in life. There is just as much (or more) inequality outside school as in it. Jencks argues, "adequate school funding cannot, then, be justified on the grounds that it makes life better in the hereafter. But it can be justified on the grounds that it makes life better right now."[15] "Eliminating these differences [in the quality of schools] would not do much to make adults more equal, but it would do a great deal to make the quality of children's (and teacher's) lives more equal. Since children are in school for a fifth of their lives, this would be a significant accomplishment."[16] True "equal access," then, depends on how the issues of housing, busing, decentralization and financing are resolved.

Busing and integration

The implications of those findings are evident in the problems relative to integration which have emerged in recent years. Most southern school districts have complied, *de facto* and *de jure,* with the 1954 Court decision. In 1968, 68 percent of the South's blacks still were in 100 percent black schools, while only 18 percent attended schools that were predominately white. By 1971, only 9 percent of blacks went to all-black schools, and 44 percent were enrolled in predominantly white schools.[17] Yet the continuing *de facto* segregation of residential neighborhoods meant that school segregation persisted.

Figure 6–1   Distribution of black school enrollment in public elementary and secondary schools, 1971

	Total	Northern & Western States	Border States & Washington, D.C.	Southern States
Total students (in thousands)	44,692	29,300	3,840	11,552
Negro students (in thousands)	6,725	2,913	672	3,139
Percent Negro:				
Of total students	15	9.9	17.5	27.2
By minority group enrollment of schools				
Under 50 percent	35.6	27.8	30.5	43.9
80–100 percent	45.9	57.1	60.9	32.2
100 percent	11.6	11.2	24.2	9.2

With the black population migrations from the South to northern urban centers in the 1950s and 1960s, the makeup of many cities changed radically. By the hundreds of thousands, whites moved from the cities to the suburbs, while the blacks settled in the "inner-city," usually the oldest and most run-down section. This pattern repeated itself across the entire country; as a consequence, society now faces the problem of desegregating city school systems which have 40 to 60 percent black enrollment. In many ways, the solution seems to be more difficult now than it was twenty years ago. Since white parents have continued to resist integration by leaving the cities for generally more expensive (hence white) suburbs, the courts have ordered school districts desegregated by taking a whole region into account: city and suburbs are to be considered together, with busing of children the mode of achieving the desired result. In 1969 and 1971 decisions, the courts have called for "good faith compliance" to the desegregation law by ordering school boards to include whole metropolitan regions in their busing plans.[18]

The case for equalizing the distribution of schooling and cognitive skill derives not from the idea that we should maximize consumer satisfaction, but from the assumption that equalizing schooling and cognitive skill is necessary to equalize status and income. This puts egalitarians in the awkward position of trying to impose equality on people, even though the natural demand for both cognitive skill and schooling is very unequal.

Christopher Jencks

Some prominent metropolitan busing cases, are still unsettled. Court-ordered busing programs have proved largely unsuccessful, often because (as in the case of Detroit) the Board "created and maintained optional attendance zones in racially unstable areas which allowed whites to escape desegregation."[19] Major cases have been before Federal courts for more than two years, but little actual progress has been made. Prior to the 1972 Presidential election, national debate was so heated that President Nixon was able to push a bill through Congress stipulating that for eighteen months no court-ordered desegregation may be effected until all judicial appeals are exhausted.

Busing children within a large metropolitan district to achieve racial integration will continue to be a volatile issue for some time. Antibusing groups assert that busing is too costly, unsafe and time-consuming. They also continue to cling to the concept of the "neighborhood school" as a cornerstone of the community and are unlikely to relinquish this concept easily. The neighborhood school is part of the American community tradition. Losing that sense of community solidarity (even though in fact it was lost long ago when school districts became centralized) is a hard prospect to accept for those Americans who moved from the cities to the suburbs in order to find just that sense of community spirit. They want a neighborhood school. So, in fact, do many blacks who are opposed to busing.

Statistically, pro-busing arguments are more to the point. According to the Department of Transportation, out of the almost 19 million children—43.5 percent of the total public school population—who are transported to school daily, *less than 1 percent* are bused to achieve integration.[20] Thus, the busing problem is really a question of how deeply rooted our commitment to integration is, or how strongly we feel about our own community or neighborhood.

Education writer Gordon Foster notes: "Desegregation is not so much a technical as a political, education, and moral concern."[21] The experience of Central High in Little Rock, Arkansas, in 1957, George Wallace's "guarding" the door at Ole Miss in 1962, the boycotts and bombing of buses in Pontiac, Michigan, in 1971, all illustrate that desegregation is an issue so complex that it may take decades to resolve.

If full integration of class and race is to be achieved in the school systems, either the communities themselves must change and become more equal, or the idea of the neighborhood school must be abandoned as hopelessly out of date. Integration is a treasured principle for many people; but too few of them are actually willing to go through the steps necessary to achieve it in a manner that might really equalize education for all. Integration per se, as the social scientists note, is not synonymous with equality.

Financing education

One of the biggest problems facing public education today is finance. Public education at all levels is paid for by tax dollars, with most of the burden falling on the state and local communities. There is a widely held belief that if the Federal government plays too large a role in paying for education, it may also want to dictate what will be taught. So each state and local government must raise sufficient funds to pay for its schools. Because communities vary greatly in wealth, gross inequities in the quality of school facilities and programs have plagued American education.

States provide about 40 percent of all public school funding; 10 percent comes from the Federal government and the remaining 50 percent comes from local school districts and is almost wholly derived from property taxes.[22] In general, Federal aid is used primarily to assist states when gross deficiencies are apparent and cannot be eliminated through state or local revenues.

The richer states have an obvious advantage. The higher the per capita income, the greater the amount of money which can be spent on schools. For instance, the estimated public school expenditure for 1972 per pupil in New York was $1,466; in Arkansas it was $601.00.[23] Yet it is within each state that the most blatant inequalities exist. As the Fleischmann Report on the financing of education in New York State states: "It is unconscionable that a poor man in a poor district must often pay local taxes at higher rates for the inferior education of his child than the man of means in a rich district pays for the superior education of his child. Yet, incredibly, that is the situation today in most of the 50 states, and that is the case in New York."[24] While an attempt is made to distribute state aid fairly, the fact is that in most states, the districts that pay the highest property taxes get the most money. The following example illustrates the result. Two school districts on Long Island, N.Y., only 10 miles apart, vary greatly in revenue. Great Neck, a wealthy community with an enrollment of 9869, spends $2,077.52 on each of its students per year. Levittown, far less wealthy, with an enrollment of 17,280 students, spends only $1,189.37 per student each year. The state provides $764.48 per student per year in Levittown to supplement the expenditure per student of $410.31, and gives each Great Neck student $364.16 to supplement the much larger expenditure of $1,684.07 per pupil.[25] Thus the inequality will never be made up unless (1) the state gives far more money to the poorer community, or (2) the property tax revenue-raising system is thoroughly overhauled.

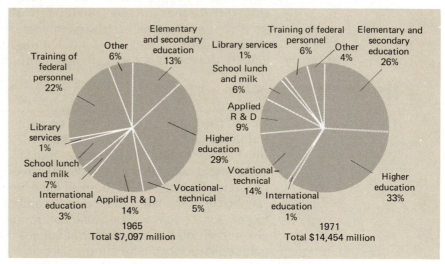

Figure 6–2   Federal outlays for education for the years 1965 and 1971

Differences between cities and suburbs are even more striking. While rich suburbs are able to build sprawling facilities complete with the newest educational aids, city schools are generally decaying. Since the white migration to the suburbs during the 1950s and 1960s was followed by the migration of corporations, the tax base of most urban centers fell enormously. Again, the suburbs gained while the cities, where money is most urgently needed for new buildings and programs, lost. Attempts to change this situation have met with mixed results. In a landmark case, the California Supreme Court recently ruled that the state's system of public school finance (property taxes) "denies children the equal protection guaranteed under the Fourteenth Amendment, because it produces substantial disparities among school districts in the amount of revenue available for education."[26] The ruling is applicable only in California, but it set the stage for further litigation. In a 1973 case involving Texas schools similar to the California one, however, the United States Supreme Court ruled that education is *not* one of the rights guaranteed by the United States Constitution, thus declining to interfere with the state's use of property taxes for education. The case was momentous because had the Court ruled education to be a right, nearly all of the nations's $50 billion structure of public school finance would have had to be changed.[27] The California decision still holds for that state, but the only avenue now open to overhaul the system is through each state's highest court.

Clearly, this problem must be solved before the issue of equal access can be decided. In view of the discrepancies in facilities, teachers' pay and physical plants, "quality" public education for all is still only a myth. Since the Federal government continues to be reluctant to increase its role in funding, the responsibility falls on the states to legislate new ways to apportion funds in a more equal manner. Either state aid for poor school districts will have to increase, or, more radically, each state may have to take full control of educational revenues in order to guarantee equality in distribution.

The financial problems of colleges and universities are of a different nature. In public universities, Federal and state funds supply most of the money for operating costs, while private grants finance specific projects. The 1950s and 1960s saw an increasing emphasis on technological and scientific research and development, due mainly to government fears that the Soviet Union might outstrip us in those fields. Growth and financial outlay were enormous. In 1957, expenditures for all institutions of higher education in the United States were 4.9 billion; by 1967, they had risen to $18.3 billion.[28] Much of this increase was due to the necessity of training scientists and technicians, and also to the enormous costs of new hardware such as lasers and computers.

The outflow of government monies to higher education began to decrease during the Vietnam War, and slowed even further during the recession that began in 1970. Research grants were cut drastically, and even though Congress has passed Education Apportionment bills, President Nixon has vetoed them as "inflationary." In 1969, the government granted $239 million for research purposes; by 1972, the figure had dropped to $166 million.[29]

Public institutions will survive these cutbacks because state monies will continue to underwrite operating expenses. Although universities desperately need Federal funds for programs that are too expensive for the state to maintain, they can still offer adequate educational programs, even at the graduate level, despite the loss of revenues.

The situation for private colleges is very different, because these institutions depend entirely on private donors and on grants from foundations and the government. Having grown in response to government outlays, many private institutions have recently found themselves overextended because government aid has been withdrawn. Only a few top colleges and universities have stable endowment funds that generate money through interest accumulation and stock market growth; most of the rest are running on a one-to three-year cash supply.

Private institutions have always been more costly for students than state colleges. Even though operating costs are roughly the same, private colleges must necessarily rely far more on tuition monies than the state-supported schools. In 1958, the average tuition for full-time students in private colleges was $729 per year; in state colleges the average was $192. By 1968, tuition in private colleges had increased by 97 percent, to $1,436, while that of state institutions rose 55 percent to $298 per year.[30] Unless private universities continue to raise tuition each year (thus pricing themselves out of the reach of many able students) or receive aid from foundations or the government, many will be forced to shut down in this decade.

Teaching and teachers

For a variety of reasons, the cost of education has skyrocketed since World War II. Building costs have soared, and expenditures for facilities such as language labs, audiovisual equipment, scientific equipment and sophisticated machinery like computers mount each year into the billions of dollars.

During the past few decades, many Americans believed that our sophisticated technology could solve any problem, including how to teach children. More and more, emphasis was placed on gadgets rather than on people. The dehumanizing consequences of this concept were a prime cause of the student rebellions of the 1960s. They demanded teaching relevant to present-day social conditions, teaching they felt neither machines nor the personnel on college and high school faculties could provide.

In America, teachers in the public schools and in most universities, though they perform an important social function, have never had very high social status. Although they are considered professionals, teachers earn much less than doctors or lawyers. In 1972, the average salary for a public school teacher in Arkansas was $7,021; in New York, one of the best paying states, the average was $11,404. In Arkansas, only 1.3 percent of teachers earned over $11,500; in New York, 43.5 percent earned over this figure.[31] Teachers' low salaries are often justified by reason of their long vacations; but even when this factor is taken into account, their remuneration is low in comparison with other occupations despite the amount of training they must undergo.

Wage inequity was even worse a decade ago,[32] when teachers were given a salary by their board of education and had no power to bargain for higher pay. But in the last ten years, teacher unions, both state and municipal, have taken a much firmer stance during contract talks. Twenty years ago a teacher's strike would have been unthinkable. But during the past ten years, almost every large American city has experienced a teachers' strike, even though such strikes are illegal under most state laws. And on the whole, teachers' demands for more equitable wages and working conditions have been met by their local districts. They are beginning to feel, and act, like professionals. Their unions, once ineffective and docile, are now powerful tools in the collective bargaining process.

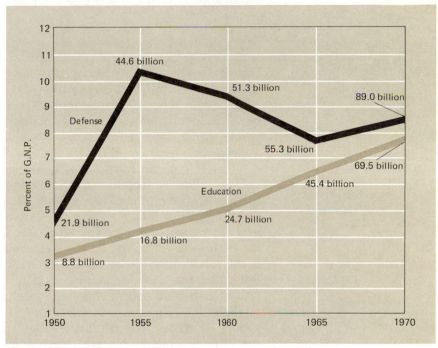

Figure 6-3 Federal government expenditures for defense and education compared in billions of dollars: 1950–1970

Until the escalation of the Vietnam War drove many young men into teaching in order to get deferments from the draft, America suffered from a chronic teacher shortage, mainly in elementary and secondary schools. Traditionally, the younger grades have been the woman's domain, and few men taught in the elementary schools. But with the shift in society's values towards more equality in all areas, more and more men have entered the elementary schools to teach, and more women have been admitted to college and university faculties. The old stereotypes about teachers are beginning to fade away, and the man who teaches first grade is not as hesitant to say so as he might have been ten years ago.

Yet many problems remain. Urban teachers are affected by violence in the schools. Boards, administrations and many teachers themselves are notoriously rigid in their methods and objectives, with an aversion to change.

Teachers will continue to press for higher salaries in the future, and suburban schools, with their greater financial resources, will be able to meet teacher demands. But urban centers will be hard-pressed to compete, unless revenues are increased considerably. Urban teachers face many problems in the classroom, and unless city governments can come up with the cash to pay higher wages, they will have little incentive to subject themselves to these problems. Even if they do, neither conditions nor sentiments are likely to alter the fairly authoritarian approach of the profession's majority.

Curriculum and educational policy

During the twentieth century, the scope of education has grown tremendously, and its diversity today is reflected in the curriculum of nearly every school and university. The frontiers of knowledge have been expanded in many areas of the sciences and social sciences. The whole world is open for study. Yet students continually complain about a dull, boring and irrelevant school experience.

What is missing from the school curriculum at all levels? Who decides what is important, and how much say should students themselves have in deciding what to study?

Until fairly recently, education was controlled by a relatively few administrators who were therefore also instrumental in determining the purpose of schooling. There was also a reasonably firm consensus in the values most parents wished the schools to teach their children. But during the 1960s, curriculum and authority in the schools became issues for heated debate. Minority groups called for more emphasis on their own concerns in the classroom, from elementary to graduate school. High school students questioned the value of their studies and the heavy emphasis placed on attending college. And all over the country college students were rebelling, challenging administrations and faculty, demanding reforms in curriculum, admissions and broad educational policy. The response of many educators and reformers is summed up by Charles Silberman in his introduction to *Crisis in the Classroom:* "Our bias, it should be emphasized, was not that everything that was being done was necessarily wrong; it was simply that everything now being done needs to be questioned."[33]

Elementary schools

Learning basic skills is important, of course, but getting along with others, being friendly and succeeding, have always been primary goals of the American educational system. Hence, emphasis on socialization is the core of elementary education in America.

But all along, reformers have been saying that this focus is wrong.

Important questions lie at the heart of the long-standing controversy between authoritarian and progressive educators: Should schools experiment and change, and try to change society? Or are they merely vehicles for providing society with its necessary workforce, making experimentation and learning for its own sake irrelevant? Should we teach children what society wants them to learn, or should we teach them to think for themselves?

Reformers have always called for more freedom of choice in elementary education. They believed that a happy child who has learned to think for himself will benefit society far more than one who has been force-fed facts and pushed into the "real world" without ever learning how to think. Philip Brenner puts the argument this way:

> In an authoritarian school, children learn submissiveness as well as mathematics if they are to "succeed." In most schools they learn to direct their energies to future goals—"It will be useful some day, you'll see." They learn that the world is made up of right answers, and that those in authority always have the right answers. They learn that they can be reduced to a quantified equivalent, to a graded profile, and that this is the way to judge people. Finally, they learn to ignore their intuition and real feelings, and to replace them with strategies of "faking"—in [John] Holt's terms—in order to receive acceptance and approval.[34]

Progressive educators stress the factors that authoritarians ignore: their emphasis is on the needs of the individual child, rather than on adherence to a rigid curriculum; they favor the development of creative, questioning minds, rather than obedient, dull ones, that are content to accept the answers provided by others.

Many students, especially those who are poor, intuitively know what the schools do for them. They school them to confuse process and substance. Once these become blurred, a new logic is assumed: the more treatment there is, the better are the results; or, escalation leads to success. The pupil is thereby "schooled" to confuse teacher with learning, grade advancement with education, a diploma with competence, and fluency with the ability to say something new.

Ivan Illich

Critics of public elementary education in the 1960s suggested new alternatives to the structured or teacher-oriented classroom. "Open classrooms" were debated; the teacher was to become a "resource person" who offered the children many activities from which to choose. The British system, whose open corridors and classrooms have worked very well, was studied by thousands of American educators eager to institute it at home.

A number of young teacher-writers launched attacks on the United States educational system in other areas. Jonathan Kozol's *Death at an Early Age*[35] documents the harm done to children by repressive, overly bureaucratic systems. John Holt's major thesis is basically that the schools are ruining children by teaching the wrong values, overemphasizing trivia and not giving a freer rein to a child's innate potential for expression.[36] Herbert Kohl, in *Thirty-Six Children*,[37] claims that the educational needs of blacks and other minorities are not being met by the standard curriculum.

For black children deprived of equal status in America *because* they are black, education in exclusively "white" values, "white" history and "white" views of America is clearly psychologically damaging. It is only in recent years that the civil rights movement, broad educational reforms and enlightened thinking by a few educators have brought about some improvement in the education of minority groups. By 1969, bilingual education programs had been initiated in seventy-six school districts for children who spoke little or no English.[38] Black studies have become a part of many curricula, and other minorities are increasingly active in getting school districts to implement courses focused on different ethnic cultures. The habit of American education—to force the culture of the majority on everyone—has slowly begun to change.

Thus, in elementary education, the focus is slowly shifting from the controlled, teacher-dominated classroom to a more open, diversified setting where children will be allowed to question more, to explore their individual interests and to learn at their own pace. Most public schools are still years from the realization of that goal, but the change in thinking and values is becoming more and more evident.

reading: Gerry Rosenfeld
LEARNING NOT TO LEARN

If one examined the average school day at Harlem School he would discover various educational procedures that are found in other schools. Some approaches seemed standard, even immutable. Yet, the implications of these procedures for learning were not as readily perceived. It seemed to me that the very format for the instructional sequence followed each day encouraged children to see subject presentation as tenuous and tentative. The children saw no connecting link among the fragments of material offered them. Rarely was a child permitted to bring his involvement in subject matter to an extensive probing. His passions were not brought to bear in any meaningful engagement in the content of learning. This can be illustrated by drawing out the events on an average school day.

Children flock to school each morning and line up outside the gates. They get to their classrooms shortly thereafter and become incorporated in the routines prescribed for them. Various norms, sometimes unstated, govern their actions. For example, it is not expected, not permitted, that a child be immediately allowed to go to the bathroom upon arrival in the morning. Similarly school culture prescribed that when a boy has gone to the bathroom during the day, only a girl may go next—as if this were to "preserve democracy" in the classroom. These procedures are not seen as mysteries by teachers or children; they are carried out as "natural" and normal events. Thus, it seems altogether proper that reading and writing lessons predominate as these are seen as requirements for effective later participation in a literate culture.

Customarily the teacher attempts to capture the collective imagination of the children at the outset of each day with a group assignment—penmanship, let us say. While the children practice their letters, they are summoned in groups for reading. The groups may be given names to distinguish reading achievement levels and to help children derive a sense of common membership with others in the group. One teacher at Harlem School named the three reading groups in her class the "Sharks," the "Barracudas," and the "Flounders." These were, of course, allegorical for the "Bright," the "Average," and the "Dull." The children interpreted the meaning of these labels quite easily, just as they had been able to understand the meaning of footprints on the binding books. Even the "Dull" knew they were so perceived, and so refused to read as an objection to their designation, often complaining, "We never get any interesting stories to read."

As each group is brought forth, a child may complain that he has not yet finished his penmanship assignment. The teacher, however, insists he join the group. During the reading this same child might not be called upon nor get actively involved over the proceedings. It may not be "his turn" to read on this day, leaving him with only a peripheral interest in what is going on. Soon thereafter he and his classmates might be involved in a continuing variety of subject explorations, including arithmetic, social studies, art, science, music, and more. None of those is ever brought to completion, but is postponed until that subject time is rescheduled.

Mixed in with these wanderings may be an unplanned itinerary that would include messages from the school office, a dispute over a pencil, the collection of milk and cookie money, even an occasional fire drill. At other times during a day there are an assembly period, a gym period, recess, and so on. These repeated partial excursions into the nature of subject matter render the child only partially aware and almost wholly uncommitted to that subject matter. It is as if he is being told that the bits of learning he is presented with are after all only temporary, and that he must be ready to relinquish his accruing insights at any given time in order to go on to other involvements. He learns in this way to "play it cool," knowing that his feeling for his subjects cannot be intense or lasting.

This appraisal may be denied by some, but at Harlem School the proof of it was evident, just as it is evident in the junior and senior high school where the fragmenting of learning is built into a format of brief fifty-minute periods for the various subjects. The constant clanging of bells punctuates the day to reassert this arrangement. In college, continuing this accepted pattern, students and subject material become even more anonymous in oversize classes, where a student's grades often become the only proof of his existence. What made Harlem School a bit more unique was that these practices—and children's subsequent underachievement—were given a mythical rationale. Teachers had a common agreement that "those" children had to be presented with material in short bursts, as it were, because they "couldn't concentrate for long." It occured to me, however, that the children's concentration was obviously shortened by the very procedures employed in teaching them. A commitment to subject content was not built up, but denied. "Lack of readiness," as it was alleged in behalf of children, was really a lack of readiness among teachers. A child could not extensively pursue a topic to a satisfactory conclusion, perhaps because teacher's own knowledge of the topic was limited. Elementary school teachers are generalists who usually do not have a particular subject specialty for which they have prepared in formal training. They may indeed be jack-all-trades, master of none.

When such procedures prevail, one's success with children cannot be measured by the children's internalizations of knowledge or their personal investments in content fields, for these do not occur. Instead, children are evaluated and estimated for their worth on a behavioral basis. That is why discipline is so important in the slum school. One can excuse his ignorance of subject matter by translating this ignorance into some alleged dysfunction in children's conduct. I learned soon enough that the administrators at Harlem School would more likely evaluate my own teaching efforts, not by what children learned, but by my bulletin board display, my disciplinary techniques, or the class play we performed in the assembly during the year.

An example of this kind of thinking came at the end of my second year at Harlem School. None of the children in my "average" fifth-grade class read at grade level; some of the children began the year reading at second- and third-grade reading levels. I had worked very hard with two children in particular, Ronald and Charlene, to bring them close to grade level. I felt myself successful with them at the end of the school year, though they had attained only fourth-grade reading level. They had begun the year reading just beyond the primer stage. This represented to me a distinct effort and capability on the part of the two children, and I was confident that they would subsequently reach expected attainment standards. Thus, I was very surprised when Mr. Green told me that Ronald and Charlene would not be promoted. When I asked why this had to be, I was told that it was undesirable to pass children on to the next grade if they were two years behind in reading. I protested that the work of Ronald and Charlene was satisfactory in other subject areas and that they had shown deliberate improvement in reading as well. It would be punishing them, I submitted, for their hard work and effort, and it would be penalizing me for the investment I made in their potential and demonstrated desire to improve. My arguments were fruitless. There was an established pattern at Harlem School: records counted more than feelings. If children were disappointed, one could understand why. They often lost conviction in their own desires and abilities and learned not to try too hard so that they would not be repeatedly denied in their efforts. If you are going to fail, you may as well not try hard to succeed.

In another effort to help Ronald and Charlene I was again overruled. I had learned who the children's teachers would be the next year after placements had already been made. It was customary to do it this way at Harlem School. When children were placed in new classes, it was not with any specific thought in mind that certain teachers can work better with certain children. In this instance I thought that Ronald would do better with Charlene's teacher and that Charlene would fare better with Ronald's assigned teacher. I spoke to the two teachers in question, and they agreed that we should switch the children for the next year. I told Mr. Green of the agreement and formally requested the change. Mr. Green told me it would be "too much trouble" to switch them because rosters had already been made out. When I pleaded on the basis of sound educational principle he told me, "You can switch a boy for a boy, or a girl for a girl, but never a boy for a girl."

I was stunned by this. He saw the children as statistics, not people. His explanation was that too much clerical revision would be necessitated. For example, if there were seventeen boys and fourteen girls in a class, the roster would read "17 + 14," One could switch a girl from another class in place of a girl and the roster would still indicate "17 + 14"; but if a girl were switched for the removal of a boy, the roster would have to read "16 + 15". The administrative upheaval would be too great. This is indeed hard to believe, but this is how the situation ended.

From
Shut Those Thick Lips by Gerry Rosenfeld
(New York: Holt, Rinehart, Winston, Inc., 1971) pp. 39-42

Secondary education

The American high school student, too old to be treated as a child, yet too young to be given full responsibility for his life, is caught in a dilemma. For the most part, the secondary schools do not resolve it; in fact, high school is often the most painful part of a young person's education. As Silberman states, "Because adolescents are harder to 'control' than younger children, secondary schools tend to be even more authoritarian and repressive than elementary schools; the values they transmit are the values of docility, passivity, conformity, and lack of trust."[39]

Perhaps because of this, during the 1960s, student restlessness filtered down from colleges, and some high schools became as frenetic as the stormiest campus; and because the high school system was so much less open to change, the damage was more apparent. Dress codes and length of hair became important issues; drugs among high school students became a national problem; grades, rules, college entrance exams—all became targets for student revolt. Efforts to update curriculum and school procedures often took the form of investment in more technological means to accomplish a discredited task, rather than reexamination of the purposes of secondary education. What millions of students and a notable number of parents and teachers wanted was a whole new way of looking at the school's role in society and at its responsibility to provide usable education. Many educators agreed, as Silberman says:

> That it is not just the curriculum that will have to change [if schools are to improve], but the entire way in which high schools are organized and run. Students at present are hardly permitted, let alone encouraged, to confront either their teachers or themselves. They are given little opportunity, and no reason, to develop resolute ideas of their own about what they should learn, and in most schools they are actively discouraged from trying to test those ideas against their teachers'.[40]

In his book, *Inside High School,* Philip A. Cusick lists nine important sociocultural characteristics of the school which, taken together, provide a good overview of the repressive nature of secondary education:

1. Subject matter specialization

2. Vertical organization

3. Doctrine of adolescent inferiority

4. Downward communication flow

5. Batch processing of students

6. Routinization of activity

7. Dependence on rules and regulations

8. Future-reward orientation

Cusick found that these structures and attitudes prevail in most American high schools, whether urban ghetto or middle-class suburban.

Nor is the problem confined to the issue of choice in curriculum. The quality of teaching itself is often so bad that little could be accomplished even with the best curriculum. Trained in bureaucratic systems, most teachers, until recently, have seen little advantage in disrupting the institutions that support them by encouraging innovation in subject matter or teaching technique. According to numerous observers, classes are boring and deadening.[42]

In the majority of school systems, curriculum plans are forced upon each school in the system. The city of Minneapolis, for example, has eleven high schools. Curriculum and policy for all are decided by the Board of Education, although each school does have a certain degree of latitude in deciding what will or will not be studied in each class. The teachers, however, are given little choice in the matter. They may make suggestions, but the power of decision rests almost entirely with the board. Much the same situation prevails throughout the country: a relatively small group of educators and administrators makes all decisions concerning what students are required to learn.

A great deal of the energies and monies of school districts throughout the country have gone into building expenditures rather than into improving the human environment. Since students spend so much time in schools, a comfortable and attractive environment is important, yet new buildings alone have not been able to provide it. Clearly, upgrading the condition, values and spirit of education itself must occur if secondary education is to have any positive effect on students' lives.

reading: **Philip A. Cusick**
FRIENDS AT HIGH SCHOOL

In sum, the students' active and interested involvement centered not around teacher-initiated, academic issues or even around the issues that were nationally centered. Instead, they concerned themselves with the procedures of fulfilling institutional demands, the cafeteria food, and their private in-group interactions. In general, what they did in school they did with their friends. For instance, if in class a teacher asked them to divide into groups and discuss some matter, they scurried around and found their good friends with whom they talked not about anything academic, but about their out-of-school activities.

Of course this made it extremely important for students to have friends. In fact, it may have been the single most important thing in school. To not have friends was to have no one to be with in the corridors and classrooms, no one to walk with to class, or to carry on with before, after, and even during class, no one to eat with. The students spoke easily of this phenomenon. As Ken said, "When I didn't have any friends, I hated this place so much I couldn't stand to come." or Dick, "In school we groove with our friends, that is, those who have friends, and most kids do." Or Pete, "You can't go to high school without friends."

After discovering this it became necessary that I begin to examine more closely the students' friendship patterns. If that is what they spent their school time doing, then that was my topic. And upon examination it became apparent that those friendship patterns were rigidly divided. One just did not hang around with anyone, or go to class with anyone, or eat with anyone. He talked to, walked with, ate with, and spent as much time as possible with his few friends and literally did not pay attention to those who were not in his group.

Therefore, the class was not simply an undifferentiated mass of students, but was a series of dyads, tryads, cliques and groups. In fact, one did not even see those with whom he did not directly associate. That may sound odd to teachers who are used to thinking of students in terms of batches of not less than twenty or thirty, but it was strongly substantiated every day. If I were talking to a member of one small group and a friend of mine who was in another group approached, I might find myself in two isolated conversations since the two students would not even recognize each other's presence. In the cafeteria it was particularly noticeable. In fact, the rush to the cafeteria at noon was probably more to assure one a seat at the proper table with one's friends than it was to satisfy hunger. If one did not sit with his friends, he literally sat alone. Once when I was with Jean she mentioned that, "The worst thing that can happen is that you have to walk around the halls alone."

"What about the cafeteria?"

"Oh, that's even worse. Kids would rather not eat than eat alone."

Thereafter I frequently asked informants, "Which would you rather do, flunk a test or eat alone in the cafeteria?"

Invariably the answer was, "Flunk a test!"

I asked one of the athletes, Greg, about associating with those not in his group. The thought did not make any sense to him. "You know like if you came here and didn't hang around with us, I wouldn't even know you."

Apparently the teachers did not see this. When asked, some admitted that the students hung around, but they thought of students in terms of [groups]. Or sometimes they spoke of the academics and the locals, or those who were and those who were not active in extracurricular activities. Neither the teachers nor the administrators saw the class as a series of rigidly differentiated friendships. This is understandable, of course, since the teachers have their own interests.

There was an important question about those who apparently did not have any friends. One person in particular was a boy named Nick who would frequently stand around the student lounge by himself. In the first few minutes I knew him, he volunteered, "You probably noticed that I'm not too popular. I don't have many friends."

Of Nick and others like him, Bill said, "Them, they're just standing around leaning against the wall. They're out of it." Which, as far as I could see, was a good description of what Nick did. I occasionally asked others about students who had no friends and would mention Nick as an example. Although he had been in the class for years they would say, "Who? Who do you mean?" They did not even see him, and I found that as I became closer to the membership of one particular group, I, too, stopped seeing Nick.

From
Inside High School By Philip A. Cusick
(New York: Holt, Rinehart, Winson, Inc., 1972) pp. 64-68.

Colleges, universities and graduate schools

American colleges and universities are not often referred to as "finishing schools" (a term associated with fancy girls' schools); yet in some ways they serve a similar function. First, those who make it through the higher education system are generally thought of (and treated) as being ready to take on life in the "real world." The degree grants a certain amount of respect. Conversely, those without a college education are treated with less respect professionally and are almost always relegated to a lower social and economic status.

The departmentalized and specialized college curriculum has a great deal to do with the "finishing school" image. During the 1960s, this structure came under attack from students and faculty alike. The impersonal "multiversity" or "human factory" became the target of bitter criticism. Too often, students found themselves locked into the rigid structure of their "major," without a chance to study other areas of interest. The "scientific" approach to education had clearly preempted other possibilities even in the humanities courses. Frustrated and disenchanted, thousands of students rebelled or dropped out.

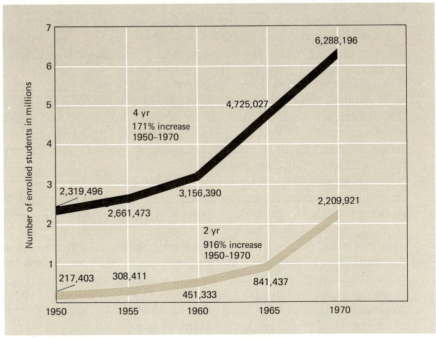

Figure 6–4   Enrollment in two-year and four-year institutions of higher education: 1950 and 1970

The colleges and universities were caught in a dilemma. After the Russian Sputnik launching of 1957, most universities had enlarged and improved their scientific and technological departments at a fast pace. America, it was felt, must never be caught offguard again, and the universities were given the responsibility of insuring our scientific and technological preeminence. The growing complexity of technological hardware demanded more and more highly trained people to operate, improve and invent still more complex machinery. A graduate degree became almost mandatory for getting a good job. Technology was seen as the key to the future; the humanities and the arts took second place.

The student revolt

Many events led to the alienation and ultimate rebellion of students during the last decade. Inspired by the civil rights movement, students by the thousands began to join forces and make their opinions known. The "Silent Generation" of the 50s gave way to the social and political activists of the 60s.

The first major disruption occurred in 1964 at Berkeley, where the Free Speech Movement pitted students against the bureaucratic administration in open confrontation. Students demanded the right to recruit members for political causes and to raise money on campus. When the administration refused permission, the first major student strike began.

As the Vietnam War escalated under the Johnson Administration, student protest became louder and more vociferous. Several campuses were disrupted when producers of war chemicals and the Armed Forces sent recruiters to interview students. The draft issue affected most college-age young men, and campuses became a natural center for resistance. ROTC, the college training program for military officers, became an important symbol for protestors, and many colleges discontinued or modified the program in the face of possible shutdowns.

By 1968, a number of campuses across the country were in a state of near-siege. Students were being joined by prominent public officials in their denunciation of the war and its ill-effects on American society. Students for a Democratic Society, a radical group that showed its power briefly towards the end of the decade, shut down Columbia University in April, 1968. With cries of "racism," "complicity in the war" (through contracts with the Defense Department) and "an unmoving unsympathetic bureaucracy," Columbia and several other colleges were struck by large numbers of students and faculty. It was not just a strike, the organizers asserted, it was a revolution.

In a decade's time, many students had moved from silence to bitter protest. Society was changing rapidly, and all during the 1960s, college students contributed greatly to the change. Anthony Mullaney wrote in 1970:

It is not strange that students demand an education which is more relevant to their values, that they abhor war as an instrument of national policy, that they identify with oppressed peoples, that they are communitarian and anti-authoritarian. These qualities, together with the beginning attempts to work out their implications in choice of life-style and in choice of careers, disprove the claim frequently voiced by officialdom that students want only to tear down—that they provide no alternatives, nothing positive. Students are filled with more anguish than rage.[43]

The current counterculture of college youth also demands a more flexible structure, but in a less rebellious fashion. Emphasis on future occupation and orientation towards technological fields still forms a large part of the college curriculum; but the upheavals of the 1960s have convinced administrators of the need for flexibility, and their more liberal orientation is already being reflected in curriculum changes and newly defined goals of higher education.

Moves toward equal access

The problem of equal access to quality education will be with us for some time to come, but some improvement in the situation can already be noted. Education and employment opportunities for minorities have risen sharply during the past decade. Much still remains to be done to wipe out discrimination, but as long as the majority of the population remains aware of the need, progress will continue. Since education in America is almost synonymous with the concept of social mobility, the issue of equal access will have to be resolved in the schools first.

The precise effects of equal access to quality education on students are too nebulous to measure today, but Christopher Jencks and David Riesman offer an interesting analogy:

> How much of the difference between the uneducated and the educated should be attributed directly to school experiences and how much to external factors such as upbringing, intelligence, personality? A good portion of the apparent impact of schooling is, we would suggest, anticipatory socialization. Sending a child to school may be like telling him he has a rich maiden aunt and will eventually inherit a fortune. The aunt and her money have no direct effect on the child's life or growth. But the idea of the money—even if it is nonexistent—may have a considerable effect, for the child may feel he has special opportunities and responsibilities. So, too, with schooling. What actually happens from day to day in a school or college may have relatively little effect on the students—though it certainly has some effect. But a good student's knowledge that he can go to college, and that a college degree will be a passport to a good job and a comfortable standard of living, may have a significant effect on him. He is more likely to adopt the attitudes and acquire the skill he thinks he will need in the world he expects to enter.[44]

Thus, equal access to education is the beginning of a long-term, difficult social reordering, as well as an end in itself.

In the elementary and secondary grades, busing is likely to continue to be the main method of achieving integration and equal access. Recent court cases attest to government commitment to integration. In June, 1973, the Supreme Court ruled that the Denver School Board discriminated against black children by gerrymandering them into a few schools. The Court's decision clearly stated that within city boundaries, the school board must begin to bus more extensively to combat segregation. But the real question—busing within a whole metropolitan area, city and suburbs alike—has yet to be decided. In May, 1973, the Court tied 4-4 on the issue of metropolitan busing in Richmond, Virginia, thus upholding a lower court decision against that busing plan. How the Court will vote on subsequent cases is unknown, but many observers feel that the present Court may move away from the strong stand against discrimination taken by the Warren Court.

Equal access at the college level has always been another matter. Colleges pick and choose on merit or talent, test scores and a host of other criteria. Higher education has traditionally been reserved for the elite or most able. But changes are occurring here, too.

The Open Admissions Policy in New York City and California substantially increases the chances of poor black or white students to attend college. New York City's program, instituted in 1970, has been heatedly debated. Enrollment in the City University of New York swelled enormously after Open Admissions was instituted. The first year's dropout rate was 36 percent, which was very high for CUNY, but about average for the country. Everyone seemed to have trouble adjusting to the new program, and many of the problems are not resolved; but real changes in attitude have taken place. According to the Fleishmann report open admissions lifted morale in the high schools whose failures made the program necessary. At Benjamin Franklin High School in East Harlem, only 10 percent of the seniors bothered to apply to CUNY at first and only 1 percent were accepted. As the students discovered that they stood a real chance of getting to college, 76 percent applied.[45]

Reforms in educational financing

Reducing the inequities in educational funding throughout each state will have to be the goal if opportunities for children are to be equalized. Since the Supreme Court has ruled that each state must find its own method of dealing with the financial problem, revision of existing laws will undoubtedly become necessary.

The Fleischmann Report offers two alternative means of financing education as feasible for New York State, which are, generally speaking, applicable to other states as well. The first involves a statewide uniform-rate property tax earmarked for the financing of education. The authors of the report suggest that if this type of reform is decided on by the state, it should be undertaken as a gradual movement over a five-year period. This seems like an equitable way of beginning to solve the problem.

The second alternative concerns the role of existing nonproperty taxes in education finance. "By nonproperty taxes we mean existing state taxes on personal income, corporate net and gross income, retail sales tax, unincorporated business tax and miscellaneous state taxes."[46] These revenues, which are not usually allocated for education, could substantially improve equality in all school districts if they could be used throughout the state.

Both of these systems make sense, but there is opposition from many quarters. Many critics claim that statewide distribution of funds would considerably decrease local control. However, it is not inevitable that state control of funding interfere with local control of policymaking. In fact, states generally desire to have communities control their own schools.

Along with revenue revision, some states are also trying to simplify and streamline the bureaucracy of public education. By decentralizing large school systems into smaller autonomous districts, it is hoped that local action in the schools will increase and communities will take more responsibility for the direction of their schools. Thus, each small district will be able to have control over curriculum, teachers and administrators. The decentralization plan in New York City, although still in need of much work, enables Harlem to adopt one set of curricula and policy for its schools, while the Chinatown area can decide on other routes to improve education. The future of decentralized systems is not clear; but they constitute an attempt to give the schools "back to the people," and should be given a chance to prove their worth.

Educational vouchers

A much-discussed alternative to local property tax funding of public schools is the educational voucher idea. Very simply, this concept would enable parents to choose a school they liked for their child, and "pay" for enrollment with a state tax voucher. The parent would not actually pay for the education vouchers because state taxes would supply the revenues. The voucher system could therefore equalize opportunities for all children in public and private schools.

But there are many problems. Advocates claim that the voucher system would have to be highly regulated, to avoid discrimination and inequality. Yet others want the system wide open to encourage maximum variety of educational alternatives.[47] Still others maintain that low-income children should receive more money credit.

Opposition to the voucher concept is presently widespread. The public school community as a whole is opposed to the idea, as are numerous other groups. They want funding to remain the same as it is now, primarily because any radical change in the system would directly affect the public school community's control over education expenditures and policy.

Three voucher plans have been put into effect in the last year with Federal assistance from the Office of Economic Opportunity (OEO is in favor of the concept and so is the Nixon Administration). In June, 1973, the reports from Alum Rock, California, one of the experimental sites, were mixed but generally favorable. In that district, all children received vouchers and could choose from a variety of schools—some traditional, some innovative. Parents reported that they liked having the choice, but the majority still chose the school closest to home. The experiment will run from five to eight years, so it is far too early to draw any definite conclusions.

One of the main issues in the debate over vouchers is whether both public and private schools are to be included in the plan. If all community schools are involved, the greatest possible choices would be available to parents and children. However, numerous legal complications would have to be overcome before a communitywide voucher system could be permanently accepted.

Changes in curriculum

The 1960s were a troubled time in American education. Amid the general chaos, however, many people were undertaking experiments and trying out projects designed to reform or revolutionize the existing system.

At the preschool level, Head Start programs (started in 1965 during the Johnson Administration) have aroused mixed reactions from observers. But most people who have worked with the program feel that it has improved socialization, as well as reading level scores, for the participating children, without requiring such strict adherence to the norms of society at large to dampen individual cultural initiative.[48]

At the elementary level, many school systems experimented successfully with "open classrooms." The open classroom, however, is not easy to achieve; teachers are required to rethink their roles completely, and many older teachers react negatively to relinquishing the control they have in the traditional teacher-oriented class.

At the high school level, the 60s saw the opening of "free" or "street" schools in several urban areas. Students, teachers and parents, disenchanted with the public school system, broke away and formed their own schools. These "free" schools are generally progressive, open-minded and experimental in both curriculum and structure.[49] Many "street" schools have sprung up in ghetto areas in an attempt to provide a relevant education for blacks who had dropped out of public schools. With foundation grants and free teaching help, they offer the best chance for advancement for many minority youths without other access to an education.

Some changes have also taken place within the public high schools. Minority studies programs are now standard in most urban areas, bilingual classes are more prevalent, classes in sex education, drug education and vocational training are more widely available than they were a decade ago. In most high schools, both the curriculum and grading systems have become more flexible. The usual A to F grading system is being modified in many communities to a more moderate "pass-fail" system designed to take much of the intense competition out of the classroom.[50] Grades have come under massive attack by reformers and pupils, because too often the grade in a course is made more important than the learning experience. By making marks less crucial, it is hoped that emphasis in education will turn more towards learning and exploring.

Curriculum alternatives have become more realistic in other areas as well. High school systems are now offering more useful courses for non-college-oriented students. Instead of a curriculum geared entirely toward preparation for college, technical and vocational classes are available for students who will seek employment after high school.

At the college and graduate levels, students have gained a voice in many programs and activities that directly affect them. There seems to be a more open climate on campuses today; curriculum remains in the control of the faculty and administration, but here, too, student demands for a loosening of the structure in their major study fields have not gone unnoticed.

Programs leading to advanced degrees have mushroomed enormously in the past two decades. And as our society continues to become more complex, graduate programs will have to continue to meet the increasing demand for highly trained people in all fields.

Numerous universities have expanded their adult or continuing education programs in response to the heavy demand from people of all ages who want to take courses either for a degree or just for the enjoyment of learning.

All the changes, reforms and improvements in our educational system are basically responses to an ever-increasing demand by society for a better life. While there is conflict over what the "good life" and the "American Dream" really are, it is safe to say that most Americans work toward their idea of that goal. Education continues to be regarded as the best vehicle in support of that endeavor.

Notes

[1] Joel H. Spring, *Education and the Rise of Corporate State* (Boston: Beacon Press, 1972) pp. 62.

[2] Lawrence A. Crimin, *The Transformation of the School: Progressivism in American Education 1876-1957* (New York: Random House, 1961) passim.

[3] James S. Coleman, *et al.*, "Equality of Educational Opportunity," U.S. Department of Health, Education and Welfare, Washington D.C., 1966.

[4] Arthur Jensen, "How Much Can We Boost IQ and Scholastic Achievement," *Harvard Educational Review*, Vol. 39, 1969, pp. 1-123.

[5] Christopher Jencks, et al., *Inequality* (New York: Basic Books, 1972).

[6] Federick Mosteller and Daniel P. Moynihan, eds., *On Equality of Educational Opportunity* (New York: Random House, 1972).

[7] Section 402 of the Civil rights Act of 1964.

[8] Coleman, *op. cit.*

[9] *Ibid.* p. 3.

[10] *Ibid.*

[11] Jencks, *op. cit.*

[12] Godfrey Hodgson, "Do Schools Make a Difference?" *Atlantic Monthly*, March 1973, p. 37.

[13] *Ibid.*

[14] *Ibid.*

[15] Jencks, *op. cit.* p. 29.

[16] Jencks, *op. cit.* p. 256.

[17] Gordon Foster, Desegregating Urban Schools: A Review Of Techniques," *Harvard Educational Review*, February 1973, pp. 5–35.

[18] *Ibid.*

[19] *Ibid.*

[20] William Taylor, "Busing: Realities and Evasions," *Dissent*, Fall 1972, pp. 586-594.

[21] Foster, *op. cit.*

[22] Newsweek, April 2, 1973, p. 97.

[23] *Statistics of Public Schools*, U.S. Office of Education, Washington, D.C., Fall, 1971.

[24] Manley Fleischmann, et al, *The Fleischmann Report on the Quality, Cost, and Financing of Elementary and Secondary Education in New York State* (New York: Viking Press, 1973) *Vol 1*, p. 57.

[25] *Ibid.*, p. 58.

[26] *Ibid.*, p. 54.

[27] Newsweek, *op. cit.*

[28] Abbot L. Ferriss, *Indicators of Trends in American Education* (New York: Russell Sage Foundation, 1969) p. 254.

[29] *Federal Funds for Research, Development, and other Scientific Activities*, U.S. National Science Foundation, Washington, D.C.

³⁰ Ferriss, *op. cit.,* p. 256.

³¹ *Statistics of Public Schools,* U.S. Office of Education, *op. cit.*

³² Average pay for all U.S. teachers in 1960 was $4,995. By 1972, the figure had risen to $9,690.

³³ Charles Silberman, *Crisis in the Classroom* (New York: Random House, 1970), p. 5.

³⁴ Philip Bremer, "Political Knowledge and Experience in Elementary Education," in Martin Carnoy, ed., *Schooling in a Corporate Society* (New York: David McKay, 1972) p. 225.

³⁵ Jonathan Kozol, *Death at an Early Age* (Boston: Little, Brown & Co., 1968).

³⁶ John Holt, *Why Children Fail* (New York: Pitman, 1967).

³⁷ Herbert Kohl, *Thirty-Six Children* (New York: Random House, 1968).

³⁸ "Projects Under the New Bilingual Education Program," *American Education,* October 1969, pp. 26-28.

³⁹ Silberman, *op. cit.,* p. 324.

⁴⁰ *Ibid.,* p. 336.

⁴¹ Philip A. Cusick, *Inside High School (The Student's World)* (New York: Holt, Rinehart, and Winston, 1973) p. 217.

⁴² See Silberman, *op. cit.,* Cusick, *Ibid.,* and Carl Nordstrom, Edgar Z. Friedenberg, and Hilary A. Bold, *Society's Children* (New York: Random House, 1967).

⁴³ *Time,* November 29, 1971, pp. 50-52.

⁴⁴ Christopher Jencks and David Riesman, "On Class in America," *The Public Interest,* Winter 1968, pp. 58-65.

⁴⁵ Fleischmann, *op. cit.,* p. 74.

⁴⁶ *Ibid.*

⁴⁷ George R. La Noue, *Education Vouchers: Concepts and Controversies* (New York: Teachers College Press, 1972) pp. v-vii.

⁴⁸ Marshall Smith and Joan Bissell, "Report Analysis: The Impact of Head Start," *Harvard Educational Review,* Winter 1970, pp. 52-105.

⁴⁹ Jonathan Kozol, *Free Schools,* (Boston: Houghton Mifflin, 1972); see also: "Another Look at Student Rights and the Function of Schooling, The Elizabeth Cleaners Street School," *Harvard Educational Review,* November 1970, pp. 596-627.

⁵⁰ Howard Kirschenbaum, Sidney B. Simon, and Rodney W. Napier, *Wad-Ja-Get? The Grading Game in American Education* (New York: Hart Publishing Company, 1971).

Summary

The need to assimilate diverse groups of immigrants into the mainstream of society helped give rise to the public school system in the United States. Authoritarian control has played a prominent part in American public education, and, despite reformist efforts, success has often been measured by how closely a student adhered to the values and ethics of those who ran the school system. These were geared to a doctrine of upward social mobility. The expansion and development of the educational enterprise has also led to impersonal bureaucratic school organization. Parents and communities have lost direct control of education, while students and teachers are seeking fundamental changes.

Three of the most important problems at issue are equal access, financing, and curriculum. Equal access and financing are both aspects of inequality in education. Equal access means the chance to attend a school offering an education as good as any other in the society. Inequities in the financing of school systems in different areas are among the causes of inequality of educational opportunity. Studies have indicated that equal education alone will not create equal opportunity for social and economic progress, however.

Segregation has always blocked equal access to education. Although the Supreme Court outlawed segregation in 1954, it continues to the present day, and is now more prevalent in the Northern urban areas than in the South. The solution most often offered for this problem is busing. Opponents of busing base their opposition on the neighborhood school concept. The contradiction between this concept and integration is at the heart of the access problem. If neighborhoods remain closed and restrict their schools, integration and equality in education seem impossible.

Since schools rely heavily on the property tax for financing, the amount of money spent per student becomes a function of his state's tax system and his neighborhood's property value. A pupil from a poor district will have much less spent on his education than a student in a wealthy neighborhood.

The costs of public education have risen sharply in recent years. With city tax bases eroding, the unionization of teachers to gain higher wages has placed big city school systems in a particularly difficult situation. Recently, the Supreme Court ruled that equal education is not one of the rights guaranteed by the Constitution. This decision throws the problem of equalizing revenue available for education in different districts back on the states. New York State's Fleischmann report has proposed a statewide property tax for education finance, and the use of nonproperty taxes as solutions.

Colleges and universities face a different type of funding

problem. Federal expenditures to institutions of higher education have grown enormously since the late 1950s. Because of national priorities in the present tight economic situation, large cutbacks have been made recently, affecting private schools more severely than public institutions.

In American education today, there is great disagreement over how students should learn, and what they should learn. In elementary schools, authoritarian control is weakening. Many teachers are encouraging their students to express themselves by offering a more open, more relaxed, and more diversified setting in which to learn. Street school, mini-schools, decentralization of control, and the use of educational vouchers are all being investigated as means to a better way of learning.

As student discontent has filtered down from the universities, many high school students have come to find their curricula irrelevant and dehumanizing. Administrators normally seem to see problems as matters of control and discipline; rarely have they upgraded curricula or examined the values which shape the human environment of their students. Innovations such as minority studies programs, sex education classes and better vocational training are more available now than they used to be, but the high schools remain for the most part rigid agencies of socialization.

Student revolts of the 1960s merged political and educational issues. Today, however, many students are working with administrators to develop more flexible curricula. Adult education programs have expanded, as have experimental programs for work-study and open admissions in higher education.

chapter

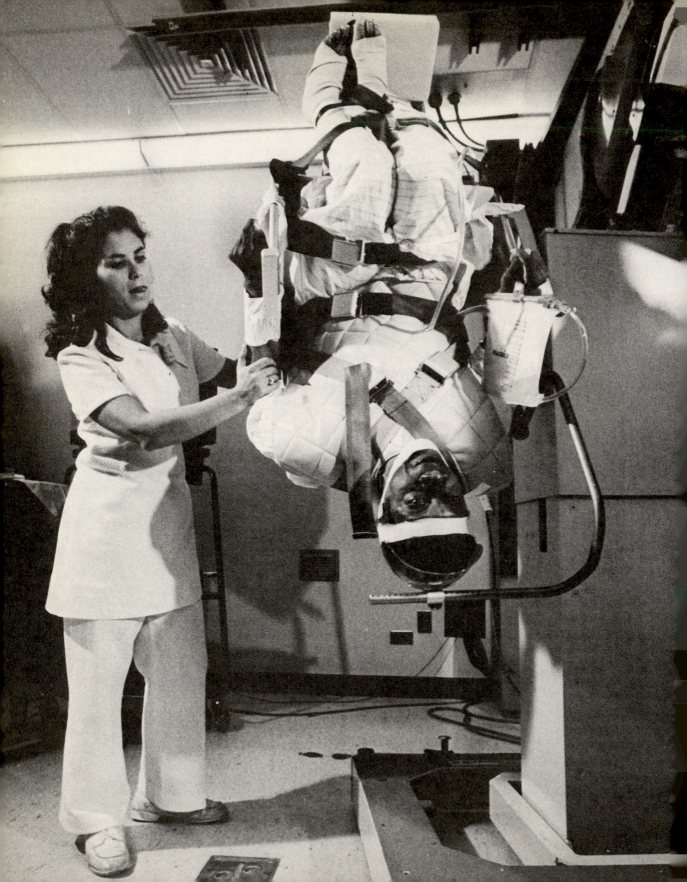

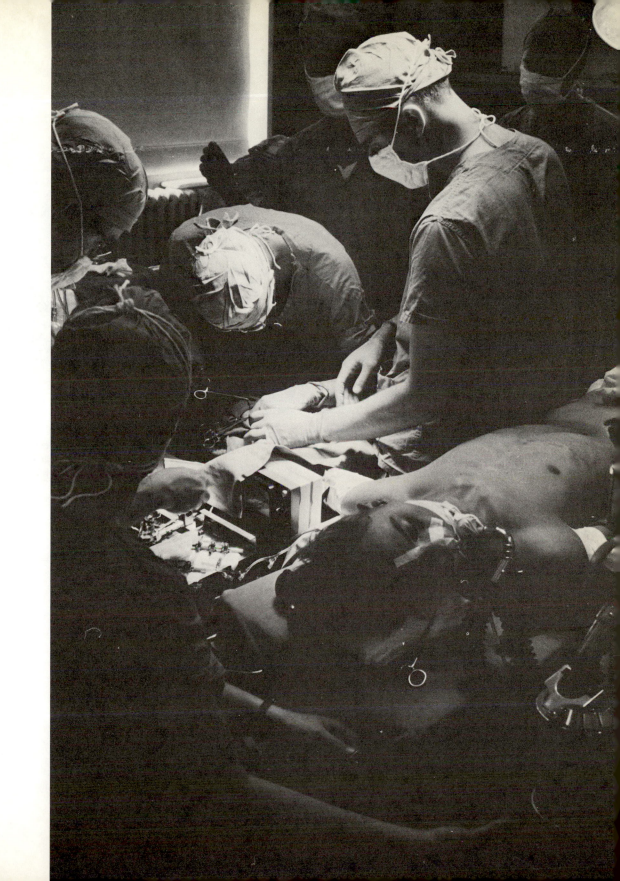

health care

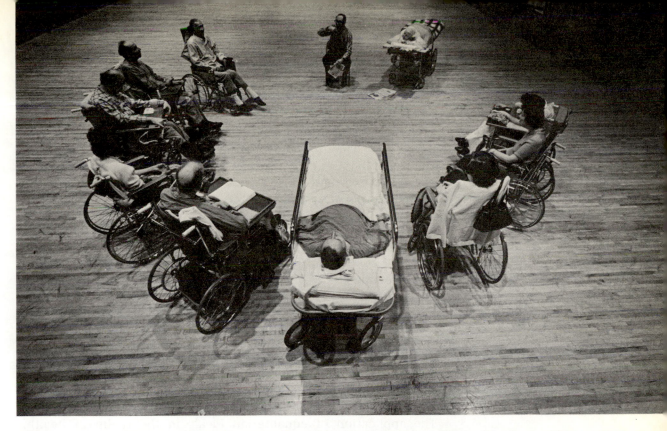

The impact of social change on American life is nowhere more apparent than in the deep-seated problems now confronting the nation in the area of health care. At first glance the situation seems a paradox. The scientific competence of our medical profession and the technological sophistication of our medical facilities are unsurpassed. The capacity of medicine to prolong life and enhance human functioning continues to expand with new advances in the understanding and treatment of disease. The United States invests more money in health care than any other nation in the world.[1] Yet we are in the midst of a health care crisis of mounting proportions. Providers and consumers of health services, public officials and scholarly authorities all agree that something is drastically wrong.

Diagnoses of the problem as well as remedies for dealing with it may vary, but the symptoms are hardly in dispute. The major issues have grown in prominence concurrently with the growth of medical expertise and the accompanying increase in national expenditures and health consciousness. They include poor levels on vital health indices, where other countries, expending smaller proportions of their Gross National Product on health services, surpass us in the results achieved. Our ranking on infant mortality, for instance, has declined steadily since 1950, until by 1970 we had dropped to fifteenth place.[2] Despite improvements, our maternal mortality rate was still 2.9 per 1000 live births in 1966, compared to England's 2.6 and Sweden's 1.1.[3]

These levels of performance are only one gauge of the problem, however. American health care is presently exorbitantly expensive and its service is discriminatory. At the same time personal care is unsatisfactory, which may be partly due to the fact that America is suffering a crucial shortage of physicians and other medical workers.

It is easy enough to locate the immediate causes of these serious shortcomings. They originate not in the deterioration of American medicine but in its enormously improved technical proficiency which has produced exorbitant costs, rising expectations and a bureaucratic reorganization of the medical enterprise. At the same time, private practice has remained locked in an unrealistic entrepreneurial approach which treats health care as a marketplace commodity and makes impossible the equitable distribution of its enhanced capacities.

There remains, however, another element which is perhaps more crucial than any other. A high assessment of health and the prolonging of life, and a belief in the equal worth of all individuals, the efficacy of science and the power of men to control their destiny through rational action are articles of faith entrenched in American attitudes. Commitment to these values constitutes the underlying source of our dissatisfaction with the medical care system in this country. The ultimate origin of the health crisis lies in the belief that health and therefore access to medical care are basic human rights.

The application of equalitarian ideals in the realm of health, however, is on a collision course with contradictory trends also deeply imbedded in the American value system. If the state of good health as a basic human right is a goal with which few would quarrel, the right of access to medical care is not. In direct opposition is the view long maintained by organized medicine that health care is a privilege to be dispensed in exchange for payment or as an act of deliberate charity. To treat it otherwise, according to this ideology, entails an infringement on the right of medical practitioners to operate as autonomous professionals, as well as an intrusion on the doctor-patient relationship.

To some authorities, however, the continuing strength of the privilege concept of medical care is directly responsible for the current health services crisis. According to sociologist Milton J. Roemer:

> Even when we have taken steps to improve medical care for the poor, as under Medicaid, or for the self-supporting, as under voluntary health insurance plans, we have used a systematized flow of money simply to purchase the services of physicians or hospitals in the open market. We have not organized the provision or "delivery" of health services in the way that other services deemed essential to society have been organized, such as education or protection against fire.[4]

By assessing past attitudes in America to health care, and by outlining the systematic changes that have led to the present problematic situation, it may be possible to gain some perspective on the suggestions for solution now being offered.

The problems of progress

Of all the changes accompanying the economic and social revolutions of the late eighteenth century, none was more profound than the transformation it effected in the most basic aspects of the human condition—the impact of disease and the duration of life itself. The average life span increased by twenty to thirty years and age-old scourges lost their power to kill. Other changes related to health followed. One was the emergence of new disease patterns and new problems of disease control. Another was the enhancement of expectations for health and longevity. They escalated with succeeding medical breakthroughs and are undoubtedly the most important factors in an ever-mounting demand for medical services. A third change, which has become more and more prominent with increasing technological complexity, has been an alteration in the nature of medical care and the organization of the medical profession.

While major credit for the dramatic health gains of the past hundred or more years must be assigned to scientific discoveries, these cannot be seen in isolation from the economic, intellectual and social milieu that produced them. Similar improvements in mortality indices have occurred in other countries experiencing industrialization; the gains in health seem to be closely associated with the advances in nutrition, sanitation and education that accompany rising levels of economic production.

The striking contrast between the mortality and disease patterns of peasant societies in underdeveloped areas and those of industrial societies gives some indication of the extent to which modern problems of health care have been generated by medical and social progress. In preindustrial societies, astronomical infant mortality rates, ranging from 150 to 400 per thousand live births (compared with 21.8 for the United States in 1968) are due in the main to nutritional disorders and infections. In general, major causes of death are epidemic diseases like typhoid, typhus, cholera and plague; or endemic killers like malaria, tuberculosis and syphilis. Chronic noninfectious diseases are responsible for only a minor proportion of total deaths.

The leading causes of death and major health hazards in industrial societies today, on the other hand, are the degenerative diseases associated with the aging process. Sociologist Odin Anderson comments:

> When a country or social class within a country attains the status of heart disease being the leading cause of death followed by cancer, stroke and accidents, obviously profound social and medical transformations have taken place in that the controllable scourges of the past have been displaced as the leading causes of death.[5]

The solution of old problems, however, has brought new ones into prominence. The disease pattern characteristic of an industrial society centers around the chronic disorders that increase markedly at middle age and are long-lasting. Many of these disorders require continuing care and so far have no ready solution.

In addition, medicine is now expected to concern itself with new classes of behavior as well, including alcoholism, obesity, modes of sexual intercourse, pregnancy and child development. The conditions of modern life are held responsible for the emergence of new epidemic diseases such as lung cancer, coronary heart disease and peptic ulcer. Ironically, medical advances have themselves produced health hazards. Whatever other physical disorders threatened preindustrial man, penicillin poisoning was not among them. Another health hazard resulting from progress has proved to be hospital care itself. According to studies, 10 to 20 percent of the patients who enter hospitals can expect to suffer from a condition induced by their stay and treatment.[6]

phototopic: AGE

As the number of elderly people in America has grown, their isolation from family and community has grown as well. Many older people are now treated not as functioning members of society, but as problems, to be provided for in the same way society provides for the ill or the mentally disturbed, through institutions rather than in the home. In a society where medical costs are spiraling, Medicare and Medicaid have been especially helpful to those living on fixed incomes. Both government and private organizations have moved to provide badly needed facilities and programs for the aged.

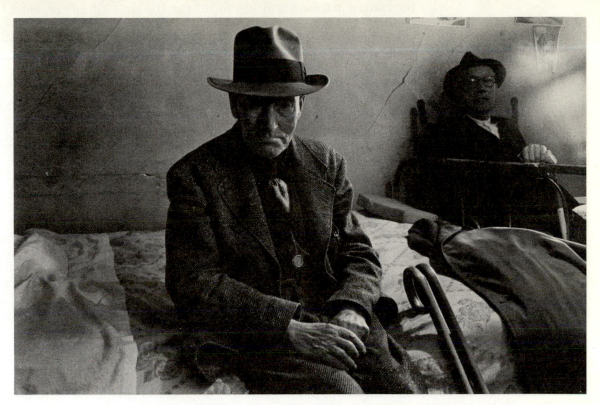

Many of the elderly now spend retirement in housing designed
for them, where sports and community facilities provide a
life-style similar to that of a resort, or settle into communities
which have grown up with the mobile home. For others, however,
age may be a decline into loneliness and despair, uncomforted
by family or by pleasant surroundings.

Rising expectations and demand

The health care crisis in the United States does not, however, stem
from the occasional failures of medical science but from its great
accomplishments. Particularly over the last forty years, these accomplishments stimulated an unprecedented demand for medical care. It
is hard to realize the radical change that has occurred in people's
attitudes toward illness and their expectations from medical science.
A new health consciousness has developed that has made medical
care a top priority and resulted in a rush on health services. People
now seek preventative care and care for relatively minor conditions.
The value of health checkups and early attention to symptoms has
been urged on the public for many years, but there has recently been
discussion and concern over what is being called "overutilization."
The admission rate to general hospitals rose from about 60 per 1000

population in the early 1930's to 109 per 1000 in 1950 and reached 145 per 1000 in 1970.[7]

Large as the rising demands for health services have been, there are good indications that they would rise much higher if financial and social barriers limiting access to medical care were removed. The consumer explosion produced by the passage of Medicare and Medicaid, which for the first time made available to the poor both medical purchasing power and the dignity of private medical service, made it clear that the new health consciousness crosses socioeconomic and ethnic lines.

reading: **Rene Dubos**
HEALTH, DISEASE AND CIVILIZATION

Clearly, health and disease cannot be defined merely in terms of anatomical, physiological, or mental attributes. Their real measure is the ability of the individual to function in a manner acceptable to himself and to the group of which he is a part. If the medical services of the armed forces which seem more successful than their civilian counter-parts in formulating useful criteria of health, this is due not to their greater wisdom but rather to the fact that their criteria are more clearly defined. On the whole, effective military performance requires attributes less varied and less complex than the multifarious activities of civilian life. But criteria of adequacy change even in the military world. The soldier of past wars who marched or rode his way to victory through physical and mental stamina might not be the most effective warrior in the push-button operations of future conflicts.

For several centuries the Western world has pretended to find a unifying concept of health in the Greek ideal of a proper balance between body and mind. But in reality this ideal is more and more difficult to convert into practice. Poets, philosophers, and creative scientists are rarely found among Olympic laureates. It is not easy to discover a formula of health broad enough to fit Voltaire and Jack Dempsey, to encompass the requirements of a stevedore, a New York City bus driver, and a contemplative monk.

One of the criteria of health most widely accepted at the present time is that children should grow as large and as fast as possible. But is size such a desirable attribute? Is the bigger child happier? will he live longer? does he perceive with greater acuity the loveliness or the grandeur of the world? will he contribute more to man's cultural heritage? or does his larger size merely mean that he will need a larger motorcar, become a larger soldier, and in his turn beget still larger children? The criteria of growth developed for the production of market pigs would hardly be adequate for animals feeding on acorns in the forests and fending for themselves as free individuals. Nor are they for man. Size and weight are not desirable in themselves, and their relation to health and happiness is at most obscure. In his essay "On the Sizes of Things or the Advantages of Being Rather Small," Boycott concluded, in fact, that an animal about as big as a medium dog has the best possible size for our world!

Curiously enough, the assumption that human beings should grow fast and large has never been examined closely as to its validity and ultimate consequences. Its only certain merit is that weight, size and a few other physical traits can be measured readily, provide objective and convenient characteristics on which to agree, and can be on the whole readily achieved.

There is no evidence, however, that these criteria have much bearing on happiness, on the development of civilization, or even on the individual's ability to adapt to the complex demands of modern technology. The specifications for man's body and mind may have to be reformulated in order to meet with greater effectiveness the exigencies of the mechanized world.

Human goals, which condition social changes, profoundly affect the physical and mental well-being of man. And, unfortunately, the most worth-while goals may have results as disastrous as those of the most despicable ambitions. Industrial imperialism was responsible for an enormous amount of misery among children during the early nineteenth century. But, as we have seen, the present philosophy to assure the survival of all children and to protect them from any traumatic experience also is likely to have unfortunate consequences by interfering with the normal play of adaptive processes.

Philosophical and social doctrines have been the most influential forces in changing the human ways of life during historical times. The high regard in which the human body was held by the Greco-Roman world certainly played a role in the development of hygiene and medicine during the classical times of Western civilization. In contrast, the emphasis on mystical values and on eternal life, the contempt for bodily functions, which characterized certain early phases of the Christian faith, probably led to the neglect of sanitary practices during medieval times—even though it did not necessarily decrease the enjoyment of sensual pleasures by normal men and women. Today, as in the past, the relation that man bears to his total environment is influenced by values of which he is not always aware. A civilization that devotes page after page of its popular magazines to portraying the rulers of the business world is bound to produce men very different from those taught to worship Confucian wisdom, Buddhic mysticism, or Blake's poems—even if that worship often does not go far beyond mere lip service. To feel at ease among the neon lights of Broadway demands a type of body and mind not conducive to happiness in the mists of a Taoist moonscape. . . .

To discover, to describe, to classify, to invent, has been the traditional task of the scientist until this century; on the whole a pleasant occupation amounting to a sophisticated hobby. This happy phase of social irresponsibility is now over and the scientist will be called to account for the long-term consequences of his acts. His dilemma is and will remain that he cannot predict these consequences because they depend on many factors outside his knowledge or at least beyond his control—in particular on the exercise of free will by men.

To become worthy of his power the scientist will need to develop enough wisdom and humane understanding to recognize that the acquisition of knowledge is intricately inter-woven with the pursuit of goals. It has often been pointed out that the nineteenth-century slogan "Survival of the Fittest," begged the question because it did not state what fitness was for. Likewise it is not possible to plan man's future without deciding beforehand what he should be fitted for, in other words, what human destiny ought to be—a decision loaded with ethical values. What is new is not necessarily good, and all changes, even those apparently the most desirable, are always fraught with unpredictable consequences. The scientist must beware of having to admit, like Captain Ahab in Melville's Moby Dick, "All my means are sane; my motives and objects mad."

From
Mirage of Health by Rene Dubos
(New York: Harper & Row, 1959)
pp. 261-263, 268-269, 271-272

Changing practice of medicine

Steadily mounting demands for health services have encountered a medical care system with a built-in incapacity for satisfying the demands. The very scientific advances largely responsible for rising expectations have also entailed fundamental alterations in the institutional organization of medicine and the procedures involved in the delivery of medical services. Among other changes, this has meant a shift to the practice of limited specialities rather than all-encompasing personalized care and to reliance on costly hospital technology for treatment as well as diagnosis. The free enterprise ideology of organized medicine has consistently been employed against innovations designed to modify the traditional system controlling access to the new modes of care.

An idealized model of the doctor-patient relationship supports this ideology. Sociologist Monroe Lerner's description of the model points up the unrealistic nature of its essential components. The physician is seen as a family doctor who, functioning alone, is able to provide excellent primary care to patients in their homes as well as in his private office. Motivated by altruistic concern and possessing high technical expertise, he is not only available for house visits and night calls but bestows his services on all who need them, whether rich or poor and regardless of race or creed. This benevolence and conscientious concern are dictated by the ethical requirements of his profession as well as by his own sense of dedication and compassion. In sum, they are not merely personal attributes but firm obligations.

The obligatory condition for fulfilling these obligations is the absence of regulation, with the physician completely autonomous and the patient unrestricted in his choice of doctor. Lerner describes the situation in this way:

> The patient in this idealized model selected his physician on the basis of "free choice"; if dissatisfied, he could always choose another physician. Because of this, the physician tried very hard to please his patient. He charged on a fee-for-service basis, discriminating only in accordance with the patient's income. Thus, he charged the poor little or nothing, and gave much free service in the hospital. The doctor made up for this in Robin Hood fashion by "soaking the rich". . .[8]

From a contemporary perspective, the preeminence of the individual physician as the all-authoritative source of health care seems rooted in tradition. It was not until the reform of medical education after 1910, however, that medical knowledge and technique advanced sufficiently to establish the general physician's monopoly over healing. As sociologist Eliot Freidson puts it: "The nostalgic and sentimental image of the old-fashioned family doctor who was all things to all men is based upon the fleeting period in history when folk practice had declined but medical specialization was still in an incipient state."[9]

The high point of the concentration of medical authority in the independent generalist occurred in the generation just prior to World War II. This was the heyday of the health care system built around the solo practitioner with specialists and hospital resources providing an important but secondary back-up to his expertise. Yet signs of an impending change were already unmistakable. The expanding base of medical knowledge was placing increasing emphasis on the role of the specialist; the growing complexity of diagnostic procedures and treatment was making the use of hospital facilities both more important and more expensive. In addition, the problem of hospital costs had, by the early 1930s, already forced the institution of a limited form of voluntary health insurance, a first departure from the principle of direct payment by the consumer for services rendered.

Specialization, hospitals and hospital insurance

After World War II, the knowledge base and technological capacities of medical science advanced with a quantum leap, forcing a drastic and apparently irreversible reorganization of medicine's professional structure, prestige hierarchy and treatment procedures. The hospital with its indispensable and costly equipment, technicians and consultants, now became the center of the medical system, replacing the home and physician's office as the locus for treatment and nursing care. As medical care grew vastly more specialized and dependent on technology, the generalist descended to the position of low man on the totem pole of medicine both in number and rank and solo practice grew to be more and more of an anachronism. Describing the changes that took place during this period that laid the foundation of many of the problems of American health care today, Freidson writes:

> Clearly, with the rise of modern medicine, it became difficult to practice alone and, what is more positively unrealistic, to attempt to handle the whole range of human ills. Over the past fifty years, general practice has declined and practice limited to particular organs, specific illnesses, or special procedures has increased remarkably. In 1923, for example, only 11 percent of all physicians were engaged in limited practice. By 1967, however, the proportion of all active physicians engaged in giving patient care in some specialty had risen to 71 percent.[10]

Through the 1950s and 1960s, these trends accelerated and intensified, leading to further emphasis on the science rather than the art of medicine, and on the role of scientific expertise developed and concentrated in large institutions with little public accountability. New medical schools and the major teaching hospitals affiliated with them became the bases of great research-oriented medical centers—"medical empires" they have been called—which replaced the individual hospital as the basic unit of the medical system. Bolstered by massive federal funding, these institutions trained a new medical elite geared to specialized practice and research. The results have been path-breaking medical discoveries, elaborate treatment and diagnostic equipment, a need for more technicians and other hospital personnel and, in addition, sky-rocketing costs and an increasing movement of medical manpower away from primary noncrisis medicine and comprehensive care. This in part accounts for America's surprisingly high patient-to-doctor ratio.

Throughout the period during which these profound alterations were taking place, the organized medical profession retained the fee-for-service, laissez-faire philosophy which defined medical care as a privilege and precluded any interference with the autonomy of the medical profession or the individual professional. Control of the system for the provision of personal health services remained firmly in its hands. Compulsory health insurance, expansion of medical manpower, prepaid group practice and other innovations designed to widen the scope and availability of health services did not become viable possibilities until the health care crisis of the mid-1960s made a reassessment unavoidable. A 1932 statement by the American Medical Association (AMA), attacking a proposal for medical reform has become a classic statement of a position that many critics have characterized as reactionary:

> The alignment is clear—on the one side the forces representing the great foundations, public health officialdom, social theory—even socialism and communism—inciting to revolution; on the other side, the organized medical profession of this country urging an orderly evaluation guided by controlled experimentation which will observe the principles that have been found through the centuries to be necessary to the sound practice of medicine.[11]

At the same time, organized medicine gave its approval to voluntary health insurance as a means of providing service benefits for hospital care. This approach, according to the AMA, would "preserve personal relationships and the free choice of physician and hospital." In 1932, the American Hospital Association not only endorsed but helped organize the Blue Cross system of voluntary hospital insurance as "one of the most effective ways to offset the increasing demand for more radical and potentially dangerous forms of national or state medicine."[12] A major impetus behind this move was the serious financial situation of voluntary hospitals during the early days of the Great Depression, when philanthropic contributions had dwindled and patients were unable to meet what were already very considerable bills for hospital care. The Blue Cross thus became a "third party" acting as agent between consumer and provider of health services for the payment of fees for services rendered. Shortly afterwards, it was followed by Blue Shield, a prepayment plan to cover in-hospital surgical and medical care. Later commercial insurance companies joined medically initiated and controlled plans in the third party role. Although a variety of coverage plans are now available, all have been criticized for their high costs.

The medical care system and its problems

No society can survive unless the individuals composing it enjoy a minimal life span and state of health, sufficient at least to insure the continuity of generations and the effective performance of essential tasks. All societies develop mechanisms for meeting this need and the American system of medical care serves the same fundamental functions in this respect as that of any other social collective. Compared to preindustrial societies or even to the situation existing within this society in the fairly recent past, however, our medical care system occupies a much more strategic place within the large institutional structure. Not only does it serve the economy by helping to maintain a high level of worker productivity, but it is itself a major component of the economy, accounting for over 7 percent of the Gross National Product.[13] Not only does it support the family and religious institutions in their care and solace of the sick, but it has become the major agency performing that function.

With the major contagious and parasitic diseases under control, medicine's assignment is not simply to alleviate illness but to prevent it and, more, to produce an optimum condition of health. The magnitude of this last assignment is indicated by the statement of the United Nations World Health Organization, often quoted in this connection, which defines health as a "state of complete physical, mental and social well-being and not merely the absence of disease and infirmity."[14] In addition, the social control and supportive function assigned to the medical care institution have expanded.

The advanced medical care system charged with this enhanced and complex role is, however, marked by a lack of coordination among its components, which have developed without reference to any overall, rational plan consistent with social realities. The problems now facing the "ailing" system are attributed by many critics to this fact, as well as to failures within the components themselves.

Doctors in the United States

According to 1970 figures, of 278,500 physicians engaged in patient care only 20 percent were in general medicine, with the other 80 percent divided among 61 specialties.[15] Significantly, almost 30 percent of these were in surgical specialties; close to 2500 of them neurosurgeons. In comparison, 48.3 percent of physicians active in England during 1967 were engaged in general practice.[16] Another way of considering the professional distribution of physicians is in terms of the administration of primary care. One analysis, which defines the primary care physician as a pediatrician, internist or general practitioner, found that there is now one primary care physician for every 2200 individuals as against one per 1000 individuals in 1930 when the ratio of medical doctors to the overall population was smaller than it is today.[17]

Private practice tends to be concentrated in middle-class urban and suburban areas and especially in the vicinity of the great medical centers with their wealth of treatment resources and available medical expertise. One extreme example of this tendency is to be found in Durham County, North Carolina. Although the county has one of the highest doctor-patient ratios in the country due to the location there of two large medical schools, an entire third of the county area is without a single practitioner.[18]

In the current solo-practice-dominated system, efforts to improve quality require clumsy compromises that are more concerned with maintaining the providers' existing style of life than with assuring quality care to the people. Even at best they often offer fast and sporadic reviews of diagnoses and treatment, rather than ongoing interchanges among physicians during diagnoses and treatment in an environment which encourages continuing education and professional growth.

Senator Edward M. Kennedy

The dependence of the modern physician on colleagues and hospitals for consultation and treatment facilities is probably more responsible than prestige and financial inducements for the geographical maldistribution, however. The realities of medical practice as it is conducted today reflect the pressures moving the conscientious physician away from professional isolation. The proportion of doctors engaging in solo practice is steadily decreasing.[19] Moreover, as Freidson points out in his analysis of the organization of medical practice, true solo practice is actually a rarity. Rather, private practice is typically marked by informal but well-integrated cooperative arrangements with a "colleague network" and a reliance on hospital ties.

In a further departure from the solo practice ideal, physicians are increasingly joining forces in legal partnerships and group practices which explicitly involve an interdependent team relationship among three or more full-time doctors. Besides the advantages that group practice offers the physician with respect to expenses, equipment, consultations and patient referrals, it has been strongly advocated as a means of counteracting the fragmentation of medical care. Although still a minor feature of the medical scene, group practice is growing steadily and now involves 15 percent of the nation's physicians.[20]

The professional orientation of the nation's physicians must be viewed against the background of their training. Those who have received their training since World War II are the products of a medical education that has stressed federally supported biomedical research and specialized knowledge. During this period, interest in effective means of delivering health care has taken second place to interest in effective ways of treating disease; the clinician has taken second place to the research scientist; the provider of primary care to the specialist. It is only in the past few years that medical schools and their affiliated hospitals have begun to emphasize training in family medicine and community-based ambulatory care. Pressures from both society and the more recent crop of medical students are held responsible for this move.

Overall, in terms of minimal federal standards calling for one physician per 1500 people,[21] we are presently suffering from a nationwide deficit amounting to 50,000. Even were that gap filled, however, it would be of only minor help if the present trends in geographical concentration and specialization continue. A simple increase in numbers will meet the needs neither of those in rural and inner-city areas where few private practitioners venture, nor of those in metropolitan and suburban areas where specialists may be plentiful but a physician offering primary care hard to find.

Sociologically, the problem of the doctor shortage can be viewed from a conflict perspective as the manifestation of an intrinsic contradiction between the self-defined interests of two opposed groups within an institutional system. Patient expectations and professional intentions have grown increasingly incompatible under the pressure of social change. The expectations, ironically, derive much of their force and legitimacy from the ideal doctor-patient model traditionally promoted by organized medicine, and from the enhanced potentialities of medical science. Doctors, on the other hand, are now confronted with the imperatives of a vastly altered professional milieu which no longer bestows rewards on the basis of the old norms and role definitions.

The character of the shortage dilemma that has emerged out of this conflict is illustrated by the situation in the State of New York. Here, in a state with one of the highest physician-to-resident ratios in the country, an intensive study of the "doctor shortage" was undertaken during the summer of 1973. Figure 7-2, showing the distribution of physicians within subregions of the state with a breakdown by primary care, reflects a pattern even more prevalent throughout the country. First, there is a wide range in physician-resident ratios throughout the state, from 2.54 per 1000 in New York City to .76 per 1000 in western Wyoming County. Secondly, whatever the overall ratio, the proportion of practitioners offering primary care is typically one-third less than those in a limited specialty practice. Interestingly, the two exceptions are the regions with the lowest physician density.

The origins of the numerical doctor shortage are clear. Acting, it has been suggested, in the classic pattern of an economic monopoly, the organized medical profession undertook and succeeded in sharply limiting new entrants into the ranks of medicine. The American Medical Association, late in the nineteenth century, persuaded state legislatures to set up procedures for licensing the practice of medicine. Then the AMA conducted a successful legislative campaign to force medical schools of poor quality out of business. With this accomplished, standards of medical training were raised and admissions curtailed.

For several decades, the ratio of physicians to the population continued to decline; then in the 1940s and 1950s it stabilized at a comparatively low level. During this time, despite greatly expanded demand, the AMA continued to press its opposition to any increase in the output of doctors under the argument of "protecting quality." The first cautious shift in this position came in 1958, but it was not until the early 1960s that the AMA admitted there was a doctor shortage.[22]

During the past decade, efforts have been made to augment the nation's supply of physicians but their scope remains limited and results still lag far behind the need. This is so much the case that graduates of foreign medical schools, many of them Americans denied admission to schools in the United States, are now welcomed as additions to the nation's pool of physicians. According to Roemer, they presently comprise about 25 percent of new medical licentiates each year.[23]

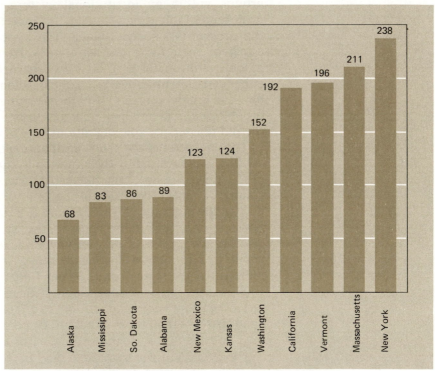

*Figure 7-1   Density of registered physicians per hundred thousand population in United States regions, 1970;
Estimated number of physicians engaged in family practice, general practice or internal medicine*

The numerical shortage is critical because of the trend to specialization that has accompanied it. While the manpower pool has remained comparatively constant, the balance within it has shifted sharply, with ever-decreasing proportions of physicians involved in primary care. According to many medical authorities, the resulting professional distribution is marked by an actual oversupply of physicians in certain medical and surgical specialties and consequent "overdoctoring." Dr. John Knowles claims that if "unnecessary surgery were reduced by 50 percent, there would be a glut of practicing surgeons and a glut of surgeons in training—all of whom would then have to move into other areas where shortages are, in fact, real."[24]

Closely linked with the dynamics of the doctor shortage are problems of the quality of care. The lack of continuity, impersonality and fragmentation widely noted and criticized in the delivery of health services can be attributed as much to the dearth of primary care physicians as to the emphasis on restricted specialty practice. In addition, the scarcity of practitioners oriented to comprehensive care makes it increasingly difficult for patients to find a point of entry into the system, a problem which obviously becomes crucial in an emergency and hinders the early detection and treatment of disease. As the Robert Wood Johnson Foundation has stated in a recent report, "In simple terms, there are not enough physicians and their associates willing and able to handle frontline, preventive, run-of-the-mill complaints or emergency."[25]

Hospital boom

Today's medical care system centers around the short-term general hospitals, which are largely nonprofit institutions controlled by private citizens and sectarian groups. The most prestigious are those affiliated with medical schools as teaching hospitals. These are the so-called voluntary hospitals, as distinguished from the proprietary variety, which is operated for profit. The short-term general hospital. providing treatment for patients with acute conditions that involve a stay of less than 30 days, has been the component of the medical care system that has changed most in the past forty years; it is the key factor in the organization and financing of personal health services. Of the approximately 7000 hospitals about 5800 are of the short-term general type,[26] a figure which includes a comparatively minor proportion of proprietary and nonfederal governmental facilities.

The growth of the general hospital for inpatient care has been dramatic and rapid. Much of the complex technology now taken for granted, for instance, was nonexistent only fifteen years ago. Among such innovations are cardiac care units, therapeutic radiation services, advanced laboratory tests of body fluids, computerized consultation services, kidney dialysis units and so forth.

Voluntary hospital personnel, in a development linked with technological advance, grew from less than 500,000 in 1950 to over 1 million in 1965 and in 1968 had reached a million and a quarter. Financial assets have increased fivefold since 1950 and have doubled since 1960. Current expenses have multiplied by ten since 1950, when they were approximately one and a half million dollars.[27] Costs to the patient have, of course, greatly increased in a snowballing process involving indirect payment procedures, operating expenses and expanded use.

In terms of the delivery of medical care, the most relevant aspect of all this growth is the great increase in hospitalization it entails. Whereas 1 out of every 10 persons in the population was admitted to a hospital for inpatient care in 1946, the figure had risen to 1 out of every 6.5 persons by 1966.[28] From 1950 to 1968 there was a 63 percent increase in admissions, from a total of 16,663,000 in 1950 to a total of 27,276,000 in 1968.[29]

More recently a number of other trends seem to indicate a new development in the hospital's role. One has been the increased use of outpatient facilities as clinics by all sectors of the community. From 1960 to 1969, outpatient visits in the United States increased by 64 percent,[30] a change which may be tied to the short supply of primary care physicians with hospitals filling in the gap.

Another trend is the growth of programs for providing health care on an ambulatory basis to surrounding neighborhoods. While many of these "outreach" operations are still experimental, they reflect a greater commitment by voluntary hospitals, especially those affiliated with medical schools, to community medicine. To a large extent, this new commitment is emerging in response to vociferous consumer demands for realistic attention to their health needs and for representation on the decision-making bodies of community hospitals.

Paying for medical care

Health care costs have risen constantly; inflation is only part of the answer. From 1960 to 1970 medical prices increased at a rate more than double the rate of inflation for consumer goods. During this period in which the consumer price average rose 30 percent, physicians' fees rose 60 percent and hospital daily service charges were up 170 percent. By 1972 inpatient costs in some areas were running as high as $150 a day and outpatient care at $40 a visit. Hospital charges, rising at the rate of 15 percent a year, are now out of reach of even the affluent unless they have hospitalization insurance, which itself is becoming increasingly expensive and restrictive.

Depending on the viewpoint of the writer, the financing of personal health care in the United States has been described as "pluralistic" or "chaotic." It is marked by diversity in the sources of payment and the procedures for payment, as well as by considerable controversy over the appropriate rationale for financing arrangements. Chief features of the situation at present are the increasing proportion of government as against private funds as the source of payment, the dominance of voluntary insurance as against direct payment for meeting hospital expenses and the importance of hospital care as an item of expense. The principle which, with minor exceptions, shapes the system of financing remains the fee-for-service approach.

	All Physicians	Primary Care Physicians*
Total for N.Y. State	1.92	.66
New York City	2.54	.86
Mid–Hudson	2.09	.72
Upper–Hudson	1.61	.57
Nassau-Suffolk	1.60	.56
Genesee–Finger Lakes	1.59	.58
Western	1.48	.53
Central	1.46	.45
Lake Champlain–Lake George	1.31	.58
Southern Tier East	1.31	.52
Upper Mohawk Valley	1.28	.48
Southern Tier Central	1.26	.49
Black River–St. Lawrence	1.05	.44
Southern Tier West	.99	.46
Wyoming County	.76	.42

Figure 7–2 Physician density per thousand population in New York State, 1970

Alternative approaches are receiving new attention because of the health care crisis, but they are still of minor significance in the overall picture. One method reimburses the physician with a fixed salary. Another provides payment on a "capitation" basis under which the physician receives a stated fee for each patient for whatever services are required over a set period of time. With a growth in prepaid group health plans, these systems of payment should become more widespread. The fee-for-service principle still predominates, however, whether in the form of direct payment by consumers or indirect payment through voluntary or public insurance. Whatever the source of funds or the procedures used for their transmission, they are disbursed for specific services rendered. This applies to expenditures made under the government's Medicare and Medicaid programs as well as to private payments. The difference between the two lies in the onus of responsibility for making the payments. The great breakthrough made by Medicare, and the reason for the intense controversy surrounding it, was the assumption of government responsibility for financing the health needs of the aged population regardless of ability to pay. Medical care for 10 percent of the total United States population was now to be considered not a privilege but a right.

The key characteristic of our pluralistic financing system is the high proportion of expenditures channeled to the providers of health care through third parties. This represents a considerable shift from the past. While over 57 percent of all health payments in 1950 came directly from the consumer at the time of service, in 1969 the proportion of payments made in this way had gone down to 35 percent.

The increased importance of government funds and voluntary health insurance accounts for the difference. Government funding rose from 28 percent in 1950 to 38 percent in the late 1960s, chiefly because of the Medicare and Medicaid programs. The proportion of total payments made through voluntary health insurance rose from 9 to 19 percent. When expenditures in the private sector are examined separately, the enlarged role of voluntary insurance becomes striking. Direct patient payments in the private sector have diminished from 80 percent of the total in 1950 to 56 percent in 1969; third party payments through voluntary health insurance have risen from 13 percent to over one-third[31] of the total.

The explanation for this shift is not difficult to discover. It is clearly to be found in the increasing use of hospital facilities and the rising costs of these facilities. Almost 80 percent of private hospital charges are now met by voluntary health insurance, as against 35 percent in 1950. About 40 percent of physician charges are met by private health insurance, mainly those for surgeons and hospital-related specialists.[32] An analysis by Anderson and Anderson of national allocations for personal health services on a per capita basis for the fiscal year 1969 points up the high proportion of the total devoted to hospital care.[33]

Health insurance

The focal point of organized health care financing, then, is voluntary health insurance geared to hospital expenses, just as the focal point for the organization of health services is the voluntary general hospital. Voluntary health insurance is, in fact, almost wholly limited to inpatient surgical and medical care. It does not cover such nonhospital connected services as preventive health examinations, ambulatory care or extended home care. Approximately 85 percent of the population under age 65 is now covered by voluntary hospital insurance and almost 78 percent by insurance for surgeon's fees.[34] About two-fifths of the coverage is under the medical association-sponsored Blue Cross and Blue Shield plans and the rest divided among industrial and union programs, independent plans and commercial insurance companies.[35] The national network of nonprofit Blue Cross and Blue Shield plans, largely controlled by hospital administrators and physicians, are, however, the dominant force in the voluntary insurance field. They account for 50 percent of benefit payments and exert considerable influence in medical decision making.

A number of additional facts about voluntary health insurance are relevant to current health care problems. Voluntary health insurance is primarily group insurance, with nonaffiliated subscribers penalized by high premiums and less extensive coverage, a situation that discriminates against the disadvantaged. Until recently insurance payments have been made to hospitals on the basis of "reasonable" costs without regard to efficiency in hospital administration, a method charged with rewarding inefficiency and contributing to runaway costs. Close to three-quarters of the cost of group health insurance is contributed by employers as a fringe benefit that is now a standard item in collective bargaining negotiations. This makes rising insurance costs a matter of increasing concern to both management and labor.

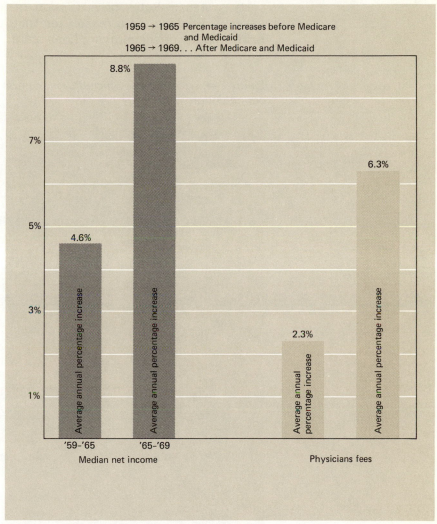

1959 → 1965 Percentage increases before Medicare and Medicaid
1965 → 1969. . . After Medicare and Medicaid

8.8%

7%

6.3%

5%

4.6%

3%

2.3%

1%

Average annual percentage increase

Average annual percentage increase

Average annual percentage increase

Average annual percentage increase

'59–'65   '65–'69

Median net income

Physicians fees

Figure 7–3   Comparative increases in median income and physician's fees, 1959–1969

The problem of rising medical care prices is primarily the problem of rising hospital costs. According to a widely held view, a major factor responsible for hospital costs is the third party system of funding, which in its present fee-for-service form encourages excessive use of inpatient care, unnecessary treatment, irresponsible investment in elaborate technology with limited application which often duplicates facilities already available and inefficient hospital management. Voluntary health insurance benefits, since they are almost wholly limited to inpatient care and hospital-related expenses, exert pressure on both patients and doctors to use hospital facilities. In contrast, prepaid group plans, where physicians work on salary and patients are covered for all kinds of services, show a 20 percent lower rate of hospital utilization than under the fee-for-service third party system.[36] Rates of admission to hospitals are considerably lower in England. One reason for the difference seems to be the British policy of encouraging home care.

Figure 7–4   Health care expenditures in gross and per capita dollars, 1950–1971

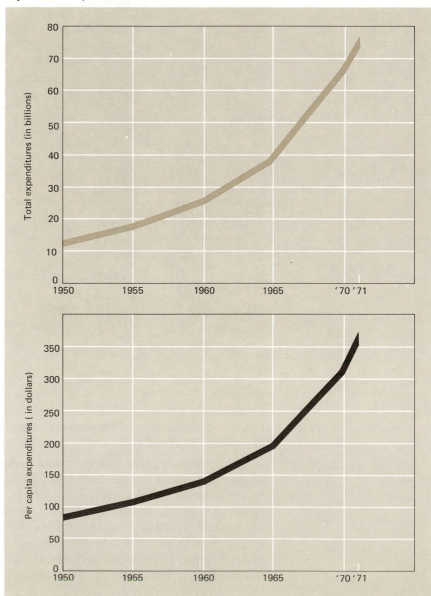

In addition, extensive hospitalization is held responsible for a great deal of unnecessary treatment, especially surgery. In Britain, prepaid groups based on capitation arrangements have reduced hospitalization utilization days and the amount of surgery done by as much as 50 percent.[37] In America estimates indicate that fee-for-service arrangements finance 86 percent more appendectomies and more than 150 percent more tonsillectomies and adenoidectomies per 100 patients than the prepaid plans.[38]

Hospital procedures

An even more basic question has been raised regarding the value of the complex medical equipment associated with rising hospital costs. The expensive procedures involved are helpful to comparatively few patients, yet the cost of maintaining them must be shared by all. Furthermore, it is argued, the new facilities may often be used unnecessarily. Sociologist Leonard Magnani offers a provocative example with regard to various diagnostic laboratory tests:

> A hypothetical serum analysis might show chemical imbalance indicative of specific pathological conditions for which "cures" exist. The analysis may be expensive but may also be routinized—results back in 12 hours or less. This laboratory analysis "saves lives," but whether it will help a given patient is uncertain. A small minority of patients are known to benefit from the laboratory procedure. But the medical practice in the modern hospital is to order this analysis for a majority of the patients *each day.* Ten years ago these tests were not available (i.e., routinized in hospitals or private laboratories); at that time related but more laborious analyses were rarely prescribed. Now the tests are available and are frequently used, increasing the cost of medical care.[39]

Finally, the fee-for-service third party system of financing is charged with boosting hospital costs by promoting what sociologist David Mechanic has called "persistent and profound inefficiencies." The fact that funds have been transmitted by third party agents, both governmental and private, with scant regard for cost control or accountability has in effect invited fiscal irresponsibility. The rapid infusion of Medicare and Medicaid funds have exacerbated these inflationary trends even further. Third party pressures have recently moved hospitals to develop record-keeping systems that permit an accurate cost-benefit analysis. Interestingly enough, when this attempt has been made hospitals have discovered in many cases that they literally did not know what various services cost, nor did they know how to evaluate alternative methods of providing the same service. Computerized systems and techniques are now being called on to cope with the problem, an undertaking which in itself involves considerable expense.

Apart from the inflationary effects of third party funding, medical advances have undoubtedly made a large contribution to rising costs by the increasingly sophisticated methods of treatment they involve.

Not only do these call for costly equipment but for an expanded and expert staff. The fact that hospital payroll expenses rose 147 percent during the period between 1960 and 1969 is attributed to the new personnel needs accompanying medical progress as well as to wage boosts for hospital staff at all levels.[40]

The inequality problem

One of the differences between the poor and nonpoor is their respective levels of health. Key indices leave no doubt that poverty is associated with significantly lower levels of health, especially when it is paired with minority racial status. Another difference is in the health care they receive. The poor not only receive less of it but what they do receive is inferior in kind, being largely outside the mainstream of private medicine. Economic barriers clearly impose effective limitations on access to services, which is scarcely surprising in a system that dispenses these services as market commodities. Differentials in levels of health and receipt of services are indisputable. What is a matter of debate, however, is the degree to which there is a cause-and-effect relationship between them.

Two arguments call such a relationship into question. One holds that the conditions of life experienced by poverty populations may be more accountable for health deficiencies than inadequate medical care. Housing, sanitation, nutrition and recreational resources are among the factors cited in this connection. The other holds that noneconomic cultural factors are also crucial in shaping patterns of behavior relevant to health apart from access to medical care. These include norms regarding illegitimacy and childrearing practices, as well as attitudes toward sickness that influence people to seek medical care.

The force of these arguments is, however, diminished by the size of the poverty-linked differentials in both health levels and health services. Anderson, evaluating factors responsible for the wide discrepancy between white and nonwhite mortality rates in the 25 to 44 year age range, where the nonwhite rate is more than two and a half times greater than the white, notes that "the differential is probably too great to be explained by social conditions and undoubtedly reflects an actual difference in available care."[41]

Social class differences in health are, of course, not unique to the United States. As sociologists M. Susser and W. Watson point out, the effect of social class in modern industrial society is nowhere more evident than in the distribution of health and disease, showing up most strongly in infant mortality rates, stillbirth rates and death rates of men from respiratory tuberculosis, rheumatic heart disease, pneumonia and bronchitis.[42] What is unique to the United States is the extent of the differences when analysis focuses on racial comparisons. The 1968 estimates of life expectancy for white males, for instance, is 71.1 years, whereas for nonwhite males it drops to 63.7

years.[43] The dramatic contrast between white and nonwhite infant mortality rates has been often noted, as well as the "phenomenally high" nonwhite maternal mortality rate. In 1966, the infant mortality rate was 2.9 per 10,000 live births for white mothers compared to 7.2 for nonwhite mothers.[44] Nonwhite infant mortality rates, although improving over the past two decades, are largely responsible for the poor standing of the United States relative to England on this index.

Inequality based on income and race dominates participation in our medical care system whether judged by frequency of use or quality of service. When average number of physician contacts is estimated by age, for instance, a strong pattern of economic differentials emerges particularly for the childhood years.[45] Significantly, poor people, and especially nonwhites, are admitted to hospitals less frequently than those more favored economically and socially, but, when admitted, they remain for longer periods. It seems probable that they have developed more serious conditions and require more extended treatment because their illnesses have not been treated.

Many [poor] families, living in the midst of poverty and disease, don't expect anything else. . . . Many think that if they come . . . and can't pay, they won't be cared for, and so they don't bother coming. Some go to municipal hospitals and sit all day and then go home, afraid of losing jobs because the boss will think they are deadbeats. A mother waits for her husband to come home to take care of the other children while she takes one to the clinic, and then finds there is no evening clinic . . .

Dr. John Knowles

The facts show that, with the exception of the elderly now subsidized by Medicare, the low-income population remains outside the mainstream of private health care. The sources of their medical care are, rather, hospital outpatient and emergency departments and health department clinics. Hospital emergency departments are, in fact, the only or primary source of care for many inner-city households. Here they receive episodic treatment seldom geared to a comprehensive approach. According to sociologist Mary Herman, health services for the poor suffer more than others from depersonalization, disorganization and inadequate emphasis on health counseling. She attributes this situation to the continuance of charity attitudes in the conduct of clinic services. Like others concerned with health care inequalities, she advocates providing sufficient financial support so that everyone can be a "paying patient," able to choose among health services.[46]

So far, government efforts to open up access to medical care for the low-income population have been somewhat limited. Since 1967, about 63 neighborhood health centers originally funded through the Office of Economic Opportunity have been set up to offer comprehensive care in poverty areas. They have reached only small numbers at a high cost and the extension of the program, much less its expansion, is now in question.[47] The federal government also disburses grants to states, localities and private sector institutions for a variety of specific purposes, including maternal and child health services, services for crippled children and infant care.[48] In addition, the Medicaid program, established by Congress in 1965, provides benefits to those defined as needy under widely differing state formulas through a system of matching state and federal funds. The benefits can be applied to private treatment. The program has been criticized for the low eligibility levels and elaborate red tape characterizing the separate state plans as well as the inflated medical fees and fraud it has produced.

The most successful and far-reaching attempt to reduce economic barriers to health care is the Medicare program for people 65 and older. It pays up to 80 percent of "reasonable charges," after the first $50 in each calendar year.[49] Medicare does not involve a means test. For the first time, it makes medical benefits available as a right to a major segment of the population, excluding only those not under Social Security.

reading: **Daniel Schorr**
CHICAGO, ILLINOIS: WELFARE DOCTOR, WELFARE PATIENT

Chicago is the medical capital of America. It is the headquarters of the American Medical Association, with an annual budget of $34 million. Chicago has eighty hospitals and five medical schools. But in the West Side ghetto, with 300,000 people and disease rates three to four times the national average, people have to travel miles and wait for hours for access to one charity hospital that must take them in—Cook County, the nation's largest general hospital.

Cook County, on the day of our visit, was bursting at the seams. More than a thousand persons daily crowd into its registration and emergency room for treatment. They are not necessarily emergency cases, but for many it is the only way to see a doctor. Many, discouraged by the wait, leave before they are attended. Others, who need a hospital bed, are sent home because no hospital bed is available. For those who are admitted, there may be waits of three to four hours for X-rays, even in emergencies. They are crowded into medical wards where there is one registered nurse for a hundred patients. Of those admitted, one out of every six dies.

Those who run Cook County Hospital grieve about the situation but have no solution. [We] witnessed one frustrated consultation that must have happened hundreds of times. Dr. Hunter Cutting, director of medicine, talked to Dr. Jeb Boswell, director of admissions, estimating that he had one bed for every three persons needing a bed.

"Listen, is there anything we can do because we have six beds left in medicine, and there are a lot of them out there?"

Dr. Boswell said, "Well, you're going to get about seventy or eighty admissions today. And I think our standing agreement is that if you don't have beds in medicine, you send them off to general surgery."

Dr. Boswell went on, "This may be the night. We don't have enough technicians to give

blood counts. We can't give them blood chemistries. We have this turnaround time in X-ray.

We take a look at the X-ray delay times and say, 'Well it's better that they get under treatment without an X-ray than to keep them down there an additional three or four hours.' That is for emergency X-rays."

Dr. Cutting left him, muttering, "I don't know, frankly, where we're going to put that crowd out there."

The crowd "out there" in the receiving room was not as big as it could have been. Many from the West Side ghetto are reluctant to go to Cook County, even in dire need. They would prefer to go to a neighborhood doctor, but there are few neighborhood doctors in the ghetto. There are empty offices of physicians and surgeons who have long since left for richer territory. We found more doctors in one medical office building in the comfortable North Side than in the entire West side ghetto.

Dr. Jean Bernier is one of the few who stayed, and he is branded by many of his colleagues with the epithet, "welfare doctor." Dr. Bernier often sees more patients in a day than his colleagues see in a week—as many as 150 in a twelve-hour day. And he told us how it is to be a "welfare doctor."

"You get complaints from organizations. You get complaints from your own physician friends. You get complaints from the hospitals. I'm afraid the doctors and hospitals need more education about the problems. For example, when you bring a patient to the hospital, they say, "Well, here's Bernier with another welfare patient!" In other words, like it was something else, you know. Well, sometimes they are a little different because they're a little dirty. They're all alone and they haven't been able to wash themselves. They're senile. They may be a little more of a problem. But they need hospital care, and you can't send everybody to County. Many times you can't send people to County because they won't go. I've seen people die because they refused to go to County."

There are few hospitals that will take the poor, and there are few Dr. Berniers to try to send them. Frank Brown is a community health worker in Kenwood-Oakland, a community that has one doctor for every 15,000 people—less than one-tenth the national average. Brown became a health worker when his daughter died because he couldn't get her into a nearby hospital in time to save her.

[We were] present when Brown called the welfare office from the home of an elderly woman, Mrs. Ivory Montgomery, whose legs were paining her from the hips down. Brown's end of the conversation went like this:

"Well, I don't know what happened. Only thing I know is that she can't walk and she needs a doctor. You know of no doctor who will come into the home? Doesn't public aid have working agreements with doctors where doctors will come to see patients who can't get about? You'll check with the medical department? The only thing I am interested in is that the lady is very sick and trying to get a doctor to see her . . .

"Let me ask you this—isn't it the obligation of public assistance to send in medical help when a person is quite ill? She needs to see a doctor now—right now! You know, I've been calling for about an hour-and-a-half and, you know, everyone has the same story that the doctor just won't come out. . . ."

The doctor did not come to Mrs. Montgomery that day. Nor did an ambulance come to the home of Mrs. Laura Hayes, whom Brown found with a doctor's note saying that she needed immediate hospitalization. Nor did any help come in time to two other homes, where persons were found dead.

"We're already a sick society," says Brown, "and we'll become a sicker society simply because people just don't care. They're more interested in perpetuating wars, more interested in getting to the moon. They just aren't interested in people's health. I've been in

281

homes where people are ill to the point where they need to be hospitalized, and hospitals will tell you that they're filled to capacity. There's no room. That's how people get to feel dehumanized. . . ."

From
Don't Get Sick in America by Daniel Schorr
(Nashville: Aurora Publishers, Incorporated, 1970)
pp. 44-48

Proposals for change

It must be kept in mind that problems of health and those of care are not necessarily identical. It is probable that changes in life-styles and living conditions as well as public health measures are at least as important as personal medical care for improving health outcomes today. The failure of mortality rates to decline further in this country during the past fifteen years despite advances in medical science is attributed by many experts to the determining influence of cultural and environmental factors.[50]

If optimum health rather than health care is the objective, then items requiring action should include, among other things: nutrition and diet; exercise; the misuse of alcohol, drugs and tobacco; environmental pollution control; unemployment; housing and urban renewal; accident prevention and recreation. Some of these are matters to which a medical care system can address itself directly. Others belong in the domain of economic and social policy and programs. Still others are rooted in cultural patterns that are highly resistant to planned change.

The widespread perception of health as a social problem, however, focuses on the transparent failure of the medical care system to match the delivery of health services with its potential. Remedies for that failure range from the cautious to the visionary, covering a spectrum from slight modifications of the status quo to a complete restructuring of the present system into some variety of national health service. On a practical level, proposals for change have three principal targets—financing, manpower and the organization of practice.

National health insurance

Rising costs have created a receptive climate for the idea of federally financed health insurance. This development is clearly related to the wide diversity of groups whose interests are now affected—industry and labor, hospitals and insurance companies, consumers at all levels. At least five major bills are presently before Congress, and it seems inevitable that a national health insurance program of some kind will be enacted in the very near future. Sponsors of the bills run the gamut from organized labor to organized medicine. They include the President and the health leadership of his administration, the insurance industry and leading Republican and Democratic senators.

Beyond the common objective of meeting the cost crisis, the bills vary widely. They differ as to population coverage, range of benefits, method and source of financing and the degree to which a voluntary or compulsory system is called for. Not surprisingly, the weakest are the AMA and insurance company proposals that provide for federal subsidy of voluntary insurance payments. The strongest is the labor-sponsored bill introduced by Senator Kennedy that provides for compulsory, federally financed coverage of all United States residents, the most comprehensive range of benefits and no deductibles or cost-sharing.[51] In addition, it attempts to institute far-reaching reforms within the health care system. The Administration proposal involves both compulsory and voluntary plans, a wide range of benefits and substantial co-payments by the patient.

Whatever form it takes, a program of national health insurance must face the specter of even greater price inflation as the result of its expenditures. The Medicare experience provides a pointed lesson in the need for stringent cost control when demand mushrooms without any associated change in the system. Whether or not the proposals now on the table have handled this problem realistically is an open question.

Prepaid group practice

After a long uphill fight for acceptance, prepaid group health plans have been given a green light. Increasing numbers are being established with the help of federal grants and foundation subsidies by medical schools, hospitals, labor unions, community groups and insurance organizations, frequently in cooperation with each other. Almost all the major proposals for the national health insurance, including the Administration's measure, contain some provisions for encouraging prepaid plans, or health maintenance organizations, as they are currently called, as an alternative way of payment for health services. The one exception is the AMA proposal. After years of fierce opposition, however, organized medicine now seems prepared to permit if not to promote what has been described as a basic revolution in the relationship between patients and those who treat them.

Prepaid group health plans are advocated on the grounds of quality and economy. On the one hand, evidence from ongoing programs shows lower hospitalization rates and consumer costs. Even more impressive, they have at the same time delivered continuous comprehensive services stressing preventive medicine and primary care. The fact that members of HIP (Health Insurance Plan of Greater New York) have 25 percent fewer hospital admissions than other Blue Cross members is, for instance, attributed to the effective preventive care they have received.[52]

Prepaid programs vary in size and organizational details, but their common format involves the elimination of fee-for-service payment and solo practice. Instead, in return for a fixed annual fee the consumer has available the services of a group of salaried doctors, specialists as well as general practitioners. Most plans cover virtually all health needs, including hospital and home care, diagnostic and laboratory procedures and even drugs. An important innovation marking many of them has been consumer participation in policy decisions and management. Most frequently cited as a successful model of prepaid group practice is the Kaiser Permanente organization with 2 million members, 2000 doctors and a network of hospitals and outpatient clinics in California, Oregon and Hawaii.

Medicare is a revolution. . . .
It is an explosion altering in drastic ways the entire status quo of the health professions. By guaranteeing payment of actual costs, it alters the system of piratical socialism by which doctors and hospitals have been shoving the burdens of those who can't pay onto the shoulders of those who can. By the very terms of this guarantee, it assumes the necessity to check on the legitimacy of costs.

Fred J. Cook

Although the prepaid idea is being hailed as the hope of the future, organizations operating along these lines presently make up only a tiny proportion of the medical care scene. About 96 percent of all Americans still pay for their medical care through the familiar fee-for-service system, and only 4 percent through prepaid plans.[53] To change that proportion significantly is clearly no overnight undertaking. The process seems to have begun, but its success is doubtful.

Solving the doctor shortage

Opening the door to medical care through national health insurance cannot help but make the doctor shortage even more severe. Prospects for reducing this shortage seem dim without positive steps to alter the present situation. The remedies proposed so far, however, seem a long way from meeting the realistic problem.

The most obvious approach, training more doctors, has been taken to a limited degree. Since the early 1960s, there has been a continuing expansion in medical education largely promoted through government grants. Since 1963, when some 8500 students entered 81 medical schools, the number of students has grown to 11,000 and the number of medical schools has increased to 107.[54] Unfortunately, the scale of this increase hardly begins to match the magnitude of present and impending needs, particularly with the dominant emphasis on specialization. A number of schools have, therefore, begun to experiment with ways of speeding up medical education by consolidating graduate and undergraduate training and by conducting year-round classes. Meanwhile, efforts to add to the number of new medical schools and students continue.

A more innovative approach and, according to many authorities, a more promising one is to develop mid-level health professionals who can replace the physician for certain tasks. New kinds of medical personnel are now being trained along these lines both to work on their own and under the direct supervision of a doctor. These include physicians' assistants, nurse practitioners and child health practitioners. Some programs are building on the skills of former medical corpsmen who are trained to take over routine work in clinics and physicians' offices. Other programs provide nurses with traditional training which equips them to function on their own or in teams with the back-up of supervising physicians. A new five-year program in Colorado is producing Child Health Associates qualified to give diagnostic, preventive and therapeutic services to about 80 percent of the children seen by physicians.

The problem of geographical distribution remains one of the most difficult and controversial. Yet past experience indicates that whenever it comes to anything approaching direct action knotty issues arise. Medical educators, for instance, expressed strong opposition to a recent New York State bill requiring that state medical schools reserve vacancies for students who agreed to practice in underdoctored communities.[55] Despite their avowed support for its goals, opponents argued that the bill would reduce the caliber of medical students, increase already tight competition among superior applicants (who presumeably would not agree to the terms) and create two classes of students. There would seem, then, to be a basic conflict between the norms and values dominating professional medicine and the felt needs of the larger public.

Interesting evidence of ambivalence on this score is to be found even within organized medicine. One example was the published reaction to a recent proposal of the AMA president for subsidized medical education as part of a campaign to solve the maldistribution of doctors. In return, the graduating doctor whose education had been financed would spend three years in areas short of medical services, receiving a limited license that permitted him to practice only where he was assigned. The article reporting this plan in the publication of the Medical Society of the County of New York makes the following comment:

> Some 20, 10 or even 5 years ago such a suggestion by the President of the AMA might have been unthinkable—indeed impeachable—but times have changed . . . Thus Dr. Hoffman's ideas are today tolerable, if not yet wholly acceptable. . . .
>
> As Dr. Hoffman states his plan would be a most radical concept for most of the medical profession but it is one that might be tried to see how it works. Somehow the unequal distribution of physicians must be overcome.[56]

As to the lopsided balance between specialists and primary care physicians in the medical care system, various small-scale programs for dealing with it are undergoing trial runs. As noted earlier, medical schools have initiated specialties in family medicine, for instance, and training in community-based ambulatory care. A more drastic reorganization of medical education has been urged to produce increased numbers of primary care physicians. The medical mainstream, however, is apparently still headed in the opposite direction.

Notes

[1] David Mechanic, "The English National Health Services: Some Comparisons with the United States," *Journal of Health and Social Behavior,* 12, 1, March, 1971, p. 18.

[2] Helen Rowan, ed., *Carnegie Quarterly,* Carnegie Corporation of America, Vol. 18, No. 3, Summer, 1970, p. 1.

[3] Odin W. Anderson, *Health Care: Can There Be Equity?* (New York: John Wiley & Sons, 1972) p. 149.

[4] Milton I. Roemer, "Nationalized Medicine for America," *Transaction,* Vol. 8, No. 11, September, 1971, p. 31.

[5] Anderson, *op. cit.,* p. 152.

[6] M. W. Susser & W. Watson, *Sociology in Medicine* (New York: Oxford University Press, 1971) p. 39.

[7] Anderson, *op. cit.,* p. 129.

[8] Monroe Lerner, "Health as a Social Problem," in Erwin O. Smigel, ed., *Handbook on the Study of Social Problems* (Chicago: Rand McNally, 1971) p. 301.

[9] Eliot Freidson, "The Organization of Medical Practice," Howard E. Freeman, Sol Levine & Leo G. Reeder, eds., *Handbook of Medical Sociology* (Englewood Cliffs, N.J.: Prentice-Hall, Inc., 1972) 2nd ed., p. 344; Lerner, *op. cit.,* pp. 291-292; Roemer, *op. cit.,* pp. 31-32.

[10] Freidson, *op. cit.,* p. 345.

[11] Anderson, *op. cit.,* p. 68.

[12] Ibid., p. 69.

[13] Leonard L. Magnani, "Health Institutions: A Brief Introduction," Dorthy Flapan, ed., *American Social Institutions,* (New York: Behavioral Publications, Inc., 1972) p. 281.

[14] John H. Knowles, "Is There a Doctor Shortage?" mimeo. of remarks, p. 2.

[15] Sylvester E. Becki & Alan W. Heston, "Introduction," *The Annals of the American Academy of Political and Social Science,* January, 1972, p. x.

[16] Anderson, *op. cit.,* p. 232.

[17] Magnani, *op. cit.,* p. 283.

[18] *Carnegie Quarterly, op. cit.,* p. 1.

[19] Barbara and John Ehrenreich, *The American Health Empire: Power, Profits, and Politics,* A Health-PAC Book (New York: Random House/Vintage Books, 1971) pp. 29–39.

[20] Roemer, *op. cit.,* p. 32.

[21] M. A. Farber, "Study Will Explore State's 'Doctor Shortage'" *The New York Times,* June 15, 1973, p. 39; p. 75.

[22] Anderson, *op. cit.,* p. 95.

[23] Roemer, *op. cit.*, p. 32.

[24] Knowles, op. cit., p. 4.

[25] The Robert Wood Johnson Foundation, Annual Report, 1972, (Princeton, N.J.: The Robert Wood Johnson Foundation, 1972) p. 12.

[26] Sydney H. Croog & Donna F. Ver Steeg, "The Hospital as a Social System," in Freedman, Levine, & Reeder, eds., *op. cit.*, p. 275.

[27] *Statistical Abstract of the United States, 1970* (Washington D.C.: U.S. Bureau of the Census, 1970), p. 70.

[28] Croog & Ver Steeg, *op. cit.*, p. 278.

[29] Anderson, *op. cit.*, p. 131. *Statistical Abstract*, 1970, *op. cit.* p. 69.

[30] Croog & Ver Steeg, *op. cit.*, p. 277.

[31] Anderson, *op. cit.*, p. 117; p. 214.

[32] *Ibid.* p. 113.

[33] Odin W. Anderson and Ronald M. Anderson, "Patterns of Use of Health Services," Freeman, Levin & Reeder, eds., *op. cit.*, p. 387.

[34] *Statistical Abstract 1970, op. cit.*, p. 462.

[35] Paul B. Horton & Gerald R. Leslie, *The Sociology of Social Problems,* 4th Edition, (New York: Appleton-Century Crafts, 1970) p. 550.

[36] Anderson & Anderson, *op. cit.*, p. 400.

[37] Knowles, *op. cit.*, p. 3.

[38] W. W. Holland, "Experiences of Medical Care in the United States," *The Lancet,* July 25, 1970.

[39] Magnani, *op. cit.*, p. 124.

[40] Croog & Ver Steeg, *op. cit.*, p. 277; Barbara & John Ehrenrich, *op. cit.*, pp. 138-139.

[41] Anderson, *op. cit.*, p. 151.

[42] Susser & Watson, *op. cit.*, p. 111.

[43] Becki & Heston, *op. cit.*, p. xi.

[44] Anderson, *op. cit.*, p. 149.

[45] Lerner, *op. cit.*, p. 305.

[46] Mary Herman, "The Poor Their Medical Needs and the Health Services Available to Them," *The Annals, op. cit.*, p. 21.

[47] Roemer, *Ibid.*, p. 33; Herman, *op. cit.*, p. 17.

[48] *Statistical Abstract*, 1970, *op. cit.*, p. 275.

[49] Horton & Leslie, *op. cit.*, pp. 556-557.

[50] *New England Journal of Medicine, op. cit.*, p. 78. Anderson, *op. cit.*, p. 142.

[51] Roemer, *op. cit.*, p. 33.

[52] Horton & Leslie, *op. cit.,* p. 553.

[53] "Group Health Plan Passed by Senate," *The New York Times,* May 17, 1973 (By Associated Press).

[54] Howard S. Becker, Blanche Geer, & Stephen J. Miller, "Medical Education," Freeman, Levine & Reeder, eds., *op. cit.,* p. 191.

[55] Farber, *op. cit.,* p. 39; p. 75.

[56] "Solving the Maldistribution of MD's" *New York Medicine,* Official Publication of the Medical Society of the County of New York, February, 1973, pp. 56-60.

Summary

The United States spends more of its national income on health care than any other nation, yet some industrial nations with a much smaller investment, such as Sweden and England, achieve better health care results. The exorbitant costs, the discrimination in service, and the lack of quality treatment characteristic of the present American health care system are conditions which have grown up at the same time that American medicine has made its most dazzling technical advances. The promise of better health today has also meant that more people want more and more types of care, at a time when there are neither enough doctors nor adequate health facilities to go around. Americans have come to view health care as a right, but physicians' services and care facilities are still organized on a fee-for-service basis.

Modern medicine has become largely a matter of specialist treatment in technologically sophisticated facilities. The personalized doctor-patient relationship, though touted by organized medicine in support of its free enterprise medical ideology, has largely disappeared from the scene. More hospital care has meant more and higher medical costs, which in turn have forced Americans to rely on third-party medical insurance concerns to help pay their medical fees. Some observers see the third party fee-for-service funding system as responsible for encouraging excessive use of facilities, unnecessary treatment and irresponsible investment.

The shortage of doctors and other medical personnel is not only a shortage in numbers, but is related to geographical distribution and distribution among the medical specialities. The shortage is most critical in rural and inner-city locations, and in the area of primary care.

The poor, especially minorities, are less healthy than the non-poor; they live in areas where doctors and hospital facilities are likely to be scarce or too expensive. They receive less health care and what they do receive is inferior. Federal aid in the form of medicare and medicaid have alleviated this situation somewhat for older citizens.

Numerous proposals for national health insurance programs have been put forward as attempts to remedy the problems of the health care system. Any national health program would cause the demand for medical care to mushroom. Cost control of some form, and better management of available resources, will be necessary to hold prices in check and avoid declining quality of care in the future. A reorganization of the systems of payment has also been proposed, with physicians being paid fixed salaries, or stated fees for each patient for whatever services are required over a fixed period of time.

part

2
deviant behavior

chapter

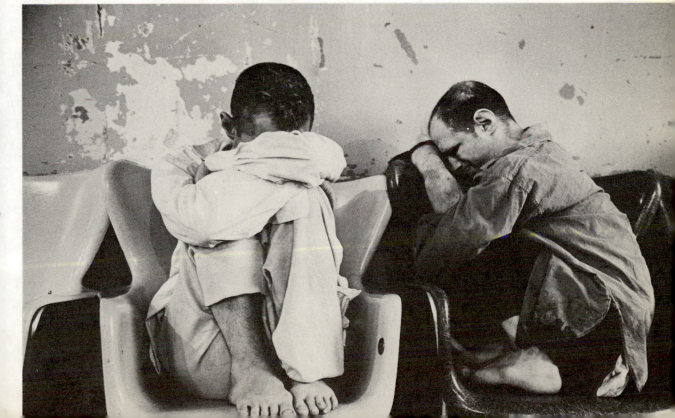

mental disorders

It has recently become the fashion to speak of crime, drug abuse, corruption as evidence of a "sickness" in our society. The word "sickness" has become a catchword for any dysfunction or break-down, any unhappy departure from the normal. We now freely apply the schizophrenic's word, "unreal," to events around us; the alienation of self characteristic of many forms of mental illness thus becomes a metaphor for the alienation of man from his society.

To the sociologist, this use of language and the "sickness" metaphor is more interesting for what it says about our attitudes than for what it says about the "real world." As our language suggests, we have come to perceive mental illness, and a variety of other phenomena, as social problems that can be diagnosed, treated and possibly cured. We are no longer willing to accept drug abuse or corruption (a healthier society would have less of this), and we are not willing to sentence and ignore the disturbed among us. In most cases we feel that the disturbed person is treatable. At any rate, he is very much among us, and we are not so likely as former generations to claim an inevitable difference between him and ourselves. Indeed there is no basis for such a distinction. Some sociologists have estimated that a majority of the population suffers from disorders that prevent them from being fully secure, adaptable, natural and happy.

Perhaps because so many of us are perceived to be afflicted in some way, we have come to place a good deal of the onus for mental illness on society or environment. We recognize that there may be social situations to which maladjustment is the most appropriate response. "What shall we think of a well-adjusted slave? A well-adjusted prisoner?" asks psychologist Abraham Maslow.[1] Can we expect disturbed behavior in given circumstances, or as the result of certain social strains? And can we prevent it? The answers to many of these questions will come in large part from social psychology. We are better equipped, and more willing, than past generations to seek sociological definitions and explanations for mental illness.

Definitions of mental illness

Definitions of mental illness vary, each representing a specific orientation and frame of reference. Before considering the ways in which they differ, it is worth noting that they share a common viewpoint: all view the problem in relative rather than absolute terms and none can define in any absolute sense the difference between a "sick" and a "normal" person.

Clinical definition

Because the mentally ill are often treated by physicians, it is not surprising that one of the earliest clinical or pathological definitions grew out of the medical tradition. According to the medical model, mental disorders involve aberrant behaviors that result from a diseased or disordered state within the individual. This state is evidenced and diagnosed on the basis of "symptoms" observed in a clinical setting—such as the twitching of facial muscles or perhaps the confused use of language. Although the clinical definition relies on objective observation, it is not entirely free of social judgments. Two observers might concur on the existence of a facial twitch: but, given different backgrounds, they might meaningfully disagree on what constitutes confused language or inappropriate laughter.

Statistical definition

A second definition, along statistical lines, is purely descriptive and devoid of social judgment. According to the statistical approach, whatever strays far from the normal is, quite simply, abnormal. The definition is based on the bell-shaped "curve of normal distribution," which graphically portrays the relative frequency of a given trait in the general population. Most people tend to cluster around the high middle of the curve, and the statistical viewpoint maintains that these people are in the majority and therefore may be considered "average" or "normal." The normal range of the curve encompasses the middle two-thirds of any group of subjects under study. People outside the range are considered statistically "deviant"—those to the far right show an excess or above average endowment of the trait that is being measured, while those to the left show a deficiency.

There are several difficulties in using the statistical approach to define mental illness. First, the approach is more dependable when simple, tangible traits, such as age, sex, height and weight are described than when psychological factors are assessed. After all, it is more difficult to measure intelligence, aggressiveness, jealousy and the like. Second, the definition is not applicable to a large number of traits and behaviors, for we have come to accept statistical divergencies without question. We do not conclude that people who are left-handed are abnormal or mentally ill just because the average person is right-handed. Third, that which is most frequent is not necessarily most "normal." If practically everyone in our society were to come down with the measles, we would not rush to the conclusion that this is a normal state of affairs.

Social definition

The social definition does not look closely at the actual frequency of traits or behaviors, but rather at the behavioral norms that a society approves and upholds. The social definition assigns the label of "abnormal" or "mentally ill" to many behaviors and attitudes that are not generally approved by society, and over which the individual has little or no control. Although this is the most arbitrary of definitions, it is not applied to the same extent as in the past. Today, for example, we do not resort to burning witches at the stake. Nevertheless we still use it; we do not hesitate to say that any parent who repeatedly beats a child is abnormal or sick, for we think child-beating indicates inability to control aggressive impulses. There are many such definitions that people in American society implicitly share, as well as some that are more controversial.

Practical definition

Still another definition of mental illness derives from purely practical criteria: Can the person function at home or on a job? Does he have access to his own capabilities most of the time? A person who cannot function is more likely to be labelled mentally ill than one who displays many of the same symptoms, but has nonetheless managed to maintain a position in society. A man who behaves strangely, talking to himself or to passersby in public, is apt to be called "crazy," especially if he is unemployed, broke and alone. But if such an individual happens to be an artist or scientist, with a regular income and a respectable social position, he may well be thought a genius.

Mental health and mental illness

All definitions of mental illness presuppose some understanding of positive mental health. However, there is no generally agreed-upon definition of what constitutes good mental health. Many of the theories on mental health that have emerged over the years suffer from an overdependence on specific cultures or periods and are therefore limited in their validity.

One useful definition, developed in the early 1950s by A. H. Maslow and B. Mittlemann, postulated ten criteria for a normal personality; that is, for one possessed of mental health.[2] The Maslow-Mittlemann list was subsequently modified by other authorities, but its basic tenets still suggest the consensus on mental "normalcy" which is characterized as follows:

1. An adequate feeling of security

2. A realistic self-evaluation

3. Attainable life goals based on realistic self-evaluation

4. Adequate contact with the everyday world of reality

5. Self-consistency

6. The ability to profit from experience

7. A judicious degree of spontaneity

8. Emotionality appropriate to the occasion

9. A judicious balance between ingroup cooperativeness and maintenance of individuality

10. Appropriate physical desires gratified in appropriate ways

Of course, not all these qualities are present to an equal degree in all mentally healthy persons at all times. It is the general profile that can be useful to us.

Another useful definition of mental health that preceded the one offered by Maslow and Mittlemann was proposed by a Commission of the 1948 International Congress on Mental Health. This commission defined mental health as a quality that operates at both the individual and societal levels:

1. Mental health is a conditon which permits the optimal development, physical, intellectual and emotional, of the individual, so far as this is compatible with that of other individuals.

2. A good society is one that allows this development to its members while at the same time ensuring its own development and being tolerant toward other societies.[3]

According to K. Soddy,[4] adjustment is the critical quality for mental health. Soddy's definition states, among other criteria, that "the healthy minded person has the capacity to live harmoniously in a changing environment." H. C. Rumke, however, points out that adaptability, consistency and balance in all things are more characteristic of mature individuals than of children or adolescents, and may not necessarily mean the latter are mentally unhealthy.[5]

As common as any of these definitions is the notion that mental health is equivalent to "happiness." Even if this were so, it would not be helpful from the standpoint of definition, for happiness, like mental health, is a quality often conspicuous by its absence. Probably happiness on a long-range basis is not possible without mental health; but mental health can certainly exist separately from feelings of happiness.

Types of mental disorders

For over 4000 years, man has been observing and classifying disturbed behaviors and attitudes that have come to be called mental illness. Not surprisingly, the disturbances that accompany the aging process were among the first to be noted, as were alcoholic disorders. The ancient Greeks studied and described a number of physical ailments that seemed to spring from mental disturbances. Their descriptions, although somewhat simplistic, helped to lay the ground for a medical orientation toward mental illness that predominated for many centuries.

In some periods, for example in the Middle Ages, the medical model was supplanted by a belief in supernatural causes. The disturbed person was thought to be "obsessed" by an external devil or "possessed" by one from within. He was regarded less as a patient than as a sinner. Progress to a more scientific consideration of mental illness occurred during the eighteenth and nineteenth centuries, when asylums first brought large numbers of the mentally ill under the systematic observation of doctors. From the 1840s on, first under the leadership of Dorothea Dix, Americans, whose intentions were humane, began to build asylums. In France, Philippe Pinel initiated the practice of taking case histories and keeping records on patients. He formulated a simple classification system on the basis of his observations. Similar work was undertaken in the United States by Benjamin Rush, the "Father of American Psychiatry," author of this country's first treatise on mental illness.

With the advent of the first psychological laboratory in Leipzig, Germany took the lead in psychiatric and psychological inquiry. Emil Kraepelin, the man responsible for the first modern classification system, emerged out of this background in the second half of the nineteenth century. His work, like Pinel's, centered around asylum practice. A major contribution was his observation that the symptoms of the mentally disturbed usually form clusters, or syndromes. He regarded these as symptomatic of specific mental conditions, and on this basis he worked out the first modern classification. With the development of more sophisticated research and clinical techniques, further refinements in diagnosis became possible.

The first statistically based nomenclature was set up in 1917 by the organization that subsequently became the American Psychiatric Association. Naturally, the nomenclature has been periodically revised in accordance with new research. Some of the most important categories will be briefly described here.

The psychoses

The most debilitating of the emotional disorders are the psychoses, including schizophrenia, paranoid psychoses, manic-depressive psychoses, involutional melancholia and a number of related disorders. All are characterized by unusual behavior, distortion of reality and an inability to function, either all or part of the time. The psychotic patient is more likely than others to be institutionalized. Usually he is committed because he threatens harm to himself or others, is unable or unwilling to attend to his basic needs or because his behaviors have become intolerable to family and friends. If he is afraid of self-destruction, he may admit himself voluntarily. It is not unusual for a patient who is diagnosed as psychotic—particularly if he is old or improverished—to be permanently institutionalized. Nevertheless, it is estimated that, at any given time, there are as many psychotics in the community at large as in the institutionalized population.[6]

Schizophrenia

The most prevalent of the psychoses, schizophrenia, accounts for more than 50 percent of all chronic mental hospital cases. Its principal symptoms include delusions, hallucinations (especially inner "voices"), bizarre response and withdrawal from personal relationships. Often the schizophrenic has no understanding of his own behavior, but during periods of lucidity he may appear perceptive and normally intelligent.

In the course of a schizophrenic retreat, the psychotic . . . may come to know the exaltation of a union with the universe, transcending personal bounds: the "oceanic feeling," Freud called it. Feelings arise, then, too, of a new knowledge. Things that before had been mysterious are now fully understood . . . our schizophrenic patient is actually experiencing inadvertently that same beatific ocean deep which the yogi and the saint are ever striving to enjoy: except that, whereas they are swimming in it, he is drowning.

Joseph Campbell

The schizophrenic is one for whom the real environment in which he lives has become too painful. Therefore, he proceeds to develop a variety of delusions about the world; gradually, he constructs an "unreal" self to deal with others. If he is a paranoid schizophrenic, he may believe that hostile forces influence the weather, political events, the deaths of famous people and so on. Despite his bizarre behavior, the schizophrenic is frequently understandable in rational terms. It is possible, for example, to understand why the institutionalized patient, who receives no letters or visits from a family that professes to love him, will accuse the nurses of an elaborate plot to steal his mail and refuse entrance to his visitors.

Inasmuch as schizophrenic behavior appears to be a rational attempt to escape an unbearable family or social environment, there is much to be gained from a psychological-sociological approach that concentrates on the environment, its meaning to the patient and its effect in precipitating and sustaining the illness. Intensive research is underway in such areas as the modes of interaction in the schizophrenic-producing family, the effect of peer relationships and so forth. These studies often produce results that are meaningful in sociological terms. One recent study, reported by David Hamburg,[7] notes the presence of distinctive interaction characteristics in families with schizophrenic members and shows that these characteristics are independent of socioeconomic status and racial background.

The problem of schizophrenia has also been investigated from a biological perspective. Studies of identical twins have attempted to separate genetic and environmental factors and, simultaneously, to trace their interdependence. H. L. Newbold describes how biochemical work has concentrated on abnormalities of neuroregulatory agents and blood proteins, with inquiry into the related role of diet and nutrition; for example, the deficiency or malabsorption of Vitamin B_{12} is a possible causative factor.[8] Recently, a research group isolated an enzyme, monoamine oxidase, that is a possible indicator of vulnerability to schizophrenia.[9]

Paranoid psychoses

In paranoid reactions, the dominant diagnostic feature is suspicion, and the degree varies in accordance with the extent of personality disorganization. This disintegration is mild to moderate in paranoia and the paranoid states, but is severe in paranoid schizophrenia. Central to paranoid reactions is an internally consistent system of delusions based on feelings of persecution or grandiosity. This involves no hallucinations or impairment of intelligence.

Ullman and Krasner state that no definite cause has been established for paranoid reactions, although a number of theories attempt to explain their dynamics. Freud's formulation, for instance, postulates a defense mechanism—projection—which is present in all individuals, but excessively so in neurotics and psychotics.[10] Traits unacceptable in oneself are projected onto another person or persons.

Sociologically, Lemert's formulation is more significant. Lemert argues that the individual's suspiciousness may be a realistic, rather than delusional, response to a situation that is itself misunderstood by the patient.[11] Suppose, for example, that the family of the disturbed person has noticed increasing oddities of behavior. Their own reaction is to accelerate their watchfulness over him. They may compare observations among themselves and fall silent whenever he appears. The disturbed person, unaware of his family's concern, notices only the secret watching, the furtive conversations. Based on these correct observations, he makes the incorrect but logical assumption that he is the victim of a conspiracy. Lemert's formulation calls for the investigation of the paranoid reaction as a function of the environment in which it occurs. Significant in terms of his theory is the fact that paranoid patients often come from changing inner-city neighborhoods that offer much material for paranoid delusion.

Manic-depressive psychosis

States of high excitement and elation alternate with depression and melancholia. These states were recognized as a single illness by Kraepelin, who named the syndrome manic-depressive psychosis. The illness is characterized by rapid mood swings of sudden onset and equally sudden disappearance. It tends to recur at intervals, sometimes as long as several years, with approximately one in two hundred people affected. Patients, most of them in their middle years, exhibit one of three distinct reaction types: depressive reaction, manic reaction and mixed or circular reaction.

Involutional melancholia

Unlike the depression phase of manic-depression psychosis, involutional melancholia almost always appears during or after middle age, without previous history of depression or violent mood alterations. It is responsible for about 4 percent of all first admissions to mental hospitals. Decidedly more prevalent in women, it often accompanies the menopause.

Psychosomatic disorders

Since the second half of the nineteenth century, when Freud, among others, pointed to the possible psychological roots of certain physical diseases, the number of disorders labeled "psychosomatic" has been steadily growing. Current research suggests that the development of psychosomatic disease may be more complex than formerly believed. Animal experiments indicate that some widely differing conditions, for example, viral infection and a form of cancer, may be at least partly due to the interaction of early life experience and current environmental stress.

Hans Selye has pointed out that stress may act nonspecifically and may lead to widely differing pathological results.[12] Similarly, Margaret Mead, as early as 1947, stated her conviction that, far from being an extraneous factor, culture is a vital component in the development of sickness. The disease-producing responses of an individual are not separable from the stresses to which society subjects him.[13]

Neurotic disorders

Unlike the psychotic patient, the neurotic is involved in the real world; he desperately wants to succeed in his relationships, but consistently chooses the wrong strategies. Self-defeating in the extreme, the neurotic is so inflexible as to appear to have no real choice in some of his behaviors. Although there are many differing manifestations of neurosis, common to most of them are inflexibility, anxiety over change, no matter how small, and unrealistically high or low aspirations, with consequent discrepancy between the neurotic's "image" and his role in the world. When anxieties become too great, the neurotic may be hospitalized and is sometimes described as having a "nervous breakdown."

According to Freud, the major causative agent of neuroses is the sexual instinct, followed in importance by aggression and the death instinct. Suppression of these drives, particularly as a result of painful childhood experiences, results in unconscious conflicts of which the neurosis is the symbolic expression. To be sure, sexual repression, which Freud found so overridingly prevalent among his own patients, may have been more characteristic of the Vienna of his day rather than of the nature of neuroses.

The extent of mental illness

Until fairly recently, the extent of mental illness was extremely difficult to determine with any accuracy because of the imprecision of definitions and the confusion in nomenclature and classification. Beginning in the 1950s, a number of studies were undertaken to provide more dependable estimates of the relative prevalence of various mental conditions. One such study was Dr. Benjamin Pasamanick's 1961 survey of mental diseases in the population of Baltimore, Maryland, which was latter applied to American urban populations in general.[14]

"Is this person crazy? Is this person mad?" I'm often asked that question by people who seem to think it's very important to them to decide who's crazy. . .In other societies, madness versus sanity never seems to worry people particularly. When I was living in India, there were people there in all sorts of states of mind, and no one brought up that binary distinction. . .Some fit in with the expectations of our system as to what experience is, and what behavior is, what is approved and tolerated. And some don't.

R. D. Laing

Pasamanick's study confirmed some figures suggested by earlier surveys. Considering all forms of mental disturbance together, it appears that approximately 12.5 percent (1 in 8 persons) of the total urban population of the United States suffers from some form of mental or emotional affliction. The affliction rate among the rural population is believed to be slightly lower. Of this total, 1 percent suffers from acute brain syndromes. Between 7 and 8 percent (or approximately 1 percent of the total population) is acutely psychotic, and a staggering 75 percent or more is neurotic to some degree.

Pasamanick, as well as other private researchers and government agencies, provides further breakdowns of these figures on the basis of demographic characteristics, such as race, sex and age. They have studied the prevalence and incidence of mental illness, both in institutional environments and in the community at large.

Two key concepts in the epidemiology of disease, whether mental or physical, are prevalence and incidence. Prevalence denotes the percentage of cases of an illness existing within a population at a given point in time. Incidence refers to the proportion of new cases that occur within a population during a given period. Thus, prevalence indicates how widespread the problem is, whereas incidence reveals how quickly the problem is growing or disappearing. After estimates on prevalence and incidence are established, the figures are broken down in accordance with several variables in order to make them more meaningful. In the epidemiology of mental illness, the most important variables have been found to be social class, occupation, age, sex and race and ethnic background.

Social distribution

Recently studies have been undertaken jointly by sociologists and psychiatrists to determine the prevalence of certain mental illnesses in various socioeconomic classes and in different situations (hospitals, outpatient facilities, private facilities and the like). A clear relationship emerged between the type of illness and the patient's socioeconomic status, as well as between the social status and form of the treatment administered.

Schizophrenia was found to be more prevalent in the lowest socioeconomic groups. Treatment for all mental conditions in these groups was usually administered in a hospital or clinic setting, often by electroshock or other medical therapies. Patients of higher socioeconomic standing were much more likely to be treated privately by some form of supportive or reconstructive psychotherapy. The outlook of the patient and his family for eventual recovery sharply differed from class to class, with disadvantaged patients displaying far more pessimism and negativism toward psychiatric intervention than those who were more affluent.[15]

One of the earliest and most significant studies was made by A. B. Hollingshead and F. C. Redlich in New Haven, Connecticut, during the period 1950-51.[16] These investigators considered all persons receiving psychiatric treatment during a five-month period. They divided this population into five social classes. Class I represented the community's business and professional leaders; Class II, the managerial class; Class III, those in administrative or clerical jobs; Class IV, members of the skilled working class; Class V, semiskilled and unskilled laborers with no more than an elementary school education.

The result indicated a higher rate of psychoses, especially schizophrenia, in Classes IV and V and a majority of neurotics in Class I. However, these findings were not regarded as conclusive, since the authors also found a marked tendency for patients from a disadvantaged background to be kept longer in those mental institutions where psychotic, rather than neurotic, disorders are common. Thus, the rate for psychosis among those on the lower-income scale may be higher than it would be where patients of all socioeconomic classes were perceived and treated in like manner.

Unfortunately, a patient's social class makes a great difference in the way he is treated. Hollingshead and Redlich found that persons in Classes I and II were more likely than others to be seen by private psychiatrists who use the most respected methods. Such patients were institutionalized mainly in private hospitals. Those in Classes III, IV and V were likely to be in public institutions.

The quality of treatment varied correspondingly. While nearly all the Class I patients saw a therapist for the standard fifty-minute session, less than half the Class V patients were so fortunate; many saw a therapist for less than thirty minutes at a time, and virtually none received continuous treatment for a significant period of time. Because treatment varies with social class, Hollingshead and Redlich concluded that observed "relations between sociocultural variables and the prevalence of treated disorders do not establish that the former are the essential and necessary conditions for the etiology of mental disorders." It therefore cannot be concluded that just because we find so many Class V psychotics in mental hospitals, poverty is invariably the cause of psychoses.

The Hollingshead-Redlich study also provided much related information on the education, occupation and income of mental patients, findings substantiated by later studies. Several, for example, have discovered a higher rate of first admissions to mental hospitals among patients from lower occupational categories. This seems to hold true for all mental illnesses. In 1969, a Department of Health, Education, and Welfare study, for one, demonstrated an inverse relationship between educational level and admission rates to state and county outpatient psychiatric services.[17] The higher the occupational status, the less likely is the prospect of hospitalization.

Occupational status, or the lack of it, also seems to be related to the kind of illness involved. The unemployed, and those in unskilled and semiskilled occupations, show a greater tendency toward schizophrenia than toward other psychoses. Manic-depressive psychosis, on the other hand, is higher among the leading professional and business groups. One interesting study, made by sociologists Jacob Tuckman and Robert J. Kleiner, suggested that the relative incidence of schizophrenia is high for patients who experience a discrepancy between their educational background and occupational status.[18]

Some general correlations exist between a patient's age and the type of his mental illness. Patients under 18 are most often admitted as a result of acute, temporary reactions to stressful situations, while for those above the age of 65 the most probable diagnosis is chronic brain syndrome. Some additional generalizations appear justified on the basis of governmental surveys and private research.

Except for mental retardation, few major disorders appear during the childhood years; the psychoses seldom manifest themselves before late adolescence.[19] From that period to early middle age, the incidence rises steadily and the most likely diagnosis is schizophrenia. During the ensuing twenty years, the psychoses of middle age—manic-depressive psychosis and involutional melancholia—are most common.

The neuroses also seem to appear most frequently during the middle years. The trend begins to manifest itself among those in the 18- to 24-year group; for them neuroses and personality disorders constitute the most frequent admission diagnosis in outpatient facilities. These disorders predominate to about age 60 or 65, until the onset age for senile disturbances and other syndromes of advanced age.

What about sexual differences? Generally speaking, there are no major ones prevalent in mental illness. Minor trends do appear in the statistics; for example, a slightly higher hospitalization rate for psychoses among males, probably connected with the greater frequency among males of mental conditions related to alcoholism and syphilis.[20] However, this trend is partly offset by the slightly greater frequency of involutional psychoses among women of postmenopausal age.

In the under-18 age group, differences between the sexes are somewhat more marked. The government's 1969 data for outpatient psychiatric services reveal that, among males of that age group, over 25 percent of the cases were classified as hyperkinetic reaction (abnormal restlessness) and 29 percent as unsocialized aggressive reaction. No such trend appeared among female patients. Their diagnoses were rather evenly divided among the subcategories of childhood behavior disorders, except for an exceptionally low incidence of hyperkinetic reactions.

Institutionalized populations

A foremost critic of mental institutions is the sociologist, Erving Goffman, who defines a total institution "as a place of residence and work where a large number of like-situated individuals, cut off from the wider society for an appreciable period of time, together lead an enclosed, formally administered round of life. Prisons serve as a clear example, providing we appreciate that what is prison-like about prisons is found in institutions whose members have broken no laws."[21]

Goffman points out that when an individual is admitted into a mental institution, he is subject to mortification and to assuming a "disidentifying role" in the daily life into which he has been thrust. His privacy has been violated; his environment is invaded; he is required to divulge facts and feelings about himself to strangers whom he invariably regards as hostile. Constantly within sight and earshot of someone (if only fellow inmates), he is kept behind locked doors. He must adapt to collective sleeping arrangements, and doorless toilets.[22]

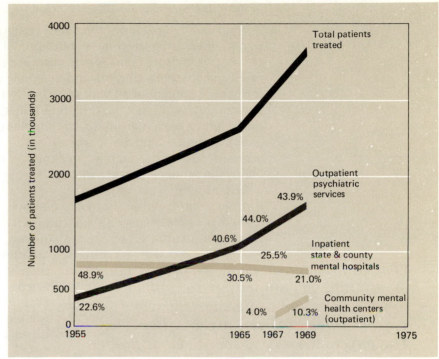

Figure 8–1   Mentally ill patient by type of facility, 1955–1969

Such measures are not likely to relieve feelings of anxiety. In an effort to emerge from his prisonlike existence and remain physically and psychologically undamaged, the inmate attempts to adjust to his alien environment. Eventually, a mental patient may accept the hospital staff's view of himself and try to assume the role of the "perfect inmate." If he has been previously institutionalized in an orphanage, reformatory, jail, military compound or religious retreat, Goffman believes that his adjustment will not be so difficult; his previous experiences will enable him to learn adaptive techniques. Most inmates of mental hospitals feel that the time spent in such an institution has been wasted and that, in effect, they have been "exiled from living." Goffman agrees that a patient does not gain values in an institution that can be transferred to life outside. Many patients become apprehensive when they are about to be released and wonder if they can "make it" in the outside world.[23] As Goffman puts it:

Mental patients can find themselves in a special bind. To get out of the hospital, or to ease their life within it, they must show acceptance of the place accorded them, and the place accorded them is to support the occupational role of those who appear to force this bargain. This self-alienating moral servitude, which perhaps helps to account for some inmates becoming mentally confused, is achieved by invoking the great tradition of the expert servicing relation, especially its medical variety. Mental patients can find themselves crushed by the weight of a service ideal that eases life for the rest of us.[24]

Statistically speaking, the great majority of institutionalized patients suffers from the more debilitating disturbances; that is, psychoses, brain syndrome and severe mental deficiency. Between the ages of 25 and 65, schizophrenia and alcoholic disorders together account for over 50 percent of all patients admitted to state and county mental institutions. After age 65, organic brain syndrome predominates. As noted previously, the youngest population—patients under 18—is usually admitted for temporary disorders that occur as a result of stressful situations, such as a change in role and responsibility or a change in family structure (death of a parent or perhaps marriage of a close sibling).[25]

In evaluating these figures, we should remember that many disturbed persons, especially in rural areas, do not seek or receive treatment and therefore are not counted. Moreover, statistics based on admission diagnoses are not in themselves completely accurate. Even the present classification system leaves considerable room for clinical interpretation. Sometimes, too, the psychiatrist is motivated by nonclinical considerations. He may be reluctant to stigmatize a bright middle-class girl with the label "schizophrenic"; on the other hand, the withdrawn older man, who has been admitted mainly because there is nowhere else to put him, may be routinely diagnosed as schizophrenic.

Statistics on admission and discharge of mental patients are probably less troublesome than those based on diagnosis. For the past seventeen years, there has been a clear decrease in the total number of mental hospital inpatients. The rate of decrease has accelerated each year since 1964, and since 1970 the number of net releases has exceeded the number of admissions to state and county mental hospitals. During the same period, however, there has been an overall 5.5 percent increase in admissions. This means that, while the hospital population is decreasing, more patients are admitted each year.

> *[The first insane asylums] represented both an attempt to compensate for public disorder . . . and to demonstrate the correct rules of social organization. . . . The psychiatrists . . . conceived of proper individual behavior and social relationships only in terms of a personal respect for authority and tradition and an acceptance of one's station in the ranks of society. In this sense they were trying to re-create in the asylum their own version of the colonial community. The results, however, were very different. Regimentation, punctuality, and precision became the asylum's basic traits, and these qualities were far more in keeping with an urban, industrial order than a local, agrarian one.*
>
> *David J. Rothman*

One reason for this trend is that the aged are increasingly referred to facilities other than the mental hospital—to geriatric hospitals or nursing homes. This results in a younger patient population in the mental hospital and contributes to the general decrease in total patient population. Another factor is a reduction in the length of the hospital stay, made possible by new drug therapies and better after-care facilities. The introduction of community mental health centers has also been significant in reducing new admissions and in preventing the rehospitalization of patients who have been discharged.

reading: ## Dorothy H. Miller
FAILURE TO ADJUST

During the past decade important and radical changes in the length of hospitalization for the mentally ill have taken place. Seldom is there confinement for life. The majority begin their "careers" as mental patients with a relatively short stay in the hospital followed by outpatient care and treatment. In California today, 85 percent of patients admitted to hospitals are released within six months. Half are discharged; the rest are put on "leave of absence," which means that they are supposed to receive outside care by psychiatrists and psychiatric workers.

We have found, in our study of 1,405 California patients on leave of absence, that what allows a mental patient to stay out is not primarily the severity of his medical diagnosis and prognosis. It depends on whether he has been able to (or has been helped to) construct a social and psychological world that will support him and allow him to function adequately in the outside world. Let us examine some of the characteristics of the patients.

They were state mental hospital patients, placed on leave of absence with the Oakland Bureau of Social Work from California state hospitals in 1956. (Between 80 and 85 percent of the mentally ill are cared for in state or federal institutions.) In general, they had not come voluntarily—they had been "committed" by the family or the community, and so started out with a legacy of despair and feelings of betrayal. They had not sought nor paid for their care while in the hospital. Most of them, after release, did not consider themselves "free." The "leave of absence" status seemed to them more like a parole, depending on good behavior and obedience to orders, rather than proof of recovery and discharge.

Looking backward, we found that some of the patients had histories of disturbances covering most of their lives. All cases were followed for at least five years (1956-61). Of the total sample, 71 percent had returned to the hospital at least once during those five years, and 24 percent had been rehospitalized an average of 4.4 times. About 85 percent stemmed originally from the poorest class and 65 percent had never finished high school. After release, only 26 percent were able to find any job; and 27 percent had to rely on public welfare.

In our country, man achieves most of his identity, and his apparent place in society, through two functions: family and work. He is a parent, spouse, child, or some combination; worker or merchant, employed or unemployed, laborer, white collar worker or housekeeper. The great majority of these ex-patients were on the fringes of both of these worlds. Few could find jobs available that amounted to anything, or support themselves; few were considered any longer to be important to their families.

In California, 85 percent of all adults are married; only 48 percent of these released patients were. The majority of them had only marginal or casual connections with their families—they were not heads of houses, nor did they have important roles in family affairs, maintenance, or support. In general they were on the fringes, dependent and "extra," often unwelcome guests in other people's homes. Before hospitalization about one-third of them had important family positions but these had been lost or reduced, so that a released patient was likely to live alone. Generally, they were important to nobody . . .

Many lived alone. Typically, these stayed in skid row hotels and were on relief. Some, though adult, moved back with parents—who were very frequently aged and infirm, barely able to take care of themselves, subsisting mostly on state welfare and social security. Those who lived with other relatives generally found themselves becoming Cinderellas in other people's chimney corners.

Among those who were married, 69 percent were women. They each had, during the study, on the average, the care of two to three children apiece. Yet 40 percent of them were unable to care adequately for their homes or their families. Among released husbands, over half were unemployed and four out of five were serious drinkers; after release they often became the dependent and passive partners in the marriages. Fifty-five percent of all married ex-patients were having extreme marital troubles and conflict; and 30 percent of all children of ex-patients were in trouble with school or juvenile authorities.

In short, these mental patients lived in, or with, the kinds of families that make up the hard core of social case work—disrupted, problem-ridden, often apparently hopeless. Their mental and domestic troubles were inseparable, being so closely intertwined that cause and effect were seldom clear. Often their return to the mental hospital was just one more result of social and family disruption. . . .

Their histories continually emphasized breakdown in communication—and even open rejection—not only between patient and family, but between patient and professionals (social workers). There were few spontaneous welcomes, little respect for the patient and his capabilities for recovery—and not even much simple trust. Breach of faith was common. For example, one-third of the patients did not even know that they were being rehospitalized— frequently the social worker and the spouse had arranged it privately, and "conned" the patient into unwitting cooperation.

We asked 249 consecutive returning patients why they were being rehospitalized. . . . Forty-two percent said they felt they had to return because of too much stress from families or the outside world. But their families did not agree. The families claimed that the fault lay with the patients themselves, in their mental trouble or antisocial behavior. In only 16 percent of cases did all three respondents (family, social workers, patient) agree on the reason for return. . . .

Almost all mental patients are eventually released, most within a fairly short time. Our findings, based on Goffman's model, indicate that what is needed to keep the great majority of them out are things so simple that most of us take them for granted: adequate livelihoods; indications from doctors, employers, and other professionals that they are well, competent, respected; a life partner to extend affection, share burdens, lend support; a consistent, structured, reassuring self-image and world. Yet our findings also show that most released patients do not have these things. Their outside careers are fragmented, marginal, depressing, disillusioning.

From
"Worlds that Fail," by Dorothy H. Miller, in
Anselm Strauss, ed., *Where Medicine Fails*
(Chicago: Aldine Publishing Company, 1970) pp. 86-97.

Noninstitutionalized populations

Researchers have always been interested in pinpointing the prevalence of mental illness in that portion of the population which is not, and may never be, institutionalized. Some of the best data in this area may be found in a comprehensive study undertaken at the University of Michigan.

The aim of the investigators[26] was to study a representative sample of people in a given community and to obtain results that would permit generalizations about other communities. To this end, 2460 men and women were interviewed in their homes, and their responses were entered on an extensive questionnaire. Statistical analyses and interpretations of all these data resulted in a number of useful generalizations.

The researchers found that one in five of those interviewed claimed to have suffered a "nervous breakdown" at least once. Two-fifths of this group felt that the breakdown had been caused by external events, while the remaining three-fifths cited internal psychological causes. One in four persons considered himself to have emotional problems so serious as to require professional help, but only one in seven actually sought such help. Women sought help more often than men, younger people more often than older ones and the more educated more often than the lesser educated. Of those in search of professional guidance, 42 percent first went to clergymen; 29 percent saw physicians other than psychiatrists; 18 percent consulted psychiatrists and clinical psychologists; and 10 percent sought out social agencies and marriage clinics.

Many factors appear to influence a person's decision to seek private treatment (and thereby become one of those counted in prevalence surveys). These include education (the sufferer's realization that his difficulty is treatable); financial status (ability to pay for treatment); geographic location (availability of professional help); and social outlook (the degree of stigma that the sufferer and his peers attach to psychiatric treatment).

Ethnic distribution of mental illness

Both outpatient and inpatient admission rates of institutions for the mentally disturbed show a preponderance of admissions for nonwhite races. This correlates with the finding that the psychoses predominate in the lower-income groups, of which nonwhite people form a large percentage. Although the most frequent psychosis among both blacks and whites is schizophrenia, black patients who suffer from this disorder outnumber white patients in hospitals by a ratio of 2.28 to 1.00. The same trend is also observable in the mental disturbances of advanced age.

Another trend that has been noted is that Jews have a lower overall rate of first admission than other whites, mostly due to the low incidence of organic mental disorders. But the incidence of other mental disorders among Jews is higher than the incidence among other whites.[27]

Irish-born whites generally have a higher incidence of mental disturbance than native-born American whites for all major mental disorders except manic-depressive psychosis and general paresis (a disorder caused by syphilitic infection). The incidence of alcoholic psychoses in this ethnic group is especially high. Italians, on the other hand, not only have a very low overall rate of mental disturbance, but an especially low one for alcoholic psychoses—even lower than that of Jews. Only their general paresis rate proved higher than that of other native or foreign-born whites.

The spread in incidence among ethnic groups is much greater than between the sexes. It has not yet been determined whether this is due to biological or social factors; a combination of both is likely.

Sociological explanations of mental illness

Sociological explanations of mental illness differ from organic and psychological explanations in that its cause is stipulated as external rather than as coming from within the individual. Focusing on aspects of the social environment thought to contribute to individual pathology, sociologists have identified conditions such as social isolation, the improper perception or improper performance of social roles and the labeling of certain behaviors as deviant from a system of social norms as influential in the growth of mental illness. It has not yet been possible to explain why some people within a society or culture are more susceptible to mental illness than others who exist under the same conditions, but the wide extent of emotional disturbances within American society would seem to indicate that these sociocultural factors have some authority.

Social isolation theory

Isolation from one's fellows is a well-known factor in the development of emotional disturbance. Even well-adjusted persons may become more or less disturbed if they are forced to exist in seclusion for any length of time. Isolation has proved its effectiveness in breaking the resistance of prisoners of war; it is equally effective in breaking the spirits of the old and lonely.

R. E. L. Faris was the first to present evidence of the role of isolation in the development of schizophrenia.[28] His theory was subsequently expanded by H. Warren Dunham, who made a detailed study of the personality patterns of schizophrenics. Dunham found social isolation a particularly important variable in the development of at least one schizophrenic type, the catatonic schizophrenic.[29]

The catatonic schizophrenic experiences isolation at a very early age. His self-consciousness and anxiety cause him to stay close to his mother and to shy away from social contacts with his peer group. Because he so actively avoids company, the process of social isolation begins earlier for him and is more devastating than for other schizophrenics.

On the other hand, the paranoid will generally attempt social relationships. Because of his domineering or otherwise disturbing personality, he is actively rejected by his peer group—but only *after* having been a member. Once rejected, his need for an audience motivates him to seek new social contacts. His sense of grandiosity allegedly makes rejection less painful. Although he may end up equally alone, his isolation usually does not begin as early as that of the catatonic, whose dread of leaving home largely precludes the initiation of social contacts in childhood and throughout life.

Dunham's detailed observations argue well for the importance of isolation in the development of the schizophrenic syndrome. But while there is little question that social isolation worsens the schizophrenic's condition, it does not suffice to explain it. Dunham himself stresses the purely descriptive nature of his observations.

Role theory

Role theory views the individual not only in the broad context of his interaction with the environment, but in terms of the separate interpersonal relationships of which he is a part. Each of the roles a person plays supposes the existence of a separate social self. Thus, a man's role within the husband-wife or marriage unit demands quite another self than the role he assumes within the office unit (further subdivisible into his roles as superior, colleague and subordinate); still other roles are assumed as father, son and friend.

Social psychologists and psychiatrists sometimes use the levels of performance in each of these roles as indices of mental health. Leo Srole has proposed the yardsticks of role "amplitude" and "congruence" to measure these performances.[30] Congruence refers to the degree to which performance parallels society's expectations or fits the programmed components of the role. The magazine quizzes designed to determine "Are You a Modern Mother?" are, in their own way, measuring congruence.

Amplitude, on the other hand, measures the level of competence; for example, the success with which a man supports his family. Minimum amplitude designates a performance level that is just enough to get by; below that level lies role failure. The inability to support one's family can lead to a disruption of an individual's personal life and, in many cases, to a nervous breakdown or other manifestations of mental illness.

In recognition of the fact that an individual's performance level may vary considerably from role to role, Harry Stack Sullivan proposed the related concept of interpersonal competence.[31] It has been suggested that for some people the stress involved in playing many, often contradictory, roles is great enough to cause a nervous breakdown or even manic-depressive psychosis.

There is some reason to believe that the complex and competitive nature of modern society is responsible for the development of personal and interpersonal conflicts. Karen Horney pointed out that competitiveness almost by definition involves hostility and resultant insecurity.[32] Her comments primarily referred to the development of neurosis and preceded the work of the role theorists by some twenty years. But some recent studies—notably one comparing schizophrenics and nonschizophrenics in the poorer sections of San Juan, Puerto Rico—indicate that escalating role and social conflicts may also play a far from negligible part in the development of schizophrenia.[33]

Labeling theory

There is a certain disadvantage to being labeled a schizophrenic, an alcoholic, or even a former mental patient, as shown by Senator Thomas Eagleton's damaging experience during the 1972 Presidential race. Such "labeling" has been studied by sociologist Thomas J. Scheff, who finds in this phenomenon the basis for a sociological explanation of mental illness.[34] Scheff and others concerned with deviant or abnormal behavior conclude that the labeling process itself results in an intensification of the deviant role. For example, Lemert, in a study of paranoid patients, noted that once an individual is designated mentally ill, those around him feel free to disregard their social obligations to him, thereby exacerbating, if not actually causing, the deviant behavior patterns. This leads to feelings of exclusion which the patient soon generalizes until he feels himself to be, as Lemert puts it, "a stranger on trial in every group."[35]

Such pressure, of course, negatively affects his condition, which, in turn, provokes further negative reactions from those in his environment. The reason the patient was labeled deviant in the first place may be relatively trivial, but the assumption of the deviant role will have long-standing and unhappy consequences.

In order to be labeled deviant—schizophrenic, for example—a person need only engage in conspicuous rule-breaking, whether it be a breach of manners or a serious crime. Although he may not break any recognized rules, his behavior may be in violation of society's expectations. As Scheff notes, there is "a residue of the most diverse kinds of violations for which the culture provides no explicit label"[36] and this may be called residual rule-breaking. There is no particular rule against a man's posting himself near a subway turnstile and making computations based on the number of people passing through, but at least one man was quickly and involuntarily committed to a mental hospital for doing just that. Such residual rule-breaking, when it comes to the attention of a policeman or other authority, may lead to being labeled mentally ill.

The theory that labeling itself is responsible for much disturbed behavior is not particularly congenial to proponents of the medical model. Perhaps more significant is the criticism leveled against the theory by some of the more sociologically oriented researchers. One of these is Walter R. Gove, who feels that Scheff exaggerates the effect of labeling (both inside and outside the mental hospital setting), as well as the degree to which former inpatients suffer from the stigma of having been confined for a mental disorder.[37] Gove, and others, focus on the rather important question of why a deviant commits the acts that invite the undesirable "mentally ill" label.

An intact human being is sound in mind and body. This includes sight, sanity, hearing, and continence. But a distorted one is insane, or blind, or deaf, or incontinent, and so on. . . . the word "distorted" seems to me to convey better than any other the inner meaning to us of such misfortunes. For what most people in our culture experience in contact with distorted people is not compassion or annoyance at some anticipated burden, but the cold sweat of revulsion.   **Jules Henry**

In addition, Gove notes that the labeling process itself is not so rigorous. Studies show that the family of a mentally ill person, far from imposing this label, may go to extraordinary lengths to deny the bizarre nature of his behavior. Even within the mental hospital setting, patients often are not regarded as mentally ill, either by themselves or by their associates. Moreover, an increasing proportion of patients admit themselves voluntarily, which implies that they labeled themselves as mentally ill before anyone else did.

In Gove's opinion, the evidence strongly suggests a reverse cause-and-effect relationship from that postulated by Scheff and others. Although he concedes that in the long run the expectations of doctors, parents and other key figures may be an important determinant of a person's behavior, in the short run it is the person's behavior that determines the expectations of those around him.

"Myth of mental illness"

Some medical and social scientists have posed the question of whether or not there really is such a condition as "mental illness." In various forms, and from different vantage points, this provocative question has been asked with increasing urgency in recent years. Among the earliest and most controversial of the questioners is the psychiatrist, Thomas Szasz, who answers with a resounding "No."[38]

An opponent of the "medical model," Szasz believes that mental deviations do not constitute illnesses, but rather disturbances due to faulty learning—disturbances that result in a distorted self-image and, finally, the assumption of the "patient" role. According to Szasz, the very person whose function it is to correct this faulty view—the therapist—plays no small part in causing and reinforcing it. By placing the disturbed person in the patient role, he encourages him to accept further distortions of his self-image.

To Szasz the doctor-patient relationship is a tragic partnership in which each member endlessly reinforces the faulty concept of the other. At best, these relationships are altruistically motivated; at worst, they represent an exploitation of the most callous kind, the therapist satisfying his own needs at the patient's psychological and financial expense.

Szasz maintains that although there is nothing to "heal" since no one is sick, there is much to learn. An individual with an information deficit must learn to adjust to the world. Since environment is a powerful teacher, the patient in the hospital does, indeed, proceed to learn: from the moment of admission, he learns to be a mental patient. Other observers, notably R. D. Laing and Erving Goffman, acknowledge this side of hospitalization. So do the many mental patients who claim that they are sick because they are in the hospital, rather than the reverse.

It is too early for a comprehensive evaluation of Szasz's contribution, but his influence has already borne fruit in a number of areas. One of these concerns the rights of mental patients, whether institutionalized, noninstitutionalized or in the process of changing from one status to the other. A gradual decline in infringements on these rights is making itself felt, together with a lessening of the authoritarian, and often downright punitive, aspects of confinement for allegedly mental reasons. Apparently, many Americans are judged incompetent on insufficient grounds and are unnecessarily committed to mental institutions. As a result, stringent tests have now been developed to determine competency and to guard against unnecessary hospitalization. In addition, hospitalized patients, along with mental health associations, have brought charges against governmental agencies on the ground that their civil rights were violated. Recent civil rights legislation now allows patients to institute court suits in such cases.[39]

Responses to mental illness

For a problem so large and broad in scope as mental illness, many approaches are needed to meet the needs of those affected and to attempt to lower the incidence of such dysfunctions. As attitudes toward mental illness change, new ways to deal with the problems emerge.

Preventive psychiatry

Intensive research into the causes of mental illness has suggested innumerable causative factors. Moreover, it was shown that timely crisis intervention can often prevent mental disorder, even under stressful conditions. The accumulation of so many promising insights resulted in the development of what came to be called preventive psychiatry. Its aims are: to reduce the incidence of mental disorder (primary prevention); to shorten the duration of disorders that cannot be forestalled (secondary prevention); to reduce the degree of impairment that may result from mental disorders (tertiary prevention).

Preventive psychiatry focuses on the physical, psychosocial and sociocultural "supplies" that people need in order to function adequately at various stages of their development.[40] In the psychological area, these "supplies" are roughly synonymous with "satisfaction of interpersonal needs"; for example, the need for parental attention and peer group support in adolescence. Preventive psychiatry seeks to provide or restore those supplies without which mental illness may occur. Of equal importance is an interest in personal crisis as a stage when a person may be actively helped to avoid mental illness.

At present, the scope of preventive psychiatry encompasses teaching on the individual, familial and broad social levels; consultation in contexts ranging from personal to governmental and international; research and development of diagnostic tools and treatment techniques; and finally, community planning.

The community mental health movement

Strongly interrelated with preventive psychiatry are the community mental health services. Recent enthusiasm for these services is the result of a general reaction against the isolation of mental patients from their families and society at large. It is now generally agreed that the mentally disturbed person should, if at all possible, be treated in the community to which he belongs. Availability of community help will result in his obtaining treatment for his illness as early as possible. In the event that he becomes institutionalized, treatment within the community context can ease his readjustment period following discharge.[41]

Ideally, public mental hospitals should operate within the framework of the local community mental health program, but at present very few public institutions are so organized; nor are they usually equipped to provide the variety of services to which the community mental health movement is committed. These services include everything from outpatient psychiatric clinics to day centers and halfway houses. An indication of the scope of services available in different communities can be found in Figure 8-2.

Therapy

If one subscribes to the view that mental disturbances are due to faulty learning, it follows that therapy must be a process of reeducation. Such is indeed the view of many therapists of widely different orientations, including, interestingly enough, a number of proponents of the medical model. The fact is that most therapeutic approaches, whether predominantly supportive or reconstructive, contain a large educational component. Among the few that do not are psychosurgery, electroshock treatment and drug therapy; of these, drug therapy is by far the most widely used.

Since their development in the 1950s, the ataractic drugs or "major tranquilizers" have become the dominant form of treatment in mental institutions. This therapy is largely responsible for the fact that many such institutions now report more discharges than admissions in any given year, as well as a marked decrease in length of hospital stay.

1   Inpatient psychiatric services in general hospitals
    These are usually self-contained units in general hospitals, although the successful use of the psychotropic drugs has resulted in some dispersal of mental patients throughout the other hospital wards.
2   Outpatient psychiatric clinics
    These are independent, nonhospital-connected units for the diagnosis and treatment (usually by individual psychotherapy) of metal disorders in adults and children.
3   Community metal hospitals
    These include the small, experimental institutions organized as "therapeutic communities," which are by and large still in a state of flux.
4   Community mental health centers
    Development of these units is high on the list of priorties of mental hygiene planners. In concept they resemble the community mental hospitals, except for the fact they do not accept certified patients.
5   Day hospitals and night hospitals
    These modern developments constitute useful alternatives to full hospitalization. Day hospitals provide patients with a full range of diagnostic and therapeutic services while allowing them to return to their homes and families at night. The reverse obtains in night hospitals. These are useful for patients well enough to hold down a job and function in society during the day, but still require the support of a hospital environment when their structured workday is over.
6   Community day centers
    These facilities offer rehabilitative services for former mental hospital inpatients.
7   Halfway house
    Originally designed for much the same purpose as the day centers, these services have now been expanded to include functions such as the gradual separation of patients from their families preparatory to hospitalization.
8   Sheltered workshops
    These small, nonprofit business ventures are designed to equip or re-equip individuals for functioning in a normal work environment, and also to provide employment for the permanently handicapped who cannot compete in the open job market.
9   Day treatment or training centers for children
10 Residential treatment centers for emotionally disturbed children
    Both these specialized facilities are devoted to the care of children too disturbed or retarded to function within the regular school environment. They combine education with clinical treatment.

Figure 8–2   Community mental health services

Drug therapy has proven most beneficial in the treatment of the psychoses. A given dosage may make schizophrenic "voices" disappear and render the patient accessible to other forms of therapy. For the outpatient, drugs have the advantage of being self-administered and less expensive than other therapies. However, the actual therapeutic effects of the major tranquilizers have been questioned. One critic, J. O. Cole, asserts that they "can produce a pharmacological strait jacket in which the patient is so stiff and sedated as to make any type of behavior, disturbed or otherwise, impossible."[42] In addition, some of the tranquilizers produce serious side effects in certain patients.

The psychotherapies attempt to treat mental illness in psychological terms rather than through purely medical means. Freudian psychotherapy (called psychoanalysis) relies on intensive sessions between analyst and patient, generally extending over a three- to four-year period. During these sessions, the patient becomes aware of early childhood experiences and conflicts that may be unconsciously affecting his present behavior. The analyst encourages him to talk freely without inhibition, that is, to free associate; and he guides the patient in the growing self-awareness that results from analysis of his thoughts and memories. Psychoanalysis is a costly therapy, requiring great commitment on the part of the patient as well as considerable verbal skill. It is a therapy that has been most useful to the educated middle and upper classes.

Other forms of psychotherapy, less intensive than analysis, do not extend over such a long period. Generally, a non-Freudian therapist (a psychiatrist or clinical psychologist) will take the present behavior problem of the patient as a starting point, drawing on unconscious memories of early childhood less than the Freudian analyst does. Most psychotherapists guide the patient toward self-awareness and shun directly giving advice; non-Freudian psychotherapists are somewhat more directive than the Freudian analysts, for they are more often in the position of helping the patient overcome an immediate stress or problem. There is an exceedingly wide variety in the techniques employed by psychotherapists today.

A therapy that differs in approach from traditional psychotherapies is behavior modification. According to behavior modification theory, a person is maladjusted because he has learned or been taught maladjusted behaviors. A therapist can teach him to substitute new responses for those that he has displayed to his own disadvantage in the past. The therapy more or less dismisses the unconscious and its motivations and addresses itself solely to current behavioral problems that can be objectively described. For example, the behavior modification therapist does not concern himself with the symbolic meaning of a patient's peculiar walk or the unconscious conflict it may portray. Instead, he tries to get the patient to change his walk, reinforcing him whenever he approaches the desired gait and posture.

Within a limited sphere, behavior modification has been very successful. Perhaps because it refuses to consider behavioral maladjustments as symptomatic of deeper problems, its success has so far been confined to the alleviation of very specific, concrete disorders, such as phobias and compulsions.

Group therapies have grown up around many different therapeutic orientations. From a sociological viewpoint, their most important feature lies less in the therapist's orientation than in the group's effectiveness on each individual member.

In group therapy, the patient becomes a member of an ingroup and gains a sense of belonging. He learns how to respond to others and how others are likely to perceive and react to him—a long step toward healthy interpersonal relations with society at large. Finally, the group, although supportive, is less inclined than outsiders to tolerate interpersonal dishonesty or pretense. The maladjusted individual, who may have "turned off" his associates on countless occasions without knowing why, gets instant feedback on a specific subject from his peers. This feedback may prove painful, at first; however, as the individual learns to profit from it, such occasions become less frequent. Moreover, his interpersonal relations with all groups in which he finds himself become correspondingly healthier and more satisfying.

reading: **Charles Kadushin**

COMMUNITY ATTITUDES AND COMMUNITY THERAPY

The growth of the community mental-health concept underscores two fundamental developments in modern psychiatry. First, modern experts do not feel that mental hospitals ought to be asylums, placed away from and outside the community. Emphasis is now placed on the treatment of mental patients within the community, in facilities ranging from office and outpatient treatment to "halfway houses" and recreation centers, day hospitals, and night hospitals. Second, the nature and degree of the emotional disturbances in which psychiatrists are interested have changed. Since Freud, there has been increasing concern not only with psychoses and gross overt disturbances in functioning, but in unhappiness and in problems of living. Both treatment within the community and concern with the less dramatic disorders of everyday living have focused attention on outpatient psychiatry in the community mental-health movement.

Each of these two trends has been championed, by and large, by a different movement in the mental-health field. The more traditional mental-health or mental-hygiene movement has been particularly concerned with mental hospitals. Founded in 1908 by Clifford Beers, a former mental-hospital patient, the mental-hygiene movement stressed the humane treatment of persons suffering from obvious psychotic disorders. The lay members of this movement often espoused a middle-class "Protestant Ethic" morality and felt that the unfortunate ought to become better adjusted. Interested in improving facilities as well as in developing more tolerant attitudes toward present and former mental patients, leaders of the mental-hygiene movement give the impression that their concern is for other persons who have problems, not for themselves. Professionals in this movement, psychiatrists interested in developing new methods of treatment and in raising professional standards, founded such famous hospitals as the State Psychopathic Hospital at the University of Michigan (1907) and the Boston Psychopathic Hospital (1912); discovered the connection between syphilis and paresis (1913); pioneered in various forms of shock therapy; and developed tranquilizers and antidepressants (1950's). They also became increasingly interested in social psychiatry—in viewing the mental hospital as a "therapeutic community" and in developing psychiatry as an effective factor in the community outside the walls of the hospital. Unlocked wards, home visits, and concern with the families of patients are all part of these newer trends, many of which were first developed in England. The type of psychiatry we have just described was called "directive and organic" by Hollingshead and Redlich, although perhaps it should now be called "directive-organic-social." The impression remains, however, that the mental-hygiene or health group is generally concerned with the more disruptive, bizarre, and antisocial mental disorders.

The second movement within the mental-health field [we describe as] the Friends and Supporters of Psychotherapy. The name is our own invention, for unlike the mental-hygiene group which is a self-defined, conscious group with a formal name and a formal membership, the Friends and Supporters of Psychotherapy is an informal social circle noticed by us but not necessarily by its members, with no official name or official membership list. Initiated by Freud, and interested primarily in the psychodynamics of office patients, this movement recruits laymen of quite a different type from those attracted by the mental-hygiene movement. As we have shown, these people tend to be intellectuals, artists, and professionals, often of a literary bent, and frequently Jewish, whereas the Protestant businessman is more characteristic of the lay leadership in the mental-hygiene group. Most important, the Friends and Supporters of Psychotherapy almost invariably see themselves as suffering from the types of mental disorder recognized by their movement, and these disorders tend to be less bizarre and more like the tensions experienced at one time or another by almost everybody. . . .

Self-involvement also allows the Friends and Supporters of Psychotherapy to function in a less formal fashion than the mental hygiene group. Perhaps because of their proselitizing they form a social circle rather than a formally constituted group, and rather than being limited to the single profession of psychiatrist many diverse professionals such as ministers, psychologists, and social workers first undergo and then come to practice psychoanalysis and psychotherapy.

Although the type of patient seen by most psychotherapists is different from the type dealt with by traditional psychiatrists, this situation is changing. Originally concerned only with neuroses, professional psychoanalysts and analytically trained psychotherapists have increasingly expanded their interests and techniques to include working with schizophrenics and other psychotics. Like the directive organic group, they have become more interested in social systems and group processes, and especially in group and family therapy. They have also entered the domain of psychiatric hospitals, once the exclusive province of the directive-organic psychiatrists; . . .

The mental-hygiene movement and the circle of Friends and Supporters of Psychotherapy have both contributed to the concept of a community mental-health center. . . . [But] the consequence of failure to recognize the difference between the mental-health movement and the Friends and Supporters of Psychotherapy is an excessive reliance on the existing system of mental-patient care, which at its best was geared to meet the ideology of mental hygiene alone. The state hospital system is not, of course, the only vested interest—there are many others including child guidance and family service agencies, corrective institutions and general hospitals. Most of these existing systems, insofar as they deal with outpatients, are more like hospital psychiatric clinics than like analytic or religio-psychiatric clinics. . . .

Part of the problem, which reliance on existing organizations engenders, is that the mental-health movement tends to regard mental problems as medical illnesses. As a leader in mental-health planning has pointed out, "Control of mental disorders is a public-health problem."

The medical model contains at least two incorrect assumptions from which a dangerous conclusion logically follows: It assumes that physicians can distinguish between those who are mentally well and those who have varying degrees of mental illness and that specific disease entities can be expressed in a standardized diagnostic vocabulary. Second, the **325** medical model assumes that the sick person's own actions roughly correspond to the physician's diagnosis of his state of illness, that is, that persons who are more sick are more likely to seek medical help. The implied conclusion is that public psychiatric facilities should turn away those who are not very sick if they do apply and instead seek out those who are more ill who might not have even considered applying. . . .

The second assumption, that the more medically ill are more likely to seek treatment, is also wrong. The Friends and Supporters of Psychotherapy are more likely to seek treatment than others. They go mainly for help with "psychoanalytic" problems, which tend to be less bizarre and less obvious than other psychiatric symptoms. And to average Americans, the most significant personal problems are family problems, not the traditional medically noted psychoses. Neither of these groups tends to select psychiatric facilities in mental or general hospitals where working-class outpatients do come with the more "medical" types of problems. . . .

The implications of offering one form of treatment in public facilities and another form in private care are most profound. In the first place, this distinction destroys the medical model that public-health officials advocate. In medicine poor people and rich people suffer from the same illness, are presumably treated in the same fashion; for the same physical condition, the same form of operation is generally effective for both rich and poor people. In psychiatry, however, this may not be true. Although they may have the same diagnosis as wealthier persons, lower-class applicants to psychiatric clinics tend to have quite different problems, and more limited expectations of treatment, as we have seen. It may very well be, therefore, that unique forms of treatment more suited to their nonpsychodynamic orientation will be more effective with poorer persons.

Whether new therapies are developed for the nonmember of the Friends, or a division of labor among existing psychiatric clinics . . . is expanded and perpetuated, the ultimate result will be to reinforce that tendency in the treatment of the mentally disturbed which has been the most criticized—namely, the two-track system. The two-track system has been a notable characteristic of mental health facilities since Bethlehem Hospital was publicly investigated in eighteen-century England. There has always been one form of treatment for the rich and another for the poor. Now the rich have by no means always had the best of it, since in eighteenth-century England, for example, the rich in private madhouses seemed relatively worse off than the poor in county workhouses. Nevertheless, whether they are kept in attics, bled, beaten, or given psychotherapy, whatever the rich get is generally deemed better than what the poor receive. And so, if those who can afford private treatment obtain psychoanalysis and if those who cannot pay for it are given something else, then psychoanalysis is, *ipso facto,* thought "better" than any other form of treatment. . . . If public facilities are to be used to give an "inferior" form of treatment to the poor and the culturally deprived, these facilities will, in this day and age, be subject to vigorous attack, for the canons of evaluation are at least, in part, social.

From
Charles Kadushin, *Why People Go To Psychiatrists*
(New York: Atherton Press, 1969) pp. 319-328

Notes

[1] Abraham H. Maslow, *Toward a Psychology of Being,* 2nd ed. (New York: Van Nostrand Reinhold, 1968) p. 8.

[2] A. H. Maslow and B. Mittlemann, *Principles of Abnormal Psychology,* revised ed. (New York: Harper and Row, 1951) pp. 14-15.

[3] René Dubos, *Mirage of Health* (New York: Harper and Row, 1959) p. 71.

[4] K. Soddy, *International Health Bulletin of the League of Red Cross Societies 2,* No. 2, "Mental Health," 1950.

[5] H. C. Rumke, "Mental Health in Public Affairs," in a report of the Fifth International Congress on Mental Health: *Solved and Unsolved Problems in Mental Health* (Toronto: University of Toronto Press, 1954) p. 157.

[6] Benjamin Pasamanick, "A Survey of Mental Disease in an Urban Population," *Archives of General Psychiatry,* Vol. 5, 1961, pp. 59-63.

[7] David Hamburg, ed., *Psychiatry as a Behavioral Science* (Englewood Cliffs, N.J.: Prentice-Hall, 1972) Chap. 2.

[8] H. L. Newbold, "The Use of Vitamin B-12-b in Psychiatric Practice," *Orthomolecular Psychiatry,* First Quarter, Vol. 1, No. 1, 1972.

[9] "Schizophrenia Clue," *Behavior Today,* Vol. 4, No. 12, March 19, 1973.

[10] Leonard P. Ullman and Leonard Krasner, *A Psychological Approach to Abnormal Behavior* (Englewood Cliffs, N.J.: Prentice-Hall, 1969) p. 437.

[11] Edwin M. Lemert, *Human Deviance, Social Problems, and Social Control* (Englewood Cliffs, N.J.: Prentice-Hall, 1967) pp. 197-211.

[12] Hans Selye, "The General-Adaptation-Syndrome in its Relationships to Neurology, Psychology and Psychopathology," in A. Weider, ed., *Contributions Toward Medical Psychology: Theory and Psycho-diagnostic Methods* (New York: Ronald Press, 1953) pp. 234-74.

[13] Margaret Mead, "The Concept of Culture and the Psychosomatic Approach," *Psychiatry,* 1947, No. 10, pp. 57-76.

[14] Pasamanick, *op. cit.,* pp. 59-63.

[15] Jerome K. Myers, Lee L. Bean, and Max P. Pepper, *A Decade Later: Follow-up of Social Class and Mental Illness* (New York: John Wiley & Sons, Inc., 1958).

[16] August B. Hollingshead and Fredrick C. Redlich, *Social Class and Mental Illness* (New York: John Wiley & Sons, Inc., 1958).

[17] Richard Redlich, "Admissions by Highest Grade of School Completed, Outpatient Services-1969," *Statistical Note 46,* National Institute of Mental Health (Washington, D.C.: Department of Health, Education, and Welfare, 1971).

[18] Jacob Tuckman and Robert J. Kleiver, "Discrepancy between Aspirations and Achievement as a Predictor of Schizophrenia," *Behavioral Science*, Vol. 7, 1962, pp. 443-447.

[19] Walter R. Gove, "Societal Reactions as an Explanation of Mental Illness: An Evaluation," *American Sociological Review*, Vol. 35, 1970, pp. 873-830.

[20] Carl A. Taube, "Admissions to Outpatient Psychiatric Services, 1969 by Age, Sex and Diagnosis," *Statistical Note 48*, National Institute of Mental Health (Washington, D.C.: Department of Health, Education, and Welfare, 1971).

[21] Erving Goffman, *Asylums*, (New York: Doubleday/Anchor, 1961), Intro., unpaged.

[22] *Ibid.*, "Characteristics of Total Institutions," pp. 22-25.

[23] *Ibid.*, p. 70.

[24] *Ibid.*, "Medical Model and Mental Hospitalization," p. 386.

[25] George F. Koons, "Change in the Median Age of the Resident Patient Population in the State and County Mental Hospitals, 1955-1973," *Statistical Note 9*, National Institute of Mental Health (Washington, D.C.: Department of Health, Education and Welfare, 1969).

[26] Gurin, Vedoff and Feld, *Field Study in the Prevalence of Mental Illness*, (Ann Arbor, Michigan: University of Michigan Press, 1961).

[27] Benjamin Malzberg, "Mental Disorders in the United States," in Albert Deutsch and Helen Fishman, eds., *The Encyclopedia of Mental Health* (New York: F. Watts Co., 1963) pp. 1064-1065.

[28] R. E. L. Faris, "Cultural Isolation and the Schizophrenic Personality," *American Journal of Sociology*, Vol. 39, September, 1934, pp. 155-169.

[29] H. Warren Dunham, *Sociological Theory and Mental Disorder* (Detroit, Michigan: Wayne State University Press, 1959).

[30] Leo Srole, et al., *Mental Health in the Metropolis: The Midtown Manhattan Study*, Vol. 1 (New York: McGraw-Hill, 1962).

[31] H. S. Sullivan, *The Interpersonal Theory of Psychiatry* (New York: W. W. Norton & Co., 1953).

[32] Karen Horney, *The Neurotic Personality of Our Time*, revised ed. (New York: W. W. Norton & Co., 1937).

[33] Lloyd H. Rogler and August B. Hollingshead, *Trapped: Families and Schizophrenia* (New York: John Wiley & Sons, Inc., 1965).

[34] Thomas J. Scheff, *Being Mentally Ill: A Sociological Theory* (Chicago: Aldine Publishing Co., 1966).

[35] Ullman and Krasner, *op. cit.*, p. 433.

[36] Scheff, *op. cit.*, pp. 33-34.

[37] Gove, *op. cit.*, pp. 873-883.

[38] Thomas Szasz, *The Myth of Mental Illness* (New York: Hoeber-Harper, 1967).

[39] "Elsewhere on the Legal Front," *Behavior Today*, Vol. 4, No. 12, March 19, 1973.

[40] Gerald Caplan, *Principles of Preventive Psychiatry* (New York: Basic Books, Inc., 1964).

[41] Leigh M. Roberts, Seymour L. Halleck, and Martin B. Loeb, eds., *Community Psychiatry* (Madison, Wisconsin: University of Wisconsin Press, 1966).

[42] J. O. Cole, "Behavioral Toxicity," in L. Uhr and J. G. Miller, eds., *Drugs and Behavior* (New York: John Wiley & Sons, Inc., 1960), pp. 100-183.

Summary

The mentally ill are no longer considered a radically distinct segment of the population. The great prevalence of mental disorder in modern society, and the development of explanations for it, have resulted in efforts to curb its serious social effects and to cure the affected individuals.

Definitions of mental illness vary. The clinical or medical definition holds mental illness to be a diseased state observed within an individual. Statistically, mental illness can be viewed as a deviation from the norm in any quality relating to mental functioning. Socially, mental illness is a quality sometimes ascribed to those whose behavior or attitudes are not approved by the larger society. A practical definition would hold mental illness to be a condition which causes difficulty in an individual's functioning at home or at work. Although there is no general agreement on a defintion of mental *health* either, there is agreement about some characteristics a mentally healthy person should have, among them an adequate feeling of security and adequate contact with the real world.

Many varieties of mental illness are normally classified according to their symptoms. Of the most debilitating psychoses, the most prevalent form is schizophrenia, which is characterized by delusions, hallucinations and withdrawal from personal relations. Other psychoses are paranoia, characterized by suspicion, and manic-depressive conditions, characterized by rapid changes between high exuberence and deep depression. Psychotics are more likely to be hospitalized than other mentally ill individuals.

Less debilitating, but still seriously damaging, are the neuroses, compulsive behavior patterns that interfere with everyday functioning. Most mental disorder in the population is of this sort.

The type of mental illness a person suffers has been shown to be related to his socioeconomic status. Psychoses are more prevalent among the poor and minorities; neuroses are more prevalent among the middle class and those of higher socioeconomic status. The type of mental illness a person suffers may also be related to his age or occupational status.

Mental hospitals, which for a century have provided the principal mode of treatment for mental disorders, have recently been heavily criticized. Sociologist Erving Goffman has argued that these institutions actually require the kind of behavior that leaves a person unable to get along anywhere except inside a mental institution. Some modifications of organization within mental hospitals have been made in response to such criticism. There are many more disturbed persons in the population who are not hospitalized, however. One study revealed that while one of every four people interviewed thought he needed professional help for a disturbed condition, only one out of seven sought it.

Sociological explanations of mental illness look for causative factors in conditions outside the individual. One factor is prolonged isolation from social contact. Role theory deals with mental illness caused by the strain of social roles too numerous or ambiguous to be played successfully. Labeling theory evaluates the extent to which calling someone "mentally ill" actually contributes to his illness.

As ideas of what causes mental illness have changed, new ways of dealing with it have emerged. Preventive psychiatry acts on the causes of mental illness at an early stage. The community mental health movement attempts to treat people in their own environment. Various forms of therapy hold faulty learning during childhood responsible for mental illness and attempt a reeducation process as a cure.

chapter

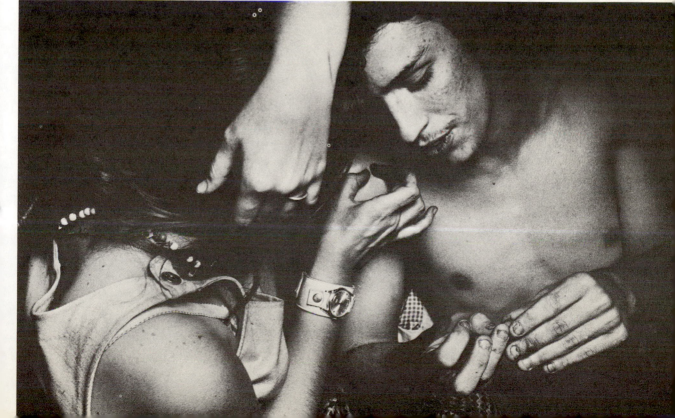

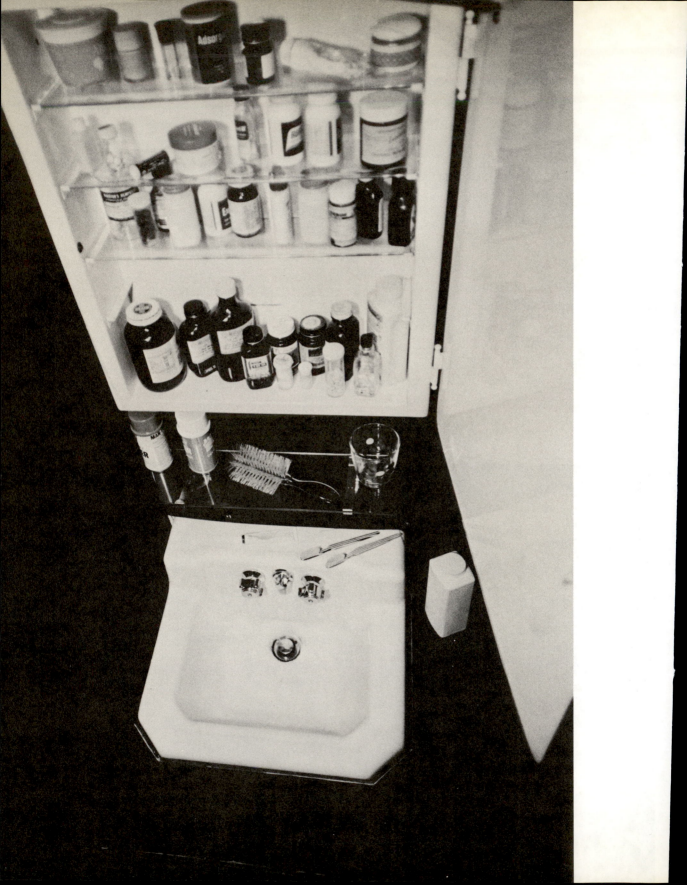

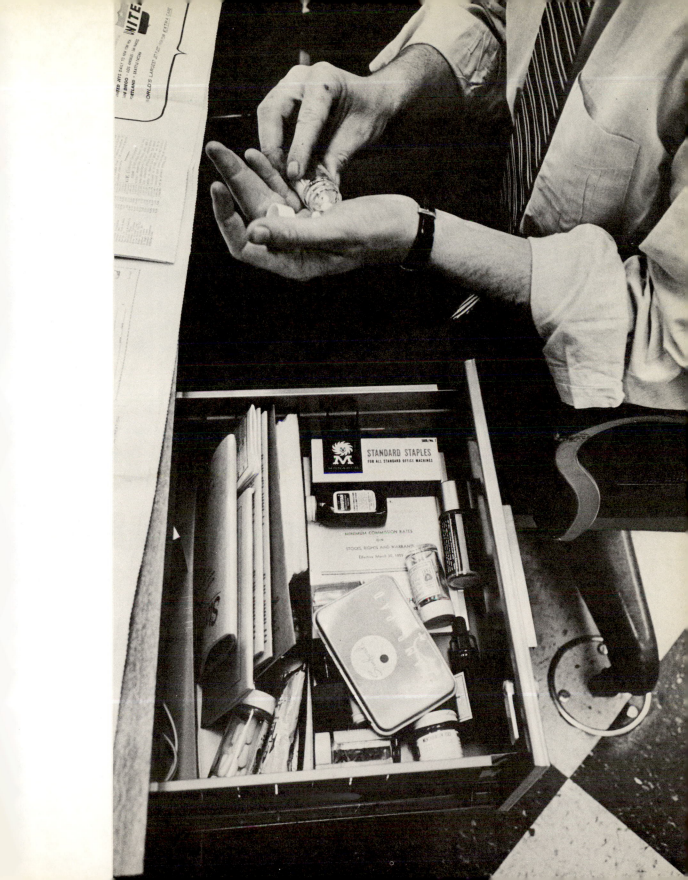

drugs
and
alcohol

The existence of any social problem, including that of alcohol and drug use, depends to a great extent on certain social definitions held within a given society at a given time. These definitions in turn depend on current and past social attitudes and behavioral norms, which are reflected in and reinforced by law and government regulations. Currently, considerable conflict exists within American society concerning the appropriate use of drugs. This conflict is manifested in the lack of consensus about the nature of the drug problem.

There has been a great deal of public debate recently about the use of marijuana, narcotics and hallucinatory drugs by middle-class youth. Citing the illegality of such use and the harm to individuals and society that it causes, President Nixon has stated that he feels drug abuse is the nation's number one public enemy. Yet the National Commission of Marijuana and Drug Abuse, which was appointed by the President and Congress to study the problem and make recommendations for policy, concluded "Dependence on alcohol is without question the most serious drug problem in the country today."[1]

Part of the disagreement over the appropriate use of drugs and alcohol is a reflection of our social attitudes and values. America is a chemical-ingesting society. We smoke, drink and take pills at an ever-increasing rate, often to induce pleasant physical or psychic states. Yet studies have shown that a large majority of the population disapproves of the use of drugs for nonmedical purposes. In response to a survey conducted recently in New York, 90.3 percent of the ople interviewed disagreed with the statement that "Everyone nould try drugs at least once to find out what they are like." And nearly 76 percent disagreed with the statement that "People can find out more about themselves through drugs."[2] "Appropriate drug use" would seem, then, to be defined by the source of the drug and the purpose for which it is used rather than by the chemical change effected by the drug itself.

n all its varieties—legal, l and illegal—needs far more gation. If drug experiences somehow t or are related to social settings we t note specific settings and determine eir exact effects on participants. We must also look further at the role of power and knowledge in each setting: knowledge of whether to take a drug, how to take it and what to expect of it; and power over distribution of the drug, knowledge about it, and over the decision to take or not to take it.

Howard S. Becker

Appropriate use is also a function of who is taking the drug. In the past, when the majority of illegal drug users belonged to "outcast" groups such as criminals, prostitutes, nonwhites and the urban poor, the drug laws reflected and reinforced public attitudes that illegal drug use undermined moral restraints, led to crime, violence and other forms of deviance and was generally un-American. In the late 1960s, however, when illegal drug use spread to the middle and upper classes, particularly to the youth of these classes, there was a startling increase in awareness and alarm concerning the "drug problem." The new users have elicited some changes in social attitudes and definitions. To many people, "appropriate drug use" has been redefined and extended to include the use of marijuana, and has resulted in a call for change in the drug laws. To others, the young from respectable classes who use drugs have been consigned to the stigmatized groups formerly associated with drug use.

Similar shifts in public mood concerning drugs have in the past taken place with regard to alcohol. Once illegal, alcohol is now legally and generally available to any adult within the society. Its problematic aspect is no longer its criminal taint, but rather the social costs alcohol use exacts—in lost employment, family breakup, social disorder. Illegality would seem to be only one aspect of the matter, to judge by the use and abuse of alcohol which continues to take place under present legal arrangements.

Definition of terms

Nowhere is the conflict of values and attitudes that surrounds the subject of drug and alcohol use more apparent than in the way terms are defined. What, for example, is a "drug"? According to a basic text for physicians and medical students, "a drug is broadly defined as any chemical agent that affects living protoplasm"[3] This includes coffee, alcohol and cigarettes, which are pharmacologically, but not socially, defined as drugs. The term "drug abuse" is also variously defined. Law enforcement officials consider it any illegal use of drugs. For the American Medical Association, it is any nonmedical drug use.

Addiction and abuse

Describing and defining the phenomenon of drug dependence is problematic for the medical sciences. In the 1950s, the World Health Organization (WHO) drew a distinction between "addiction" and "habituation." Addiction meant compulsive use, a tendency to increase dosage, psychological and physical dependence and detrimental effects to the individual and society. Habituation meant a desire for the drug, no tendency to increase dosage, no dependence and only personal detriment. Then, in 1969, WHO abandoned this distinction, suggesting that the term addiction be dropped in favor of the more specific terms "physical and psychological dependence."[4]

Yet the term "addiction" is still used. Sociologist Jerome Jaffe defines addiction as ". . .a behavioral pattern of compulsive drug use characterized by overwhelming involvement with the use of a drug, the securing of its supply and a high tendency to relapse after withdrawal."[5] Jaffe believes that one cannot state precisely when compulsive use becomes addiction, and that it is possible to be physically dependent without being addicted and to be addicted without being physically dependent.

Physical dependence can be deduced from definite clinical indices, and its deduction is an objective judgment. The clinical signs of physical dependence are the occurrence of withdrawal symptoms once the concentration of the drug in the blood has decreased. Psychological dependence must be inferred from the user's mental or emotional states and behavior patterns and involves a value judgment on the part of the observer.

Alcoholism

Alcoholism, like drug addiction, is also variously defined. Researcher E. M. Jellinek, who began his studies in the early 1940s, describes many different patterns, or kinds, of alcoholism, two of which he considers to be diseases. In both these disease patterns, the user is alcohol dependent. But in one pattern, the user cannot control the amount of his drinking; in the other, the user cannot abstain from drinking.[6]

Mark Keller of the Rutgers Center of Alcoholic Studies stresses Jellinek's concept of the user's loss of control, defining the alcoholic as "one who is unable consistently to choose whether he shall drink or not, and who, if he drinks, is unable consistently to choose whether he shall stop or not."[7] Still another definition is preferred by sociologist Robert Straus, who holds that alcoholism is "the use of alcoholic beverages to the extent that it repeatedly exceeds customary dietary use or ordinary compliance with the social drinking of the community, and interferes with the drinker's health, interpersonal relations or economic functioning."[8] Alcoholism has also been defined in terms of the degree of dependence, complications connected with nutritional deficiencies or in terms of the quantity of alcohol consumed.

Government regulation of drugs and alcohol

The Food and Drug Administration, a federal agency, tests all drugs intended for sale in the United States. Their evaluation is made not solely in terms of the drug's safety; they also must determine whether it will be beneficial in the treatment of the health conditions for which it is intended. The FDA determines which drugs may be sold over the counter and which may be obtained only by a doctor's prescription. State and federal laws make illegal the nonprescription use of certain narcotic-containing drugs and barbiturates, amphetamines, tranquilizers and other drugs classified as dangerous. It is presently illegal to sell, possess or use heroin, opium, cocaine, marijuana and the various hallucinogens. These drugs may not even be prescribed, although physicians with government permission may use hallucinogens in carefully controlled research and cocaine as a local anaesthetic. Certain narcotic drugs such as morphine, codeine, meperidine, the barbiturates and some amphetamines may be obtained legally with a doctor's prescription.

Although the potential danger of alcohol and tobacco, especially cigarettes, is well-documented, their sale and consumption are subject to minimal control. Cigarettes may not be sold to anyone under eighteen, but since they are freely available in vending machines, this prohibition is unenforceable. Liquor sales are legal to adults in all states—the regulations varying from place to place. Now that the voting age has been lowered, some states are lowering the age of persons who may buy or be served liquor from twenty-one to eighteen. Liquor and cigarettes are heavily taxed and provide considerable revenue at all levels of government.

Social attitudes and social control

In the early days of America's history, people drank primarily wine and beer, although distilled alcohol in the form of rum was popular with the colonists. Drinking then was subject to strict family, community and religious control. However, as the young nation opened new frontiers westward, as immigrants with different drinking habits swelled the population, as the cities grew in size, American drinking patterns changed. This change is indicated by a New York City police report of 1852 in which out of 180,000 arrests, 140,000 were related to drinking. By the mid-nineteenth century, drinking in the United States had surfaced as a social problem.

Concern about the problem prompted the reform movement of the early nineteenth century to attempt to eliminate drinking and its associated evils. The American Temperance Union, founded in 1826, distributed vast quantities of antiliquor propaganda in its attempt to persuade people to reform. Until the mid-1840s, religious organizations and local temperance societies continued to urge moral reform. When this proved generally unsuccessful, they turned to political action. By the time of the Civil War, eleven states had passed antiliquor laws.

The crusading Women's Christian Temperance Union regarded the use of alcohol not only as sinful but as the root cause of all social ills. Mainly rural, upper class and Protestant, they felt it their calling to teach the new immigrants of the city the evils of drink. In 1870 the Anti-Saloon League began a political movement against alcohol. This new reform movement culminated in the passage in 1919 of the Eighteenth Amendment, creating Prohibition. The amendment had no effect on decreasing the consumption of alcohol; rather the demand for illegal alcohol during Prohibition fostered crime on a scale and to an extent of organization not hitherto known in the United States. By the time of the repeal in 1933, the attitudes toward liquor had changed. The respectable classes no longer considered drinking an evil; without their support antiliquor laws proved unenforceable.

The use of drugs for inducing changed mental states is not confined to any one society or any particular historical age. For centuries, American Indians used peyote, a type of cactus that grows in the Southwest and Mexico, in their tribal religious ceremonies. Peyote was considered the most powerful and sacred of the various hallucinogenic plants in common use among the tribes, and was used by initiates for healing, prophecy and divination. Various tribal peyote groups continued to use the drug until 1964, when California ruled the religious use of peyote illegal.

Opium was used in Asian countries for centuries and became a serious problem in China in the early 1800s. Although many Chinese immigrants brought the use of the drug with them to the United States, opium was not an unknown drug in America. It was the major ingredient in many patent medicines in the nineteenth century. Morphine, an opium derivative that was not at first thought to be addictive and was considered a miracle drug when first introduced as a pain reliever in the early 1800s, was widely used during the Civil War in the medical treatment of wounded soldiers.

Prior to World War I, there were an estimated 200,000 to 500,000 addicts in the United States, many of whom had become addicted through the use of patent medicines containing morphine. These medicines were widely advertised to cure "female troubles" and many other diseases, and were available over the counter in any drug store. A majority of the user population was white, middle class and female. "Long Day's Journey Into Night," an autobiographical play by Eugene O'Neill, dramatizes his mother's addiction and the family's heartbreaking attempts to deal with it. The user of laudanum, as morphine was often called, was often not aware that it was addicting nor that he was an addict. Narcotic drugs and addiction were not yet viewed as a personal or social problem.

In the 1920s and 30s, new addicts were largely white males who frequented areas where illegal drugs could be purchased—the disorganized areas of the largest cities, areas characterized by overcrowding, crime and other social problems.[9] In fact, narcotics use may actually have declined during the period between the two world wars. It was found that one of every 1500 draftees in World War I was a narcotics addict as opposed to one of every 10,000 draftees in World War II. By the early 1950s, new population groups, primarily blacks and Puerto Ricans, were taking up residence in the slum areas where illicit drugs had long been available. Adolescents and young adults thus had access to drugs in their home neighborhoods. By 1960, in some neighborhoods as many as 10 percent of all males in late adolescence were officially recorded as drug users. In recent years nearly three-fourths of all addicts recorded on the register of the Bureau of Narcotics have been black, Puerto Rican or Mexican-American, marking a shift in the racial character of the drug problem.

A major change in drug use patterns occurred in the mid-1960s, when young people, particularly white middle-class students, began smoking marijuana and taking nonnarcotic drugs such as barbiturates, tranquilizers, amphetamines and hallucinogens for their euphoric effects. The boom in psychedelic drugs began as early as 1954 with the publication of Aldous Huxley's *The Doors of Perception,* in which he describes his visions and insights under the influence of mescalin. "Beat" writers such as Allen Ginsberg, William Burroughs and Ken Kesey began writing about their drug experiences. In 1960, at Harvard University, Drs. Richard Alpert and Timothy Leary began using mescaline, psylocybin and LSD in a research project, and were later dismissed from the university. Leary established a psychedelic cult, declaring it was time to "tune in, turn on, and drop out." By the late 1960s and early 1970s, the consumption of heroin and cocaine had risen, including very high use in the armed services, particularly among troops in Vietnam.

The drug experience

Attitudes toward drugs have changed over time; the patterns of use among different segments of the population have varied over the years. To understand the phenomenon of drug and alcohol use, it is helpful to analyze drug-using behavior from a variety of perspectives. These include the pharmacological properties of drugs and their effects on the physical functioning, emotional state and behavior of the user. Each of these factors is influenced by the particular user's perception of drug use.

9 *chapter*
Drugs and alcohol

Psychoactive drugs—sedatives, stimulants, narcotics, hallucinogens and marijuana—affect the central nervous system (CNS) (the brain, brain stem and spinal cord) in such a way that physical functions, emotional states and consciousness are altered. Physiologically, alterations occur because a molecule of the drug penetrates a cell or cell membrane and causes certain chemical changes.[10] This is called the *action* of the drug. The action triggers a series of biochemical and physiological reactions that are called the *effects* of the drug. The primary effects of the psychoactive drugs are that they depress or excite the level of activity in the brain.

Sedatives	Stimulants	Narcotics	Hallucinogens	Marijuana
Alcohol	Caffeine	Opium	LSD (lysergic acid diethylamide)	Hashish
Barbiturates	Nicotine	Opium derivatives	Peyote	
Luminal		Morphine		
Amytal	Cocaine	Heroin	Mescaline	
Nebutal	Amphetamines	Codeine		
Seconal	Benzedrine	Hydomorphine	Psilocybin	
Pentathol	Dexadrine			
	Methedrine	Synthetic narcotics	DMT (Synthetic derivatives	
Tranquilizers	Desoxyn	Methadone	DET of psilocybin)	
Thorazine	Preludin	(Dolophine)		
Compazene	Dexamyl	Meperidine	THC (chemical deriv-	
Stellazine		(Demerol)	ative of	
Reserpine	Anti–depressant drugs		marijuana)	
Barbituratelike tranquilizers	Tofranil			
Doriden	Elavil			
Miltown				
Librium	Amphetaminelike drugs			
Quaalude	Nardil			
Somnes	Parnate			
Nectoe				

Figure 9–1   Table of drug classification

Statements about specific drug actions are always partly theoretical, because very little is known about the cellular biochemistry and physiology of the central nervous system. Medical researchers have long thought that brain cells have certain chemical structures or receptors into which the drug molecule fits.[11]

The effects of drugs on the physical and mental states of the user cannot be predicted with complete accuracy. In general, the size of the dose and the consequent level of drug concentration in the blood are the major determinants of effect. With small doses, many other factors may also come into play. These include individual sensitivity, which varies according to body temperature, inherited blood or enzyme deficiencies, sex and age; the rate at which the drug is absorbed, broken down into chemically inert substances and eliminated by the body; the presence of other drugs in the body; body weight; and the route of administration. Drugs are absorbed most quickly if they are injected into a vein, more slowly if injected under the skin or inhaled and more slowly still if swallowed and absorbed through the intestinal tract. Factors such as personality, mood, previous experience with the drug, expectations of drug effects and the circumstances under which a drug is taken also influence effects.[12] These are particularly important with the hallucinogens.

Drugs are classified according to similarity of chemical structure and, more generally, similarity of effects. Figure 9-1 on page 343 shows the classification of drugs used by the Haight-Ashbury Free Medical Clinic in San Francisco.

Sedatives

The sedative drugs depress activity in the CNS and are often prescribed for their sleep-producing or calming effects. The tranquilizers, also called antipsychotic drugs, are prescribed for anxiety and have been used widely in treating schizophrenics.

Sedatives are capable of depressing a wide range of functions. The progressive effects include conceptual disorganization, feelings of euphoria, release from anxiety and a lessening of inhibitions. With higher doses, the user loses control of speech articulation and coordination. Still higher doses depress body temperature and cause sleep. In massive doses of sedation, suppression of cardiovascular and respiratory control can cause coma and death.

Alcohol, the barbiturates and the barbituratelike tranquilizers, when taken in small doses, produce a "tolerance," or a resistance to the effects of the drug which may lead the user to increase the dose. These drugs all cause physical dependence, and when taken together or within a short time of one another, they are much more potent than when taken alone. Many accidental deaths as well as suicides have been attributed to the combination of alcohol and barbiturates.

Withdrawal symptoms reverse the effects of these sedatives. The symptoms range from a mild "hangover" through extreme agitation, insomnia, anxiety, nausea, vomiting and delirium. Convulsions are common with barbiturate withdrawal, and hallucinations with alcohol withdrawal. When these drugs wear off, the user becomes more tense, anxious or agitated than he was before taking the drug.

The tranquilizers, in contrast to other sedatives, are selective depressants. They do slow down responses to stimuli and decrease anxiety and tension, but do not produce euphoria. Nor do they produce tolerance or physical dependence.[13]

Stimulants

Stimulants step up activity in the CNS. The general progressive effects include depression of appetite, a more rapid flow of thought, heightened sensitivity to sensory stimuli, a decrease in reaction time, an increase in motor activity and the suppression of drowsiness or fatigue. The rate of the heartbeat and the respiratory rate are considerably increased, which, in the case of an overdose, can lead to convulsions, coma, cerebral hemorrhage, respiratory collapse and death. Large doses of cocaine and the amphetamines often produce a psychotic state accompanied by visual and auditory hallucinations. Users may have paranoid feelings of being persecuted or attacked, and because they also may feel abnormally powerful, they often can harm others.

Many users of stimulants, particularly the amphetamines, also use barbiturates to counteract the effect of coming down or "crashing." This cyclical drug use is extremely disorienting and harmful to the user, physically as well as psychically.[14]

With the exception of the milder antidepressants, stimulants produce a strong tolerance and the dosage must be increased to attain the desired effect. The depression and exhaustion that follow the use of these drugs are considered withdrawal symptoms by some researchers and a natural result of loss of sleep by others.[15]

reading:

Anonymous
AMPHETAMINE

The whole operation of giving yourself a shot is a very sexual sort of thing. It's like a very exhibitionistic rite, you know. Okay, so you finally get the blood into the works, and you squeeze the stuff into your vein, and then you pull the needle out, and you go about cleaning out the works. Now, just about the time you get the works in the water, which is maybe five to ten seconds, ten seconds at the most, you get this thing coming up the back of your neck, this zing, when your skin starts to prickle, and it goes to your head and explodes, and then you get a huge smile on your face, and all of a sudden your mind has never been so awake in your life, and you start singing or start talking or something. Now, if you had a good shot, you get a hot feeling in the back of your throat. You cough, or have to breathe very deeply, because your heart is all of a sudden beating much faster, so you have to catch up with it. Now, if you had a really good shot, you can't walk. You're just sitting there—sssshhhh—the blood's all over your arm, you can't see very well or anything. That goes away in a few minutes. Now, the rush is when it zooms into your head and floats your head. It's one of the nicest feelings on earth. It's beautiful. And nothing—nothing—can hurt this big, wonderful thing. If you're really high, you couldn't care less about anything. But if you're not that high, you've got this little thing in the back of your mind which comes closer and closer: you realize that you haven't got any more. And that'll throw the whole thing. And before long, you're out on the street, looking for more. So you get high. Your high is like—you build delusions in your head. You're really happy. If you're with anyone else, you talk an awful lot. You talk incessantly when you're high. You're incredibly active. You're also a little bit unaware of things, so you'll knock things over and not know it, but all the while, you think you've got control over everything. But if you take an awful lot, the reaction is just about the opposite. Your mind gets, just gets quiet, and you sit around dreaming. Okay. Five people, let's say, have just shot. All right. Now then, there isn't just five people sitting around. There's five different little things going on. Someone's cleaning up the rug, rearranging the house a little bit. Someone else is sitting down to write something in their book. Somebody else is babbling and someone else isn't listening. Someone is painting a picture. Someone else is being uptight because whoever it is that he wants to be concerned with is high, and not concerned with him. All right. So that's a good cross-section: someone's unhappy, someone's being an idiot, someone is having fun, and someone is just high. Everybody's exuberant for maybe an hour. That's what you always aim for is that first hour or so. Then you're high and things are okay. After three hours, after four hours, after five hours, depending on how much you had, things ain't so okay, more and more, so that after six or seven hours, things are downright nasty. That's the time you go out and want more. There's a thing. There's a very simple physical principle. To get high, you gotta come down. No question about it. And the higher you get, and the better your high, the worse it's gonna be when you come down. With the exception of one funny little thing which you keep in the back of your mind. And that is, if you stay high for long enough, you'll be able to sleep right through coming down. Now for the comedown. The amphetamine starts to go away. Wears off. You're still awake. And you can't get to sleep. You start to come down. And it's the worst feeling in the world. It's not as physical as heroin withdrawal, although if you've been using a lot of it for some time, you start to have convulsions and things like that just because you know, your heart has been going too fast, and your body has been moving so fast, that when you stop, you are so worn out that your body just can't function. But it's not an actual physical withdrawal. It's a mental withdrawal, when all these illusions you've been having high come crashing down. It's like a celebration of disillusionment. All of a sudden, nothing in the world is right, nothing—absolutely nothing. Usually you just sit there with all your nerves burnt out, with your stomach shrunk, with your lips and mouth too dry to be comfortable so that you're always chewing, your eyeballs twitch, you're pretty nervous, but at the same time, you're too depressed and too nervous to do anything, you just sit there feeling miserable. It's the kind of thing you wanna cry, but you can't usually cry. It's the kind of thing that the only relief you can see is would be, like, really, really desperate crying. Sometimes you can cry, and you just go into some room and get underneath a pillow and cry. It's a good thing to do, but usually you can't do that, and so you just have to sit around and be the dregs. From people who have seen others when they're coming down, the normal reaction is that they look like they're dead, 'cause that's what you look like. Your extremities are deprived of blood. Your nose is freezing cold, your cock shrivels up, 'cause your blood can't reach out into the extremities. . . .Usually it's a lot nicer to be high, you know. But meanwhile you have to live a certain way. You don't eat. You lose an incredible amount of weight. You become very thin, very gaunt. Vitamins are burnt out of you. Because of your metabolism, you become sort of disinterested in sex, at least for the time being. And you get sick very easily. The common cold is deadly—it can kill you, you know, because of the condition your body is in. You're probably one-quarter as defensive against the conditions of nature. Like, when you're walking around in the streets in the wintertime, high, you don't know that you're being frozen to death. And you get colds. Like, I had a cold once for three months, and I deserved it. I just had to live with it. It could have wiped me out, you know, really easily. When you stay awake for a couple of days, your mind isn't working very well and you become paranoid very easily. Anything you want to be true and ugly, will be true and ugly. It develops into where you're hallucinating. People start coming out of trees and stuff. It's really horrible.

From
Drugs in American Society by Erich Goode
(New York: Alfred A. Knopf, Inc., 1972) pp. 138-142

Narcotics

Narcotics, which are the only effective drugs in relieving severe physical pain, act as selective depressants on the CNS; some, but not all, brain functions are slowed. The general effects of moderate doses are relief of pain, drowsiness, euphoria, difficulty in concentration, apathy, a decrease in appetite, scratching and sometimes nausea and vomiting. Narcotics do not produce slurred speech or impair physical coordination, as do alcohol and barbiturates. Narcotics are a poisonous substance to the body and if a tolerance is not built up or the dosage is too large, there is the danger of respiratory failure.

Junk is the ultimate merchandise. The junk merchant does not sell his product to the consumer, he sells the consumer to the product. He does not improve and simplify his merchandise, he degrades and simplifies the client.

William S. Burroughs

Narcotics produce a rapid and strong tolerance and are strongly addictive. Narcotic withdrawal symptoms are similar to those of alcohol and barbiturate withdrawal. They include chills and trembling, sweating, abdominal cramps, diarrhea and muscle spasms—the classic "cold turkey" syndrome. The average street dose of heroin is so mild, however, that the physical withdrawal symptoms are often no worse than the symptoms of a bad cold.[16] The intensity of narcotic withdrawal symptoms appears to be influenced by a number of psychological factors. In two therapeutic communities, Synanon in California and Daytop Village in New York, the withdrawal symptoms experienced by resident addicts are relatively mild, a situation attributed to the fact that in a community of former addicts, status is gained through being drug free, rather than through the size of one's habit and the severity of withdrawal.[17]

Hallucinogens

Hallucinogens produce changes in mood and perception and make users extremely sensitive to their emotional and physical environment. The intensity of the reactions depends on the size of the dose. However, the reactions themselves are idiosyncratic and depend on the user's personality, emotional state, expectations of effects and immediate surroundings. The physiological effects include increased pulse rate, heartbeat and blood pressure, and also irregular breathing, shivering, nausea and loss of appetite—although these effects are usually mild and are not significant for most users.[18]

Moderate or large doses of hallucinogens cause distortion of the perceptual constants of space, time, solidity of objects and body image. A minute may seem like hours, sound may be seen as colors or colors heard as sound. Many users feel that their bodies are melting or that they no longer exist as physical beings. In some people this dissolution of ego boundaries produces a religious feeling of union with God, Nature or the cosmic consciousness. For others, this feeling can be extremely frightening, causing panic, depression or periodic flashbacks of perceptual distortions.[19]

There are no withdrawal symptoms with hallucinogens and therefore no physical dependence. Although LSD is by far the most potent of the hallucinogens, researchers have recently concluded that no evidence exists to show that normal doses of pure LSD cause chromosome damage or birth defects. However, in 1966, the only producers of LSD, in Switzerland, stopped shipment to the United States. It is assumed, therefore, that most of the LSD in this country comes from clandestine sources and may be mixed with other substances which may be harmful.[20]

Marijuana

Marijuana is a mixture of the leaves, stems and resinous flowering tops of the female hemp plant, *Cannabis sativa,* which grows wild throughout the world. Researchers disagree on its pharmacological classification; it has been classed as a mild hallucinogen, a sedative whose effects are similar to those of alcohol and as a "mixed stimulant-depressant."

The effects of smoking marijuana, which does not cause physical dependence, are extremely subtle and subjective and usually must be learned in order to be experienced. The primary effects are emotional and perceptual. The user experiences feelings of elation and well-being; time and distance appear elastic and sensory stimuli are intensified. Smoking marijuana increases the appetite and often induces a deep sleep. With larger doses, users usually become absorbed in their own experience of the drug. Some become sleepy; others become more active and talkative.

Acute toxic reactions of anxiety or psychosis are rare, but they do occur and appear to be related to the user's expectations and setting. Also, studies have shown that young people with positive expectations can get high smoking placebos.[21]

Drug users

While drugs of all kinds are being consumed by Americans in the 1970s in large amounts—Figure 9-2 on page 352 shows the rate of nonmedical drug use in the United States based on 1972 data—it is extremely difficult to determine the number of drug users and drug addicts in the United States. All users who come to the attention of the authorities in any way are reported to the Drug Enforcement Administration and officially listed. However, the clandestine nature of illegal drug use makes such statistics difficult to compile and keep up-to-date. It is just as difficult to discover the number of alcoholics in the general population, because authorities do not agree on a definition of alcoholism. Still the statistics that are available can suggest associations between a particular behavior and the factors against which it is being measured.

Alcohol

A 1964-65 survey of American drinking practices examined a variety of factors such as age, sex, education, race, religion, socioeconomic class, region of residence and size of community and correlated these variables with drinking.[22] The study concluded that persons most likely to be social drinkers are college graduates of high social and professional status, residents of Eastern suburban cities and towns, Jews, Episcopalians and those whose fathers were foreign born. According to this survey, those most likely to be heavy drinkers were of a lower educational and occupational status. These people were most likely to reside in large cities, in the East and in the Pacific states. Their marital status was single, divorced or separated, and they were Protestants, Catholics or had no religious affiliations.

The authors classified 6 percent of the people interviewed as "heavy escape" drinkers—those who drink to escape "problems of everyday living." They differed from other heavy drinkers in being older, of lower social status and income, more pessimistic and alienated. This group included an above average percentage of nonwhites.

The above distinctions are not very clear-cut, and it can be seen that it is difficult to derive population characteristics for alcoholics. The literature of Alcoholics Anonymous stresses that alcoholism cuts across every social variable. This point is made by Mark Keller when he stated that "The investigation of any trait in alcoholics will show that they have either more or less of it." And he concluded that "alcoholics are different in so many ways that it makes no difference."[23]

A few studies have investigated race or ethnic background variables in alcoholism. Studies of alcoholism in New York City have found the highest rates in ghetto areas, and higher rates among blacks and Puerto Ricans than among whites.[24] Several studies have found that, although rates of drinking are high for Jews, Irish and Italians, the rates of alcoholism are very high for the Irish and very low for Jews and Italians. The differences are attributed to cultural differences in attitudes about drinking.[25]

Drugs other than alcohol

As with alcohol, drug use in general cuts across social variables. It appears, however, that certain groups of people are more likely to use certain drugs and to use drugs frequently. A 1967 study of a random sample of 600 students in a West Coast college found that 21.2 percent smoked marijuana and that the typical user was a single or engaged male atheist from an upper-income family.[26] They found the strongest indicator of drug use, however, to be adherence to a "'hang-loose' ethic which attempts to cut itself loose from the traditional 'establishment' and to develop freedom from conformity and the search for new experiences."[27] A 1971 survey of 3500 liberal arts college students in the New York City area showed the following racial differences in drug use: black students were more likely to have tried heroin or cocaine, whereas white students inclined to the amphetamines and to hallucinogens.[28]

A 1971 study by the New York State Narcotic Addiction Central Commission of medical and illegal drug use in New York State based on interviews of householders over the age of fourteen found a prevalence of drug use among white, middle-class women over thirty-five who use prescription drugs.[29]

The findings of the New York State study showed that of the 1 percent of people reporting heroin use, only .2 percent used it regularly. Of the regular users, race was not a significant variable. Fifty percent were employed and 15.6 percent were middle class. Thirty-four percent were students, 50 percent had finished high school and 15 percent had at least some college. None had dropped out of high school and only 12.5 percent could not maintain employment.

The study noted that these findings are inconsistent with the findings of other studies of known addicts, which show that only one-third had completed high school and from 70 to 80 percent could not maintain employment. The researchers believe that the discrepancy is due in part to their own sampling procedure, which excluded people having no regular address, those living in rooming houses or those seldom at home. Their projected population of heroin users, for example, is 147,000, but they believe that a better estimate would be three times that, or 441,000.

Reasons for drug use

Many hypotheses have been formed to explain why people use drugs. An individual may drift into the use of drugs or alcohol through the influence of his peer groups; or he may have easy access to a supply, as do doctors or nurses; or there may be psychological or physical factors predisposing an individual to alcohol or drug use. Explanations of how and why people start to use drugs or find themselves drinking to excess may be quite different from explanations of why they continue; all explanations depend on a complex combination of physical, social, environmental and cultural processes.

Alcohol

In investigating the causes of alcoholism, the major theories contain transformations and combinations of the following factors: biochemical reactions to alcohol; low tolerance for stress and the consequent benefit of alcohol in reducing anxiety; cultural predisposition; learned response to various stimuli.

Biochemical sensitivity to alcohol may well be a factor in the development of alcoholism in an individual, but so far a causal connection has not been proved. Such sensitivity does develop in some people with the high, continuous intake of alcohol, but it may be a product of the intake rather than a preexisting condition.[30]

A similar objection can be raised to the theory that alcoholism is the product of the "alcoholic personality," whose supposed qualities are low self-esteem, chronic anxiety and emotional dependence. Studies have shown that this type of person does not inevitably or even usually become an alcoholic. Some alcoholics do show this repeated neurotic pattern of behavior, but it may be that this pattern is caused or increased by alcoholism rather than being the cause of alcoholism.[31]

Psychological and social factors working together appear to be important. Studies have consistently shown, for example, that the prevalence of drinking is greater and the incidence of alcoholism is less among Jews and Italians than among the Irish.[32] A 1946 study of alcoholism among Irish-American males found a cultural pattern of dependence, intense frustration, hostility and sexual prohibition for single men. This was combined with social approval of frequent and excessive drinking by single men and a tendency to substitute alcohol for food. The drinking was further exacerbated by the anxiety caused by low economic status and a need for single men to be independent. The study concluded that a combination of all these factors resulted in the high rate of alcoholism among Irish-Americans.

E. M. Jellinek, in his studies, concluded that psychological and sociocultural factors accounted for the heavy drinking that paved the way to alcohol addiction.[33] However, he believed these could not explain the addictive process itself—which was characterized by what he found to be a loss of control phenomenon. He felt this could best be explained by biochemical factors and that researchers should study tissue metabolism and reactions to stress as well as possible inherited or developed abnormalities.

Mark Keller extended the concept of loss of control to include the consistent inability to either abstain from drinking or to control the amount consumed at a given time and made this broader concept the basis of alcoholism per se.[34] Keller attributes loss of control to conditioning; the alcoholic responds to certain cues which, for him, have become strongly associated with drinking. Alcohol itself, or the particular blood-alcohol level, may become the cue.

Other drugs

Most researchers relate compulsive or addictive drug use to underlying psychological problems and environmental stress. A few, notably Drs. Marie Nyswander and Vincent Dole, the developers of the methadone treatment for heroin addicts, believe that addiction is purely physiological and probably results from a metabolic deficiency, but a direct causal relationship has not been proved.[35]

According to sociologist Alfred Lindesmith, it is not the pleasurable sensation of the drug which makes an addict continue its use, but rather his fear of what would occur should he stop using it.[36] To become addicted, the user must identify his withdrawal distress specifically with the drug, however. Lindesmith's formulation helps explain the process of becoming "hooked" on drugs.

Sociologist Howard Becker views drug addiction as the product of a learning process, which takes place through a user's participation in a drug "culture" of other addicts.[37] In the process, the user first learns to experience the pleasurable effects, as defined by the culture, of the drugs taken. His use is subsequently reinforced by the "specialness" of his habit; he learns a new language relating to drugs, and engages in new behaviors which are part of the addict role, most of them centering on supplying himself and his associates with the needed drugs. Since his drug use has normally made him a social outcast, he clings more tightly to the drug culture of which he has become a part.

	Youth (12–17)		Adult (18 and over)	
	Percent	Population	Percent	Population
Alcoholic beverages*	24	5,977,200	53	74,080,200
Tobacco, cigarettes*	17	4,233,850	38	53,114,120
Proprietary drugs** (sedatives, tranquilizers, stimulants)	6	1,494,300	7	9,784,180
Sedatives**	3	747,150	4	5,590,960
Tranquilizers**	3	747,150	6	8,386,440
Stimulants**	4	996,200	5	6,988,700
Marijuana	14	3,486,700	16	22,363,840
LSD, other hallucinogens	4.8	1,195,440	4.6	6,429,604
Glue, other inhalants	6.4	1,593,920	2.1	2,935,254
Cocaine	1.5	373,575	3.2	4,472,768
Heroin	.6	149,430	1.3	1,817,062

*within the last 7 days
**nonmedical use only

Figure 9–2   Reported experience with drug use for recreational and non-medical purposes by American youth and adults

Though Becker studied marijuana use, most older theories about addiction focused on young heroin addicts in urban ghettos or those addicts in institutions. It was believed that the addict was either psychotic or neurotic and that drugs provided relief from anxiety and were a way to withdraw from the stress of daily existence in the ghetto. The portrait of addiction was that of passive adaptation to stress, in which drugs allowed the user to experience fulfillment and the satiation of physical and emotional needs. Early studies done in the ghettos tended to support this theory. It was concluded that ghetto youth who experienced "double failure," who could not succeed in the gang subculture or in the legitimate larger culture, turned to drugs as a way of finding a place for themselves in society.

> *To the experienced smoker, marijuana seems quieting, rather mild, sometimes amusing, usually trivial, and often downright dull. But society defines what he considers a commonplace and harmless act as deviant, dangerous, and illegal. . .He does not constantly ruminate about this, of course, but it always exists, in the back of his mind, as a reservoir for anger and suspicion, a basis for doubting the validity of many other laws and attitudes.*
>
> Harrison Pope, Jr.

More recent studies of drug use in urban settings have found that many different patterns of drug use exist. Many habitual users avoid addictive drugs or are weekend users. Because the street dose of heroin is relatively low in potency, many addicts are able to control their habits. They may work or attend school and must exhibit energy and resourcefulness in order to support their habits. Today, the drug use pattern is one of different kinds of drug use which are integral parts of ghetto life and through which users gain status and respond to the goals and beliefs of their drug subculture.

Sociologist Edward Preble and economist John Casey, Jr., in a study of New York street addicts, make the point that for the average ghetto youth, a career as an addict is much more rewarding and satisfying than any other he is likely to achieve. One research subject declared:

> "When I'm on the way home with the bag safely in my pocket, and I haven't been caught stealing all day, and I didn't get beat and the cops didn't get me—I feel like a working man coming home; he's worked hard, but he knows he done something, even though I know it's not true."[38]

This is not the earlier depiction of a psychologically disturbed young man unable to cope with his social environment.

Investigations of the more recent phenomenon of drug use among middle-class youth have found that the majority tend to avoid hard drugs such as heroin and cocaine, generally come from stable homes and are not psychologically disturbed. For these people, drug use appears to be a response to their environment, a way of dissenting from middle-class values and life-styles and a way of affirming their own values. A middle-class youth who is an illegal drug user may reject the values of society. This rejection may be either a result or a precondition of illegal drug use. But whether antiestablishment values encourage drug use or result from it, drug use probably reinforces these values.

In investigating drug use among college students in the 1960s, psychologist Kenneth Keniston concluded that the primary motives for drug use are exploration of the self and a desire to find meaning in life.[39] He distinguishes between "seekers" and "heads." Seekers are those students who are neither deeply involved in drugs nor alienated from straight society. Heads, who make drug use a central part of their lives, have become alienated by the extreme pressures of academia and temporarily drop out into the drug subculture.

Some researchers, however, still believe that, in some cases, underlying psychopathology is the primary reason for drug use. A study by Smith and Luce stresses the severe degree of psychological impairment that they found in the Haight-Ashbury hippie community. Finding characteristics of unstable childhoods and low self-esteem, they concluded that the more damaged a person is psychologically, the more likely he is to become deeply involved in drug use. They note that hippies themselves are aware that they use drugs in order to gain self-esteem and status. While drugs may help maintain the illusion of mastering anxiety and depression, they mask psychological chaos by creating chemical chaos.

phototopic: YOUTH

Youthful rebellion against American society has recently been felt in especially strong forms, from the upsurge in the use of drugs to demonstrations against the Vietnam War, social conditions in the cities, and the policies of educational institutions. The constitutional amendment granting 18-year-olds the vote was one response to this rebellion. Increased public discussion of changes in social norms concerning drugs, sex, political action and educational arrangements were others. None has stopped the youthful search for alternatives to the present organization of American society.

Education, which some think the best means available to integrate American youth into society, is viewed by others as the source—for good or ill—of the strife that presently characterizes much public debate. Youthful idealism is often evoked for commercial purposes by the communications media; its capacity actually to influence events is still being tested.

Social effects of drug use

The abuse of alcohol and other drugs has a disruptive and destructive effect on the functioning of society. Moreover, the use of alcohol and drugs is associated with certain kinds of socially disapproved behavior. The relationship of organized crime and other criminal elements to the procurement and distribution of narcotics and the necessity of criminal behavior on the part of drug addicts to ensure their supply of drugs, has certainly contributed to the deterioration of our cities. Just as the adoption of alcohol by members of the middle class changed attitudes toward drinking, so the adoption of drugs by some members of the middle class has changed attitudes toward the use of drugs. This does not turn the problems of drinking or drug taking into nonproblems. A reassessment of social problems is a healthy process, but not to the extent that it makes a social problem disappear at the expense of many lives and the fate of some segments of society.

The risk that drug taking by the middle class will lead to a coverup of the effects of drug use does not seem great at the present time, for the subject of drugs and their effects is currently a commodity bought and distributed widely by the electronic and print media. Yet once a social problem ceases to impinge directly on those who possess power in society, chances are good that public perceptions of the problem will decline. If social norms relax to the point where marijuana is made legal, and narcotics may be acquired easily and legally by prescription, the result may be a lessening of public outcry against drugs. As can be seen with alcohol, however, the dysfunctional effects of drug taking are likely to continue, even though lowering of public perception makes evidence of these effects more difficult to gather.

Drug used	Characteristics of users
Barbiturates	White, middle-class high school graduate over fifty
Tranquilizers, amphetamines, (excluding methedrine), prescription narcotics	White, middle-class housewife over thirty-five who has at least finished high school
Anti-depressants	White middle-class high school graduate under twenty-five
Marihuana	Upper middle-class male under twenty-five who is employed and/or a high school or college student
Hallucinogens	White, upper-middle or middle-class male student who also smokes marihuana
Methedrine	Male high-school or college student who also smokes marihuana
Cocaine	White, male high school or college student from a lower-middle or lower-class family who also smokes marihuana and uses pep pills
Heroin	Lower-middle or lower-class male between the ages of eighteen and twenty-four who is employed and/or a student and who smokes marihuana and uses barbiturates

Figure 9–3   Profile of typical regular drug users in New York State (at least six times a month), 1971

Alcohol

Alcoholism is definitely associated with other kinds of deviation from social norms. Alcoholics have difficulties in holding jobs and in establishing and maintaining personal relationships and in fulfilling personal roles. They have more accidents and illnesses than other people and they die sooner.

With the exceptions of public drunkenness and drunken driving, drinking alcohol or being drunk are not crimes. Studies have shown, however, that drinking and drunkenness are associated with both crime and suicide. The nature of the relationship between alcohol and crime is not clear. In an extensive review of studies relating alcohol and alcoholism to crime, the Rutgers Center of Alcohol Studies concluded that the alcoholic is usually too debilitated to commit any crime other than public drunkenness. The studies showed that drinking has nothing to do with professional crime; they did note that drinking is a correlate to some crimes, such as arson, in which the lessening of inhibitions is a factor. But this behavior also occurs without drinking, and in most cases, drinking is not followed by any crime at all.

Public drunkenness ranks second as a major crime in our society, and its control involves considerable amounts of money. Laws against public drunkenness are variously enforced. The people most often arrested are derelicts and other people of low status. Some question now exists about the constitutionality of these laws, which can be construed as cruel and unusual punishment. The Supreme Court has so far upheld these laws, in part because there are no institutional alternatives to jail.

Other drugs

Illegal and habitual drug use is positively correlated with social disorganization. Many studies have shown that where family and community structures are weak, drug abuse is high. The dollar costs of drug abuse are great. The federal government has budgeted 419.1 million dollars for law enforcement, prevention and treatment in 1974. It spent 239.3 million dollars on these activities in 1972, and estimates show that the same amount was spent by state governments.

The current and major public concern, however, is that drugs cause crime. This is true, but the causal relationship between drugs and crime is not simple and direct. A user is not incited to criminal acts by the taking of a narcotic drug; in fact the reverse is the case. The narcotics, as their name implies, act to induce relaxation and contentment. The strategies necessary to procure drugs is another matter. Each time a connection is made between a dealer and a user, a crime is committed. Heroin is expensive. An addicted young ghetto resident may have to generate from $10 to $50 a day, every day, to support his habit. Some of this money may be earned legitimately, but sooner or later he is going to turn to criminal behavior, either by dealing himself, or by stealing and selling stolen goods to others. For women, prostitution, which is also illegal, is a major means of obtaining cash for drugs.

According to the Federal Strategy Commission on Drug Abuse and Drug Traffic, all the various estimates that have been made of property loss due to drug-related crimes are at least a billion dollars a year. The Commission also states that the best estimates of drug-related crime are that 35 percent of the people arrested for property crimes in urban areas are narcotic users and that about 25 percent of "addict crimes" are against people.

This relationship between crime and drug abuse has led to the point of view that government regulation of drugs should be abandoned— legalize drug distribution and take it out of the hands of the pusher. It is argued by some that the elimination of drug-related crimes might be one way to halt the deterioration of our cities.

Figure 9–4   Frequency of signs of developing alcoholism as reported by supervisors of alcoholics and alcoholics themselves

Type	Supervisors	Alcoholics
I Noticed early and frequently thereafter	Leaving post temporarily Absenteeism: half day or day More unusual excuses for absences Lower quality of work Mood changes after lunch Red or bleary eyes	Hangover on job Increased nervousness/jitteryness Hand tremors
II Noticed later but frequently thereafter	Less even, more spasmodic work pace Lower quality of work Hangovers on job	Red or bleary eyes More edgy/irritable Avoiding boss or associates
III Noticed fairly early but infrequently thereafter	Loud talking Drinking at lunch time Longer lunch periods Hand tremors	Morning drinking before work Drinking at lunch time Drinking during working hours Absenteeism: half day or day More unusual excuses for absences Leaving post temporarily Leaving work early Late to work
IV Noticed late and infrequently thereafter	Drinking during working hours Avoiding boss or associates Flushed face Increase in real minor illnesses	Mood changes after lunch Longer lunch periods Breath purifiers Lower quality of work Lower quantity of work

Social control of drug and alcohol use

Attempts at social control of drug and alcohol abuse have involved educating the public by means of programs in the schools and churches, campaigns in the mass media and social pressure in the family and among friends. Treatment of alcoholics and addicts has varied in medical and penal institutions, depending upon attitudes toward the alcoholic or addict. If such behavior is viewed as a moral failure, the addict or alcoholic will be treated punitively. If it is seen as a behavior pattern for which the individual should not be held directly responsible, the treatment may be more humane. American society has tended to treat the middle-class alcoholic in a medical or psychiatric setting and the lower-class user in the more punishing milieu of a penal or state mental institution.

Alcohol

Ever since the failure of Prohibition, no real attempt has been made to limit the supply of or demand for alcohol. Instead, voluntary, educational and government institutions have made great efforts to educate the public to view alcoholism as an illness and to develop a public health approach to the problem.

The public health approach has not had great success. The American Medical Association has officially defined alcoholism as a disease, and in 1956 the Association urged doctors and hospitals to treat alcoholics. In general, however, the medical profession and medical institutions have been slow to respond. Most hospitals do not have adequate bed space for alcoholics, nor do they provide detoxification services. The skid-row alcoholic is still arrested for public drunkenness and thrown in jail to dry out. Derelicts cannot get health insurance, usually they cannot get state welfare assistance, and they are excluded from many federally supported programs as well.

Community detoxification and treatment centers were recommended in 1969 by the President's Commission on Law Enforcement and the Administration of Justice and were written into an Act of Congress. As yet, however, only three programs are under way: federal projects in Maryland and Washington and the Manhattan Bowery Project in New York City. The latter is funded by a private foundation and cares for only fifteen men a day.

The most effective organization so far in rehabilitating alcoholics has been Alcoholics Anonymous, with its concept of alcoholics helping one another. AA employs no health professionals, keeps it own bureaucracy to a bare minimum, makes no racial or class distinctions, accepts no public funding and bases it technique on altruism and faith in God.

reading:
Selden D. Bacon
PREVENTING ALCOHOLISM

To my own way of thinking the culture and social activation of drinking forms, together with alcohol itself, is the crucial factor in the emergence of alcoholism; I do not feel, however, that this is the best target for those concerned with the prevention of alcoholism. The culture and social activation of drinking cover a far, far wider field than that of alcoholism. The impact of an attack in this area will require a long, long time before it can be measured. Many values only distantly related to alcoholism will be involved, and the attempts to change such values may instigate conflicts which would seem pretty irrelevant and hardly worth the effort to those concerned specifically with alcoholism. Preventive work on this level is in some ways analogous to preventive work concerned with mental health. Unless changes occur, alcoholism will presumably continue. Certainly preventive work on alcoholism will aid preventive work in the field of social and cultural disorganization related to the use of alcohol. Cooperation, perhaps integration, with any working on those problems would probably be a wise step. . . .

And so we come to [what] I believe to be the target of choice: That part of the culture and its social activation which relates to chronic deviations from the drinking culture, especially the deviations called alcoholism. The phenomena referred to are those behaviors and expressed attitudes both of individuals and groups which repeatedly occur in patterned fashion as responses to what is called alcoholism. In addition, for purposes of more extensive and more intensive understanding, one should consider repeated, patterned responses in the society to other deviations and irritations which are in any way similar to alcoholism. This will allow us to see the cultural items and social mechanisms which are available but which are not recognized or at least are not used in this particular situation.

. . . The most obvious response is perhaps that of avoidance, both an intellectual and a physical avoidance. Individuals, families, unions, business management, insurance companies, the military, the healing and health professions, and on and on have been avoiding perception of the problem. Much of this is passive avoidance; some of it is active avoidance. By "active" I mean that positive steps requiring money, time, energy and personnel are utilized to block recognition or action.

A second phenomenon occurs after recognition of the fact of chronic irritating deviation directly related to alcohol usage in an individual can no longer be avoided. This phenomenon is the use of mislabeling. It may be conscious or unconscious, based upon ingenuity or ignorance. The label may be the common cold, "nerves," emotional instability, sowing wild oats, grief, accident or kidney disease. The label may be applied on a death certificate, in a disciplinary hearing, in a cocktail conversation or by an alcoholic himself in utilizing some alibi which he all too shrewdly perceives will be accepted by many in the society.

A third phenomenon, one which also appears after recognition can no longer be avoided, but which accepts the idea that deviant consumption of alcohol is an important factor in the situation, is to fall back on archaic and useless responses such as cursing, ridiculing, beating, hiding, covering with maudlin sympathy, arguing with, lecturing at, pleading with, firing, fining, imprisoning, ostracizing, shaming, and putting into operation all the quack-therapy activities temporarily available in the society.

This is enough to indicate what is meant by repeated and patterned responses to the occurrence of chronic painful deviation related to consumption of alcohol in a given individual. If going to alcoholism clinics, to physicians active and able in this field, and to A.A. is a more satisfactory response, then it is very doubtful if as much as 10 percent of the estimated number of alcoholics has shown this response in the last 20 years, doubtful that 1 percent show it any one year. . . .

I would first like to indicate the impact of the typical responses and typical attitudes on the therapeutic process. A study by Trice on acceptance and rejection of A.A. is directly relevant to this subject. Mr. A and Mr. B, both alcoholics, come to the alcoholism clinic or to a physician or to an A.A. group. Let us state that they each have made four visits during a period of 10 days. Each has a wife, each has a close friend, each has a relationship with another individual who is a supervisor or close associate on the job. These three people are emotionally and behaviorally significant others. This, of course, puts them in a remarkably different spot than that occupied by the therapist who is not only a stranger but a threatening stranger, one who is going to steal from the alcoholic his great satisfaction in life and who is going to analyze him as if he were a bug on a pin and who is going to try to ram some esoteric philosophy, perhaps called religion or psychiatry or an adjusted life, down his gullet.

If Mrs. A and A's buddy and A's workaday associate or boss all agree that the clinic or A.A. group or that a doctor or an individual A.A. are no good, hypocritical, stuffed-shirt meddlers who can't do Mr. A any good and if they further indicate that Mr. A is a weakling, a sissy and no friend of theirs if he continues visiting these people, there is a very good chance that Mr. A will not be a good bet for recovery through the clinic, the physician or the A.A. approach. Let me postulate that Mr. B is psychologically, socially, physically and drinking experience-wise as identical with Mr. A as possible, but that Mrs. B, B's buddy and B's business associate or supervisor think that his new therapeutic venture is just about the smartest thing he ever did, that it is pretty sure to work and that he has gained new and significant respect from them because of this action. Then I think there is a very good chance for Mr. B's recovery.

This example relates to the social mechanism as it directly affects the individual alcoholic after he has been recognized as a chronic problem drinker. Now let us turn to the cultural setting and the social mechanisms on a less direct level. From this level we may get insight into the factors lying behind and supporting the positions of the two sets of wife, buddy, business associate and the accepting target of their actions. Mr. A's church, the druggist or old gentleman down the street or popular columnist or even doctor who serves as Mr A's fountainhead of health knowledge, Mr. A's dear old mother and Mr. A's one-time social drinking cronies implicitly or explicitly agreed that a drunk was a weak-willed or weak-witted excuse for a human being or was inevitably a particularly nasty type or was someone who "inherited bad blood and that was that" or who was a strong-willed sinner. Or they may have quite clearly expressed the belief that a great many men were "that way" and it wasn't particularly surprising and only nosy-Parkers and cops bothered about it anyway: Why shouldn't a man get plastered and throw his weight around a bit every once in a while?

These are common responses in our society. They reflect social values and they reflect perceptions of cause and effect in human behavior which are directly in conflict with current therapies for achieving recovery from alcoholism. These general responses can be strongly backed up by incidents and by the reporting of incidents which are interpreted in ways harmonious with the theory or value. They can be further reinforced by the absence of counter-values, counter-explanations and counter-incidents, especially when such counter-views are present and are active and are recognized in closely related problems. However, when there are doctors and nurses and clinics and when there are chronic cases who have gotten well through their advice and service and when industry, unions, management, and the armed forces and the church effectively spread these counter-values, explanations and their success, when the druggists and popular cartoonists and columnists and movie stars express these counter-views, then the power of the attitudes and behaviors which block acceptance of therapy are reduced.

I am emphasizing by indirection a definition of alcoholism which goes beyond the usual orientation suggested, if not, indeed, explicitly posed by usual psychiatric explanations. I am saying that alcoholism, at least its persistence through time, is a product of social interaction. This does not deny, nor is it incompatible with, descriptions of alcoholism given in terms of individual psychic or emotional process. However, I will go out on a limb and state that I believe in 90 percent of what is called alcoholism that without the social interaction favorable to its origination and persistence, alcoholism will not occur, or, if it should start, will be easily stopped. I will pick out another limb and state that social interaction and cultural settings with only the most minor and fleeting psychic maladjustments are the major factor in perhaps 25 percent of all those conditions commonly called alcoholism.

From
Realizing the Potential in State Alcoholism Programs by Selden D. Bacon
(Hartford, Conn.: Connecticut Commission on Alcoholism, 1959)
pp. 11-17.

Other drugs

In the control of drug use, public policy continues to emphasize law enforcement. Currently, many government officials are pressing for more stringent drug laws and, at the federal level, a reorganization of drug control programs to place more control with the Attorney General. Although the projected federal government programs will include research, education and treatment, the bulk of federal funds for 1974 are allocated to law enforcement.

Through the years, only token medical treatment facilities have been available for drug addicts. The Public Health Service has maintained two resident treatment centers since the 1930s; and most major cities and states with high addict rates do offer hospital treatment, but bed space is extremely limited. Some states, notably New York and California, have civil programs under which people arrested on drug offenses can be committed to a drug-free treatment program rather than jail.

The Synanist leans heavily on his own insight into his own problems of personality in trying to help others find themselves, and will use the weapons of ridicule, cross-examination, and hostile attack as it becomes necessary. . . . The Synanist does not try to convey to another that he himself is a stable personality. If fact, it may very well be the destructive drives of the recovered or recovering addictive personality embodied in a Synanist which makes him a good therapeutic tool—fighting fire with fire.

Charles E. Dederich

Hospitalizing addicts has been notoriously unsuccessful in helping them to maintain abstinence. Recognizing that such programs are repeatedly used by addicts to cut down rather than cure their habits, many cities began methadone maintenance programs in the mid-1960s. Such programs allow addicts, after a brief detoxification and stabilization period, to live at home and continue maintenance on daily oral doses of methadone, a synthetic opiate that blocks heroin effects. Patients report to a clinic for their methadone and also receive psychological and job counseling. Currently, about 85,000 people are enrolled in such programs around the country. Methadone was initially hailed by many drug-abuse specialists as the answer to heroin addiction. Now, however, it has become a popular street drug, and reports of deaths from overdoses are becoming frequent.

Another recent phenomenon is the drug-free resident addict community. The first, Synanon, was started in California in 1958 by a former alcoholic who applied the philosophy of Alcoholics Anonymous to a small group of drug addicts on a 24-hour-a-day live-in basis. The Synanon technique aims at restructuring the addict's personality by breaking through his emotional defenses by means of group confrontation with other addicts.

Critics of the American approach to drug abuse often compare it unfavorably to the so-called British System. In Britain, drug users may register at a central government office and then receive their drugs at little or no cost from government-licensed clinics or physicians. Yet, in the mid 1960s, the British experienced a surge in all categories of drug use. After much public debate and in a climate of extreme social disapproval of nonmedical drug use, Britain voted to maintain the system it had been using since 1920, which is a medical one. Accordingly, cocaine, amphetamine and narcotics users may use these drugs, but only under the supervision of medical doctors. The British System still operates on the premise that any nonmedical drug use is abuse.

American emphasis on law enforcement, even with a limited use of the medical model, will not change social attitudes toward illegal drug users. On the contrary, we have created a huge drug-abuse control bureaucracy of experts in the fields of medicine, social science and law enforcement. These people have a professional interest in a large population of illegal drug users, and are often more interested in their own careers and expertise than in helping drug users.

Figure 9–5   Interrelationships among systems affecting drug use

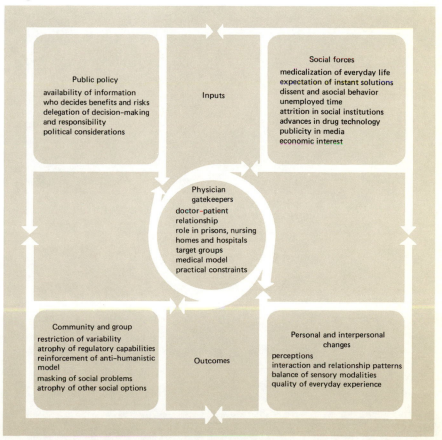

Future prospects

The problem of drug and alcohol abuse and the attendant problem of social control are deeply enmeshed in our attitudes and culture, and any solution in the near future seems unlikely. Moreover, signs indicate that drug use in general will increase. Researchers see a trend toward quiescence in American society. Raymond Shafer, who headed the National Commission on Marihuana and Drug Abuse, concluded, after its last report, that "Many persons have come to regard very real and fundamental emotions and feelings as abnormal, avoidable, socially and personally unacceptable, and worst of all, unnecessary."[40]

If drug use does increase, society will more than ever need new and better definitions and policies concerning drug abuse. Perhaps if the majority of future drug users and abusers are middle-class, following the model of the history of alcohol abuse, a more rational system may evolve. But it seems extremely unlikely that attitudes will change in regard to drug use by the poor and the outcast.

Notes

[1] Warren Weaver, Jr., "U.S. Drug Study Stresses Treatment, Not Penalties," *The New York Times,* March 23, 1973.

[2] Carl D. Chambers, *Special Report No. 2 Drug Use in New York State,* New York State Narcotic Addiction Control Committee, June 1971.

[3] Edward Fingle & Dixon M. Woodbury, "General Principles," in *The Pharmacological Basis of Therapeutics,* 3rd ed., Louis S. Goodman and Alfred Gilman (eds.) (New York: Macmillan, 1965) p. 1.

[4] *World Health Organization Technical Report,* Series # 407, WHO Expert Committee on Drug Dependence, Geneva, 1969.

[5] Jerome Jaffe, "Drug Addiction and Drug Abuse," in Goodman and Gilman (eds.) *op. cit.,* p. 286.

[6] E. M. Jellinek, *The Disease Concept of Alcoholism* (New Haven: Hill-House Press, 1960) p. 35.

[7] Mark Keller & Mairi McCormick, *A Dictionary of Words About Alcohol* (New Brunswick: Rutgers Center of Alcohol Studies, 1968) p. 12.

[8] Mark Keller & John R. Seeley, *The Alcohol Language* (New York: University of Toronto Press, 1958) p. 58; quoted in Robert Strauss, "Alcohol and Alcoholism," in *Contemporary Social Problems,* Robert Merton and Robert Nisbet (eds.) (New York: Harcourt, Brace, Jovanovich 1971) p. 181.

[9] Isidor Chien, Donald L. Gerald, Robert S. Lee, and Eva Rosenfeld, *The Road to H: Narcotics, Delinquency, and Social Policy* (New York: Basic Books, Inc., 1964).

[10] John A. Clausen, in the *International Encyclopedia of the Social Sciences,* Vol. 4 (New York: Crowell, Collier, and Macmillan, 1968) p. 300.

[11] Fingle and Woodbury in Goodman and Gilman (eds.) *op. cit.,* p. 3.

[12] *Ibid.* p. 17; p. 18.

[13] Fingle and Woodbury in Goodman and Gilman (eds.) *op. cit.,* pp. 24-26.

[14] Seth K. Sharpless, "Hypnotics and Sedatives," and Murry E. Jarvik, "Drug Used in the Treatment of Psychiatric Disorders," both in Goodman and Gilman (eds.) *op. cit.*

[15] J. Murdoch Ritchie, Don W. Esplin, and Barbara Zablocka, "Central Nervous System Stimulants," in Goodman and Gilman (eds.) *op. cit.*

[16] Helen Nowlis, *Drug on College Campus* (New York: Anchor Books, 1966) p. 90.

[17] Jerome Jaffe, "Narcotic Analgesics," in Goodman and Gilman (eds.) *op. cit.*

[18] Guy Endore, *Synanon* (New York: Doubleday, 1968); Daniel Casriel and Grover Amon, *Daytop* (New York: Hill and Wang 1971).

[19] Nowlis, *op. cit.,* pp. 101, 102; Jarvick *op. cit.,* pp. 205-208.

[20] David E. Smith and John Luce, *Love Needs Care* (Boston: Little Brown, 1971) pp. 90-96.

[21] Discussed in Erich Goode, *Drugs in American Society,* (New York: Knopf, 1972) pp. 117-118.

[22] Smith and Luce, *op. cit.,* pp. 87-88.

[23] Don Cahalin, Ira H. Cisin, and Helen M. Crosley, *American Drinking Practices* (New Brunswick, N.J.: Rutgers Center of Alcohol Studies, 1969) p. 189.

[24] Mark Keller, "The Oddities of Alcoholics," *Quarterly Journal of Studies on Alcohol,* Vol. 33, December, 1972, p. 147.

[25] *New York City Alcoholism Study: A Program Analysis,* Health Services Administration, Jan. 1972, pp. 6-16.

[26] Robert Freed Bales, "Cultural Differences in Rates of Alcoholism," *Quarterly Journal of Studies on Alcohol,* Vol. 6. 1946, pp. 480-499.

[27] Edward A. Suchman, "The Hang-Loose Ethic and the Spirit of Drug Use," in *Youth and Drugs,* John H. McGrath and Frank R. Scarpitti (eds.) (Glenview, Illinois: Scott, Foresman, 1970) p. 109.

[28] *Ibid.* p. 116.

[29] National Commission on Marihuana and Drug Abuse, *Marihuana: A Signal of Misunderstanding* (New York: New American Library, 1972) p. 58.

[30] Chambers, *op. cit.*

[31] Jellinek, *op. cit.,* pp. 99-110; Mark Keller, "On the Loss-of-Control Phenomenon in Alcoholism," *The British Journal of Addiction,* Vol. 67, 1972, pp. 153-166.

[32] Jellinek, *op. cit.,* pp. 55-57.

[33] Bales, *op. cit.*

[34] Jellinek, *op. cit.,* pp. 154-155.

[35] Keller, "On the Loss-of-Control Phenomenon in Alcoholism," *op. cit.,* pp. 159-163.

[36] Alfred Lindesmith, *Opiate Addiction* (Bloomington, Indiana: Principia Press, 1947). "A Sociological Theory of Drug Addiction," *American Journal of Sociology,* Vol. 43, 1938, pp. 593-613.

[37] Howard S. Becker, *Outsiders: Studies in the Sociology of Deviance* (New York: The Free Press of Glencoe, 1963), Chapters 3 and 4.

[38] Richard Cloward and Lloyd Ohlin, *Delinquency and Opportunity* (New York: The Free Press of Glencoe, 1960), pp. 178-186.

[39] Kenneth Keniston, "Heads and Seekers," in McGrath and Scarpitti (eds.) *op. cit.,* pp. 112-126.

[40] National Commission on Marihuana and Drug Abuse. *op. cit.,* Intro.

Summary

Recent public concern with drugs has focused on the use of drugs other than alcohol, although a national commission appointed to study marijuana and drug abuse concluded that alcohol dependence was America's most serious drug problem. Alcohol was once seen as the cause of criminal behavior, but today it is primarily the individual and social costs associated with alcoholism that are decried. The recent shifts in the use of drugs other than alcohol, from use by the urban poor, to use by portions of the middle class, has created public concern over drug control and the social effects of drug abuse.

Medically a drug can be defined as any chemical agent that affects living tissue. "Drug abuse" is therefore defined as any nonmedical drug use, but law enforcement officials consider it to be any illegal use of drugs. Addiction is generally equated with physical and psychological dependence, although these are variously defined. Alcoholism may be the inability to abstain from drinking or to control the amount of drinking.

Government regulation of drugs and alcohol derives from differing social attitudes to their use. In America, control of the use of alcohol became a social issue in the mid-nineteenth century, when new immigrants became the target of moral reform efforts. Political action against alcohol use culminated in 1919, with the passage of a constitutional amendment prohibiting its sale. Demand for liquor during the Prohibition led to an extensive criminal organization which supplied it. This criminal element persisted even after the repeal of the Prohibition amendment in 1933. Although taxed and regulated, alcohol is now legally available to all adults in the population.

Most of the narcotic drugs derived from opium were put under strict control by the Harrison Act of 1914. At that time, there were perhaps half a million narcotic addicts in the United States; most of them were white middle-class women, who became addicted through patent medicines containing the drugs. After World War II, the use of illegal drugs became a phenomenon of urban slum areas, where the principal users were the poor, blacks and Puerto Ricans. By the 1960s, however, many members of the military and middle-class white youth had begun to use marijuana and other drugs, a situation which prompted both stricter law enforcement and discussion of possible changes in the drug laws.

The nature of the drug experience is a function of the properties of the chemical, its effects on the brain, dosage and the characteristics individuals bring to it. Sedative drugs depress the activity of the central nervous system, can produce a physical dependence and build up a tolerance requiring increasing dosages. Narcotics, which are strongly addictive and produce high tolerances, are selective depressants used medically to minimize pain. Stimulants excite the nervous system; hallucinogenic drugs produce mood, sensory, emotional and perceptual changes; marijuana is classified as a mild hallucinogen whose effects are similar to those of alcohol.

The extent of American alcohol and other drug use is difficult to determine because no accurate statistics are available. Studies of the social variables involved in alcoholism have been inconclusive, although racial and ethnic background seem to have some significance. Middle-class drug usage seems primarily to be of nonnarcotics, while black and other minority group members use "hard drugs" with greater frequency.

Theories that explain alcoholism and drug use in terms of psychological and social factors seem the most persuasive. Hypotheses concerning biochemical sensitivity to alcohol or the "alcoholic personality" do not explain the evidence well. In the case of other drugs, self-definition and the positive aspects of involvement in a deviant subculture can be seen as adaptations to the stress and anxiety of ghetto life. Among middle-class youth, drug usage appears to be seen as a mechanism of self-exploration, escape and dissent from the dominant value norms.

The current stress on "law and order" in metropolitan areas is, in large measure, a response to the crimes committed to support drug habits. The exact relationship of alcohol to crime and suicides is less clear, but the costs in unemployment, family strife and social welfare efforts are great.

Solutions to the social problems of drug and alcohol abuse are in short supply. The public health approach to alcoholism education has been a failure, and while community detoxification centers are talked about, few have been set up. The most effective means of treatment has been the self-help group, Alcoholics Anonymous. Law enforcement has been the primary means of controlling the use of other drugs, although group interaction programs on the model of Synanon are widely used for rehabilitation of drug users. Medical treatment and drug maintenance programs have generally been rejected by policymakers, who persist in seeing the issue as one of law enforcement.

chapter

crime
and
justice

Page one of a big city newspaper headlines the discovery of a third rape murder victim in another city. Page three details some local news: three people have been robbed at knifepoint, a young boy has been shot and killed by "an unknown assailant," and a policeman is in critical condition after tangling with a killer. Page five tells the story of a bank robbery in which hostages were taken to insure the safety of the bank robbers. Page seven quotes a police official saying that three recent murders are the result of a feud between rival drug traffickers. Page twenty reports that a prison riot has been suppressed in a distant state, and a feature article on page thirty-two advises ways of burglar-proofing one's home.

In the same newspaper are reports of other crimes that arouse no fears. A man is arrested for falsifying income tax returns. A financier flees the country after defrauding investors of many millions of dollars. A case is documented against local judges who are suspiciously benevolent to organized crime figures who appear before them. An automobile manufacturer has knowingly ignored a defect in its cars that may cause thousands of highway accidents.

Americans fear crime on a selective basis. They are frightened and outraged by the crimes in the first category—crimes of violence and crimes against personal property. But the fleeing financier may be regarded by many as a clever rascal, and the cheating taxpayer may be perceived as an unlucky Joe. These are the crimes of the wealthy and middle classes, and a certain amount of hypocrisy is involved in criminal behavior and in attitudes toward crime. The individual who fears street crime and hates criminals may think nothing of taking some office supplies; he does not think of *himself* as a criminal.

Clearly, when citizens vote overwhelmingly for a politician who promises to get tough on crime by stricter law enforcement and harsher criminal penalties, they do not expect him to enact stricter laws against price-fixing or industrial espionage. The politician and the voters understand that what is wanted is a crackdown on crime in the streets, not crime in the executive suites.

Defining crime

Crime may be defined legally in terms of a body of law which codifies a society's rules about proper and improper behavior. The American legal system includes both civil and criminal codes. The civil code defines certain kinds of behavior as civil wrongs entitling those offended to compensation or redress; the civil courts act only as arbiters between private parties. A libel suit or a suit demanding compensation for a work-related injury are examples of civil suits.

Criminal law governs behavior that is described as an offense against the state; essentially, criminals are considered threats to public order. Criminal law involves penal sanctions imposed by the state. Someone who breaks a criminal law can be arrested, brought to trial, and penalized by fines or imprisonment. (Until the recent Supreme Court decision abrogating the death penalty, the criminal might also be penalized by loss of life.) Criminal statutes are very specifically worded, outlining the exact nature of the offense, the different ways in which it may be committed and the penalties attached. A felony is defined as a crime serious enough to warrant imprisonment for more than a year, whereas a misdemeanor is a lesser offense warranting a fine or imprisonment for less than a year. Hence simple assault is a misdemeanor, while assault with a deadly weapon, a more serious offense, is a felony.

Crime may also be considered in a cultural or social context. In our society bigamy is illegal; in a Moslem society a man may have as many as four wives. In some Communist countries free enterprise is illegal; the free enterprise system is a solid tradition in the United States, and many American laws reinforce this system.

Every society makes laws that reflect its values and traditions. In small-scale societies, laws may go unchanged for generations; there may be little crime because every member of the society understands and accepts the society's rules. In a rapidly changing society, values may change very swiftly, leaving a gap between old laws and new values. For example, some of our present laws reflect what many consider to be a repressive, Puritanical attitude toward sexual relations and other "pleasurable" activities such as gambling or the use of alcohol and other stimulants. Conflicts often develop between groups that adhere to the old values and those that have adopted new values, and the conflicts are often expressed in terms of agitation to change the laws in one direction or another. Thus, a number of Americans think present laws are too permissive, while other Americans feel equally strongly that they are too repressive.

Americans in the last decade were often told that the criminal was not responsible for his crimes against society, but that society was responsible. I totally disagree with this permissive philosophy. Society is guilty of crime only when we fail to bring the criminal to justice. When we fail to make the criminal pay for his crime, we encourage him to think that crime will pay.

Richard M. Nixon

Current conflicts over the causes and prevention of crime are partly a reflection of old and new attitudes toward crime. Traditional interpretations involve the perception of criminals as an essentially separate class of people whose behavior can be explained in religious terms ("Criminals are evil, possessed by the devil"), or biological terms ("You can tell a criminal by the shape of his head," or "Black people are just naturally inclined to crime"), or social terms ("Only lower-class people engage in crime"). Traditional solutions to crime are simple and punitive: criminals should be locked up and punished; if the punishments are harsh enough, criminals will be afraid to break the law. Newer attitudes toward crime involve an essentially sociological perspective which locates the causes of criminal behavior in environmental factors such as poverty, overcrowding, frustration over racial discrimination and cultural norms favoring violence and aggression. Viewed in this perspective, crime rates can be reduced only by changing the environmental conditions that influence criminal behavior.

The dimensions of the crime problem

The major source of statistical information on crime in the United States is the set of *Uniform Crime Reports* published annually by the Federal Bureau of Investigation. To compile these figures, the FBI relies on statistics submitted by local police departments. A crime index is issued based on certain offenses thought to serve as a weather vane for all crime: murder, nonnegligent manslaughter, forcible rape, aggravated assault, robbery, burglary, larceny and auto theft. Property crimes usually account for more than 85 percent of all crimes committed in the United States.[1]

The *Uniform Crime Reports* for 1971 reveal an increase over 1970 in every specific crime contributing to the index. A comparison between 1971 and the 1960 index suggests a phenomenal growth in crime over the past decade, ranging from a 95 percent increase in the total number of murders to a 269 percent rise in the number of larcenies.[2]

These figures seem to justify the growing fear of crime in this country. However, there are indications that the present and past figures do not reflect a true picture of the crime situation. For instance, many crimes are never reported to the police. Forcible rape is rarely reported because the victims are unwilling to endure the painful processes of investigation and trial. Many minority group victims mistrust the police and are afraid to get involved in a police investigation. Many people fail to report crimes because they don't believe the police will find the offender.

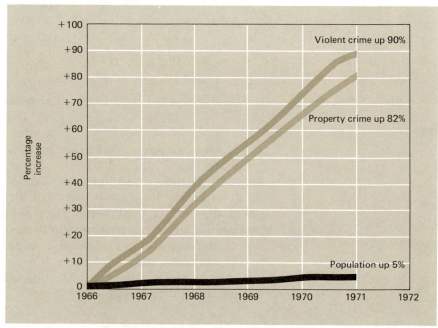

Figure 10-1   Comparison of percentage increase in crime with percentage increase in population, 1966–1971

Other factors may distort the crime picture. Police departments do not necessarily record all the crimes reported to them or include them in statistics sent to the FBI. In the past, crimes committed in the ghetto, or by one minority group member against another, have not been considered important enough to be recorded or investigated by police. High crime rates have always been associated with the slums, but dramatic increases in crimes reported from these areas may represent changes in reporting rather than changes in actual crime rates. A rise in reported crimes may also reflect increased police efficiency. A low crime rate may mean that many crimes are undetected and therefore unreported; higher rates may mean improved methods of detection and reporting.

All these considerations indicate that the FBI's official records offer a somewhat misleading view of the extent of crime today and in the past. In a sense, it is impossible to obtain really accurate measures of the extent of crime, since many crimes go completely undetected and unreported, and we have no way of telling how much crime this represents. Statistically, most crimes occur in ghetto areas, and research suggests that ghetto residents are indeed worried about their personal safety. Yet the same research points out that residents of low crime areas (such as wealthy suburbs) are even *more* fearful than residents of high crime areas. The people who express the most fear about crime also report the most apprehension about changing social conditions—particularly racial integration.[3] In analyzing the "crime problem" in the United States, it may be more useful to examine who commits crimes and how those crimes are perceived than to consider the actual extent of crime.

Demographic analysis of crime

To the people who live in comfortable suburbs, it may seen obvious that crime is a city problem. To a policeman investigating gambling and prostitution, it may seem that organized crime is behind the crime problem. To a ghetto dweller, the police themselves may seem like criminals. Where does crime occur, and who are its perpetrators? Sociological studies of criminals often focus on five major demographic variables: sex, age, race and ethnicity, social class and geographic location.

Sex

Males are far more likely to engage in criminal behavior than females. Statistics from 1971 show that male arrests outnumbered female arrests by 6 to 1. Males committed 94 percent of all auto thefts, 86.7 percent of all aggravated assaults and (not surprisingly) 100 percent of the forcible rapes reported. The only serious crimes for which women account for more than token percentages are murder (16.3 percent female offenders) and larceny (28.1 percent).[4]

There are some indications that the trend is shifting. FBI statistics from 1966 to 1971 show male arrests for major crimes increased 39 percent while female arrests showed an increase of 80 percent.[5] The greatest increases have been in property crimes such as larceny, but there are also more female narcotics violations and robberies. In a society that traditionally encourages active and aggressive behavior in males and passivity in females, these differences are not suprising. The recent increase in female crimes may be partiallly attributable to the greater activism of women today in all areas of national life.

Age

Teenagers and young adults have sustained higher crime rates than other groups for as long as studies have been conducted. FBI statistics for 1971 indicate that persons under 15 comprised 10 percent of the total police arrests for that year. Persons under 18 comprised 26 percent of the total arrests made, and person under 21 accounted for 51 percent of all arrests.[6] Although young people are seldom involved in sophisticated or career criminality, they are overrepresented in property crimes, vandalism and the offenses that apply only to juveniles, such as curfew violations. Of course, the number of arrests of young people for drug violations has increased sharply in recent years. In 1971, 52 percent of the arrests of persons under 21 were for Narcotics Drug Law violations; 62 percent of the arrests for marijuana possession involved persons under 21.[7]

Figure 10-2   Percentage increase in number of arrests by sex, 1970–1971

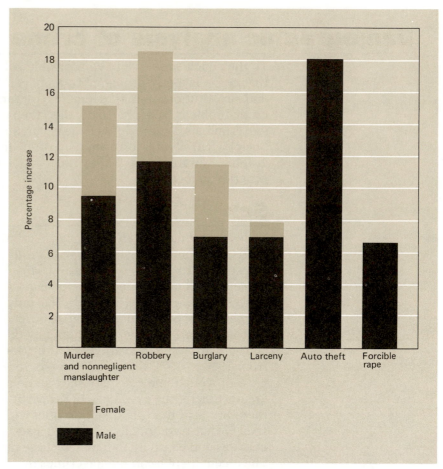

Race and ethnicity

The ethnic differences in criminal behavior have been somewhat politicized in recent years, and the sociological evidence is often conflicting. Blacks, Mexicans, Puerto Ricans, and American Indians all maintain high crime rates, whereas the rates for both Jews and

Orientals remain much below the average for all groups. Yet these differences are subject to closer scrutiny. The black crime rate is estimated to be two to five times as high as the black distribution in the population, but this could be largely a result of differential enforcement by police agencies. Studies have demonstrated that blacks are usually arrested, brought to trial and convicted more often than whites who commit the same crime. Once blacks are convicted, they are also less likely to receive probation, parole or a suspended sentence.[8] Race and social class also overlap; blacks tend to belong to the lower socioeconomic groups which are strongly prone to higher crime rates. In the past, immigrants and the children of immigrants—who were usually very low on the socioeconomic scale—had very high crime rates. In fact, the attitude of the middle class towards these new immigrants—the Irish, Italians, Greeks and others—was very similar to the middle-class attitude toward blacks and Puerto Ricans today. As the children and grandchildren of immigrants moved up the economic scale, the high crime rates associated with those ethnic groups disappeared. Middle-class blacks and Puerto Ricans show the same relatively low crime rates as middle-class people from any other ethnic group.

Social class

As might be expected, most criminals come from low socioeconomic backgrounds. This is particularly true with younger offenders. One study of 1000 juvenile delinquents concluded that three-quarters of the subjects lived below a level of comfort.[9] But there is another view, supported by self-report studies involving subjects of all socioeconomic groups, that lower-class people are simply more likely to be arrested and convicted, whereas middle- and upper-class offenders often manage to avoid arrest and particularly conviction.[10] Consider the staggering amount of white-collar crime in this country—a higher socioeconomic activity than the blue-collar crimes of assault, robbery and burglary—and this theory seems quite plausible; even for their crimes, the poor pay more.

Geography

For a variety of reasons, cities seem to produce and nurture considerably more crime than rural areas. Suburban crime rates are higher than rural rates, but still considerably below urban rates. One reason for the high urban rates is the presence of slum or ghetto areas with their poverty, unemployment and overcrowding—all conditions associated with crime.[11] As the distance from this "inner city" increases, the crime rate tends to go down. Cities also attract people in search of anonymity; those who commit crimes usually fall quite neatly into this group. In addition, crime that is not too serious may be handled informally in rural areas, and sometimes in suburban areas. If a rural youth gets into trouble, he will probably be dealt with by police officials who know his family; the police are more likely to solve the problem by talking it over with the family than by making an arrest. Urban police, of course, cannot take such an individualized approach to criminal offenders.

Urban/rural differences are the most significant factors in the geographic distribution of crime. For obvious reasons, states with large urban centers usually have higher crime rates than rural states. There are slight regional differences in types of crime committed, with western states supporting the highest property crime rates and the South particularly noted for homicide.[12] Obviously, there are no simple correlations between crime and sex, geography, race and ethnicity or even social class. More elaborate theories of criminal behavior have been developed by criminologists who use the methods of the behavioral sciences.

Explaining crime

Crime has always been a part of Western culture, and the most popular explanations of crime have been those which somehow distinguish criminals from the rest of society. Until the end of the Middle Ages, a criminal was usually considered to be someone who was willfully evil, possibly even possessed by demons. After the Middle Ages, theological explanations became less popular, and theories of criminality based on class distinctions gained support. People with social position and property were responsible citizens; lower-class people were rough, ill-bred and inclined toward crime. When an upper-class person committed a notorious crime, this was seen as an aberration of nature; sometimes the explanation was offered that he must have had a low-born ancestor. Upper-class people used this idea to justify strong legal controls exercised over the lower classes. Nineteenth century debates on the extension of voting privileges revolved in part around the question of whether or not the lower classes, with their criminal tendencies, could be trusted with voting power.

During the nineteenth century, theories based on physiological and mental abnormalities became popular. The Italian criminologist Lombroso launched this approach by studying the skulls of criminals and identifying a criminal "cranial type" characterized by traits approximating primitive men and lower animals. Physicians studied criminals to see if physical illness had something to do with behavior. Biologists looked for hereditary differences between criminals and noncriminals. Freudian theorists viewed crime as still another unconscious effort to resolve psychic conflict.

Underlying all of these approaches is a fundamental belief that criminals are aberrant individuals, possessing some quirk of mind or body that is not present in the rest of us. However, psychological theories of criminal behavior have proved inadequate, and the search for physical causes of criminal behavior was even less successful. Certain brain tumors may cause violent and aggressive behavior, but this is a rare condition and does not really explain criminal behavior.

If we are to deal meaningfully with crime, what must be seen is the dehumanizing effect on the individual of slums, racism, ignorance and violence, of corruption and impotence to fulfill rights, of poverty and unemployment and idleness, of generations of malnutrition, of congenital brain damage and prenatal neglect, of sickness and disease, of pollution, of decrepit, dirty, ugly, unsafe, overcrowded housing, of alcoholism and narcotics addiction, of avarice, anxiety, fear, hatred, hopelessness and injustice. These are the fountainheads of crime. They can be controlled.

Ramsey Clark

Finally sociologists began to investigate environmental factors as causes of criminal behavior; this approach has been the most successful so far in explaining the differences between criminals and noncriminals. Sociological theories assume that social variables, not individual differences, are responsible for criminal behavior. Early studies identified high crime rates with overcrowded inner-city poverty areas.[13] No matter what racial or ethnic group established themselves in certain slums, crime rates continued to be high. People had always associated high crime rates with slum-dwellers, but the sociologists had for the first time identified crime with the slum environment rather than with the particular people who lived there. This change in perspective was important because it implied that crime could be eliminated by changing factors in the environment which engendered criminal behavior. Today, there are many sociological theories which attempt to explain the cause of crime. Social structure, delinquent subculture, differential association and labeling theories are the most widely accepted explanations.

Social structure theory

Searching for an explanation of suicide rates in different cultures, the sociologist Emile Durkheim developed the concept of *anomie*.[14] This French word translates roughly as normlessness, or a state of confusion produced by sudden or dramatic changes in the social structure. Robert Merton, a contemporary American sociologist, takes this concept one step further in studying crime. He points out that American society sets cultural goals that revolve around material success, but severely limits the opportunities for various social, ethnic and racial groups to achieve this kind of success. Merton maintains that where a disjunction between cultural goals and institutionalized means for their achievement exists, a condition of anomie prevails.[15] When this happens, acute problems of crime and delinquency follow. Conversely, when a society provides fairly equal access for all to its material benefits, anomie and crime are not as prevalent. The Scandinavian countries, for instance, have largely homogeneous populations with no great extremes of poverty and wealth, and crime rates in these countries are far lower than in the United States.

American culture places great emphasis on achieving success and acquiring a wide range of material possessions. Advertisements present new products as seductively as possible and urge people to buy: buy a house, buy a car, buy new clothes, buy a swimming pool, buy an electric toothbrush. Most of us cannot afford all these luxuries, but we come to *want* them. So some people turn to crime: a little shoplifting, evading income taxes or armed robbery. The poorest in our society are likely to be the most frustrated. The unemployed ghetto youth may hold up a liquor store or start selling drugs. Out of rage and frustration he may engage in random violence and vandalism.

Delinquent subculture theory

To explain the phenomenon of juvenile crimes which are counterproductive to achieving material success, Albert Cohen offers a delinquent subculture approach.[16] Although he agrees with Merton that juvenile crime usually emanates from lower-class neighborhoods, he feels that it represents a reaction to values imposed by social agencies such as schools. Since a lower-class youth is unprepared to measure up to middle-class standards of ambition, deferment of gratification and control of aggression, he will develop status anxiety. To escape this anxiety, he subscribes to the norms of the delinquent subculture—a different set of standards which repudiate middle-class values.[17] Other researchers have isolated three types of subcultures: the criminal type (money-oriented), the conflict type (gang-oriented) and the retreatist type (drug-oriented). Criminal subcultures exist where illegal operations are condoned by community values. Conflict patterns occur where there are no effective controls on young people of any sort, and retreatist subcultures include those who cannot adapt to criminal activity or enter into a conflict pattern, but simply escape into drugs or alcohol.[18]

One difficulty with subculture theory is that only lower-class males are accounted for. Another is that delinquent youths, especially in gangs, may engage in activities that characterize all these subcultural types—crimes, gang fighting and drugs.

Differential association theory

Differential association theory explains a wider range of criminal behavior than any discussed so far. Developed by Edwin H. Sutherland, a noted criminologist, it stresses the conviction that criminal behavior is learned through interaction with a group that offers rewards to the learner and helps him to build an identity. This learning process involves both specific techniques for committing a crime and a "specific direction of motives, drives, rationalizations, and attitudes."[19]

A new salesman may be surprised to learn from his fellow salesmen that he is *expected* to cheat on his expense account. Since the company can count expense account payments as tax-deductible business expenses, company officials would rather have their employees "adjust" their expense accounts than ask for raises in salary. If he has any doubts, friendly company accountants assure him that it is accepted practice and even help him fill out the forms.

In the ghetto, a youth may learn early in life that certain criminal behaviors are not only condoned but encouraged by his peers. An older brother or a friend may instruct him in the fine arts of purse-snatching or breaking-and-entering, lend him a gun or knife and recruit him into a gang. The "drug culture"—in which drugs are readily available and the taking of drugs is condoned or encouraged—was once confined mostly to ghetto areas. Today it has spread to middle-class areas, particularly among young people. Young people are particularly susceptible to social pressure from their peers; when the peer group is engaged in criminal behavior, the individual is unlikely to resist the pressure to conform.

In prison, convicts overwhelmingly identify with other convicts. Criminal behavior becomes the norm, and the first offender may leave prison with an increased commitment to crime and greater knowledge of criminal techniques—thanks to the encouragement and advice of more experienced criminals.

Labeling theories

Some criminologists argue that once a person is labeled as a criminal, he will tend to live up to his reputation. In Howard S. Becker's view, deviance (or criminality) is not a quality of one's behavior but a consequence of the way society treats an offender.[20] In other words, the nature and implications of criminal acts are determined by our social handling of them. The trial procedure is an example of a "status degradation" ceremony, in which a person's law abiding status is taken away and a criminal status is substituted. And, as Edwin Lemert suggests, once an individual begins to perceive himself as a criminal, he may use this deviant behavior to cope with the problems created by the societal reaction to him.[21] In the same way that a student whom teachers have labeled a behavioral problem fulfills their prophecy, a person labeled "criminal" accepts this identity and behaves accordingly.

There is no shortage of theories about criminal behavior, and each of the concepts discussed offers some important insights. It is probably impossible to develop one major unifying theory of crime that would help us devise specific ways of attacking the problem. It is not enough to be aware that a delinquent subculture may exist in ghetto neighborhoods, or that some people may use criminal behavior as a means to achieve material success. For crime in the United States involves a widely disparate group of lawbreakers who do not always behave according to our sociological explanations.

Some types of crime

A full catalog of criminal activities would include violations ranging from adultery to abduction and from selling beer to a minor to skyjacking. Clearly, the diversity of criminal behavior makes a comprehensive list impossible. Our concern in this section is with law-violating behaviors reflecting patterned interaction or a purposeful degree of social organization. These patterns are juvenile, professional, organized and white-collar crime.

Juvenile crime

The sheer growth of crime committed by persons under 18 troubles everyone concerned with criminology. FBI statistics show that from 1960 through 1970, arrests of juveniles more than doubled, while arrests for all criminal violations increased only 31 percent. During this period the crime rate for people under 18 rose four times as high as the population increase in the 10 to 18 age group.[22] Also, a dramatic growth in crimes committed by juveniles *under 15* has been noted by the National Commission on the Causes and Prevention of Violence. In the period from 1958 to 1967, there was a 300 percent increase in assaults by 10 to 14 year olds and a 200 percent increase in robberies by members of this age group.[23]

Juvenile crime is usually termed "delinquency," and juvenile delinquincy could be defined legalistically as those offenses committed by minors which may or may not be punishable if they are committed by adults. In other words, different rules apply to offenses committed by juveniles, and these offenses are handled by juvenile courts. The violations for which minors may be arrested include the ones applying to adults in the same jurisdiction, but also a series of vague categories such as habitual vagrancy, sexual promiscuity, incorrigibility and deportment endangering morals, health or general welfare of the child. The vagueness of many offenses classified as juvenile is intentional; judges are expected to be flexible in judging young people and devising ways of rescuing them from lives of crime. The system has been abused, however, because many judges have provided differential justice to various categories of juvenile defendants. Some judges consistently sentence girls accused of sexual promiscuity to reform schools, while dismissing cases in which boys are involved. Others tend to release middle-class youngsters in the custody of their families while sentencing poor minority youth charged with the same offenses to correctional institutions.

Much delinquency involves behavior which is considered criminal for any age group. Auto theft and drug abuse are particularly prevalent now, and to an extent these offenses cut across social, regional and racial distinctions. Teenage gangs still flourish in most major cities. Some gangs have become more sophisticated and better organized—and thus more dangerous. Although most of the members are juveniles, the leaders are often men in their twenties. Some of the gangs have been connected with drug traffic and gunrunning. Other gangs, however, have been credited for positive activities such as keeping neighborhoods free of drugpushers, alcoholics and prostitutes.

Professional crime

The attitudes and behavior of professional criminals distinguish them from other criminals. These people make their careers in larceny, forgery, robbery, confidence games or some other illegal activity, and approach their work with the same sort of professional standards as do doctors and lawyers. They are usually skillful enough to make crime an economic livelihood, and are seldom apprehended because nothing illegal is attempted before either the police or the court (or both) have been paid off to ensure safety.[24] Even in the more hazardous occupation of robbery, professional criminals are considerably more prudent than amateurs and are less likely to be caught. Professional criminals also maintain a status system, with the highest prestige attached to "confidence schemes." These operations begin with the premise that most conventional citizens are basically out to earn a fast dollar; the "mark" is approached with some dishonest plan for making a great deal of money and is ultimately relieved of some of his own money by the confidence man. Unwilling to admit that he was duped, or that he was engaged in plans for some shady activity, the mark rarely reports his losses to the police.

Because professional criminals take great pains to protect themselves, their social visibility is low and their total contribution to crime in the United States remains uncertain.

Organized crime

Some of the wealthiest American criminals lead quiet, respectable lives in exclusive suburbs. They are often good family men who attend church regularly and are fond of their grandchildren. They are successful businessmen, but their "business" is crime and their business methods often include torture and murder. They are the leaders of organized crime. Organized crime is distinguished from other types of crime by its hierarchical structure, monopolistic control and influence, dependence upon violence for enforcement, immunity from the law through the corruption of police and judicial processes and incredible financial success.[25]

The structure of organized crime, as outlined by the President's

Commission on Law Enforcement and the Administration of Justice in 1967, reflects both the "extended family" of traditional societies and an army.[26] There are apparently some twenty-four "families" operating in large urban centers, each composed of a boss, a counselor or assistant, some "lieutenants" and a large number of ordinary members or "foot soldiers." Each family is independent, but a commission of nine to twelve bosses from the most powerful families may act to arbitrate disagreements between families. The "five families" of New York seem to be the most powerful in organized crime.

Their activities are threefold. One involves traditionally illicit services such as gambling, narcotics, loan sharking and prostitution. A second concerns infiltration of legitimate businesses—from advertising to scrap surplus sales. These businesses are bought and controlled through a number of procedures, such as investing concealed income from illegal activities, extortion and foreclosing on usurious loans. The third major enterprise is racketeering—essentially the extortion of money from legitimate businesses on a regular basis.

Organized crime remains arrogantly resistant to all efforts to disorganize it. Witnesses are difficult to come by, people who use the "services" seldom complain, and few law enforcement agencies are equipped to tackle this huge criminal conglomerate. Consequently, there is no indication that major gains will be made in the near future.[27]

White-collar crime

The criminal behavior that has been labeled white-collar crime accounts for enough violations of law to dwarf burglary, larceny and other conventional crime by comparison. Yet here a strange principle applies; people tend to tolerate white-collar crime because they are sometimes involved in it.[28] The criminals are doctors, accountants, public officials, TV repairmen, corporate executives and people who sell term papers to college students. In other words, white-collar criminals are the people responsible for determining and supporting the community standards which lawbreakers supposedly violate.

There are actually two kinds of white-collar crime, occupational and corporate. The *occupational* variety consists of violations committed in the course of one's work and offenses by employees against their employers. One example is the disclosure that two out of every three New York surgeons split their fees with the doctor who recommends a patient to them.[29] The high incidence of employee thefts from retail stores, warehouses, docks and the trickier crime of embezzlement are all familiar examples of occupational white-collar crime.

Corporate white-collar crime involves a somewhat different process—offenses committed by corporate executives for their corporation and offenses attributed to a corporation itself. Edwin H. Sutherland conducted a study of the seventy largest corporations in the United States and found an average of eight negative court or commission decisions for each over a period of eight years. The violations were for false advertising, unfair labor practices, infringements of trademarks and patents and illegal monopoly.[30] Since federal law recognizes the corporation as a legal entity, it is seldom that the officials of corporations, the people who make the actual decisions that result in law violations, are punished. More typically, the corporation itself is fined by a court or a commission, and its officials evade censure.

But the problems of prosecuting white-collar crimes are deeply imbedded in our socioeconomic values; we still tend to see them as more comparable to traffic offenses than to larceny or burlary. Most Americans fear and hate street crime, but are almost indifferent to white-collar crime.

The American system of justice

In a completely just society, the innocent would be protected and those guilty of a crime would be apprehended, separated from society if necessary and reformed if at all possible. The American system of justice falls far short of this ideal vision. Hundreds of thousand of crimes—including violent crimes—go unsolved every year. Justice is unevenly administered: convicted of the same crime, one person may receive a heavy prison sentence while another is released on probation. Prisons do not rehabilitate. The prison experience itself may turn a first offender into a lifetime criminal. The three major elements of the American criminal justice system are the police, the courts and the correctional or penal system. To understand why the system is not working, we must first understand how each of these institutions is supposed to function and why they are failing.

The police

To the speeding motorist or the inner-city drug pusher, the policeman is The Law. The policeman often sees himself as a soldier in the front lines of a war against crime—a soldier who is often betrayed not only by his commanders, judges and lawyers, but also by the people he is supposed to protect. The police are asked to prevent crime, protect innocent citizens and property and apprehend criminals. In the course of duty they are also asked to respect individual rights and to use no unnecessary force. Herein lies a major difficulty. In recent years judges have ruled that suspected criminals cannot be coerced into confessing. They have a right to a lawyer's help even if they cannot afford it. They must be informed of their rights at the time of arrest.[31] Finally evidence obtained through illegal search and seizure cannot be used in court.[32] These court decisions were based on documented evidence of police abuses, and most thoughtful citizens recognize the importance of protecting constitutional rights. But the average policeman feels these rulings coddle criminals and handcuff the police, and he deeply resents rules that keep changing.

The police have other reasons for feeling resentful. For the most part, they are ill-paid and short of manpower. In a society in which violence is common and guns are readily available, their jobs are dangerous. Between 1967 and 1971, 452 policemen were killed in the line of duty; 95 percent of those killed were killed by guns.[33] The ordinary middle-class citizen loudly demands police protection against violent crime, but he is often contemptuous of the individual policeman—particularly when he is charged with a traffic violation. The policeman is asked to deal with victimless crimes—drunkenness, drug abuse, gambling, prostitution and illegal sexual behavior. The fact that large segments of the population engage in or condone such behavior induces a certain cynicism in the average policeman.

Middle-class citizens generally expect and get polite treatment from the police even when they are being arrested for such white-collar crimes as fraud or embezzlement. People who live in inner-city slums invariably expect and sometimes get police treatment that is biased, brutal and belligerent. In one study, researchers reported that police used abusive language in 14 percent of their contacts with victims, witnesses and defendants in cases of suspected crime. Members of the research team also observed a considerable amount of physical abuse.[34] One can only wonder about the frequency of such abusive police behavior when observers are not present. New training programs to sensitize police to the needs of community members and police-community relations programs are an indication that some effort is being made to correct this problem.

In the past decade a number of major cities have experienced scandalous revelations of police corruption. In New York City, the Knapp Commission uncovered the involvement of hundreds of policemen—some of high rank—in criminal protection rackets involving gambling, drug trafficking and prostitution. In Chicago, widespread involvement in extortion and outright burglary was uncovered in certain police districts and a small group of policemen were indicted for dealing in drugs and murdering several people to protect their activities. In its Task Force Report on *The Police*, the President's Commission on Law Enforcement and the Administration of Justice reported that "a significant number of officers engaged in varying forms of criminal and unethical conduct."[35]

Most policemen start their careers with high ideals; many of the policemen caught committing crimes claim that they gradually became disillusioned by the corruption they saw all around them among politicians, businessmen and other policemen. Organized crime figures offer huge sums of money as bribes; the ill-paid policeman needs great strength of character to turn down such money when he is asked merely to look the other way. Once corrupt practices become entrenched in a police district or a whole department it is difficult to root out. The honest newcomer in the department is under severe pressure to accept bribes himself or at least to keep quiet about his colleagues' activities. Since he is often not sure just how high up in the department such corrupt practices extend, he may be afraid to inform his superiors and thus jeopardize his career.

Many, perhaps most, policemen are honest, dedicated and hardworking. They perform difficult tasks, hampered by inadequate resources and manpower, archaic administrative procedures and the ambiguous attitudes of many citizens toward law enforcement. The flaws in the justice system tend to harm the individual policeman as well as the accused criminal and members of society at large. Many of the flaws are found not in police operations but in the two other institutions of the justice system—the courts and the penal system.

---

reading: **Albert J. Reiss, Jr. and David J. Bordua**
THE POLICE IN THE LEGAL ORDER

Liberal democratic societies stemming from the English tradition formally organize enforcement of the laws and the maintenance of order *within* the society in both the military and the police but principally in the police. The extension of the role of law in legality, due process, the exercise of discretion, and enacting justice when accusations or arrests are made is formally organized in the public prosecutor and the courts. This functional separation of powers in which ordinarily the police are expected to enforce the law and the judiciary to determine the outcome of events creates problems for both organizations and appears to account for some aspects of police organization and work.

Although the police formally organized to enforce the law and maintain public order, it is apparent they are involved at the same time in enacting justice. It is important to note that all three key terms—order, legality and justice—are ambiguous terms in any social system. But what philosophers, social scientists, and lawyers have argued over for centuries, the police must do every day. The point requires little documentation. A policeman on duty, for example, when confronted with a situation of law enforcement or threat to public order must make decisions about the evidence and whether the act violates the law. Decisions to hold for investigation, to arrest or release, or to enforce order likewise require the extension of legality. His decision may, and often does, involve him at the same time in dispensing equity. Police, in short, make important decisions that affect outcome. They either do justice or limit the judicial function of courts, particularly by determining the nature of the evidence.

Court decisions to dismiss charges are often viewed by the police as a rejection of their decisions. Such decisions may be particularly galling to the officer, since he regards his rules of knowing as more valid than the court's rules of evidence in making decision. Furthermore, court decisions to dismiss offenders or to return offenders to the community often affect police work, as released offenders frequently create problems for continued law enforcement. The most obvious examples of this kind occur in police work with juveniles, vagrants, and habitual drunks. Police dissatisfaction with rehabilitation workers such as probation officers likewise stems in part from the fact that they have been unable to control disposition of the case; today's probationers are not infrequently tomorrow's work.

Police dissatisfaction with the administration of justice by the courts results in their doing justice, a tendency to settle things outside the courts to be sure that "justice is done." Nowhere is this more apparent than when police are expected to continue law enforcement involving violators that the court sends back to the community. The police then may take the law in their own hands and dispense justice, even if it means using violence. The continuing conflict between the police and the courts over admissibility of evidence, techniques of interrogation, the status of the confession, and the use of force, together with their separate definitions of justice, are likewise consequences of the separation of powers.

Transactions among police officers, public prosecutors, and the judiciary not infrequently have the effect of subverting the goals of law enforcement, since each is in a position to sanction the other's behavior. That individual or collective sanctions do not always achieve the intended goal is clear when the effect of sanctions of one part on another is examined. A single example may serve as an illustration.

Judges often negatively sanction police officers for failing to develop cases that meet court standards. It is not uncommon for a judge to criticize publicly from the bench an officer new to the service with a terse statement that fails to explain the grounds constituting an effective case. This judicial practice leaves the young officer in a quandary that often leads him to turn to the informal police system for advice about responses to judicial practice. Not infrequently this course of action leads to poor police technique and the development of cases where there is no intention to prosecute. Such responses lead to further judicial criticism that department administrators may ultimately perceive as an unwillingness by the court to convict. At this juncture, however, police practice may have deteriorated to the point where the court could not convict, if it would. Negative sanctions by the court and prosecutors thus lead to a deterioration of police practice which subverts judicial goals. . . .

The legally defined end of a police department is to enforce the law. The measure of success of a police department is presumably some measure of the degree to which it has in fact enforced the law. There are two major ways that success gets defined for departments. The first kind is a measure of aggregate success, whether of a crime rate, arrests, crimes cleared by arrest, convictions, or value of stolen property recovered. The second is the success it has in meeting public demands to solve a particular crime problem as, for example, when a crime outrages the public conscience.

Police are relatively free to define their own criteria of success in crimes known to them, arrests made, and crimes cleared through arrest, despite national attempts to standardize the criteria. They can determine a successful arrest per se and satisfy themselves when a case has been cleared by arrest. They can recover stolen property incident to arrest and clearance, or independent of it, as is often the case for stolen autos. Their productivity record in these areas, however can be compared with that of other cities through the uniform crime reporting system organized through the FBI. The media of communication hold the local police system accountable for its record in this system.

So far as the public is concerned police departments generally have a low success rate in the proportion of crimes cleared through arrest. Only about one in four offenses known to the police is generally cleared by arrest. Clearance through arrest is greater for crimes against persons than crimes against property and for misdemeanors such as vagrancy, drunkenness, and disorderly conduct, though the latter bring few credits in the public ledger. The low success rate in crimes cleared by arrest creates a dilemma for the police administrators in their efforts to maintain a public image of themselves as productive in a market oriented society. . . .

The dilemma created by the necessity to maintain a public image of success in the face of aggregative measures of lack of success can readily lead to the manipulation of the statistics to create a favorable public image. Police departments, in fact, build up their *volume* of production largely out of misdemeanors rather than felonies, out of crimes against property rather than against persons, and in these days from juveniles and traffic. . . .

The separation of enforcement from outcome creates additional dilemmas for the department in defining its success rate. Assuming legal police conduct, it is through convictions only that the penal sanctions presumed efficacious in reducing crimes can be forthcoming. And it is also through conviction only that the police's sense of justice can be vindicated. The conviction rate, however, is subject to police control only within narrow limits. Both prosecutors and courts intervene. The courts do so with the avowed purpose of scrutinizing police conduct, especially when legality as well as violation of the law is defined as an issue. While department arrest figures may define the policeman's success, acquittals in court may define his failures. . . .

Police concern for clearance of crimes through arrest is not infrequently a response to immediate public pressures that they maintain a safe community as well as to the more general and continuing one that they are an effective and efficient department. The police, for example, may come under fire when a neighborhood is plagued by a series of assaults or strong-arm robberies or when the "public" is offended by any specific crime. Police concern then shifts to clearing up these particular crimes so that they may reduce public pressure by an announcement that the perpetrators have been brought into custody.

Police administrators are confronted with a dilemma in their effort to manipulate the image of crime in the community. To justify increases in manpower and budget before municipal agencies, they are compelled to emphasize the high volume of crime in the community and the difficulties they face in meeting it with the resources available to them. At the same time, this emphasis can easily be interpreted as failure.

The individual policeman likewise is production oriented; his successes are arrests and acquittals are his failures. The successful policeman quickly learns what the police system defines as successes. These become his arrests. When he is not supported by the judicial system for what he regards as right action, he tends to take the law into his own hands, often by making a decision not to arrest or by making an arrest where there is no intention to prosecute. In this way the police officer sanctions the judicial system for what he defines as its failure to make him a success.

Separation of enforcement from outcome also has an effect on police attitudes. The refusal of the courts to convict or of prosecutors to prosecute may rest on what seem to the police the most artificial of formalities. Police are aware as well that this lack of support attributes failure to them. Their sense of justice may be outraged. Collective subcultural modes of adjustment are a common protective response to such dilemmas and contradictions. For the police this adjustment consists in part in the development of a collective identity wherein the police are viewed as the true custodians of morality and justice. In the words of one police administrator:

> Police get conditioned to the idea that we are the only people with our finger in the criminal dike in this country. They feel that everyone else "lets him go." Police differ from the D.A. The D.A. is satisfied with the conviction, finding him guilty. But police want him punished. They become outraged when the result of their work is ignored. "What if they let him off, I get him tomorrow: those bastards kiss him on the cheek and let'em go," is their attitude of how the D.A. and the judge handle their cases.

395 Thus the police want an outcome that signifies for them that their effort has been appreciated and that morality has been upheld. This for them is what is meant by justice being done.

From
Albert J. Reiss, Jr. and David J. Bordua, "Environment and Organization,"
in David J. Bordua, ed., *The Police: Six Sociological Essays*
(New York: John Wiley and Sons, Inc., 1967), pp. 32–37.

The courts

The primary function of the courts is to provide justice to those who have been accused of a crime. Through the legal processes of the courts, the innocent are presumably acquitted and freed and the guilty are fined, released provisionally or imprisoned. Court processes include an adversary system of prosecution versus defense and a system of determining guilt or innocence that may involve a judge alone or a judge and a jury of the accused's peers.

The American court system includes federal, state and local courts. (Local courts are under the jurisdiction of the states.) A person convicted in a lower state or federal court may appeal his conviction to a higher court until he reaches the Supreme Court, whose decision is final. With a few exceptions, such as kidnapping and bank robbery, most criminal activity falls under the jurisdiction of the state courts. Since each state enacts its own criminal code, an activity that may be severely punished in one state is only lightly punished in another. Before abolition of the death penalty, for instance, forcible rape was punishable by the death sentence in several southern states; in Maine forcible rape may be punished by a $500 fine.

Embedded in our Constitution are a number of rights which pertain to persons accused of a crime—among them the right to a swift trial and due process of law. The President's Commission on Law Enforcement and Administration of Justice discovered that most accused criminals could expect far less than this constitutional ideal.[36] A major problem is overcrowding. As they are now set up, the criminal courts cannot possibly handle the volume of defendants awaiting trial and some defendants have to wait several years before their cases are heard. The problem is especially acute for poor people, since those who cannot afford bail must usually remain in jail until their trials are scheduled. In some instances, people have spent several years in jail and then been acquitted. Those who cannot afford a lawyer are provided with the services of a public defender, but public defenders carry very heavy case loads and can spend only a little time on each client. Through sheer lack of time, the public defender may present a wholly inadequate case for his client. Finally, the poor defendant may be persuaded to accept plea bargaining as a resolution of his case. Plea bargaining means that the defendant agrees to plead guilty to a lesser crime—simple assault rather than assault with a deadly weapon, for instance—instead of waiting for a trial in which he may be found guilty of the more serious offense. Many judges and prosecutors approve of plea bargaining because it helps to clear the backlog of cases awaiting trial. The problem is that an innocent man who has spent many weeks or months in jail awaiting trial may choose plea bargaining out of a sense of desperation.

The Commission has been shocked by what it has seen in some lower courts. It has seen cramped and noisy courtrooms, undignified and perfunctory procedures, and badly trained personnel. It has seen dedicated people who are frustrated by huge caseloads, by the lack of opportunity to examine cases carefully, and by the impossibility of devising constructive solutions to the problems of offenders. It has seen assembly line justice.

President's Commission on Law Enforcement and Administration of Justice

The quality of American trial judges obviously has an effect on the judicial system. Judges alone often decide the innocence or guilt of a defendant and in most states determine the sentence. In jury trials, judges sum up the evidence and instruct the jury on the legal points on which they must make a decision. Unfortunately, judges are often political appointees; they do not necessarily have great knowledge of or experience with criminal law. Then too, some judges are corrupt, narrow-minded or unsympathetic to defendants from different social and cultural backgrounds than themselves. Many judges do their best, but are hampered by their middle-class cultural indoctrination or inexperience. The problem is compounded by the fact that there are no systematic training programs for judges. They are expected to know their jobs automatically upon appointment to the bench.

Many judges, prosecutors and other court officials are in the forefront of movements for court reforms. Thoughtful officials realize that the processes with which they are involved affect the defendant's life in the most serious way possible: will he go free, or will he be sentenced to a term of imprisonment?

The penal system

At various times and places crimes have been punished by hideous tortures and mutilations. In eighteenth century England, a man or woman might be hanged for stealing a watch or a pocket handkerchief. The American Constitution forbade such cruel and unusual punishments, but many people consider our present penal institutions barbarous and inhumane. Former Attorney General Ramsey Clark described the results of a 1966 investigation into two prison farms in Arkansas:

> . . . discipline was basically maintained by prisoners themselves—trustees with shotguns—with only a handful of paid employees supervising. Allegations, at least partially verified and largely credible, included the murder of inmates, brutal beatings and shootings. Shallow graves with broken bodies were uncovered. Food unfit to eat was regularly served.

Forced homosexuality was openly tolerated. Extortion of money by wardens and sexual favors from families of inmates to protect their helpless prisoner relatives from physical injury or death were alleged. Torture devices included such bizarre items as the Tucker telephone, components of which were an old telephone, wiring and a heavy duty battery. After an inmate was stripped, one wire was fastened to his penis, the other to a wrist or ankle, and electric shocks were sent through his body until he was unconscious.[37.]

Although this is an extreme example, the pattern of brutality is common in most prisons. Many prison administrations try very hard to prevent brutality on the part of the guards or between prisoners. Yet even the best conventional prisons release prisoners who are hostile and embittered at the system and likely to commit further crimes. When a man enters prison he loses all freedom of action, privacy and many other rights that people in the outside world take for granted. Our society places great value on individuality and freedom of choice, yet the new prisoner is placed in a situation in which his every move is dictated by rigid, and often arbitrary, prison rules.[38] Many prison customs are humiliating and degrading: the strip search, a security measure, means that a prisoner is ordered to strip naked and is then physically searched by a guard for weapons or other contraband. In our culture, a man who is humiliated and oppressed is expected to fight back, verbally or physically. But the prisoner who rebels is likely to find himself in solitary confinement, and continuous rebellion will destroy his chances for early parole.

Figure 10–3   Disposition of persons formally charged by police in 1971

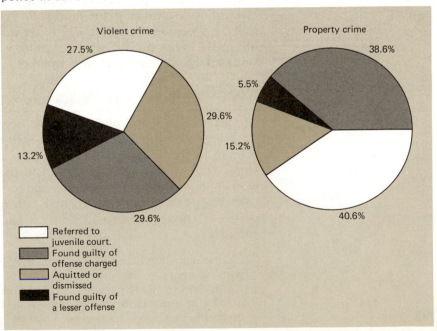

Part of the underlying problem in the penal system is indecision on the part of society concerning the basic purpose of imprisonment. Is it to separate the criminal from society, thereby protecting society from his antisocial behavior? Is it to punish him for his crime? Or is it to rehabilitate him, to change him from being a danger to society into a valued citizen? Criminologists and other experts would overwhelmingly choose the third goal, but unfortunately many Americans seem to be concerned only with the first and second goals. A 1966 survey of penal institutions revealed that in 65 percent of the nation's short-term prisons (in which sentences of one year or less are served) there were *no* rehabilitation programs.[39] The study also showed that occupational training programs and psychological counseling and guidance were almost nonexistent. Where vocational programs do exist, they rarely teach skills that are valuable in the outside world. Most Americans desperately want to reduce crime rates, yet by failing to demand massive prison reform they support a system which tends to reinforce criminal behavior and turn first offenders into hardened criminals.

reading: **Donald R. Cressey**
INMATE ORGANIZATION

Although prison guards and other officers have some control over much of an inmate's overt behavior, mostly in the form of authority and power to punish for deviation, their control is negligible compared to control by the prisoners themselves. In a system of friendships, mutual obligations, statutes, reciprocal relations, loyalties, intimidation, deception, and violence, inmates learn that conformity to prisoner expectations is just as important to their welfare as is conformity to the formal controls imposed by "outsiders."

Powerful prisoners insist that most inmates be orthodox in their statements and actions most of the time. An orthodoxy is more important in prisons than in outside life, because in outside life a person has freedom of mobility not possible in prisons. Conformity is promoted by rewards and punishments, with the latter emphasizing gossip and ridicule but also including beatings, knifings, and killings. Informal control may be seen in the persistence of the fundamental principles of prisoner organization, called "the code." The chief tenets of the code can be classified roughly into five major categories.

First, there are those maxims that caution: *Don't interfere with inmate interests.* These center on the idea that inmates should serve the least possible time, while enjoying the greatest possible number of pleasures and privileges. Included are directives such as, *Never rat on a con; Don't be nosey; Don't have a loose lip; Keep off a man's back; Don't put a guy on the spot.* Put positively, *Be loyal to your class, the cons.*

A second set of behavioral rules asks inmates to refrain from quarrels or arguments with fellow prisoners: *Don't lose your head; Play it cool; Do your own time; Don't bring heat.*

Third, prisoners assert that inmates should not take advantage of one another by means of force, fraud, or chicanery: *Don't exploit inmates.* This injunction sums up several directives: *Don't break your word; Don't steal from cons; Don't sell favors; Don't be a racketeer; Don't welsh on debts. Be right.*

Fourth, some rules have as their central theme the maintenance of self: *Don't weaken; Don't whine; Don't cop out* (plead guilty). Stated positively: *Be tough; Be a man.*

Fifth, prisoners express a variety of maxims that forbid according prestige or respect to the guards or the world for which they stand: *Don't be a sucker; Skim it off the top; Never talk to a screw* (guard); *Have a connection; Be sharp.*

There is no question that the code is frequently violated, just as the formal legal code is violated. Nevertheless, its effects can be seen everywhere in the prison community. It helps inmates avoid some of the conditions of punitive deprivation which the prison is supposed to impose on them. Yet it should not be assumed that the code is "anti-administration" in emphasis as it seems to be. On the contrary, the code reflects important alliances between inmate leaders and prison officials, as we shall see in the next section. Three principal categories of inmates can be found in any prison. Their ways of behaving—their subculture—are quite different. The three kinds of inmates adjust to each other, and to the guards and other personnel, and the three subcultures mesh in various ways. The outcome of the adjusting and the meshing is the organizational character—the "inmate culture"—of a particular prison.

First, there is the subculture of the "thief." Prison "right guys" or "real men," as they are called, participate in this subculture, which thrives on the street as well as in institutions. These men have the highest status among the inmates in any prison. This is no accident, for the prisoner's code is really the code of the "right guys." They subscribe to the code and promote it because it is their benefit to do so. On the street, any man deserving of the title "thief" is a man known to be "right," "solid." The "right guy" in a prison is this thief locked behind walls and bars. Gresham Sykes and Sheldon Messinger a few years ago summarized the "right guy's" relations in prison as follows:

> In his dealings with prison officials, the *right guy* is unmistakably against them, but he doesn't act foolishly. When he talks about the officials with other inmates, he's sure to say that even the hacks with the best intentions are stupid, incompetent, and not to be trusted; that the worst thing you can do is to give the hacks information—they'll only use it against you when the chips are down. A *right guy* sticks up for his rights, but he doesn't ask for pity; he can take all the lousy screws can hand out and more . . . He realizes that there are just two kinds of people in the world. Those in the know skim it off the top. Suckers work.

Then there is the culture of the "convict." It is oriented to manipulating the conditions of prison life, not to an honorable and proud life as a thief. Prison argot identified some of the men participating in this subculture as "merchants," "peddlers," "shots," "politicians." Nowadays prisoners tend to call them, simply, "convicts." Not all inmates are "convicts." Prisoners playing this role do favors for their fellow prisoners in direct exchange for favors from them, or for payment in cigarettes, the medium of exchange in most prisons. Many if not most of the favors involve distribution of goods and services which should go to inmates without cost—the "merchant" demands a price for dental care, laundry, food, library books, a good job assignment, etc. Their central value is utilitarianism, and the most manipulative and the most utilitarian individuals win the available wealth, privileges, and positions of influence.

Also oriented to the "convict" subculture and to manipulating prison life are men who exhibit highly aggressive behavior against other inmates or against officials. They are likely to be called "gorillas," "toughs," "hoods," "ballbusters," or some similar name, depending on the prison they are in. The terms are all synonyms, and they refer to men, likely to be

diagnosed as "psychopaths" by psychiatrists, who hijack their fellow inmates when the latter are returning from the commissary, who attack guards and fellow inmates verbally and physically, who run any kangaroo court, who force incoming inmates to pay for cell and job assignments, who smash up the prison at the beginning of a riot. These "convicts" offer "protection" to weak inmates for a fee but, like the "merchants," they actually exploit other inmates while seeming to help make prison life easier for them.

A final category of inmates is oriented to legitimate subcultures. Prisoners with this orientation are called "straights," "square Johns," "do-rights," etc. When they enter prison they are not members of the thief subculture. Further, while they are in prison they reject both the values of the thieves ("right guys") and the values of the convicts ("merchants," "gorillas"). These men are oriented neither to crime nor to prison. They present few problems to prison administrators. Like "dings" (psychotic or highly eccentric inmates), they isolate themselves—or are isolated—from the thief and convict subcultures. There are great differences in the prison behavior of men oriented to one or the other of the three subcultures. As indicated, the hard-core member of the convict subculture seeks status through means available in the prison. But it is important for an understanding of inmate conduct to note that the hard-core member of the thief subculture seeks status in the broader criminal world of which the prison is only part. Similarly, a man oriented to legitimate life is, by definition, committed to the values of persons outside the prison.

Numerous studies have documented the fact that "right guys," many of whom can be identified as leaders of the thieves, not of the convicts, exercise the greatest influences over the total prisoner population. The influence is the long-run kind stemming from the ability to define what is right and proper. The thief, after all, has the respect of many inmates who are not themselves thieves. He acts, forms opinions, and evaluates events in the prison according to the "right guy" values of the code, and in time he in this way determines the basic behavior patterns in the institution. In what the thief thinks of as "small matters"—getting job transfers, enforcing payment of gambling debts, making cell assignments, stealing and selling food, and acquiring symbols of status such as specially tailored clothing—members of the convict subculture run things.

Most inmates are under the influence of both the thief subculture and the convict subculture. Without realizing it, inmates who serve long prison terms are likely to move toward the middle, toward a compromise between the directives coming from the two sources of deviance. A convict may come to see that thieves are the men with the real prestige; a thief or even a do-right may lose his ability to sustain his status needs by outside criteria.

The thief subculture scarcely exists in institutions for women and some institutions for juveniles. In places of short-term confinement, the convict subculture is dominant, for the thief subculture involves status distinctions that are not readily noticeable or influential in the short run. At the other extreme, in prisons confining only long-term men, the distinctions between the two subcultures are likely to be blurred. Probably the two subcultures exist in their purest forms in institutions holding inmates in their twenties, with varying sentences for a variety of criminal offenses. Such institutions, of course, are the typical prisons of the United States.

Perceiving that the prison community is made up of three principal subcultures helps make sense of prisoners' behavior after they are released. Because "square Johns" are oriented to a "straight" life, we should expect them to have a low parole violation rate, and we should further expect this rate to remain low no matter how much time was served. We should expect "right guys" to have a high violation rate that decreases markedly as time in

prison increases—the continued incarceration tending to sever the thief's connections with the thief subculture on the outside, thus increasing the probability of successful parole. Finally, we should expect "merchants" to have a low parole violation rate if their sentences are rather short, but to find the rate increasing systematically with time served—with continued incarceration they should learn to wheel, deal, exploit, and manipulate in ways that get them right back into prison. A number of sociological studies have found the violation rates of "straights," "thieves," and "convicts" to be almost exactly as expected.

From
Donald R. Cressey, "Adult Felons in Prisons," in Lloyd E. Ohlin, ed., *Prisoners in America* (Englewood Cliffs, N.J.: Prentice-Hall, 1973) pp. 133–138.

Responses to the crime problem

If we wish to reduce the incidence of crime, there are certain obvious steps that might be taken. Some steps involve administrative reform and the investment of more resources; others, however, involve difficult changes in attitudes and customs. Unfortunately, many Americans do not see these reforms as obvious or necessary, and political leaders often respond by proposing only simplistic solutions to the problem of crime.

Legal reform

Most criminologists strongly recommend that we "decriminalize" certain categories of behavior that are now considered crimes. These include "victimless" crimes such as gambling and unconventional sexual behavior between consenting adults. Many experts also agree that alcoholism and narcotics addiction should be treated as medical problems instead of crime problems. In 1972, the President's Commission on Marijuana and Drug Abuse recommended that marijuana should be legalized. The decriminalization of these categories of behavior would enable police forces to devote more manpower and resources to the investigation of crimes against people and property. Such reforms would eliminate the problem of selective enforcement for political reasons or because of bias against an individual, and police and judicial corruption. Most important of all, perhaps, these reforms would greatly reduce the revenues of organized crime, which revolves largely around popular but illegal vices. If a heroin addict could obtain a sufficient dose of heroin or a substitute from a doctor, he would not need to buy it at exorbitant prices from an illicit dealer. The addict would also not have to resort to robbery or prostitution to support an expensive habit; this in itself would probably help reduce crime rates.

Agreement to these reforms is unlikely in the near future; present attitudes are very strong and many people are unsympathetic to decriminalizing such behavior. Politicians, forced to cater to their constituents, are unlikely to take the lead in demanding such reforms, for they do not wish it to appear that they are in favor of "vice."

Another legal reform that might greatly reduce crime rates is gun control legislation. FBI statistics for 1971 show that in 50 percent of all murders and in 40 percent of all robberies handguns were used by the perpetrator.[40] Gunowner lobbying efforts may prevent passage of a strong federal gun control law, but many local government bodies have already passed laws regulating the sale and registration of guns.

Administrative reforms

Both the police and the courts would benefit greatly from increased funding. The federal government has attempted to help by providing money through the Law Enforcement Assistance Administration. However, a study by the National Urban Coalition showed that almost all of the $25 million disbursed by the agency in 1969 went to local police departments for the purchase of communications equipment and other hardware. Only $750 thousand went to the courts.[41] Increased funds may be used to enlarge a police force, and the presence of more police personnel may deter some crime, especially in crowded inner-city areas. Additional computers and other technological devices would improve recordkeeping and information retrieval systems. Reform of internal structure and jurisdictional overlap would also promote greater efficiency. For instance, many metropolitan areas include within their boundaries independent city, state, county and township police forces; centralized control would provide better police service for the entire area.

But increased efficiency, however necessary, may have little effect on the *quality* of the services provided by the police and court system. In this connection, experts' recommendations have centered around reforms of recruitment and training programs. Recommended police reforms include the raising of educational standards and the attraction of better-educated recruits through increases in the minimum and maximum salaries, increased hiring of recruits from among minority groups and the use of tests and interviews to screen out people who are essentially unsuited to police work. It has been suggested that a good policeman has integrity, openness, flexibility and a reluctance to use force except when it is unavoidable. The corresponding negative traits would, of course, include a tendency toward dishonesty, rigidity, bigotry and violent and aggressive behavior. Present police training programs tend to be brief and concerned primarily with technical procedures at the expense of human relations aspects of police work. Suggested reforms include longer training programs with greater emphasis on the constitutional rights of suspects and police relations with all segments of society.

The selection of judges is now largely a political process, and the fate of the accused often depends solely on the discretion of the presiding judge. Many of the judges themselves, including Chief Justice Burger of the Supreme Court, are vitally interested in judicial reform. One goal of the reformers is to reduce political influence in the selection of judges. This might be accomplished by some variation of the "Missouri Plan": a short list of candidates would be selected on a merit basis by local bar associations and from that list a judge or judges would be elected or appointed. Through research and consultation, judges and bar associations would draw up uniform codes to guide judges in setting bail, conducting a trial and sentencing the convicted criminal. (The proposed codes generally include guidelines to help judges determine which accused criminals may be safely released without bail when they cannot afford it; thus the "safe risk" would not have to spend days, weeks or months in jail awaiting trial.) Reformers have also suggested an introductory training program in judicial processes for newly selected judges. Conferences and refresher courses would provide continuing education for judges.

One stage of the criminal justice system which desperately needs reform is sentencing. At present, judges determine sentences on the basis of limited information about the defendants and the crimes committed. In addition, sentences vary from judge to judge, jurisdiction to jurisdiction and case to case. In one study, fifty-five judges were asked to determine the sentences they would impose on a criminal in a hypothetical case. The judges were given information such as probation reports which they normally use when sentencing an actual criminal. Approximately 50 percent of the judges said that they would place the defendant on probation or fine him; the other 50 percent said they would sentence him for a term of one year or more.[42]

Even if radical reforms take place in law codes and in police and judicial administration, there still remains the problem of the penal system. No area of the system of justice has a greater traumatic effect on the convicted criminal; to a great extent the nature of the prison experience will determine whether the released convict will resume criminal activities or go on to achieve a productive life.

Penal reform

A variety of reforms have been suggested to make the present penal structure more humane. Overt brutality and verbal abuse might be eliminated by more careful selection of guards and administrators, prison rules might be changed to allow more individuality and freedom of action, and the physical architecture of the prison might be improved. Psychologists have discovered that human beings have a basic need for a certain amount of space and privacy. Overcrowding and lack of privacy, conditions that are characteristic of modern prisons, often lead to increased tensions, hostility, riots and violence. Physical redesign of prisons might prevent riots and lesser forms of violence.[43] Greater educational opportunities and personal guidance might be provided, particularly to young inmates.

Many reformers now believe, however, that the essential nature of the correctional process must be changed if true rehabilitation is to take place. The principle behind the new reform ideas is that rehabilitation cannot take place when the convict is completely separated from normal society. (Some criminals, especially the mentally disturbed, obviously must be separated from society until such time as they are no longer dangerous.) The goal in regard to most convicts, however, is to return them as quickly as possible to an environment in which they can live and work as normal citizens. Some propose housing convicts in homelike, frequently coeducational, institutions where new skills and attitudes can be learned prior to release. Work-release programs would permit the convict complete freedom to go to school or work during the day; he is then expected to return to the prison at night. Halfway houses would grant convicts almost complete freedom under the loose supervision of a correctional official. Finally, a convicted criminal might be released directly after conviction on a probational basis. The role of the probation officer would be increased; today he often has difficulty just keeping track of probationers. Under the new system he would be expected to provide extensive and sympathetic counseling services.

These new systems are in dramatic contrast to the traditional correctional approach. So far the techniques have been tried only on a limited basis with carefully selected convicts, but the results are encouraging. Few of the convicts in the experimental groups betrayed the trust placed in them. There are, of course, many problems that must be solved in connection with the proposed new systems. Techniques that work well with essentially middle-class convicts may not work at all with hostile inner-city youths or with older, "hardened" convicts. To return a slum dweller to his own environment would probably be disastrous. Most businesses are still highly reluctant to employ ex-convicts. The most serious problem of all is probably public reactions to these programs. The idea of releasing convicts under these circumstances is likely to cause an uproar among people who believe in a punitive correctional system. In fact, public opinion now seems to favor harsher treatment of criminals. The new breed of penal reformer believes that if people are treated like animals they will behave like animals, and if they are treated with dignity and respect they will behave like human beings. Crime is not a simple matter of "us against them." Every American is involved in the cultural values that make some crimes more respectable than others—and some people more likely to be arrested and convicted than others. Most Americans deplore violent crimes, but many of those same Americans are not willing to deal adequately with the potential causes of crime—poverty, oppression and overcrowded slums. Present judicial and penal systems have demonstrably failed to reduce crime, yet some Americans call for more of the same. Until some of the basic contradictions in American society are resolved, there is little chance of real reduction in crime rates.

Notes

[1] Federal Bureau of Investigation, *Uniform Crime Reports, 1971* (Washington, D. C.: Government Printing Office, 1972) p. 60.

[2] *Ibid.*, p. 61

[3] Frank R. Furstenburg, "Public Reaction to Crime in the Streets," *American Scholar,* Vol. 4, Autumn 1971, pp. 565–752.

[4] *Uniform Crime Reports, 1971*, p. 125.

[5] *Ibid.*, pp. 34–35.

[6] *Ibid.*, p. 34.

[7] *Ibid.*

[8] Sidney Axelrad, "Negro and White Male Institutionalized Delinquents," *American Journal of Sociology,* Vol. 57, May 1952, pp. 569–574.

[9] Sheldon Glueck and Eleanor T. Glueck, *1000 Juvenile Delinquents* (Cambridge: Harvard University Press, 1934).

[10] Edwin H. Sutherland, *White Collar Crime* (New York: Dryden Press, 1949) pp. 3–13.

[11] Robert H. Gordon, "Issues in the Ecological Study of Delinquency," *American Sociological Review*, Vol. 36, December 1967, pp. 927–944.

[12] *Uniform Crime Reports, 1971*, p. 35.

[13] Clifford R. Shaw and Henry D. McKay, *Delinquent Areas* (Chicago: University of Chicago Press, 1929).

[14] Emile Durkheim, *Suicide,* trans. by John A. Spaulding and George Simpson (New York: The Free Press, 1964).

[15] Robert K. Merton, *Social Theory and Social Structure* (New York: The Free Press, 1968) pp. 183–214.

[16] Albert K. Cohen, *Delinquent Boys* (New York: The Free Press, 1955).

[17] Edwin H. Schur, *Our Criminal Society* (Englewood Cliffs, N. J.: Prentice-Hall, Inc., 1955).

[18] Richard A. Cloward and Lloyd E. Ohlin, *Delinquency and Opportunity* (New York: The Free Press, 1960).

[19] Edwin H. Sutherland, "Theory of Differential Association," in Rose Giallombardo (ed.), *Juvenile Delinquency* (New York: John Wiley, and Sons, Inc., 1972) pp. 81–83.

[20] Schur, *op. cit.*, pp. 115–117.

[21] Edwin Lemert, *Human Deviance, Social Problems and Social Control* (Englewood Cliffs, N.J.: Prentice-Hall, Inc., 1967) p. 17.

[22] *The New York Times,* November 4, 1971.

[23] *Ibid.*

[24] Edwin H. Sutherland, *The Professional Thief* (Chicago: University of Chicago Press, 1937) pp. 197–215.

[25] Marshall B. Clinard, *Sociology of Deviant Behavior,* 3rd ed. (New York: Holt, Rinehart and Winston, Inc., 1968) pp. 282–283.

[26] President's Commission on Law Enforcement and Administration of Justice, *The Challenge of Crime in a Free Society* (Washington, D. C.: Government Printing Office, 1967) p. 192.

[27] *Ibid.* p.190.

[28] Donald J. Newman, "Public Attitudes Toward a Form of White Collar Crime," *Social Problems,* Vol. 4, January 1957, pp. 228–232.

[29] Clinard, *op. cit.,* p. 271.

[30] Edwin H. Sutherland, "Is 'White Collar Crime' a Crime?" in Marvin E. Wolfgang, Leonard Savitz, and Norman Johnston, (eds.), *The Sociology of Crime and Delinquency* (New York: John Wiley and Sons, 1962) pp. 20–27.

[31] *Miranda* vs *Arizona,* 384 U. S. 436 (1966).

[32] *Mapp* vs *Ohio,* 367 U. S. 634 (1961).

[33] *Uniform Crime Reports, 1971,* p. 43.

[34] Bruce J. Terris, "The Role of the Police," *Annals of the American Academy of Political and Social Science,* Vol. 374, November 1967, pp. 65–66.

[35] President's Commission on Law Enforcement and Administration of Justice, *The Police, Task Force Report* (Washington, D. C.: Government Printing Office, 1967) p. 208.

[36] *The Challenge of Crime in a Free Society, op. cit., p. 128.*

[37] Ramsey Clark, *Crime in America* (New York: Simon and Schuster, Pocket Books, 1971) pp. 193–194.

[38] Bruce R. Jacob, "Prison Discipline and Inmates' Rights," *Harvard Civil Liberties Law Review,* Vol. 5, April 1970, pp. 227, 235–240.

[39] National Council on Crime and Delinquency, *Corrections in the United States* (Washington, D.C.: Government Printing Office, 1966).

[40] *Uniform Crime Reports, 1971,* pp. 8, 15.

[41] National Urban Coalition, *Law and Disorder II, State Planning and Programming under Title 1 of the Omnibus Crime Control and Safe Streets Act of 1968,* Vol. 2, p. 5.

[42] *Report of Hearing Before the Subcommittee on National Penitentiaries of the Committee on the Judiciary,* U. S. Senate, January 22, 1964, pp. 281–285.

[43] Edward T. Hall, *The Hidden Dimension* (Garden City, N. Y.: Doubleday and Company, Anchor Books, 1967) pp. 165–178.

Summary

Crimes in the United States are acts in violation of the law. Our social system creates the law by codifying rules to govern behavior. There are two kinds of law, civil and criminal. Criminal law differs from civil law in four ways: criminal law must be enacted by duly organized political bodies; criminal law uses state-imposed penal sanctions; criminal statutes are specific; and criminal statutes apply to everyone living in a particular jurisdiction.

There are two types of crime, felony and misdemeanor. A felony is a serious crime punishable by more than one year's imprisonment. A misdemeanor is a lesser offense usually punishable by a fine or local imprisonment for one year or less.

Widely accepted sociological explanations of crime include: social structure theories, which attribute crime to a state of confusion produced by sudden changes in social structure; subculture theories, which attribute crime to the "status anxiety" prevalent in a delinquent subculture; differential association theory, which attributes crime to a process of learning techniques and attitudes through intimate contacts; and labeling theory, which attributes crime to a person's living up to his criminal label and reputation.

Four types of crime are: juvenile crimes, committed by minors; professional crimes, committed by career criminals; organized crimes, committed by organizations with hierarchical structure, monopolistic control and influence, dependence on violence for enforcement, immunity from the law through corruption and extraordinary financial success; and white-collar crimes, committed by employees in the course of their work and by corporate executives in the name of the corporation.

The American criminal justice system consists of police, courts and prisons. The system is not working: police are hampered by inadequate resources and manpower, archaic administrative procedures and ambiguous attitudes toward law enforcement; courts are hampered by overcrowding, understaffing and a lack of uniform sentencing codes; prisons are hampered by violence and society's indecision as to the purpose of imprisonment.

Proposed legal reforms include "decriminalizing" certain behavior, treating alcoholism and narcotics addiction as medical problems and passing gun control legislation. Proposed administrative reforms include increasing police and court funds, improving recruitment and training programs and reducing political influence in judge selection. Proposed penal reforms include carefully selecting prison personnel, redesigning prisons and maintaining closer ties between the convict and society.

chapter

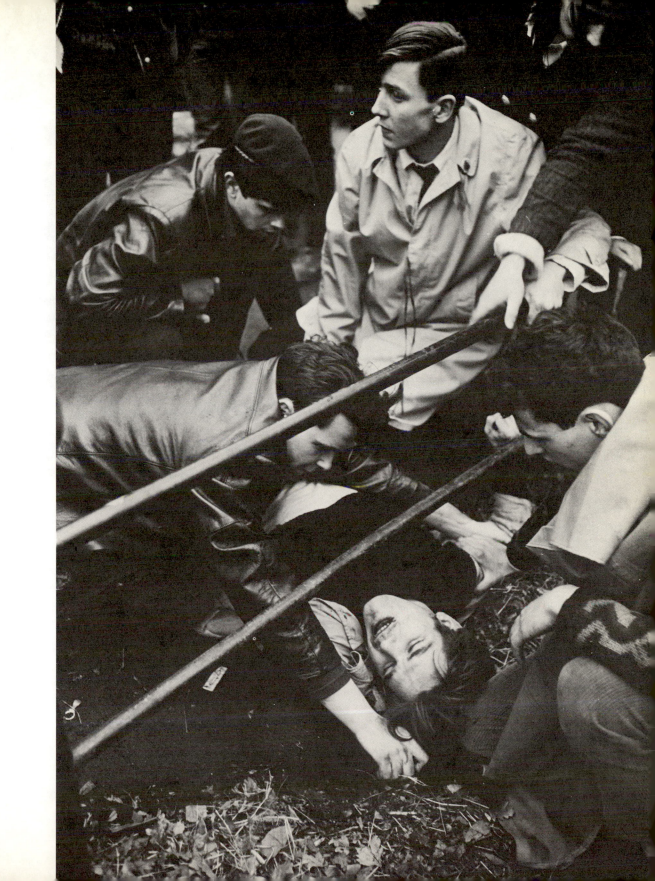

violence

Every society known to man exhibits violence in one form or another. Although violence is by no means new to Americans, the war in Vietnam, rioting in the black ghettos, unrest on the campuses, assassinations and fears about crime in the streets in the 1960s have caused many Americans to focus their attention on the problem of violence for the first time. In this chapter, we will be discussing in detail the causes and forms of violence in contemporary American society.

The history of violence in America begins before the earliest efforts of settlers to push the frontier westward and extends beyond the most recent incidence of police overreaction to a campus demonstration. Violence in America has assumed forms ranging from suicide—the taking of one's own life—to war—the institutionalized violence of one society against another—with countless variations in between. In our study of violence as a social problem, we will be concerned not only with these forms and their causes but with possible alternatives to violence as well.

In what sense are we justified in speaking of violence as a social problem? First, it is a social problem because of the large number of people who are affected by it every day. If the occurrence of violence were restricted to an occasional suicide or an infrequent homicide, we could perhaps leave it to the psychologists to discover the reasons why people sometimes do harm to themselves and to others. Unfortunately, acts of violence are by no means so rare; indeed, few of us are lucky enough not to encounter some form of violence in our lives every day. With the waging of war, the anger and hostility which most of us encounter daily may be blown into earth-shaking proportions. Each of us, from the soldier fighting abroad to the most dedicated pacifist at home, is affected in countless ways by the climate of violence in American society.

Secondly, violence is a disruptive force within society. Every society creates institutions designed to achieve certain ends—elections are held for the choosing of leaders, a court system is established to administer justice, and so forth. Violence is a means of short-cutting normal institutional functions. A man who murders another man in anger or frustration is ignoring those ways of resolving disputes which are approved by society. By taking justice into his own hands, he is—in a small way—expressing contempt for the normal legislative and judicial processes. On a larger scale, every act of violence, from assault to armed revolution, detracts to some degree from the authority normally vested in society. Violence is a social problem in that it is the cornerstone of anarchy and lawlessness.

Who are the perpetrators of violence in American society? None of us is entirely untainted. Those who have witnessed or participated in ostensibly nonviolent peace rallies know that good intentions are, at best, an inadequate basis for the eradication of violence. A problem cannot be solved until it is first thoroughly understood. Perhaps the first step in undermining violence is to work toward a fuller understanding of the roots and forms of violence in American society today.

Causes of violence

Every society, from the simplest hunters and gatherers to the most complex industrialized nations, has found it necessary to establish institutions to control and minimize acts of violence. Whether or not the tendency toward violence is a genetic inheritance of man is a question still open to debate. In this section, we will consider some of the theories which have been offered to explain that tendency.

Biological theories

Is man compelled to perform violence by biological factors beyond his control? The ethologist Konrad Lorenz finds that, while many animals kill for food, only rats and men kill their own kind in anger.[1] Although an animal may be equipped with potentially lethal teeth and claws, he does not turn these weapons against others of his species. Lorenz suggests that the inhibiting mechanisms which prevent a species from endangering its own survival seem to be poorly developed in *Homo sapiens.* As Lorenz observes, "Human behavior . . . far from being determined by reason and cultural tradition alone, is still subject to all the laws prevailing in all phylogenetically adapted instinctive behavior."[2]

An interesting biological theory of human behavior involves the effort to establish a causal link between violent behavior in man and a specific genetic anomaly. Although preliminary research has disclosed the presence of an extra sex chromosome among some criminals, mentally ill, and retarded individuals, control data on the incidence of this anomaly in the general population has yet to be developed. Until more conclusive evidence can be produced, we must continue to assume that there are no "natural born" violent individuals.[3]

Psychological theories

Psychologists have devoted a great deal of attention to the problem of the violent personality. Freud believed that human violence is linked to man's desire to return to the inorganic state, known as the "death instinct."[4] According to Freud, the "death instinct" is centered in the id and must be controlled by the ego—the self—and the super-ego—that portion of the mind concerned with social norms. Although the Freudian hypothesis may serve to explain cases of individual deviance, it fails to take into consideration the social and environmental variables which are believed to elicit violent behavior.

According to Erich Fromm, human aggression stems from the character of individual personalities, determined mainly by incidents in the individual's personal life history. Fromm describes three types of potentially aggressive personality types: the *sadistic,* who compensates for real or imagined impotence through his need for absolute control over others; the *necrophiliac,* who is driven to destruction and annihilation by his hatred for life; and the *bored,* who displays a lack of interest not only in other people and things but in himself as well.[5] It is the bored personality to which Fromm ascribes the cause of most contemporary aggression and violence. Fromm's theory emphasizes the role of the parent in shaping the personality of the child. The seeds of violence are planted early in life.

In their analysis of violence, some psychologists have attempted to consider the influence of social factors on personality development. The frustration-aggression theory maintains that violent behavior results from the frustration of purposeful activity.[6] Factors which may turn frustration into aggression include ethnic discrimination, poverty and emotional deprivation. Although this theory makes a valuable contribution to the study of violence, it ultimately fails to account for the fact that repeated frustration may produce violent behavior in one individual and not in another.

Anthropological theories

Recognizing that violence is present in some form in every known society, anthropologists have addressed themselves to examining some of the ways in which various societies maintain social order. In most societies, order is maintained not through the threat of force but rather through the establishment of norms which are accepted by the majority as proper standards of behavior. Unlike most societies, however, the United States is a nation of many different regional, ethnic, racial, religious and economic sub-cultures, each with its own standards of acceptable behavior. The same regional differences which led to the Civil War over a century ago and which later motivated Northerners to support the civil rights struggle in the South are still causing tension and internal conflicts today. It is frequently misleading to generalize the causes of violence in a society as complex and varied as that of the United States.

Subcultural differences within a region may involve the exclusionary tactics of the dominant class; that is, the group with the greatest amount of power may segregate itself in restricted neighborhoods and private clubs while ethnic minorities live together in ghetto areas. In America, blacks, American Indians, Mexican-Americans and other minority group members stigmatized because of race or religion often find it difficult to find work for which they are qualified or homes in neighborhoods which they can afford.

Discriminatory practices resulting from cultural variation often create inequities which are long-lasting in their effects. When regional norms are not held in common by the society as a whole, the legitimacy of such inequities may be strongly questioned by the stigmatized groups. Eventually, feelings of frustration and injustice will usually result in violence.

Sociological theories

In studying violence, sociologists have concerned themselves with the phenomenon of violence as it occurs within the context of the ordered society. Weber argued that the legitimate use of violence is restricted to the State;[7] Durkheim maintained that some degree of punishment is necessary to integrate the conforming members of society by defining the limits of acceptable behavior.[8]

When a large portion of the members of a society adopt violence as a means of achieving their ends, the bonds which normally hold that society together begin to disintegrate. Excessive violence may be evidence of the need to restructure some social institutions.

Sociologists warn against accepting as satisfactory those institutions which are contributing to social disruption. In dealing with civil violence, generalized abstractions rarely offer adequate solutions to a very real social problem. Ascribing violence to "tension" or "strain" does nothing, according to sociologist Jerome Skolnick, to "explain the specific injustices against which civil disorders might be directed; nor does it help tc illuminate the historical patterns of domination and subordination to which the riot is one of many possible responses."[9]

In order to understand the alienation of lower-class youth from conventional social norms, sociologists have devoted a great deal of attention to the phenomenon of the juvenile gang. In his work on delinquent gangs, Albert Cohen described the gang as a delinquent subculture in revolt against middle-class values and behavioral standards. The subculture of the gang espouses its own life style, traditions, and focal concerns, with status generally gained through the judicious use of violence. To be tough, to live by one's wits, and to hustle for survival are the norms which determine social conformity among the youthful gangs of the urban poor.[10]

According to sociologists Cloward and Ohlin, members of lower-class gangs adhere to the social goals of wealth and upward mobility but find access to them blocked by racial and class discrimination.[11] The delinquent gang provides an alternative route to success by offering an opportunity to prepare for a rewarding career outside the law. A crucial part of this training is an education in the use of violence.

The effort to maintain social control through shared norms and values may be unsuccessful for a number of reasons. Chief among these is inconsistency of interpretation and enforcement of sanctions. "Plea bargaining," in which the accused is put in the position of negotiating the seriousness of his offense, and the failure to prosecute white-collar crime are two examples of the inconsistent administration of justice. The contradictory and discriminatory application of social norms may contribute significantly to the frustration of those who find themselves the victims of injustice.

A variety of social causes of violence emerge from these sociological theories. As discriminatory practices close off access to socially approved life-styles, the ensuing frustration frequently leads to antisocial attitudes and violence. Among young people, the alternative of gang membership offers support to a nonconforming life-style and an opportunity for an alternate form of success through illegal activities. When they lack fairness and consistency, the institutions of law and justice may serve to encourage and perpetuate disorder and violence.

Abundant models for learning violent behavior are available to an individual growing up in America. Parental aggression, the portrayal of violence in the media, and the various forms of violence ensuing from racial prejudice are all significant elements in the development of the violent personality in America. Furthermore, the ambiguity of society's attitude towards violence may contribute heavily to such development. In condoning violent repression by the military and police establishments, society may unwittingly encourage individuals or groups of individuals to adopt violent tactics as a legitimate means of achieving their goals.

Viewed from a sociological viewpoint, violence is the outcome of many variables encountered by an individual throughout the socialization process and complicated by the conflicting values of society. In dealing with the problem of human aggression, acts of violence—

whether committed by individuals or by groups of individuals—must be viewed within the specific context in which they occur. The casual repression of violence is a poor substitute for the study of its underlying causes. To control violence without discovering and treating its sources is ultimately to invite more violence.

Forms of violence

So far, we have spoken of violence as if it were a single isolated social phenomenon. In actuality, violence may assume many different forms ranging from the violence of an individual against himself to the violence of one society against another. Let us now consider some of these forms and examine their relevance to the problem of violence in American society.

Suicide

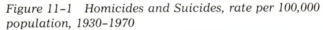

Perhaps the most elementary form of violence is the taking of one's own life. In the United States, over twenty-two thousand persons are definitely known to have taken their own lives in 1970.[12] Since 1958 the suicide rate has remained at almost 10 per 100,000 population. In his classic study, *Suicide,* Emil Durkheim observed that "so long as society remains unchanged the number of suicides remains the same;"[13] that is, the suicide rate of a given society seems to vary directly with the integration of the structure and fabric of that society. In describing fundamental categories of suicide, Durkheim stressed that each has causes attributable to society rather than to the individual.

Figure 11-1   Homicides and Suicides, rate per 100,000 population, 1930–1970

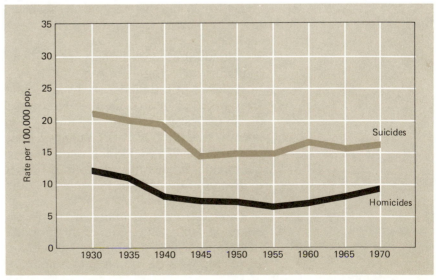

Egoistic suicide is personally motivated and is an indication of a lack of group unity and identification. This type of suicide is most common when interpersonal relations do not bind a person to others.

Altruistic suicide involves the sacrifice of one's life for the sake of some higher cause or power. Such suicides usually involve religious, political, or military allegiences.

Anomic suicide results from the failure of society to properly regulate the individual. Economic changes which cause previously accepted norms to be inoperative maximize conditions for anomic suicide. Sudden wealth or proverty sometimes act as catalysts for suicide when the individual is unable to cope with his suddenly altered status. Divorce is another major factor in anomic suicides. With the removal of the regulatory mechanisms of marriage, an individual may feel lost and alone. Suicide rates among divorced men and women are considerably higher than among married ones.

Durkheim directed his attention to suicide rates rather than confining his study to individual psychological circumstances, then correlated them with other social phenomena. Although the factors of changing norms and societal integration discussed by Durkheim do not entirely explain available suicide statistics, they do offer valuable insights into the phenomenon. In keeping with Durkheim's theories, the rate of suicides in the United States rises sharply with advancing age and is twice as high for males as for females. On the other hand, there seems to be no significant variation in the suicide rate between urban and nonurban areas. Furthermore, white Americans are statistically more prone to commit suicide than nonwhite Americans.[14] Despite this national tendency, a study by Herbert Hendin of suicide in New York City indicates that "among blacks of both sexes between the ages of twenty and thirty-five, suicide is decidedly more of a problem than it is in the white population of the same age."[15] Recalling Durkheim's definition of anomic suicide, it seems likely that what has been called the "revolution of rising expectations" may account for the disproportionately high suicide rate among young urban blacks; the social structure has failed them; it does not offer them the minimum economic, emotional and psychological support needed to integrate them into a productive role in society.

> *... tendencies of the whole social body, by affecting individuals, cause them to commit suicide. The private experiences usually thought to be the proximate causes of suicide have only the influence borrowed from the victim's moral predisposition, itself an echo of the moral state of society. To explain his detachment from life the individual accuses his most immediately surrounding circumstances; life is sad to him because he is sad. Of course his sadness comes to him from without in one sense, however not from one or another incident of his career but rather from the group to which he belongs.*
>
> *Emile Durkheim*

Crimes of violence

Although crimes against property—such as theft and embezzlement—are statistically more common than crimes of violence, it is the increase in violent crime which has been most distressing to the American public in recent years. Between 1960 and 1968, the national rates of criminal homicide, aggravated assault, and forcible rape have all increased.[16] Although a change in police reporting procedures may play some small part in the increased rates of reported crimes, there is considerable evidence to suggest that the incidence of violent crime in America has risen substantially over the last several years.

The most under-reported of all crimes is that of rape. A number of special problems arise in connection with the reporting of rape. Many women are reluctant to report rape to the police due to embarrassment and social pressures, especially in cases where the rapist is a relative or friend. Furthermore, women who report rape are frequently subject to the harassment of male police and justice officials who may prefer to believe that the rape victim was in actuality the provocateur. Finally the requirement in most states that the victim produce corroborative evidence of the crime makes conviction on a rape charge close to impossible.

Although most violent crime in America takes place in large cities, the occurrence of such crimes is not evenly distributed throughout each city. Rates of violent crime are disproportionately higher in the black ghettos; and urban arrest rates for assault and rape are ten times higher for blacks than for whites and sixteen times higher for robbery and homicide. In a study of seventeen cities, a Victim-Offender Survey found that 90 percent of urban homicides, assaults, and rapes involve victims and offenders of the same race[17] and that most victims and offenders are males, poor persons, blacks and youths. The Survey further indicated that most homicides and assaults occur between relatives and friends, often provoked by family quarrels, disputes over money, jealousy or other personal matters. The difference between homicide and assault sometimes rests more with the offender's choice of weapon than with his intent. Assaults generally involve knives while homicides usually involve handguns.[18]

Young males at the bottom of the socioeconomic scale are the most frequent perpetrators of violent crime. In 1968, the rate of males arrested for homicide was five times higher than that of females, with most offenders falling in the 18-24 age group.[19] Although arrests for rape, robbery, and assault are concentrated in the 15-24 age group, there has been a marked increase in the arrest rate of 10-14 year olds. Local studies indicate that the poor and the uneducated are most likely to commit crimes of violence. Studies involving Philadelphia police data show that the unemployed, skilled and unskilled laborers constitute 90-95 per cent of the criminal homicide offenders, 90 percent of the rape offenders and 92-97 percent of the robbery offenders.[20]

Studies clearly indicated that the crowded conditions, high unemployment, sub-standard housing and low educational level which characterize the urban slums are related to the large percentage of violent crimes which occur there. The gap in crime rates between the middle-class white and ghetto black cannot be explained on a racial basis; rather, it should be clear that inequality of opportunity makes for inequality of social behavior. Almost invariably, violent crime is the result of desperation.

Family violence

A great deal of violence in America occurs within the home. Normally, members of a family are bound by the exchange of love, respect and personal services. When one member begins to feel that his contribution to the family outweighs the benefits he derives from the other members, quarrels may arise. When both parties to a quarrel feel they are already giving more than they are receiving, it may be difficult for either of them to conceive of a resolution of the argument.

Because the emotional investments both in the family relationship and in the argument of the moment are too great and the costs of leaving too high, it may become difficult for quarreling family members to terminate a dispute. Ultimately, because intimates cannot retreat behind the polite masks they wear for the rest of society, family members may be unable to find a suitable alternative to physical violence.

Locked in but suffering from it couples may engage in fighting that is savage and even lethal. Many men and women have finally come to the conclusion that homicide is a cleaner, neater solution than the dragged out acerbic destruction of ego and dignity that is inherent in breaking off.

William C. Goode

A more dramatic problem than marital conflict is that of child abuse. A recent study of this problem indicates that poverty, broken families and other environmental factors may not be as significant as earlier studies had suggested.[21] Instead, the investigators concentrated on a number of remarkable parallels in the backgrounds and personalities of child-abusing parents. Often deprived of tenderness in their own childhood, such parents tend to demand an unreasonable level of performance from their child at an age when the child is too young to understand or comply with their demands. In many cases, the abusive parent also expects the child to supply him with the kind of loving comfort his own parents failed to give him. Typically, the discrepancy between what is demanded and what is received leads to acute frustration and, ultimately, violence. In every case studied, the abusive parents were found to have been abused themselves as children. This pattern, by which abused children grow into abusive adults suggests a certain rigidity in the learning of the social role of parent. As a child learns his own role in the family, he incorporates the role of his parents into his learning process. Ultimately, it is the behavior of his own parents which he will re-enact in his relationship to his own children. In this way, the pattern of child abuse may thus be perpetuated until some element of change can be introduced.

Juvenile gangs

Not unlike the family, the juvenile gang is a social microcosm, a group bound together by close ties of loyalty, obligation, personal service, respect and the bond of mutual defense. Essentially an urban lower-class phenomenon, gangs range from a spontaneous group of some twenty or thirty boys to a complex structure of sub-groups comprising hundreds of boys in various age brackets.

Most researchers have described gang leaders as relatively stable, "cool" youngsters who have earned their leadership status through fighting prowess, verbal facility and levelheadedness. The gang provides its members with a structure within which self-esteem and self-expression can be developed. In a subculture where the conventional means of achieving status may be closed, the gang provides a setting in which a young person can acquire a sense of pride and belonging. Although gang violence is a very real problem, it is possible that the media have exaggerated the intensity of delinquent behavior. Malcolm W. Klein comments:

> Gangs are *not* primarily assaultive or violent in their delinquent behavior and, what is more, the greatest part of their time is spent in non-delinquent activity . . . Assaults are more often minor than major; gang fighting seldom involves massive confrontations between warring hordes; robbery often means purse snatching or veiled threats accompanying theft; rape is often an invited act, subtly or otherwise; gang vandalism often means writing gang names on playground walls or throwing stones at the windows of condemned tenements.[22]

The same writer observes that "the gang more commonly does nothing so much as wonder what to do."

Assassination

An interesting aspect of American violence is the phenomenon of politically motivated homicide. In a study of eighty-four countries over a twenty-year period (1948–1967), the United States ranked fifth in frequency of political assassinations.[23] Studies indicate that assasination is closely linked to internal political violence, systemic frustration, external aggression, minority tension and high homicide rates.[24] The high level of tension among ethnic, racial, linguistic and religious groups in the U.S. may be a significant factor in explaining the high incidence of political violence in America.

The Presidency, a highly visible center of both symbolic and actual power, is a prime target for those who would express their resentment of authority through assassination. A survey of the personalities of the assassins of Lincoln, Garfield, McKinley and Kennedy, as well as the would-be assassins of Jackson, Theodore Roosevelt, Franklin Roosevelt and Truman, reveals a number of striking similarities.[25] All were men who had difficulty making friends, and special difficulty in developing satisfactory relationships with women. Most came from broken homes in which at least one parent was either dead or unresponsive to the child's needs. All had been unable to work steadily for at least a year prior to the assassination, and most were aligned with some political or religious cause although not members of any organized movement. All but Oswald—Kennedy's alleged assassin—used a handgun, and nearly all made their attempts on the President's life while he was appearing in a crowd. The psychological profile which emerges is that of a man who feels alienated from his fellow human beings and from his society—a failure who feels compelled to perform a public deed of great significance in order to assert his own value as a human being.

Parents preach, and children with the natural vitality of their first decade listen. Soon, all too soon, at ten, at twelve or fourteen urban death or rural degradation takes them. Growing awareness brings feelings of humiliation. Growing needs reveal the cramped frustration of life. Infants and young children can be taught goodness and compliance, but such lessons do not stick fast to youths in search of jobs not to be had, and dignity constantly refused.

Robert Coles

Although the assassin himself is usually a highly disturbed personality, the act of assassination carries grave political implications. The frequent performance of antisocial acts by disturbed individuals may indicate a significant level of social and political unrest within American society. The act of assassination frequently sets off a chain of events in which other individuals, inspired by the assassin, may resort to violence to redress their grievances—sometimes legitimate, sometimes not—against society.

The civil rights movement

A critical period in the history of American violence stems, ironically, from the nonviolent boycotts, marches, and sit-ins led by Martin Luther King and other advocates of civil rights legislation in the 1960s. With the death of King the move toward militancy grew as the black cause became increasingly identified with the struggles of the revolutionary activities of all oppressed peoples. As it became more apparent that riots in the ghetto were a means of achieving quick, albeit transitory, results, the use of militant violence as a revolutionary tactic became the main thrust of the new movement.

At the close of the 1960s, peaceful integration was no longer the dominant theme of the black movement. In its place were "self-defense and the rejection of nonviolence; cultural autonomy and the rejection of white values; and political autonomy and community control."[26] These values, represented in varying degrees by various organizations and individuals, reflect certain common goals in the black community. Through violence, militant blacks are struggling for "a measure of safety, power, and dignity in a society that has denied them all three."[27]

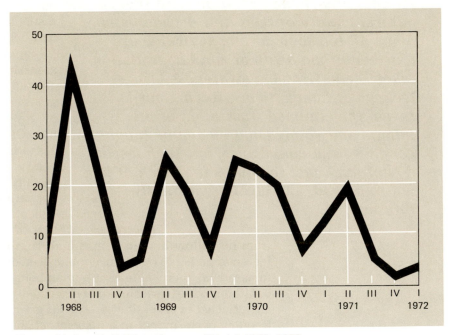

Figure 11-2   Civil Disturbances (Riots) 1968–1972, quarterly
I   — January–March
II — April–June
III — July–September
IV — October–December

The ghetto riots which followed the death of Dr. King served two principal functions. While providing an outlet for the repressed anger of the black community, the riots also called attention to the injustice of widespread discrimination against blacks. In some case, middle-class blacks have benefited from the ghetto riots by achieving better employment, higher pay scales, and greater access to a college education. For the most part, however, black militancy and the violence which has accompanied it has had the effect of polarizing attitudes of both blacks and whites. The liberal support of the black cause, inspired in part by the pacifism of Dr. King, has been replaced in many instances by fear and suspicion. "Law and order" has become a euphemism for the old repressive tactics used against members of the black community in the past. In too many cases, civil violence has been met by still greater violence on the part of the law enforcement establishment.

The anti-war protest movement

In many ways, the protest movement directed against the war in Vietnam closely paralleled the civil rights movement in its effort to achieve its goals through the use of nonviolence. Both movements, despite their original motivation, were forced to escalate their tactics gradually in the direction of increased violence. For the most part, violence in antiwar demonstrations was instigated by over-zealous police who were unaccustomed to dealing with the thousands of young middle-class people who assembled for the demonstrations. The demonstration was a new form of political expression to many Americans, and certainly one which the police were unprepared to handle. In many cases, inappropriate methods of riot control served to antagonize demonstrators and further polarize pro- and anti-war factions. The pitting of violent repression against nonviolent protest caused alarm even to some of those whose goals opposed the efforts of the demonstrators.

The effects of middle-class dissent on American society have been far-reaching. In questioning traditional institutions and in developing a new political awareness, anti-war protestors may have served as the *avant garde* for major changes yet to come in American social structure.

War

The most devastating form of violence known to man is the institution of war. Although few societies in the world have not experienced war at some point in their history, the ultimate causes of war have yet to be fully understood. It is believed by some that the waging of war is an integral feature of human society. To a large degree, war in modern industrial societies may be understood in terms of political and economic factors. War may erupt due to intensive competition for power and influence in the exploration of underdeveloped lands. The war in Vietnam illustrates this phenomenon. Most Americans did not know why their nation was involved in a war in Asia. Modern warfare often involves a conflict between the governments and not the people of nations.

War performs a number of secondary functions. By socializing the young men of a warring nation into the mystique of killing, war contributes to a climate of violence which may linger long after hostilities have ended. At the same time, war may serve to unite people by providing them with a common enemy. Londoners who survived the German bombardment of 1940 recall the event as a time when people helped each other and pulled together in their common cause. Class barriers collapsed and people talked to each other as equals. Studies show that crime and suicide rates go down in time of war as well. War may provide a sense of belonging and purpose to soldiers and civilians alike.

In America, war has sometimes been blamed on the "military-industrial complex". Without war, the manufacturers of war goods and the military establishment would find themselves out of business. Furthermore, governments may use war to unite the people or to distract them from internal problems. As long as there is profit to be made from institutionalized violence, war will continue as a part of the American way of life.

reading:

Hannah Arendt
VIOLENCE AND POWER

Violence is by nature instrumental; like all means, it always stands in need of guidance and justification through the end it pursues. And what needs justification by something else cannot be the essence of anything. The end of war—end taken in its twofold meaning—is peace or victory; but to the question And what is the end of peace? there is no answer. Peace is an absolute, even though in recorded history periods of warfare have nearly always outlasted periods of peace. Power is in the same category; it is, as they say, "an end in itself." (This, of course, is not to deny that governments pursue policies and employ their power to achieve prescribed goals. But the power structure itself precedes and outlasts all aims, so that power, far from being the means to an end, is actually the very condition enabling a group of people to think and act in terms of the means-end category.) And since government is essentially organized and institutionalized power, the current question What is the end of government? does not make much sense either. The answer will be either question-begging—to enable men to live together—or dangerously utopian—to promote happiness or to realize a classless society or some other nonpolitical idea, which if tried out in earnest cannot but end in some kind of tyranny.

Power needs no justification, being inherent in the very existence of political communities; what it does need is legitimacy. The common treatment of these two words as synonyms is no less misleading and confusing than the current equation of obedience and support. Power springs up whenever people get together and act in concert, but it derives its legitimacy from the initial getting together rather than from any action that then may follow. Legitimacy, when challenged, bases itself on an appeal to the past, while justification relates to an end that lies in the future. Violence can be justifiable, but it never will be legitimate. Its justification loses in plausibility the farther its intended end recedes into the future. No one questions the use of violence in self-defense, because the danger is not only clear but also present, and the end justifying the means is immediate.

Power and violence, though they are distinct phenomena, usually appear together. Wherever they are combined, power . . . is the primary and predominant factor. The situation, however, is entirely different when we deal with them in their pure states—as, for instance, with foreign invasion and occupation. . . . the current equation of violence with power rests on government's being understood as domination of man over man by means of violence. If a foreign conqueror is confronted by an impotent government and by a nation unused to the exercise of political power, it is easy for him to achieve such domination. In all other cases the difficulties are great indeed, and the occupying invader will try immediately to establish Quisling governments, that is, to find a native power base to support his dominion. The head-on clash between Russian tanks and the entirely nonviolent resistance of the Czechoslovak people is a textbook case of a confrontation between violence and power in their pure states. But while domination in such an instance is difficult to achieve, it is not impossible. Violence, we must remember, does not depend on numbers or opinions, but on implement, and the implements of violence . . . like all other tools, increase and multiply human strength. Those who oppose violence with mere power will soon find that they are confronted not by men but by men's artifacts, whose inhumanity and destructive effectiveness increase in proportion to the distance separating the opponents. Violence can always destroy power; out of the barrel of a gun grows the most effective command, resulting in the most instant and perfect obedience. What never can grow out of it is power.

In a head-on clash between violence and power, the outcome is hardly in doubt. If Gandhi's enormously powerful and successful strategy of nonviolent resistance had met with a different enemy—Stalin's Russia, Hitler's Germany, even prewar Japan, instead of England—the outcome would not have been decolonization, but massacre and submission. However, England in India and France in Algeria had good reasons for the restraint. Rule by sheer violence comes into play where power is being lost; it is precisely the shrinking power of the Russian government, internally and externally, that became manifest in its "solution" of the Czechoslovak problem—just as it was the shrinking power of European imperialism that became manifest in the alternative between decolonization and massacre. To substitute violence for power can bring victory, but the price is very high; for it is not only paid by the vanquished, it is also paid by the victor in terms of his own power. This is especially true when the victor happens to enjoy domestically the blessings of constitutional government. Henry Steele Commager is entirely right. "If we subvert world order and destroy world peace we must inevitably subvert and destroy our own political institutions first." The much-feared boomerang effect of the "government of subject races" (Lord Cromer) on the home government during the imperialist era meant that rule by violence in faraway lands would end by affecting the government of England, that the last "subject race" would be the English themselves. The . . . gas attack on the campus at Berkeley, where not just tear gas but also another gas, "outlawed by the Geneva Convention and used by the Army to flush out guerrillas in Vietnam," was laid down while gas-masked Guardsmen stopped anybody and everybody "from fleeing the gassed area," is an excellent example of this "backlash" phenomenon. It has often been said that impotence breeds violence, and psychologically that is quite true, at least of persons possessing natural strength, moral or physical. Politically speaking, the point is that loss of power becomes a temptation to substitute violence for power—in 1968 during the Democratic convention in Chicago we could watch this process on television—and that violence itself results in impotence. Where violence is no longer backed and restrained by power, the well-known reversal in reckoning with means and ends has taken place. The means, the means of destruction, now determine the end—with the consequence that the end will be the destruction of all power. . . .

. . . Power and violence are opposites; where the one rules absolutely, the other is absent. Violence appears where power is in jeopardy, but left to its own course it ends in power's disappearance. This implies that it is not correct to think of the opposite of violence as nonviolence; to speak of nonviolent power is actually redundant. Violence can destroy power; it is utterly incapable of creating it. Hegel's and Marx's great trust in the dialectical **429** "power of negation," by virtue of which opposites do not destroy but smoothly develop into each other because contradictions promote and do not paralyze development, rests on a much older philosphical prejudice: that evil is no more than a privative *modus* of the good, that good can come out of evil; that, in short, evil is but a temporary manifestation of a still-hidden good. Such time-honored opinions have become dangerous. They are shared by many who have never heard of Hegel or Marx, for the simple reason that they inspire hope and dispel fear—a treacherous hope used to dispel legitimate fear. By this, I do not mean to equate violence with evil; I only want to stress that violence cannot be derived from its opposite, which is power, and that in order to understand it for what it is, we shall have to examine its roots and nature.

From
"On Violence" in *Crises of the Republic* by Hannah Arendt,
(New York: Harcourt Brace Jovanovich, Inc., 1972)
pp. 142–155.

The climate of violence

So far we have examined some of the causes and forms associated with the phenomenon of violence. What is it about American society that encourages these manifestations of violence to thrive and grow? What must be done to turn the tide? Where shall we look to put an end to the climate of violence in America? Perhaps the most significant factor in the shaping of the American consciousness is the public communications media. Although representations of violence in books, newspapers and films are of undeniable influence, the most significant contribution to media violence has been television. While warning against the type of facile judgment that would brand television as the scapegoat for widespread domestic violence, the National Commission on the Causes and Prevention of Violence stated that it was nevertheless "deeply troubled by television's constant portrayal of violence, not in any genuine attempt to focus artistic expression on the human condition, but rather in pandering to a public preoccupation with violence that television itself has helped to generate."[28] According to the Commission's Task Force on Media, avid television viewers, particularly young children and adolescents, witness repeated acts of violence which, in the absence of social sanctions, appear to them as acceptable means of gaining desired ends. The violent world of television fiction has come to serve as a warped mirror of reality for much of the American public.

Studies have shown that youngsters spend as much as half their waking hours before the television set and view, on the average, twenty acts of violence per hour in cartoon shows and more than six per hour in dramatic shows.[29] Furthermore, the unacceptability of violent behavior is rarely stressed by these presentations. Consequences of arrest and trial were depicted only 20 percent of the time in the world depicted by television, and pain as a consequence of violence only 25 percent of the time, suggesting that violence is neither painful, bloody nor messy, although it may result in death or injury.[30] The conclusion of the Commission was that present television fare may have an adverse effect on impressionable young people. Whether or not television can be blamed for the gang phenomenon or for any specific act of violence is still open to debate.

Another factor contributing to the climate of violence in America is the misguided encouragement of sexual stereotypes. Violence is inevitable in a society which equates femininity with gentleness and masculinity with physical strength and brutality. In such a society, the occurrence of rape and the organizing of gangs as an expression of masculine power should not be surprising.

Compulsive masculinity is prevalent in urban homes in which boys may grow up without the presence of a father figure. A perverted notion of masculinity may contribute to the development of a violent personality. Superior strength and readiness become the norms of the violent subculture "concentrated in segments of the American population having little opportunity to wield symbolic power—among adolescents rather than adults, in the working class rather than the middle-class, among deprived minority groups rather than among white Protestant Anglo-Saxons."[31] When the accepted "masculine" roles cannot be played out, alienated individuals may choose violence as a convenient alternative.

A controversial aspect of American violence is the question of gun control. One out of every two households in the United States is armed; there are an estimated 90 million firearms in private hands. Although the majority of sportsmen and collectors are careful and responsible individuals, the general availability of cheap handguns may be seen as a significant factor in our climate of violence. The skyrocketing of gun sales after major ghetto riots, instigated in part by white and black extremist groups, is evidence of this contention.

Opposition to the regulation of gun ownership is led by the National Rifle Association. It is difficult to dispute the NRA's position that the right to bear arms is clearly guaranteed by the Constitution. Nevertheless, the abuse of this right has resulted in intolerable acts of violence and death. The United Nations World Health Organization reports that the United States leads all industrialized nations in all categories of deaths due to firearms, including accidents, suicides and homicides.[32]

Once we have noted some of the underlying causes of violence in America, we are left with the difficult question of determining what— if anything—can be done about them. Out of the presidential commissions on civil disorders and violence have come many recommendations for legal and social reform. The National Commission on Violence has advocated expansion of the 1968 Gun Control Act's curb on the importing of "junk" guns to include domestic production and sale as well as recommending state and local registration of handguns and long guns. The Commission further recommended the drastic overhaul of law enforcement and judicial procedures in order to insure the equal administration of justice. Although little action has been taken on these recommendations to date, several of the Commission's suggestions have been implemented. The reduction of violence on television and the introduction of a rating system for films are examples of the influence of the Commission on the communications media. The Commission also expressed the belief that the integration of youth into the American political process may have a significant effect on the incidence of unrest and violence. Subsequently, the voting age has been lowered to 18.

Among its social recommendations, the Commission urged that aggrieved groups be granted their constitutional right to protest and that institutional flexibility be insured to promptly correct injustices which have been perpetrated. The Commission urged that schools "emphasize in American history and social studies classes the complexities and subtleties of the democratic process; shun the myths by which we have traditionally made supermen of Presidents, 'founding fathers,' and other prominent persons; and restore to history books a full and frank picture of violence and unrest in America's past, in the hope that children can be educated to repudiate violence and recognize its futility."[33]

Can violence ever be eradicated from American society? Anthropologist Margaret Mead expressed the belief that peace can be established by

> reducing the strength of all mutually exclusive loyalties, whether of nation, race, class, religion, or ideology, and constructing some quite different form of organization in which the memory of these loyalties and organizational residues . . . cannot threaten the total structure.[34]

Ultimately, the end of violence may depend on man's ability to structure a society based not on competition and power but on human equality and mutual respect.

Notes

[1] Konrad Lorenz, *On Aggression* (New York: Bantam Books, 1971) p. 229.

[2] *Ibid.*

[3] Donald J. Mulvihill and Melvin M. Tumin, eds., *Crimes of Violence*, staff report submitted to the National Commission on the Causes and Prevention of Violence, (Washington, D.C.: U.S. Government Printing Office, 1969) pp. 419–424.

[4] Sigmund Freud, *Civilization and its Discontents* (New York: Doubleday Anchor, 1956).

[5] Erich Fromm, "The Erich Fromm Theory of Aggression," in *New York Times Magazine,* February 27, 1972, pp. 14 ff.

[6] John Dollard, Leonard W. Doob, Neal E. Miller, O.H. Mowrer and Robert R. Sears, *Frustration and Aggression* (New Haven: Yale University Press, 1939).

[7] Julien Freund, *The Sociology of Max Weber* (New York: Pantheon Books, 1968).

[8] Emile Durkheim, *The Rules of Sociological Method* (Glencoe: The Free Press, 1956).

[9] Jerome H. Skolnick, *The Politics of Protest* (New York: Ballantine Books, 1969) p. 338.

[10] Albert Cohen, *Delinquent Boys: The Culture of the Gang* (Glencoe: The Free Press, 1955).

[11] Richard Cloward and Lloyd E. Ohlin, *Delinquency and Opportunity* (Glencoe: The Free Press, 1961).

[12] *Statistical Abstract of the United States 1972* (93rd edition.) Washington, D.C. 1972, p. 59.

[13] Emile Durkheim, *Suicide,* translated by John A. Spaulding and George Simpson (Glencoe: The Free Press, 1951) p. 304.

[14] Mulvihill and Tumin, eds., *op. cit.,* p. 104.

[15] Cited in *Ibid.,* p. 102.

[16] National Commission on the Causes and Prevention of Violence, *To Establish Justice, to Insure Domestic Tranquility* (New York: Bantam Books, 1970) p. 16.

[17] *Ibid.,* p. 21.

[18] *Ibid.*

[19] Uniform Crime Reports, 1968 (Washington, D.C.: U.S. Government Printing Office, 1969).

[20] *Ibid.,* p. 20.

[21] Brant F. Steele and Carl B. Pollock, "A Psychiatric Study of Parents Who Abuse Infants and Small Children," in R. Helfer and C. Henry Kempe, eds., *The Battered Child* (Chicago: University of Chicago Press, 1968) pp. 103–113.

[22] Malcolm W. Klein, "Violence in American Juvenile Gangs," in Mulvihill and Tumin, eds., *op. cit.* pp. 1444–45.

[23] James F. Kirkham, Sheldon G. Levy and William J. Crotty, eds., *Assassination and Political Violence,* staff report submitted to the National Commission on the Causes and Prevention of Violence, (Washington, D.C., United States Government Printing Office, 1969) pp. 163–166.

[24] *Ibid.*

[25] *Ibid.*

[26] Skolnick, *op. cit.,* p. 150.

[27] *Ibid.*

[28] National Commission, *op. cit.,* p. 160.

[29] *Ibid.,* pp. 161–166.

[30] *Ibid.*

[31] Jackson Toby, "Violence and the Masculine Ideal: Some Qualitative Data," *The Annals of the American Academy of Political and Social Science,* Vol. 364, 1966, p. 22.

[32] *Associated Press Almanac* (New York: Almanac Publishing, 1973) p. 147.

[33] National Commission, *op. cit.,* pp. 231–232.

[34] Margaret Mead, "Alternatives to War," in *War: The Anthropology of Armed Conflict and Aggression* (New York: Natural History Press, 1968) p. 224.

Summary

After the civil disorders and rising rates of violent crime of the 1960s, the violence of American history began to seem more characteristic of the country than its periods of social peace. The social disorder spawned by violence and the large number of persons affected by it—from suicide on the one hand to war on the other—warranted its emergence into the public consciousness as a social problem of importance.

Violence occurs in almost every human society. Various theories have arisen to explain its persistence. Biological theories of violence stipulate that man's violence is instinctive, as is the violent behavior of animals, or that it is caused by genetic irregularities. The frustration-aggression theory posed by psychologists traces violence to the frustration of purposeful activity. Psychological character, made up both of inborn and experiential elements, is also held to explain the violence of certain individuals. Anthropologists, in accounting for violence, stress the differing cultural norms which govern the functioning of one group within a society as against another. Although sociologists draw on many of these theories in explaining violence, they focus primarily on the social environment as the cause of violent behavior, seeing in friction between classes, discrimination and other social factors the keys to violent behavior.

Suicide in the United States has not increased markedly in recent years, though regional differentials may indicate it to be more characteristic of areas with fewer traditional social bonds of family and community (supporting Durkheim's characterization of some suicide as resulting from lack of integration within a society.)

The rates of violent crime—rape, robbery, aggravated assault and homicide—have recently risen alarmingly. For psychological, social and legal reasons, rape is probably significantly underreported. Violent crime occurs most often in large cities, though again there are regional differences. There is a significantly higher rate of homicide in the south, for instance, than in other regions. Most of the violent crimes in the cities are committed by poor and uneducated young men, and are disproportionately centered in ghetto areas. Accordingly, arrest rates for blacks are considerably higher than for whites. Studies have shown that the racial and other characteristics of most victims are similar to those of their attackers.

Family violence is also widespread in American society. The close ties of a family sometimes make its members unwilling or unable either to escape or to submit during an argument, and violence results. Child abuse seems to have much to do with the way parents were treated when they themselves were children. Parents who were abused abuse their children. Changing attitudes to parental authority over children have increased awareness of child abuse as a social problem.

The group violence of juvenile gangs is primarily an urban, lower-class phenomenon. Gang organization appears to compensate for social disadvantages by providing opportunities for adolescent achievement of self-esteem, self-expression and status.

Political assassination, although it has significantly altered our history over the last century, seems in America to be most often the work of disturbed individuals, rather than a feature of the American political system. The civil violence of ghetto riots, however, has been viewed as an explosion of black rage against victimization by a white-controlled social and political system. Preceded by the nonviolent protests of the Civil Rights Movement primarily directed against these same abuses, the riots were paralleled first by nonviolent, and later by violent protest against American involvement in violence abroad, the Vietnam war. In some instances the violence of such demonstrations was perpetrated by police, who possess society's authority to commit violence in pursuit of public order.

Violence by legally constituted authority, including war, the most institutionalized of modes of violence, has dominated recent history and, indirectly, American society. The imperatives of a society at war, which sometimes contribute to social cohesion, in the 1960s had the opposite effect. Mass media broadcasts of violence, both in news-related and entertainment programming, may have had the effect of desensitizing many Americans to the effects of violence, thus creating more tolerance for violent behavior when it occurred but was not personally felt. Social conventions which connect violence and manliness may also contribute to indifference to violence. Alienated from society's mainstream, denied the accepted "masculine" role characterized by physical prowess or material success, many choose violence as a means of proving masculinity. The large-scale American commitment to individual ownership of firearms is based partly on an interpretation of the Constitution, partly on a tradition of individualism and self-defense. Private ownership of guns, unregulated by the law, has recently been criticized by many as promoting violence. Moves against violence include policies of gun control, the lessening of violence in broadcast programming, and efforts to involve the poor and racial minorities more closely in the society by means of work programs and changes in other social attitudes.

chapter

sexuality

In dealing with social conduct, sociologists speak of "norms," meaning types of behavior not only approved of and legally sanctioned, but presumably practiced by the vast majority of the society. However, in the realm of sexual behavior, every teenager growing up in America becomes aware that practice varies widely from precept.

By way of illustrating this, it is only necessary to cite one primary "norm" of Western society: that sexual intercourse take place only between a female and a male legally married to one another. The number of deviants from this norm, or individuals engaging in nonconforming sexual behavior at one time or another in their lives, constitutes a majority of the population.

This may indeed have always been the case, but certainly in the years since World War I, American society has increasingly been engaged in a discussion and reassessment of its sexual norms. Sexuality has been accepted as a suitable topic for debate from the pulpit and podium, in the popular press and the mass media. The new outlook has been guided and directed by a steadily swelling stream of scientific investigations into sexual conduct and its motivations.

The new tolerance reflects in part the organized attempts by deviants themselves to win social and legal recognition; more importantly, it reflects changes in society itself. In the twentieth century, with a greater proportion of the population living in urban centers, individuals are less subject to the pressures of conformity that have historically been enforced in folk and small-town communities. The rising literacy level has similarly led to a greater degree of open-mindedness and understanding, two world wars have contributed to the breakdown of traditional values, and the changes in social structure wrought by industrialization and greater affluence lessen blind adherence to established codes. Widespread acceptance of Freudian psychology, with its concept of sexual desire as normal and natural, has led to less guilt, shame and embarrassment in the discussion and expression of that desire. Because of these recent developments, it is crucial that we reexamine the norms that have guided sexual conduct; in many instances, current legal restrictions seem out of step with social attitudes.

Attitudes toward sex in America

The twentieth century has rebelled against the Victorian ideal of sexual love only within marriage. The Victorians have been criticized, not so much for this ideal, but for the double standard and hypocrisy which living up to the ideal entailed. While "good" women were considered virtuous and free from physical cravings, men were recognized to have strong and not necessarily licit desires. Hence, in order to protect the good women and sanctity of the home, prostitution was tolerated and condoned in Europe, Great Britain and the United States.

Sexuality and industrialization

Victorian morality was essentially a middle-class phenomenon, a barrier thrown up to protect individuals against pressures of rapidly industrializing society. As Arno Karlen observes in his history of *Sexuality and Homosexuality,* mill girls in factory towns were often forced to prostitute themselves to their employers if they wished to keep their jobs.[1] The way out of situations of this sort was the control of impulses, even under provocation, so that one's reputation as a "good woman" guaranteed a position in the lower middle class, at least.

The greater mobility and freedom of frontier society in America provided some alternatives. Although prostitutes in Eastern cities with "red-light" districts were looked down upon and socially ostracized, in the West "bad" women, as the first settlers, sometimes enjoyed unprecedented prestige. Between 1860 and 1875, in Virginia City, Nevada, the great silver boom town, ladies of easy virtue were the only ladies in town. They assumed integral roles in community life, nursing the sick, doing charity work and organizing picnics and parades. Only after the arrival of respectable wives and schoolmarms in the late 1870s were informal pressures exerted to drive the painted ladies out of community affairs.[2]

Certain nineteenth century religious communities also sought to channel or restrict the sexual drive. The Shakers practiced celibacy, with males and females segregated in separate dormitories.[3] The Oneida Community of John Humphrey Noyes engaged in free love, or rather a strictly regulated form of intercourse between unmarried members of the community.[4] The Mormons who settled Salt Lake City legalized polygamy, but were forced to repeal it to enable Utah to become a state.

Pornography, like prostitution, was technically illegal—and flourished. Although the existence of homosexuality in America is not widely documented, it apparently existed—among other reasons, because in frontier societies so few women were around. Homosexuality, in fact, was known to exist not only throughout Europe but also, according to travelers' memoirs, in the Near East, Far East and in primitive societies. The laws in Western Europe and America condemning it were essentially carryovers from medieval canon law, which had condemned not only "sodomy" but every other "crime against nature," including masturbation.

The modern era

The first scholarly examination of Victorian sexual behavior began in the latter half of the era with the studies of Richard von Krafft-Ebbing, Havelock Ellis and Sigmund Freud. Coincident with some of this work were the social and technological upheavals that exerted a liberalizing force on that behavior. In the years after World War I, women became "emancipated," seeking jobs outside the home, cutting their hair, smoking and drinking like men and demanding an end to the double standard. The introduction of the automobile provided for the first time an all-weather living room, secure from prying eyes of parents and neighbors. Cheap and effective contraceptives for both men and women became widely available. Yet, for all the talk of emancipation, it was hard to tell how many men and women were altering their traditional patterns of sexual behavior.

The uninhibited atmosphere of the 1920s was in part a by-product of its affluence, and with the coming of the Great Depression, something of a reaction set in. With many men unemployed and their wives forced to take menial jobs to support the family, traditional roles of the sexes were often reversed. Nevertheless, books and movies of the period eulogized romantic, conjugal love. During World War II, a comparable situation prevailed. The reality was that families were parted, servicemen overseas engaged in casual affairs and prostitution near Army bases increased. All the same, national interest dictated that popular literature and movies celebrate hearth and home, portraying men and women alike displaying undying fidelity.

The postwar era saw the publication of Alfred Kinsey's studies of sexual behavior in the American male (1948) and female (1953). For the first time, Americans were given a statistical picture of the activities they actually engaged in—and the statistics were startling.

Regardless of the moral and legal strictures against such practices, nearly half of American females had engaged in premarital coitus;[5] fully 37 percent of the men had experienced homosexual contact to orgasm;[6] 69 percent of the men had patronized prostitutes.[7]

Kinsey's studies were greeted with a barrage of criticism, most of it purely emotional but some of it based on legitimate scientific arguments. It had been difficult for him and his colleagues at the Institute for Sex Research in Indiana to find subjects to interview. The method he used to get a cross section of the population was to approach leaders of community organizations and persuade them to enlist the cooperation of their memberships. Thus, as the sociologist Ira Reiss has pointed out, in the upper-class level, Kinsey's samplings are heavily weighted with the kind of people who join voluntary organizations—the PTA, church groups and so forth. Their attitudes towards sex may be somewhat more conservative than the attitudes of nonjoiners in the same social class. For lower-class samplings, on the other hand, Kinsey was forced to rely heavily on prison populations—a segment well known to be more heavily permissive.[8]

Kinsey's findings may therefore not represent a totally accurate picture. Nonetheless, considering the problems he encountered, it is remarkable that his studies were as comprehensive and informative as they were. Since their publication, behavioral scientists and sociologists attempting to improve on Kinsey's methods have produced new material. Meanwhile in the public arena, debate over just what constitutes permissible nonconforming behavior has increased.

Pornography

One of the greatest controversies in the area of sexual permissiveness has concerned the publication or public performance of sexually explicit books, magazines, plays and films. From prehistoric times, man has sought to depict and comment upon human sexuality, whether in the form of Paleolithic fertility images, the Kama Sutra or ribald comedies by Aristophanes. Throughout most of human history, such activity has been more or less unchecked by legal authorities. Even the ecclesiastical censorship of the Roman Catholic Church before and during the Reformation was concerned primarily with the suppression of sacreligious and anticlerical expressions of sentiment.

Only toward the beginning of the nineteenth century did the common law of England evolve to the stage where it began to be applied in some cases to prohibit purely sexual works that did not attack or libel religious institutions. Obscenity legislation was first enacted in England as part of the Vagrancy Act of 1824, which outlawed exposing an obscene book or print in public places. More extreme prohibitions were enacted in 1853 and 1857. In America, which derives its common law from England, no legislation was enacted before the nineteenth century except in Massachusetts in

1711. There were no prosecutions under this statute until 1821, when a publisher of *Fanny Hill* was found guilty of disobeying it.

Legal attitudes

The nineteenth century, with its Victorian crusaders active in such organizations as the Committee for the Suppression of Vice, witnessed the growth of legal prohibitions in the United States as well as in England. Federal laws enacted in 1842 and 1865, and broadened in 1873, prohibited both the importation of obscene publications and their dissemination through the mails. By the end of the century, some thirty additional states had statutes. In all cases, the definition of "obscene" was based on an 1868 English ruling, where a magistrate named Hicklin defined the test of obscenity as:

> Whether the tendency of the matter charged as obscenity is to deprave and corrupt those whose minds are open to such immoral influences, and into whose hands a publication of this sort may fall.[9]

In the twentieth century, United States judges began redefining "obscenity" and broadening the range of permissible literature. As early as 1913, Supreme Court Justice Learned Hand was already questioning the Hicklin test, noting that:

> However consonant it may be with mid-Victorian morality, [it] does not seem to me to answer to the understanding and morality of the present time.[10]

In 1933, the United States District Court Judge John Woolsey issued significant new guidelines when he permitted the publication of James Joyce's *Ulysses*. In rejecting the "most susceptible persons" aspect of the Hicklin rule, he became the first to argue that the objective effect of a work should be determined by its effect on "the average person." Moreover, he was the first to take the literary quality of the book into consideration. He wrote that:

> In *Ulysses,* in spite of its unusual frankness, I do not detect anywhere the leer of the sensualist. I hold, therefore, that it is not pornographic.[11]

In 1957, the United States Supreme Court, incorporating the important portions of the Woolsey ruling, issued the first broad guidelines concerning obscenity. Material was actionable if:

> to the average person, applying contemporary community standards, the dominant theme of the material taken as a whole appeals to prurient interest . . . (and is) utterly without redeeming social importance.[12]

In the decade that followed, further rulings limited the definition of obscenity still more rigidly. In 1959, the state of New York attempted to prohibit the showing of the movie, *Lady Chatterly's Lover,* on the grounds that the theme was immoral. The Court said the film could be shown, because forbidding "ideological or thematic obscenity" was unconstitutional.

In 1964, the Court faced the question of defining "contemporary community standards." The state of Ohio had tried to prohibit the showing of *Les Amants,* a French picture that had been widely exhibited (and acclaimed) elsewhere. The Court held that national, not local, standards were applicable and the picture could be shown. In 1966, the Court added a further limitation to the definition of obscenity. In permitting the publication (at long last) of *Fanny Hill,* it ruled that to be considered obscene, material must be not only "prurient" but also "patently offensive."

Given not only the increased liberality of the Court, but also the widening measure of public acceptance, books, magazines, Broadway plays and movies sought to portray nudity and sexual behavior more explicitly than ever before. Local citizens' groups complained of the swelling volume of "hard-core" pornographic magazines and sex exploitation films. Such forms of erotica customarily avoided the possibilities of legal action by including texts or sound tracks of "educational" value. This enabled their owners and promoters to claim "redeeming social importance."

The national commission

Finally, in 1967, declaring the traffic in obscenity and pornography to be "a matter of national concern," Congress appointed a National Commission to investigate "the gravity of the situation and determine whether more effective methods should be devised to control the transmission of such materials."[13] When the Commission rendered its report in 1970, its findings must have come as a surprise to many Congressmen. Far from recommending more effective methods of control, the Commission advocated fewer and less stringent ones. It based its case on one of the first genuinely thorough and scientific studies of pornography's social and psychological effects.

The Commission found that, despite legal prohibitions, the vast majority of United States citizens had access to sexually explicit material—with no apparent harm to themselves or society at large. Approximately 85 percent of adult men and 70 percent of adult women, the Commission reported, had been exposed at one time or another to pornography. From one-fifth to one-quarter of the adult male population had had somewhat regular experience with materials as explicit as the depiction of heterosexual intercourse.[14]

Citizens themselves, when interviewed, were ambivalent over what they considered to be the effects of such exposure. They believed that sexual materials, for example, could lead both to moral breakdown and to improved sexual relations between married couples. However, individuals were more likely to report having personally experienced desirable rather than undesirable effects.[15] Surveys of psychiatrists, psychologists, sex educators, social workers, counselors and similar professionals conducted by the Commission revealed that large majorities of such groups believed that sexual materials were not harmful to either adults or adolescents. On the other hand, a survey of police chiefs found that 58 percent believed that obscene books played a significant role in causing juvenile delinquency.[16]

The evidence examined by the Commission did not support this belief. In Denmark, where laws regarding the sale of pornography had been greatly liberalized, analysis of Copenhagen police records showed a "dramatic" decrease in reported sex crimes.[17] Statistical analysis of such records for the United States provided a more complex picture. During the period when there had been a marked increase in the availability of erotic materials, some specific rates of arrest for sex crimes had increased (forcible rape, for instance) and others had declined. In sum, the Commission concluded:

> The massive overall increases in sex crimes that have been alleged do not seem to have occurred.[18]

In examining the reasons for the popularity of pornography, the Commission found that a large majority of sex counselors and educators felt that adolescents turned to such material out of a perfectly healthy curiosity. If sex education programs in schools, homes and churches were to provide more adequate information, the interest in pornography would be reduced. Accordingly, the Commission recommended that a massive "sex education effort" be launched, and that "federal, state and local legislation prohibiting the sale, exhibition or distribution of sexual materials to consenting adults should be repealed." Restrictions prohibiting sales to young people and guarding adults against undesired solicitation (through advertising mailers) should be kept.[19]

Congress did not act upon the recommendations of the Commission, and in 1973, the Supreme Court, in a series of five decisions, offered broader definitions of obscenity, rather than narrower ones. Reversing the 1964 ruling on *Les Amants,* the Supreme Court held that "community standards" could mean the local community in which books are sold or movies shown.[20] The way thus became open for state and local authorities to challenge nationally distributed publications and films.

It is still too early to tell to what extent the promulgation of explicit sexual materials will be limited by the Court's 1973 decisions. Public opinion obviously remains divided on the issue.

Sexual permissiveness

The commonest form of sexual deviance, or nonconforming sexual behavior, is intercourse between a male and female not married to one another. To read the popular magazines of the day, one might conclude that—especially among young, unmarried people—everybody engages in this particular form of deviance. Yet how recent and widespread is the "sexual revolution" in reality?

The ideal of chastity before marriage has always been accorded more deference in principle than in practice. In folk societies, especially in northern Europe, older people frequently overlooked or even encouraged the engaged couple who consummated their relationship before the church ceremony; a pregnant bride was looked upon as a sign that the marriage would be fruitful. As long as the man was ready and able to marry his pregnant girlfriend, premarital permissiveness did not act against the social goal of the creation of homes for rearing the young.

The twentieth century's development of contraceptives and the acceptance of the Freudian belief that sexual expression is desirable in itself have seemingly broadened the opportunities and incentives for premarital sex. However, the traditional belief in sex only with or as a prelude to marriage is deeply ingrained, not only in external strictures but also in internal codes. It is allied to the Judaeo-Christian, and more especially Puritan, belief that only sexual experience conducted between two people in love is important or socially valuable.

Surveys of permissiveness

Statistical surveys vary widely in their assessment of the situation. Kinsey found that nearly 50 percent of American women had engaged in premarital coitus. Sociologist Robert Sorenson, in his 1973 study, *Adolescent Sexuality in Contemporary America,* found that 72 percent of the boys and 57 percent of the girls between the ages of 16 and 19 that he interviewed said they were not virgins.[21] On the other hand, the sociologists Harold T. Christensen and Christina F. Gregg found a less extensive pattern. In 1968, they interviewed students at three colleges: a conservative Mormon college in the western United States; a moderately liberal middle western college; and a liberal college in Denmark, where the society is known for permissiveness. In the western college, they found only 37 percent of the males with premarital coitus experience and 32 percent of the females. In the middle western college, 50 percent of the males and 34 percent of the females had such experience. In Denmark, the figures were 95 percent and 97 percent.[22]

Various explanations for the wide discrepancies in the statistics can be advanced; most of them center on the variance in conduct and attitudes of different segments of the population. Ira Reiss has correlated attitudes on sexual conduct with other characteristics and related attitudes on conduct in general. He found no parallel between social class and sexual permissiveness; instead, Reiss found that persons who were divorced, infrequent churchgoers or Jewish, living in towns of 100,000 or more, low on romantic beliefs, living in New England or the Middle Atlantic region and believing that their standards did not apply to others were more likely to have liberal sexual attitudes regardless of their level of education.[23]

Obviously, the trend toward city living and the decline in national church attendance have to some extent been related to the overall increase in permissiveness. Although statistics may vary on the actual extent of premarital sexual activity, they agree on the direction of the trend. Kinsey found that among females in his sampling born before 1900, less than half as many had had premarital coitus as among females born in any subsequent decade.[24] Christensen and Gregg, whose 1968 survey was preceded by a similar study in 1958 at the same three colleges, found that the percentage of males with premarital sexual experience remained stable. However, the percentage of females with such experience had tripled at the western college, nearly doubled in the middle western college and even in Denmark increased by 50 percent.[25]

Thus it appears that the first wave of "emancipation" did in fact occur with the generation of women who came to maturity after World War I. The second wave occurred in the 1960s. For men, the change in women's attitudes has primarily meant a change in the types of partners.

More tolerant attitudes on the part of parents must to some extent contribute to the change, although not all parents are equally permissive. The surprisingly broad extent of experience revealed by the Sorensen study, for example, may be somewhat weighted by the fact that out of his initial selection of 839 adolescents only 508 sets of parents gave consent to have their children interviewed.[26] It can be argued that the parents who refused were probably less permissive in their attitudes—and their children correspondingly less experienced.

Contemporary America has escalated depersonalized sex almost as though it were resisting sexual intimacy for those who could benefit from it. . . . A father is often seen as one who will very likely reject a sexual experience for his daughter but will not reject his daughter's exposure to a movie replete with sexual sadism or his son's military indoctrination to kill. In this context, sex has become a social issue with many adolescents who indulge in sex not to combat parents or society but to seek intimate personal relationships.

Robert C. Sorensen

Other factors play a role in the changing situation. Seeking to combat the decline in church attendance, progressive clergymen are beginning to take a less restrictive attitude. Another important development has been the introduction of the birth control pill. A third consideration has been a growing rejection of conventional middle-class values by many members of the younger generation who believe that love can be better expressed in a free union, or even that sex itself can be undertaken without a need for permanent commitment or deep emotional engagement.

Christensen and Gregg asked their subjects to what extent they believed it necessary to be engaged or feel a strong affection for their sexual partners. As measured by Christensen and Gregg, the percentages had lessened in the decade.[27]

Evidence of the new life-styles favored by the young are the communes, where unmarried groups of males and females live together, or the "swinging singles" complexes of apartment houses in some parts of the country. Coeducational dormitories are a recent innovation on college campuses, although this does not mean that all college students actually share beds or rooms with members of the opposite sex. Many young adults in cities have begun to share apartments with roommates of either sex.

Swinging

The younger generation's attitude is conditioned by overall change, by sexually explicit movies, best-selling sex manuals and even advertisements that portray sexual situations with increasing candor. The increase in divorce rates, together with the greater sexual freedom permitted divorced persons by society, helps to create an atmosphere in which experimentation is encouraged. In addition, the past decade has seen the development—or at any rate, the mass media's discovery—of adulterous behavior sanctioned by marital partners and engaged in by both husbands and wives. These alternate patterns of more or less accepted conduct represent an attempt to incorporate the new approval of the need for sexual satisfaction into a society still organized around the nuclear family.

The practice of "swinging," consensual exchange of marital partners for sexual purposes, in theory affords husbands and wives a chance to find other sexual partners, yet still maintain the economic stability and social prestige of a household. In practice, swinging may not represent a radical departure from established norms. Extramarital experience by husbands, like premarital sex between engaged couples, has long been tacitly accepted by society as a way of ensuring the continuance of households. What is new in swinging is that wives are expected to join their husbands on the assumption that women need sexual satisfaction as much as men do. The assumption may not always be founded on fact. In a study of Toronto swingers by the Canadian sociologist Anne-Marie Henschel, 68 percent of the husbands had made the initial suggestion to swing.[28]

Swingers, while considering themselves "with it" or "where it's at," do not necessarily represent a cultural avant-garde in other aspects of their lives. In a study of group sex by "mid-Americans," sociologist Gilbert D. Bartell examined 280 swingers. He found that his subjects were often Republicans, with better than 40 percent Wallaceites (interviews were conducted during the 1968 Presidential campaign). The swingers were antiblack, strongly antihippie and opposed to the use of marijuana. When couples met to exchange partners at parties, mini-skirts and bell-bottomed trousers were avoided by the women, few beards were seen on the men and the stereo music was low-key fox trot, not infrequently Glenn Miller.[29]

By and large, while the twentieth century, and more especially the

1960s, have seen an increase in extramarital heterosexuality, it has expressed itself in various ways. For some sections of the population, it has meant greater freedom to explore personal relations and to reconcile the relationship between love and sex. But not everyone has adopted the new life-styles, totally or even in part. Every year, millions of young couples still fall in love, go steady and get married in a fashion not far removed from the tradition of their parents and grandparents.

Prostitution

Prostitution—"the world's oldest profession"—continues to flourish in an era when, theoretically, it should be out of date. For purposes of this discussion, a prostitute may be defined as a woman who accepts money in return for granting a man sexual favors. Although male prostitutes, who sell themselves to women, have likewise existed, they have been rare by comparison with female prostitutes. That in itself is an indication that the sociological phenomenon of prostitution is intimately related to the status of women in society.

Historical perspectives

In the nineteenth century, prostitution was condoned because single men had no outlet for their sexual drives with women of their own class. Married men might respect their wives but be unable to find sexual satisfaction with them. But today, in this period of "sexual revolution," single men should be able to have sex with "respectable" girls; frustrated married men presumably have other options—seek advice from sexologists, "swing" or get a divorce. Perhaps the fact that millions of American men still feel the need or desire to pay women for sexual favors illustrates that society is engaged in evolution, rather than revolution.

Certain aspects of prostitution, to be sure, have changed very markedly. There are, and always have been, two classes of prostitutes: the lowly streetwalker, or brothel inmate, who accepts "a trick" at a time, and the more elevated courtesan or mistress. In preindustrial societies, where a woman's means of finding a legitimate occupation outside of marriage or engaging in social or intellectual activities was limited, courtesans might enjoy relatively high social status. The *hetairae* of ancient Athens were among the best-educated women of Greece; they maintained salons distinguished for wit and intellectual inquiry to which philosophers and statesmen flocked. The mistresses of Louis XIV and Louis XV held official positions at the French Court, counseled their lovers in affairs of state and were fawned upon by courtiers eager for political advancement.

Prostitution has been legal in many countries and eras. It was often the "fallen woman's" only way of supporting herself. However, since the nineteenth century, prostitution has become increasingly outlawed—in France and Italy, specifically due to the pressure exerted by newly enfranchised women voters, who consider the profession demeaning and offensive. With women increasingly able to find other jobs and ways of achieving prominence in the arts and professions, both the economic incentives to engage in prostitution and the "glamor" of being a courtesan have lessened. Although the occasional high-class call girl, such as Christine Keeler or Xaviera Hollander, continues to make headlines, prostitutes are now more likely to be studied by psychologists and sociologists as "deviant" personalities. Research is directed toward finding out how and why they continue to constitute a sizeable subsection of the community.

As late as 1945, the Encyclopedia Americana estimated that there were perhaps 600,000 women in the United States engaged in prostitution as a full-time occupation, with another 600,000 women who could be categorized as occasional prostitutes.[30] This number was probably exaggerated by the period of wartime; there is consensus that men make use of prostitutes less now than in the early years of the century.

Kinsey found that the frequency of premarital sexual relations with prostitutes was more or less constantly lower in the younger generations he studied, at all educational levels. In most cases, the average frequencies of intercourse with prostitutes were down to two-thirds or even one-half of what they were in the previous generations. Kinsey attributed this decline to the extensive educational campaigns linking prostitution with venereal disease, plus the fact that police vigilance had largely eliminated organized "houses."[31]

In addition, the class of patrons today appears to be more predominantly lower class and lower middle class than was formerly the case. Author Vance Packard conducted a survey of 200 sexually experienced males at one university in 1966. Comparing his findings with Kinsey's 1940s figures, he found that the percentage of college-educated men who had patronized a prostitute by the age of 21 had decreased from 22 percent to 4 percent.[32]

Prostitutes and prostitution in modern America

Who are the prostitutes? In a study conducted in 1965 at three correctional institutions in Minnesota, sociologist Nanette J. Davis found that a history of familial instability was typical for sixteen of the seventeen white girls studied, and eight of the twelve blacks. Such instability included a drunken, violent or absentee parent (usually the father), extreme poverty or families larger than the parent could cope with. More than half of the informants had spent one year or more of their childhoods in foster homes, living with relatives or in other separations from the nuclear family.[33]

Prostitutes characteristically drift into "the life" in their early teens, having first engaged in a series of casual sexual experiences in which money was not a consideration. Frequently, they are initiated into prostitution by a boyfriend who wants to live off their earnings. While many prostitutes live with their pimps, and turn over a substantial portion of their earnings to him, lesbian relationships with women are also common. The lesbian prostitute finds that her sexual relations with men are depersonalized or exploitative, and turns to women for affection and tenderness.

Since prostitution in the United States is illegal, except in Nevada, prostitutes are subject to frequent police harassment and arrest. (By contrast, patrons of prostitutes, or "johns," are seldom liable.) For protection, prostitutes have traditionally relied on bribes to the police or turned to organized crime for support. However, the evidence does not suggest that at present big-league criminal organizations, such as organized crime, are affiliated with most prostitutes. The profits are too meager, the competition from amateurs too great.

The professional prostitute being a social outcast may be periodically punished without disturbing the usual course of society. . . . The man, however, is something more than partner in an immoral act: he discharges inportant social and business relations, is as father or brother responsible for the maintenance of others, has commercial or industrial duties to meet. He cannot be imprisoned without deranging society.

Abraham Flexner (1920)

If prostitution is less widespread than it used to be, at the same time it has—in the permissive atmosphere of the 1960s—become increasingly evident. Streetwalkers in Manhattan may be observed plying their trade on Park Avenue, and at conventions in most large cities it is not too difficult to make arrangements with "party girls." Many spokesmen for public opinion still find prostitution immoral and offensive and encourage police to crack down on it. On the other hand, a sizeable number of lawyers and criminologists argue that prostitution is a "crime without victims." Since it endangers neither property nor life, police could be more constructively occupied devoting their energies to serious crime. Criminologist Norval Morris has suggested that the United States would do well to follow the British example. In England, street solicitation is illegal, but prostitutes to satisfy all demands and purses are discreetly available to those who want them.[34]

---

reading: **Gail Sheehy**
REDPANTS AT THE BEGINNING

On the all-night Greyhound from Detroit to New York she changed professions six times. Beautician, salesgirl, cocktail waitress . . . then dreaming in loftier circles . . . dancer, fashion designer, model. As a pretty black girl in 1968 she was bringing up the rear of America's consumer ethic. Her expectations derived from television commercials. And from vacuous

Sidney Poitier movies and the promises after riots. If a pretty black girl puts her mind and body together and *gets down,* that is, insinuates her full powers on the unsuspecting city, here at the epicenter of a culture which celebrates killers and whores (so long as they can be exploited by the merchandisers and the media), well, Johnny, anything can happen. . . .

From the Port Authority building, she walked directly to Miss Dixie's Employment Agency in Times Square. A cardboard suitcase slapped against her long legs and she was feeling as reckless as a kite. They told her she could do day work.

When she came out of Miss Dixie's, he was in position. A voluptuous figure of a man, radiantly clothed and well-displayed against what looked like a metal rhinoceros (in fact it was a custom El Dorado with a Rolls-Royce front mounted with Texas steer horns). He was grinning.

"What you want to wash Whitey's floor for?"

"I'm a model, thank you." And she huffed off.

He was in the same spot the next day and the next. "How's the modeling business?" His arrogance was insufferable. She knew the type, a dope pusher, most likely. Yet for a black man so young, his prosperity was impressive. Fitted in the finest vines and kicks of the day, pepper silks and Alpaca fronts and Halloween socks matched to his half-gaiters, he lounged against his metal rhinoceros without a flicker of exertion. . . .

"Sugarman digs you, baby. Men are all suckers 'cause they looking to protect their glands. Women run this joint. A smart girl can make any man her bloodhound. Sugarman has nothin' but respect for a girl like you."

It takes her a while to understand that Sugarman always speaks of himself in the third person. By then the car is spinning through the East Side and he is doing his father-daughter routine. "Men have always roughed you around, right? If you was my girl I'd touch you like velvet, drink you like champagne. You could cry to Sugarman."

"I'm not interested in sex," she lies. "I need money."

He is in the modeling business himself, he says. "All the girls in my agency are white but—" he flips back her coat—"you shine like brass. Accordin' to Whitey's color scheme you'll pass, jus' fine. But you can't go out with Sugarman dressed like that!"

In the back room of an East Village boutique a small Indian man brings on a selection of exotic clothes. The girl swoons over the mirrored boleros and chooses a pair of crimson velvet pants. "I can cut the legs off when it gets hot."

"You know your assets, honey." Sugarman builds her up and up. "Legs is what a man looks for, not faces, and you got one *hellifying* pair of legs." He walks around her, mumbling, "Hey, I got you a professional name. Redpants."

"Quite so," the Indian man says. . . .

The Indian was what they call an easy trick, which is how the smart street pimp eases his girls into the trade. (It also pays for the clothes.) From there he drives Redpants up Third Avenue and introduces her to the rest of his stable.

"Say hello to Horseface, she's my French import. Rotten face but a body like creampuffs." Horseface is a pubescent girl from the Canadian provinces whom Sugarman recruited in Montreal. She smiles dumbly.

"This here's Kimp. She got four kids and she brought herself a big house in Philadelphia. I saw the deeds. Kimp, she comes to work for me and makes herself a coupla grand and stays away awhile, and comes back again. Got herself a husband now. He don't know nothin' about her professional life. But she came back to Sugarman, isn't that so?"

Kimp nods her red Marie Antoinette wig. She is about 35 and her face appears to be bolted over steel plates. Only one complaint from Kimp—her teenaged sons are beginning to ask what kind of work she does up in New York. "I tell them I work for the city."

Sugarman beckons Redpants across the hall of this modern high-rise in the Murray Hill section where he keeps his gals. He pays the $350 rent; two girls share an apartment and at least one generally has a child with her. He lives in a better pad on a higher floor but in the same building, for purposes of surveillance.

"Now you're gonna meet the hustlingest dame in Sugarman's agency. College girl, real class. She was a track star at this dum-dum nun's school of hers. She can outrun anybody—cars, cops, anybody 'cept Sugarman of course."

He rings. "Road Runner?"

A pair of dark eyes, painted beneath with zebra stripes, peer around the door. "Hello, you bastard. I'm busy."

A child is crying in the dimness behind Road Runner. The young woman is nude except for a Catholic medal on a chain.

"Redpants here needs employment." Sugarman spins the new girl around by the hair. "She's a model."

The eyes narrow in appraisal. How old? Is she clean? Any habit? Any experience on the street? Sugarman answers for his probationer, whose attention is wholly distracted by the apartment. Though sparsely furnished and humorless, it is, in the eyes of a girl from a rooming house in Detroit, the quintessence of glamor.

Road Runner reaches for the girl's cardboard suitcase. "I'll try her out in the Lindy tonight and see what she's got." The door shuts. . . .

In strong terms [Road Runner] lays out the philosophy:

The working girl is honest; the rest of the world is the con. Straight women exchange sex for financial security and the respected social status of marriage. You have no status, no power, and no way to get it except by using your snapper. You give it away, why? You're sitting on a gold mine! We prossies provide a product in more demand than the world's best-selling book. *Don't let life just happen to you.* Get out there and hustle for yourself!

The outlook of this once-Catholic refugee from the California suburbs is simply a direct application of American capitalism, circa 1960s: fast, aggressive, confident of the growth of urban lust and prepared to indulge it, manipulate it and cash in on it. . . .

Nothing in the room but a glass night lamp on a table and, set flat out under the windows like a cheap placemat, the bed. Above it rattle curtains of plastic brocade. Fluorescence intrudes; across the street is a block of windows framing eccentric postal workers at their night labors. Fixing on those windows, she bites down on the plastic brocade curtains and gives him fifteen minutes for 30 dollars.

Redpants learned the games of her trade very quickly.

The Badger Game. She lures a man up to a hotel room. As the pair disrobe, Sugarman bursts in taking the part of the outraged husband. She whimpers to the john that they both will be killed unless he hands over his money, which he usually does.

Variation on the Badger Game. Horseface and Kimp are waiting in the closet when Redpants enters with a trick. He pays in advance. When she has him wholly engaged, the other girls creep out and relieve his trousers of excess bills. "If he misses his bread, we'll jump him," Road Runner says. "If that doesn't work, cut him up a little."

Redpants balks at using her knife. "It's your insurance policy," the experienced hooker instructs. "These johns are all married men. They're going to have a hard enough time explaining a few blade marks when they get home. Even if they call the cops in the heat of the moment, they are never going to get up on that stand and tell the judge they got stung by three hookers in a hotel room. It's giving the wife a gift divorce case! Another thing, never forget the stud complex. These johns are jellyballs or they wouldn't be sniffing around chippies in the first place. They can't stand admitting women can get down and do raw deeds. . . ."

It gets in the blood. All night long peeking and hiding, zipping and lacing. Hustling bucks and ducking the Third Division boys, those earnest young plainclothesmen assigned to the vice squad who work out of the 17th Precinct on the East Side. The pace itself, the sheer velocity of risk, is a drug. And then a girl *controls* the situation with her tricks. (Not so in allied fields such as modeling and acting, Sugarman points out.) She sets the price and delivers the pleasure, or doesn't, pretending submission while all the time she is in control. Can it be sensed by anyone straight, the exhilaration of a young street hooker? If she is fast, and Redpants is very very fast, the payoff can never be duplicated. It gets in the blood like gambler's fever. . . .

From
"Redpants and Sugarman," by Gail Sheehy, in *New York Magazine,*
March 12, 1972.

Homosexuality

Another form of sexual deviance that has received extensive publicity within the last decade is homosexuality. A homosexual may be defined as a person feeling erotic attraction for persons of the same sex; homosexual desires may be experienced by a person whose primary orientation is heterosexual. The degree to which the individual acts out his desires or allows them to influence his life-style varies widely.

Kinsey found that 37 percent of the males in his sampling had at some point in their lives had homosexual experience to orgasm. However, the vast majority of these men practiced heterosexual behavior predominantly. Only 4 percent of white males were exclusively homosexual throughout their lives.[35] Psychoanalyst Robert Lindner similarly estimated the extent of "genuine inversion" in the United States at 4 to 6 percent of the male population.[36]

Female homosexuality, known as lesbianism, is thought to be only half as frequent as male homosexuality. Males also have more frequent homosexual experiences than females, continue their activities over a greater number of years and are more promiscuous.[37]

Since the Middle Ages, homosexuality has been regarded as a sin. American laws against fellatio, anal intercourse, cunnilingus and mutual masturbation (all included in the general category of "crimes against nature") represent carryovers from religious law. In theory, they apply to heterosexual relations as well, even between married persons. The Judeo-Christian opposition to "crimes against nature" stems from the principle that sex ought to occur only in the family context, for the purpose of begetting children.

The conventional nineteenth century Victorian looked down upon homosexuality with fear, disgust and anger. The psychological literature of the early twentieth century treated the homosexual as emotionally crippled. In recent years, more sympathetic studies have attempted to analyze the extent to which individual homosexuals are deviant only in their sexual behavior—the assumption being that other aspects of their lives conform to norms of social usefulness.

In addition to statutes specifically directed against deviant sexual practices, in force in every state except Illinois, homosexuals are liable to prosecution in all states for offenses such as lewdness, solicitation for unnatural copulation, vagrancy, loitering near a public toilet, procuring and prostitution (of a male by another male). Known homosexuals may be fired from their jobs and ostracized in small communities. The degree of acceptance is higher in large communities and in sophisticated intellectual circles where individuality of any sort is respected. Accordingly, since the mid-nineteenth century, cosmopolitan centers in both Europe and America have had certain quarters and meetingplaces—bars, pubs, restaurants and nightclubs—where homosexuals may congregate and live "the gay life."

Popular opinion has held to a stereotype of the male homosexual: a mincing, flamboyantly dressed person with "artistic" predilections. Scholarly research, however, indicates that not all homosexuals conform to the stereotype. Either for reasons of personal preference or for fear of social castigation, most dress and act much like other men. Sociologists Maurice Leznoff and William A. Westley studied sixty homosexuals in a large Canadian city. On the basis of their findings they were able to describe the characteristics of both secret and overt homosexuals in the area. Leznoff and Westley reported:

> The mode of adaptation is largely dependent upon the extent to which identification of the individual as a homosexual is a status threat. . . . Thus, there are many occupations, of which the professions are an obvious example, where homosexuals are not tolerated. In other areas, the particular occupation may have traditionally accepted homosexual linkages in the popular image or be of such low rank as to permit homosexuals to function on the job. The artist, the interior decorator, and the hairdresser exemplify the former type; such positions as counter-man or bellhop, the latter. Thus we find a rough relationship between form of evasion and occupation. The overt homosexual tends to fit into an occupation of low status rank; the secret homosexual into an occupation with a relatively high status rank.[38]

What makes a homosexual? Arno Karlen, in *Sexuality and Homosexuality,* surveys the various explanations, including genetic, biological, psychological and sociopsychological. There is little evidence that genetics are the cause.[39] Prenatal factors, either genetic, gonadal or hormonal, can cause individuals to be born with imperfectly formed sex organs—for example, a genetic female possessing both ovaries and testicles. However, such a child identified by the parents at birth as a girl will grow up thinking and acting like a normal woman.

In considering the small number of transsexuals, that is, individuals who had undergone operations to achieve a change in sex, Karlen relies on the findings of Dr. Harry Benjamin, the endocrinologist and author of *The Transsexual Phenomenon*. Karlen found that:

> In most cases, the male transsexual is physically normal, without disorders of the genes, hormones or sex organs. But he believes that he is a woman. . . . He probably had strong feelings of being a female early in life.[40]

By contrast, the male homosexual is reared by a family that thinks of him as a boy—although commonly in homes with parents suffering from severe emotional problems. Dr. George Henry's 1941 study, *Sex Variants*, chronicled the case histories of eighty homosexuals, half of them male, half of them female. In both cases, sexual education was ignored or implicitly rejected; mothers were often found to be stiff, unhappy and reserved—yet also domineering and overprotective; and fathers were angry and destructive, or else negative, withdrawn ciphers. Both parents usually fought each other to win the affection of the child.[41]

Not all children growing up in such circumstances, however, become homosexuals, and many changes in social attitude have occurred since Henry's study. Further research is needed, and is being done, to find specific factors that lead a child to identify more strongly with the parent of the opposite sex than his own. It is increasingly thought that social as well as psychological factors are important. The homosexual characteristically discovers his deviant erotic direction in puberty or adolescence. Sociologist Barry M. Dank, in studying fifty-five admitted homosexuals, found that on the average, there was a six-year interval between the time of first sexual feelings toward a person of the same sex and the decision that one was a homosexual. This decision is known as "coming out."[42]

Dank studied the circumstances under which individuals "came out." He found that 50 percent did so while associating with other homosexuals: in bars, at private parties or in single-sex situations that provide convenient locales for homosexual activities, such as the life of prisons, mental homes, and the military services or public men's rooms. Another 15 percent discovered their true identity while reading about homosexuality.[43]

It is during the period of "coming out" that sociocultural factors, as opposed to psychological ones, play a key role in the homosexual's development. The period of "coming out," as the sociologists William Simon and John A. Gagnon note, is apt to be the period:

> that many homosexuals go through a crisis of femininity; that is, they "act

out" in public places in a somewhat effeminate manner; and some, in a transitory fashion, wear female clothing, known in the homosexual argot as "going in drag."[44]

It is during this period, usually when the homosexual is between the ages of 16 and 30, that he is most likely to become a member of the homosexual subcommunity. This is known as "secondary deviance," rather than "primary deviance." As defined by the sociologist, Edwin Lemert,

> secondary deviance refers to a special class of socially defined responses, which people make to problems created by the societal reaction to their deviance.[45]

Although America as a whole places a high premium on youth, the homosexual undergoes "the crisis of aging" at an even earlier age than the heterosexual. Homosexuals over 40 are often derisively known as "aunties" and have difficulties in finding partners. Moreover, as they move up the social ladder, homosexuals are apt to become progressively more conservative about revealing their deviance. They are more apt to prefer the atmosphere of private parties to that of the "gay" bar, more likely to refuse to recognize overtly homosexual friends they meet on the street.

In these respects the case of the transvestite parallels that of nontransvestite homosexuals. As described by the anthropologist Esther Newton in *Mother Camp*, transvestites fall into two classes: amateur "street fairies," who are usually young and wear effeminate garb in public, and professional female impersonators. The latter, frequently older men, wear "full drag" only while doing their acts in gay bars or nightclubs. Offstage, they dress in casual sports clothes and avoid being seen with obviously effeminate men.[46]

If many male homosexuals therefore fail to capture the public eye, lesbianism is even less conspicuous. While some female homosexuals affect the role of "butch" or "bull-dyke," with mannish clothes and straight, short hair, the vast majority prefer the role of "femme," dressing and acting like ordinary women. Lesbians patronize their own gay bars, but to a lesser extent than male homosexuals patronize theirs. Rather than seeking a variety of casual sexual encounters, they are more apt to fall in love with another woman and set up a more or less stable "home."

Only in Spain, Austria and the state of Georgia are lesbian activities specifically legislated against, and lesbians are not prosecuted to the same extent as men. This tendency has been variously interpreted. Some authorities see it as a sign that male homosexuality, with its rejection of the dominant, aggressive personality typically thought "male," constitutes more of a threat to established modes of social behavior. Others, however, say it is simply evidence that society is in general less concerned with protecting or defining the status of women.

The twentieth century as a whole and the postwar years in

particular have witnessed both the growth of literature depicting the homosexual condition sympathetically and organized attempts to gain legal and social respectability for homosexuals. The most publicized protest has been that created by homosexuals themselves, through such organizations as the Mattachine Society, the Gay Activists' Alliance and the Daughters of Bilitis. On June 27, 1971, some 5000 homosexuals marched uptown through Manhattan to Central Park to demonstrate "Gay Power." Not only were adult homosexual organizations represented, but also college campus organizations, including those from Harvard, Columbia, Rutgers and Penn State.[47]

Homosexuality is only part of the frequently tragic search for real experience in a world which, to many people seems to have been stripped of all that once supported their humanity from outside. Man stands alone now; class, rank, family, even the fundamental sex role no longer props him up. He must choose the very basis of his existence.

Hendrik M. Ruitenbeek

In 1967, Britain's Parliament, by an overwhelming majority, repealed the ancient statute making homosexuality between consenting adults a criminal offense. The decision was based in large measure upon the recommendations of the Wolfenden Commission's 1957 report, which argued that crime was not the same as sin. Britain's laws were thus brought into conformity with those of other European countries regarding this issue. The decade between the Wolfenden report and the change in the law indicates, however, that such changes of attitude in society are not instantaneous. As yet, legal changes in America have been minimal.

reading: David McReynolds
PUBLIC THOUGHTS ON PRIVATE MATTERS

Months ago, . . . I had decided, for reasons that remain as mysterious to me as the seasons, that I had to make public the fact that I am homosexual. Originally, I was simply going to "drop the remark" into a longer political article, noting that times had changed so greatly that I could deal with my own sexual life thus briefly. But things are not, after all, that easy. . . .

I have a hunch that younger people will not even grasp my qualms at this point—and they will be right—for they have not yet confused a concern with honesty and directness with a concern for preserving an organization committed to honesty and directness. . . .

It is not, of course, that I have been dishonest. There is not a single one of my friends who is unaware that I am queer. . . . The entire matter of my queerness would be much safer to discuss if I were not *really* queer, but neatly repressed, confessing to a life of sin buried in the past. Happily for me, but perhaps not so happily for those groups with which I am associated, I am an active, unsublimated homosexual whose private life is such that it entitles me to something close to an infinity of prison terms. I am a walking ton of potential prison terms. I come into your church to talk to your youth about morality, and they have a right to have the goods on me. If the law is no damn good (and, in this case, it is neither good nor effective—I feel no guilt at all for my sexual conduct, which is everywhere illegal except in Illinois—yet often feel tremendous guilt for being lazy, wasting time, and so forth, activities that are everywhere legal, including Illinois), let us violate it with a certain honesty. And I do not find it honest to let my personal friends and working associates know I am queer, while keeping that fact a secret from those to whom it might matter most deeply as they seek to evaluate my advice and counsel—the youth I urge on to action against this government. My life must be all of a piece, or it is shoddy.

As for the argument that every man's private life is his own to live as he chooses, I am not sure that applies to public figures, and I know it does not apply to a pacifist who believes in truth and honesty. I have to say to you, the congregation of men and women that I encounter day by day, that I will be perfectly happy to live my sexual life in secret at such time as it is legal, but it is impossible for me, finally, to continue to play a game which makes me a kind of Establishment Queer, keeping silent in public because I know I shall be left alone in private. . . .

How do I explain that I am not sophisticated, but part of Middle America; that my religious life began in the fundamentalism of the Baptist Church and the temperance movement; that I am part of that America that elected Nixon; that my grandparents, still alive, came to California from Kansas by covered wagon at the turn of the century; that my great-grandmother was an evangelist to the Mexicans, and my father and grandfather are both colonels; that I was not raised on Dr. Spock; that I am of American stock so old and proper, even in its poverty, that my late aunt Ettamae was the first of the family ever to be divorced; that no one smoked, and the family was privately scandalized because my aunt Alice and uncle Don were known to serve an occasional glass of port to friends and had once even offered it to Grandfather?

That is my own universe, where I was the first-born child on both sides of the family, destined to be all those things the first child of two large families must be, and becoming instead pacifist, socialist, and queer. . . . To put this in writing is almost to mock my ancestors, but, much more, it is to be cut off from the generations to come. Some will understand. Most will not.

The homosexual minority is different from any other. It is a basic mistake to think of the queer as another variety of Negro, Catholic, or Jew. Other minorities are visible. Blacks stand out, can be segregated, kept from certain jobs. Even Catholics and Jews *choose to be identified*. We know these minorities because of which holy days they take off, which food they eat and which they forego. Of course, Jews and Catholics can "pass" into the general population, and blacks cannot, but, if Jews and Catholics "pass," they have been assimilated and cease being Jews and Catholics.

Now we come to queers. Everyone—hopefully—realizes by now that most queers are not obvious. . . . With the exception of a small handful of homosexuals, we are invisible. We are not black. We eat fish on Friday. Pork doesn't bother us. We wear no yarmulke, no cross. There is literally no personality test most of us could not pass. Therefore, we are unique as a minority. We are—in five out of six cases—absolutely normal in appearance, invisible, omnipresent, occurring in upper and lower classes, among blacks, Jews, Catholics, Puerto Ricans, and so forth. (With the exception, it seems, of the Asians, among whom I have, in this country, encountered few homosexuals.) We do not, contrary to belief, even recognize each other on the street by some secret sign. Often, it is only in the bar that we meet an old high school or college friend and turn, saying, "My God, Frank! I never thought I'd see you here!"

463   Some of the militant gay kids think the cause of queers *must* be linked with that of blacks, because "if they can cut down the blacks now, they'll get us later." Nonsense. Homosexuals have survived the most rigorous of persecutions without difficulty. It turns out we always have friends in very high places. The brotherhood touches everywhere. One supports black liberation because it is moral and right to do so, but never because these two minorities are almost the same.

Homosexuals are a reminder of the dark side in every man, the repressed parts of his psyche. We know from a study of psychology that men have homosexual drives, that these are generally absorbed into nonsexual channels, such as male friendships, men's clubs, and so on. The homosexual makes visible this hidden aspect of every man, and he is, therefore, feared precisely by those men who cannot come to terms with their own inherent sexual ambiguity.

Homosexuals do not, incidentally, represent the "feminine" in men. It is a myth that homosexuality is feminine. Homosexuals represent a wide range of male and female characteristics, not only as a group, but within each homosexual. The man who is today, in one relationship, aggressive and dominant (that is, "masculine"), may be, the next day with another partner, passive and yielding (that is, "feminine"). The reason drag queens don't convince us they are women is simply their failure to project the veiled strength that is a basic part of "womanness," just as the "bull-dyke" lesbian strikes a false note because she is too tough and misses that which is essential in the normal male—a strange, astonishing gentleness.

The normal male wants to think queers are feminine, because that reassures him of the distance between himself and the queer. The race survives and the family exists because, early on in the man's life, there is a fixation on the sexual role he will play, which is that of husband and father. Playing that role demands that most men repress other possible sexual roles. The "straight" or normal male can engage in homosexual relations only with a very feminine man—someone so obviously a faggot that the "straight" man does not feel threatened. . . .

Homosexuals do not need to be forgiven. To forgive them is an insult, for it assumes that sin is involved. There is a notion in some circles that most homosexuals rather willfully "choose" to be queer, the implication being, oddly, that queerness is really more fun than straightness. Most of us didn't choose this particular bed of nails and would have preferred it otherwise. We have come to terms with it. . . .

One major point I had meant to make in this nonarticle is an attack on gay society. "Homophiles" and gay publications are always compiling lists—Socrates, Caesar, Alexander the Great, Hadrian, Leonardo Da Vinci, Michelangelo, Walt Whitman, and so on, who were queer. Yes, sure, and so what the hell. I can make up a list too, of A. J. Muste, Norman Thomas, Ernest Hemingway, Albert Einstein, Sigmund Freud, Karl Marx, Charles Darwin, Eugene O'Neill, George Bernard Shaw, Pablo Picasso, and they weren't queer, and so where does that leave us?

When homosexuals compile themselves into a ghetto they are sterile. The black ghetto had, and still has, tragic power, because it is involuntary, coerced from outside, and out of the rage and sorrow of what blacks faced in white America came—among other things— jazz. There is *nothing* in the history of mankind that homosexuals *as a group* have contributed. Allen Ginsberg is a poet, and his homosexuality is not central to that fact. Allen's poetry is not homosexual poetry, but the poetry of a homosexual—and there is a world of difference. . . .

Look. First of all, why do we expect honesty only of poets and crackpots and misfits like

Allen Ginsberg and Paul Goodman and, then, excuse the bureaucrats and politicians like myself? Why should we preach honesty but fail to practice it "in order to protect the organization." If the Aquarian Age has begun it has to liberate and touch even us.

Second, I don't believe in leadership. We need fewer leaders and more leaders. If that makes sense. I was criticized when, some years ago writing in *Liberation,* I admitted to being a coward. "Leaders," I was told, "don't admit such things." Right, I said. They don't. The point, friend, brother, sister, is that, if cowards and queers can be in the movement, so can you. If I can somehow find the courage to write this article, which is one of the genuinely courageous things I've done in my life and one of the very few things of which I am deeply proud, then why not you? The job is to open the radical movement to all of us. To normalize radicalism. To humanize resistance to inhumanity. . . .   (1969)

I did not know, until after the article was written and out of my system, the degree of self-hatred my homosexuality had involved. . . . In fact, I had, over the years, largely accepted society's definition of the homosexual as queer, pervert, and sinner.

Life can be hard for all of us, and one reason I'm never much impressed when some black militant says, "you shouldn't talk—you have no idea what it is to have a black skin," is because I want to say back, "And you have no idea what it is to be queer." But the lesson that every minority should learn (and we are all part of some minority) is that the human condition is such that it involves great (and usually hidden) pain for all of us and, in different ways, for each of us. Life is a joyously hard, painfully sweet, bitterly happy experience. You are black; I am queer; she is ugly; he is a moron; his wife got killed on their honeymoon— I suggest we all bear such a freight of pain with us, that no one, poor or black or queer, should dwell too long on his own problems. . . .   (1970)

From
"Notes for a More Coherent Article" by David McReynolds,
in *We Have Been Invaded by the 21st Century*
(New York, Praeger Publishers, 1970) pp. 115–131.

Changing sex roles

At the root of much of the discussion surrounding each of the nonconforming forms of sexual behavior lies the fact that the norms themselves are seriously under question. What is a "normal" male? A "normal" female? Once, we like to think, the answers were simple: warrior, breadwinner and governmental leader; homemaker and childrearer. In today's society, some of these roles seem to appear less rewarding and desirable to the sexes traditionally assigned to them.

The changing attitudes have meant some realignments in family structure, which were discussed in Chapter Two. Here we shall consider the broader changes being wrought in social attitudes and behavior. These changes are of recent date, indeed they frequently represent goals set for the society rather than goals achieved. To a researcher as recent as Freud, "anatomy is destiny." Freud argued that women, by virtue of being physically weaker and equipped for bearing children, were naturally passive and designed to stay at home and be mothers. Only in later years has scholarly research been directed toward discovering the extent to which "masculine" and "feminine" behavior is socially conditioned, rather than biologically determined.

Although the biological differences certainly exist, and to a greater extent than in any other animal, *Homo sapiens* is conditioned by postnatal influences. No instinctual, programmed responses are engineered into his brain. He must be taught to feed himself, to protect himself, even to procreate. He must be taught which sex he belongs to, though the learning begins at an early age. Studies show that a majority of two-and-one half-year-olds do not answer the question, "Are you a little boy or a little girl?" correctly. However, by the age of 3, two-thirds to three-fourths have their sexual identities straight.[48]

Traditional sex roles are taught in the childhood years, for the most part automatically by parents. Girls are encouraged to be passive and obedient, boys aggressive and demanding. In a study conducted by the Norwegians, Eva Eckhoff and Jakob Gauslaa, parents claimed they believed the sexes should be raised identically. However, in practice, boys were treated with more emotional "warmth," given in to more easily and punished less severely than girls.[49]

Boys are encouraged to prepare for professional careers, for example, through academic achievement in mathematics and the sciences. Studies have shown that in preschool and primary years, there is little difference in science achievement between boys and girls. However, during junior and senior high school years, boys do better than girls in science. Psychologists believe the difference develops because girls are less motivated and have been taught to believe they are less competent. Cultural definitions of the female sex role have placed more emphasis upon the ability to attract and maintain a love relationship than on academic skills.[50]

By the time they reach maturity, therefore, both men and women are prepared for their respective roles. However, with the achievement of suffrage and the greater proportion of women attending college, an increasing number of women are seeking employment outside the home. They have become increasingly restive with a society that dictates "careers" for married men but only "jobs" for married women, and with the discrimination they encounter in seeking emotionally rewarding employment. At the same time, men have been finding some aspects of the male role unsatisfying. Until the twentieth century, much prestige was attached to aggressive, warlike temperaments. However, with the nuclear age, the soldier has become a suspect figure rather than an admired one. The occupations of farmer, woodsman, frontier trapper and explorer utilized and exemplified traditional male attributes—but these occupations are becoming obsolete. Even nineteenth century factory labor required masculine brawn. But the types of white-collar jobs that the twentieth century male must increasingly seek—whether as computer analyst, certified public accountant or "organization man"—require the very qualities traditionally considered "feminine": patience, the ability to get along with people and the capacity for routine detail.

As larger numbers of women enter the working force, men find their traditional dominance threatened. The situation can be overstated, of course. Whereas women represent a substantial proportion of all employees in teaching and clerical occupations, these are for the most part lower-paid and lower-status jobs. The percentage of women in college teaching, the professions, top-level management and political office is still small, especially by comparison with their percentage in the population. Nor, except in the field of journalism, has the percentage changed much over the last decade, despite the well-publicized activities of women's liberationists. Salary levels in general are still well below those of men.

phototopic: WOMEN

Woman's traditional role in America has been that of wife, mother and upholder of conservative social values. Recently many women have begun to question this conception of their social role. For a long time women have formed a significant portion of the labor force, working for low pay in subordinate positions. Despite their better education and training, many women find limited career opportunities available to them; if they have achieved high status in the professions, they have in general suffered discrimination and endured social restrictions not imposed on most of their male counterparts.

The women's organizations formed during the last decade have stimulated a great deal of public discussion. Partly through their activity, laws permitting abortion and requiring equal pay for equal work have been passed, but public attitudes continue to be hostile to more radical aspects of the movement, including those that threaten traditional conceptions of sexual roles.

Nevertheless, the very fact that more women work has combined with their changing sexual conduct and social attitudes to create an atmosphere in which men wonder what they must do to define themselves as men. In the nineteenth century, virility could be demonstrated by sexual prowess; now, women are expected to be almost as experienced as men. Once, a couple considered a sexual relationship satisfactory if the male alone achieved an orgasm; now, the expectation is that women will derive as much satisfaction from sexual activities as men. Once, women were expected to play a receptive role in both sexual relations and professional ones. Now a small but perhaps growing percentage of women initiate sexual relationships; a much larger percentage pursues careers at even higher levels in the work hierarchy. If the role change sought by so many women has tended to demoralize some men, it has liberated others to engage in activities traditionally considered "feminine." In the present context, males may take up cooking or sewing as a hobby and not be considered effeminate.

Notes

[1] Arno Karlen, *Sexuality and Homosexuality* (New York: W. W. Norton and Company, 1971) p. 167.

[2] Marion Goldman, "Prostitution and Virtue in Nevada," *Society,* November/December 1972, pp. 32–58.

[3] Rosabeth Moss Kanter, *Commitment and Community: Communes and Utopias in Sociological Perspective* (Cambridge, Massachusetts: Harvard University Press, 1972) p. 91.

[4] *Ibid.,* p. 88.

[5] Alfred C. Kinsey, Wardell B. Pomeroy, Clyde E. Martin, and Paul H. Gebhard, *Sexual Behavior in the Human Female* (Philadelphia: W. B. Saunders Company, 1953) p. 286.

[6] Alfred C. Kinsey, Wardell B. Pomeroy, and Clyde E. Martin, *Sexual Behavior in the Human Male* (Philadelphia: W. B. Saunders Company, 1948) p. 650.

[7] *Ibid.,* p. 597.

[8] Ira L. Reiss, *The Social Context of Premarital Sexual Permissiveness* (New York: Holt, Rinehart and Winston, 1967) pp. 66–67.

[9] Cited in *The Report of the Commission on Obscenity and Pornography* (New York: Holt, Rinehart and Winston, 1967), pp. 66–67.

[10] Cited by Marc Schnall in "The United States Supreme Court: Definitions of Obscenity," *Crime and Delinquency,* Vol. 18, January 1972, p. 61.

[11] *Ibid.*

[12] *Ibid.,* p. 62.

[13] *The Report of the Commission on Obscenity and Pornography, op. cit.,* p. 1.

[14] *Ibid.,* pp. 23, 26.

[15] *Ibid.,* p. 27.

[16] *Ibid.*

[17] *Ibid.,* p. 31.

[18] *Ibid.*

[19] *Ibid.,* pp. 43–72.

[20] *The New York Times,* June 22, 1973, p. 1. et seq.

[21] Robert C. Sorensen, *Adolescent Sexuality in Contemporary America: Personal Values and Sexual Behavior, Ages 13–19* (New York: World Publishing, 1972) p. 441.

[22] Harold T. Christensen and Christina F. Gregg, "Changing Sex Norms in America and Scandinavia," *Journal of Marriage and the Family,* Vol. 32, November, 1970, p. 621.

[23] Reiss, *op. cit.,* pp. 61–63.

[24] Kinsey *et al., Sexual Behavior in the Human Female, op. cit.,* p. 298.

[25] Christensen and Gregg, *op. cit.,* p. 621.

[26] Sorensen, *op. cit.,* p. 464.

[27] Christensen and Gregg, *op. cit.,* pp. 624–625.

[28] Anne-Marie Henschel, "Swinging: A Study of Decision-Making in Marriage," in Joan Huber (ed.), *Changing Women in a Changing Society* (Chicago: University of Chicago Press, 1973) p. 126.

[29] Gilbert D. Bartell, "Group Sex Among the Mid-Americans," *The Journal of Sex Research,* Vol. 6, No. 2, May 1970, pp. 113–130.

[30] *The Encyclopedia Americana,* "Vice-Regulation Of," Vol. 28 (1945) p. 58.

[31] Kinsey *et al., Sexual Behavior in the Human Male, op. cit.,* p. 411.

[32] Vance Packard, *The Sexual Wilderness: The Contemporary Upheaval in Male-Female Relationships* (New York: David McKay Company, 1968) pp. 163–164.

[33] Nanette J. Davis, "The Prostitute: Developing a Deviant Identity," in James M. Henslin, (ed.), *Studies in the Sociology of Sex* (New York: Appleton-Century-Crofts, 1971) p. 303.

[34] Norval Morris, "Crimes Without Victims: The Law is a Busybody," *New York Times Magazine,* April 1, 1973, p. 61.

[35] Kinsey, *et al., Sexual Behavior in the Human Male, op. cit.,* p. 651.

[36] Robert Lindner, "Homosexuality and the Contemporary Scene," in Hendrik M. Ruitenbeek, (ed.), *The Problem of Homosexuality in Modern Society* (New York: E. P. Dutton and Company, 1963) p. 61.

[37] Kinsey, *et al., Sexual Behavior in the Human Female, op. cit.,* pp. 474–475.

[38] Maurice Leznoff and William A. Westley, "The Homosexual Community," in Ruitenbeek, *op. cit.,* p. 328.

[39] Karlen, *op. cit.,* p. 337.

[40] *Ibid.,* p. 372.

[41] *Ibid.,* pp. 324–327.

[42] Barry M. Dank, "Coming Out in the Gay World," *Psychiatry,* Vol. 34, May 1971, p. 182.

[43] *Ibid.,* pp. 183–184.

[44] William Simon and John A. Gagnon, "Homosexuality: The Formulation of a Sociological Perspective," *Journal of Health and Social Behavior,* Vol. 8, September 1967, p. 345.

[45] Edwin Lemert, "The Concept of Secondary Deviance," *Human Deviance, Social Problems and Social Control* (Englewood Cliffs, N. J.: Prentice-Hall, Inc., 1972) p. 73.

[46] Esther Newton, *Mother Camp: Female Impersonators in America* (Englewood Cliffs, N. J.: Prentice-Hall, Inc., 1972) pp. 7–19, et seq.

[47] *The New York Times,* June 28, 1971, p. 23.

[48] Lawrence Kohlberg, "A Cognitive-Developmental Analysis of Sex-Role Concepts," as abridged in Arlene S. Skolnick and Jerome H. Skolnick (eds.), *Family in Transition* (Boston: Little Brown and Company, 1971) p. 226.

[49] Sverre Brun-Gulbrandsen, "Sex Roles and the Socialization Process," in Edmund Dahlstrom (ed.), *The Changing Roles of Men and Women* (Boston: Beacon Press, 1962) pp. 64–65.

[50] Joy D. Osofsky and Howard J. Osofsky, "Androgyny as a Life-Style," *The Family Coordinator,* Vol. 21, October 1972, pp. 412–413.

Summary

Social norms governing sexual behavior have been called into serious question in the twentieth century. The double standard of the Victorian era, when official morality insisted on the sanctity of the home but prostitution and other varieites of nonconforming sexual behavior flourished outside it, came under serious attack near the end of the nineteenth century. This was due partly to the studies of Freud and others who saw it as contributing both to private suffering and social disorganization. Increased communications, new technology—especially the automobile—and changed social conditions worked together to loosen both sexual habits and the social attitudes of Americans toward sexual behavior. The extent and variety of American sexual behavior, as revealed by the Kinsey reports of 1948 and 1953, astonished many, however, and Kinsey's methods and findings came under attack. Attitude changes in the years since the reports were published is evidence that the findings of his study, as well as later research on sexual behavior, have been widely accepted. Changes in sexual norms have definitely occurred in America, although there is still much disagreement about the effects of such changes.

Pornography is a case in point. Throughout most of human history sexuality has been written about, depicted and commented on without legal restraint. In the nineteenth century, however, legal restraints on the distribution of such work grew, especially in the United States and England. Until recently, twentieth century judicial decisions were narrowing the definitions of obscenity and broadening the range of permissible literature. Recent Supreme Court decisions have reversed this trend, however, removing "redeeming social importance" as protection for pornographic literature, and allowing local communities to decide for themselves what is obscene. The findings of a recent National Commission on Pornography, which found most pornography relatively innocuous, were thus rejected by the courts, as they had earlier been rejected by other government officials.

The most common form of nonconforming sexual behavior is intercourse between unmarried couples. Premarital intercourse has always been accepted to a certain extent, provided couples were married by the time a child was born. In the twentieth century, contraceptives and a belief that sexual expression is desirable in itself have broadened the opportunities and incentives for premarital sex. Increased city living, a decline in religious influence, the post-World War I "emancipation" of women and candid portrayals of sexual situations in films and books are other contributing factors. Emerging sexual permissiveness within marriage, involving the exchange of marital partners, is a more recent development.

Despite greater permissiveness, prostitution continues to flourish, although there is a slight decline in activity from earlier decades. Prostitution remains illegal in most states, but it is more out in the open in today's permissive society. Prostitutes are frequently harassed and arrested, though, and turn to bribery and organized crime for protection and support.

Of all nonconforming sexual behavior, homosexuality has received the most public discussion over the past decade. It is estimated—following Kinsey—that perhaps 4 to 6 percent of American men are homosexual, although many more have had homosexual experience. Female homosexuality is thought to be about half as prevalent. Until recently, male homosexuality was strongly condemned for religious reasons and because it was thought to undermine the institution of the family. Only male homosexuality has been extensively legislated against.

There are numerous psychological theories about the causes of homosexuality: most center on the family situation in which a child is raised. During the period in which a homosexual characteristically realizes his deviance, however, sociocultural factors shape his development. Attempts are currently being made to legalize homosexual behavior and to prevent the stigmatization of individuals because of their homosexuality.

Sex roles in American society are currently changing considerably. Women are breaking out of their traditional role as wives and mothers and moving into the work force at levels of skill and responsibility formerly the prerogative of males only. They now argue for general equality in all areas of social life. While some men have been intimidated by this change, others have been liberated by it. Male roles too have shifted, partially because modern society has less need of traits formerly thought "masculine." "Masculine" and "feminine" tendencies inherent in all humans are increasingly being acted out in society.

part

3

technology and social change

chapter

communications

Of the effects of technological development, perhaps the most pervasive in our society are the communications media. Movies, recordings, the press, radio and television—the mass media—are read, heard and seen by millions. The information they dispense affects our daily lives and is woven into our perception of the world. The telephone, data transmission systems and the computer make possible business and private arrangements which in earlier centuries would either have been impossible or would have taken years to accomplish, from rapid inventories of stock to plans for large-scale construction. Former Federal Communications Commissioner Nicholas Johnson calls the media's presence a "communications mosaic," which includes

> a Defense Department hotline, a child tranquilized before a TV set, a ringing telephone, a politician campaigning by radio, a news service teletype, a fog-bound ship's radar, a hidden microphone in a business meeting, satellites, and computerized airline reservations.[1]

Communication between individuals or groups in our complex society would not be possible without the mediation of highly organized systems. A "breakdown in communications" is viewed as a serious matter that can affect the entire society's functioning. It would be hard to calculate the chaos that the Northeast blackout of 1965 might have caused if the radios had not continued to operate, informing people of efforts to correct the situation.

Increasingly, however, breakdowns in communication are occurring even when the media seem to be functioning properly. "Credibility gaps" have become common; information transmitted is not believed. Individuals find it impossible to discover what is known about them by the FBI or by a credit agency; or the general public is denied information on numerous matters for reasons of "national security." False information is promulgated, as in some advertising in the mass media. Information may be managed—the communications industries' primary goal is to entertain rather than to inform—and the presentation of events or ideas is hardly ever "straight." The problems are simpler to state than to resolve: to an unprecedented degree, information in modern America is being suppressed, altered or even manufactured out of whole cloth, while the public is effectively being denied access to procedures and instruments that would allow it to correct the situation.

The reason for this massive tampering is that information and its manipulation have been recognized as potent means of social control.

Few facts in consciousness seem to be merely given. Most facts in consciousness seem to be partly made. A report is the joint product of the knower and the known, in which the role of the observer is always selective and usually creative. The facts we see depend on where we are placed, and the habits of our eyes.

Walter Lippmann

As Commissioner Johnson observes, "We have moved from an age when political and economic power were measured in land, or capital, or labor, to an age in which power is measured largely by access to information and people."[2]

Furthermore, in a nation such as ours—where the power to dispense information is vested not only in government, but in the networks and other public media, as well as in segments of private industry such as advertising agencies, credit bureaus and public relations firms—all these agencies seek to influence not only the public at large but also each other. The explosion of stimulation as the mass media and diverse interest groups vie for attention seems both impossible to rationalize and increasingly difficult to control. In order to devise and enforce adequate safeguards—to verify the truth or fairness of what we hear, see and read, and to monitor the actions of the agencies and industries that provide it to us—we must first understand the historical forces that shaped our present communications problems.

Development of the media

The ascendancy of the mass media is largely an event of the last century. Although Johann Gutenberg invented movable type in the 1450s, print was little used to disseminate news until the eighteenth century when newspapers became common. Because there were few means to supply news rapidly from distant places, early newspapers confined themselves generally to local affairs and opinion. With the invention of the telegraph in 1837, however, newspaper coverage became less local and more general, providing rapid dissemination of news from distant places. At the same time, newly developed presses made multiple reproduction much easier than it had been before. As more and more newspapers were founded in the growing towns of the new nation, the entire country came to know what was happening in the capital and on the frontier almost as soon as it took place. Technological developments had brought print alive.

Forty years later, Alexander Graham Bell's invention of the telephone ushered in the era of instant private news transmission. The telegraph and telephone were the electric technologies of America's age of territorial and industrial expansion. They were soon followed by other communication technologies. Wireless telegraphy, developed by the Italian Guglielmo Marconi, Lee DeForest and others, did away with the cumbersome lines of the telegraph. But its capacity as a one-way medium of broadcasting was soon taken up with equal interest, and radio came into being.

By the turn of the century, America had attained a national life, with national patterns of production and distribution and national organs of communication. The heyday of the mass magazine was soon to come, and the technologies of entertainment—motion pictures and recordings—developed by Thomas Edison, among others, were soon to be available on a national scale as well. Even the newspapers, once proudly local or regional, had been gathered by such men as William Randolph Hearst and Joseph Pulitzer into chains whose editorial viewpoints had national importance. Hearst is reputed, not without reason, to have provoked the Spanish-American War almost single-handedly through his newspapers.

Radio, the first broadcast medium, soon grew to be national in scope. By 1927, the Columbia Broadcasting System was operating a sixteen-station network. The motion picture industry, institutionalized in Hollywood, was integrating sound with film. The industry of advertising had also established itself and was working with both print and broadcast media. As the problems of American industry shifted from production to distribution, advertising, working through the media, provided the means for widespread dissemination of product information and new methods of consumer persuasion.

Television, developed largely by the companies that controlled radio (the 1941 patent for television was granted to the Radio Corporation of America), led to even further integration of the communication technologies, combining elements of the newspaper, motion picture, radio and recordings.

The trend to integration can also be seen in the electronic technology of computers. Originally introduced in the 1940s as a means of performing rapid mathematical calculations, the computer has evolved at a dramatic rate into a device for the storage and retrieval of information. At present the electronic technologies have to a great extent involved almost every member of society in a network of information and communication activity.

Control of the media

As integration proceeded in media technology, some amount of concentration of ownership and control also took place. The concentrated power that characterizes other sections of the American economy has not come about, but the power groupings that emerged have significantly influenced the character and variety of information the media provide.

The newspaper business, once so competitive, has become less so in recent years. There are actually more daily newspapers in the country today—1750—than there were at the end of World War II, but the number is down from newspaper's great days; in the years before World War I there were 2000 dailies. Large metropolitan areas have suffered a loss of competing papers, and where a morning and an evening paper exist today in the same city, they are likely to have the same ownership. But dailies in suburban communities have grown, and overall circulation has kept pace with the increase of population. The long established national wire services, Associated Press and United Press International, together with news feature syndicates, have made the average newspaper less local in orientation and more national.

Constantly rising costs and the competition of other media have made newspapers, at least papers in the old mold, increasingly difficult to establish, and although publishers still look to local advertisers for most of their revenue, they are increasingly buying properties across the media. Newspapers now own 25 percent of all television stations in the country and 8 percent of the AM radio stations. Many also own book publishing companies and magazines. A recent introduction to mass communications notes "A Minneapolis citizen . . . can find the Cowles family members in ownership situations affecting both his morning and evening newspapers, his leading radio station, his CBS television network station, and his subscription to *Harper's* magazine."[3]

Concentration of ownership and control was once the pattern of the film industry. In 1949, the films produced and distributed in the United States came mainly from five Hollywood studios. Sociologist Melvin DeFleur predicted the demise of Hollywood because of the competition of television and the necessity for the major studios to sell their theatrical outlets because of an antitrust judgment delivered in the mid-50s.[4] Since then the film industry has reorganized, however, with studios providing funds for independent producers and acting as TV production units. The major consolidation in the period since film became established, and perhaps the most important in terms of control of access to date, has been that of the integrative medium—television.

Radio and television stations are regulated by the Federal Communications Commission (FCC) set up in 1934 to grant licenses to local stations based on their services in the public interest. (Since the number of stations that can operate and broadcast within a vicinity is limited by problems of wave interference, some regulatory mechanism was necessary to provide good service.) They are owned, much like newspapers, by businessmen in the communities where they are located. There is thus no antitrust problem, as there was with the

Figure 13-1 Advertising expenditures by medium

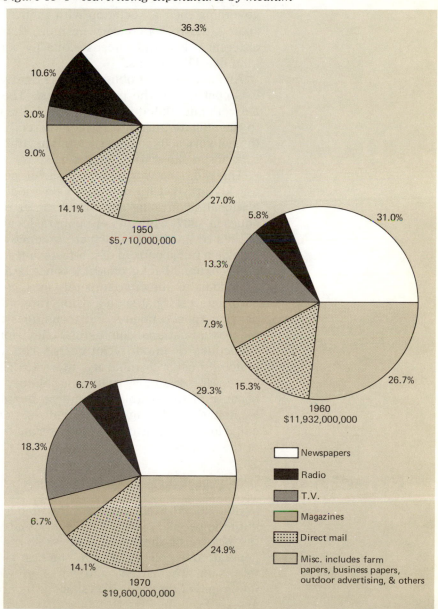

movie industry's ownership of theatres. Yet the means for consolidation of control in radio and television go beyond ownership.

While diversity of viewpoint, style and tone are today available in media such as the press and films, three television networks currently dictate what Americans will see on prime time, the evening hours, which provide most of the advertising revenues that support national television. Since, strictly speaking, it is the individual stations that broadcast over the public airways, rather than the networks, the networks are not subject to the formal authority of the FCC. However, the FCC regulates the networks indirectly by setting the rules governing their association with their subscribing stations or affiliates. A network may own no more than five television stations in different cities. And a licensee of a TV station also may own no more than five TV stations.[5]

An affiliate is not obliged to carry network programming if it feels it is contrary to the public interest. The arrangement between the network and affiliate is one in which the network gives its programs to the affiliate in return for commercial time on the program which the network sells to advertisers. The affiliate makes its money on the spot ads at the station breaks.

The radio networks, which developed television as a medium, quickly grasped its potential as a medium of national advertising. National advertising accounted for 81 percent of all television revenues in 1967, while in newspapers, local advertising was 81 percent of their revenues.[6] To reach an audience of 50 million people that will include a full spectrum of interests, ages, and social, religious, ethnic and economic backgrounds, it is necessary, according to author Ben Bagdikian, to obey two imperatives. One is to find common denominator interests that span a whole range of people and the other is to develop special talents and techniques to maintain attention. This means that national commercial television must largely ignore whole collections of minority interests.[7] This is not true of newspapers, which do cater to minority interests. The New Bedford *Standard-Times,* for example, will print almost any news about Portugal because of the sizable Portuguese population in that city. Only on local stations during news broadcasts or unpopular viewing hours could local stations do this. Prime time television is the true medium of the masses.

Effects of the media

Writer Robert Stein says that the media "furnish our consciousness with the people, places, and events that we agree to call reality"[8]— the picture of the world that we carry around in our heads. The generation in college today is the first generation that grew up with television. The extent and ways in which this latest and most integrated of the media has shaped their reality has not yet been fully assessed.

It is generally conceded, however, that the mass media have created what we call "mass culture." Normally, the term is used together with another, "mass society." Growth in population alone does not create a mass society, of course. India's many languages and cultural traditions, still functioning as essential media of communication in the country's numerous regions, prevent that country from being labeled a mass society. The British anthropologist Edward Shils characterizes mass society as one in which there is diminished sacredness of authority, a sense of the personal dignity of each member of the society, and individuality, which he partially defines as "openness of experience . . . a sensitivity to other minds and personalities." [9]

The Canadian cultural critic, Marshall McLuhan, contends that the electronic media introduced in the last two hundred years are major "transformations" of man, which inevitably affect man's way of thinking about himself and society. [10] Finding the effects of Gutenberg's invention of movable type in the altered political, social and literary life of Europe following the diffusion of printing, McLuhan ascribes similarly sweeping alterations in modern social structure, such as the telephone, television and the photograph.

The media are factors, but obviously not the only factors, in social change that have encouraged mass society; industrialization and urbanization have also contributed to the alteration of American society.

Attitudinal change

Sociologists have generally been much more cautious than McLuhan in ascribing social change to the media. The most important changes to be studied are probably those concerning opinion and behavior. A classic study, *The People's Choice,* [11] based on the 1940 presidential election, observed the process of voter decision-making over a period of several months with the aim of discovering the extent to which the media—at that time, primarily radio and the print media—influenced votes. The important discovery was that the media did not directly determine voters' decisions, but that most people turned to someone they knew and trusted—an opinion leader—to interpret the messages they were receiving via the media. Interpersonal relationships intervened in the communication process. This was called the "two-step" flow of communication. Its findings have received support in later work, such as the 1967 study *The New Media,* which concludes that in the absence of a face-to-face relationship between an individual and some authority figure, such as a parent or teacher, no substantive changes in behavior or attitude can be ascribed to the media. [12]

Many studies indicate that persuasive mass communication functions far more frequently as an agent of reinforcement than as an agent of change. Media reinforcement works by a process of selective exposure, selective perception and selective retention. The individual in the mass audience is not an automaton to be readily manipulated, but a person with his own fully formed picture of the world in his head. He is most likely to choose programs that are consonant with his reality. He is more likely to attend to the message of a program if he agrees with it and to remember the message if it conforms to his own reality. *The People's Choice* noted that values derived from religion, socioeconomic status and rural or urban residence were the most important factors in predicting voter preference.[13]

The process of reinforcement as an effect of the media depends on an audience made up of individuals who belong to stable groups in the society, however, and leaves the mechanism of social change unexplained. Attitudinal change is difficult to map because it requires longitudinal studies, but some work has been done.

It is often said that the media bring people into contact with each other. We must be more literal. The media only transport symbols. They do not bring people together. On the contrary, the media stand between people. The media may invite subsequent interaction, but they do not and cannot provide it.

Gerhart D. Wiebe

Before television, blacks in the rural south, for example, had little access to news and what they did receive was strictly censored by local radio stations and newspapers. In the 1950s, with the advent of television, this situation changed radically. Millions of blacks in the deep south heard direct and unfiltered racial news for the first time. Even illiterate blacks quickly developed detailed knowledge of the civil rights movement.[14] The institutional and social changes that occurred in the 1960s obviously had other sources than this knowledge, but it is likely that television was important in attitude change.

Today television permeates American society. Ninety-seven percent of the households own television sets, and, on any one day, the television audience has been calculated to be 81 million people or 66 percent of the population 18 years and over.[15] One hundred and seven million or 87 percent of the adults comprise the television audience who watched at some time during a given week. The average number of hours a day that an American television set is turned on is six hours and thirty-eight minutes. The audience for dramatic public events is enormous. The 1968 Democratic convention was seen by 50 million households, 88 percent of the total number. Television coverage of John F. Kennedy's assassination and funeral was seen in 96 percent of all television homes, where it was watched an average of 31 hours and 38 minutes.

The effect of television on children, the members of society most vulnerable to the media, has often alarmed parents and educators. Spokesmen for the broadcast industries contend that little is definitely known or can be proved about the effects of TV on children. Numerous studies indicate, however, that television is a powerful part of every child's environment and that the media can and do teach children about the world they live in. The average American child has spent more hours watching television by the time he enters kindergarten than he will spend in college classrooms.[16]

Differences in social class are important factors in television's impact. A middle-class child who is exposed to violence on television is more likely to see it as fantasy, unconnected to his personal experience at home and school, whereas to a lower-class child, the lesson of violence may be confirmed and reinforced by his experience in the street. Research has confirmed earlier findings that viewers who are predisposed toward violence will tend to select television programs featuring violence. Many specific instances of juvenile crimes have been traced to television programs. As television scholar Harry J. Skornia notes, there is no longer any question of whether the media teach; it is a question of what they teach, either intentionally or unintentionally.[17]

Figure 13-2   Number of media voices, 1880–1970

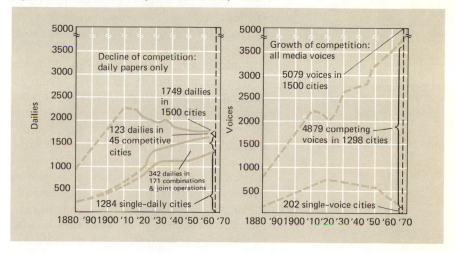

Media content

Both print and broadcast media have come under fire for their programming policies and the way they handle information. Because of the pervasiveness of the broadcast media and the fact that the number of outlets is limited, licensed and regulated by the Federal Communications Commission, criticism by government and individuals and groups has had more effect on the content of the broadcast media over the years than it has had on the content of the press, whose free functioning is guaranteed by the First Amendment.

Entertainment

After forty years of corporate management of the broadcast media, the public has been conditioned to find its programming normal; most people can scarcely think of other kinds of broadcast systems and uses. In the United States, when the decision was made to allow radio, then television, and now satellite communications to be handled by corporate enterprise, the groundwork for programming and advertising consonant with the interests of the business community was laid. Television programming and advertising is primarily directed toward selling the American consumer a mythical image of American life which emphasizes material consumption, often ignoring problematic or controversial issues.

The critic Marya Mannes, writing of television commercials, suggests some long-range consequences of TV's constant portrayal of stereotypical Americans: ". . . the dimunition of human worth, the infusion and hardening of social attitudes no longer valid or desirable, pervasive discontent, and psychic fragmentation."[18] Until recently, the television presented only the white, middle-class American milieu. Even now commercials and programs featuring the contemporary scene make only token references to racial and ethnic minorities. They foster the image of the well-to-do in gleaming suburban houses at the expense of the poor in crowded city apartments, and the image of beautiful, active young people at the expense of older members of the society.

Additionally, most programming is fragmented by constant interruptions for commercials that often obscure and distort program content. While such practices are not always the case, the "selling pitch" normally takes precedence over artistic, educational and informational content. Great care seems to be taken not to interrupt the playing of the game in sports events, however.

Bland situation comedies, Westerns depicting the conflicts of a bygone era, stories of crime, espionage and violence fill the nighttime hours. The rationale of the television industry in putting together these programs, and of big corporations in sponsoring them, is that television ratings show that this is what people choose to watch, presumably reflecting lower- or middle-class tastes. A mass medium requires a mass audience. At least one study found that lower-class respondents watch television 108 minutes a night as opposed to sixteen minutes by upper-class persons.[19] One reason for this, of course, is that television doesn't cost its audience as much as other entertainment. Programming that has been proven to be profitable, can be cheaply repeated and is confined to successful formulas is safer for both the television industry and its sponsors.

Edward Shils notes that much of the content of television programming has a certain merit:

> It often has elements of genuine conviviality, not subtle or profound perhaps, but genuine in the sense of being spontaneous and honest. It is often very good fun. Moreover, it is often earnestly, even if simply, moral.[20]

Much the same was said of film in its heyday in the earlier part of the century. The normal product of the film industry then was just as likely to be trivial in content and conventional in the attitudes presented as the television and radio shows of the present day. Film today, released to a certain extent from the requirement to be a mass medium, is generally held to be a more serious artistic and expressive medium than it was in the 1930s and 1940s, when its object was obviously mass entertainment. The attitudes presented in today's films are much more unconventional than in earlier times.

Few deny the high level of skill and imaginative work that goes into television production, but the necessity to hold the mass audience and satisfy the advertising needs of American industry seems to compel ever more absurd variations on conventional formulas.

In the 1950s, the early days of TV, "high culture" as opposed to "mass culture" was represented on TV by live dramatic presentations—but as the medium became more organized and institutionalized and the programming more expensive to produce, such specialized programming became rare. Drama, art, music and the dance on television have been given some exposure through educational TV, which first developed at the community level, but has itself since been institutionalized as the Public Broadcasting Corporation. For the most part, American business has shown interest in sponsoring "cultural" programming only when such activity can enhance corporate prestige. The recent increase of industry-sponsored "specials," both on educational television and the regular networks, includes a wide variety of educational and cultural programming, though critics continue to characterize programs on issues such as ecology sponsored by large corporations as a public relations effort designed to blur issues rather than clarify them.

reading: **Paul F. Lazarsfeld and Robert K. Merton**
SOME SOCIAL FUNCTIONS OF THE MASS MEDIA

The mass media undoubtedly serve many social functions which might well become the object of sustained research. Of these functions, we have occasion to notice only three.

The Status-Conferral Function. The mass media confer status on public issues, persons, organizations and social movements.

Common experience as well as research testifies that the social standings of persons or social policies are raised when these command favorable attention in the mass media. In many quarters, for example, the support of a political candidate or a public policy by the *Times* is taken as significant; this support is regarded as a distinct asset for the candidate or the policy. Why?

For some, the editorial views of the *Times* represent the considered judgment of a group of experts, thus calling for the respect of laymen. But this is only one element in the status-conferral function of the mass media, for enhanced status accrues to those who merely receive attention in the media, quite apart from any editorial support.

The mass media bestow prestige and enhance the authority of individuals and groups by legitimizing their status. Recognition by the press or radio or magazines or newsreels testifies that one has arrived, that one is important enough to have been singled out from the large, anonymous masses, that one's behavior and opinions are significant enough to require public notice. The operation of this status-conferral function may be witnessed most vividly in the advertising pattern of testimonials to a product by "prominent people." Within wide circles of the population (though not within certain selected social strata), such testimonials not only enhance the prestige of the product but also reflect prestige on the person who provides the testimonials. They give public notice that the large and powerful world of commerce regards him as possessing sufficiently high status for his opinion to count with many people. In a word, his testimonial is a testimonial to his own status.

The ideal, if homely, embodiment of this circular prestige pattern is to be found in the Lord Calvert series of advertisements centered on "Men of Distinction." The commercial firm and the commercialized witness to the merit of the product engage in an unending series of reciprocal pats on the back. In effect, a distinguished man congratulates the man of distinction on his being so distinguished as to be sought out for a testimonial to the distinction of the product. The workings of this mutual admiration society may be as nonlogical as they are effective. The audiences of mass media apparently subscribe to the circular belief: "If you really matter, you will be at the focus of mass attention and, if you *are* at the focus of mass attention, then surely you must really matter."

This status-conferral function thus enters into organized social action by legitimizing selected policies, persons and groups which receive the support of mass media. We shall have occasion to note the detailed operation of this function in connection with the conditions making for the maximal utilization of mass media for designated social ends. At the moment, having considered the status-conferral function, we shall consider a second: the enforced application of social norms through the mass media.

The Enforcement of Social Norms. Such catch phrases as "the power of the press" (and other mass media) or "the bright glare of publicity" presumably refer to this function. The mass media may initiate organized social action by "exposing" conditions which are at variance with public moralities. But it need not be prematurely assumed that this pattern consists simply in making these deviations widely known. We have something to learn in this connection from Malinowski's observations among his beloved Trobriand Islanders. There, he reports, no organized action is taken with respect to behavior deviant from a social norm unless there is public announcement of the deviation. This is not merely a matter of acquainting the individuals in the group with the facts of the case. Many may have known privately of these deviations—e.g., incest among the Trobrianders, as with political or business corruption, prostitution, gambling among ourselves—but they will not have pressed for public action. But once the behavioral deviations are made simultaneously public for all, this sets in train tensions between the "privately tolerable" and the "publicly acknowledgeable."

The mechanism of public exposure would seem to operate somewhat as follows. Many social norms prove inconvenient for individuals in the society. They militate against the gratification of wants and impulses. Since many find the norms burdensome, there is some measure of leniency in applying them, both to oneself and to others. Hence, the emergence of deviant behavior and private toleration of these deviations. But this can continue only so long as one is not in a situation where one must take a public stand for or against the norms. Publicity, the enforced acknowledgment by members of the group that these deviations have occurred, requires each individual to take such a stand. He must either range himself with the nonconformists, thus proclaiming his repudiation of the group norms, and thus asserting that he, too, is outside the moral framework, or, regardless of his private predilections, he must fall into line by supporting the norm. *Publicity closes the gap between "private attitudes"* and *"public morality."* Publicity exerts pressure for a single rather than a dual morality by preventing continued evasion of the issue. It calls forth public reaffirmation and (however sporadic) application of the social norm.

In a mass society, this function of public exposure is institutionalized in the mass media of communication. Press, radio and journals expose fairly well known deviations to public view, and as a rule, this exposure forces some degree of public action against what has been privately tolerated. The mass media may, for example, introduce severe strains upon "polite ethnic discrimination" by calling public attention to these practices which are at odds with the norms of nondiscrimination. At times, the media may organize exposure activities into a "crusade."

The study of crusades by mass media would go far toward answering basic questions about the relation of mass media to organized social action. It is essential to know, for example, the extent to which the crusade provides an organizational center for otherwise unorganized individuals. The crusade may operate diversely among the several sectors of the population. In some instances, its major effect may not be so much to arouse an indifferent citizenry as to alarm the culprits, leading them to extreme measures which in turn alienate the electorate. Publicity may so embarrass the malefactor as to send him into flight—as was the case, for example, with some of the chief henchmen of the Tweed Ring following exposure by the *New York Times*. Or the directors of corruption may fear the crusade only because of the effect they anticipate it will have upon the electorate. Thus, with a startlingly realistic appraisal of the communications behavior of his constituency, Boss Tweed peevishly remarked of the biting cartoons of Thomas Nast in *Harper's Weekly:* "I don't care a straw for your newspaper articles: my constituents don't know how to read, but they can't help seeing them damned pictures."

The crusade may affect the public directly. It may focus the attention of a hitherto lethargic citizenry, grown indifferent through familiarity to prevailing corruption, upon a few, dramatically simplified, issues. As Lawrence Lowell once observed in this general connection, complexities generally inhibit mass action. Public issues must be defined in simple alternatives, in terms of black and white, to permit organized public action. And the presentation of simple alternatives is one of the chief functions of the crusade. The crusade may involve still other mechanisms. If a municipal government is not altogether pure of heart, it is seldom wholly corrupt. Some scrupulous members of the administration and judiciary are generally intermingled with their unprincipled colleagues. The crusade may strengthen the hand of the upright elements in the government, force the hand of the indifferent and weaken the hand of the corrupt. Finally, it may well be that a successful crusade exemplifies a circular, self-sustaining process, in which the concern of the mass medium with the public interest coincides with its self-interest. The triumphant crusade may enhance the power and prestige of the mass medium, thus making it, in turn, more formidable in later crusades, which, if successful, may further advance its power.

Whatever the answer to these questions, mass media clearly serve to reaffirm social norms by exposing deviations from these norms to public view. Study of the particular range of norms thus reaffirmed would provide a clear index of the extent to which these media deal with peripheral or central problems of the structure of our society.

The Narcotizing Dysfunction. The functions of status conferral and of reaffirmation of social norms are evidently well recognized by the operators of mass media. Like other social and psychological mechanisms, these functions lend themselves to diverse forms of application. Knowledge of these functions is power, and power may be used for special interests or for the general interest.

495

A third social consequence of the mass media has gone largely unnoticed. At least, it has received little explicit comment and, apparently, has not been systematically put to use for furthering planned objectives. This may be called the narcotizing dysfunction of the mass media. It is termed dysfunctional rather than functional on the assumption that it is not in the interest of modern complex society to have large masses of the population politically apathetic and inert. How does this unplanned mechanism operate?

Scattered studies have shown that an increasing proportion of the time of Americans is devoted to the products of the mass media. With distinct variations in different regions and among different social strata, the outpourings of the media presumably enable the twentieth-century American to "keep abreast of the world." Yet, it is suggested, this vast supply of communications may elicit only a superficial concern with the problems of society, and this superficiality often cloaks mass apathy.

Exposure to this flood of information may serve to narcotize rather than to energize the average reader or listener. As an increasing amount of time is devoted to reading and listening, a decreasing share is available for organized action. The individual reads accounts of issues and problems and may even discuss alternative lines of action. But this rather intellectualized, rather remote connection with organized social action is not activated. The interested and informed citizen can congratulate himself on his lofty state of interest and information, and neglect to see that he has abstained from decision and action. In short, he takes his secondary contact with the world of political reality, his reading and listening and thinking, as a vicarious performance. He comes to mistake *knowing* about problems of the day for *doing* something about them. His social conscience remains spotlessly clean. He *is* concerned. He *is* informed. And he has all sorts of ideas as to what should be done. But, after he has gotten through his dinner and after he has listened to his favored radio programs and after he has read his second newspaper of the day, it is really time for bed.

In this peculiar respect, mass communications may be included among the most respectable and efficient of social narcotics. They may be so fully effective as to keep the addict from recognizing his own malady.

That the mass media have lifted the level of information of large populations is evident. Yet, quite apart from intent, increasing dosages of mass communications may be inadvertently transforming the energies of men from active participation into passive knowledge.

The occurrence of this narcotizing dysfunction can scarcely be doubted, but the extent to which it operates has yet to be determined. Research on this problem remains one of the many tasks still confronting the student of mass communications.

From

"Mass Communication, Popular Taste and Organized Social Action" by Paul F. Lazarsfeld and Robert K. Merton, in *The Communication of Ideas,* edited by Lyman Bryson (New York: Harper and Row, 1948).

Information

Although television news programming serves as the major source of information about current affairs for some 65 percent of the American population,[21] with very few exceptions, broadcasters tend to follow the lead of the printed news and siphon off the results in a few short items that are presented in stereotyped form. The national networks maintain specialists who cover a few major national and international categories, but seldom do the broadcast stations assign a reporter to systematic coverage of a special area in a way that originates new information.[22]

In his recent study of TV network news, *News From Nowhere,* Edward J. Epstein notes that news is structured on television according to organizational demands such as budgets, time slots and general policies concerning content. Network procedures, systems and policies are formulated primarily to reduce the uncertainties of news.[23]

. . . the law of news is that it is a daily affair. Man can never stand back to get a broad view because he immediately receives a new batch of news, which supersedes the old and demands a new point of focus . . . To the average man who tries to keep informed, a world emerges that is astonishingly incoherent, absurd, and irrational . . . As the most frequent news story is about an accident or a calamity, our reader takes a catastrophic view of the world around him.

Jacques Ellul

With the interspersion of commercials, news segments on the evening news programs of a major network are rarely more than five minutes long, and the news must conform to the FCC requirements of the Fairness Doctrine, which requires that each side of any issue of national importance be given equal time. These conditions are met within a format based on the assumption that the audience knows absolutely nothing about any subject. The result is a production in which events are presented primarily as stories of conflict, where certain picture symbols are used for "instant meaning." The more controversial the story, the greater attention is paid to the careful presentation of each side, which is usually followed by an inconclusive synthesis by the newscaster who's presenting the material.

Epstein found most NBC Evening News presentations of campus disturbances in the late '60s to be stories "depicting bloody melees between two sharply drawn sides" which "usually began with mounting protest, a confrontation, the climactic battle, then a tapering off of, the actions."[24] In interviews the leaders articulated their positions, and the newscaster gave an account of causes for the disturbance in which the theme was mostly the same: the students wanted more freedom, and the administrators wanted to maintain the status quo. Epstein notes that there were hundreds of student actions at the time which neither led to bloody confrontations with the police nor showed a campus at war with itself. But the format used was easier for the news staff to handle and, supposedly, for the audience to understand.

If television news often simplifies the events it chooses to report, the television documentary remains a powerful instrument for the investigation of particular topics. The documentary was a prominent feature of early television, but with growing commercialization and institutionalization of the medium, documentary programs are often relegated to time slots where they will be seen by a small audience; often documentary production is less well-funded than TV's "entertainment" component. In 1971, however, the CBS documentary, *The Selling of the Pentagon,* which dealt with the system of military procurement and its abuses, inspired congressional criticism and subpoenas of network officials, the program itself and the film edited out before the program was shown (outtakes). The courts eventually voided the subpoenas for the outtakes.

What was once a public service function of the communications media, the reporting of government activity, has become more and more a media event in itself. Historian Daniel J. Boorstin[25] has described much of the activity covered by the media as pseudo-events—planned, rather than spontaneous, occurrences, arranged for the convenience of news media. Their relation to real events is at best ambiguous, so their news value can be heightened and prolonged with little trouble. Much local television news reporting has this flavor as well. Political parties and candidates spend increasing amounts of money for radio and television time, and networks invest millions in coverage of political conventions and campaigns.

Journalism is governed by many of the same factors that govern television news. Like the broadcast media, newspapers and magazines are businesses that exist to make a profit. They depend on advertising revenue for support, and advertisers generally measure a newspaper's effectiveness by its circulation. Sociologists Joseph Bensman and Robert Lilienfeld suggest an additional factor they feel has come to influence the way in which the media delivers information to us: the journalistic attitude.[26] This is comprised of time limitations imposed on journalists, the necessary relationship of the journalist to his audience, which dictates reporting of "human interest" stories above all others and the element of re-creation that reporting involves. In manipulating the symbols—verbal or visual—of the reality reported, the reporter tends, according to Bensman and Lilienfeld, to feel that all events, whatever their appearances, are fraudulent, warped and engineered. The images presented of the reality observed thus are highly conditioned by the organizational requirements of the media in a way that compromises full and complete coverage of any event or issue.

Government and media

A plethora of communications can produce either an open or a closed society. During the regimes of Hitler, Mussolini and Stalin, all communications media were used to present a uniform, unvarying point of view. Democratic political life in America, on the other hand, is dependent on the free and open exchange of ideas on the basis of all available information. Recently, however, the First Amendment guarantees of freedom of the press and speech have come into sharp conflict with the desire of government to withhold some information from the public. The privacy of a reporter's sources has also been questioned, and government attempts to regulate the presentation of opinion on the broadcast media—something the networks and advertisers have done in their own interest for years—have become matters for executive policy decisions.

reading: Gaye Tuchman
WHAT ARE FACTS?

. . . Newspapermen must be able to identify "facts," even though some truth-claims are not readily verifiable. For instance, a U.S. senator may claim that America lags behind the Soviet Union in the development of a specific type of missile. A reporter certainly cannot check that claim in time to meet his deadline, and it is even possible that he could never locate adequate information with which to assess the extent to which the claim is a "fact." The reporter can only determine that the senator stated "A." Newspapermen regard the statement "X said A" as a "fact," even if "A" is false.

This creates problems for both the reporter and the news organization. First, the news consumer supposedly wants to know whether statement "A" is a "fact," and one function of news is to tell the news consumer what he wants and needs to know. Second, since the senator's claim to truth cannot be verified, the news consumer may accuse both the reporter and the news organization of bias (or of "favoring" the senator) if an opposing opinion is not presented. For instance, if the senator is a Democrat and the president is a Republican, the news consumer might accuse the newspaper of bias favoring the Democrats, because the only "fact" reported was that the Democratic senator said "A." The newsman would feel his ability to claim "objectivity" in the face of anticipated criticism had been endangered.

Although the reporter cannot himself confirm the truth of the senator's charge, he can contact someone who can. For instance, he can ask the Republican secretary of defense whether the senator's charge is true. If the secretary of defense states the charge is "false," the reporter cannot prove that the secretary's assessment is "factual." He can, however, write that the secretary of defense stated "B." Presenting both truth-claim "A" attributed to the senator and truth-claim "B" attributed to the secretary of defense, the newsman may then claim he is "objective" because he has presented "both sides of the story" without favoring either man or political party. Furthermore, by presenting both truth-claims, the "objective" reporter supposedly permits the news consumer to decide whether the senator or the secretary is "telling the truth."

Calling this practice a procedure fostering objectivity is problematic. In this simple example, it could equally well be labeled "providing a sufficient number of data for the news consumer to make up his mind." The procedure may grow increasingly complex. For instance, while asserting truth-claim "B," the secretary of defense may charge the senator is playing politics with national defense. The chairman of the House Arms Committee, a Democrat, may then counter the secretary's charge, stating that the Republican administration is endangering national safety through inadequate intelligence and cavalier treatment of the military budget for arms development. The next day, the national chairman of a peace group may call a press conference to accuse all parties to the controversy of militarism, overemphasizing weapons development to the detriment of a determined exploration of a diplomatic search of world peace and security. A spokesman for the president may then condemn the leader of the peace group as a communist sympathizer.

At this point, there are five persons (the senator, the secretary, the committee chairman, the peace group leader, the presidential spokesman) making nonverifiable truth-claims, each representing one possible reality. Analyzing the marijuana controversy, [sociologist Erich] Goode . . . refers to such a morass of opinions purporting to be facts as the "politics of reality." While this notion is sociologically relevant, it is useless to newsmen faced with the dilemma of identifying and verifying "facts." However, by pairing truth-claims or printing them as they occur on sequential days, the newsmen claim "objectivity." As the newsmen put it, the news consumer may not be presented with all sides of a story on any one day but he will receive a diversity of views over a period of time.

As a forum airing the "politics of reality," the newspapermen's definition of the situation goes beyond the presentation of sufficient data for the news consumer to reach a conclusion. A morass of conflicting truth-claims, such as those hypothetically introduced, might more profitably be viewed as an invitation for the news consumers to exercise selective perception, a characteristic reaction to news. Indeed, the invitation to selective perception is most insistent, for each version of reality claims equal potential validity. Inasmuch as "objectivity" may be defined as "intentness on objects external to the mind," and "objective" as "belonging to the object of thought rather than the thinking subject" (both dictionary definitions), it would appear difficult to claim—as newspapermen do—that presenting conflicting possibilities fosters objectivity. . . .

From
"Objectivity as Strategic Ritual: An Examination of Newsmen's Notions of Objectivity,"
by Gaye Tuchman,
in *American Journal of Sociology*, Vol. 77, No. 4 (January, 1972) pp. 665–667.

National security

With the advent of the cold war, concern for national security led to the justifiable withholding of information by government from the press and broadcast media. The move was a continuation and extension of the policy that existed during World War II. With increasing detente, however, the concept of national security has come under fire, partially because it was widely viewed by the press during the Vietnam War as a means for withholding facts about U.S. conduct of the war that the American people had a right to know. Extension of the concept to sensitive information relative to domestic issues and internal political dissent has also been questioned. The strained relations between the government and media in recent years have other sources as well: the high visibility of the actions of government leaders through television and the use of television as a forum for courting the voter or explaining national policy, for instance. If information withheld at a news conference or press briefing is subsequently revealed by sources other than government—usually investigative reporters for newspapers, magazine and the broadcast media—the effect is often resentment and disenchantment throughout the society, measured by polls which are then reported by the media. When such events are frequently repeated, the result is an escalating "credibility gap," which manifests itself in cynical disbelief of all government communications.

Conflict between government and press has always existed in America, and has been viewed as healthy, on the whole, for the society. But in the context of the vast increase in the scope and rapidity of communication, and in relation to topics such as the conduct of foreign relations, it has become increasingly bitter. What does the public have "a right to know"? The publication of the "Pentagon Papers," a compilation of secret government documents which traced the history of United States involvement in the Vietnam War, was viewed by the federal government as damaging to the peace negotiations then taking place in Paris. The press countered that the events presented in the Pentagon Papers were known to the participants at the peace conference, but not to the American public. They further contended that these were historical events, not strategic plans, and, as such, their revelation did not threaten national security. Although the government sought legal redress in the matter, no definitive settlement of the issues was achieved, paving the way for future litigation in similar cases.

Confidentiality of sources

Another recent problem relative to the free exchange of information has been the conflict between the government and the media over the issue of the confidentiality of sources. Newsmen are insistent on their right to protect the confidentiality of their sources and to decide what information to present. During the late 1960s and early 1970s, federal and state prosecutors have issued a series of subpoenas compelling reporters to reveal confidential information and the identity of previously unnamed sources.

For example, during a recent investigation of housing in Newark, New Jersey, the grand jury subpoenaed reporter Peter Bridge of *The Newark Evening News,* who had written of housing scandals in the city. He answered a number of their questions but refused to divulge the names of individuals who were allegedly involved in a bribe offer to the housing commissioner. The material had not appeared in the articles he wrote concerning housing, and Bridge considered the material privileged information. He was held in contempt for refusing to answer, and sent to prison for the time the jury sat on the case.

Earl Caldwell, investigative reporter for *The New York Times,* also refused to testify before a grand jury investigating the activities of black militant groups. He, like the others, contends that the right to withhold information is guaranteed under the First Amendment and also argues that to reveal names and other information would indirectly deprive the public of its right to information by seriously undermining his ability to obtain further information in the future. In 1972, the Supreme Court ruled Caldwell had to testify.

Government officials themselves often leak news to the press to gain publicity for some program or event or to plant a rumor advisors believe will be to their advantage. During the administration of President Kennedy, news leaks were legion, and the practice has continued, not only at the national level, but also in state and local politics. A more recent development has been the leaking of testimony from grand jury proceedings, which some observers feel gravely undermines the fair administration of justice. Often "backgrounder" interviews are given to the press by government officials (or other prominent leaders) to be used for reportage without specific attributors, rather in general terms such as "informed sources state," or "according to one authority."

Were it left to me to decide whether we should have a government without newspapers or newspapers without a government, I should not hesitate to prefer the latter. Thomas Jefferson

Newspaper editors contend that the government manipulates reporters by means of leaks and backgrounders, causing them to serve as unwitting mouthpieces for the government. According to A. M. Rosenthal, a senior editor of *The New York Times*:

> . . . Often the real purpose (of non-attribution) is simply to float trial balloons or to present an attitude or a policy without taking responsibility for standing behind them. . . . The result often is concealment of sources not on the basis of real need for confidentiality but to suit the political or diplomatic convenience of the government or political sources.[27]

Regulating the broadcast media

The First Amendment guarantees freedom to the press and forces government to use indirect methods such as those detailed above to regulate the press, but the FCC is able to regulate broadcasting to some extent by means of its licensing power. Theoretically, the policies of the FCC are based on three broad assumptions: the right of the public to be informed, the maintenance of a diversity of information sources and the need for stations to present information of local interest. In practice, these are normally translated into the following: (1) information—broadcasters must devote 5 percent of air time to news, of which 1 percent must be of local interest; (2) diversity—single ownership cannot exceed five stations, which must be in different geographical areas; and (3) locality—networks may not require local affiliates to use network programs.

Because the FCC holds the power to grant or cancel a station's license, however, the government can exert some control over programming. As the owners of affiliated stations are primarily businessmen who wish to earn a profit, they will tend to identify with governmental interests to protect their licenses. As a result, news presentations tend to avoid controversial issues, and the networks, in an effort to earn a profit on public affairs programs, must be able to sell them to their affiliated stations.

For most of its history the FCC, like many other government regulatory agencies, has responded favorably to the concerns of the industry it regulates. It has not lost this bias, but recent developments have made the FCC more critical of media content than in earlier years. In 1970, President Nixon created the Office of Telecommunications Policy (OTP). The OTP was not to become directly involved in regulation, but rather in researching long-range broadcasting policies.

When the Corporation for Public Broadcasting was created by Congress in 1967, it was intended to be insulated from government control and influence over content and to preserve local station autonomy. Financing and programming were to be independent functions. Under policies developed by the OTP, however, the original intent of Congress for public broadcasting has been voided. The functions of financing and programming have been joined, and the content of programs is now subject to pre- and post-broadcast review.

In a society ruled as much by what is believed as by what is known, even without regulation, the OTP had the effect of dampening media content it disapproves of. Focusing on the principle of locality, Clay Whitehead, the chief of OTP, declared in 1973 that local stations should reject those network programs that did not reflect local community interests. The result was an almost immediate softening of media coverage of controversial issues.

As new media develop, regulatory powers are extended. Cable television, developed in the 1960s, theoretically offers unlimited channels for access to television and could eliminate the relative monopoly of television by the present networks. In 1971, the FCC decided to remove its previous restrictions on access to programming by cable operators, and to permit the transmission of at least two long distance signals to urban subscribers. When the broadcast industry vehemently protested, the OTP interceded and required the FCC to restrict cable television from transmitting long distance signals into the one hundred largest television markets.[28] Overall, the principal effects of government regulation of television have been to encourage the least controversial programming, to increase the scope of its regulatory control in the area of public broadcast and to strengthen the existing network monopoly of television.

Computer technology and the flow of information

While the American public is being saturated by the flow of stereotyped and standardized information from the media, information about private citizens is being processed in an easily accessible form and preserved in the interlocking data banks of government agencies, public institutions and private businesses. Any individual in the United States old enough to have a driver's license or a social security number may be the subject of a computerized dossier.

In August 1973, a story in *The Los Angeles Times* reported that on a slow night, a deputy sheriff ran his family through the computer of the National Crime Information Center of the FBI.[29] Ten out of eleven of the family were listed. His mother was listed because when she was 18, neighbors complained of a noisy sorority party. His stepfather, a respected businessman, was listed because he complained to the police that he had received a bad check. There was no criminal conduct and no criminal record. The significance of such occurrences is real. Access to files is not controlled; information in dossiers is random and not according to strict categories; data in files tend to remain there, without any cutoff point in time; and the information itself may be inaccurate.

Computers today store information fed to them on a memory device that contains a large number of cells, each of which holds a single piece of information. Memory banks can accommodate a billion bits of information in a single system, and input and output terminals can be located as far as necessary from the central processor and storage devices. Since computer systems can be linked together, the result is a communications network similar in scope to the media networks or the telephone system. Into the system are fed the minute details that govern our interaction in society, as well as the data that support the research and development characteristic of our technological society. Political scientist Harold Lasswell, commenting on this accumulation of information, sees no sign that it will abate:

> I suspect that there is no limit to the data that may be regarded by some scientist as of research importance . . . Only think of all the psychologists, sociologists, physicians, nurses, welfare workers, child specialists, educators, tax collectors, police officers, salesmen, creditor agents, personnel administrators (and so on and on) who will continue to collect and collect and collect.[30]

How will this information, especially that relating to individuals, be used?

Data banks and their uses

Historically, governments have kept three different kinds of records on individuals.[31] *Administrative* records—birth certificates, marriage licenses, passports—are usually the result of a transaction and, when kept by governments, are accessible to public scrutiny. *Statistical* records are typically created in a population census or a sample survey, and the data are separated from the individual subject. The statistics that result may be published but the individual sources are anonymous. *Intelligence* records, kept by government agencies such as the FBI and private companies who sell credit information, are normally secret. The information gathered is usually from informants and investigators and tends to circulate only among intelligence gathering organizations.

Today numerous government data banks store such information in computer systems. The Department of Transportation operates a National Driver Register Service which contains the names of 2.5 million drivers whose licenses have been denied, revoked or suspended within the last six months. Routinely most states process driver applications through this file. (The file each day incorrectly matches about 125 applicants, who must then prove that they have not had their licenses revoked.) The Secret Service maintains a data bank on citizens along guidelines that include such loose designations as "information on gate crashers, information regarding civil disturbances, information regarding anti-American demonstrations, information on persons who insist on personally contacting high government officials for the purpose of redress of imaginary grievances, and so forth." [32] The Bureau of the Customs has a central automated data bank which includes information on informer, fugitive and suspect lists. The Federal Bureau of Investigation National Crime Information Center (NCIC) is a computerized clearing house of wanted persons, stolen property and criminal history records. In private industry, extensive records are maintained by credit bureaus who sell the information they gather on private citizens. Banks are required by law to make a reproduction of every check drawn along with the social security number of each customer. Employers and schools are also collectors of information.

The new technology has removed the quality of mercy from our institutions by making it impossible to forget, to forgive, to understand, to tolerate. When it is used to intimidate and to inhibit the individual in his freedom of movement, associations, or expression of ideas within the law, the new technology provides the means for the worst sort of tyranny.

Senator Sam Ervin

Undoubtedly, the information accumulated by both government and business serves legitimate purposes. The number and variety of services provided by government and business make it necessary to keep records of a population that is constantly on the move, and whose transactions, inaccurately recorded, would become hopelessly tangled. Yet concern in recent years has focused on the invasion of privacy such record-keeping requires and the problems of abuse that complicate the whole system of computerized record-keeping; once in existence, the data are inevitably used.

According to some sociologists, computerization of record-keeping has now cut across the uses, categories and access to the records kept by government and private agencies. More often than not, information which might in the past have been regarded as statistical or administrative assumes the character of intelligence, for much of it reveals deviation from social norms. The current state of computer technology, according to sociologist Robert Bogaslaw, "requires an insistence upon a uniformity of perspective, a standardization of language, and a consensus of values that is characteristic of highly authoritarian social structures." [33]

Accuracy and access

When computers have the power to eliminate distinctions, the problem of accuracy is a serious one. Records of the intelligence variety, gathered by investigators in the field who may question neighbors, employers and friends, are necessarily of a hearsay nature. There is also always the possibility of confusion of names and errors due to incomplete information. The Fair Credit Reporting Act, which went into effect in 1971, gives some redress to consumers. It forces a company refusing credit to disclose the name of the credit bureau that furnished the information on which the decision was based. However, the credit bureau need not reveal the source of its information, so there is no check on accuracy.

Mr. William D. Ruckelhaus, former interim director of the FBI, admitted that much of the information in FBI files may be inaccurate. Information is kept in what Ruckelhaus called a raw file and is in many instances rank hearsay—unverifiable allegations against people.[34]

As important as the accuracy of the information stored is the matter of access to data banks. Who can use such repositories?

A Kansas police department has used its computer terminals for the benefit of local apartment owners who wanted to check on tenants.[35] The FBI is permitted to send its records to federally chartered or insured banks and other institutions on the approval of the Attorney General. Defense contractors can secure records from the Department of Defense. A Senate subcommittee has found that federal investigators have access to 264 million police records, 323 million medical histories, 279 million psychiatric reports and 100 million credit files. The Treasury Department is allowed to share information received from banks with other government agencies, such as the FBI. The information on the FBI network is available to 40,000 federal, state and local law enforcement agencies.[36]

The ad hoc arrangements for controlling the use of such information, then, are none too careful with respect to individual privacy. Researcher Alan Westin notes that there are great difficulties in applying constitutional standards to the information process, since there are no clear-cut legal definitions of personal information; the traditions of free circulation of information that apply to such media as the press and the traditions of confidentiality and secrecy are equally strong.[37] There are no legal procedures to protect against improper collection of information, storage of false data and interorganizational use of data. Westin suggests a legal ruling based on the First Amendment, which he construes as permitting "silence" by a citizen as well as free speech, but he notes that America is barely entering the debate over data and its treatment. In regulation of information in the media, traditions of law at least provide a precedent for action. One comment Westin makes about data storage is almost equally applicable to information handling problems in other media, however: "The fact is that American society wants both better information analysis *and* privacy."[38]

The technological developments that have enabled Americans to communicate with each other directly on a scale never before known in history have also created a politics of information control which only public awareness and legislation can resolve.

Responses to communication problems

A study in the sociology of communications in the Soviet Union showed that, the higher an individual is on the social scale, the more likely he is to depend on rumor as a channel for communication.[39] Among top government officials and intellectuals, rumor was found to be practically the sole source of information considered reliable. Informal social networks, such as those necessary to support the circulation of rumors, have operated in all societies as an alternative to institutionalized communication, and they show a distrust of the less personal forms of communication that is hardly unique to the Communist world. The distrust of impersonal voices is one of the major elements in the communications problems discussed above. Is it possible to create, within institutionalized communications media, more responsive arrangements than exist at present?

Alternative media

When the mass media have not responded to the needs and desires of the American public or a segment of it, it has normally been possible for other voices to make themselves heard. In the late 1960s, for example, the underground press served as an important means of communication in the counterculture, providing news of radicals, drugs, rock music and other antiestablishment subjects. As these elements of content have been picked up by the mass media and laundered for mass consumption, the underground press has faded, but the fact that it was able to flourish for a time is important. Such media are often facilitated by a new technology—the underground press grew partly because of the development of new and inexpensive methods of printing, which made it possible for individuals with very little money to print and distribute their work.

Cable TV (CATV) has been perhaps the most important new development of this sort in recent years. Developed to bring clearer pictures to individual communities by means of a powerful community antenna to which local inhabitants subscribe, it also provides a large number of channels hitherto unavailable to television viewers and television producers. The first efforts of such stations, which functioned primarily as arms of antenna companies, were amateurish and unimaginative, but it was soon seen that the numerous channels of CATV provided many segments of the community with access to a medium of wider range than had hitherto been possible. As noted earlier in this chapter, the government, together with the broadcast networks, intends to maintain CATV primarily as a supplementary system to the normal commercial channels, but the question is as yet unsettled, and the possibility remains that CATV will become a powerful and responsive medium for the presentation of local issues and the views of groups within the society that have no other means of presenting their point of view. Again, technology will help. The development of inexpensive TV taping equipment has put TV production within the reach of many segments of society.

FM radio and Public Television are also means through which messages not carried on the networks or in the press can be broadcast. FM stations, relatively inexpensive to operate, have long been a fixture at universities. During the 1967 student strike at Columbia University, the best source of news was the FM radio station sponsored by the university. Placed close to the action on campus, it was able to provide a service the network news could not supply. An experiment in listener sponsorship of FM radio, the Pacifica Foundation, has been broadcasting since 1959 and presently has FM stations in four of the nation's major cities. Supported mostly by small donations from listeners, the Pacifica stations produce their own news programs with no set time limitation and with the express purpose of presenting news not regularly heard on other stations. They have also opened programming to third world groups, women's and gay liberation groups, the Young Americans for Freedom and other groups who ask for radio time.

Programming on public television had its inception when the FCC kept an outlet in each city for a noncommercial station to serve community interests. Public broadcasting was initiated in many cities by universities and supported by grants from major foundations. Now, with financial backing from the federal government, the Public Broadcasting System offers national programming of an educational nature to its local stations. Despite the threat of content control, public television usually provides a viewpoint different from that of the major networks on many issues. In addition, the public stations provide time for programming of interest to local communities, and give minority groups an opportunity to reach wider audiences.

Changing values

There are, then, alternatives to the mass media. Many of the social problems concerning the mass media are not solved by alternatives, however, because of mass media's pervasiveness in American society. Messages transmitted by network television and radio are often reinforced by magazine advertising, outdoor advertising and by journalistic attention to entertainment programs and personalities. The effect is to create a widespread consciousness of mass media and their presentations that has had its effect on social and political life alike.

The antiwar movement and the civil rights movement learned in time to exploit television news in order to get their message aired. Since TV coverage tends toward violent or unusual subjects, however, events planned with an eye toward the TV cameras have the unintended consequence of highlighting the bizarre aspects of a course which otherwise merits serious attention.

Value change in other areas of society, however, has begun to have its effect on the media as well. Growing concern for the environment and for product safety has put many corporate advertisers on the defensive and has forced them to develop completely new rhetoric of persuasion. As political currents within the society have shifted, so have the values of TV programming. Despite the many criticisms made about it, such a program as *All in the Family* would not have been broadcast in the late 1950s, before the social movements of the 1960s altered the climate of opinion to permit more frank discussion of social conflicts. TV is the mass medium most immediately subject to shifts in social attitudes, because it depends on the good will of its mass audience for its efficacy. While it seldom cultivates social change, it has been called the "great reflector" of social attitudes. In simplified symbolic form, its programming recreates the value struggles that daily go on within society.

Legal moves

The regulatory controversies and legal wranglings of government and media have been discussed earlier in this chapter. In issues involving the control of information, the government and media have both made suggestions for change, especially with respect to establishing legal standards to determine privacy of information.

Confidentiality of information was an important issue in the investigations of the Watergate affair conducted by the special government prosecutor and the Senate committee headed by Sam Ervin. The confidentiality of both the President's official and unofficial conversations raises serious constitutional questions; allied to it are questions regarding the use of national security as a designation under which information may be denied the press and public.

On the press's side, shield laws for reporters have been passed in numerous states to guarantee the confidentiality of news sources. Many observers think such laws redundant, since they hold that the First Amendment to the Constitution already guarantees the confidentiality of a reporter's sources. Court decisions which have gone against reporters, like the Caldwell case, however, indicate that in the short run shield laws could be helpful.

Recently there has been much discussion about the matter of government and private dossiers on individual citizens as well. A 1973 report to the Department of Health, Education and Welfare, *Records, Computers and the Rights of Citizens,* notes that "The net effect of computerization is that it is easier for record-keeping systems to affect people than for people to affect record-keeping systems,"[40] and suggests the enactment of a federal code on fair information practice guaranteeing citizen access to records and placing safeguards on the distribution of material in dossiers.

The technology of modern communications has made possible the greatest possible interpenetration of public and private life the world has yet known. The organization of these technical capacities in our social system has become increasingly problematic; in the face of so much information, of so many differing sorts, discrimination breaks down, and the ability to judge the importance or validity of communication is compromised. Marshall McLuhan suggests that, while we may not now perceive individual items of information we at least perceive the pattern.[41] In taking this position, however, he lays the groundwork for an entirely different society from the one we now know and are trying to maintain. Somewhere between the determinism that makes us victims of the media and those who control them and the social ignorance which today is the lot of those deprived of the media, perhaps a balance can be found.

Notes

[1] Nicholas Johnson, *How to Talk Back to Your Television Set* (Boston: Atlantic, Little, Brown, 1970) p. 131.

[2] *Ibid.,* p. 140.

[3] Edwin Emery, Philip H. Ault, and Warren K. Agee, *An Introduction to Mass Communications,* third edition (New York: Dodd, Mead and Company, 1971) p. 135.

[4] Melvin L. De Fleur, *Theories of Mass Communication,* second edition (New York: David McKay Company, Inc., 1970) p. 42.

[5] Edward J. Epstein, *News From Nowhere* (New York: Random House, 1973) p. 51.

[6] Ben H. Bagdikian, *The Information Machines* (New York: Harper and Row, 1971) p. 172.

[7] *Ibid.,* p. 173.

[8] Robert Stein, *Media Power* (Boston: Houghton Mifflin, 1972), p. xi.

[9] Edward Shils, "Mass Society and its Culture," *Daedalus,* Vol. 89, No. 2, Spring 1960, pp. 288-314.

[10] Marshall McLuhan, *The Gutenberg Galaxy* (Toronto: University of Toronto Press, 1962); *Understanding Media* (New York: McGraw-Hill Book Company, 1965) passim.

[11] Paul F. Lazarsfeld, Bernard Berelson, and Hazel Gaudet, *The People's Choice* (New York: Columbia University Press, 1948).

[12] Wilbur Schramm, *The New Media* (UNESCO, International Institute for Educational Planning, 1967).

[13] Lazarsfeld, Berelson and Gaudet, *op. cit.,* p. 73.

[14] Bagdikian, *op. cit.,* p. 18.

[15] Bagdikian, *op. cit.,* pp. 57–59.

[16] Harry J. Skornia, *Television and Society* (New York: McGraw-Hill Book Company, 1965) p. 100.

[17] Skornia, *op. cit.,* p. 143.

[18] Marya Mannes, "Television: The Splitting Image," *Saturday Review,* November 14, 1970, pp. 66-68.

[19] Harold M. Hodges, Jr., *Social Stratification: Class in America* (Cambridge, Mass.: Schenkman Publishing Corporation, 1964).

[20] Shils, *op. cit.*

[21] Survey done by the Roper Organization for the Television Information Office (TIO), New York City, 1967.

[22] Bagdikian, *op. cit.,* p. 139.

²³ Epstein, *op. cit.,* p. 240.

²⁴ *Ibid.,* p. 254.

²⁵ Daniel J. Boorstin, *The Image* (New York: Atheneum, 1961) pp. 42–43.

²⁶ Joseph Bensman and Robert Lilienfeld, "The Journalistic Attitude," in Bernard Rosenberg and David Manning White (eds.) *Mass Culture Revisited* (New York: Van Nostrand Reinhold, 1972) pp. 131–149.

²⁷ *The New York Times,* December 17, 1971, p. 26.

²⁸ *On the Cable,* Report of the Sloan Commission on Cable Communications (New York: McGraw-Hill Book Company, 1971) pp. 28–29; *OTP,* The Network Project Notebook, Number 4 (New York, 1973) pp. 20–23.

²⁹ *The Los Angeles Times,* August 17, 1973, p. 1.

³⁰ Harold D. Lasswell, "Policy Problems of a Data-Rich Civilization," in International Federation for Documentation, *Proceedings of the 1965 Congress* (Washington, D.C.: Spartan Books, 1965).

³¹ *Records, Computers, and the Rights of Citizens,* Report of the Secretary's Advisory Committee on Automated Personal Data Systems (Washington, D.C.: U.S. Department of Health, Education and Welfare, 1973), pp. 5–7.

³² *Uncle Sam Is Watching You* (Washington, D.C.: Public Affairs Press, 1972) p. 6.

³³ Robert Bogaslaw, *The New Utopians* (Englewood Cliffs, N.J.: Prentice-Hall, Inc., 1965) p. 186.

³⁴ Tom Wicker, "Reflections of Ruckelshaus: Inside Report on the F.B.I.," *The New York Times Magazine,* August 19, 1973, pp. 24–30.

³⁵ Michael Sorkin, "The F.B.I.'s Big Brother Computer," *The Washington Monthly,* September, 1972.

³⁶ *Ibid.*

³⁷ Alan F. Westin, "Legal Safeguards to Insure Privacy in a Computer Society," in *Communications of the A.C.M.,* Vol. 10, No. 9 (September, 1967) pp. 533–537.

³⁸ *Ibid.*

³⁹ Raymond A. Bauer and Dan B. Gleicher, "Word of Mouth Communication in the Soviet Union," *Public Opinion Quarterly,* 17, pp. 297–310.

⁴⁰ Records, Computers and the Rights of Citizens, *op. cit.,* p. xx.

⁴¹ McLuhan, *Understanding Media, op. cit.,* p. vii.

3 *part*

**Technology and
social change**

Summary

In our society, many of whose functions are coordinated through a "communications mosaic" created by the electronic media, information is often suppressed, altered and manufactured, to the detriment of political and social life. Control of information media in American society is a potent means of social control.

Since the invention of the telegraph and the proliferation of newspapers, developing communications techniques—the telephone, radio, film, television and computers—have increasingly involved almost every citizen in a web of communications activity. By 1900 newspapers were national in scope, and though their number is down from earlier days, their circulation has kept pace with population growth. For most of the public, newspapers are the conventional medium of information. Newspaper owners have increasingly bought properties across the media—television stations and book publishers. The film industry, once consolidated under the control of a few Hollywood studios, has lost both its centralized organization and its social influence to television, the most integrated of the electronic media, whose programming is nationally centralized in the three major networks, though ownership of individual stations is dispersed.

Mass media have helped to create mass society, which is characterized by both social homogeneity and the idea of individualism. Sociologists doubt that mass media are as effective in changing attitudes as they are in reinforcing them, but TV especially has added to the general population's knowledge of the world at large, a process that has undoubtedly had some effect on the direction of social change. The effect of television on children is an issue hotly debated. Effects seem to differ in relation to social environment.

Mass media content tends to emphasize American middle-class values. These values also provide the background for the advertising whose revenues largely support media operations. Vigorous consumption of the products of American enterprise is the keynote. Television programming runs to variation on tried and true formulas—westerns, situation comedies, espionage stories—which networks and sponsors decide will find the largest audience. Educational presentations and cultural programs are becoming more frequent, however. Formula affects television news presentations as well. Engineered to minimize the uncertainties of news reporting, they often simplify complex issues. Similar organizational considerations affect print journalism. Political life has recently been influenced by the media; "pseudo-events" staged for media presentation have become commonplace.

Because of media's pervasiveness, however, conflict between media and government has intensified recently. Confidentiality, of government information related to national security on the one hand, of newsmen's sources on the other, is the primary issue, and cases focusing on it are still being debated in the courts. While the press has constitutional guarantees as a shield, broadcast media, because they use the public airwaves, are subject to government regulation and so liable to indirect constraints on their programming by government.

The growth of computer technology has led to concern about the confidentiality of information on private individuals gathered by government and by private industry. Computer systems tend to treat all information uniformly and thus demand a consensus on values that tends to uphold and solidify the claims of social norms. Individuals neither have the access to check the accuracy of information about them held in dossiers, nor can they deny access to the files to a wide range of public and private agencies with different purposes. Legal and administrative procedures to guarantee privacy have yet to be developed.

Despite the pervasiveness of conventional mass media and the control exercised over them by owners and advertisers, a number of alternative media are available. Some serve special audiences, such as the underground press, but some—cable television, FM radio, public television—allow small groups within the society a wider hearing than ever before. Changing values within the society have begun to affect the mass media as well, as evidenced by television's quick enthusiasm for environmental protection in the light of public concern. Legal moves are under way, to resolve issues between government and media with respect to regulation and confidentiality and to guarantee individual privacy in the light of computerized record-keeping.

chapter

the
corporate state

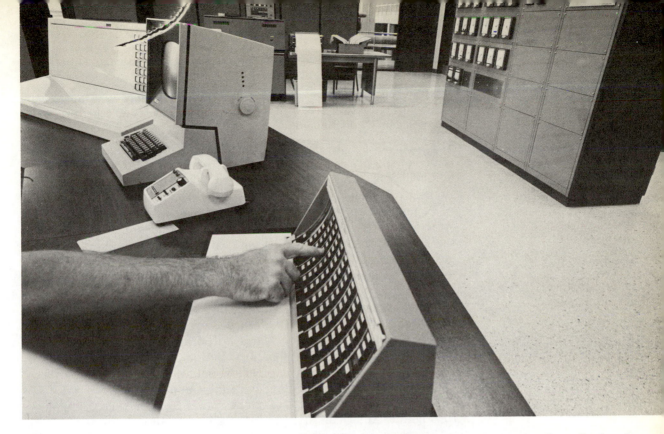

Of the United States in the 1830s, a country in the first flush of democratic fervor, the Age of Jackson and his successors, the French writer Alexis de Tocqueville commented:

> . . . Men there seem on a greater equality in point of fortune and intellect, or, in other words, more equal in their strength, than in any country in the world, or in any age of which history has preserved the remembrance.[1]

Despite a political system organized to give individuals both proper representation for their point of view and a basis for redress of grievances, one of the more prevalent attitudes found among contemporary Americans is a sense of powerlessness to affect the direction of their lives meaningfully, or even to control some of the petty annoyances of daily life. De Tocqueville's promising view of American society seems not to have been fulfilled.

The feeling of impotence is not confined to the poor, the elderly, the unemployed and uneducated, or the young, but is shared by a large portion of America's middle class and working class. The growth in recent years of public interest groups such as Common Cause, Ralph Nader's investigating groups and many other environmental, safety and consumer organizations, is one response to the growing feeling of powerlessness. The more despairing responses are less obvious, but social scientists are now examining such behavior as shoplifting, "white collar" crime, wild-cat strikes and automobile malfunctions due to sabotage in assembly plants in this light.

Citizens' groups and concerned individuals are asking, as political scientist Robert A. Dahl did:

> In a political system where nearly every adult may vote but where knowledge, wealth, social position, access to officials and other resources are unequally distributed, who actually governs?[2]

The answer is that, especially at a national level, where so many issues of the present are decided, it is not those who vote but those who possess "knowledge, wealth, social position," and especially "access to officials," who are able to determine priorities.

To many it appears that government and business, especially the American large corporations, are collusive, and not necessarily for the benefit of the public. At any rate, decision makers in both government and business are protected by bureaucracies and customer relations departments, which, though unable to effect remedies, manage quite competently to shield from the public those who can effect them. There seems also to be a revolving door whereby the top officials of government and large corporations frequently alternate positions. A lawyer for a large corporation may be appointed to a regulatory agency which has jurisdiction over the activities of his former employer. Former cabinet officials turn up on the boards of companies which had dealings with their departments.

Such practices certainly are not new; they have been commonplace throughout American history and at all levels of government. There is, however, an important reason for them to be regarded critically today. Within the last 30 years or so the federal government has gained extensive control over large areas of the country's enterprise. Its relations with other countries and with domestic organizations now have the potential for a much greater impact on the welfare of the nation than ever before. In this shift of power, it often seems that the private individual has lost his ability to affect either the economic or the political system. In the words of Walter Lippman, the eminent American political commentator,

> The private individual today has come to feel rather like a deaf spectator in the back row. . . . He knows he is somehow affected by what is going on. Rules and regulations continually, taxes annually, and wars occasionally, remind him that he is being swept along by great drifts of circumstance.
>
> Yet these public affairs are . . . for the most part invisible. They are managed, if they are managed at all, at distant centers, from behind the scenes, by unnamed powers. As a private individual . . . he lives in a world which he cannot see, does not understand, and is unable to direct.[3]

Large-scale business organizations in America

In 1971, James M. Roche, then Chairman of General Motors, America's largest private corporation, attributed America's "high levels of education, health and individual opportunity" to "our free competitive economic system." Economist John Kenneth Galbraith views the delivery of such platitudes as a basic function of the modern corporate board chairman, who is expected

> . . . to act as emissary to liberal learning; and to affirm, on appropriate occasions, faith in free enterprise, the social responsibility of business and the continuing relevance of ancestral virtues.[4]

The "free, competitive economic system" of which Roche speaks is in fact a myth, and hardly applicable to the conditions that prevail at the present day. The early capitalist who took calculated risks in an insecure competitive market has passed from the scene, as has the market in which he built his empire. Even the economic power of such individual and financial giants as Henry Ford, Sr., John D. Rockefeller and J. P. Morgan has been passed on to a group who possesses the specialized knowledge and experience to make the decisions appropriate to a highly interdependent industrial system, rather than a free and competitive economic system.

Despite all its theoretically laudable qualities, the market system of the mid-nineteenth century presented the entrepreneur with many problems. Raw materials had to be bid for competitively; finished products had to be sold to highly independent distributors who in turn were affected by fickle consumers. The main goal of late nineteenth and early twentieth century entrepreneurs was to gain control over these market insecurities. Through absorption of suppliers and distributors, the forerunners of many of today's corporate giants were able to gain a better economic foothold than their competition. Rockefeller's oil mergers of the 1870s are a classic example.

The corporation

In the twentieth century, the consolidation of the automobile industry through centralization of control and administrative expertise is the representative example. In 1904 there were 35 American producers of automobiles. In 1909, a year after William Durant had formed General Motors, the prototypical corporation, GM controlled 20 manufacturers of cars and auto accessories. In 1921, the costs of entry into the automotive industry were still low enough so that there were as many as 88 companies involved in the industry. Three years later, there were only 43. Although some independents held out against the economics of centralization until well after World War II, there are today only four major auto producers, who control everything from natural resources at one level of the manufacturing process to auto insurance companies at the other.

The domination of an industry by a few producers creates an oligopoly, a situation in which competition is limited, and the consumer can no longer choose between different products at different prices dictated by free competition. The oligopolies are so large and control so much of the business done in the country that they have a vested interest in maintaining not only sales levels but the conditions in the larger society that keep sales levels high.

Another important consequence of oligopolistic growth is the increasingly national character of big business: when local or regional companies became divisions of national corporations, community relations and company personnel practices came to be less subject to local conditions and more dependent on the decisions of corporate executives far removed from the centers of production and distribution.

The corporate technostructure

Leadership in the oligopolistic corporation is realized by a group which is known as the corporate technostructure. Galbraith describes the structure as:

> A collective and imperfectly defined entity; in the large corporations it embraces chairman, president, those vice presidents with important staff or departmental responsibility, occupants of other major staff positions, and, perhaps division or departmental heads not included above . . . It embraces all who bring specialized knowledge, talent or experience to group decision making. This, not the management, is the guiding intelligence—the brain of the enterprise.[5]

The technostructure of the modern industrial corporation includes elements of the earlier entrepreneurial corporations and financiers, and has added scientists, technicians, lawyers and other specialized personnel. It differs from the older corporate form in that the wielder of power is no longer an identifiable person like Ford or Morgan, but rather an anonymous group of specialists. Decisions are no longer made by individuals, but by groups. An impersonal face is thus presented to the public.

In corporate life, organization is nearly everything. The complex array of jobs, of positions and duties, can be pictured as standing apart from the temporary human inhabitants, a kind of social landscape that provides a setting little affected by the petty affairs of transients. . . . there is a sense in which the homely aphorism, "organization is people," represents a greater distortion than the view that organization is either super-human or non-human.

Wilbert E. Moore

Since World War II, an even newer type of corporate giant has emerged. Early corporations like General Motors were content with an oligopolistic position in basically one industry. The new corporations, and even some of the older ones, are now diversifying. It is common for corporations like the International Telephone and Telegraph Corporation (ITT) to be involved not only in telecommunications but in the baking of cupcakes. In both the oligopolistic giants, such as General Motors, General Electric, and U.S. Steel, and the more diversified conglomerates, ITT, Litton Industries and Liggett and Myers, for example, corporate power lies within the technostructure. Oligopolies and conglomerates dominate the American economic scene, and the anonymity of their technostructures has allowed them to do business almost without regard for the problems of private citizens or of individual communities.

The most obvious characteristics of the American corporate system are its size and concentration. The five largest industrial corporations of the United States owned 11 percent of all assets used in manufacturing in 1969; the top fifty had 38 percent; and the largest 500 owned 74 percent. The five largest employed 11 percent of all workers engaged in manufacturing, and in combination with the next twelve had 20 percent of the industrial workforce on their payrolls. The General Motors Corporation has annual revenues exceeding the revenues of any government except the United States, the United Kingdom and the Soviet Union. Unlike government, which, at least in theory, is controlled by the citizenry, GM is privately owned and dedicated to the continued profits of its stockholders alone, rather than to any public benefit.

Corporation and consumer

The size and concentration of American corporations has many ramifications for the citizenry. Large corporations, no longer challenged by massive competition, feel little pressure to lower prices, nor do the products need to be innovative in any but the most superficial sense. Rather, emphasis is placed on maintaining the firm's share of the market. In the oligopolistic market the firms involved are large enough to absorb short-term losses in a price war; no one firm will lower prices when this will cause its competitors to do likewise. All, however, may very well raise prices, even if only one of their competitors does. The net effect on the consumer is that he has lost any power to influence prices.

That price is often high partially due to the cost of advertising. Advertising is important to the giant corporations because it often represents the only way it can distinguish its product from the very similar products offered by its competitors. Corporations are usually unwilling to take the market risks involved in manufacturing a truly different product, so they must create the difference artificially through advertising. The consumer is asked to "taste the difference" or told he can "see the difference." But the satisfaction he receives from one product as opposed to another is largely psychological, the result of imagined differences rather than actual differences. Moreover, investment in advertising reduces the money available for product improvement, further diminishing the consumer's return on his dollar.

The use of advertising by large corporations is not limited to creating imagined differences among very similar products, however. Advertising is utilized to create a demand for the product in the first place, and to contrive demand for the new varieties of consumer goods which companies seek to manufacture and market. The telephone industry has no need to create imagined differences. As a government-authorized monopoly, it has no competition which offers comparable service. Yet the telephone industry spends millions of dollars in advertising to convince the consumer to buy more of its service. In the case of a new product, a carefully planned advertising campaign is usually launched well before the product itself is widely available. The implication is that demand will need to be contrived—and this indeed seems to be true.

In earlier times, demand was largely confined to commodities that satisfied physical needs—food, shelter, clothing, and attendant goods. While these needs obviously exist in today's consumer society, they have been supplemented by a host of contrived needs which far exceed the physical necessities of life. Advertising, to a greater or lesser degree, has exploited or played upon human psychological desires such as the desire to belong, to feel sexually adequate, to be always young, and so on. With these appeals, some contend, advertisers have partially stripped the consumer of his very power to decide whether or not to buy.

Advertising simply accepts the world as it is, and then makes it even more so.

Joseph Bensman

The net effect of contrived consumer needs has been to reduce the consumer's decision-making capacity. The exercise of America's vast industrial strength in this direction has led to corruption of a character and at a rate that has become a burden for society. The multiplicity of so-called "convenience" appliances so routinely sought by modern consumers has already resulted in a tremendous burden on energy resources, for instance. The archetypal consumer product, the automobile, is so involved with other aspects of American life that it has massive effects on air quality, on the physical layout of cities and towns and on the employment of a good portion of America's working force.

The acquiescence to contrived demand—and the conspicuous consumption of unnecessary products—is, of course, as much a result of personal selfishness as of corporate design. The satisfaction obtained by one person from the continued use of a dishwasher or of a second and third car must be weighed against the cost to society should electricity in hospitals become curtailed because of a power shortage.

Large-scale government

As business organizations have grown in size and scale, so has government, most notably at the federal level. The federal government in the United States has normally refrained from direct participation in commercial enterprise. This is not to say that government has refused a national economic role, but its role in earlier eras was not a comprehensive one, stemming from any single defined policy. In the nineteenth century government did attempt to create a uniform stable currency, to protect burgeoning industry, to promote agriculture and education. However, such actions were taken in response to immediate concerns, and seldom represented any long-range planning of the economic, social or political direction of the country. Furthermore, the states retained a good deal of power so that prior to World War II, various regions were easily distinguishable in terms of their economic, social and political features, a situation not unlike the regional development in the business world prior to the mergers which gave industry a national nature.

In the period between 1890-1925 Populist and "muck-raking" pressures gave rise to regulatory agencies at the national level such as the Interstate Commerce Commission, Federal Trade Commission and Federal Power Commission, but governmental operations were largely unchanged. The specialized agencies, like the Cabinet departments, were designed to deal with specific problems. As such they often had overlapping jurisdictions, and the policies of one often conflicted with those of another. One could describe the United States Government in this period as a feudal system comprised of petty fiefdoms of agencies, commissions and departments employing a cumbersome bureaucracy.

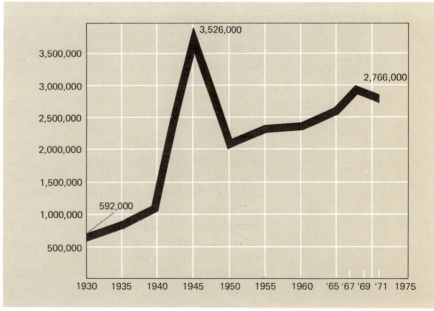

Figure 14–1   Increase in number of federal employees, 1930–1971

The crisis of the Great Depression necessitated a different arrangement. Planning, although still toward limited ends, then became a permanent preoccupation of government, as did the scientific management already common in the private sector. The administrators whom President Franklin D. Roosevelt brought to Washington to govern the country were not so much political cronies as they were technocrats. Far from successful in curing the Depression, they did manage to streamline and refine government bureaucracy; the United States was relatively well prepared administratively to engage in World War II. During the war and in the postwar period the ranks of this bureaucracy (and also of the bureaucracies supporting state governments) swelled to an astonishing degree (Figure 14-1). New departments of the federal government include Defense, Health, Education and Welfare, Housing and Urban Development, Transportation. The specialized agencies are almost numberless; they include the Central Intelligence Agency, the Office of Economic Opportunity, the Office of Management and Budget and many more. It is often difficult to separate cause from effect in delineating the events which shaped the growth.

The post-war partnership

World War II witnessed major cooperation between big business and government. A War Production Board coordinated all industrial efforts toward wartime needs. Its director, a former business executive, reported directly to the President. Coordination succeeded not only because of the emergency, but also because the technostructures in business and government were speaking the same language.

The World War II partnership between business and government was continued into the postwar era by legislation such as the Full Employment Act (FEA) of 1946 and the National Security Act (NSA) of 1947 which greatly expanded the specific and implied activities of government in the national economic sphere. The FEA instructed the government to use "all practicable" means to maintain a high level of employment and low rate of inflation. The NSA, especially through its National Security Resources and Research and Development Boards, has been used to rationalize governmental actions that amount to nothing less than the financial rescue of otherwise failing firms.

This expansion of government control of the economy necessitated increased planning and coordination with corporate giants. The National Resources Board, for example, has designated certain materials (aluminum, nickel, rubber) as those critical to the nation's defense effort. To ensure the availability to these resources, it has instituted a policy of stockpiling, which requires coordination with the several large corporations that might use them for the production of consumer goods. Similarly, many studies related to defense capability, and to the effectiveness of public programs (such as job training and education) are contracted out to private firms. Some of these firms are quasi-governmental—The Rand Corporation, for example, is well subsidized by the Air Force—while others, such as ITT's Research Institute, have been established to service government research and development contracts.

Primarily in the interest of national security, the federal government has become active in certain areas of the economy, and industry, which once jealously guarded such prerogatives as production decisions and price policies, has in many instances relinquished power to various government control boards. In turn, it has received greater protection from market insecurities. The increased size and technology of government and business have resulted in an alliance with increasing power over what Americans buy, and how they live.

---

reading: Jacques Ellul

MODERN BUREAUCRACY

A modern state is *not* primarily a centralized organ of decision, a set of political organs. It is primarily an enormous machinery of bureaus. It is composed of two contradictory elements: on the one hand, political personnel, assemblies, and councils, and, on the other, administrative personnel in the bureaus—whose distinction, incidentally, is becoming less and less clear. Tradition accords great importance to deliberative bodies, councils, votes, and the designation of political leaders. Political thought revolves around this; from the point of view of democracy, the people's sovereignty operates here. This goes hand in hand with the well-known pattern, the classical and reassuring schema of administration; administrative personnel are named by the politicians: such personnel therefore depend entirely on them. It constitutes the ranks of government employees, who have no latitude whatever with regard to the state as, in another day, the officer corps had. At best they have freedom to look after their professional interests. The administration exists in order to execute the decisions of the political leaders—that is its only role. It is activated by the decisions of its central brain. Thus the vast administrative body is nothing without the political center, which is everything. Against this administration, the citizen can be and is being effectively protected: he can have recourse to channels. But more than that, the citizens are the masters, thanks to elections, councils and assemblies. They can act upon the state's decisions and therefore upon the administration. The latter is nothing but a relay mechanism, a transmission belt.

This very simple and classic view includes, without being aware of it, both the Hegelian concept of administration as a relay between the state and society, and the Marxian concept of administration as a means of the state. This also explains the insufficient importance most people attribute to the study of the administration proper (except for administrative law). There are very few sociological studies on government administration. Yet, in reality, the state is gradually being absorbed by the administration. A façade or appearance of political power still clings to some man or council; but it is only a façade, even in authoritarian regimes. The true political problems, those concerning the daily lives of the nation and affecting the relationship between citizen and public power are in the hands of the bureaus. In them resides the reality of the modern state.

First, governmental administration has acquired considerable weight and complexity. It is all well and good to claim that the corps of functionaries can be reduced to some simple rules or statutes, the administration to some general structure. That takes no account of reality. On the contrary, one would have to penetrate into the endless mass of bureaus and their competences, the hundreds of services under a cabinet member, the divisions, the hierarchies, and above all the liaison organs. Relations among administrative sectors have become incredibly complicated, so much so that liaison organs had to be created. A dossier must go through five, ten, twenty services, with each adding something and attesting to having taken note of it. As those services are subject to different chiefs, and even belong to different ministries, the channels are not clear. The liaison organs know the proper channels, and put one bureau in touch with the other. We must not condemn the bureaucracy's expansion—its complexity is the mirror image of the nation's complexity and the diverse tasks entrusted to the state. Nobody can have exact knowledge of this vast machinery, and, to my knowledge, no organizational chart detailing the various interrelationships exists. Even if there were a chart for one minister's department, it would not amount to much, as it would not indicate the horizontal relations with other departments and administrative organs. Nobody can grasp the whole, and in reality nobody controls it.

But this bureaucracy penetrates the entire state. A cabinet member amounts to nothing without his bureaucratic infrastructure. A ministry in turn is an enormous administrative organism. The bureaucracy penetrates the top levels of the government, which in turn is reduced to being a bureaucratic complex, except for some personalities whose function is not always clear. It will be objected that the minister makes the decisions, and if he does not know all his bureaus or his department's entire administrative structure, he does know the various section chiefs. These chiefs are well acquainted with their subordinate chiefs, and so on; with the result that as one descends the hierarchy, everyone at each level knows his immediate subordinates and the offices under his command, and the well-regulated machinery ultimately depends on the man at the top. That, too, is an entirely theoretical view of the matter. From the very moment that a general policy decision has been made by the minister, it escapes his control; the matter takes on independent life and circulates in the various services, and all depends eventually on what the bureaus decide to do with it. Possibly, orders will eventually emerge corresponding to the original decision. More frequently, nothing will emerge. The decision will evaporate in the numerous administrative channels and never really see the light of day. Everyone knows of ministerial orders getting nowhere simply because they were blocked—purposely or not—somewhere along the line. We know the even more frequent case in which a basic decision is couched in a one-line decree, with the addendum that another decree for its implementation will follow. These implementation decrees never see the light of day. They depend entirely on the bureaucracy. In France a major and essential order issued in 1945 was never applied. Twice, in 1951 and in 1959, a minister gave orders to implement the decision, but to no avail. Was this simply a question of disorder? Complicity? The chief's inability? The jungle of offices? Laziness? Actually, the phenomenon is much more important; the bureaus by now have taken on an independent life; the bureaucratic administration has powers of decision and censure *outside* the elected political powers, and obeys special interests (though it does that at times) and person pressures (which is very rare) much less than inexorable operational laws. What is frequently overlooked is that the administrative machinery's complexity precludes any decision by a single center and that the bureaucracy's—inevitable—weight makes it impossible for a chief to activate the whole mechanism transmitting orders.

Does that mean the state is paralyzed, impotent? Not at all. What we see is a transformation of central importance: what used to be a system of transmission has progressively turned into a system of decision; what used to be a ministry (literally, service) has turned into a power. But we do not have here a real range of *diversified* centers of decision-making in opposition to one another; rather we see here a multitude of interrelated decision-making centers, none directly responsible, all included in the same machine. Today, **530** *that* is the state. This emerges even more clearly if we consider that not one, but, every day, at various levels of the various organisms, hundreds, sometimes even thousands of decisions are made. These decisions are not the work of an individual. It cannot even be said that they form even *one* general decision of which the other decisions are only implementations; even when these decisions reach back to fundamental choices taken, these thousands of partial decisions will lend that basic choice its particular coloration, value, efficacy. The basic decision amounts to very little. . . .

From
The Political Illusion by Jacques Ellul, trans. by Konrad Kellen
(New York: Alfred A. Knopf, Inc., 1967) pp. 141–144.

Government and corporation

Products for private consumption are only one aspect of modern corporate output. Most of America's firms also produce goods and services that are purchased by the government. Corporate sales to the Department of Defense are the most visible, but the government is closely connected with industrial, chemical and agricultural corporations also. Much of the country's crop parity program is based on storage contracts with large concerns like Continental Grain Company. Litton Industries is not only a large defense contractor but has been involved with Job Corps training programs under the auspices of the Department of Labor. A government with so much to manage has a keen interest in the economic survival of the corporations which supply it with so many goods and services. It is thus less likely to effect policies which might detract from continued profits and sales for these firms, or to attempt to alter their production priorities. This attitude may in part explain why government has often been mild in their regulation of the oligopolies which have economic control of the market. The client-customer relationship between government and business works against the consumer's ability to exercise his power in the market, and also it influences considerably the capacity of government to represent the concerns of individual citizens effectively.

Defense and industry

Nowhere is the partnership of large corporations and the government more in evidence than in the defense establishment. In 1967, 100 firms, many of them among the largest 500 manufacturers in the country, had two-thirds of all prime defense contracts.[6] Of the thirty largest prime contractors, nineteen rank among the top sixty-five manufacturers in terms of sales. In 1972, there were almost 1.1 million civilians employed by the Department of Defense. This amounted to 38 percent of the total civilian employment in the Federal government. The nongovernment employment generated by defense contracts with the private sector was estimated to be over 3 million in 1970.[7] Nearly 31 percent of President Nixon's "peacetime budget" for 1973, as proposed, was allocated for the national defense. Defense is an important component of the American economy.

Shortly before leaving office in 1961, President Eisenhower warned the nation of the dangers of a "military industrial complex," an interested cooperation between the industries of defense, and the military arms of government. Although the term came into general use as a result of Eisenhower's warning, the institution of which he spoke had its roots in the period immediately following World War II. The United States could not, as in 1918, retreat into isolation at the close of hostilities. World War II had severely crippled the economies and industries of much of the world. Two new superpowers, the United States and the Soviet Union, stepped into the military-economic void. Each had an ideology which it wanted the rest of the world to accept. And each adopted military and defense goals as a means of demonstrating its power.

The Cold War both accelerated and was in turn sustained by defense expenditures. The more each country spent on armament, the greater was the perceived threat, a threat which could only be met by another round of spending. The economic results are easily measured. Much of American industry has become dependent on government outlays on defense and has exerted tremendous effort to continue the outflows.

During the Cold War period Charles E. Wilson, President Eisenhower's Secretary of Defense, declared that "What's good for General Motors is good for the United States." Mr. Wilson, previously President of General Motors, is a famous example of a corporate executive who moved from supplier of military hardware and services to procurer of military hardware and services. Several years later, Robert McNamara, President of the Ford Motor Company, made a similar move under President Kennedy. Wilson and McNamara were not exceptions. Wisconsin's Senator William Proxmire, a frequent critic of the defense establishment's excesses, discovered in 1969 that 100 firms which were involved in defense contracts employed more than 2000 ex-officers who had retired from the military at the rank of colonel (Army), captain (Navy) or above. Lockheed Aircraft, one of the perennial defense giants, employed 210 such ex-officers alone.[8] Obviously, the ex-officers have rather easy access to the Pentagon and the chambers of the House Armed Services Committee. Sociologist Stanley Lieberson wrote of this tendency,

> Personal contact between high ranking officers and their former colleagues can affect negotiations, particularly when the military officers themselves may soon seek employment from the corporations after their military retirement.[9]

The contrived demand that operates in the private sector is just as prevalent in the defense industry. How much of our defense demand is contrived and how much is real is a question for the experts. But most of the experts are employed by the combined technostructure of the large corporations and the Defense Department. Thus decision-making in the defense establishment is carried out within a close group of specialists with essentially common interests.

What happens when a nonspecialist private citizen speaks out on foreign policy or defense expenditures? Even if he is highly respected, as were Dr. Benjamin Spock, or Martin Luther King, he is said to be entirely out of line, speaking on matters he knows little about. Sociologist Mark Pilusuk and activist Tom Hayden point out that William P. Rogers, President Nixon's first Secretary of State, was a corporate attorney with no previous experience in foreign affairs.[10] Either Dr Spock and Mr. Rogers are equally unqualified to speak out on foreign policy, or corporate legal departments have more at stake in foreign policy than a private citizen has.

Not only are the opinions of the defense industries upheld; their economic well being is nurtured. If national survival is dependent on the various weapons systems developed by large corporations, then the economic survival of these corporations is also thought to be in the national interest. During World War II, when Ford Motor Company proved to be using inefficient production methods, the government came close to putting it in receivership.[11] In 1971, however, the government made a $250 million loan to Lockheed Aircraft to avert its economic failure. The rationale for the loan was that, if Lockheed failed, the government could not obtain certain types of military hardware without a time-consuming and expensive tooling-up of another company.

The loan to Lockheed represents, at least for the present, an extreme example of the limits to which government is willing to go to sustain its suppliers, but it raises some important concerns regarding the relationship between defense production and the civilian economy. Part of Lockheed's economic difficulties arose from its inability to meet production deadlines on its civil aircraft production, particularly the L1011 Tri-Star. Although the loan was ostensibly made to keep Lockheed alive for defense production, it in effect allowed the firm to continue in civil aviation production. Such arrangements have been characterized by economist Robert L. Heilbroner as "a love affair" between the Pentagon and Lockheed Aircraft. Says Heilbroner, "It is the scandal of the military industrial interlock that the big contractors are now protected by the Pentagon."[12]

The alternative to bailing out Lockheed may very well have been the loss of almost 75,000 civilian jobs. Heilbroner has estimated that if the Department of Defense were dismantled, and no other governmental agency spending similar amounts were installed, there would be a threefold increase in unemployment.[13] This increased unemployment would not be found primarily among ex-officers, but among workers employed on defense-related projects. Were the tap to suddenly run dry, big industry's high degree of dependence on defense expenditures would result in a cataclysmic economic dislocation. Cutbacks in government spending in 1970 and 1971 had severe effects on the aerospace industry of the west coast, centered in Los Angeles. The expense of a defense establishment is no longer justified solely on the basis of national security; the country's very economic survival is dependent on it.

Priorities within government

Defense expenditures are sizeable, but nevertheless two-thirds of the national budget is designated for non-defense related endeavors. Yet in terms of priorities, the government is relatively neglectful of human services, unless they can be related to national security, national prestige or the continued growth of large corporations. Priority is put on those programs which are amenable to technological solutions and thus utilize the resources of the technostructure.

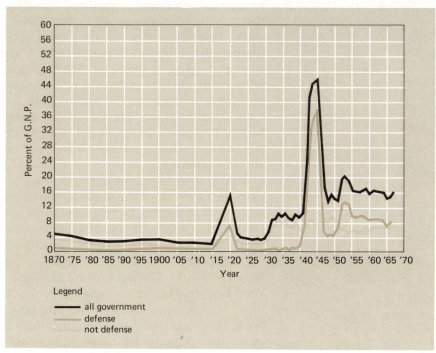

*Figure 14-2   Expenditures of the federal government as a
percentage of the GNP, 1869-1967*

When internal unrest demands it, war is declared on poverty. Solutions to poverty are not yet subject to technical methods, as is, for example, the construction of a new bomber. Progress is likely to be slow; there may be no return on investment which can be easily measured. In comparison with a public endeavor which promotes national prestige, such as the space program, solutions to poverty have little interest for technicians accustomed to results and thus to renewed funding by government. Once a technological goal such as placing a man on the moon is achieved, however, another often follows in its wake. Not to have one would threaten the economic survival of major American industries. When matters having to do with the public welfare are involved, concern over the nation's prestige sometimes evaporates. The United States is the only industrial nation without a national health plan.

Even in agriculture, technological problems are researched while human needs go unanswered. Government funds are spent for improvements in productive capacity—for example on developing special strains of hard tomatoes that are easy to harvest mechanically though not so pleasant to eat—but at the same time billions more are spent to keep a lid on agricultural production. Corporate profit-taking pervades the arrangement as well. We are accustomed to an agricultural surplus, which for years has been sold to foreign nations through corporate intermediaries, yet millions of Americans are malnourished and underfed. Only after sales in large supermarkets began lagging were Food Stamps sold to the poor. Here again, we see that the economic well-being of organizations rather than human needs provides the stimulus for government programs.

Profit-taking in human oriented programs also affects America's foreign relations. Many foreign assistance programs are contingent on the purchase of American products. A case in point was the Alliance for Progress, in essence an international development bank for Latin America, whose deposits were supplied by the United States. If a government, say Peru, wanted to borrow money to buy bulldozers, the bulldozers had to be purchased from a United States firm, even if they could be bought more cheaply from West Germany. What on the surface was hailed as an example of America's humanity was actually a profit-making venture.

Such a system is relatively benign, however, when compared to the standard operations of many multinational corporations. Numerous American companies have subsidiaries and major operations in foreign countries. Many of them have been able to pay little or no taxes on their holdings under arrangements with local governments. When such governments are replaced by a new group, the American firm is often in danger of losing its preferred tax status. The corporation thus has an interest in keeping certain officials in power. The allegations that ITT attempted to enlist the CIA in preventing the election of a Marxist President in Chile is only a recent case in point. The CIA was admittedly involved in overthrowing a socialist government in Guatemala in 1956; an executive of the United Fruit Company flew in with the new President once the revolution was successful.

The individual in corporate society

The size, complexity, and interdependence of business and government are factors which minimize the exercise of political control by the voter. Sociologist Irving S. Horowitz suggests that in America policy-making has replaced politics; it is, he says, "A system in which expertise (real or imaginary) displaces elective office in the legitimation of power . . . and elective offices are giving way in importance to appointive offices."[14] Few elected officials have had the power and prestige of the Secretaries of Defense and State in the Kennedy and Johnson administrations or of Presidential aides in the Nixon administration. Government by appointed experts ceases to be either accountable to the voter, or responsive to his suggestions for change.

In the light of recent developments in business and government, serious questions are being raised concerning the American political system. Are individuals able to affect decisions about national priorities in any way? How can individuals as consumers and as citizens successfully seek redress for various actions taken by business and government?

Voting for officials of one's choice is the traditional means in our society of choosing the priorities and policies of government, and informing those officials of needs and desires. Recent changes in the law, from the Voting Rights Act of 1965 to the Constitutional amendment lowering the voting age to 18, have opened the political process to more of our citizens than ever before. Yet America's voters stay away from the polls in droves on most election days. Many do not know the names of their representatives once they are seated, and make few attempts to influence the voting of their representatives one way or another.

The result is that the lobbyists of various special interest groups have the ear of the legislature. None of this is new in American society, but as government, federal and state, has come to rule and regulate wider and wider areas of the national life, government decisions are moved further and further away from the individual citizen, and are made on the basis of a choice between expert opinions.

For instance, few members of Congress are specialists in any legislative area. When deciding on legislation, they often need to rely on outside information. Such advice is very readily offered by well-paid lobbyists representing major corporations and industries. The costs of lobbying are tax deductible. Though some individuals belong to groups that can afford to send delegations to consult with their Congressmen about pending legislation, most do not. The result is that too few Congressmen solicit the views of their constituents except at election time. Rather they rely on the advice of corporations, labor unions, farm associations and the like. These to some extent represent the interests of the people, but the size and scope of corporate interests often override the legitimate demands of individuals or of groups with little economic power.

It is true the Congress was designed to balance local and national interests, and lobbying for legislation can to some extent be justified. The Chief Executive, on the other hand, is chosen to represent the people as a whole. Yet the President is counseled by a Cabinet, and works within a White House bureaucracy which has grown rapidly in recent years, especially in the administrations of Kennedy, Johnson and Nixon. The proliferation of special executive agencies and the increase in the size of the executive bureaucracy—to 2.8 million in 1972—has spurred the concept of decision by "experts," many of whom come from the technostructure of corporate America, and are relatively unresponsive to individual needs, depending instead on informal structures of influence. As sociologist Suzanne Keller notes, "The tyranny of the expert over the unenlightened, though different from that of the haves over the have-nots, is nevertheless a tyranny." [15]

It is difficult to view current governmental operations without skepticism. The rhetoric of popular sovereignty is still abundantly used, but the system of government is one in which congressmen look to corporate advisers and supporters, where the President receives advice and much of his campaign backing from corporate executives and experts, and where regulatory commissions accede to the demands of corporate pressure.

The Federal courts in the fifties and sixties were a means by which the citizen could reaffirm his Constitutional rights, but the use of the courts by the ordinary citizen is a lengthy and costly procedure. In cases where an important legal principle was involved, the American Civil Liberties Union, the legal division of the National Association for the Advancement of Colored People and other groups have represented what they felt was the public interest. The Supreme Court has used its power to interpret the Constitution to make policy decisions—in the school desegregation case, in cases involving the rights of accused prisoners, wiretapping and bugging, abortion, the right of indigents to counsel, miscegenation, denial of passports and other significant issues.

Without well-run organizations our standard of living, our level of culture, and our democratic life could not be maintained. Thus, to a degree organizational rationality and human happiness go hand in hand. But a point is reached in every organization where happiness and efficiency cease to support each other.

Amitai Etzioni

There is no doubt that the lack of effective institutionalized means to affect government policy was a major cause of the demonstrations and riots of the 1960s. With few resources beyond their indignation, people took to the streets in an effort to express their sense of injustice and to influence public opinion.

The relationship of the citizen as consumer to the power of the corporations which serve him is analogous to that between the voter and his representatives. Galbraith argues that "the consumer is managed by those who, nominally, exist to serve him—a tendency toward producer instead of consumer sovereignty." [16] It is necessary, Galbraith says, for large industrial concerns to have control over demand and prices, if they are to engage in the long range planning required by the extensive use of advanced technology and the related scale and complexity of organization. The key to management of demand is "effective management of the purchases of the final consumers"[17] by means of the communications and advertising industries. This results in a control over the market in which the consumer has little choice and the producer is neither accountable nor responsible to anyone. The citizen as voter or consumer has become the object of manipulation by organizations.

In his role as a consumer, however, the citizen deals with a variety of producers of goods and services. Sociologist Amitai Etzioni puts forward a continuum of institutions that are responsive in varying degrees to the "countervailing power of the consumer." He makes a distinction between consumption of goods and services and control as represented by direct financing, and then he shows that consumer power varies according to the degree of separation between control and consumption. The countervailing power of the consumer on the continuum is large for retail shops and small-scale private services; smaller for large, bureaucratized enterprises, especially those depending only partially on the mass of individual consumers; and even smaller for the rest of the economy, including organized professionals, private and public monopolies. Organized activity of consumers remains rare, although attempts are increasingly being made. Etzioni's conclusion is that "the consumer seems to be the one taken advantage of rather than the one served by the economy."[18]

---

reading: **Norman Birnbaum**
POLITICS AS ADMINISTRATION

The rise of the state technicians, then, does not mean the elimination of ideology from politics. The current debate on the sources of American poverty, with urbanists, economists, sociologists, psychologists, and a host of other experts at each other's throats, is evidence for the continuing ideologicization of politics. Arguments about the role of familial structure in engendering attitudes to work, about local or national control of poverty programs, about the incorporation of capitalist enterprise in an anti-poverty program (or about the incorporation of a program in the agenda of capitalist enterprise), about the role of an autonomous black population in state and society, are not simply technical differences. They call into play fundamental notions of social order, of the good society, and refract and express fundamental and conflicting social interests. The state technicians, here as elsewhere, exercise power.

The exercise of power by state technicians, however, is not identical with the domination of a society by a uniform elite of technocrats. That technicians have risen to directing posts in the economy, in public institutions (whether publicly administered or not) like educational systems and the media of communications, is clear. They subserve interests, however, other than their own; indeed, they frequently define their own interests (as I have just suggested above) in terms derived from their alliances with other groups. In particular, much has been made of the substitution of impersonal forms of corporate property for direct private ownership of the sort characteristic of industrial property in the early entrepreneurial epoch of capitalism. It follows, for some, that the managers of corporate property are in effect the civil servants of advanced capitalism. The analogy may be correct, but its exegesis allows a conclusion other than that of the existence of a technocratic elite uniform in its composition and monolithic in its politics. The property managers' interests are in the maintenance and extension of the privileges which accrue to property, and these often enough conflict with the interests served by the state technicians. That a long-term balance of power may align the two, in certain societies (certainly in the United States up to now) does not exclude short-term conflicts or differences. Furthermore, that the technocrats constitute an elite element in a society and a political system increasingly technicized does not render them spokesmen for the intermediate sectors of the technical intelligentsia: the interests of the engineers who work for a large corporation and of those with engineering degrees who sit on its board of directors or occupy its executive posts continue to differ. Quite apart from their relationships within the boundaries of the enterprise itself, these groups may pursue political interests (with respect to fiscal policy, government expenditure on social services, and even foreign policy) of a quite different kind. We are still obliged to understand industrial politics as the interpenetration of state and property systems.

For the United States (as for Imperial Britain before it), property and state systems coalesce most obviously in the conduct of foreign affairs. Foreign affairs, in the industrial epoch, include far more than relationships between sovereign states: they encompass investment abroad, the exercise of political and economic influence in other countries by agencies other than governmental ones, the covert intervention in the affairs of other nations effected by clandestine official agencies, and ostensibly nonpolitical cultural activities. (It will be recalled that the American Central Intelligence Agency financed a cultural organization which had the effrontery to use these funds to establish "independent" journals in a number of countries, all of them extolling the virtues of political pluralism.) Domestic spending for the varied activities categorized as "defense" and overseas investment constitute important components of the American economy: state and economy are nowhere so intertwined as in these spheres. The frequent movement of technicians and politicians (if the two categories can be kept apart) between posts in the state agencies dealing with foreign affairs and the private sector have reinforced a similarity of perspective re conventional definitions of the national interest. The description by a prominent social critic of anti-Communism as a racket may well apply to certain intellectuals; as far as the private sector is concerned, it is good business. The enormous resources at the direct disposition of the state in these spheres, the inertial force of certain policies (anti-Communism has been more quickly modified by the American elites than by a public indoctrinated over decades), the necessity for delegating authority to the state in times of crisis, do combine to endow the state with a very considerable short-term autonomy in the conduct of foreign affairs. That there is a long-term consonance of state and property interests in the conduct of foreign policy seems clear. What is less clear is the extent to which certain features of America's internal politics can be attributed to this consonance. Here, an enumeration may be helpful. Man power is planned (through mechanisms like government educational policies and the workings of Selective Service) with a view toward strengthening the nation in international competition; economic policies and social investment generally are adjusted to "defense" spending (consider the enormous stupidity of the moon race, with its distorting effect on the entire nation's technological resources); above all, the limits of national consensus have been set at those compatible with a rapid psychological mobilization of the population in the defense of a schematic notion of the national interest.

America's young (and old) radicals consider the adventure in Vietnam more than a miscalculation or a mistake; they think of it as the supreme expression of a polity organized internally for external repression. The recent popular revulsion for the war, and its electoral consequences, would seem to refute them; at the very least, we may say that the internal consensus on violent anti-Communism is not immovable. This popular revulsion followed a considerable current of doubt and disillusionment about the war amongst political and economic elites. These elites have utilized their command positions in the foreign policy apparatus to legitimate themselves as servitors of the national interest: the distinction between its own interests and those of these elites, with respect to foreign affairs, has proven up to now practically impossible for the populace to make.

It is true that considerable economic benefits accrued to a good proportion of the entire population as a result of American foreign relations. In this connection, it is suggestive that the rhetoric of the two Kennedy brothers, their insistence that only a more equitably organized American society can effectively prosecute a global mission, represents an enlightened version of American imperialism. As the examples of Bismarck's Germany and Lloyd George's Britain showed, an enlightened imperialism remains imperialism. At any rate, the sphere of foreign affairs is precisely the sphere in which the interpenetration of state and property seems to have advanced the furthest; it remains to be seen what role property will play in the new fields of gigantic state intervention in America—education, health and welfare services, and urbanism. The preliminary evidence suggests that corporate enterprise envisages a certain collaboration with the state in these areas, possibly involving the nationalization of risk, but certainly involving corporate profit.

From
"Power" in *The Crisis of Industrial Society* by Norman Birnbaum
(New York: Oxford University Press, 1969) pp. 82–86.

Sociological explanations

The values of growth and productivity that are traditional underpinnings of corporate enterprise in America have, for the economic and political reasons described above, become wed to the government's concept of its role as well. Corporate executives point to higher profits and sales in their annual reports; the government points to a rising Gross National Product (GNP), and to high levels of employment as measurements of the country's performance. The evidence is impressive, but it does not take into consideration the social costs of growth or of corporate and governmental policy decisions, nor does it account for the powerlessness of individuals who wish to change these decisions through the political system. A number of sociological explanations for the present state of affairs have been put forward.

Bureaucratic institutionalism

Many sociologists see the close relationship between business and government as stemming from the increasingly similar structures of the two institutions. Growth in size and concentration resulted in bureaucratic organization in both business and government. At the turn of the century Max Weber, a founder of modern sociology, noted that bureaucratic organization is one means by which institutions can efficiently collect information, arrive at decisions and implement those decisions. The bureaucratic form of organization, Weber believed, was the structure most suited to the modern legal-national state which requires the universal application of rules, rather than standards based on tradition and loyalty.

> The more complicated and specialized modern culture becomes, the more its external supporting apparatus demand the personally detached and strictly 'objective' *expert,* in lieu of the master of older social structures, who was moved by personal sympathy and favor, by grace and gratitude. Bureaucracy offers the attitudes demanded by the external apparatus of modern culture in the most favorable combination.[19]

In the course of arriving at their present tremendous size and concentration, however, both government and business bureaucracies underwent a transformation. Efficiency and rationality in pursuit of a goal have given way to an effort to preserve the bureaucratic structure itself, so that rather than serving simply as a means to achieving profits (in the case of the corporation) or delivering services (in the case of government) bureaucracy became an end in itself. For the new bureaucracy of the corporate technostructure, profit became a means to its own preservation, rather than an organizational goal.[20] For the government bureaucracy, the end became a continual increase of jurisdictions for governmental action; so long as it can sell its importance to the public, its legitimacy and preservation are assured. Professor Norton Long, one of the leading analysts of the public bureaucracy, has described this phenomenon:

> A major and most time-consuming aspect of administration consists of the wide range of activities designed to secure enough 'customer' acceptance to survive and, if fortunate, develop a consensus adequate to program formulation and execution.[21]

Neither our welfare bureaucracies, our narcotics units, or our government departments really want to go out of business. They have a vested interest in the persistence of the problem they were formed to control or eliminate.

Elitism

Another explanation for the cooperation of government and business derives from an elitist conception of power. Those who adhere to this conception believe that a small and select group exercises power in society, more or less behind the scenes. As originally described by the late sociologist C. Wright Mills, the power elite in America is not a conspiracy. Rather, the elite assume power through common associations which inevitably lead to common ways of perceiving and reacting to issues. According to Mills,

The rise of the elite . . . was not and could not have been caused by a plot . . . But once the conjunction of structural trend and of personal will to utilize it gave rise to the power elite, then plans and programs did occur to its members and indeed it is not possible to interpret many events and official policies . . . without reference to the power elite.[22]

While the elitist theory of power has fed the fantasies of many, it has also stimulated the investigation of many scholars. One of these, Gabriel Kolko, has shown that through corporate investments and interlocking directorships, American corporations are effectively controlled by a relatively small number of individuals.

Corporate investments enable one corporation to determine the structures and decisions of another by voting its stocks at shareholder meetings. Kolko points out that as early as 1955 the 200 top non-financial companies directly owned 43 percent of the total assets of 435,000 non-financial corporations; these 200 were effectively controlled by a maximum of 2500 men.[23] This concentration has probably become even greater in recent years.

A second mode of functioning for the elite is the interlocking directorate, the presence of directors and executives of one corporation on the board of directors of others. A good case is the executive structure of the Chase Manhattan Bank. Chase is the third largest bank in the United States in terms of its assets, deposits and loans. In 1970, it was number two in the first two categories. In 1970, Chase had among its 24 directors, the directors and/or top executives of 6 of the top 60 manufacturers in terms of sales (1970 ratings). Three of these were the Chairmen of the 1st, 6th, and 8th ranking petroleum companies. In addition, sitting on Chase's Board was the Executive Vice President of AT&T, America's leading corporation in terms of assets. Moreover, many of these members had previously held governmental office. Among the better known board members were: David Rockefeller, Chairman of Chase and brother of New York's Governor; John T. Connor, Chairman of Allied Chemical and Secretary of Commerce under President Johnson; C. Douglas Dillon, Chairman of U. S. & Foreign Securities Corp., a State Department official and then Secretary of Treasury under Presidents Kennedy and Johnson; James A. Perkins, Chairman of International Council for Educational Development and former President of Cornell University; and William R. Hewlett, Chairman of Hewlett-Packard, an executive for a top defense contractor, and partner of David Packard, who served as Deputy Secretary of Defense under President Nixon.

Chase's Board of Directors is not unique; its make-up is comparable to that of other corporate giants. Kolko notes that the actions taken by the elite, whether socially beneficial or not "would not be the results of social control through a formal democratic structure and group participation."[24] That is, society as a whole does not suggest the decisions of the elite. If valid, this would be a serious indictment of an economic and political system that is theoretically based on consumer and citizen sovereignty.

Responses

The problems of concentration and bureaucratization in business and government and the powerlessness for significant numbers of the population which results from them have elicited numerous responses. Some suggest changes in corporate policy and structure; others point to change in governmental structure and political life.

Social responsibility of the corporation

One suggestion for relief of the situation is that corporations voluntarily devise their own standards of social responsibility. The libertarian school of economics acknowledges that corporations can take steps to improve the quality of life, but only if these steps can be rationalized in terms of increased profits, over the short or long run. As stated by Milton Friedman, this school's most prominent spokesman, ". . . few trends could so thoroughly undermine the very foundations of our free society as the acceptance by corporate officials of a social responsibility other than to make as much money for these stockholders as possible."[25]

Friedman's neoclassical picture of corporate responsibility is too pure for many scholars. Daniel Bell, for instance, notes that the corporation is more than just an institution for carrying out monetary transactions; in addition it has a number of social functions.[26] Therefore it must endeavor to strike a balance between its economic role of producing goods at least cost and its social obligation to contribute to the improvement of the quality of life. Bell offers no formula for arriving at the balance, but he does suggest areas in which corporations should weigh their responsibilities, including minority employment and responsibility to communities.

reading: **Daniel Bell**
SOCIOLOGICAL IMPLICATIONS OF THE CORPORATION

The economizing mode [of conceiving the corporation] is based on the proposition that *individual* satisfaction is the unit in which costs and benefits are to be reckoned. This is an atomistic view of society and reflects the utilitarian fallacy that the sum total of individual decisions is equivalent to a social decision. Yet the aggregate of individual decisions has collective effects far beyond the power of any individual to manage, and which often vitiate the individual's desires. Thus, every individual may value the freedom and mobility which a personal automobile provides, yet the aggregate effect of so many autos on the roads at once can lead to clogged transportation. We might all accept, in the abstract, the principle that the automobile has become a vehicle of uglification; yet lacking a social decision about which alternative modes of transportation might best serve an area, I might have, willy-nilly, to go

543

out and buy a car. Each of us, individually, may see the consequences of an individual action, but lacking a social mechanism to assess it, we become helpless, drift, and accelerate it.

In effect, in contrast to the economizing mode of thought, one can specify—I apologize for the heavy-handed clumsiness—a sociologizing mode, or the effort to judge a society's needs in more conscious fashion, and (to use an old-fashioned terminology) to do so on the basis of some explicit conception of the "public interest."

Two fundamental questions are involved.

First, the conscious establishment of social justice by the inclusion of all persons *into* the society. If the value system of a society is made more explicit as a means of guiding the allocative system (pricing) of a society, this value system must also establish, however roughly, the "right" distribution of income in the society, the minimum income available to all citizens, etc.

The second is the relative size of the public and the private sector. Economic goods, to put it in textbook fashion, are of two types, individual and social. Individual goods are "divisible"; each person buys the goods or services he wants—clothes, appliances, automobiles—on the basis of free consumer choice. Social goods are not "divisible" into individual items of possession, but are a communal service—national defense, police and fire protection, public parks, water resources, highways, and the like. These goods and services are not sold to individual consumers and are not adjusted to individual tastes. The nature and amounts of these goods must be set by a single decision, applicable jointly to all persons. Social goods are subject, therefore, to communal or political, rather than individual demand.

A man cannot ask for and individually buy in the market place his share of unpolluted air, even if he were willing to pay extra for it. These are actions that have to be taken in coordinated fashion through public channels. We can assign the costs of air pollution to its source, whether industrial, municipal, or individual, in order to force culprits to reduce the pollution, or we can use the money for remedial measures. In the same way, the laying out of roads, the planning of cities, the control of congestion, the organization of health care, the cleaning up of environmental pollution, the support of education—all these, necessarily, become matters of public policy, of public concern and often (though not necessarily) of public funding.

To say, in effect, that the public sector of the society has to be expanded, is not to assume, naively, that the failures of the market will now be remedied. Each arena has its own problems, and the beginning of political wisdom is to recognize the ineluctable difficulties in each. Public decision-making can easily be as irrational and counter-productive as private decision-making. The major sociological problem ahead will be the test of our ability to *foresee* the effects of social and technological change and to *construct alternative courses* in accordance with different valuations of ends, at different costs.

A considerable amount of planning goes on already. Every major corporation today necessarily operates in accordance with a one-year fiscal plan and a five-year market strategy in order to meet competition or to expand its size. Each company plans singly and each introduces its own new technologies—yet no one monitors the collective effects. The same is true of the planning of various government agencies. In considering social effects, one finds this kind of planning unsatisfactory.

The first flaw is the fallacy inherent in single-purpose planning itself. Most engineers, developers, industrialists, and government officials are single-purpose planners. The objective they have in mind is related almost solely to the immediate problem at hand—whether it be a power site, a highway, a canal, a river development—and even when cost-benefit analysis is used (as in the case of the Army Corps of Engineers) there is little awareness of,

544

and almost no attempt to measure, the multiple consequences (i.e., the second-order and third-order effects) of the new system.

The second is the failure to make the necessary distinction between, as Veblen put it, the technological and institutional processes, or, in the terminology used by a panel of the National Academy of Sciences, between the "technologies" and "the supporting system." The automobile, the SST, pesticides, drugs—all these are technologies in the physical engineering sense of the term. The support system is the organization of production and distribution, or more generally the economic and legal matrix in which the technology is embedded. The simple point is that there is no "technological imperative," no exact one-to-one correspondence between a particular technology and a specific supporting system. As Jack Burnham pointed out in a pungent way: "When we buy an automobile we no longer buy an object in the old sense of the word, but instead we purchase a three-to-five year lease for participation in the state-recognized private transportation system, a highway system, a traffic safety system, an industrial parts-replacement system, a costly insurance system . . ."

One may, therefore, depending on the problem, seek to change either the technology (the gasoline engine) or the support system (unrestricted private use of the roads). But what this allows us to do is to compare alternative modes, at alternative costs, and to design better systems to serve social needs. This, in turn, suggests a need for national "technology assessment." With few exceptions, the decision about the future use of a technology today is made by the economic or institutional interests who will primarily benefit from it. But as the panel of the National Academy of Sciences argues: "Decisions concerning the development and application of new technologies must not be allowed to rest solely on their immediate utility to their sponsors and users. Timely consideration must be given to their long-term sacrifices entailed by their use and to potentially injurious effects upon society and the environment often remote from the places of production and application."

In rather inchoate fashion, assessment and decisional systems already exist in the federal government. The Federal Water Pollution Control Administration, the National Air Pollution Control Administration, and the Environmental Control Administration, all are empowered to make studies of consequences; but they have less power to establish controls. Some agencies, such as the Atomic Energy Commission both promote new technology (e.g., nuclear power) and assess the consequences. But what may be needed are *independent* boards to make assessment and propose remedial actions to the executive or to Congress. Whatever the final structures may be, it is clear that some social decision mechanisms will have to emerge in the next few years to make such assessments of second-order effects of technological and social change.

And for the private corporations, a new principle in the relation of corporations to public policy will soon be emerging. Just as it has been public policy to provide tax inducements to help corporations expand plant capacity (by investment credits, or more rapid depreciation allowances), so it will be public policy to provide tax penalties either to force corporations to bear the burdens of social costs generated by the firm, or to favor an alternative technology or supporting system if the social costs can be minimized by the alternative system or the social benefits enhanced. Given the collective effects of private decisions, this involvement of public policy in corporate policy is inescapable.

From
"The Corporation and Society in the 1970's" by Daniel Bell
The Public Interest 24 (Summer, 1971) pp. 17–21.

Reform of regulatory agencies

The interlocking directorates described earlier do not violate current antitrust or antimonopoly laws. So long as competitors do not sit on each other's boards or on the boards of suppliers or customers, they may sit on the boards of putatively neutral third parties. It might be possible, through revision of the antitrust laws, to reduce the level of concentration the interlocking directorates make possible. Congress might also consider the composition of the regulatory agencies.

Federal legislation has recently been put forward to create a new independent agency, a Federal Consumer Protection Agency with no regulatory power of its own, to represent consumer interests before other Federal agencies that do have regulatory power. Robert Pitofsky, former director of the Federal Trade Commission's Bureau of Consumer Protection, testified before Congress on "the consumers' woeful lack of clout in the corridors of Federal power." The consumer's interest is fragmented and grossly under-represented in ordinary regulatory business.

People's lobbies and class action

The government's taxing power might also be reassessed in terms of the way it affects public interest groups. The Daughters of the American Revolution, which lobbies for many causes which it deems patriotic, is granted tax-free status, but the Sierra Club, which lobbies for environmental causes, has had its tax free status rescinded.

In general, tax policy might be revised to give an even break to the recently developed people's lobbies, such as Common Cause and the Center for Responsive Law. Under the present system a large corporation may deduct lobbying as a business expense, but the private citizen who donates to a "people's lobby" which challenges the corporation may not deduct this contribution from his taxes.

The technique of the class action suit came into fashion in response to the high cost of justice and the rather wide ranging effects of corporate and government actions. For instance, automobiles come off the assembly lines in a series. If one has a defective brake system, it is likely that the other 9999 in that series will also have this defect. It is also likely that no single purchaser among the 10,000 will be able to afford the court costs to successfully pursue this grievance against the manufacturer. Through the use of class action suits, a consumer organization can sue on behalf of all 10,000. If the court finds in their favor, the manufacturer is obligated to make amends to all.

Before the recent court decisions that turned back such cases, class actions had had both direct and indirect effects on corporations. Not only were several cases for product callbacks won, but several more were avoided by voluntary callbacks and rollbacks of defective and unsafe products. Government was just as liable to such action. For example, curtailment of assistance programs by administrative fiat or state legislative actions contrary to Federal law were successfully challenged by Community Action Legal Services, a branch of the Office of Economic Opportunity. If such activities are to continue, the class action technique must be sustained.

Government reorganization

Another solution that might be considered involves government reorganization: return of some decision-making power to states and localities, for instance. Under revenue sharing, recently enacted, the national government redistributes some of its revenues to state and local governments for them to use as they determine, rather than in ways defined in Washington. If revenue sharing is to be successful, however, state and local governments must also be made more responsive to citizen input. When the national government provides a Public Service Employment Program to a locality, local governments may be allowed to hire personnel to perform functions which the local government feels are necessary, e.g. police protection, education and beautification programs. In hiring employees and deciding on what must be done, local governments have until recently been required by Federal guidelines to give greater attention to the needs of the hard-core unemployed, minorities, youth, welfare recipients and veterans. Under revenue sharing, the national guidelines might prove difficult to enforce.

The administration of programs which are not delegated to the states and localities might also be reformed, of course. National budget determinations, environmental quality standards, development of desirable levels of agricultural production, and so forth, involve policies which must be performed at the national level, but they are often left to competing agencies and departments. The Presidency has developed a greater span of control over the activities of the countless bureaus and agencies which plan and carry out government programs. But it cannot be denied that the federal bureaucracy is often so elephantine as to be ineffective in fulfilling its functions.

The imposition of tighter controls on campaign spending and increased disclosure of campaign contributions might somewhat lessen the power of wealthy individuals and organizations on legislators. Proposals have also been made to limit the level of donations which any one contributor may make. Open disclosure of campaign contributions certainly subjects the motivations—real or suspected—of contributors to public investigation. The campaign disclosure laws which went into effect in 1972 have already had the effect of clearing the air. It has also been suggested that income tax credits be granted to all who contribute to political campaigns, a move which might be an incentive to individual citizens to contribute and thus become more involved in the political process.

Notes

[1] Alexis de Toqueville, *Democracy in America*, vol. 1 (New York: Alfred A. Knopf, 1945) p. 55.

[2] Robert A. Dahl, *Who Governs? Democracy and Power in an American City* (New Haven: Yale University Press, 1961) p. 1.

[3] Walter Lippmann, "What's Democracy?" in Karl M. Schmidt, ed., *American Government in Action* (Belmont, California: Dickenson Publishing Company, Inc., 1967) pp. 2–3.

[4] John Kenneth Galbraith, *The New Industrial State,* 2nd ed. (New York: New American Library, 1971) p. 104.

[5] *Ibid.,* p. 84.

[6] *Ibid.,* p. 88.

[7] Morton Mintz and Jerry S. Cohen, *America, Inc.* (New York: Dell Publishing Co., Inc., 1971) p. 27.

[8] Ralph E. Lopp, "Military-Industrial Complex," *The New York Times Encyclopedic Almanac 1970* (New York: New York Times Company, 1970) p. 736.

[9] Stanley Lieberson, "An Empirical Study of Military-Industrial Linkages," *American Journal of Sociology,* Vol. 76, January 1971, p. 564.

[10] Marc Pilisuk and Tom Hayden, "Is There a Military-Industrial Complex that Prevents Peace?" *Journal of Social Issues,* vol. 21, No. 3, pp. 67–117.

[11] Peter Drucker, *The Practice of Management* (New York: Harper & Row, 1954) pp. 113–114.

[12] Robert L. Heilbroner, "Controlling the Corporation," in Robert J. Heilbroner, et al., *In the Name of Profit* (New York: Warner Paperback Library, 1973) pp. 211–212.

[13] Robert L. Heilbroner, "Military America," *New York Review of Books,* July 23, 1970, p. 2.

[14] Irving L. Horowitz, *Three Worlds of Development,* rev. ed. (New York: Oxford University Press, 1972) p. 149.

[15] Suzanne Keller, *Beyond the Ruling Class* (New York: Random House, Inc., 1963) p. 278.

[16] Galbraith, *op. cit.,* p. xv.

[17] *Ibid.,* p. 200.

[18] Amitai Etzioni, *The Sociology of Organization* (Englewood Cliffs, New Jersey: Prentice-Hall, Inc., 1964) p. 106.

[19] H. H. Gerth and C. Wright Mills, eds., *From Max Weber: Essays in Sociology* (New York: Oxford University Press, 1958) p. 216.

[20] Charles M. Bonjean and Michael D. Grimes, "Bureaucracy and Alienation: A Dimensional Approach," *Social Forces,* Vol. 48, March 1970, pp. 366–367.

[21] Norton Long, "Power and Administration," in Schmidt, *op. cit.,* p. 203.

[22] C. Wright Mills, *The Power Elite* (New York: Oxford University Press, 1959) p. 293.

[23] Gabriel Kolko, *Wealth and Power in America* (New York: Praeger Publishers, 1962) pp. 56–57.

[24] *Ibid.,* pp. 68–69.

[25] Milton Friedman, *Capitalism and Freedom* (Chicago: University of Chicago Press, 1962) p. 133.

[26] Daniel Bell, "The Corporation and Society in the 1970s," *The Public Interest* 24, Summer 1971, p. 170.

Summary

In the past thirty years, the scope of American government has grown so wide, its administration so technical, and its relations with American business so close, that the power of the citizen to influence governmental policy, or even to affect the direction of his own life, has been minimized.

In America the competitive market system has given way to a national economic life dominated by corporations. Corporations were able to absorb suppliers and distributors, thus gaining control over market insecurities. As corporations became larger, they also became more complex. Specialized technostructures took over each function within corporations' far-flung operations. Corporations once restricted their operations to a single industry, but since World War II they have bought up diversified industries, formed conglomerates and extended their operations abroad. Relatively few corporations control a large portion of the nation's assets and employ a large percentage of its workforce. The size and concentration of American corporations has effectively eliminated competitive pricing and seriously affected consumer choice. Much of present-day industrial production serves product needs contrived by an aggressive advertising program sponsored by industry.

Since the time of the Depression the size and scope of government operations have risen to match that of business. At that time President Roosevelt streamlined the governmental bureaucracy with technocrats. The result was a technostructure similar to that of business, which expanded as the economic and administrative roles of government grew wider.

Following World War II, when the cold war caused American defense expenditures to mushroom, the largest corporations received major shares of defense contracts. Over time, the corporate economy has become highly dependent on government defense outlays. Interpenetration of the business and defense technostructures is typified by the large number of former military men entering business, who greatly influence the placement of defense outlays and contracts.

Besides expenditures for defense, priorities in government spending tend to go to those projects related to national prestige, such as the space program, and to those which are amenable to technical solutions. In fields such as agriculture, where technology has solved problems of production, government policy maintains attitudes toward distribution based on corporate profit-taking, rather than on human need. Problems not readily yielding to technical solutions, such as poverty or the improvement of health care, are often downgraded, unless political currents demand their solution.

Multinational corporations, seeking tax havens and special benefit in operations abroad, also have a large potential for influencing American foreign policy.

The monetary and organizational power of technostructures in business and government have seriously affected the American political system. The political system depends on a legislature and executive responsive to citizens. Policy decisions are increasingly dependent on the technical opinions of experts, rather than matters for public debate and political decisions, and lobbying by organizations with vested interests exists on a large scale: factors which limit the effectiveness of Congress and the executive branch. Lack of institutional response to demands for changes in government and corporate policy has led to public demonstrations and to the formation of consumer movements striving for greater governmental and corporate accountability.

Theories of bureaucracy explain the present system as the attempt by organizations to perpetuate themselves. Elitist theories contend that interlocking directorates between top officials of major corporations and banks, many of whom have served in government as well, place major decisions about social goals in the hands of a small group of powerful people.

Increased social responsibility on the part of corporations is suggested as one method of alleviating the social effects of business size and concentration. Reform within the regulatory agencies of government, to give them greater power to operate in the public interest, is also suggested. Consumer movements and legal moves such as class action suits are attempting to make corporations and government more responsive to individuals. Moves for government decentralization, such as revenue-sharing, are also suggested, together with reforms in the tax system.

chapter

work

Most adults in the United States spend forty years or more of their life working eight hours a day, five days a week, with two weeks vacation and six paid holidays. Their satisfaction, or lack of it, with the work they do and the income they receive is the central experience of their lives. In earlier eras, the family, community and religious activities were expected to give meaning to work. Today, we expect work to give meaning to other areas of life. There is no other aspect of a man's life that provides as much social continuity as does work. The work people do determines the material comfort and economic security that they and their families enjoy, the social milieu in which they live, and, as a result, their identity—their sense of themselves and their view of the world they live in.

The primary function of work is economic: work is the means toward the end of earning a living. Income is necessary for survival in a money economy, and without the income from their jobs most people would not be economically self-sufficient. Unions have long recognized this, and negotiations usually begin with wage and salary demands. Money is a necessary reward of work, but is by no means the sole meaning and purpose of work.

The kind of work a man does and the amount of income he receives locates the worker and his family in the class structure of society. His income determines the areas of the community in which he will live and, therefore, the schools to which he will send his children. Because his job regulates the hours of his daily life, he is able to associate with some people but not others. Further, a person's friends may often be members of the group with which he works.

A man or woman's self-esteem is closely interwoven with work. If a job is providing something worthwhile to an organization and a community, this is clear evidence to the worker and others of his value and is an important source of self-esteem. Also, as he achieves mastery of his work, he develops feelings of accomplishment, which, in turn, lead to self-confidence. The worker to a degree has control over his surroundings. Work, then, fulfills individual psychological needs.

For these three reasons—economic, social and psychological—lack of work or absence of meaningful and challenging work can lead to serious problems for the worker.

Society also feels the effects of work and work problems and unemployment constitutes the largest work problem today. The economic ramifications of unemployment reach not only the worker, who must then be provided by society with some means to support himself and his family in the form of welfare or unemployment benefits, but those who contribute taxes to this support. If unemployment becomes widespread in an area, the ramifications are felt by local shopkeepers, banks and property owners. In slum areas where unemployment is a constant problem, the attendant ills of poverty, crime and unstable family life constitute a state of social disorganization. When there is not enough work or when the work that does exist increasingly frustrates the workers' attempts to satisfy basic needs, the society pays high economic and social costs.

Besides unemployment, another important problem in our rapidly changing technological society is worker dissatisfaction. People care profoundly about the quality of work, and significant numbers of American workers are dissatisfied with the dull, repetitive form most work tasks have assumed. They offer little challenge or autonomy.

The callous palms of the laborer are conversant with finer tissues of self-respect and heroism, whose touch thrills the heart, than are the languid fingers of idleness.

Henry David Thoreau

Although a worker may have a job, if he believes the work itself is meaningless or if he does not consider himself an integral part of the total operation or have opportunity for advancement based on achievement, he is discontent. Job dissatisfaction leads to lower productivity on the part of the worker as measured by absenteeism, turnover rates, wildcat strikes, sabotage and poor quality of work. Today a general increase in education and economic status has placed American workers in a position where an interesting job is as important as the income it produces. Pay is still important, but it will not, by itself, produce satisfaction with the job. The growing awareness of the importance of meaningful work is a fairly new social problem and reflects an overall concern with the quality of life. Examination of the vital problems of unemployment and the quality of work as they relate to blue-collar and white-collar workers, to men and women, to workers of various ages and races and to society will here be followed by discussion of some recent attempts to solve problems related to work in America.

Attitudes toward work

In America, ideas about work have been derived largely from the Protestant Ethic of the early settlers. This work ethic, derived from Calvinist doctrine the Puritans brought to America, held that thrift, diligence and deferring pleasure were virtues; work was man's highest duty; idleness was evil; and worldly success was proof of salvation. Although the specific tenets of the work ethic may have had diminished impact on workers' motivation in later years, work is still seen as a righteous means to achieve the benefits of wealth. The Protestant immigrants from northern Europe in the early part of the nineteenth century also were imbued with the same ethic of hard and constant work, saving and deferred gratification. Later immigrants saw work as the primary means to make a better life for themselves and, particularly, for their children. In America, the dream of life, to move upward in society, was to be achieved by hard work.

The progression of different systems of production, from subsistence farming to cybernation, demanded different patterns of work and ownership from Americans. As the technology became more and more complex, the individual worker learned new skills and conformed to the kinds of jobs required by the economy.

Work in the colonies

During colonial days 95 percent of the population lived on farms. The subsistence farm encouraged individualism, with each farmer and his family working autonomously, making their own decisions and consuming the products of their labor.

The mercantile system of the eighteenth century fostered small individual businesses. In the North, many tradesmen—merchants, artisans, craftsmen—were self-employed. In the South, owners of large tracts of land commanded the labor of indentured white servants and black slaves, but with the exception of the slaves, few men were employees.

Industrialism

By 1840 there was a marked proliferation of small mills and the industrialism which was to characterize American life was beginning to take shape. The Civil War hastened the consolidation of small, individually owned businesses into giant enterprises. Such men as Andrew Carnegie, John D. Rockefeller and the railroad organizer James J. Hill were the instruments of a vast money power that reorganized and enlarged America's industrial capacity. During the course of this expansion, these industrial giants and others like them provided jobs for natives and immigrants alike. And apart from those who gave up their independence in enterprise with reluctance, Americans generally greeted the industrial age with optimism.

The character of work changed with early industrialization and imposed certain constraints on the worker. He was no longer his own boss and had to spend a required amount of time in his assigned place, usually performing a repetitive task. Working conditions were generally poor or unsafe, hours were long, and wages were low.

Mechanization and automation

As technology progressed, the factory system became more sophisticated. Early in the twentieth century Henry Ford introduced a new kind of work organization which greatly increased the efficiency of assembling the components of a manufactured article. The assembly line he developed in 1913 to produce automobiles more rapidly and cheaply has since been adopted by most manufacturing and processing industries.

The assembly line consisted of three basic features. First, workers remained stationary and performed their operations on parts that were moved to them at optimum speed. Second, parts and partially finished products were delivered to workers mechanically on a conveyor belt in a calculated progression; for example, an automobile interior was trimmed after the car body was fastened to the chassis. Third, each operation was broken down into the simplest possible motions because a worker could develop maximum speed by repeating only a few movements again and again.

Automation has further refined the assembly line and added nonhuman control mechanisms to work. An article about the Ford Motor Company in *American Machinist* in 1948 defined automation, using the word in print for the first time, as:

> the art of applying mechanical devices to manipulate work pieces into and out of equipment, turn parts between operators, remove scrap, and to perform these tasks in timed sequence with the production equipment so that the line can be wholly or partially under pushbutton control at strategic stations.[1]

Cybernation, the result of adding computers to automation, changed work even further. Cybernation can be defined as the "simultaneous use of computers and automation for the organization and control of material and social processes,"[2] and for the manipulation of symbols and material objects. Computers perform clerical jobs such as billing and payroll work, as well as monitoring production quality and performing welding and machining operations.

Automation and cybernation have relieved workers of many tiresome tasks and freed them from certain kinds of drudgery. On the other hand, workers must now be more subservient to machines, keeping up with the pace of the machinery and attempting to match the accuracy of the devices around them.

Technology

In our twentieth century employees economy, technology has changed the kinds of work available, the organization and institutions of work and the security of the worker. It used to be assumed that a person would work his whole life in one trade or craft. Rapidly changing technology now makes that an obsolete concept. A man who began his work life in the manufacture of 78 rpm records twenty years ago must now be able to work with tapes. To continue work in the sound reproduction business, he will probably have to learn about quadrophonic systems.

Automation has revised work in several ways. First, it has eliminated many jobs. Elevator operators have virtually disappeared. Dock workers and coal miners have been replaced by automated machines. Jobs in manufacturing decreased from 34 percent of the total employment in 1950 to 26 percent in 1972. Second, automation requires a staff of technical and service personnel who have new skills and more education. Third, there is greater bureaucratization of work and the ranks of middle managers have swelled because their knowledge of a specialized area has given them new authority. Technocrats and scientists have also moved into the business hierarchy at nearly the same level as managers. Along with that increase, the percentage of industrial workers has gradually declined since 1955.[3]

Worker insecurity is integral to the nature of work today. Not only does technology make old skills and jobs obsolete, but the dynamics of the American economy also affect the job market.

The burgeoning of employment in the space and defense industries in the 1960s, followed by a sudden and massive shrinkage of jobs in those fields in the early 1970s, came about largely because of shifts in the pattern of federal spending. As the national government attempts to combat inflation by controlling wages and prices, the job market will be still more unsettled. Automation has given employers new choices in the use of machines to do work. One of the important strains within industrialized society is uncertainty. Workers at all levels must live with the possibility of displacement from the work force. At best, anyone who sets out with plans to work in a specific occupation may have to adjust to a different career.

The work force

According to figures released in March, 1973, the total labor force of the United States in 1972 numbered 88 million persons, including members of the Armed Forces. The proportion of people working to the total population has remained fairly constant since 1947 which means the labor force has increased at a rate roughly the same as the rate of total population increase.

While the percent of men in the population who work has dropped slightly from a high of 83 percent in 1950 to 75 percent in 1972, the percent of women in the population who work has gone up from 33 percent to 43 percent. Moreover, as many women were "keeping house" (and, therefore, were not counted as working) as were in the work force in 1972, which would indicate that women may do far more work than the percentage in the work force would indicate.

The number of nonwhites in the work force is about nine and a half million. The percent of nonwhite men in the population who work is slightly less than the percent of white men. In 1972, 69 percent of nonwhite men worked as compared to 75 percent of white men. However, a greater percent of nonwhite women work than white women—48 percent as compared to 43 percent.

White-collar workers totaled over 39 million in 1972. The majority of them, over 14 million, were labeled by the Bureau of Labor Statistics as clerical workers, but nearly as many, over 11 million, were at the top status level, professional and technical workers. More than 8 million were managers and administrators; only 5 million were listed as sales workers. Publications of the United States Department of Labor indicate that "About a fourth of all employed women were in five occupations—secretary-stenographer, household worker, bookkeeper, elementary school teacher, and waitress."[4]

Blue-collar workers numbered over 28 million in 1972. More than 13 million were factory operators. Craftsmen and kindred workers numbered well over 10 million, while nonfarm laborers numbered 4 million. Just 3 million were listed as farm workers.

The Bureau of Labor Statistics lists "service workers" in a category separate from white- and blue-collar workers. Medical, health, hotel and personal services were performed by 11 million workers in 1972. The total of white-collar and service workers is about 50 million, which means that over half of all workers are engaged in nonmanufacturing jobs. Although the marketplace is swelling with increasing production, fewer workers are producing the tangible goods. The trend is toward increases in the number of government employees and far more workers in services than in production.

Criticism of labor statistics

The Bureau of Labor Statistics is empowered with the important task of regularly collecting and reporting statistics on the labor force. The methodology of the BLS has been criticized, particularly in regard to the figures on unemployment. While unemployment will be considered later in this chapter, it may prove useful to explore briefly at this point objections to procedures both of counting and labeling the unemployed. One aspect of the criticism is that nonprofessional persons with political interests have been employed by the BLS to release findings to the press. The consensus among economists and other social scientists is that official statistics must be collected and compiled without bias or any suspicion of manipulation.

The other criticism is that the methods and definitions employed by the BLS to compile statistics on unemployment, while above criticism of secret manipulation, systematically undercount unemployed people. The BLS collects its statistics by means of regular surveys of a sample of the population who are asked certain questions by interviewers. The answers are then tabulated according to the classifications of employed or unemployed. The criticism centers around the wording of the questions, which favors a higher count of people employed. For example, people who have worked at any time during the period of the survey are counted as employed whether they are working or not. Workers who are on strike, on vacation or ill are classified as employed whether or not they are receiving pay. Seasonal workers are considered employed even if the survey covers a period in which they are not working. People who have been unemployed for over twenty-eight days and are not looking for work during the survey period are not included in the labor force as either employed or unemployed. Definitions actually serve to increase the number of people employed and decrease the number who are jobless.

More difficulties attend the figures on unemployment of minority groups. Spanish-speaking peoples are included with the white labor force, thereby making the difference between white and black unemployment in New York City, for example, not as great as it actually is. Similarly, Asiatic peoples are considered nonwhite. In San Francisco, where Japanese-Americans have very high rates of employment, they boost the official employment rate of chronically unemployed blacks.[5]

Classification and status

Although the classification of jobs into professional, white-collar, blue-collar and laborer categories is a device of the Bureau of Labor Statistics, it is descriptive of the social and economic class hierarchy in this country. Rank in the hierarchy is related to an individual's income, social prestige and quality of life. Despite egalitarian ideals and a semblance of democratic informality at the top of the hierarchy, the listing of work categories by the statisticians conforms so closely to the realities of the class structure in American life that socioeconomic status can be predicted from job classifications.

Professionals have the highest job status and are at the top of the classification hierarchy. A professional's occupation involves general systematic knowledge, authority over clients, community interest as well as self-interest, symbolic as well as monetary rewards, self-determination of tasks and recognition by the public and law (through licensing) of professional status.

Occupations do not remain constant with respect to professional standing. As the requirements for the licensing of clergymen becomes more a matter of conscience and conviction than of seminary education and training, that occupation becomes less professional. On the other hand, nurses and social workers, as well as doctors, have developed organizations that guard the status of the occupation as a profession and set standards for professional status and the privileges and prerogatives of members. Such groups have become more professional in recent years. In general, white-collar workers differ from professionals in that they are employed by an outside agency, use practical skills and exercise much less self-determination.

Generally, white-collar workers work for annual salaries rather than hourly wages, perform tasks requiring some amount of advanced education and are not as likely to be subject to layoffs as less prestigious blue-collar workers. Although the salaries of clerical workers and salespeople are lower than those of the better paid blue-collar workers, the close association with management, the more attractive atmosphere of the place of work and even the clothing worn to work confer greater social prestige on the white-collar worker.

Blue-collar workers perform work that demands training and perhaps skill or craftsmanship but not higher education. They have no subordinates unless they move up to positions as foremen or line supervisors. Such positions are usually the limit of their upward mobility, and they expect no more. One study showed that nearly half of all factory workers interviewed believed that they were stuck in their jobs no matter how well they performed. Only the combination of seniority, built up over the years, and exceptional good luck could help them advance.[6]

A steel handler, interviewed by Studs Terkel in "The World of the Blue-Collar Worker," said that he felt he was looked down on by others because he was a manual laborer.

> It's the nonrecognition by other people. To say a woman is *just* a housewife is degrading, right? . . . It's also degrading to say *just* a laborer. The difference is that a man goes out and maybe gets smashed. It isn't that the average working guy is dumb. He's tired, that's all.[7]

Other interviews with blue-collar workers "revealed an almost overwhelming sense of inferiority: the worker cannot talk proudly to his children about his job, and many workers feel that they must apologize for their status."[8]

Still lower in status than blue-collar workers are the unskilled manual laborers, or day laborers. One group in this category is migrant workers. Although farming is respectable, farm labor is not.

Lowest on the social ladder, migrants receive the least pay, are excluded from social security or unemployment benefits, are paid only for hours worked; their working conditions are not under government control.

The problems of unemployment

At all levels and in all categories of the work force, there are people who can't find work. Unemployment is the most serious problem of the work structure in America. While federal officials assert the tolerability of 4 percent unemployment, the human fact is that during 1972 close to 5 million people on the average were denied income through lack of work.

To assess fully all of the human factors of unemployment, we must add to the number of unemployed the millions who earn so little that their earnings fall below the established poverty line. To these we must also add those who are underemployed. Underemployment, another facet of the unemployment problem, is the term used to describe the worker who is working less than full-time, at a job below his level of skill or training and for wages that are insufficient to support himself or his family. Those whose primary support is derived from welfare or who are out of the labor force but wish to work must also be included. The aggregate of these three groups total between 10 and 30 million people who are not accounted for in the official Bureau of Labor Statistics. As we examine the rates, kinds and causes of unemployment and the differential impact of unemployment on women, minorities, youth and other groups, we shall consider as well the impact of unemployment on society.

Unemployment statistics

The rate of unemployment for 1972 was 5.6 percent of the civilian labor force. For men over the age of 20 the unemployment rate was 4 percent, while for women over 20 years old it was 5.4 percent. For male and female members of the work force ages 16 through 19, the unemployment rate was 16.2 percent. Most statistics eliminate this age group from employment averages.

For all whites the unemployment rate for 1972 was given as 5 percent. For Negroes and other minorities it was listed as 10 percent. White men over 20 years of age had the lowest unemployment rate of all groups by age, sex and color in 1972—3.6 percent. The highest unemployment rate was that of blacks, ages 16 through 19—33.5 percent. White youths had the next highest unemployment rate, 14.2 percent of those included in the labor force. Unemployment has a differential effect on men and women. Women of all races had higher unemployment rates than men. Negro and other minority women had nearly twice the rate of unemployment as white women, despite the fact that their need to work is often greater.

The unemployment rates differ significantly among various occupations. Nonfarm laborers had the highest unemployment rate, with 10.3 percent of those so designated out of work in 1972. Operative, service workers and blue-collar workers, together, had well over 6 percent unemployment. White-collar workers, on the other hand, had much lower unemployment rate of all the white-collar categories, 4.7 percent. Managers and administrators had the lowest rate of unemployment of all groups, with only 1.8 percent out of work. Professional and technical workers also had a relatively low rate of unemployment in 1972, only 2.4 percent.

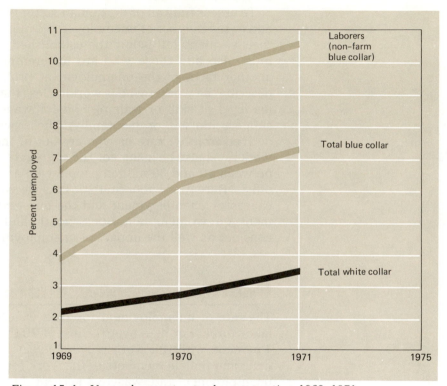

Figure 15-1   Unemployment rates by occupation, 1969–1971

These statistics clearly show that unemployment is not uniformly distributed among the total work force and reveal the inequalities of the social structure. Sex, race, age and occupation play primary roles in determining who is unemployed. A white male, over age 20, and a member of the managerial class has the highest probability of maintaining employment, while a black youth in a nonfarm or blue-collar laboring job has the highest probability of being unemployed. The higher rates of unemployment among women present another instance of discrimination.

The labor unions have little power to deal with unemployment. Many union contracts forbid firing an employee except under certain conditions, and when many workers are to be laid off, the contract will specify that layoffs be on the basis of seniority. Although layoffs according to seniority protect older union members, they discriminate against minority groups who are the "last hired and first fired."

Causes of unemployment

Many factors contribute to the unemployment problem in our society. They include shifts in consumer demands and priorities, government spending, the state of the economy, the structure of job openings, disputes between management and labor, seasonal fluctuations, automation and rapidly changing technology and discriminatory employment practices. For the purposes of this discussion, however, we shall concentrate on the effects of three: the economy and the government, automation and technology and discrimination.

Economy and government

During the period of severe economic depression that existed during the decade of the thirties, millions of workers were unemployed. However, as the unemployment statistics of 1972 clearly show, in a prosperous economic period millions of workers are still unable to find work. In the early sixties there was a change in the economic policies of the federal government, and full employment became an important priority. Employment increases with economic growth, but growth is also accompanied by inflation. Balancing the desire for full employment against the disadvantages of inflation, the federal government finally determined to hold the line on inflation and tolerate a rate of unemployment of 4 or 5 percent.

Shifts in priorities in government spending are more directly visible than changes in economic policy at the highest levels. During the 1960s billions of dollars were allocated by the federal government to related defense and aerospace industries. In many geographical areas huge plants were constructed and thousands of workers employed. Between 1969 and 1971, however, enormous cutbacks in federal funding to these industries caused them to reduce their work force severely or close their operation completely. The result was an unusual phenomenon: large-scale, long-term unemployment among professionals and technicians. Because of the high status of these people, their misfortunes were highly publicized by the news media. However, the picture of the "middle class unemployed further dramatizes the plight of the larger number of unemployed, non-skilled workers who may have to cope with unemployment often."[9]

Economic policies and national priorities bear a constant relationship to the size and composition of the work force. The conditions of unemployment among professionals is only a minor though vivid manifestation of the effects of shifts in federal spending.

Automation and technology

Workers at the administrative, professional and technical levels are generally not as likely to lose their jobs due to automation and rapidly changing technology as are workers at the clerical, blue-collar and laborer levels. When computers and automatic control devices are introduced into factories and offices, only skilled personnel are needed for their operation or maintenance, resulting in the loss of jobs for unskilled and clerical workers who may be unable to find other jobs. When coal mining was greatly mechanized during the 1950s, miners found themselves in this position. The effect of automation in a particular business situation is one in which a few highly skilled persons plus machines replace many people with low level skills.

The universal demand for happiness and the widespread unhappiness in our society (and these are but two sides of the same coin) are among the most persuasive signs that we have begun to live in a labor society which lacks enough laboring to keep it contented. For only the animal laborans, and neither the craftsman nor the man of actions, has ever demanded to be "happy" or thought that mortal man could be happy.

Hannah Arendt

Labor unions, particularly the craft unions, have tried to control the jobs of their membership by stipulating conditions of work in their contract agreements. When automation has made certain jobs obsolete, as in the railroad, printing, stagecraft and construction industries, unions have insisted that certain jobs be retained even when the work was replaced by a machine. This is called "featherbedding" and can be employed only with discretion. If the unions make work too costly, whole corporations and even undustries can go out of business.

However, automation and mechanization creates new jobs, as well as whole new industries, which come into existence to manufacture and service the machines. IBM has grown in twenty years from a small company manufacturing office equipment into one of the largest corporations in the world employing many thousands of people.

During the 1960s automation was considered a cause for alarm as it appeared to be causing extensive changes in work in America. In 1966 the National Commission on Technology, Automation, and Economic Progress issued a report that called for a manpower policy that would facilitate movement of the labor force from the farm to the city, from the South to the North, from blue-collar to white-collar positions and from manufacturing goods to producing services. These shifts were deemed necessary to meet the growing demands for skilled service personnel who could be trained to fill technical jobs in northern urban areas, as well as to prevent unemployment among the less skilled workers who might be displaced as a result of the mechanization of their jobs.

The Commission's report also assumed that those who had only simple manual skills would be unemployable in more sophisticated, technological industries and recommended that the federal government become an "employer of last resort" for these people. It was estimated that over 5 million jobs could be created for them in the areas of national beautification, urban renewal, sanitation and services in medical and educational institutions.

However, Charles Silberman suggested that:

> Automation is only a minor cause of unemployment. Over-all, however, what evidence is available . . . suggests that automation does not radically alter the existing distribution of skills. *Jobs* change, allright, but not the level of skill. . . . The work may involve a different kind of rote, but it is still rote.[10]

Current opinion is that aggregate demands for goods and services and government policy play a more important role in the employment situation than does automation.

Minorities

Members of minority groups, who would number about one out of every ten workers at all levels if parity existed, have unemployment problems of grave dimensions. One report asserts that "one out of three minority workers is unemployed, irregularly employed, or has given up looking for a job."[11]

Systematic discrimination in hiring practices throughout the American economy works a far greater hardship on minority groups than social prejudice or discrimination in housing or education, and according to Gunnar Myrdahl's classic study on racial prejudice, *An American Dilemma*, is the root cause of poverty among minority groups. Despite the recent improvement in the situation of young educated black men who are beginning to be hired on a par with their white counterparts, study after study has shown that qualified members of minority groups at every level have lower level jobs, receive less pay and have higher unemployment rates than majority groups. Even after the passage of federal legislation banning discrimination on the basis of race or sex, minority workers are not found in many unions, are usually hired for menial jobs and are among the first to be laid off.

The social costs of joblessness among these young people is primarily a loss in productivity. In a sense, they are a drain on the economy since they make no contribution. In the 16 to 19 year old group, they will be either high school dropouts or will finish high school and eventually head for a blue-collar job. Their problems will be largely personal as each one wrestles with the difficulties of finding his niche in society.

The high schools tend to concentrate on the student headed for college, and a recent survey found that high school guidance counselors spend twice as much time on college-related counseling as they do on vocational topics. Nevertheless, over half of high school graduates receive some form of job guidance, while less than a quarter of the drop-outs receive such guidance. Vocational training is a sadly neglected area in our schools and, except for apprenticeship programs in a few unions, there is little attention given to training young people in skilled work. In England and the European countries, vocational training and apprenticeship programs are offered in a great number of occupations. In *Work in America,* a study sponsored by the Department of Health, Education and Welfare, it is recognized that "where training cannot be obtained on the job, there is clearly a need for society to help young people to receive the skills they need to earn a living."[12]

Figure 15–2   Percent of civilian labor force unemployed by specific group, 1955–1972.

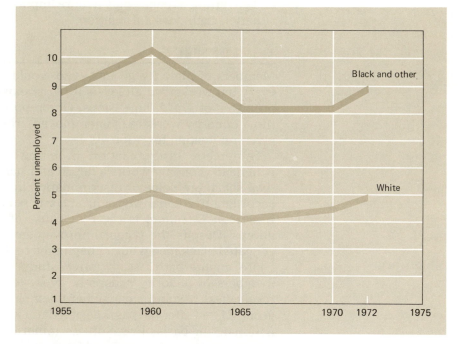

Women and unemployment

Although numerically not a minority group, women, because of discrimination against them in hiring practices, suffer from the same problems as the more clearly recognizable minority groups: unemployment, underemployment and unequal pay for equivalent jobs. Women are prevented by occupational sex-typing from obtaining jobs for which they are qualified; they are discouraged from entering occupations and professions which have traditionally been for men only; and they have been ignored in regard to promotions despite their work records.

There are 31 million women in the work force, over half of them married. For most of these women, work is a necessity, not a matter of choice. Three-quarters of all working women hold full-time jobs when they are employed, and their incomes are vital to family well-being. In 1964, well over 4 million women were heads of families.

The differential impact of unemployment on women workers is significant. Over the years they have consistently had a higher rate of unemployment than men, often nearly twice as high. In 1969, a year of low unemployment for men (2.8 percent), one of every twenty working women was without work. Single women and those separated from their husbands have the highest unemployment rates among women, and teenage single women have a higher rate than older single women.

Occupational sex-typing has limited the work women are hired to do. Sex-typing is a term applied to a situation in which traditional expectations derived from the sex roles are associated with work roles. Thus, the association of the feminine role of wife, mother and housekeeper are carried into occupational categories. Women are largely restricted to occupations such as secretary—the office wife; nurse, social worker and school teacher—the nurturing mother. Managerial pursuits associated with men's roles or occupations that require high level skills are usually closed to all but a few "token" women. Occupational sex-typing effectively closes off most jobs and crowds women into a limited number of jobs where the pressures of excess supply lowers wages below the level that would otherwise prevail. "Once such a division of labor becomes established, it tends to be self-perpetuating since each sex is socialized, trained and counseled into certain jobs and not into others."[13] And, in fact, as Abraham Gitlow noted, there is a "major structural disjuncture" between the educational tracks recommended to and popular with young women on the one hand and the labor market demands and job openings on the other hand.

According to Hanna Papanek, some American women choose to be part of a "two-person career," remaining unemployed, but experiencing achievement through participation in their husband's careers. This pattern, typical of the upper middle class, she says, "plays a particularly significant role . . . where an explicit ideology of educational equality between the sexes conflict with an implicit inequality of occupational access."[14] In fact, she finds some women find the demands of their husbands' jobs to be important in their own reluctance or inability to attempt independent careers at levels for which their education has prepared them.

Some women have been displaced by automation. The number of telephone operators dropped by almost 100,000 when direct-distance dialing equipment was installed. In spite of an expansion in telephone service, fewer operators needed to be hired. Much of the clerical work involving payrolls, inventories, invoicing and sales in the banking, insurance and department store industries has been taken over by computers, although women with appropriate training and skill can work as computer programmers, keypunch operators, tape librarians, console operators and systems analysts. The jobs available to young women just entering the work force, however, typically require only low level skills, so they have frequently been displaced by automation in some fields. Throughout the decade 1958–1968, unemployment rates for women under age 19 was above 12 percent in comparison with 4.8 percent for all women.

Federal law now requires that women be given equal pay for equal work, but in 1970 women took home only 59 percent as much income as men. Discrimination against women is evident in unequal pay as well as job segregation, and the courts have ruled that $44.5 million in back pay is due to more than 108,000 employees under the Equal Pay Act of 1963.

A different look at income discrepancies for women came from Juanita Kreps,[15] who estimated that the 1960 Gross National Product would have been $105 billion larger than it was if all housekeeping wives over age 18 without preschool children had been working outside their homes. Her claim is not that their productivity in the marketplace would have been greater than it was at home, but rather that the failure to value housewives' services as part of the GNP has had important consequences for the status of homemaking as work. Thus, subsidies to welfare mothers could well be justified as payments for work as homemakers rather than as a handout.

Unemployment as a lost resource

Unemployment represents a loss of human resources. Whether measured by the material loss of goods and services that might have been produced or by the loss entailed in human suffering, the cost of unemployment is high. Unused natural resources are banked for future exploitation. But work, the creative activity of man, when wasted, can never be recovered. Apathy attends unemployment and often inhibits a worker who should retrain and enter a different occupation. Unemployment creates anxiety and insecurity. The unemployed cease to participate in the life of the community when their associations at work are severed by unemployment. Nor do the unemployed have the energy or the disposition to make new social connections. They are, indeed, lost to the community.

Worker dissatisfaction

A problem of major proportions in our economy concerns the large number of people who are working but are dissatisfied with their jobs. The reasons for this dissatisfaction with work are that the worker feels he does not have and will not be able to gain any control over his work situation, and, secondly, that neither he nor his work has sufficient merit or importance. The immediate source of this dissatisfaction includes the mechanical arrangements of work and the routinization of tasks, the lack of intrinsic rewards from the work itself, the absence of control over the work process and the insufficiency of financial rewards. Another term to describe the dissatisfaction produced by these conditions is alienation.

As early as the nineteenth century, Karl Marx recognized the problem of alienation in factory life. Factories one hundred or more years ago were brutalizing and dangerous places where men, women and children worked long hours in prisonlike conditions. Marx, while critical of these places of work, was more concerned with the state of mind of the factory worker for whom this kind of work had no meaning. The worker could not identify with the goods produced as he tended a machine which was only a small part of the process of production. He had no control over any portion of the production process and was, in fact, a kind of appendage to the machine itself. Marx described the state when a man's deepest feelings are separated from his activities as alienation.

Certainly the methods proclaimed as efficient in terms of human movements in production processes introduced by Frederick W. Taylor in 1911 in his book *Principles of Scientific Management* only further exacerbated worker alienation as observed by Marx. Taylor's ideas were based on job analysis—breaking down each task into its simplest motions—and on time study—calculating the amount of time each movement takes. By eliminating unnecessary movements, Taylor turned men into efficient adjuncts to the machines with which they worked. One of his earliest successes was in directing every movement of a pig iron handler named Schmidt, enabling him to handle 47.5 tons per day instead of 12.5 tons. What the application of Taylor's principles meant to workers was a dissatisfaction with work—the anonymity of feeling like a piece of machinery, powerlessness over the work itself, inability to make decisions about techniques or tools to be used and an inability to identify with the finished product; in short, work became meaningless.

Alienation from work or worker dissatisfaction is seen today as a combination of four factors: (1) powerlessness—no worker control over the policies, instruments or conditions of his work, (2) meaninglessness—no feel for the relationship of a single task to the production process as a whole and no broad awareness of the utility of each operation, (3) isolation—no sense of cooperation with fellow workers and little contact with them, and (4) self-estrangement—boredom with monotonous repetitive work and the sense of being trapped.

---

reading: **Bennett Kremen**
A DOWNER DAY IN THE MILLS

Yanagan, Charlie Chan, Scatterbrain, his brother Nobrain, Measles, Big John—almost everyone in the mills gets a nickname, including me after the second week:

"Out late last night, huh?" I hear while half asleep in the labor shack, a tiny room where the men warm up in this freezing open building.

"Yeah," I tell Stash, one of the few older Polish guys still coming in here since the young blacks arrived.

"Chasin' whores, huh Ben . . . that's it—*Ben Whore!*" Everybody laughs except those still asleep, but they don't remain that way long:

"Get up—it's Biz!"

Four of my young friends leap up from their daze and dart out onto the floor away from the crotchety foreman: Stash heads upstairs where the electric furnace is blazing—and the big pay's made. I follow Yanagan, the burner, who lights up his torch and starts cutting up scrap, but only until Biz passes out of sight.

"Come on Ben Whore—let's get away from here!"

"Hey, that's some name Stash gave me."

"Yeah—he's all right."

"Why do most of those guys upstairs stay out of the labor shack, Yanni?"

"Why?—'cause they're jive-ass bigots!"

"Are the younger workers the same way?"

"Uh-uh—some of those white boys are all right—not all of 'em; but a lot are gettin' hip. We wrote a petition to get a new union man for this shop, and none of those lilly-asses upstairs would sign it, but those young dudes did."

"What about the union—you for it?"

"You gotta be—or this company'll fuck you up for good! But none of us really gives a shit about the union, 'cause no kind of big shot is goin' to make it any different in here."

"How do you want it to be different, Yanni?"

"I don't know man—just different, *real* different."

Yanagan leads me through a dark corner of the shop now, his eyes cast cautiously at the overhead cranes scooping up scrap for the insatiable furnaces upstairs.

"Psssst!! Hey!"

Hissing at us from behind a half-filled gondola car is Tommy Thumbs, and huddled uncommonly close to him are Little Joe, two vets recently back from Vietnam, and the new Italian kid.

"It's a downer day, man—let's lift it up!" Tommy passes a joint to Yanagan who draws the smoke deep, then hands it to me. For a moment I hesitate till Little Joe pats me on the shoulder and says: "What you waiting for? When you're feeling bad, you take medicine, right? Well, this place makes ye feel sick, and you got the medicine right in your hand!"

The smoke striking into my lungs sends my blood leaping. And soon the flying sparks, the hot steel, the raging, exploding furnaces above us seem like frivolities on a carnival night.

Not all the mills in the country are quite like this one, I'm told. But old hands insist they will be, as the older workers retire in the next five years.

"Maybe some big doses of economic trouble will shape these kids up," a tough-minded company man told me in Pittsburgh. "But that's liable to murder us too. And I'd hate to see too many of this breed out on the streets without jobs. I just don't think it'd be healthy." Others both in Pittsburgh and Detroit reminded me that plenty of the younger workers—indeed many I've met—are diligently paying off mortages and working hard for a second car, "and when that other type gets older and has a few kids, everything'll probably settle down." Yet when I asked what'll happen until then, I got only a shrug of the shoulders. A few clever economists, however, point out that the steel industry has invested more than $10 billion in capital expenditures since 1965, but that the expected soaring increases in productivity associated with such a huge investment hasn't materialized. The "productivity puzzle" is what this unprecedented mystery, found not only in the steel industry, is being called. And it's haunting the financial wizards of Wall Street and Washington. I recommend they spend a few days in a labor shack getting it all straight.

"Tommy—you've been out for two days. Don't you miss the bread?"

"I can get by. I rather have the time than the money."

"You know—if jobs stay tight, the company'll probably start cracking down on that."

A sudden, angry silence falls, and all the men in the shack are staring at me. But I keep on talking because after four weeks of digging choking lime from degasser pits, hooking scrap to cranes, and sweeping miles of dust and grime into neat little piles the way they do, I'm entitled to their trust. "What if they crack down, Yanni?"

"They don't own me, man! If I want a day off, I take a day off. Nothin's gonna stop that!"

"What if they fire you?"

"Then let'em fire me. I ain't seen 'em do it yet."

"Why not?"

" 'Cause the next guy who comes along is going to do the same thing I am."

Everybody in the room is laughing—not at me or Yanagan but at the company, that slightly ridiculous Goliath they so easily can thumb their noses at. For just the other day when Biz, that old Yankee workhorse, caught Charlie Chan sleeping in the locker room, he rolled his cigar in his mouth and began barking:

"Get to work! You know you shouldn't be lying around in here—go on now!"

"Fuck you Jack!" Charlie hissed up at him.

"Get your coat mister!"

"Shut up, or I'll shove that cigar right down your throat!"

"You get the hell home!"

Charlie is laughing now as he tells us how mellow it was having the rest of the day off even though he lost the pay, and how he came in ten minutes late the next morning and not a word was said.

"Don't you care at all about getting the work done, Charlie?"

"They don't care about me—whether I'm livin' or dying! Why should I give a shit about them!"

Not all these young men are so bitter, and some even work hard—when they show up. But neither whites, blacks, skilled workers, laborers, militants nor conservatives—and there are conservatives—are thankful to the company for providing them with jobs.

"Oh,—that's strictly Mickey Mouse," a young Polish millwright with hair flowing from under his hard hat said to me. "You find some guys upstairs talking that way—but not many my age. This company is using me to make money: I use them the same way. And that's all. . . ."

From
Bennett Kremen, "No Pride in This Dust," *Dissent*
(Winter, 1972) pp. 21–28.

Sources of worker dissatisfaction

The problem of worker dissatisfaction has recently been discussed in the works of Frederick Herzberg, Abraham Maslow and John Kenneth Galbraith. Each of these men classifies a system of needs and motivations which are related to worker satisfaction.

Herzberg observes that there are two different kinds of work conditions related to worker satisfaction. One set of conditions is concerned with the work environment—good pay, safe and sanitary conditions and supervision with consideration for human dignity. Even if this set of conditions is satisfactory, Herzberg notes a second source of worker dissatisfaction. The work itself must be challenging, must provide an opportunity for accomplishment and must enable the worker, himself, to feel responsible for the achievement.

Maslow[16] suggests that human needs are hierarchical and that as needs are satisfied at one level, the unsatisfied demands at the next higher level are felt as keenly as were the more basic lower level needs. He sets up the following hierarchy: first, simple physiological needs such as food and shelter; second, a need for safety and security; third, the need for friendship and affection; fourth, a desire for self-respect and esteem from other people; and fifth, at the top level, a need for "self-actualization," for the chance to develop fully one's potential. The first and second levels of Maslow's hierarchy are similar to Herzberg's environmental factors, and the fourth and fifth levels are comparable to considerations of a sense of accomplishment.

Galbraith,[17] in discussing motivation of workers in corporate organizations, outlines a four-level hierarchy. Only after the conditions of work have satisfied the motivational desires at a lower level do the desires of the next higher level operate as incentives to work.

Increasingly, the problem of exploitation is giving way to the problem of uselessness. The bitter truth seems to be that the current militancy of American Negroes is less a product of their exploitation than of their growing uselessness in an increasingly automated economy. One can bargain and negotiate and thus affect the terms and conditions of exploitation; but one can only grow desperate and overtly rebellious in the face of a sense of growing uselessness.

Alvin W. Gouldner

In Galbraith's system the lowest level of the hierarchy of motivation to work is simple fear of punishment, or compulsion. At the second level, money is a motivating force. The goods, services, comfort and status that money can obtain are so extensive that financial rewards operate as intense incentives to work. Money is certainly necessary to worker satisfaction, but it is not enough alone. The next level of motivation Galbraith postulates as "identification." As human beings evaluate their own positions in relation to those of the people around them, it becomes important to them to accept the goals of their managers and to identify with the aims of their work organization. After "identification" has become motivation for working, workers desire to adapt the goals and policies of the work group to their own values. "Adaptation" serves as an additional incentive for workers whose motivation has been satisfied at the three lower levels. Lack of satisfaction at any of these levels can lead toward worker alienation.

Feelings of alienation and dissatisfaction were already prominent in the factories of the nineteenth and early twentieth centuries where the mechanization of work made it dull, deadening and dangerous. As work became more automated, worker dissatisfaction grew more pronounced. Computer control of work now extends from heavy industry jobs through lower level white-collar jobs and even into some of the work of professionals.

Dissatisfaction among industrial workers is particularly evident in the automotive industry. In 1955 Eli Chinoy published a study of the frustrated aspirations of workers in "Autotown." In the factory he studied, 25 percent of the workers performed their jobs on some kind of conveyor line. Nearly 30 percent were operating automatic or semiautomatic equipment which is highly repetitive work. Only 5 percent were skilled workers. He found that nearly 80 percent of the men he interviewed had at one time considered leaving the factory. Chinoy sees their frustration as centered on the disparity between the American myth of success and the real limits to advancement of their jobs. Their work in the factory, he found, entailed "few clear-cut sequences of progressively more skilled, better-paid jobs. . . . instead, the men worked at carefully time-studied jobs in a highly rationalized industry [which] provide little opportunity to display either initiative or ability."[18]

In early 1972, prolonged worker dissatisfaction at a General Motors plant culminated in a 22-day wildcat strike after a speedup of the assembly line which allowed the workers only 36 seconds to perform their operations. The walkout was preceded by massive sabotage and was supported by most of GM's other assembly workers.[19] Although the growth of labor unions has secured for almost all industrial employees substantial benefits in the form of better wages, working conditions and medical and pension plans, the unions have not been able to confront the industrial corporations directly on the problems of job satisfaction. In most instances, industrial workers are stalled at the second level of Galbraith's hierarchy.

White-collar workers, too, face fragmented, repetitive, mechanical, meaningless tasks. Clerks, accountants, bookkeepers, secretaries, keypunch operators, telephone operators—these lower level white-collar employees feel cut off from advancement in dead-end jobs. They are increasingly dissatisfied with their pay, as well as with their mechanized jobs. As the size of the organizations which employ them grows, they, like production line workers, have become anonymous cogs in the bureaucratic machinery. Two signs of their discontent are a 46 percent increase in white-collar union membership between 1958 and 1968, and a 30 percent annual turnover rate.

Professionals endure a certain amount of insecurity and dissatisfaction also. Among professionals and managers, 70 percent responded affirmatively to a Gallup Poll statement that "they could produce more each day if they tried." While most workers could certainly increase their productivity, the implication of the statement reveals professional workers' perception of their own dissatisfaction. Even at this level, work could be more meaningful.

Social effects of worker dissatisfaction

Technology has invaded offices of higher management in the form of computer professionals who have more knowledge than the managers they work for. These and other scientists and technicians on whom managers depend, called "technocrats" by Galbraith, threaten the authority of managers who do not keep up with advances in technology. When profit pressures are high, older executives undergo severe tension.

Disproportionate dissatisfaction is felt among some groups of workers: women, blacks, and youth especially report to pollsters and researchers their discontent with work. For all of these groups, some of the sources of dissatisfaction are the same: rising expectations frustrated by low wages, boredom, lack of dignity, no opportunity for progressive advancement and little authority to direct their own work. These three groups are demanding equality and the chance to exercise the same rights as white male workers.

The quality of work and its vital relationship to the quality of life led to a thorough study of work in America in 1972. The resulting report, *Work in America,* offers extensive documentation linking worker dissatisfaction to economic, social and personal costs. It affects workers at all levels of society and affects society adversely. Certain costs of worker dissatisfaction are passed along to the consumer in the form of inefficient services and inferior products. According to a variety of studies in *Work in America,* mental and physical health to some degree vary inversely with work dissatisfaction. Other studies indicate that escapism through drugs or drinking, family dissension, suspicion and hostility and political apathy are all social costs of worker dissatisfaction.

Some responses to work problems

The major response to dissatisfaction with work conditions has come from the workers themselves. The trade union movement historically and right up to the present is the most important institution devoted to the problems of the worker.

Strategies for creating new jobs and enriching existing ones have also been incorporated into government programs. The programs proposed to create more jobs and to train or retrain workers in employable skills are directed toward reducing unemployment and worker dissatisfaction. The federal government, along with state and city governments, has taken on a share of the responsibility for solving work problems.

Some new methods of organization in factories that incorporate cooperation, decision-making power and greater autonomy among workers have been tried in a few companies and show promise of a viable solution to worker dissatisfaction.

The trade union movement

Unions have their historical roots in the nineteenth century. But the struggle for the acceptance of the institutionalization of the union as the legitimate representative of the workers took place in the 1930s and was characterized by bitter strikes and the hounding of union organizers by management and government alike. The early unions were organized around specialized crafts, but in the thirties whole industries, such as the automobile, mining and electric industries, were organized into single unions. The industrial unions not only bargained for higher wages and better working conditions, but felt that the improvement of social conditions for all was an integral part of their movement.

In some unions, for example the International Typographical Union of printers, the sense of community among the workers is quite strong and offers some alternatives to worker dissatisfaction. Participation in union activities and recreational activities associated with the union is high and a classic sociological study found that there was a positive relationship between participation in union activities and job satisfaction.

In many sectors of the American economy, however, workers are still without union organization. This puts nonunion workers at the double disadvantage of receiving lower wages and having to pay high prices for goods produced by industries. The craft unions, particularly in the construction industry, have closed their ranks to minority groups, effectively preventing them from learning the necessary skills or obtaining employment.

Although unionization has not fulfilled the promise of its early days, the trade union has functioned to protect the individual worker from the misused power of management. Within a given industry, the power of the union is limited by the effectiveness of its only weapon—the strike. Since strikes are as costly to union members as to the management, it is a weapon seldom resorted to. Unions have no leverage to create jobs or to change the structure of the work situation to improve worker satisfaction, despite gains they have made on other fronts.

Federal employment strategies

The goal of federal laws and policies concerning work should be, according to *Work in America*, "total employment." That situation would obtain when anyone who wishes to work is able to find a job that is reasonably satisfying. The report does not accept the economists' definition of "full employment," which permits 4 percent of the work force to be unemployed at any given time.

Federally supported work programs began in the 1930s when 25 percent of the labor force was unemployed. In response, President Franklin D. Roosevelt created jobs with public funds to employ 10 percent of the labor force. In 1946, the Employment Act committed the national government to a policy of combating unemployment in broad terms. "It is the continuing policy and responsibility of the Federal Government . . . to promote maximum employment, production, and purchasing power."[20] In spite of this policy, the rate of unemployment from 1957 to the present has seldom been less than 5 percent.

Three pieces of legislation in the early 1960s were directed at the employment problems of women and minorities: (1) the Equal Pay Act of 1963 requires that men and women receive equal pay for equal work; (2) Title VII of the Civil Rights Act of 1964 prohibits discrimination in hiring and promotions on the basis of sex, race, national origin or religion; and (3) Executive Order 11246 of 1965 is a "contract-compliance provision affecting companies which do business with the Government."[21] Every employer with a federal contract worth $50,000 or more must file a written affirmative-action plan listing the company's "utilization rate" of minority group members in each of its job categories at each of its establishments.

Later in the 1960s two programs were established for job training: (1) WIN, the Work Incentive Program, of 1967, was to provide education and job training to welfare recipients; and (2) JOBS, Job Opportunities in the Business Sector, was expected to create 338,000 jobs by June, 1970, through the joint efforts of the National Alliance of Businessmen and the government. In 1971, Richard Nixon was the first president since Franklin D. Roosevelt to endorse a general public employment law, the Emergency Employment Act. It called for investing $2.25 billion in the creation of 15,000 public service jobs. Though this program has not yet been implemented, this is an important policy determination.

These and other programs at the state and local levels have been established to alleviate unemployment among women, youth, minorities, those displaced by automation, and hard-core unemployed white males. Another group who now need help is the 350,000 veterans of Vietnam who must be absorbed into the economy.

These programs have not been too successful. In some cases trained persons have not been able to establish contact with businesses to find openings that would fit their abilities. Many who need some kind of federal assistance do not fall into the categories specified in the laws governing the programs. Some hastily drawn-up plans were put into effect haphazardly. JOBS, for example, in 1972 had enrolled only enough trainees to make up 10 percent of their 1971 goal. In 1972, WIN had only 100,000 participants rather than the expected 280,000, and only 20 percent of its trainees are actually working now. Many of them are in menial jobs which pay little more than welfare.

On the other hand, the Equal Employment Opportunity Commission and the Department of Labor have recently engaged in a landmark agreement with the American Telephone and Telegraph

Company concerning employment and promotion of women and minority workers. Some $38 million will be paid to 13,000 women and 2000 minority group males who allegedly suffered job discrimination, and to about 36,000 workers whose advancement in the company may have been impeded by discrimination. The company has also agreed to alter its system of hiring, promoting and transferring employees in order to upgrade female and minority workers and to take steps to end sexual sterotyping in job descriptions. Men will be hired as operators and women as line and switch workers.

Democracy in the factory

A movement far more conspicuous and active in Europe than in the United States is that for workers' control or democracy in the factory. The goal is not better working conditions or job enrichment, but power over production. André Gorz, a French journalist, notes that the division of labor is both technical and social. The specialization of jobs in a factory, so that no one knows enough about other aspects of the production process to be capable of taking any initiative or making decisions, is intentional. If everyone in a factory had the skills to do all the operations in a factory, they would not only understand the overall process but would be able to make decisions. Knowledge is power, as we know, and we need no longer speculate what would happen if employees were given power over the process of production and the power to hire and fire, to set salaries.

Writer David Jenkins describes several factories, one owned by Proctor and Gamble and the other General Foods, in which worker democracy has been attempted.[22] In a pet food factory in Topeka, Kansas, where there was poor quality production, vandalism and graffiti on the walls, the conditions were diagnosed as symptoms of alienation among a younger work force. The management decided to adopt a new approach which emphasized human needs—the employees' self-esteem, sense of accomplishment, autonomy and increasing knowledge. What was needed was "autonomy"—workers desired to plan the work, check the quality, change the design of jobs. They wanted real control, not just control over simple stuff such as when they took their coffee breaks.

The management cut down on the work force to make each job more challenging and omitted as many specialized functions as possible. Each worker learned every job at his own pace from another worker and proceeded up the pay scale according to his progress as judged by the other workers. Employees also took on the job of hiring and firing. The results are considerable in terms of worker satisfaction. But more suprising was the result in terms of cost of production. Overall costs of the product are considerably lower than customary in a conventional plant and quality is higher because of greater worker involvement.

At a Proctor and Gamble factory in Lima, Ohio, there were similar

results. Although the pay scale is considerably higher than is customary, overall costs are approximately half those of a conventional
plant. Furthermore, the workers take on more activities outside the
workplace. Nearly 10 percent of the work force in one democratically
run plant holds elective office in the outside community. The lesson is
important: personal satisfaction and fulfillment go hand and hand
with efficient production.

Shorter workweeks are another means of reducing worker dissat-
isfation. One study of over one hundred companies trying the four-
day forty-hour week showed increases in worker motivation and
productivity. A related concept is that of earlier retirement. At
General Motors a worker can retire anytime after thirty years of work
with an adequate pension. The Armed Forces have long had early
retirement plans.

Abbreviated workweeks and shorter working lives pose the problem of leisure, however. Finding meaning and identity in leisure may
prove as difficult as searching for autonomy and significance on the
job. Not many of us are trained for long periods of fruitful, satisfying
non-work.

---

reading: **Raymond Williams**
WORK AND SOCIAL ORGANIZATION

There is never only a work process, of the kind that is usually abstracted: a set of operations
on things. There is also, whether recognized or not, a set of social relationships, which in
experience are quite inextricable from the work. In organizing the work, these real
relationships have defined it; a change of social organization can change the definition. It
follows that we can only properly explore the meanings of work if we explore this kind of
organization: whether by asking how we come to be doing a particular job, or by asking why
it is being done in this way and not that.

Take the first question first.

If work often means that we have to do what we would never freely choose to do, what
kind of fact is that? There are obvious cases where there are unpleasant jobs to be done, that
all other things being equal we wouldn't do, and we do them, sometimes, because we see in
the end that it isn't a conflict between desire and reality, but that the desire and the reality
include each other: clearing up a mess, getting something out of the way, saying something
difficult that absolutely has to be said. All of us do jobs like this, not because we want to do
them as such, but because we see them as necessary, if the desire and the reality are to meet.
But then what is characteristic of our kind of society is that the relation between desire and
reality has been specialized and, as it seems, set beyond us. This isn't just that we can only
do what we want if we do at least some other things that other people want. Such a fact is
a condition of any society: the basis of any co-operative effort and common responsibility.
But it becomes a travesty of itself: a rhetoric surrounding an absence of meaning. What the
rhetoric covers, in our own society, is the actual source of the decisions about what work is
done and how it is to be done. To discover this real source, to follow the questions right

through, is to see the reason for the gap between what work means and what much of it has been made to mean.

What is the reason why the woman bringing up her children, the man digging his garden, the men and women running societies, are not said, conventionally, to be workers? They are *working* but not *workers* while they are doing that: a strange paradox. But the explanation is simple. They are not, though working, engaged in wage-labour for another; or in the performance of services for a salary or a fee. Some women, it is true, are in effect employed by their husbands; what they get, as housekeeping, is even spoken of as a wage by the husband. Yet that only brings this most immediate and personal of activities within the larger and dominant system: what most men and women would do anyway, looking after their children and their house, is specialized to the woman and reduced, by analogy, to the habits of thought of the impersonal system outside. This is a common and persistent degradation, in which a real desire is exploited and made to conform with an imposed and external reality. The weakness and exposure of women, while they are bearing children, has been used to impose what is not reality but a particular method of organization. Yet as such it is only a dramatic example of a common condition, in which both men and women are exposed and then used. The man who treats his wife as a special kind of wage- or fee-servant is only doing to her what has usually already been done to him. His work, springing from his desire to make his living in the world, has been accepted only on terms set by others. What he wants to give his energy to has to fit in with that system. Anything else he devotes his energy to will not, in such a society, be socially recognized as work. It will be what he does in what is called his own time.

Once again, the decision about what needs to be done, about what is worth giving his energy to, is usually not made by him, or by co-operation with others. It is made by those who, as it is usually put, have work to offer. Who are these people and how do they come to be in such a position, that they can decide what work there is and how it is to be done? The simple answer used to be the rich: if you have money, you can employ others. This is still often true, and it ranges all the way from the really rich, who can employ a houseful of servants, to the man or woman who sets aside a part of his own personal income to get some part-time service. But it isn't the possession of money, as such, that decides most work. It is the possession of a very different thing: capital, not a store of currency to be dipped into to get some service done, but a store, an organization, of labour, and of the means of labour. Most work can only be done if its means are provided: tools, materials, workplaces, outlets. But then the decision about what work will actually be done and how falls to those who own or control these means. This, fundamentally, is capitalism. The means of work have passed into the hands of the minority who own this necessary capital and who are alone in a position, in a developing society, to begin new major enterprises. What is really social capital—the product of generations of co-operative work—has passed into the hands of a small group who then, as they say, have work to offer to others; or, as they more often say, have a need for an abstract thing they call labour (the labour market—that is, the energy of other men and women—is treated factually on the same level as that other requirement for the things which are raw materials). This is the real root of the class system. What is often called a protest against class is no more than a secondary protest, about opportunities or treatment or attitudes within this system. This is an important area of tension and complaint but it must be seen as secondary to the basic process, which settles what work and what conditions of work are available at all.

The meaning of work, in such a system, is reduced, against all other human interests, to

a profitable return on the investment of capital. Labour is wage-labour, and to find the meaning of work in wages alone is a shadow—a real shadow—of this commanding fact, by which men's freedom to direct their own energies has been practically limited for so long that it can pass as a fact of nature. There has, of course, been an important and widespread revolt against such a system. Generations of men and women have fought for the recovery of the means of labour, by a system of common ownership. In some areas—education, and the social services—work has been defined as a public service, subject to democratic direction and control. This was also one of the meanings of the demand for the public ownership of industry, and it is said that this has happened in our nationalized corporations. But we have only to look at the experience of anyone working in education or the social services or in one of the nationalized industries to know that in practice the alienation is still real: this is not, all the way through, free and co-operative effort, but is still subject, sometimes grossly, to external and seemingly arbitrary controls.

The reasons for this are important. It is not only that the nationalized industries have been instructed to fit in with a capitalist economy, and to conduct their own operations on what are called ordinary commercial lines, which is to say, choosing work according to whether it is profitable rather than whether it is, on general grounds, necessary. It is also that the basic organization of work—in these new services as in the old—has been made to conform with the kind of relationships that were so deeply learned when the power to direct other men's work was factually, by the possession of capital, in minority hands. Thus an authoritarian structure—what is euphemistically called the chain of command—is imposed on areas of work which are supposed to be and in fact often are socially owned and subject to open democratic decision. Because nowadays people usually resent authoritarian methods there is, of course, a constant attempt to disguise this reality. There is talk of human relations in industry but these, characteristically, are the human relations that are possible—information, politeness, outings, sports fields, office parties, speeches—after the decisive human relations, of who decides what is to be done and how, have been settled and built in. It is even called, in the trade, man-management, which means, quite frankly, keeping people happy while they are working for you.

If we are ever to recover effective control over the direction of the energy that we call work we shall have, it is clear, to call for more than common ownership, though we shall certainly have to call for that. Common ownership will only mean anything, in practice, if it is experienced where it matters, when decisions are being made: first-order decisions, not merely their second- and third-order consequences

From
The Meanings of Work by Raymond Williams in *Work, Twenty Personal Accounts,*
ed. by Ronald Fraser,
(Baltimore: Penguin Books, Inc., 1968) pp. 292–298

Notes

[1] James R. Bright, "The Development of Automation," in *Technology in Western Civilization,* Vol. II, eds., Melvin Kranzberg and Carroll W. Pursell (New York: Oxford University Press, 1967) p. 635.

[2] Donald N. Michael, "The Impact of Cybernation," in *Technology in Western Civilization,* Vol. II, *op. cit.,* p. 655.

[3] "Where the Workers Are," *Fortune,* May 1972, p. 189.

[4] Janice Neipert Hedges, "Women at Work: Women Workers and Manpower Demands in the 1970's," *Monthly Labor Review,* June 1970, p. 19.

[5] John C. Leggett and Claudette Cervinka, "Countdown: Labor Statistics Revisited," *Transaction,* December 1972, p. 100.

[6] Robert Blauner, *Alienation and Freedom: The Factory Worker and His Industry* (Chicago: University of Chicago Press, 1964) p. 206.

[7] Studs Terkel, "A Steelworker Speaks," *Dissent,* Winter 1972, p. 11.

[8] *Work in America* (Cambridge, Massachusetts: The MIT Press, 1973) p. 35.

[9] Douglas H. Powell and Paul F. Driscoll, "Middle Class Professionals Face Unemployment," *Society,* January/February 1973, pp. 18–26.

[10] Charles Silberman and the editors of *Fortune, The Myths of Automation* (New York: Harper and Row, 1966) pp. 3, 21.

[11] *Work in America, op. cit.,* p. 51.

[12] *Ibid.,* p. 151.

[13] *Work in America, op. cit.,* p. 60.

[14] Hanna Papanek, "Men, Women, and Work: Reflections on the Two-Person Career," *American Journal of Sociology,* Vol. 78, No. 4, January 1973, pp. 852–853.

[15] Juanita Kreps, *Sex in the Marketplace: American Women at Work* (Baltimore: Johns Hopkins Press, 1971) p. 65.

[16] Abraham Maslow, *Motivation and Personality* (New York: Harper and Row, 1954).

[17] John Kenneth Galbraith, *The New Industrial State* (Boston: Houghton Mifflin, 1972) pp. 141–143.

[18] Eli Chinoy, *Automobile Workers and the American Dream* (Garden City: Doubleday, 1955) p. 21.

[19] Emma Rothschild, "GM in More Trouble," *New York Review of Books,* March 23, 1972, p. 20.

[20] Arthur Okun, ed., *The Battle Against Unemployment* (New York: W. W. Norton and Company, Inc., 1965) p. viii.

[21] Harvey D. Shapiro, "Women on the Line, Men at the Switchboard," *New York Times Magazine,* May 20, 1973.

[22] David Jenkins, "Democracy in the Factory," *Atlantic,* April 1973, pp. 78–83.

Summary

Work is the central activity in the life of every adult man and woman. People work primarily to earn a living, but the nature of the work they do also determines the socioeconomic class they belong to, gives them a sense of identity and a frame of reference from which to view the world. When the economy does not provide either a sufficient number of jobs for the working population or work is structured in a fashion unsatisfactory to the worker, the reverberations are felt throughout society. Unemployment and underemployment are a major correlate of poverty, and social disorganization and worker dissatisfaction may result in shoddy goods, sabotage and strikes.

The primary attitude toward work in America is derived from the Protestant ethic, in which industriousness and success were proof of salvation, a doctrine appropriate to a society of individual striving and small businesses. As technology grew more complex and small businesses gave way to corporations employing many thousands of people, however, workers lost their autonomy and sense of satisfaction and identification with their work; rewards no longer seem to compensate for the efforts exerted.

The number of workers, the classification of jobs and the classification of jobs on the basis of sex, age and race are contained in statistics on the working population compiled at regular intervals by the Bureau of Labor Statistics. In 1972 the work force contained 89 million people, 37 percent of them women. Half of the work force is employed in the service sector of the economy. Blue-collar workers, mostly industrial workers, now comprise only a third of the work force. Since occupation is the main indicator of social class, the categories of professional, white-collar and blue-collar are descriptive not only of differential job experience but of life-styles and social influence.

The major social problem to be considered in studying work in America is unemployment as it affects different groups. The causes of unemployment are imbedded in economic processes, which are manipulated to some extent by government control. The technological advances made in automation and computerization are also responsible for the displacement of workers. Discrimination in the hiring of minority groups and women makes them the principlal victims of both unemployment and a lower wage scale at every occupational level.

Unemployment and its attendant loss of income works untold hardships. Prolonged unemployment causes a loss of dignity and the sense of worth that comes from regular work. The unemployed tend to drop out of community life and in areas of widespread unemployment even those who are working are affected. The human resources wasted can never be recovered.

chapter

16

environment

The earth, water and air, once taken for granted as a sort of scenic backdrop for the human drama, have all become areas of intense discussion and worry. Twenty years ago, only a few alert scientists were predicting our present despair over what mankind is doing to the earth. Resources seemed unlimited, the air was fresh and clean, and rivers and oceans were seen as elements to be harnessed for power and used to dispose of waste. But in a relatively short time, we have seen the threat of a shift in the balance of nature away from its cycle of use and renewal to one of use, decay, and if we are not careful, gradual collapse.

Our environment is now a social problem, not just a problem for the sciences. With huge increases in air, water and land pollution in the past quarter century, the world we now live in poses problems of health and welfare for a large portion of the population. A dirty lake or river not only affects those who live near it, but it also affects the entire ecosphere, nature's rhythms and cycles, and the future functioning of man. A threatened environment, like a weak house close to crumbling, puts man in a precarious position: the more he produces goods that do not fit into nature's cycle (DDT, for example), the more he pollutes and thus undermines his own health and well-being.

Biologists refer to the intricate web of relationships between all living things and the physical environment they share as the ecosystem. It has been shown that each living thing plays a part in this ecosystem. There is a food chain, in which organisms that produce their own food using the sun's energy (green plants) are eaten by small animals, which in turn are eaten by larger animals. The food chain is closed by bacteria and fungi, which decompose the wastes and eventually the dead bodies of all living things, returning useful nutrients for the use of the original producers, or plants. Each element necessary for life, such as carbon, nitrogen and phosphorus goes through cycles of use and reuse; although at certain periods in the cycle the element is not available for use, it eventually reenters the cycle. Populations of all animals in the ecosystem are adjusted through natural forces, such as disease and predation, to a size in keeping with the food supplies the environment can provide.

A change in any part of the delicately functioning ecosystem carries widespread and often unexpected repercussions. An illustration can be seen in the outcome of the campaign waged in South Africa against the hippopotami, who were grazing on agricultural land along the river banks. The hippo population was successfully reduced, but new problems set in. It turned out that the movement of the hippos through the rivers kept the channels open; without them, the rivers silted up and then overflowed their banks. The floods damaged crops and homes; moreover, the resulting stagnant pools permitted a huge increase in the population of water snails which served as hosts for one stage of the life cycle of a parasite that causes the sometimes fatal disease schistosomiasis. So the net result of the attempt to stop the hippos' grazing was a shortage of food and a disease epidemic.

The damage to our environment and the harm it can bring to human and animal life resulting from injudicious alteration of the ecosystem it took billions of years of evolution to establish is now obvious. Areas devastated by one or more problems (Los Angeles with its smog, West Virginia with its strip-mining) are trying to correct the problem; other areas not yet polluted are taking measures to insure that the quality of their water, air and land is not degraded. Yet often it has taken either government or private spokesmen to point out the dangers; many communities were unaware of the threat until the late 1960s, when in many cases the problem had reached an almost irreversible point.

The question before our society, based on our new and growing perception of the effects of human pollution of the environment, is both elementary and monumental. Will we pay for the clean-up of rivers, oceans, the landscape and the air? How will we pay? Can we simply pay cash, or must we give up some of our now taken for granted machines and luxuries?

History of the problem

The problems of the environment seem to be newer than most other social problems; it has been only in the last decade that much has been written about the threats of pollution and environmental degradation. But to conclude from this that the problem itself is new is to be misled. The environment began to suffer from man's activities at least 6000 years ago.

Civilization and environment

Anthropologists believe that environmental degradation is closely linked to the rise of the city. Early man subsisted by hunting wild animals and gathering wild plants; his natural environment was also his grocery store. The fact that nature fed him freely led not only to a sense of respect for the natural world, but also to a feeling that man and nature are closely linked. This symbiotic world view remains characteristic of the few hunter-gatherer cultures still found in the modern world, such as the Guayaki of South America or the Pygmies of Central Africa.

With the development of agricultural technology, man's world view began to change. Now it was not nature that produced his food, but he himself, through his own efforts. This change in his relationship with nature led to a corresponding change in attitude. Agriculturalists tend to have an exploitative world view, seeing their natural environment as something to be manipulated for man's benefit.

Early agriculturalists posed no real threat to the environment, despite their attitude of exploitation; settlements were small, and groups frequently moved from one site to another. Real damage to the ecosystem began only when the exploitative world view was coupled with the relatively high population density of fixed urban areas. The need to produce food for a large number of people gathered in a small area led to more and more manipulation of the environment. For example, the early cities in Mesopotamia, such as Sumer and Ur, embarked on large-scale irrigation projects, diverting water from nearby rivers. The short-term result was to increase crop yield, but the long-term result was ecological disaster. The repeated evaporation of water pulled salts to the surface of the soil; eventually the salt concentration became so high that no crops would grow. Today the region remains an arid waste, for the most part uninhabitable.

The density of population in urban areas also led to a problem of waste disposal. Archeological excavations have uncovered large middens, or trash heaps, in nearly every ancient city. Written records indicate that contamination of water sources was also a frequent problem. The accumulation of wastes near cities caused frequent disease epidemics. During the Middle Ages, the epidemics were so severe that it is estimated that the population of European cities was reduced by 50 percent. Cities in the New World had similar problems; Jamestown, the first capital of Virginia, had to be abandoned when its wells became contaminated.

Historically, the solution to environmental problems has been sought in new technology. When wastes began to contaminate wells, sewers were built; when sewers began to pollute waterways, sewage treatment plants were built; when the gases from the treatment plants began to pollute the air, atmospheric precipitators were added on. Each technological solution seems sooner or later to have created a new problem.

Today we continue to look toward technology for solutions. Certainly there is reason to believe that engineers and technicians can bring about some amelioration of present problems. They can install emission-control devices on car exhausts and smokestacks; they can treat solid wastes; they can add chemicals to help purify the water. Yet all of these actions may in the long run simply serve to create new strains on the ecosystem. Many scientists and sociologists believe that a true solution must be a social rather than a technological one. Efforts to manipulate the environment will have to be tempered by an awareness of its limitations and an understanding of our dependence upon it.

reading: **Lawrence Krader**

WATER AND SOCIETY

There is an interaction between a society and its physical environment, which has a corollary: that changes in these relations will be affected by changes in the society, on the one hand, and in the environment on the other. The most obvious area in the society in which these changes are to be sought will be in the technology and economy; these, in turn, directly involve the political organization and the legal practices. Human societies have certain traits in common with societies of other living beings. All societies, plant and animal as well as human, live in determinate relations to the physical environment, relations which together comprise their respective ecological systems. The ecological systems of plant and animal societies, however, are fairly constant for the given species or subspecies; that is, the ecological relations, expressed and maintained as behavioral adaptations within each species, are not highly variant. On the other hand, the sum of ecological systems of the various human societies comprises a vast amount of variation. There are probably as many such systems as there are human societies and cultures; and although these have not been accurately counted, we may venture the guess that they number several thousand at present. . . .

The threats to our own society are set before us, not by our environment directly, but by what we have made of it in the past three centuries. These threats have only recently come to the forefront; until very recently, certainly within the memory of most adults in the United States, we had far more confidence in the natural resources of our country and far more pleasure in the physical space and recreation opportunities at our disposal. Ecological thought of fifty years ago, such as it was, would not have put forward a theory of environmental danger or threat with reference to the United States; however, we are no longer as rich or as spacious, relative to our population size, today as we then were; our resources are being depleted; the reserves of raw materials on which our civilization was founded, and on which it still depends, are reduced. There is a close relation between our theory and the national experience through which we are passing. In particular, we have to

connect the factor of population size and growth with our current stock and use of our resources and their future prospects. . . . One of the consequences that we draw is that if we were to begin over again from the base of our present stock of available resources, we could not possibly develop our industrial civilization in the way that we have; it is improbable that we could have developed an industrial and urban civilization in the first place.

The evolution of life on earth has been predicated on two processes. The first of these is the successive adaptations of the viable species to the natural environment; the second is the successive adaptations of the environment to the specific forms of life within it. The first process was originally formulated for our time by Darwin in his notion of fitness for suvival, and although it has been profoundly transformed by modern genetics and systematic biology, its outlines are still perceptible in modern theory. The second doctrine was given major impetus by L. J. Henderson, who initiated a good deal of modern thinking on how the environment itself is in adaptation to the species. Although he had a static view of the environment, we nevertheless owe to him the idea of environmental fitness which matches that of species fitness, and from this we proceed in our theory to species adaptation paired with environmental adaptation. Today, we conceive that both the species and the environment are in adaptation and readaptation, one to the other; in the case of man, the operational variable is not the species but the society. This is also the unit of planning and policy. . . .

The contrast between the inimical attitude of the hunter towards nature and the increasingly confident farmer and townsman constitutes a polarity in the adaptive systems of human societies. The opening up of the New World for exploitation by European farmers and townsmen was marked by a posture of confidence and optimism which has continued down to our era. The Industrial Revolution in this country was further based on the assumption, which it promulgated, of full trust in the bounties of nature and our ability to exploit them. This is, of course, subject to some variation, and American attitudes towards water are a case in point. It was, at one time, easier to get a law passed husbanding water resources in the western than in the eastern states. On the eastern seaboard, the common law regarding water courses has its ancient history; flowing water has long been held a common enemy to be fended off at will by the owner of the land through which it passes. In many of these jurisdictions it is difficult to find any legal remedy for damage by a neighbor's water practices, and, generally, water rules and precedents are contradictory, under the common law, over parts of our country. . . .

Every culture is an amalgam of ecological traditions, some of them internally contradictory, as we have seen in the case of our own society. Our culture has been predominately spendthrift of our water resources; yet, in a minor way, we have acted as a folk water-poor and parsimonious of our resource. Today, water of sufficient high quality for human and other purposes is an increasingly scarce and costly resource; the Great Lakes, particularly Michigan and Erie, exhibit records of depletion, mismanagement, and non-management among the most striking in world history. Our society today is, on balance, water-poor, not only in the mountain and southwestern states, but in every major urban and industrial center, not because of the physical lack of water, but because of our practices in regard to its quality and distribution. Let us contrast the practices of a traditionally water-poor culture in order to understand some of the alternatives to our own tradition.

The arid zones of Asia stretch continuously from the Red Sea to within a few miles of the Pacific Ocean at the Manchurian border of China. Within these interconnected zones, rainfall averages less than three hundred millimeters (12 inches) annually, save in the vicinity of mountains, and is insufficient to grow any cereal crops unaided. Therefore, virtually all Central Asia is a region of sporadic settlement, with great concentrations of population in the vicinity of the water-courses, and thinly settled in the steppes and deserts between. The river valleys are the natural centers of the irrigation systems for field agriculture and for town life. The rich old cities of Samarkand, Bukhara, and Khiva throve in this way. Water is here treated not as a common enemy, but as a valued resource. Land is wasted; water is not. So crucial is the role of water that it has led to theories of a single causative factor in history; here Ellsworth Huntington evolved his theory of the determining role of the geographic—*read* water—factor in history when he accompanied the archaeological expedition of R. Pumpelly to Central Asia in the years before the first World War. Water there is important as a factor in history, not directly, but through man's work. The rise and fall of cities and empires is not directly dependent on the amount and timing of rainfall; the reserves of water would eliminate the immediacy of concern with drought at any time for a season or two. The maintenance of the water system depended on the technology which was sophisticated even by contemporary standards, and on the maintenance of the civil peace. The rulers maintained the irrigation system by levies of conscripted labor, a form of tax paid in service. By these technical, social, political, and economic arrangements, the systems flourished; without them, the social systems collapsed, no matter how much rain did or did not fall or how much ground water was led up through the conduits. . . .

Under the local Islamic practices known as *adat* law, which were in force in the region from the time of the Islamic conquest in the eighth century down to the dissolution of the system by the Russians in the nineteenth, land which was waste, and hence owned by no one, could be "vivified." With official permission, a man could irrigate the waste land, and it would thereby pass into his private ownership. The importance of water was such that the practical act of irrigating the soil at once took on the symbolic significance of constituting a necessary condition for the establishment of the right of private ownership of the waste. On the other hand, no official permission was needed for cultivation of waste land with the use of natural sources of water supply, nor did such cultivation bring with it any right of ownership beyond the season of its cultivation.

The economic, technological, and legal customs of the traditional societies of Central Asia, which were and knew themselves to be water-poor, contrasts with our own tradition. In particular, we have seen how the legal and the other practices interact in Central Asia; they are plainly at variance with what we know as squatters' rights, the *jus primi occupantis* in Western society, which were in force on the early American frontier, even in areas which were and are water-poor. Here it was often found that claims to landownership were registered on the basis of occupancy alone, sometimes on the basis of some sort of improvement of the land, for instance, a house and patch of garden, dry cultivation, or fencing. The contrast between a society with a deep tradition of water-poverty and a society whose consciousness of water-poverty is recent is striking.

Thus far, we have concentrated only on one aspect of the total ecological field, the relations of society to the natural environment. However, any given human society also exists in relation to other human societies which together form its social environment. . . . So cieties with histories of strong aggressive and defensive international relations are found repeatedly to perceive their natural environments as threats. . . . It is plain that America has proceeded from a period of confidence and control over the potentialities of its natural environment and predominantly external peace to a period of environmental threat and war. Depletion of our natural resources and of our social well-being have gone hand in hand.

We focus our attention on the relations to the natural environment in these pages, contrasting the adaptive system of the present with that of the past, and, at the same time, contrasting our own with the adaptive systems of other societies. One of the reasons why I have dwelt . . . on the ecology of water supply in Central Asia is in order to advance yet another hypothesis. *Although a society may experience chronic water shortage, it does not necessarily follow that it will regard water or its lack as a threat.* In Central Asia it has been rather that the breakdown in the social arrangements (legal, political, and economic as well as technical) has been regarded as a threat, and threats to such social arrangements have been warded off, where possible, as the central issue in those societies. It is therefore not necessary to conclude that a threat to a society lies in its relations to its natural environment; these may be quite variable. On the contrary, it would follow from what we have here set forth that the threat to the society only seemingly arises from the natural ecological relations; it actually lies in the shift from one set of relations to the next. In the case of America, it is the shift from an ecology of abundance to an ecology of scarcity; it is the ecological goods that have become scarce that are now perceived as comprising a threat. There are goods that we have long taken for granted as being present or available in sufficient quantity and at the requisite qualitative level: air, fresh water, area for recreation; these are no longer perceived to be such. Our society is threatened by this shift; it is a danger which is real and actual.

From
Lawrence Krader, "Environmental Threat and Social Organization,"
The Annals of the American Academy of Political and Social Science,
Vol. 389 (May, 1970) pp. 11–18.

Environmental concern in America

The issues of environmental protection and conservation were almost nonexistent until the twentieth century. For early settlers, the American wilderness was an enemy to be conquered. Trees were not viewed as beauties of nature or links in the ecosystem, but as obstacles to the agriculture that was the only way these pioneers knew how to produce their living.

The wilderness of America—so unlike the tamed European landscape—of the eighteenth and nineteenth centuries was a challenge. The men and women who fought natural obstacles such as mountains, prairies and deserts to expand the American frontier had respect for the land; some of those who traveled westward have left moving accounts of their emotional reaction to the beauty and promise of the land they were seeing for the first time. Yet there is ample evidence to show that the speed of the westward movement caused destruction. Forests were cut or burned needlessly; fields were cleared and then abandoned to rank second growth; waterways were turned into cesspools as growing towns tried to dispose of their wastes. This disregard for the land is understandable to some degree, because the earth's goods then seemed unlimited. If progress has been the key word in the building of America, then the victim, almost from the beginning, has been the land's variety of resources. This mentality, although perhaps suitable to pioneer times, has caused the very problem we face today.

A few spokesmen in the nineteenth century saw where this disregard and unthinking misuse might lead. Henry David Thoreau today sounds like a prophet, because of his emphatic stand against rapid and unneeded expansion; his *Walden* has become a sort of Bible for the ecology movement. Theodore Roosevelt was the first president (1901–1909) actively to promote conservation of our resources and wildlife. He established the United States Forest Service to protect national forests and promote replanting of destroyed areas. The nation's waterways, the problems of flooding and soil erosion were also studied. He encouraged states to set up their own conservation commissions. But, as William G. Carleton writes, "it was soon evident that most states were much less able to resist encroachments on their public lands by private interests and to protect the national domain than was the federal government."[1]

The federal government was cautious about interfering with state's rights when it came to the question of regulating the use of natural resources. Even in areas of safety and health—such as the terrible flooding of the Mississippi and other rivers, which affected many states and at times threatened the whole economy—federal officials were slow in acting. The American ethic of private property and freedom to use land as the owner saw fit has also been instrumental in permitting misuse of the environment.

More federal regulatory agencies were established during the 1920s (such as the Federal Water-Power Commission in 1920 and the Federal Power Commission in 1930). But it was in Franklin D. Roosevelt's administration that the federal government became the primary watchdog on the environment. Although hated and suspected by many, the Tennessee Valley Authority (TVA), a federal program, created employment for thousands affected by the Depression; it reduced the flooding of the Tennessee River; and it created new hydroelectric power supplies because of the six giant dams built in the Tennessee Valley. Roosevelt also instituted federal programs concerned with protecting the soil (because of the disasters of the Dust Bowl in the early 1930s), clearing forests, dredging rivers, and generally trying to upgrade many segments of the environment. Of course, at the same time plants and factories were being built which were to cause much of the trouble we face today.[2]

The problems of pollution in the cities have an even more recent beginning than those of the country, since they are linked with the trend toward urbanization. In 1900 only about 30 percent of America's population lived in urban areas; by 1920 this figure had increased to 50 percent; and today it is about 75 percent. The great increase in population density in urban areas has created many problems of pollution control and waste disposal.

Before World War II, each community had to deal with its own—usually small—amount of air, water and land degradation. The problems didn't seem very big, and they almost never caused national concern. People who were alarmed by the amount of filth being spewed from smokestacks or into rivers were generally hushed by the community, many of whom depended on those industries for their employment. Thus in the cities, the whole problem was magnified—and became more so after the war. Cities were crowded, autos caused congestion, waterways deteriorated, and the air became foul. Yet nothing was done. Progress, growth, wealth and success were the goals. Those with economic power kept the status quo. So who cares if the water is getting a little dirty?

Probably the first major pollution scare in the country was in 1948 in Donora, Pennsylvania. Because of an inversion of hot and cold air in the atmosphere, and because Donora is surrounded by mountains, the fumes from the town's steel mill, zinc plant and sulfuric acid factory were trapped in the valley. A yellowish haze was cast on the town, and after four days, when the weather shifted and fresh air blew the smog away, over 40 percent of the town's population became ill; 20 people died as a result of the toxic pollutants they were forced to breathe. London had a similar inversion crisis in 1952, and New York in 1966. Los Angeles faces a deadly smog almost half of each year due to auto emissions and industrial smoke.[3]

Another aspect of the worsening situation in the last several decades is the change in the way many goods are produced. All manufacturing processes create waste products that must somehow be disposed of; examples are smoke from the energy sources, chemical run-off, discarded raw materials, even heat from furnaces and machines. In recent years, however, manufacturing processes have changed, so that both they and the product are more damaging to the environment.

Consider as an example the making of a sweater in 1934 and 1974. In 1934, the raw material would be wool, which takes only a few processing steps to turn from the fleece on a sheep's back into yarn. There is very little waste in the processing, and only a moderate amount of energy is required for the manufacturing. Once the sweater was used and discarded, it could be quickly broken down into chemical elements that reenter the ecological cycle. Since the molecules in wool are ones frequently found in living things, microorganisms in the soil and water possess the right enzymes to digest and break them down. The sweater made in 1974 is a very different story. It is likely to be made from a synthetic fiber, created by the processing of byproducts of the petroleum industry. Turning petroleum wastes into yarn requires many processing steps, and it takes a great deal of energy, in the form of very high heat and compression. And when a sweater of synthetic fiber is discarded, it is not easily disposed of or converted into anything else; bacteria do not have the enzymes to break down this man-made substance. Thus the new methods of producing sweaters require more energy, create more wastes, and

Clov: There's no more nature.
Hamm: No more nature! You exaggerate.
Clov: In the vicinity.

Samuel Beckett, Endgame

leave behind a product that cannot reenter the ecological cycle. Barry Commoner cites the situation very clearly:

> The technology factor—that is, the increased output of pollutants per unit production resulting from the introduction of new productive technologies since 1946—accounts for 80 to 85 percent of the total output of pollutants, except in the case of passenger travel, where it accounts for about 40 percent of the total. Most of the sharp increase in pollution levels is due not so much to population or affluence as to changes in productive technologies.[4]

Not only have most pollutants increased enormously (for instance, nitrogen oxides from automobile exhausts have risen 630 percent since 1946), but more striking are the new pollutants unleashed in our environment since the end of the war. Commoner fills out the list: smog—first noticed in 1943 in Los Angeles; man-made radioactive elements—first produced in the war; DDT—since 1944 used as a pesticide; detergents—used to displace soap in 1946; and synthetic plastics—a contributor to pollution since the war.

We now know that everything on earth is linked—often very fragilely—together within the ecosphere. We are no longer on a wild frontier, but we face a problem even more vast and difficult: how to live on our "spaceship" earth, within a closed system, and survive as well as prosper.

Environmental problems

Environmental troubles are numerous. Soil erosion, radioactivity, pesticides, and other man-made problems plague our health and existence. But by far the most visible and widespread concerns facing our society are air, water and land pollution, and the depletion of scarce natural resources.

Air pollution

Air pollution is not only ugly and uncomfortable for the eyes and lungs, it is also harmful to living things. The pollutants from automobiles, homes, industry, and power plants permeate the air from Maine to California; it is estimated that over 200 million tons of contaminants are released every year. New Jersey's oil refineries cast a dark cloud over New York City on many days; Detroit's pollutants contaminate the Canadian woods; the vast mists of polluted air encircle the entire earth daily. Although Americans are probably the leading air polluters, the task of cleaning up the air is really an international one.

About 60 percent of pollutants released into the air come from the exhaust pipe of an automobile. The major chemical component of this exhaust is carbon monoxide, known to be highly toxic. Also found in exhaust fumes are nitrogen oxides, which give the air a brown tinge.

The action of the sunlight causes these oxides to combine with waste hydrocarbons also emitted from exhausts, forming peroxyacetyl nitrate, a chemical that causes eyes to smart and water; it may also damage the lungs.

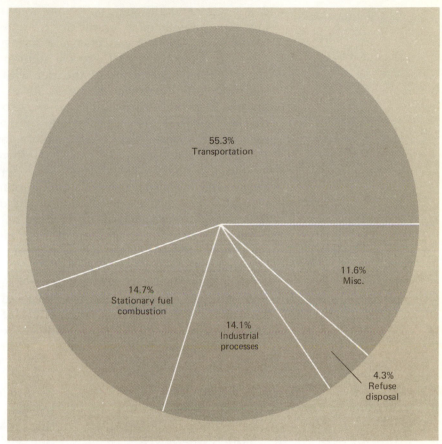

Figure 16-1   Air pollutant emissions 1970: percent of total by source

Automobiles, however, are not the only culprits. Electric utilities using low-grade fossil fuels give off sulfur oxides that cause much of the trouble; about 24 million tons are released by American industries each year. When mixed with other chemicals normally present in the air, these sulfur oxides turn into sulfuric acid. Recently rains containing large amounts of sulfuric acid were recorded over Chesapeake Bay. These problems of air pollution are worsened by occasional air inversions, in which the layer of air over low-lying cities is trapped by a layer of warmer air in the upper atmosphere. All pollutants released into the air are thus held firmly in place over the city, creating a smog and the issuance of an air quality alert.

What damage does air pollution do? It is known to kill plants; more than a million trees have died from California's smogs, and crop losses due to air pollution are thought to be high. It erodes buildings and public monuments made of stone; it causes house paint to deteriorate and clothes to need more frequent washings. It appears that air pollution is also hazardous to human health. Medical researchers have found that air pollution greatly affects the bronchitis death rate. And although pollutants may not be the cause of many illnesses, "significant relationships nonetheless were established for lung cancer, stomach cancer, heart disease, emphysema, and infant mortality. According to these calculations, cleaning the air to the same level as that enjoyed by the area with the best air would reduce the bronchitis death rate alone by 40 to 70 percent."[5] The air we breathe is so vital to our well being—yet so often taken for granted—that we tend to forget about the long-term affects of air pollution. But most doctors agree that twenty to forty years of breathing contaminated air surely leads to an earlier death.

And how do we solve the problem? Certainly some progress has been made in limiting industrial pollutants and auto emissions, but a workable and permanent solution is still decades away. Because of the close interconnection of the animate and inanimate in the ecosystem, cleaning up one part of the environment or one area of the country is not enough: the whole system must be treated in order to successfully combat the problem.

The Clean Air Act of 1970 set rather stringent requirements on the auto industry, electrical utilities, pulp and paper industries and the steel mills, as well as other major polluters.[6] Because of this Act, there has been a major effort to have "add-on" controls in automobiles by 1975 or '76 that will substantially reduce dangerous emissions.

. . . it is necessary to redress, in part, the semantic bias on "pollutants, garbage, and poisons." This usually tends to suggest vast quantities of alien substances being injected into an otherwise perfectly functioning system. Rather—pollutants are, as we perceive and designate them: poisons and natural substances "out of place," or in excess of tolerable levels.

John McHale

The answer to industrially caused pollution seems to lie in control devices that will reduce the deadly particulates and gases that are given off from these factories. Federal and local authorities have set standards in most areas, but the necessary equipment to greatly reduce pollutants has not yet been manufactured or perfected. When these devices are working, perhaps by the mid-1980s, the air will be appreciably freer of the major polluting gases.

For the electric utilities, another problem must be solved. They are major polluters, because until recently utilities depended on low-grade (high-sulfur) coal as the chief source of power. EPA and local agencies have banned the use of "dirty" coal in most regions (on the Eastern Seaboard since the late 1960s). EPA has mandated that only "clean" fuel must be burned by 1975–76, although different areas will have different standards of cleanness. The problem is, where does this fuel come from? Low sulfur coal is most abundant in the Northwest—

Montana, Wyoming, and other adjacent states. However, to get this fuel, strip-mining is usually employed, which then leads to destruction of land resources. On top of this is the simple fact that transporting low sulfur coal from this area to other parts of the country is almost prohibitively expensive, and the cost of electricity and power would rise drastically. The quest for clean fuels, whether clean coal or gas or oil, leads directly to other environmental problems.

One feature of all suggested solutions to the problem of air pollution is that they cost money. For example, in the case of auto emission controls, the public will end up paying the costs in the form of higher car prices. A "trade-off" is made: the public wants cars; they want clean air, too; it costs a great deal of money to convert old engines or develop new nonpolluting ones; therefore, the public will end up paying the bill. This same trade-off principle applies to most other forms of pollution control as well—either in the form of higher taxes or increased price of products, the average citizen will bear the largest economic burden.

Yet economists point out that we already pay many hidden costs of air pollution. Polluted air causes so much damage to humans, plants and man-made structures that American economists generally agree that in the long run it will be cheaper simply to lay out the billions of dollars necessary to clean it up.[7] When we take into account the hundreds of thousands of people who are ill and hospitalized because of respiratory diseases partially caused by air pollution, the staggering crop losses each year due in part to dirty air, the damage being done to private homes and public buildings, it becomes clear that the costs of air pollution are very high indeed.

Water pollution

Like the air we breathe, water is essential for human and plant life. It is estimated that the average person uses between 50 and 100 gallons of water a day for such things as bathing, flushing toilets, drinking, cooking and washing.[8] Yet like the air, much of the water we use is polluted. City water treatment plants add chemicals to clean the water we drink, but in many parts of the country these measures are not sufficient to counteract all the pollutants that man pours into the rivers, lakes and other water supplies, and the purity of water supplies is endangered. Water pollution is so bad in some areas that lakes, such as Lake Erie, have actually been declared "dead": they can no longer support fish and plant life, because they have been ruined by man's waste. The real danger of uncontrolled water pollution is this kind of death; if waters are not clean and fresh, then a large segment of the ecosystem is thrown out of control, thereby endangering all life.

The nation's rivers and lakes have long been the dumping grounds for many industries. Rivers transport wastes downstream, away from the various plants. Major industries—paper, steel, automobile, chemicals—depend on the water for cooling and production as well. They take water from the rivers and return it polluted and heated, thus doubly affecting aquatic life. Industries discharge various substances into rivers and oceans: solid wastes, sewage, nondegradable pollutants, synthetic materials, toxic chemicals, even radioactive pollutants. Add to this the sewage systems of towns and large cities, detergents, boat and ship spillages, oil spills, pesticide run-off from agricultural areas and acid run-off from strip-mined land, and the enormity of the problem is seen with more clarity. The fact that the Cuyahoga River, which runs through Cleveland, recently caught fire dramatizes the situation's severity.

One of the most troublesome pollutants of lakes and rivers is the phosphates from fertilizers and detergents. These chemicals "fertilize" the plant life in the water, and the algae experience a population explosion. Then food supplies run short, the algae dies, and bacteria begin to live on the remains. The growth of the bacteria uses up all the oxygen dissolved in the water, and soon it is uninhabitable for all living things. The result is a body of water that looks ugly, smells bad, cannot be used for recreation, and does not provide a living for fishermen.

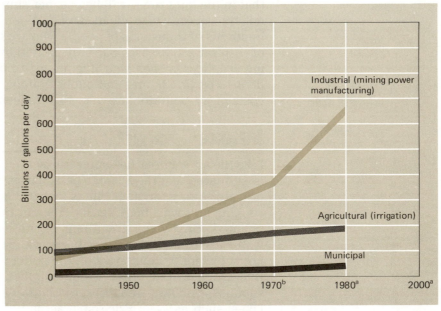

*Figure 16–2   Water use—municipal, industrial,
agricultural, 1950–2000*

The Refuse Act of 1899 outlaws the discharge of pollutants other than municipal sewage into navigable waters without a permit from the Army Corps of Engineers.[9] Then how have all the private industries been able to go on polluting our public waters? The answer is, as usual, an economic and political one. Industries that help keep the economy growing have generally had little trouble from government authorities when it comes to polluting the environment. Only recently, and only because of public awareness and outrage, has the government started fining major polluters. There are thousands of examples of this "look the other way" attitude. Even more troubling is the fact that when federal and local authorities do fine a major polluter, the industry usually continues its polluting activities. It is cheaper to pay the fine than to correct the cause.

One of the most publicized enforcement actions has been against the Reserve Mining Company of Minnesota.[10] Since 1955, this company has deposited more than 190 million long tons of taconite tailings from its iron ore processing in Lake Superior, and it adds another 60,000 tons each day. EPA finally gave Reserve 180 days to find ways of cleaning up and finding other ways of disposing of the wastes. EPA consultants suggested five alternatives; all were rejected by Reserve. The case then went to the Justice Department in 1972, and it is still under litigation. All the while, Reserve keeps pumping 60,000 tons of tailings into the lake every day.

This type of noncompliance with laws is far from rare. One or two large companies are able to seriously pollute a body of water that thousands of people use for recreation and other things—yet private interest so far is winning the battle. The authors of *Water Wasteland* see the problem this way:

> The major problem in pollution control is the vast economic and political power of large polluters. Water pollution exists, in large part, because polluters have more influence over government than do those they 'pollute.' So long as this disproportionate influence persists, so will the pollution. It is a mistake to suppose that new laws with higher clean-up requirements and tougher penalties will ultimately succeed in eliminating environmental contamination; unless new laws also tip the scales of influence over government in favor of the public, the requirements they set will be consistently violated and the penalties rarely used.[11]

The oceans are another problem, and the amount of pollutants spewed into them daily is incalculable. Oil spills from ships and off-shore wells can ruin hundreds of miles of shoreline and endanger aquatic life. Mercury poisoning in fish has also been on the increase. Thor Heyardahl, in his journey across the Atlantic in the *Ra* several years ago, said that floating debris and waste was visible most of the way. Like inland rivers, the oceans are our dumping grounds. Unless our waters are protected from industrial and energy-plant pollutants, everyone in the society will be faced with the possibility of contaminated drinking water, unusable recreation areas, and a loss of many species of fish.

Land pollution

Pollution of our land takes many forms—destruction of forests, strip-mining, build up of pesticides and herbicides in our soil, neglect of land, even the paving of highways and roads. Our dumps for waste materials and especially our habit of littering the landscape with all kinds of trash from bottles to automobiles make land pollution the most visible—and aesthetically disgusting—kind of menace.

The use of chemical fertilizers, which dramatically increases crop yields, has unfortunate side effects on our land. The more that fertilizers are used, the more the soil loses its natural capacity to produce its own nitrates. The phosphates in the fertilizers enter the water supply and cause the excessive growth of algae. Nitrates in the water can cause an often fatal disease in infants, called methemoglobinemia; many cases of the disease have been reported in the agricultural regions of the midwest.

The accumulation of pesticides in the soil is another threat to man's health. Fears of the effects of high concentrations of DDT have led to a ban on its use, but there is evidence that many of its replacements may have just as harmful an effect. The extensive use of pesticides has already threatened many species of wild life, such as the bald eagle and brown pelican, with extinction.

Because of the interlocking of all parts of the ecosystem, other serious repercussions appear with each of these problems. Animal life disappears, trees and other plant life die, the ability of the soil to retain water is diminished, erosion takes place. Flooding is more frequent and finally we have a barren, useless land. The disastrous Dust Bowl situation in the midwest and western states during the 1930s was largely caused by unchecked deforestation and overuse of the farm lands. Man had blindly neglected the very soil from which he got his wealth, food and shelter.[12]

The problems we face in the future are similar. Although some land is being set aside by the federal and local government as wilderness area and National Parks, far more will have to be allotted in the coming decades. To meet the demands for our growing population, our farmlands must be expanded and used for more diverse crops—without being depleted or overdosed with nitrate fertilizers and other forms of chemicals which cause other problems. Solid waste disposal will also multiply, and we have to find new ways of recycling our goods before a large portion of our land becomes a garbage heap. Forest lands are being used at an alarming rate; a strict program of replanting must be followed. Our need for fossil fuels and other resources will continue to skyrocket, yet strip-mining is not the ecological answer to our energy needs. Cities and suburbs continue to sprawl, destroying more land. Without care, planning and an eye towards ecological balance, what we now call land may be called wasteland by future generations.

Energy resources

Energy is essential for all production. Our industries and power plants have long relied on fossil fuels for power. But the energy crisis the world faces now is due to the simple fact that these fuels are nonrenewable and quickly running out. Once they have been used up—it will take some time, of course—mankind will have to depend on new types of energy. Yet for the past century we have been acting as if the fuel would never end, oil wells would magically refill and ore mines would regenerate themselves. Now we are faced with the prospect of rationing fuels, cutting back on some forms of energy, or turning too quickly to nuclear energy when we do not know enough about controlling the dangerous radioactive elements. As Sterling Brubaker says, "The environmental consequences of this (using nuclear fuels) are that we shall be exchanging some of our current problems, particularly in air pollution, for the problems of managing radioactive wastes. The former are mostly health and aesthetic threats while the latter are hazards to human health and genetics."[13]

phototopic: ## STRIPMINING

Surface mining of coal provides a relatively inexpensive fuel for the electric generators and steel mills that our society demands. In many localities, mines and related services constitute most of the employment locally available, with the result that residents are either forced to leave their homes to look for work or to participate in the land destruction that surface mining causes. This type of mining is normally undertaken in areas where mineral taxes are low and mined land is valued less than farmland, but the process of mining itself makes adequate land reclamation difficult to achieve.

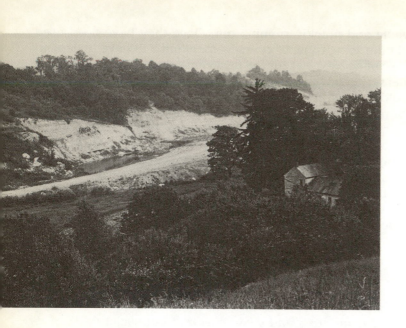

After topsoil has been removed and the layers of rock above a coal seam have been loosened by blasting, a large earth-mover moves in to scoop up the rock and pile it on one side. This creates a valley deep enough to expose the coal seam. The coal is then scooped up and loaded onto trucks to be taken away. When one section of coal has been removed in this fashion, the cycle of clearing, blasting, removal of "overburden" and loading of coal begins in another. The land left behind, however, is often severely damaged.

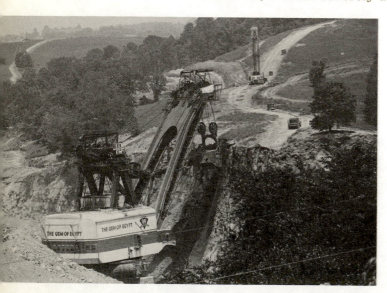

Heavy blasting disturbs foundations, wells and watercourses of nearby homes. Once watercourses have been disturbed, there is no way known to restore them to accessibility. Haphazard piling of overburden brings to the surface acid bearing rocks which poison streams and other water sources, and prevent the growth of vegetation to control erosion. Forced by recent legislation to reclaim the land, coal companies often plant only a meager growth of vegetation on unstable earth. The unreclaimed land of older mines testifies to rapacious disregard for environment.

Our current energy sources are causing great environmental dangers. The need for oil is increasing, yet we have depleted most of our own oil deposits. Thus we seek off-shore wells that are always liable to leak or explode; buy oil from the Middle East and transport it in supertankers that can sink like the *Torrey Canyon* did off England in 1967, polluting the waters with 166,000 tons of oil; or look to the Alaskan pipeline for oil, despite the hazards it poses for the environment.

The depletion of natural resources will affect every citizen in the country in the coming decades. Combustion engines may have to be limited, which would mean new sources of transportation, mainly electric, will be used. By cutting back our use of fuels in automobiles, fossil fuels would last centuries longer, and air pollution would be dramatically reduced. Many ecologists favor this idea, but then comes the question: how do we move from place to place? New forms of mass transportation would be required; perhaps electric-charged cars, buses, and trains will be the transportation of the future. Whatever form it takes, we clearly cannot continue our upward spiral of fuel consumption, air pollution and environmental imbalance indefinitely. Many changes will have to take place in society's way of thinking about unlimited production, individual transportation and the world's livelihood.

Technology may provide many of the solutions. Although it is the technological age that has caused the environmental crisis, man can harness his tools to work more efficiently in the future. We cannot replace what we have taken from the ground, but perhaps we can find new ways of maintaining society and providing for its increasing needs while still remaining committed to a safe and balanced ecosphere.

Responses to environmental problems

The scope of the environmental problems confronting us has been well established. The question is, what can the citizen do about helping to ease the burden? Action groups have been formed in many communities to insure passage of environmental legislation; ecology courses are given at many levels of the education system; and just plain watching for one's own garbage or littering is a beginning. But all of these and other measures assume a knowledge that the ecosystem is in danger. Certainly not everyone knows it or agrees to the extent that earth is scarred or the air polluted. Common public acceptance of the problem, combined with real concern, is the only way the society as a whole can deal with the costs and efforts of the clean-up ahead. Just as the ecosystem is made up of thousands of functions all dependent in some way on each other, the society, too, has to depend on all its members to treat the problem with seriousness. The minority cannot achieve a clean, healthy world; it will take a vast majority of the population to make that world a reality.

Changing values

In many ways the underlying competitive, commercial ethic of America fights against the reordering of our national priorities. We have not realized as a nation that we must start to cooperate in the task of cleaning up the environment.

In the past, we have worked together as a country to defeat similar problems. During World War II, recycling of goods was necessary and popular. No one thought twice about saving materials, returning bottles for reuse or rationing gasoline. But now the problem is either not recognized or seems too remote to matter. So we produce millions of throw-away bottles, cans and plastic containers and pretend they will just disappear after we have discarded them. Our production of goods is increasingly redundant: "more" is our slogan, but "more" is not necessarily better. Geared-up production may help the economy in the short run, but in the end it may come back to haunt us even more than now.

The ecological constraints on population and technological growth will inevitably lead to social and economic systems different from the ones in which we live today. In order to survive, mankind will have to develop what might be called a steady state. The steady state formula is so different from the philosophy of endless quantitative growth, which has so far governed Western civilization, that it may cause widespread public alarm.

René Dubos

Any real change in the situation will have to involve an accompanying change in our values. For most Americans today, the vision of "the good life" involves the ability to consume. It is two chickens in every pot, two cars in every garage, two color television sets in every household. No social scientist can say that such a vision is either right or wrong, but there are signs that it is inappropriate to the kind of future we will probably have. The production of those two chickens or television sets uses up energy resources and creates waste products that must be disposed of in the environment. As the population grows larger and increasingly dense, there is no way to do this without causing a problem of pollution.

It is clear that the value of consumption conflicts in many ways with the goal of a clean and safe environment. All solutions will therefore require a modification or replacement of this value. Writer L. Rust Hills has suggested, only half in jest, that in future we must praise not those who do things but those who undo them—the people who dismantle factories or take down bridges. This is a funny way to make a serious point about the need for a change in values.

Currently we tend to measure the state of the nation in terms of its output. Gains in the Gross National Product are viewed as a sign of social health and prosperity. But a factory that produces 10 million dollars worth of paper may also produce tons of waste that enter nearby streams; as GNP rises through increased production at such factories, so does the waste output. Economists and sociolgists both have suggested that we pay less attention to GNP and more to increases or decreases in real social welfare. A new statistical measure might distinguish between the production of goods and the production of amenities. Thus the small firm that produces a limited output while improving its environment might be rated more highly than one that produces a large volume while it degrades the environment.

There are signs that some change is taking place in values that call for more and more production, to be followed by more and more consumption, in an ever-expanding economy. As this reevaluation takes place, our ability to solve environmental problems will increase.

reading: **Edward Hoagland**

END OF THE WILDERNESS

My knowledgeability outdoors is that of a generalist—which is to say that I know very little. My guidebooks awe me, and, of course, nothing ever quite looks like its picture in a field guide. I'm rather glad not to be a scientist, though, because when there are no more bears left in the woods to study there will still be plenty of bears left in my head. In Vermont a man with a naturalist's bent can find maybe 100 meadow mice in an acre of hay, and redbacked mice, lemming mice, pine mice, and two kinds of jumping mice in the neighboring woods. Also three sorts of moles and five kinds of shrews. There's the screech owl, horned owl, snowy owl, barrel owl, long-eared owl, short-eared owl, and sawwhet owl.

I was pleased at how easy it now was for me to re-explore the mountains around my place, not leaning limp-legged against a tree wondering how I would ever get myself home—wouldn't somebody carry me, please? It was nothing to get myself up on top of one for a two-hour stroll; and I loved the new views I got of familiar hillocks, exotically green, heaving and humping like monsters of the sea. I walked to the lonely border of Canada on the Long Trail, and on the Fourth of July tramped to a fire tower which the Green Mountain Club considers the most remote in the state (it will remain nameless here). I wondered whether the towerman and I would be alone for the holiday, and found that we were; in fact, he'd had no other visitors for five or six weeks. He didn't know what to make of me; he climbed down from the tower, then scrambled up again skittishly while I slipped off my pack, got a drink, stretched my shoulders, and glanced about at the summit clearing, which seemed to abound in soft spots where I could bed down.

Domenic was 24, from Rutland. He had a mustache and wore his hair long as a mop, and since this was his fourth year in the towers, he could look out and see mountains where he'd lived before. . . .

We went up in the tower to talk. He pointed out Island Pond, a town 15 miles away across Ferdinand Bog and the Yellow Bog—a walk no one has thought to attempt for years and perhaps as difficult as any in Vermont; yet the towerman here a decade ago had made it routinely each Friday night in order to go see his girl. The prodigious topography, the Western grandeur, hundreds of thousands of acres of timberland, and the rolling, splendid, numberless mountains that might have been Asian or African and were not to be pigeonholed geographically or in altitude, ranged away to the Suttons of Quebec Province and to the sailing, ghostly looking Presidential Range, fluttering high in the south. Domenic said he occasionally saw pairs of hawks playing in the air, swooping and grasping at one another, and a pileated woodpecker would land on the frame of the tower and beat it with his bill, giving a crazy laughing cry. . . .

He was glad not to have many human visitors; he spoke with a kind of panic of what happened when trippers came, dropping pop bottles off the tower, chopping up the sawhorse for firewood and stealing the axes. "Uncontrollable," he said. He was afraid one might climb up and push him off. The towermen talked on the radio daily to each other of their troubles with black flies and visitors. Except for that period in the fall when he would have got so used to being alone that he'd feel sure he could go on forever, his favorite season was when he first snowshoed into the mountains in May, bursting to be on his own, finding rugged big drifts and bears and bear tracks on the trail—all contained within the tractable dimensions of Vermont which signify that one is not going to die, but otherwise like the great North. The bears, after all, having been asleep for half the year, are literally rediscovering the world, and one of the most fuddling discoveries they must make for themselves in their rebirth is that, as big and strong as they are, even these far mountains do not belong to them. When Domenic was manning the tower on Stone Mountain he had watched bachelor bears and bear families climb into the apple trees of abandoned farm down below; jumping on the limbs, they shook out bushels of fruit. He saw a hunt, too, in pantomime, where the tiny-looking bear caught the scent of an even tinier hunter stalking him just in time and flattened down, practically spread-eagling into the grass, and wriggled out of sight.

We leaned into the view. The fire towers of New England are in the process of being inactivated; planes, touring at statistically predetermined hours, will replace them. But the six that we could see had all been connected by a circuitous 60-mile telephone wire before radios came into use, and we tried to reconstruct its route in the swarm of space. So much space blots the eyes, the mountains in unending ridges and circles simply absorb any perspective. . . .

As the summer went on, I climbed the other fire-tower mountains in the 40-by-20-mile area that I'd staked out for myself, usually sleeping in the June-grass-and-hawkweed clearing on top, with my dog curled protectively around my head, waving his tail to shoo the mosquitoes off, and the moon out, the trees in the moonlight a mixed silhouette of heart-leaved white birch and spruces with their tops broken off by the snow and wind so they were as stunted as pitch pine at the beach. On West Pond Mountain one towerman had kept a burro to pack his groceries, and wherever he'd tethered her the grass was particularly lush and sweet. The trail climbed up through cathedral hemlock groves and parks of witch hobble and maidenhair fern, over numerous brooks, through a beech-maple forest and belts of recent logging, up into ledgy bad footing and softwood growth, to that first abrupt view of the tower, which looked like some queer sort of dynamo or tall telescope, a giddy, four-legged, laddered and bolted steel superstructure 100 feet above the mountaintop. With the cold winds of early morning blowing and the cold of the heights, the cabin looked enviably cozy to me as my sweat dried and I rested a bit. Though I was glad to meet nobody on the path, I was always disappointed if the towerman himself was not at home. But on Burke Mountain the fellow, famous for silence, went straight to his ladder as soon as he saw me and began to climb. I called to him and tried to talk, but he kept right on climbing. I began to stutter, and halfway up he turned around long enough to lock behind him a gate he'd built on the ladder. I found myself stuttering even more, like an epileptic, and he glanced down and kept on climbing coolly, until he reached the final hatch, which he closed, leaving me to my fate.

Domenic's domain looked down on the ponds, bogs, glories, and ramifications of Paul Stream. On Gore Mountain there was a young German with a seaman's beard who surveyed the complexities of the Nulhegan country: the North Branch, Yellow Branch, Logger Branch,

615

Black Branch, East Branch; and Sable Mountain, Green Mountain, Black Mountain, Meacham Swamp. Each of the towers, unexpectedly man-wrought in such surroundings, somehow had the focus and seriousness of a whole progression personified; such a climb, such a sight from the top, seemed to possess the arduousness of a life's work. The sense that I always had was that the fellow's career was just to gaze out at it all, not looking for anything so particular as smoke.

I went to the dismantled radar station on top of East Mountain which a wood-carver has bought as a kind of eccentric kingdom; and toured with the county forester and the game warden; and visited the sheriff who leads the search if people disappear, and whose territory encompasses all this fine timberland. During the hunting season I drove with Vermont's bear biologist on his rounds—he pulled a tooth from each beast that was killed to extract a cross-section for aging purposes. Usually the bear was hung up on show at the side of the road by the hunter's house, and he would lower it, pull the tooth, and then winch it up on the gibbet again. Still wet from the dew of the chase, the bear would smell doggy and seem to move with some of the ambly looseness of life while he was cranking it down and then up again, as if making a tacit plea on behalf of the rest of the race against the passion of each new spectator to shoot another. The biologist, a young man with a recent M. A., was becoming fond of bears as he went around measuring their vital statistics. He had observed that their average age declined year by year: below six, below five, towards the tender and vulnerable age of four, which is scarcely above puberty and hardly allows for a population base.

By the end of the summer, after canoeing and climbing and visiting such a great number of people across the three northern states, I found that what I'd heard in the beginning was right. There is no wilderness as such left in New England, nor any wilderness people of the sort who might miss it either, not even the handful of elderly hermits who lived in the woods through perhaps the end of the 1950s, marking the last stage of that earlier existence. I asked everywhere for them, and after trappers who really knew how to track in the snow in the old style. I inquired whether there were any Fish and Game personnel anywhere who in the pursuit of their duties still slept out overnight in the woods in good weather. No, none. Human beings adjust to change so swiftly that no change quite overtakes them. And it isn't a problem of villains, I found. It's a dilemma whereby the areas designated officially as wilderness areas become over-run because everybody gets so nostalgic and enthusiastic about them. On the other hand, any wild redoubt that isn't publicly identified will soon vanish completely, turned into cash.

There is no solution to this. I learned, though, that everybody concerned does know the measures that must be employed as a stopgap: easements or other tax breaks for the owners of undeveloped land, the loss of revenue to be made up by an expanded system of license fees which would include all outdoorsmen, the hiker as well as the hunter. Alrady the tax bite is forcing a good many timber owners to sell out or subdivide. Time is so short that there is no time, and yet it's a matter of waiting for the public's wisdom to catch up with the planners, and for all the outdoorsmen to recognize that they must pool their interests and lobby concertedly—the snowmobilers, bird watchers, and campfire buffs together, putting aside their squabbles. I learned, too, that I personally will have an abundance of deserted land to roam about in for the next decade or so. In the 40-by-20 miles, my friend Domenic and the bear biologist (getting fonder and fonder of the creatures whose carcasses he examines) and I will be pretty much on our own, except for the loggers the St. Regis Company sends in. This is the strange twist to what is happening: people are not going to bother to explore what is left. Despite all the fuss about wilderness, people nowadays don't really want to be in the woods all alone. If they did, there would be less wildness in the woods and in the end there would also be more of it. Even faster than the woods go, people are losing their taste for the woods.

From
"Mountain Towers" by Edward Hoagland in *The Village Voice*, February 15, 1973, pp. 9–10, 16.

Taking action

For an industry to curb its pollution, it must either cut back production or incur increased costs of pollution-control devices. This leads to financial problems. How do our society's industries clean themselves up and still remain in operation? It is a difficult question to answer at this time; much exploration is currently in progress.

If an industry is made to spend a large portion of its profit margin in fines, penalties or taxes because of its pollution, most will find a way to remedy the problem. If laws are strict enough, polluters will have to measure up to the regulations and stop dragging their feet. In the case of automobile manufacturers, the laws stipulated in the 1970 Clean Air Act make it clear that by the late 1970s, auto emissions have to be cut by 90 percent for California and other areas. This will be achieved with new equipment, modification of the internal combustion engine, and other add-on parts such as the catalytic converter. The consumer will probably pay the cost of such improvements.

Government sources predict that it will cost $287 billion to clean the environment in the ten year period from 1971 to 1980.[14] This is a staggering figure, almost impossible to comprehend; and most of us have trouble understanding a problem until it affects us individually. Air pollution seems to many people just a discomfort, but when the fact became known that New York City air was so bad that a resident there, just by standing on a street corner, breathed enough pollutants to equal the harmful effect of smoking two packs of cigarettes a day, people began to understand. Or when a man in Tokyo was able to develop a photograph in the city's river because the water was so contaminated with chemical wastes, people again took notice. And when the "energy crisis" hit America in 1973 and people could not buy enough gas to take a short trip, citizens began to feel the effects of our environmental problems first-hand. This growing awareness with society's previous and present disrespect for nature and its resources may cause individuals and communities to reorder their priorities for action in the future.

Government regulation

Environmental problems, by their very nature, cannot readily be solved by individual action; they require the concerted action of government intervention. Such intervention has been increasingly frequent, and its effects are beginning to be seen. Recent studies show that the air quality in New York, Chicago, Pittsburgh and other cities has begun to improve since the 1960s. The nation's rivers are not receiving as much sewage and industrial pollutants as in previous decades, because laws now prohibit this mode of disposal. Stripmining is being watched carefully, and in some parts of the country, states are ruling against huge mining operations because of the eventual depletion of resources and ruin to the land. DDT has been outlawed by Congressional approval, thus halting the deadly cycle that proved fatal to many segments of the ecosphere.

New laws and regulations, such as the 1970 Clear Air Act, the 1972 Water Quality Act, and other bills passed in Congress, are steps

Figure 16–3   Federal funds for pollution control and abatement summary 1970–1972 (in millions of dollars)

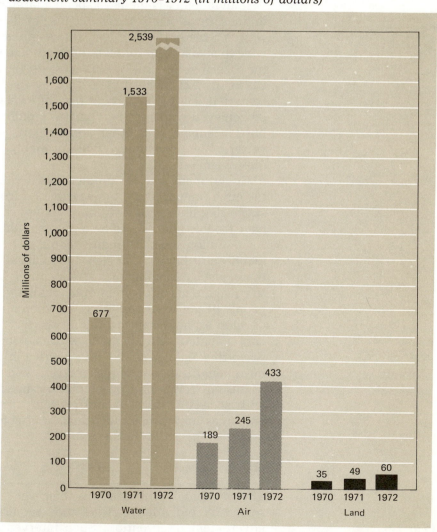

toward a solution. Effectively policing these laws is difficult, but the Environmental Protection Agency is moving ahead trying to settle disputes and insure that the laws are enforced. Yet problems of conflicting priorities still arise. When the Detroit auto makers appealed for a one year extension on meeting the law for auto emissions, the Agency was forced to grant it because of the prospect of lost jobs in Detroit; economic needs are more immediate than environmental ones in this case. We again reach a point where the society must face a difficult trade-off—lost jobs of thousands of workers (or so the auto industry claimed) or cleaner air beginning a year earlier. Given that choice, the trade-off was made on a short-term basis, as is often the case. This kind of issue-ducking and law reversal does not bode well for the long-term situation of the environment, and even though there are numerous laws on the books, environmentalists continue to worry because the laws are so often disregarded, flagrantly violated, or simply rewritten to suit the economic producers in the country.

The problem is not confined to America alone. In the past several years the United Nations has become increasingly concerned with the fate of the environment. A U.N. Conference, held in Sweden in 1972, laid some groundwork for international cooperation on ecology matters. The United States and Canada have committed themselves to cleaning up the Great Lakes, and Russia and the United States are planning to trade vital information on controlling pollution of all kinds. Scientists are moving ahead, but the various governments and their constituents must be knowledgeable and willing to follow.

There is sufficient reason for optimism, even in the face of the task ahead. We have solved many problems before, and there is no reason to believe that, given enough public support, reordering of social priorties, and money, we cannot overcome the environmental dilemma. Barry Commoner writes,

> It [the environmental crisis] is not the product of man's *biological* capabilities, which could not change in time to save us, but of his *social* actions—which are subject to much more rapid change. Since the environmental crisis is the result of the social mismanagement of the world's resources, then it can be resolved and man can survive in a humane condition when the social organization of man is brought into harmony with the ecosphere.[15]

Notes

[1] William G. Carleton, "Government's Historical Role in Conservation" *Current History,* Vol. 50, No. 346, June 1970, pp. 321-327, 365.

[2] *Ibid.*

[3] Barry Commoner, *The Closing Circle* (New York: Alfred A. Knopf, 1972) p. 7.

[4] *Ibid.,* pp. 176–77.

[5] Sterling Brubaker, *To Live On Earth* (New York: New American Library, 1972) p. 153.

[6] James Rathlesberger, ed., *Nixon and the Environment* (New York: Village Voice Book, 1972).

[7] *Environmental Quality: The Third Annual Report of the Council on Environmental Quality.* Washington: U. S. Government Printing Office, August, 1972.

[8] David Zwick and Marcy Benstock, eds., *Water Wasteland* (New York: Grossman Publishers, 1971) p. 32.

[9] *Environmental Quality, op. cit.,* p. 119.

[10] Commoner, *op. cit.,* p. 128.

[11] Zwick and Benstock, *op. cit.,* p. 395.

[12] Paul R. Ehrlich and Anne H. Ehrlich, *Population, Resources, Environment* (San Francisco: W. J. Freeman & Co., 1970).

[13] Brubaker, *op. cit.,* p. 153.

[14] *Environmental Quality, op. cit.,* p. 278.

[15] Commoner, *op. cit.,* p. 299.

Summary

The intense pressure on the natural environment of a society wedded to production and growth has created a serious social problem. The intricate web of relationships among all living things that biologists term the ecosystem has been significantly disrupted by man's attempts to master and exploit his surroundings.

Areas blighted by unthinking exploitation are now attempting to restore ecological balances, but society's awareness of the importance of such measures is not yet fully developed.

Anthropologists link environmental degradation to the rise of the city. The need to produce food for a large number of people gathered in a small area led to more and more manipulation of the environment. Density of population also led to problems of waste disposal. Historically, the solutions to such problems have been sought in new technology, but much of the new technology, especially that developed in recent years, only puts new strains on the ecosystem. Many experts now believe that the true solution to environmental problems must be social, rather than technological.

The issues of environmental protection and conservation were almost nonexistent until the twentieth century. In conquering the wilderness that was America, the early settlers destroyed the environment while they built a nation, but there were few who thought the result anything but progress. By the 1890s, however, the federal government began to establish agencies to protect the land and its resources, and to prevent such catastrophes as flooding. Federal works and power commissions and government projects such as the Tennessee Valley Authority followed, despite resistance to government activities that put limits on the rights of private property.

Until about thirty years ago, each community had to deal only with its own environmental problems. Post-World II expansion led to national environmental concerns, however, as the number of factories, goods, automobiles and people increased, and as new production processes consumed more and more energy.

Four of the major environmental problems facing American society are air, water and land pollution and the depletion of scarce natural resources. Air pollution, the product of chemical emissions from automobiles and industries, damages crops, destroys property and is hazardous to human health. It is significantly related to the incidence of many diseases, including lung cancer, emphysema and others. Over time, it can certainly shorten life. The solution to the pall of air pollution may lie in control devices that limit automobile emissions, or in the use of higher-grade fuels for industrial production; but the price of control devices will inevitably be passed on to the consumer, and high-grade fuels can only be obtained by the environmental destruction (through strip mining) of states where they are found. Any solution to the problem will cost a great deal of money, yet the social costs are so high that some move to clean up the air must be made.

Water is essential for human and plant life. Supplies of pure water for the large American population are endangered by pollutants dumped into the nation's rivers and lakes. Industrial pollution and human waste also kill aquatic life and thus throw a major portion of the ecosystem out of balance. While laws for preventing water pollution have been in force since 1899, the government has tended to be indulgent when industrial polluters important to the economic life of the nation are involved. Small fines are levied only after tortuous litigation, and the companies meanwhile continue polluting. Even the oceans have been affected by waste dumped into them from ships, by oil spills and the like.

Land pollution takes many forms—from the destruction of forests and strip mining to the litter and trash that disfigure the landscape. Chemical fertilizers, while they increase crop yields, also lower the capacity of the land to replenish its own natural elements. Pesticides kill insects, but build up to toxic levels in the tissues of other forms of life. Despite the amount of land set aside for national parks, the recreational, food and production needs of our growing population continue to put pressure on available land.

All our development has been based on the free availability of resources, but these resources—oil, for instance—are now running out, and they are not renewable. The environmental risks of drilling for oil offshore or importing it by tanker from the Middle East or by pipeline from Alaska are prohibitive. To cut back on consumption more means, among other things, doing without transportation systems which depend on fossil fuels.

To combat the environmental problems, there must first be common public acceptance of the problem. Growth and increased consumption are currently primary social values. Solution of these environmental problems requires they be replaced by values that emphasize greater regard for the public, rather than individual, welfare.

Legal changes embodying these changed values have begun to be implemented, as has government regulation of industry in areas relating to environmental pollution, although the necessity for safeguarding the economy has prevented rapid progress. The recently organized UN conference on the environment gives evidence that the problem is now recognized as an international one.

epilogue

As the chapters of this book have amply demonstrated, the social problems that face Americans are complex; they show no signs of disappearing overnight. Possible solutions for all of them have been discussed. In many cases, programs embodying the desired changes have been instituted. But true social change is a complicated process. Any attempt to solve a social problem adds to the social system new variables—and thus new problems. Better health care has ameliorated the problems of disease and early death, but its byproducts include both overpopulation and the problems of the aged.

Why is this so? The reasons are clear enough: Solutions are attempted within the context of societies and institutions too inflexible to deal with them. Values seem to change much more slowly than either technology or legislative programs. To introduce better medical care within the context of the Indian family system is to create at first not only better infant health but overpopulation; and a solution to overpopulation is likely to depend on a pronounced change in the Indian family system, which may in its turn be viewed as a social problem. American family life is already viewed as a social problem. In a context of family breakdown, better health care for all has resulted in more older people dependent, not on their families anymore, but rather on the health care system itself which is notably bureaucratic and rigid. The solution has created a social problem. The interplay of factors is endless.

In America, with the breakdown of traditional family and religious ties, solutions to social problems are now attempted within a framework of social policy set by the executive and legislative branches of government, national, state, and local. We have demanded that government undertake the solution to problems that our more traditional institutions have, until recently, handled by themselves. Too often, social policy has been unable to fulfill the goals it has set for itself. They have been ambitious goals, and some of their successes have been salutary. Yet, the result of many programs has been only to complicate the situation further. To quote Nathan Glazer:

> Their promise, inadequately realized, leaves behind a higher level of expectation, which a new round of social policy must attempt to meet, and with the same consequences. In any case, by the nature of democratic (and not only democratic) politics, again and again more must be promised than can be delivered.[1]

Glazer concludes, pessimistically, that "our efforts to deal with distress themselves increase distress."[2]

The problem is an important one for social scientists, since they are often involved in the making of government programs. They may be called on by government officials and government agencies to make studies of a specific social problem and subsequent legislation sometimes embodies the results of their research. In recent years, a series of government commissions has involved a great many social scientists in attempts to bring forth solutions to the nation's social ills.

There are numerous factors which dictate whether social science in its best form gets into social policy. Part of what Glazer laments is not that social science is inadequate, but that government and politics are inadequate to institute policy of a wide-ranging sort, for as long a time as necessary. The perspectives of the social scientist, who is free, given time and funds, to trace the problem where it leads, and the perspective of the decision-makers, whose concerns are political, often differ considerably. Some essential research is never undertaken, and some corrective actions are never pursued, because of the lack of agreement between scientist and politician on the issues involved and the goals to be attained.

The conflict between the social scientist and the politician is often a conflict between theory and practice. This conflict is exemplified by the Mobilization For Youth (MFY) experiment in New York City. MFY was a social experiment involving the full-scale implementation of Cloward and Ohlin's opportunity theory of juvenile delinquency. Because the program failed to reduce the crime rate significantly, sociological theory was strongly criticized as an inadequate approach to the solving of social problems. What critics failed to understand, of course, was that MFY was not set up to accomplish *that* goal in the first place. Its focus was at the same time wider and of longer range.

There is another reason that social policy sometimes fails. Too often, enthusiasm for technological progress has led to neglect of the dynamics of social change, which have been ignored in the design and implementation of social programs. Urban planning exemplifies this situation. In replacing slum housing with more efficient apartment complexes, planners failed to compensate for the loss of social identity that would result from the new physical arrangements. Neighbors who once congregated on front steps or on sidewalks began to lose contact with each other; crime increased in the convenient setting of labyrinthine corridors and stairwells; the unique quality of neighborhood life deteriorated, only to be replaced by a group of anonymous, hostile individuals living in an environment without the physical capacity to nourish any sense of community. Social scientists were among the first to point out the deficiencies of the new housing systems. Planners have learned from such failures, and may recommend scatter-site construction to the decision-makers in the future, but care must be taken to plan for the inevitable social disruption that new policy will bring about.

Though Americans have often been disinclined to interfere with the seemingly "natural" outcome of the democratic system, the long-cherished notion that ours is a society in which competing pressure groups can resolve the problems of advanced industrial society through peaceful democratic debate has now been relegated to myth.[3]

Ultimately, the war in Southeast Asia may serve as a tragic demonstration of the futility of technological advance divorced from meaningful political and social analysis. Vocal oposition to the war, however limited its effect on national policy may have been, has given rise to a mood of skepticism concerning governmental and corporate institutions. Will the indifference of most citizens yield to a situation in which the majority will demand that human needs be given priority over technological needs? An answer to this question may determine the quality and character of American society in the years ahead.

There have been numerous attempts made in recent years to deal with the limitations of social policy enumerated above. It might be useful to consider some of them here. The most extreme, of course, involves complete overthrow of the present political and social system, by revolution if need be. Because the term revolution has been applied so indiscriminately to drastic changes in fashion, music and sexual mores, its real meaning—the violent overthrow of governmental institutions—has been all but forgotten. The true meaning of revolution has further been obscured by those members of the power structure who have interpreted active dissent as revolution.

In an advanced technological society, it seems fairly obvious that major disruption and disorder could only lead to violent repression. The likelihood of a successful armed rebellion against the United States military establishment is small, and the death and bloodshed that would result render revolution an impractical and undesirable approach to the solution of social problems. In industrial society, the revolutionary has generally been driven in the direction of reform; indeed, yesterday's revolutionaries have frequently emerged as today's candidates for political office.

Extreme in a different way are the suggestions that involve the restructuring of human society through social engineering to eliminate conflict and disruption. Still in its infancy, this science, most closely identified with behavioral psychology, envisions a Utopian society based on scientifically-determined models of social behavior and institutions.

The behavior of every individual, some psychologists reason, is determined by the customs and institutions of his society. By eliminating such social flaws as nepotism, prejudice and human obstinacy, through the design of a culture free of human fallibility, some social scientists believe that a society can be created which will be free of social problems. Essentially, the social engineer seeks to control the social factors which determine human behavior.

Can a society succeed without the element of human options? Although none of the proponents of social engineering have as yet specified how a successful system could be designed and initiated, the main question at this point is: who would program the programmers? That is, how could we be sure that the values built into the system are the values which we want for our society? Is it possible for a heterogeneous population to agree on a universally applicable set of values? Although B. F. Skinner and others argue that culture design would lead us "beyond freedom and dignity"—presumably to a new, "freer" freedom—many social scientists remain unconvinced. Robert Boguslaw, himself an advocate of system design, cautions:

> Our own Utopian renaissance receives its impetus from a desire to extend the mastery of man over nature. Its greatest vigor stems from a dissatisfaction with the limitations of man's existing control over his physical environment. Its greatest threat consists precisely in its potential as a means for extending the control of man over man.[4]

It is impossible to predict the new problems that may arise from man's assumption of this massive responsibility.

At the opposite end of the scale of intervention is the notion of "benign neglect," which operates on the assumption that, whenever possible, social problems should be left to work themselves out.

In practice, benign neglect is rarely benign, usually because some social programs for the amelioration of conditions have already been begun. To withhold support once given is almost worse than to give no help at all. It certainly puts a brake on escalating programs of social policy that promise more and more, but it exacts a high social cost in institutional and human terms.

A great deal of federal money was given to universities in the 1960s, for example, but many educational institutions discovered that their funding disappeared just as they began developing new programs and constructing new buildings. Bloated in size by the government, the universities were left with no money to bridge the gap between planning and implementation. The result has been institutional crisis. Similarly, federally funded Upward Bound programs offered students from urban slum high schools a valuable intensive summer session of small academic classes, cultural activities and individual counseling. When no funds were made available for follow-up programs during the school year, the students who returned to the ghetto schools were no closer to achieving the educational experience they had briefly encountered than they had been the previous spring. Benign neglect may characterize the expedient solution, but it is ultimately inadequate as a basis for on-going social policy. Aimed at reducing social tension, it nevertheless increases it, since expectations have been raised, but not gratified.

The most realistic approach to social problems still seems to be that involving the traditional democratic methods of petition, legislation and the influencing of public policy. The solution of social problems through the American political process combines respect for the traditional structures of family, community, ethnic groups and institutions with an awareness of the significance of current social developments. At this point in history, the process of expressed need and legislative response has had admittedly mixed results. It has, however, yielded such valuable social legislation as social security, Medicare, civil rights legislation and the Federal Housing Administration.

In the recent past, the tendency of legislative bodies has been to serve as a rubber stamp for the executive elite, as exemplified by Congress' unwitting provision of funds for Predident Nixon's unauthorized bombing of Cambodia and its generosity with respect to defense spending, a situation which has raised the question of the government's efficacy in bringing forth valuable social legisation. However, a revival of Congressional interest in health and hospital care, abuses of executive authority and other matters would seem to indicate that there is still considerable vitality in the traditional democratic processes, and that a reorientation of priorities may be in the making.

The need for revivification of the American political system was brought out most dramatically by the widespread expression of dissatisfaction among large segments of the population in the 1960s. The legacy of skepticism of government institutions left by the Vietnam war has led many Americans to question the validity of a hierarchical social structure in which decisions are made by a few individuals at the top and are borne by many individuals at the bottom, and of a value system that stresses financial and material success over the establishment of meaningful human relationships. Some have opted to withdraw from conventional society, seeking refuge in communal living, religious experimentation, drugs and other counter-cultural alternatives. Others have turned their attention to the educational establishment, demanding a voice in the conduct of the schools and an end to school supervision of their personal lives. Women, blacks, and other oppressed groups are refusing in greater and greater numbers to accept social conditions that grant them less than equality. Each in his own way is struggling for the power to control his own life.

The success of these various groups in achieving their goals depends largely on their ability to secure some degree of political power. For an institution to represent the interests of the people it serves, the individual at the bottom must have access to some of the power held by those at the top. The effort to create an effective social policy involves the limiting of governmental power over the individual. To this end, movements such as the consumer and environmental groups and institutions such as the civilian review boards (panels through which citizens may exert a degree of control over the police), and the ombudsman—a government official who investigates individual complaints about public officials—have proven to be useful tools in restoring citizen power.

The issue of professionalism is one which invariably arises in relation to the question of individual power, and it is one with which sociologists, as professionals, ought to be concerned. The notion that the professional alone is properly equipped to deal with certain social problems gives rise to the profession's concern with its own development as a separate entity, no longer accountable to the larger community. The history of modern bureaucracy is a case in point. Efforts to counteract this deleterious effect of professionalism have generally been unsuccessful. Nathan Glazer describes how the poverty program encouraged the rise of community-action agencies as a check on the professionals, only to find that "the community organizers have become another professional group, another interest group, with claims of their own which have no necessary relation to the needs of the clients they serve."[5] The same complaint has often been made of the professionalism of the social scientist. Unless the sociologist makes an effort to circumvent the limitations of professionalism in his own work, his findings may contribute only to the containment of social conflicts, rather than their resolutions.

Sociologists have been responsive to the mood of alienation and dissatisfaction among Americans. They too are dissatisfied with purely technical measures on the one hand, and purely political measures on the other, which are used to remedy our social problems. While sociologists have not abandoned the traditional role of the social scientist, that of the dispassionate, professional observer, they have attempted to supplement it by new approaches which involve the researcher viscerally in the social reality which he is examining.

Many sociologists today are vigorously asserting that self-awareness and awareness of the social world are inseparable aspects of the social scientist's work. They reject the lofty certainty which results in social programs that succeed technically and statistically, but fail on the human level.

Max Weber, as noted in the introduction, advised sociologists to declare their biases when they present their findings. After a time in which this admonition has generally been neglected, the present tendency to participant-observer studies, which sometimes carry research to the point of autobiography, comes as a relief. The method has its own dangers, of course. Self-involvement sometimes triumphs over self-examination. But in the present moment, when the bureaucracy and professionalism of the modern age have proved inadequate to deal with many of our social problems, a sociology which attempts to cope with its own inadequacies is heartening.

Barring Utopia, it seems likely that the social problems discussed in the present text, if they are solved, will be replaced by others. But disciplined observation and analysis of social conditions and personal involvement in them can help each of us assume his share of the responsibility for making America a more truly humane society than it is at the present.

Notes

[1] Nathan Glazer, "The Limits of Social Policy," *Commentary*, September, 1971, p. 52.

[2] *Ibid.*

[3] Barrington Moore, Jr., *Reflections on the Causes of Human Misery* (Boston: Beacon Press, 1972) pp. 105–149.

[4] Robert Boguslaw, *The New Utopians* (Englewood Cliffs, N.J.: Prentice-Hall, 1965) p. 204.

[5] Glazer, *op. cit.*, p. 54.

appendix

Most people assume that in studying various physical phenomena, scientists will follow deliberate and painstaking procedures of investigation, using special scientific tools and sophisticated measuring devices. But they often fail to realize the importance and function of a similarly scientific approach in the professional study of social phenomena. To some people, social research apparently implies a pseudoscientific guessing game which lacks the precision and logic of "real" scientific inquiry. These people often claim that social research provides the same information an average person could derive from common sense, intuition and traditional authoritative sources of information.

It is quite true that the variables of social patterns and problems are, by nature, less easily controlled than those of a chemical experiment. But this does not invalidate the usefulness of a scientific approach in the study of social behavior, nor does it substantiate the notion that one person's observations about social phenomena are as good as another's. In fact, social researchers have discovered that many of the most commonly held assumptions and interpretations of social reality are merely the product of traditional prejudices, misperceptions and unenlightened guesswork which fail to concur with the knowledge gained through even the most basic methods of scientific inquiry. If knowledge is to be regarded as a prerequisite for understanding, the investigative methods of social science are means both necessary and pertinent to clarification of social problems.

The scientific method

The process of scientific investigation is more than a set of rules that guides the search for facts and relationships among them. It begins with investigator's ideas about the phenomena he wishes to study, ideas from which he formulates those questions that will define his research. If his ideas and conceptions are vague and unfocused, the scientist may decide to conduct exploratory research about a particular subject which may suggest more specific objectives for future research. On the other hand, he may have a specific hypothesis which he wishes to test, one that is based on certain elements in his overall conception of phenomena. The social researcher, for example, may have several ideas about the ways in which people relate on an interpersonal level. From these ideas, he may formulate an hypothesis which suggests a relationship among variables in human interaction—for example, that people in close proximity develop feelings of liking for one another.

The purpose of his research (whether it is exploratory or the testing of a specific hypothesis) will then determine the social scientist's research design, or the methods and techniques of investigation he considers best suited to answering the particular questions he has posited. The research design enables the social scientist to approach phenomena objectively, and to avoid making any value judgments to which he might be susceptible if he were not continually guided by a specific procedure of investigation. Furthermore, if the investigation is unsatisfactory, the researcher can use his original design as a reference in deciding which procedural changes might yield better results.

In plotting out his research design, the scientist will determine the type of study he will conduct. An *ex post facto* investigation involves sifting through data observed in past studies for factors which may at least partially account for the relationship among certain variables in presently observed phenomena. In a cross-sectional study, the social scientist observes certain variables as they operate among representative members of a population at a specific point in time. A longitudinal study, on the other hand, may examine those same variables over an extended period of time in order to determine and describe possible trends; or it may involve observations made before and after specific factors have been introduced into a social situation in order to determine their effects.

In deciding which type of study he will utilize, the researcher also considers the type of data he will search for and the ways he can control the variables in order to test his hypothesis. These are important considerations, since the researcher does not wish to be deflected by extraneous or inaccurate information. In order to actually gather the facts, the scientist may utilize one or a combination of research methods appropriate to the scope and limitations of his study. Sample surveys, questionnaires, interviews, participant-observer studies, case studies and controlled experimentation are just some of these methods. The coding of data, or the way data will be organized and systematized, is also planned in the research design and enables the researcher to analyze those factors which are pertinent to his study. The actual techniques used in analyzing data may be designed to include various mathematical computations and statistical procedures.

Equipped with his basic research plan, the scientist can finally proceed to gather his facts. In the course of doing so, he may discover that his intended methods of investigation are inadequate or that certain kinds of data are simply unavailable. He may therefore be compelled to modify his research design. In analyzing and interpreting the data, the researcher seeks to relate the facts he has uncovered to those ideas which originally inspired his research. This often involves correlating variables in order to discover what (if any) significant relationships exist among them. It is quite possible that his findings may necessitate a modification of his original hypothesis, or he might be obliged to reject his hypothesis altogether. Regardless of the outcome of his research, the social scientist realizes that he must record the facts as they have presented themselves and not fabricate or deliberately misrepresent information in order to prove his ideas. In other words, empirical evidence is the social researcher's guiding principle in formulating a generalization.

As his final task, the scientist prepares a report of his findings, taking deliberate care to choose the most precise method of presentation. Affective or colorful language is strictly avoided, since the strength of the scientist's conclusions rests on the clarity and objectivity of his findings. The report itself may be utilized by other researchers as a support for their own investigations or as a departure point for further studies on the subject. In the case of sociological research, the report may be used by policy-makers in determining which areas of the social environment demand public concern and in devising programs that are responsive to specific social problems.

Types of social research

Whatever the fundamental goal of the social researcher—whether it be to uncover basic principles and patterns of social behavior, to delineate social problems and develop practical procedures for improving the quality of social life or a combination of the above goals—he is dependent upon a research methodology that includes the collection and analysis of social data. Not all techniques of data gathering are used as frequently or successfully as others, nor are they all equally precise or applicable to the testing of certain hypotheses. The social scientist must utilize his training and experience in deciding which techniques are appropriate to his particular inquiry and in judging the validity of information gained through these techniques.

Controlled experimentation

A technique of data gathering that most people automatically associate with the scientific method is experimentation. Whether the experiment is conducted in the laboratory or the field, the fundamental purpose is the same: to arrange a comparison of two sets of circumstances that are equal (constant) in all variables except one.

For instance, in one study, researchers attempted to test the hypothesis that delinquency might be prevented in a potentially delinquent boy if he received intense friendly counseling on a one-to-one basis with an adult. The researchers set up experimental and control groups, consisting of 235 subjects each. Both groups contained an equal number of predelinquent (potentially delinquent) and non-predelinquent boys. Individual boys were matched on the basis of age, delinquency-prediction rating, health, intelligence and other relevant variables, so each group contained equivalent samples. During a period of from four to eight years, the boys in the experimental group received adult counseling, whereas the boys in the control group received no counseling. The researchers then compared official records of the boys in both groups within a few years after the end of the program. Counseling had no significant effect on delinquency.

Controlled experimentation is a powerful method for testing hypotheses which involve causal relationships among variables. While such experimentation is common in the physical sciences, only recently has it been employed by social researchers. One limitation is the expense of such research. In the delinquency study, a large staff of professionals was needed to screen the boys before adequate sample groups could be created and to provide one-to-one counseling for the experimental group. The size of the group and the length of time of the experiment required considerable sums of money. Other limitations of controlled experimentation are inherent in the nature of social research. One such limitation is the intervention of other factors which may affect other variables in the experiment. For example, some counselors left during the middle of the delinquency study, requiring a change in counselors for the boys in the experimental group. There is no way to account for the impact this change may or may not have had on individual boys. Furthermore, there is no way to make certain that each boy received the same counseling services; in fact, in this experiment, no attempt was made to standardize the counseling services provided to the subjects in the experimental group. These and other factors may limit the usefulness of any conclusions drawn from such experimentation.

Sample survey

The sample survey is a major technique for gathering empirical data on attitudes, values, opinions and behavior. It is commonly utilized by political campaigners and advertisers to obtain some indication of those qualities people are seeking in a candidate or a product, and the way people are affected by different types of campaigns and commercials. Therefore, the sample survey has been useful in quantitative analysis (for example, in estimating the number of people who will vote Democratic or Republican) and in qualitative analysis (for example, in determining the type of person who is attracted to the Democratic or Republican party.)

In social research, the sample survey has provided considerable empirical data which has been useful in conjunction with other research methods such as case studies. The term "sample" refers to any group of people who have been chosen as representative members of the population under study. In a national voting survey, for instance, the population would consist of all adult voters; the sample would consist of just those citizens interviewed.

Depending upon the availability of a sample group for survey investigations and the type and projected use of the data being sought, the social scientist will design a survey plan which may employ such data-gathering techniques as interviews, questionnaires or tests. The researcher may conduct his survey to assess public opinion in response to a specific event, such as the repeal of the death sentence or the invasion of a foreign country. Other surveys are repeated at various time intervals to determine changes in the public's attitudes or values. Americans are regularly polled by the Harris and Gallup organizations to determine their opinions of the President's job performance.

The problems and limitations associated with sample surveys are in some respects similar to those that affect other methods of social research. Briefly stated, sample groups may not be as representative as the researcher thinks or would wish them to be. The responses given during a survey investigation are not always accurate or adequate. However, other sources of information can be used to test the findings of survey studies; and the surveys may, in turn, reveal certain variables that may not be accounted for in controlled experiments or other methods of social research.

Case studies

The case study is an important technique for investigating the details of social patterns, processes and behavior. It may involve the compilation of data about the life history of a single individual or family, a detailed account of a specific event such as a political demonstration or the history of a special group of individuals—for example, the Amish community in Pennsylvania. Sometimes the personal case study is used as a scientific "wedge" into the more complex phenomena of group behavior. For example, the history, attitudes and practices of a single member of the Amish community could serve as the groundwork for more comprehensive studies and as a dramatic and illustrative accompaniment to statisical reports.

The case study is an especially useful method of gathering data when the social scientist is doing exploratory research. Although a single case study is adequate for only limited generalization, it may be helpful in formulating additional hypotheses and creating the design of related studies which employ more comprehensive and objective techniques of scientific inquiry. Furthermore, case studies of specific individuals and situations provide information essential to any practical efforts or programs that are designed to ameliorate social conditions, since broad theories and statistical reports may not indicate the special needs of the individuals within the population.

Participant-observer studies

Intimate knowledge of various social experiences and phenomena may be gained through a type of field investigation in which the researcher functions as both a participant and an observer. Used as an alternative or in conjunction with other research methods, participant-observer studies can provide valuable insights which would be difficult, if not impossible, to gain through other means.

For example, the sociologist, William F. Whyte, conducted a study of social organization in an urban slum. Whyte's hypothesis maintained that a slum area had a highly complex social organization. Previous sociological theories maintained that slum districts suffered from social disorganization. To collect his data, Whyte employed the participant-observer method of research. He lived with an Italian family in the area for eighteen months, and then took his own apartment for an additional two years. While living in Cornerville (the fictitious name of the slum), Whyte participated in many community activities. He joined clubs, dated local girls and became a campaign worker for a local politician.

Rather than study all aspects of social organization in the slum, Whyte chose to focus on the street corner gangs living in the area. He carefully observed the behavior of gang members. Sometimes he deliberately remained on the sidelines while the gang members engaged in conversation. On other occasions, he joined the conversation in order to direct it toward topics about which he desired information, such as the status relationships among gang members. Whyte found "that in every group (in Cornerville) there was a hierarchical structure of social relations binding the individuals to one another and that the groups were also related hierarchically to one another."

A major difficulty for the researcher using the participant-observer method is maintaining his own credibility as a member of the group under observation. If group members suspect duplicity or bad faith, they may become hostile or exclude the researcher from their confidences. On the other hand, if the researcher informs group members of his purpose (as Whyte did), they may consciously or unconsciously modify their usual behavior. Furthermore, there is the problem of quantitative analysis and verification of field observations. The researcher may be able to make only field notes of his impressions about the group; as a result of his own participation, he may risk emotional involvement and loss of objectivity.

Nevertheless, the researcher's training in the scientific method will lend at least some validity to his observations, and his findings may form the basis for hypotheses that inspire further studies. Participant-observer studies also enable researchers to evaluate the implementation of social programs—for example, prisoner rehabilitation programs—and to study and assess the behavior and practices of those professionals and officials who administrate such programs.

Interviews and questionnaires

Although interviews and questionnaires may be used in sample surveys, they also may be used as separate tools or in conjunction with any other methods of social research. Both provide for the systematization of the data being sought, and the significance of findings derived from both techniques is dependent, to a great extent, upon whether or not the sample of people chosen for study is truly representative.

The questionnaire is a structured instrument completed by a respondent or by an interviewer asking questions of a respondent. The design of the questionnaire is therefore of great importance to the social researcher, since he will have no personal control over the responses. The researcher must consider the socioeconomic level and educational background of his "target" population when planning the language and sentence structure of the questions. Even if the information sought is purely factual, ambiguous wording and the use of unfamiliar terminology may result in inaccurate responses by the subjects. More difficult to plan for is the psychological game-playing of the respondent. It is not uncommon for a person to try to "psyche out" the researcher's intention in asking certain questions (especially those which ask for opinions and attitudes) and to give answers which he believes are acceptable to the researcher. Or, lacking any firm opinion about a topic, the respondent may simply fabricate a response. Subtle use of repetitive or overlapping questions may expose duplicity and misunderstandings on the part of the respondent, although the researcher must be cognizant of these factors when evaluating the questionnaire.

Unlike the questionnaire, the interview provides an opportunity for the social researcher to evaluate responses and modify his questioning pattern while the interrogation is in progress. However, the researcher formulates at least a general plan of questioning prior to the actual interview. He may devise a highly structured format (similar to the questionnaire) in which the respondent is asked a series of questions and is required to choose one of several answers. He may control the order and type of questions asked, but allow the respondent to formulate his reply in any fashion he chooses. Or he may dispense with formal questions and simply follow a topic outline. This last interview format is especially useful if the researcher has little in-depth data about the subject of his inquiry. It encourages the respondent to volunteer any information he feels is pertinent to the topic and for which the researcher may not have known to ask.

The use of records

Utilizing the techniques of experimentation, survey, interview and observation, the social researcher gathers data pertaining to a single event or phenomenon in time or to social conditions and changes within an extended time period. Considerable sociological research also involves the comparison of data in the form of already existing records from different sources and time periods.

For example, a sociologist suspected that there might be a relationship between substandard housing conditions and juvenile delinquency. In his study, he correlated delinquency rates in 155 census districts in Baltimore (available from court records) and data from the Bureau of the Census relating to housing units in the same districts. By controlling different variables, such as race and income, while comparing the statistical data, he discovered that home ownership was the one variable that remained significant throughout. His conclusion was that home ownership was indicative of family stability. This was interpreted as a partial explanation for the fact that lower delinquency rates were found in areas where home ownership was the major housing characteristic.

The interpretation of data

Quantitative measurement of data is a major activity of the social researcher, no matter which of the previously mentioned research methods he employs. However, statistics and other quantified data are useful in describing and comparing phenomena only insofar as they are handled skillfully and with scientific objectivity; misinterpreted, they may suggest false conclusions and misleading generalizations. The concepts and problems associated with scientific measurement are therefore important subjects for discussion.

Averages

The term "average" is casually and commonly used by most people. Unfortunately, the "average" person often uses the term as a convenient disguise for imprecise information. The social researcher, on the other hand, recognizes it as a useful statistical device that enables him to describe and compare people, events and various aspects of social phenomena. Used scientifically, an average refers to the most central mathematical tendency of whatever group of social phenomena is being studied. There are three types of averages: the mean, the mode and the median.

The mean, commonly equated with the term "average," is the total sum of values divided by the total number of cases from which those values are derived. For example, suppose a researcher were calculating the mean annual income of a group of ten high school graduates. The income figures for this group are:

$5000 $5500 $5500 $5500 $6000
$6500 $6500 $7500 $9000 $9500

To arrive at the mean, the researcher would determine the total income of all families ($66,500) and divide by the number of cases (ten). He would arrive at a mean income of $6650.

The mean is a good indicator of the typical score (central tendency), since it utilizes all the values available from the collected data. However, the mean can be a misleading figure if the distribution of scores includes extreme cases. If the $9500 top income in the example above was $35,000, the mean income would be $9200. For this reason, social researchers often use the mode and the median as measurements of central tendency, since neither is affected by extremes in distribution.

The mode is that value in a series of scores which most frequently occurs. In the example above, the mode would be an income of $5500. The median is the midpoint in a series of numerical values when those values are arranged in a low-to-high order. The median is therefore flanked on both sides by an equal number of scores when there is an odd-numbered series of values. If there is an even-numbered series of values, the median is the mean of the two middle values. In the example above, the median is $6250, the mean of the two middle values—$6000 and $6500.

In using averages, the social researcher must determine which of the three measures of central tendency best fits his needs and the data under consideration. Unless the data contains extreme cases, the mean is the best measurement, since it takes into account the value of all cases. Like the social researcher, the student or reader of such statistics should also keep in mind the inherent limitations and advantages of each of these three types of averages.

Sampling methods

Drawing a sample can be one of the most important steps in any research program and a necessary concomitant to any of the major research methods that are used to obtain data. Information obtained from a sample is used as the basis for making inferences about the particular population group from which it is drawn. Samples are necessary because the total population is often too large to study.

There may be problems not only in planning, but also in evaluating studies based on sampling.

A common deception perpetrated on the public are "scientific" studies based on absurdly small samples. An advertiser may state that in a recent survey of doctors, nine out of ten recommended a certain brand of cough medicine. However, if the survey happens to have included only ten doctors, any self-respecting statistician would be obliged to view the results as a chance occurrence. A sample is simply not adequate unless it is large enough to preclude chance occurrences; the researcher must be able to establish that further sampling would not significantly modify the results.

More important and difficult than the problem of size is finding a sample that is truly representative. If a sample is chosen without any specific system, it will not serve a valid purpose—even if it includes thousands of cases, a high percentage of which yield positive results in support of an hypothesis. There are two basic methods the researcher may use to draw a sample: the random method and the proportional representation method. Both techniques may involve problems for the researcher.

The random sample is comprised of people who are randomly chosen from the population under study—for example, every thirtieth name in a phone book, or every other house in a particular community. In some ways, the random method is the most accurate and easiest technique for choosing a sample group. However, this method can be costly and time-consuming, especially if contact with random group members is difficult to achieve or sustain for the duration of the study. For example, some group members chosen on a random basis may have erratic work schedules that make it difficult for the researcher to interview them at his convenience.

The other technique of sampling is based on proportional representation of each type of individual in the population group under study. Residence, income, profession, ethnic background and education are some of the variables the sample may reflect in percentages comparable to the larger population group from which it is drawn. The obvious difficulty is choosing and controlling those variables that are relevant to the investigation. If the variables are not carefully considered, information from the sample group may lead to inaccurate inferences about social behavior in the larger population. Sometimes data from previous studies is available as a guide in organizing the sample group. But quite often, the researcher is obliged to expend considerable time and energy in making preliminary tests in order to determine those factors that are relevant to his study.

Correlation

Correlations are mathematical statements that indicate the degree to which two sets of variables are related. A common error is to equate correlation with causation, thereby suggesting relationships among variables that may not exist. It is true that a statistical correlation may eventually provide evidence for a causal relationship, but the relationship cannot be claimed until certain questions have been posed and satisfactorily answered.

Before a researcher can consider causation, he must establish that a true relationship between variables exists; he must demonstrate that two factors significantly vary together. The first step, then is to determine whether or not a certain factor occurs significantly more (or less) frequently in the specific group being studied than it does in the general population. For example, before a researcher could begin to determine whether or not a valid association existed between heredity and alcoholism, he would need to compare the percentage of *all alcoholics* with living or dead alcoholic relatives to the percentage of *all people* who have living or dead alcoholic relatives. The researcher might then determine the coefficient of correlation, a measurement of the two variables which involves complicated mathematical prodedures. For our purpose, it will suffice to state that there may be a positive correlation in which two factors vary together in the same direction, or a negative correlation in which two factors vary proportionately but in opposite directions. Even if a relationship between two factors seems to exist, this would not prove causation nor indicate which factor was the cause and which one was the effect. The researcher must still examine several possible relationships before suggesting a pattern of causation. For example, inherited organic malfunctions may cause alcoholism, alcoholism may cause organic malfunctions, other factors may be responsible for the incidence of both alcoholism and organic malfunctions, or alcoholism and inherited organic malfunctions may be independent factors and only coincidentally associated.

Obviously, if more than two variables are involved, establishing what is cause and what is effect is even more difficult. The complexity of the interactions may preclude any definitive statements about correlation, much less causation. Holding all but one variable constant (assuming this is possible) may suggest a correlation which is mathematically accurate, but which is only a partial and simplified description of available data. Investigation into social problems such as juvenile delinquency, for example, might yield partial correlations which suggest simple causal relationships or seem to negate the relationship between a certain factor and delinquency. However, in real-life situations, very subtle and complex interactions between variables may result in the particular social problem under study.

photo credits

15 Eva Rubinstein; **16** Arthur Tress; **17** Lucia Woods; **18** Bob D'Alessandro; **19** Patricia Walsh; **25** James Foote-Photo Researchers; **26** George W. Gardner-Photo Researchers (top) Paul V. Thomas-Black Star (bottom); **27** Alycia Smith Butler (top) Christopher G. Knight-Photo Researchers (bottom); **28** Charles Pratt; **63** Patricia Walsh; **64** Jodi Cobb; **65** Lilo Raymond; **66** Steve Schapiro-Black Star; **67** Arthur Tress; **103** Ernest Baxter-Black Star; **104** Chie Nishio-Nancy Palmer; **105** Bob Brooks; **106** Ken Heyman; **107** Julio Mitchel; **141** Kenneth Murray-Nancy Palmer; **142** Morton Broffman-Bethel; **143** David Campbell-Photo Researchers; **144** James H. Karales; **145** Kenneth Murray-Nancy Palmer; **179** Paolo Koch-Rapho Guillumette; **180** Leonard Freed-Magnum; **181** Elliott Erwitt-Magnum; **182** Fujihira-Monkmeyer; **183** Marc Riboud-Magnum; **215** Julio Mitchel; **216** Sardi Klein; **217** J. Crow-Monkmeyer; **218** Ted Cowell-Black Star; **219** Van Bucher-Photo Researchers; **251** Dan Budnik-Woodfin Camp; **252** Gordon Baer-Black Star; **253** Dan Budnik-Woodfin Camp; **254** Marc St. Gil-Black Star; **255** Julio Mitchel; **258** Allyn Z. Baum-Rapho Guillumette; **259** Lilo Raymond (top and bottom left), Barbara Pfeffer-Photo Researchers (bottom right); **260** Virginia Hamilton; **261** Ira Nowinski; **295** Bill Stanton-Magnum; **296** Jerry Cooke-Photo Researchers; **297** Jerry Cooke-Photo Researchers; **298** Mike Levins; **299** Hella Hammid-Rapho Guillumette; **333** Julio Mitchel; **334** Sepp Seitz-Magnum; **335** Ted Spiegel-Black Star; **336** Leonard Freed-Magnum; **337** Barbara Nadelman; **354** Lilo Raymond; **355** Patricia Walsh (top left), Jim Jowers-Nancy Palmer (top right), Thomas Hopker-Woodfin Camp (bottom); **356** Virginia Hamilton (top left), Hugh Rogers-Monkmeyer (top right), Bill Gallery (bottom); **357** Bob Fitch-Black Star; **373** Donald McCullin-Magnum; **374** Charles Harbutt-Magnum; **375** Donald McCullin-Magnum; **376** John Launois-Black Star; **377** Michael Lloyd Carlebach-Nancy Palmer; **411** Arthur Tress; **412** Arthur Tress; **413** Mike Levins; **414** George W. Gardner-Photo Researchers; **415** Philip Dante; **439** Bob Fitch-Black Star; **440** Bob Brooks; **411** Michael Abramson-Black Star; **442** William Ravenisi; **443** Jan Lukas-Rapho Guillumette; **467** Paolo Koch-Rapho Guillumette; **468** Mimi Forsyth-Monkmeyer (top), Roy Ellis-Rapho Guillumette (bottom left), Hugh Rogers-Monkmeyer (bottom right); **469** Enrico Natali-Rapho Guillumette (top), Ron Sherman-Nancy Palmer (bottom); **471** Sid Sattler-Nancy Palmer; **479** Dick Hanley-Photo Researchers; **480** Dennis Brack-Black Star; **481** Monkmeyer; **482** United Press International; **483** Bob Fitch-Black Star; **517** United Press International; **518** Tim Kantor-Rapho Guillumette; **519** Georg Gerster-Rapho Guillumette; **520** Robert Houser-Rapho Guillumette; **521** Charles Harbutt-Magnum; **553** Leo Choplin-Black Star; **554** Photo Researchers; **555** Ted Spiegel-Black Star; **556** Leo Choplin-Black Star; **557** Enrico Natali-Rapho Guillumette; **589** Burk Uzzle-Magnum; **590** Elliott Erwitt-Magnum; **591** Kenneth Murray-Nancy Palmer; **592** Paul Sequeira-Rapho Guillumette; **593** Rohn Engh-Photo Researchers; **609** Franklynn Peterson-Black Star; **610** Alycia Smith Butler; **611** Alycia Smith Butler.

figure sources

Figure 3-2: Mental Disorders/Suicide *(Cambridge, Mass: Harvard University Press, 1972) p. 180.*

Figure 5-4: *Bernard Berelson, "Beyond Family Planning."* Ekistics 162 *pp. 288–294*

Figure 9-1: *adapted from David E. Smith, Joel D. Fort, Dolores L. Craton,* Psychoactive Drugs: A reference for the Staff of the Haight-Ashbury Clinic, *unpublished.*

Figure 9-4: *Harrison M. Trice, "New Light on Identifying the Alcoholic Employee,"* Personnel, *Vol. 44 (1964) 18–25.*

Figure 9-5: *Lee Quinn, from Arnold Bernstein and Henry L. Lennard, "Drugs, Doctors and Junkies,"* Society, *Vol. 10, No. 4 (Mar/June 1973) p. 15.*

Figure 13-2: *Edwin Emery, Phillip H. Ault, Warren K. Agee,* Introduction to Mass Communications, *third ed. (New York: Dodd, Mead and Company, 1971) p. 133.*

Figure 14-2: *Stanley Lieberson, "An Empirical Study of Military-Industrial Linkages,"* American Journal of Sociology, *Vol. 76 (January 1971), p. 576.*

Figure 16-2: *David Zwick and Marcy Benstock.* Water Wasteland: Ralph Nader's Study Group Report on Water Pollution *(New York: Grossman Publishers, 1971).*

index

647

Ford, Henry, 164, 560
Freud, Sigmund
  on neuroses, 307
  and psychoanalysis, 323
  on psychosomatic disorders, 306
  on sex roles, 465
  view of crime, 384
  on violence, 417
Friedman, Milton
  on corporate responsibility, 543
  on negative income tax, 170
Friedson, Eliot, and doctor-patient relationship, 264, 265
Fromm, Erich, on violence, 417
Future of the Family, The (Ed. by Louise Kapp Howe), 87

Gagnon, John A., on homosexual "coming out", 460–461
Galbraith, John Kenneth
  on corporate technostructure, 524–525
  on function of corporate chairman, 523
  on poverty, 149, 150
  on producer sovereignty, 537–538
  on worker dissatisfaction, 575–576
Gangs, and juvenile crime, 389
Gans, Herbert
  on poverty, 161, 172
  on social organization of suburbs, 42
  study in Boston, 44
  on urban dweller, 32
Garvey, Marcus, on separation, 131
Gay Activists' Alliance, 462
General Motors, 522, 523
  revenues of, 525
Geography
  and criminal behavior, 383–384
  and divorce rate, 77
  and doctor shortage, 285
  and population distribution, 196–197
  and poverty, 152–153, 154
  and violence, 418
Ghetto areas
  and crime rates, 383
  drug use in, 352–353
  mental illness in, 120
  problems of, 40–42
  rise of, 29
  and violence, 116, 418
Glazer, Nathan
  on ethnic background, 130
  on government and housing, 43
Goffman, Erving, on mental institutions, 310–312
Goode, Erich, 345–346
Goode, William J.
  on family and society, 73
  on violence, 423
Government
  cooperation with business, 528–529
  and defense industry, 531–534
  economic role of, 526–528
  and environmental problems, 600, 617–619
  large-scale, 526–529
  and media, 498–503
  and medical expenditures, 273–274
  and pornography, 447–449
  and poverty programs, 161–177
  records, 504

relationship with corporations, 531–535
reorganization, 547
technological priorities within, 534–535
and unemployment, 567
and violence, 427–428
  See also City government; Federal government; State government
Government employees
  trends, 562
  worker dissatisfaction among, 579–581
Government regulation, of drugs and alcohol, 340
Group therapy, description of, 323–324
Gun control legislation, 403, 431

Hallucinogens, properties and effects of, 347–348
Hardin, Garrett, 193
Harrington, Michael, 148, 160
Hauser, Philip M., on urban crisis, 45–48
Head Start programs, 243
Health care, 254–258, 261–286
  and poverty, 172
  problems of, 257–258, 261–266
  and use of paraprofessionals, 285
  See also Doctors; Medical care
Health insurance
  establishment of, 266
  and hospital expenses, 274–277
  prepaid group, 283–284
Heilbroner, Robert L., on relationship between Pentagon and Lockheed Aircraft, 533
Herzberg, Frederick, on worker dissatisfaction, 575–576
Higher education
  and curriculum changes, 244
  financing of, 227–228
  policy of, 238–239
  See also Education
Historian and the City, The (Ed. by Handlin and Burchard), 55
Hoagland, Edward, on wilderness, 614–617
Hollingshead, A. B., on mentally ill, 308–309
Holt, John, on education, 231–232
Homosexuality, 458–465
Horney, Karen, on competitiveness, 318
Horowitz, Irving S., on policy-making, 535–536
Hospital(s)
  cost of, 277–278
  growth of, 265–266
  role of, 272
  See also Doctors; Health care; Medical care
Hospitalization, of mentally ill, 310–314
Housing, 43–45
  and poverty, 145, 156
Hutterites, communal family of, 94–95

Illegitimacy, 79–80, 91
Illness
  changing attitude toward, 261–262
  See also Health care; Medical care
Immigrants
  acculturation of, 131–133
  and American frontier, 70
  assimilation of, 130
  after Civil War, 71
  and cultural discrimination, 111
  and education, 220
  first generation, 23

and sexuality, 452–453
  See also Divorce; Family
Marx, Karl, on worker dissatisfaction, 573
Maslow, Abraham
  on mental illness, 300
  on normal personality, 302
  on worker dissatisfaction, 575–576
Mass media
  alternatives to, 507–509
  content of, 491–498
  control of, 486–488
  development of, 484–488
  effects of, 488–491
  and government, 498–503
  myth of America, 145
  regulation of, 502–503
  social functions of, 493–496
  and violence, 419, 430
    See also Communication; Journalism; News
      media
Mead, Margaret
  on mental disorders, 306
  on violence, 432
Medicaid, 280
Medical care
  inequality of, 278–282
  payment for, 272–282
  and poverty, 145–146
  proposals for change of, 282–286
  and socioeconomics, 308–310
    See also Doctors; Health care; Hospitals
Medical insurance, 272–274
Medicare program, 280
Men
  changing role of, 74, 466–467, 470
  and crime, 422–423
  in family, 82–87
    See also Children; Women
Mental disorders, 298–326
  definitions of, 300–303
  ethnic distribution of, 315–316
  extent of, 307–316
  in ghettos, 120
  institutions for, 310–314
  myth of, 319–320
  responses to, 320–326
  social distribution of, 308–310
  sociological explanations of, 316–320
  treatment of, 310–315
  types of, 303–307
Merton, Robert K.
  on social function of mass media, 493–496
  theory of crime, 385–386
Methadone, 364
Mexican-Americans, 110, 114–115, 116, 117
  See also American Indians; Blacks; Minority
    groups; Puerto Ricans
Middletown (Lynd), 34
Migrant workers, 154–155
  status of, 564
    See also Immigrants; Migration
Migration
  calculation of, 187
  and population, 185–186, 198–199
    See also Migrant Workers; Immigration
"Military-industrial complex", 428
Miller, Dorothy H., on adjustment of mentally ill,
    313–314
652 Mills, C. Wright, on elitism, 541–542

Minority groups
  and access to education, 240, 241
  and mass media, 492
  and unemployment, 569–570
  and violence against, 119–120
    See also American Indians; Blacks; Mexican-
      Americans; Puerto Ricans
Model Cities, 44–45
Moore, Barrington, Jr., on family, 90
Moore, Wilbert E., on corporate life, 524
Mormons, 69, 445
Mortality rate
  and population, 185
  white compared to nonwhite, 278
Motion picture industry, 485
  changes in, 492–493
  control of, 486
    See also Entertainment
Moynihan, Daniel
  on education, 222
  on ethnic background, 130
  on Family Assistance Plan, 170, 171
Myrdal, Gunnar, 569

Narcotics, properties and effects of, 347
  See also Drug addiction; Drug use
National Advisory Commission on Civil Disorders,
    findings of, 41
National Commission on the Causes and Prevention
    of Violence, findings of, 430–432
National Commission of Marijuana and Drug
    Abuses, 337
National Commission on Technology, Automation,
    and Economic Progress, 568
National defense, and postcivilization, 52
National health insurance, 282–283
National Organization for Women (NOW), 92
National Urban Coalition, 403
National Welfare Rights Organization (NWRO), 165
Natural resources
  depletion of, 200
  and population, 184
  threats to, 593
    See also Environmental problems
Negroes
  See Blacks
Neighborhood control, 50–51
New York City
  air pollution in, 617
  drug addiction in, 120
  income distribution of population, 37
  police corruption in, 392
  problems in, 38–49
  Puerto Ricans in, 117
News media
  and confidentiality of sources, 501–502
  decline of, 486
  development of, 484–485
  effect on minority problems, 129
  objectivity of, 499–500
  and prejudice, 129
  underground, 507
    See also Communication; Journalism; Mass
      media
New York state
  doctor shortage in, 269
  and education, 225, 226
Nineteenth century, family in, 67–71